HUMAN DEVELOPMENT
93/94

Twenty-First Edition

Annual Editions
A Library of Information from the Public Press

Editor

Larry Fenson
San Diego State University

Larry Fenson is a professor of psychology at San Diego State University. He received his Ph.D. in child psychology from the Institute of Child Behavior and Development at the University of Iowa in 1968. Dr. Fenson is a member of the MacArthur Foundation Research Network on Infancy and Early Childhood. His research focuses on early conceptual development, and he has authored articles on infant attention, symbolic play, concept development, and language acquisition.

Editor

Judith Fenson
Children's Hospital

Judith Fenson received a B.A. from Ohio University in 1963 and an M.A. from the University of New Mexico in 1965. She is the Language Data Coordinator at the Language Research Center at Children's Hospital. She has contributed to a variety of research projects in medicine, psychology, and linguistics, and has authored a variety of materials and study aids for students in psychology and child development.

Cover illustration by Mike Eagle

The Dushkin Publishing Group, Inc.
Sluice Dock, Guilford, Connecticut 06437

The Annual Editions Series

Annual Editions is a series of over 55 volumes designed to provide the reader with convenient, low-cost access to a wide range of current, carefully selected articles from some of the most important magazines, newspapers, and journals published today. Annual Editions are updated on an annual basis through a continuous monitoring of over 300 periodical sources. All Annual Editions have a number of features designed to make them particularly useful, including topic guides, annotated tables of contents, unit overviews, and indexes. For the teacher using Annual Editions in the classroom, an Instructor's Resource Guide with test questions is available for each volume.

VOLUMES AVAILABLE

Africa
Aging
American Government
American History, Pre-Civil War
American History, Post-Civil War
Anthropology
Biology
Business Ethics
Canadian Politics
China
Commonwealth of Independent States
Comparative Politics
Computers in Education
Computers in Business
Computers in Society
Criminal Justice
Drugs, Society, and Behavior
Dying, Death, and Bereavement
Early Childhood Education
Economics
Educating Exceptional Children
Education
Educational Psychology
Environment
Geography
Global Issues
Health
Human Development
Human Resources
Human Sexuality
India and South Asia
International Business
Japan and the Pacific Rim
Latin America
Life Management
Macroeconomics
Management
Marketing
Marriage and Family
Microeconomics
Middle East and the Islamic World
Money and Banking
Nutrition
Personal Growth and Behavior
Physical Anthropology
Psychology
Public Administration
Race and Ethnic Relations
Social Problems
Sociology
State and Local Government
Third World
Urban Society
Violence and Terrorism
Western Civilization, Pre-Reformation
Western Civilization, Post-Reformation
Western Europe
World History, Pre-Modern
World History, Modern
World Politics

Library of Congress Cataloging in Publication Data
Main entry under title: Annual Editions: Human development. 1993/94.
   1. Child study—Periodicals. 2. Socialization—Periodicals. 3. Old age—Periodicals.
I. Fenson, Larry, *comp.*; Fenson, Judith, *comp.* II. Title: Human development.
ISBN 1–56134–203–3   155′.05   72–91973
HQ768.A55

Twenty-First Edition

Manufactured by The Banta Company, Harrisonburg, Virginia 22801

Printed on Recycled Paper

To the Reader

In publishing ANNUAL EDITIONS we recognize the enormous role played by the magazines, newspapers, and journals of the *public press* in providing current, first-rate educational information in a broad spectrum of interest areas. Within the articles, the best scientists, practitioners, researchers, and commentators draw issues into new perspective as accepted theories and viewpoints are called into account by new events, recent discoveries change old facts, and fresh debate breaks out over important controversies.

Many of the articles resulting from this enormous editorial effort are appropriate for students, researchers, and professionals seeking accurate, current material to help bridge the gap between principles and theories and the real world. These articles, however, become more useful for study when those of lasting value are carefully *collected, organized, indexed,* and *reproduced* in a *low-cost format,* which provides easy and permanent access when the material is needed. That is the role played by *Annual Editions.* Under the direction of each volume's *Editor,* who is an expert in the subject area, and with the guidance of an *Advisory Board,* we seek each year to provide in each *ANNUAL EDITION* a current, well-balanced, carefully selected collection of the best of the public press for your study and enjoyment. We think you'll find this volume useful, and we hope you'll take a moment to let us know what you think.

Any history of the field of human development will reflect the contributions of the many individuals who helped craft the topical content of the discipline. For example, Binet launched the intelligence test movement, Freud focused attention on personality development, and Watson and Thorndike paved the way for the emergence of social learning theory. However, the philosophical principles that give definition to the field of human development have their direct ancestral roots in the evolutionary biology of Darwin, Wallace, and Spencer, and in the embryology of Preyer. Each of the two most influential developmental psychologists of the early twentieth century, James Mark Baldwin and G. Stanley Hall, was markedly influenced by questions about phylogeny (species' adaptation) and ontogeny (individual adaptation). Baldwin's persuasive arguments challenged the assertion that changes in species precede changes in individual organisms. Instead, Baldwin argued, ontogeny not only precedes phylogeny but is the process that shapes phylogeny. Thus, as Robert Cairns points out, developmental psychology has always been concerned with the study of the forces that guide and direct development. Early theories stressed that development was the unfolding of already formed or predetermined characteristics. Many contemporary students of human development embrace the epigenetic principle that asserts that development is an emergent process of active, dynamic, reciprocal, and systemic change. This systems perspective forces one to think about the historical, social, cultural, interpersonal, and intrapersonal forces that shape the developmental process.

The study of human development involves all fields of inquiry comprising the social, natural, and life sciences and professions. The need for depth and breadth of knowledge creates a paradox: While students are being advised to acquire a broad-based education, each discipline is becoming more highly specialized. One way to combat specialization is to integrate the theories and findings from a variety of disciplines with those of the parent discipline. This, in effect, is the approach of *Annual Editions: Human Development 93/94.* This anthology includes articles that discuss the problems, issues, theories, and research findings from many fields of study. In most instances, the articles were written specifically to communicate information about recent scientific findings or controversial issues to the general public. As a result, the articles tend to blend the history of a topic with the latest available information. In many instances, the reader is challenged to consider the personal and social implications of the topic. The articles included in this anthology were selected by the editors with valued advice and recommendations from an advisory board consisting of faculty from community colleges, small liberal arts colleges, and large universities. Evaluations obtained from students, instructors, and advisory board members influenced the decision to retain or replace specific articles. Throughout the year we screen many articles for accuracy, interest value, writing style, and recency of information. Readers can have input into the next edition by completing and returning the article rating form in the back of the book.

Human Development 93/94 is organized into six major units. Unit 1 focuses on the origins of life, including genetic influences on development, and unit 2 focuses on development during infancy and early childhood. Unit 3 is divided into subsections addressing social, emotional, and cognitive development. Unit 4 addresses issues related to family, school, and cultural influences on development. Units 5 and 6 cover human development from adolescence to old age. In our experience, this organization provides great flexibility for those using the anthology with any standard textbook. The units can be assigned sequentially, or instructors can devise any number of arrangements of individual articles to fit their specific needs. In large lecture classes, this anthology seems to work best as assigned reading to supplement the basic text. In smaller sections, articles can stimulate instructor-student discussions. Regardless of the instructional style used, we hope that our excitement for the study and teaching of human development is evident and catching as you read the articles in this twenty-first edition of *Human Development.*

Larry Fenson

Larry Fenson

Judith Fenson

Judith Fenson
Editors

Contents

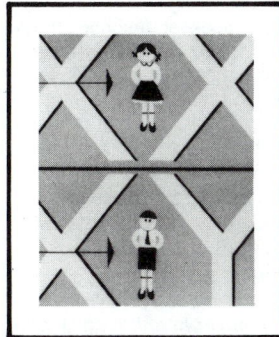

Unit 1

Genetic and Prenatal Influences on Development

Nine selections discuss genetic influences on development, reproductive technology, and the effects of substance abuse on prenatal development.

The concepts in bold italics are developed in the article. For further expansion please refer to the Topic Guide and the Index.

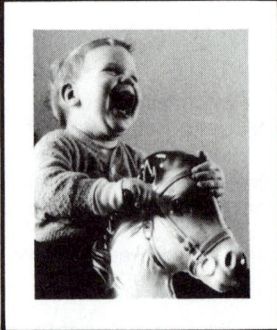

Unit 2

Development During Infancy and Early Childhood

Six selections profile the impressive abilities of infants and young children, examine the ways in which children learn, and look at sex differences.

The concepts in bold italics are developed in the article. For further expansion please refer to the Topic Guide and the Index.

Unit 3

Development During Childhood

Eight selections examine human development during childhood, paying specific attention to social and emotional development, cognitive and language development, and developmental problems.

The concepts in bold italics are developed in the article. For further expansion please refer to the Topic Guide and the Index.

Unit 4

Family, School, and Cultural Influences on Development

Thirteen selections discuss the impact of home, school, and culture on child rearing and child development. The topics include parenting styles, family structure, and cultural influences, as well as the role of education in social and cognitive development of the child.

Unit 5

Development During Adolescence and Early Adulthood

Six selections explore a wide range of issues and topics concerning adolescence and early adulthood.

Unit 6

Development During Middle and Late Adulthood

Seven selections review a variety of biological and psychological aspects of aging, questioning the concept of set life stages.

The concepts in bold italics are developed in the article. For further expansion please refer to the Topic Guide and the Index.

Topic Guide

This topic guide suggests how the selections in this book relate to topics of traditional concern to students and professionals involved with the study of human development. It is useful for locating articles that relate to each other for reading and research. The guide is arranged alphabetically according to topic. Articles may, of course, treat topics that do not appear in the topic guide. In turn, entries in the topic guide do not necessarily constitute a comprehensive listing of all the contents of each selection.

TOPIC AREA	TREATED IN:	TOPIC AREA	TREATED IN:
Adolescence/ Adolescent Development	33. Alienation and the Four Worlds of Childhood 37. Myth About Teenagers 38. Girls' Self-Esteem 39. Those Gangly Years 40. Much Riskier Passage 42. Jealousy and Envy: The Demons Within Us	Developmental Disabilities	8. What Crack Does to Babies 18. Miracle of Resiliency 22. Clipped Wings 23. Tykes and Bytes
		Divorce	1. Suffer the Little Children 27. Life Without Father 30. Children After Divorce
Aggression/ Violence	29. Children of Violence 31. Biology, Destiny, and All That	Drug Abuse	1. Suffer the Little Children 8. What Crack Does to Babies 22. Clipped Wings 40. Much Riskier Passage
Aging	45. Vintage Years 47. How Old Are You Really? 48. Don't Act Your Age!	Education/ Educators	1. Suffer the Little Children 12. Preschool: Head Start or Hard Push? 13. How Three Key Countries Shape Their Children 19. How Kids Learn 20. Head Start Does Not Last 23. Tykes and Bytes 32. Why Japanese Kids Are Smarter (or Are They?) 33. Alienation and the Four Worlds of Childhood 35. Tracked to Fail 36. Why We Need to Understand Science
Attachment	17. Your Loving Touch 18. Miracle of Resiliency 26. Can Your Career Hurt Your Kids? 44. Family Ties: The Real Reason People Are Living Longer		
Brain Organization/ Function	4. Mapping the Brain 15. Sizing Up the Sexes 46. On Growing Old		
Child Abuse	1. Suffer the Little Children 18. Miracle of Resiliency 28. Lasting Effects of Child Maltreatment	Emotional Development	14. Day Care Generation 16. The Good, the Bad, and the Difference 17. Your Loving Touch 26. Can Your Career Hurt Your Kids? 27. Life Without Father 28. Lasting Effects of Child Maltreatment 29. Children of Violence 30. Children After Divorce 31. Biology, Destiny, and All That 33. Alienation and the Four Worlds of Childhood 35. Tracked to Fail 37. Myth About Teenagers 40. Much Riskier Passage 42. Jealousy and Envy: The Demons Within Us 43. Myth of the Miserable Working Woman 44. Family Ties: The Real Reason People Are Living Longer
Cognitive Development	10. New Perspective on Cognitive Development in Infancy 18. Miracle of Resiliency 19. How Kids Learn 23. Tykes and Bytes 26. Can Your Career Hurt Your Kids? 31. Biology, Destiny, and All That 45. Vintage Years		
Competence	10. New Perspective on Cognitive Development in Infancy 11. The Child Yesterday, Today, Tomorrow 18. Miracle of Resiliency 29. Children of Violence		
Creativity	23. Tykes and Bytes	Erikson's Theory	48. Don't Act Your Age! 49. Prime of Our Lives
Culture	32. Why Japanese Kids Are Smarter (or Are They?) 34. Culture, Race Too Often Ignored in Child Studies	Ethics	6. Making Babies 34. Culture, Race Too Often Ignored in Child Studies
Day Care	1. Suffer the Little Children 26. Can Your Career Hurt Your Kids?	Family Development	14. Day Care Generation 17. Your Loving Touch 24. Same Family, Different Lives
Depression/Despair	29. Children of Violence 30. Children After Divorce 35. Tracked to Fail		

TOPIC AREA	TREATED IN:	TOPIC AREA	TREATED IN:
Family Development (cont'd)	25. Putting Children First 26. Can Your Career Hurt Your Kids? 27. Life Without Father 30. Children After Divorce 33. Alienation and the Four Worlds of Childhood 37. Myth About Teenagers 43. Myth of the Miserable Working Woman 44. Family Ties: The Real Reason People Are Living Longer	**Parenting (cont'd)**	41. Puberty and Parents: Understanding Your Early Adolescent
		Peers	33. Alienation and the Four Worlds of Childhood 41. Puberty and Parents: Understanding Your Early Adolescent
Fertilization/ Infertility	6. Making Babies 7. Sperm Under Siege	**Personality Development**	18. Miracle of Resiliency 31. Biology, Destiny, and All That 42. Jealousy and Envy: The Demons Within Us 49. Prime of Our Lives
Genetics	2. Gene Dream 3. New Genetic Code 5. Nature or Nurture? 7. Sperm Under Siege	**Piaget's Theory**	10. New Perspective on Cognitive Development in Infancy
High Risk Infants	8. What Crack Does to Babies 9. War Babies 22. Clipped Wings	**Prenatal Development**	7. Sperm Under Siege 8. What Crack Does to Babies 9. War Babies 22. Clipped Wings
Infant Development	10. New Perspective on Cognitive Development in Infancy 11. The Child Yesterday, Today, Tomorrow 14. Day Care Generation 17. Your Loving Touch	**Preschoolers**	12. Preschool: Head Start or Hard Push? 13. How Three Key Countries Shape Their Children 20. Head Start Does Not Last 30. Children After Divorce
Kohlberg's Theory	16. The Good, the Bad, and the Difference	**Psychoanalytic Theory**	33. Alienation and the Four Worlds of Childhood
Language Development	21. Now We're Talking!	**Self-Esteem/ Self-Control**	1. Suffer the Little Children 18. Miracle of Resiliency 31. Biology, Destiny, and All That 38. Girls' Self-Esteem 39. Those Gangly Years 42. Jealousy and Envy: The Demons Within Us 43. Myth of the Miserable Working Woman 44. Family Ties: The Real Reason People Are Living Longer
Learning	10. New Perspective on Cognitive Development in Infancy 12. Preschool: Head Start or Hard Push? 19. How Kids Learn 20. Head Start Does Not Last 21. Now We're Talking! 23. Tykes and Bytes 45. Vintage Years		
Love/Marriage	42. Jealousy and Envy: The Demons Within Us	**Sex Differences**	15. Sizing Up the Sexes 31. Biology, Destiny, and All That 48. Don't Act Your Age!
Maternal Employment	14. Day Care Generation 26. Can Your Career Hurt Your Kids? 31. Biology, Destiny, and All That 33. Alienation and the Four Worlds of Childhood 43. Myth of the Miserable Working Woman	**Social Skills/ Socialization**	27. Life Without Father 28. Lasting Effects of Child Maltreatment 42. Jealousy and Envy: The Demons Within Us 49. Prime of Our Lives
Mid-Life Crisis	48. Don't Act Your Age! 49. Prime of Our Lives	**Stress**	12. Preschool: Head Start or Hard Push? 27. Life Without Father 29. Children of Violence 30. Children After Divorce 33. Alienation and the Four Worlds of Childhood 35. Tracked to Fail 43. Myth of the Miserable Working Woman
Parenting	1. Suffer the Little Children 14. Day Care Generation 16. The Good, the Bad, and the Difference 18. Miracle of Resiliency 26. Can Your Career Hurt Your Kids? 27. Life Without Father 32. Why Japanese Kids Are Smarter (or Are They?) 33. Alienation and the Four Worlds of Childhood	**Teratogens**	7. Sperm Under Siege 8. What Crack Does to Babies 22. Clipped Wings

Genetic and Prenatal Influences on Development

Advances in our knowledge of human development are becoming increasingly linked to progress in the fields of genetics, biochemistry, and medicine. Among these frontiers of knowledge are new advances in our understanding of fertility. "Making Babies" describes some of these new findings, which are helping many childless couples achieve pregnancies. With new knowledge have also come a host of problems that society will have to confront, including those generated by new ways of detecting anomalies prior to birth and by improved methods for sustaining life in highly premature infants. Thirty years ago, prematurity generally referred to infants born no more than two months prior to the expected date. Today, infants born at far less than seven months gestational age are frequently brought to term with the assistance of biomedical technology. Unhappily, a substantial proportion of these children suffer from a range of serious medical problems. Many of these babies are victims of substance abuse. The effects of drug and alcohol use during pregnancy are also dependent on what stage of fetal development they were used. An in-depth look at what happens when crack crosses the placental barrier and the resulting damage to the fetus is described in "What Crack Does to Babies."

Until recently, the mother's life-style has been considered responsible for the health of the unborn child. However, as pointed out in "Sperm Under Siege," new findings suggest the father's sperm may also be affected by such factors as smoking, alcohol, drugs, radiation, and chemical exposure, all of which may lead to spontaneous abortion or birth defects.

Another long-term concern has centered on the effects of maternal malnutrition on the health of the growing fetus. The almost daily accounts of hunger in America have refocused attention on this issue. The article "War Babies" relays an absorbing tale of how researchers used public health records to assess the effects of varying degrees of maternal malnutrition in the besieged Netherlands during World War II.

Advances in genetics have created renewed respect for the role of heredity in human development. One hundred thirty years after Gregor Mendel discovered the rules of biological inheritance in "A New Genetic Code," genetics revolutionaries are showing that Mendel's laws can be broken. "The Gene Dream" describes a colossal new government-backed project that has as its target the mapping of the complete set of instructions for making a human being. This work promises to revolutionize the fields of medicine and biology and perhaps even psychology and sociology. Some scientists foresee the day when individuals can obtain a computer readout of their complete genetic makeup, along with a diagnosis, prognosis, and suggested treatment.

The three-part article "Suffer the Little Children, Shameful Bequests to the Next Generation and Struggling for Sanity" presents a forceful argument for a reordering of national priorities regarding the treatment of children in America.

The question of whether or not human behavior is controlled by genes or by upbringing is addressed in "Nature or Nurture?" There is no simple answer, and the debate goes on.

The role of the brain in personality development is explored in "Mapping the Brain." The article incorporates information about mapping the brain, brainteasers for the reader to try, and discussion of how various parts of the brain function to contribute to thought, language, and, most importantly for us, emotions.

Looking Ahead: Challenge Questions

Of the almost endless list of problems confronting the nation's children (as outlined in "Suffer the Little Children, Shameful Bequests to the Next Generation and Struggling for Sanity"), which ones seem most amenable to solutions? Which ones seem most intractable?

Almost every human development textbook lists the steps that pregnant women should take to promote healthy fetal growth. What steps should prospective fathers take? What are some factors that account for the dramatic increase in infertile couples today? What are some of the techniques that offer hope to these couples?

Consider your current beliefs about abortion, genetic engineering, and socialized medicine. How do you think these views would be challenged if you learned that your baby-to-be was expected to be profoundly retarded?

If manipulation of genetic material can prevent the appearance of physical dysfunctions, might not similar manipulations be used to engineer intellectual abilities, personality traits, or socially desirable behaviors? What factors would constrain a society that attempted to actively and explicitly practice eugenics?

Of the many issues raised in this section, for example, prenatal care, vaccination programs, sex education, prevention of child abuse, and so forth, which would you give the greatest priority to and why?

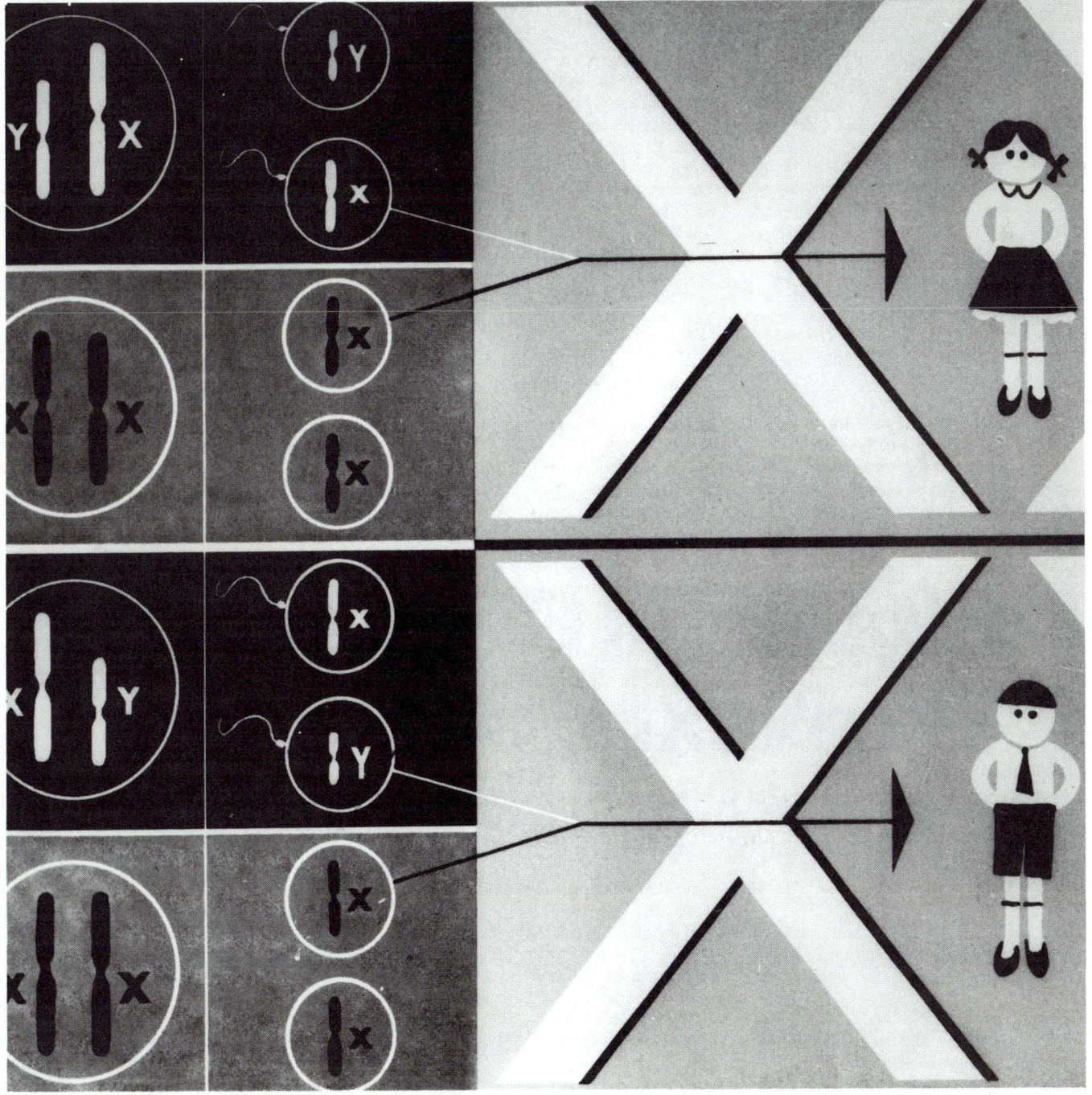

Suffer the Little Children

The world's leaders gather for an extraordinary summit and listen at last to a crying need.

Just how much is a child worth? To a father in northern Thailand, 10-year-old Poo was worth $400 when he sold her to a middleman to work in Madame Suzy's Bangkok brothel. To Madame Suzy, Poo is worth $40 a night while she's still young and fresh. But her price will soon come down.

To a quarry owner outside New Delhi, 12-year-old Ballu is worth 85¢ a day, the amount the child earns breaking rocks in an 11-hour shift. "I wanted to become an engineer," says Ballu. He glances sadly at his callused hands. "But now I have crossed the age for studies and will be a stonecutter all my life."

To local bosses in Mexico City, children are worth about $2.80 a day for scavenging food, glass, cloth and bones from three vast municipal dumps. The walls around the dumps enclose homes, families, even a church and a store. Many of the 5,000 children living there attend school in the dumps; they are not tolerated on the outside because of their smell.

Just how much is the very life of a child worth? A 10¢ packet of salt, sugar and potassium can prevent a child from dying of diarrhea. Yet every day in the developing world more than 40,000 children under the age of five die of diarrhea, measles, malnutrition and other preventable causes. An extra $2.5 billion a year could save the lives of 50 million children over the next decade. That is roughly equal, children's advocates note, to the amount that the world's military establishments, taken together, shell out every day.

Last weekend George Bush joined 34 other Presidents, 27 Prime Ministers, a King, a Grand Duke and a Cardinal, among others, at the United Nations for a meeting unlike any in history: the World Summit for Children. The leaders came to discuss the plight of 150 million children under the age of five suffering from malnutrition, 30 million living in the streets, 7 million driven from their homes by war and famine.

Shamed into action, the leaders endorsed a bold 10-year plan to reduce mortality rates and poverty among children and to improve access to immunizations and education. For once, this was more than a political lullaby of soothing promises; the very existence of the extraordinary summit held out hope to those who have fought to make children's voices heard. To lend support, more than a million people held 2,600 candlelight vigils earlier in the week—in South Korea's Buddhist monasteries, in London's St. Paul's Cathedral, in Ethiopia's refugee camps, around Paris' Eiffel Tower, in 700 villages in Bangladesh.

As the whole word directs its attention, however briefly, to those to whom the earth will soon belong, what kind of leadership can the United States offer? Americans cherish the notion that they cherish their children, but there's woeful evidence to the contrary. Each year thousands of American babies are born premature and underweight, in a country torn by neither war nor famine. The U.S. is one of only four countries—with Iran, Iraq and Bangladesh—that still execute juvenile offenders. And nearly 1 in 4 American children under age six lives in poverty. Congressmen wrestling with budget cuts, policymakers musing about peace dividends, voters weighing their options—all would do well to wonder what sort of legacy they will be leaving to a generation of children whose needs have been so widely ignored. And those needs go far beyond vigils and poignant speeches.

Shameful Bequests to The Next Generation

America's legacy to its young people includes bad schools, poor health care, deadly addictions, crushing debts—and utter indifference

NANCY GIBBS

 George Bush knows how to talk about children. With a sure sense of childhood's mythology, of skinned knees and candy apples and first bicycles, he campaigned for office in a swarm of jolly grandchildren and promised justice for all. In this year's State of the Union address, he mentioned families and "kids" more than 30 times—the electronic equivalent of kissing babies on the village green. "To the children out there tonight," he declared as he built to his finale, "with you rests our hope, all that America will mean in the years ahead. Fix your vision on a new century—your century, on dreams you cannot see, on the destiny that is yours and yours alone."

Forget the next century. Just consider for a moment a single day's worth of destiny for American children. Every eight seconds of the school day, a child drops out. Every 26 seconds, a child runs away from home. Every 47 seconds, a child is abused or neglected. Every 67 seconds, a teenager has a baby. Every seven minutes, a child is arrested for a drug offense. Every 36 minutes, a child is killed or injured by a gun. Every day 135,000 children bring their guns to school.

Even children from the most comfortable surroundings are at risk. A nation filled with loving parents has somehow come to tolerate crumbling schools and a health-care system that caters to the rich and the elderly rather than to the young. A growing number of parents with preschool children are in the workplace, but there is still no adequate system of child care, and parental leaves are hard to come by. Mothers and fathers worry about the toxic residue left from too much television, too many ghastly movies, too many violent video games, too little discipline. They wonder how to raise children who are strong and imaginative and loving. They worry about the possibility that their children will grow wild and distant and angry. Perhaps they fear most that they will get the children they deserve. "Children who go unheeded," warns Harvard psychiatrist Robert Coles, giving voice to a parent's guilty nightmare, "are children who are going to turn on the world that neglected them."

And that anger will come when today's children are old enough to realize how relentlessly their needs were ignored. They will see that their parents and grandparents have left them enormous debts and a fouled environment. They will recognize that their exceptionally prosperous, peaceful, lucky predecessors, living out the end of the millennium, were not willing to make the investments necessary to ensure that the generation to follow could enjoy the same blessings.

The natural case for taking better care of children would be made on moral grounds alone. A society cannot sacrifice its most vulnerable citizens without eroding its sense of community and making a lie of its principles. But having been left behind by a decade of political shortcuts, child advocates have adopted a more practical strategy. "If compassion were not enough to encourage our attention to the plight of our children," declares New York Governor Mario Cuomo, "self-interest should be." Marian Wright Edelman, the crusading founder of the Children's Defense Fund, goes further. "The inattention to children by our society," she warns, "poses a greater threat to our safety, harmony and productivity than any external enemy."

Spending on children, any economist can prove, is a bargain. A nation can spend money either for better schools or for larger jails. It can feed babies or pay forever for the consequences of starving a child's brain when it is trying to grow. One dollar spent on prenatal care for pregnant women can save more than $3 on medical care during an infant's first year, and $10 down the line. A year of preschool costs an average $3,000 per child; a year in prison amounts to $16,500.

But somehow, neither wisdom nor decency, nor even economics, has prevailed

with those who make policy in the state houses, the Congress or the White House. "We are hypocrites," charges Senator John D. ("Jay") Rockefeller IV, who is chairman of the National Commission on Children. "We say we love our children, yet they have become the poorest group in America." Nearly a quarter of all children under six live in households that are struggling below the official poverty line— $12,675 a year for a family of four.

In some cases the abandonment of children begins before they are even born. America's infant mortality rate has leveled off at 9.7 deaths per 1,000 births, worse

Between 1978 and 1987, spending on programs for the elderly rose 52%; spending on children dropped 4%

than 17 other developed countries. In the District of Columbia, the rate tops 23 per 1,000, worse than Jamaica or Costa Rica. Fully 250,000 babies are born seriously underweight each year. To keep these infants in intensive care costs about $3,000 a day, and they are two to three times more likely to be blind, deaf or mentally retarded. On the other hand, regular checkups and monitoring of a pregnant woman can cost as little as $500 and greatly increase the chances that she will give birth to a healthy baby.

Every bit as important as prenatal care is nutrition for the child, both before and after birth. "Of all the dumb ways of saving money, not feeding pregnant women and kids is the dumbest," says Dr. Jean Mayer, one of the world's leading experts on nutrition and president of Tufts University. During the first year of life, a child's brain grows to two-thirds its final size. If a baby is denied good, healthy food during this critical period, he will need intensive nutritional and developmental therapies to repair the damage. "Kids' brains can't wait for Dad to get a new job," says Dr. Deborah Frank, director of growth and development at Boston City Hospital, "or for Congress to come back from recess."

Congress understood the obvious benefits of promoting infant nutrition in the 1970s, when it launched the Special Supplemental Food Program for Women, In-

fants and Children. WIC provides women with vouchers to buy infant formula, cheese, fruit juice, cereals, milk and other wholesome foods, besides offering nutrition classes and medical care. It costs about $30 a month to supply a mother with vouchers—yet government funds are so tight that only 59% of women and infants who qualify for WIC receive the benefits. "A power breakfast for two businessmen is one woman's WIC package for a month," says Dr. Frank. "Why can't public-policy makers see the connection between bad infant nutrition, which is cheap and easy to fix, and developmental problems, which are expensive and often difficult to fix?"

The theme of prevention applies just as forcefully to medicine. This year the U.S. will spend about $660 billion, or 12% of its GNP, on medical services, but only a tiny fraction of that will go toward prevention. For children the most basic requirement is inoculation, the surest way to spare a child—and the health-care system—the ravages of tuberculosis, polio, measles and whooping cough. During the first 20 years after the discovery of the measles vaccine, public-health experts estimate, more than $5 billion was saved in medical costs, not to mention countless lives. And yet these days in California, the nation's richest state, only half of California's two-year-olds are fully immunized. Dallas reported more than 2,400 measles cases from last December through July, eight of them fatal, including one child who lived within six blocks of an immunization clinic.

Even parents who recognize the importance of preventive care are having a harder time affording it for their children. Most Americans over age 65 are covered by Medicare, the federal health-insurance plan under which the elderly—rich or poor—are eligible for benefits. Children's health programs, in contrast, are subject to annual congressional whims and budget cutting. Fewer and fewer employers, even of well-paid professionals, provide health benefits that cover children for routine medical needs. This means that health costs are the responsibility of individual parents, who make do as best they can, often at considerable sacrifice.

Some states and community groups are trying to help. Two years ago, Minnesota pioneered the Children's Health Plan to provide primary preventive care for children. The plan costs the state about $180 per child, but parents pay only $25: in the end everyone saves. Schools in Independence, Mo., established a health-care package to provide drug and alcohol treatment and counseling services for every child in the district. Cost to parents: $10 per child. In Pittsburgh 12,000 children have received free health care through a program crafted by churches, civic groups, Blue Cross and Blue Shield.

But too many kids are denied such care, and that starts a chain reaction. "You can't educate a child unless all systems are go, i.e., brain cells, eyes, ears, etc." says Rae Grad, executive director of the National Commission to Prevent Infant Mortality. A national survey in 1988 found that two-thirds of teachers reported "poor health" among children to be a learning problem. This is why Head Start, the model federal program providing quality preschool for poor children, also includes annual medical and dental screenings. But once again the money is not there: only about 20% of eligible children are fully served by the program.

Head Start and similar preschool strategies improve academic performance in the early grades and pay vast dividends over time. President Bush has promised enough funding to put every needy child in Head Start, which Congress says will require a fivefold increase by 1994 from the present $1.55 billion a year. Both the House and the Senate have approved higher funding levels, and lawmakers will soon meet to reconcile differences between the two bills. But as the deficit mounts, the peace dividend sinks into the Persian Gulf and the savings and loan crisis chews into basic budget items, politicians may have a hard time approving funding increases for a constituency that does not vote. Senator Orrin Hatch of Utah, a proponent of costly child-care legislation, says the outcome of the budget negotiations is "going to be terrible for kids."

Likewise, American society has, in the past generation, abandoned its commitment to providing a world-class system of secondary education. Education Secretary Lauro Cavazos himself calls student performance "dreadfully inadequate." From both the inner cities and the affluent suburbs comes a drumbeat of stories about tin-pot principals who cannot be fired, beleaguered teachers with unmanageable workloads and illiterate graduates with abysmal test scores. If they can possibly afford to, parents choose private or parochial schools, leaving the desperate or destitute in the worst public schools. Teachers, meanwhile, are aware that they are often the most powerful influences in a child's life—and that their job pays less in a year than a linebacker or rock star can earn in a week.

Across the board, people who deal with children are more ill-paid, unregulated and less respected than other professionals. Among physicians, pediatricians' income ranks near the bottom. In Michigan preschool teachers with five years' experience earn $12,000, and prison guards with the same amount of seniority earn almost $30,000. U.S. airline pilots are vigilantly trained, screened and mon-

itored; school-bus drivers are not. "My hairdresser needs 1,500 hours of schooling, takes a written and practical test and is relicensed every year," says Flora Patterson, a foster parent in San Gabriel, Calif. "For foster parents in Los Angeles County there is no mandated training, yet we are dealing with life and death." The typical foster parent there earns about 80¢ an hour.

In France, Belgium, Italy and Denmark, at least 75% of children ages 3 to 5 are in some form of state-funded preschool program

Worst of all is the status of America's surrogate parents: the babysitters and day-care workers who have become essential to the functioning of the modern family. In the absence of anything like a national child-care policy, parents are left to improvise. The rich search for trained, qualified care givers and pay them whatever it takes to keep them. But for the vast majority, child care is a game of Russian roulette: rotating nannies, unlicensed home care, unregulated nurseries that leave parents wondering constantly: Is my child really safe? "Finding child care is such a gigantic crapshoot," says Edward Zigler, director of Yale's Bush Center in Child Development and Social Policy. "If you are lucky, you are home free. But if you are unlucky, well, there are some real horror stories out there of kids being tied into cribs."

The U.S. economy has long been geared to two-income families; many families could not afford a middle-class lifestyle without both parents working. The real median income of parents under age 30 fell more than 24% from 1973 to 1987, according to a study by the Children's Defense Fund and Northeastern University. But social programs rarely reflect those economic realities. Growing financial pressure all too often translates into fewer doctors' visits, more stress and less time spent together as a family. Between 1950 and 1989, the divorce rate doubled: 1.16 million couples split up each year. That makes the need for reliable support services for children all the greater.

In place of responses came rhetoric: a 1986 Administration report on the family titled "Preserving America's Future"

called for a return to "traditional values," parental support of children and "lovingly packed lunch boxes." Time and again, Washington has failed to address the needs of working parents—most recently in June, when President Bush vetoed the family-leave bill on the ground that it was too burdensome for business. The bill would have allowed a worker to take up to 12 weeks a year of unpaid leave to care for a newborn, an adopted child or a sick family member.

That is abysmal compared with what other industrialized nations allow. Salaried women in France can take up to 28 weeks of unpaid maternity leave or up to 20 weeks of adoption leave, though they are less likely to need it since day care, health care and early education are widely available in that country. In France, as well as in Belgium, Italy and Denmark, at least 75% of children ages 3 to 5 are in some form of state-funded preschool programs. In Japan both the government and most companies offer monthly subsidies to parents with children. In Germany parents may deduct the cost of child care from their taxes. "Under our tax laws," observes Congresswoman Pat Schroeder of Colorado, "a businesswoman can deduct a new Persian rug for her office but can't deduct most of her costs for child care. The deduction for a Thoroughbred horse is greater than that for children."

If the troubles children face were all born of economic pressure on the family, then wealthy children should emerge unscathed. Yet the problems confronting affluent children are also profound and insidious. Parents who do not spend time with their children often spend money instead. "We supply kids with things in the absence of family," says Barbara MacPhee, a school administrator in New Orleans. "We used to build dreams for them, but now we buy them Nintendo toys and Reebok sneakers." In the absence of parental guidance and affirmation, children are left to soak in whatever example their environment sets. A childhood spent in a shopping mall raises consumerism to a varsity sport; time spent in front of a television requires no more imagination than it takes to change channels.

At Winchester High School in a cozy Boston suburb, clinical social worker Michele Diamond hears it all: the drug use, the alcohol, the eating disorders, the suicide attempts by children who are viewed as privileged. "Kids are left alone a lot to cope," she says, "and they sense less support from their families." Pressured to succeed, to "fit in," to be accepted by top colleges, the students handle their stress however they can. Some just dissolve their problems in a glass. In nearby Belmont, a juvenile officer finds that parents shrug off the danger. When their kids are caught drinking, he notes, "they say, 'Thank God it isn't cocaine. It's alcohol. We can handle that.' "

All too often it *is* cocaine, the poisonous solace common to the golf club and the ghetto. It is not only the violence of the drug culture that threatens children; it is also the lure of the easy money that turns 11-year-olds into drug runners. "Alienated is too weak a word to describe these kids," says Edward Loughran, a 10-year veteran of the juvenile-justice system in Massachusetts. "They don't value their lives or anyone else's life. Their values system says, 'I am here alone. I don't care what society says.' A lot of these kids are dying young deaths and don't care because they don't feel there is any reason to aspire to anything else."

Violence in the neighborhood is bad enough. Violence in the home is devastating. Reports of child abuse have soared from 600,000 in 1979 to 2.4 million in 1989, a searing testimony to the enduring role of children as the easiest victims. In New York City, half of all abuse reports are repeat cases of children who have had to be rescued before, only to be returned to an abusive home.

When two-year-old "Rebecca" accidentally soiled her underwear, her mother and the mother's boyfriend were not pleased. So they heated up some cooking oil, held Rebecca down and poured it over her. Then they waited a week or so before Rebecca's mother, unable to stand the stench of the child's legs, which were rotting from gangrene, took her to the hospital. After a month's stay that saved her legs, Rebecca was able to move to a foster home. From there she went to live with her paternal grandmother, who had plenty of room: all four of her sons were in state prison.

Around the country there are hundreds of thousands of other children who scream for help from overburdened teachers, understaffed social service agencies, crowded courts and a gridlocked foster-care system. To dismiss child abuse as a personal, private tragedy misses the larger point entirely. If children are not protected from their abusers, then the public will one day have to be protected from the children. To walk through death row in any prison is to learn what child abuse can lead to when it ripens. According to attorneys who have represented them, roughly 4 out of 5 death row inmates were abused as children.

A reordering of priorities toward protecting children would include far higher funding and staffing of Child Protective Services, the organization that investigates charges of abuse and can move to rescue children before the damage is irreparable. But even that would do little good if there is no place to put them. No solution will be possible without an overhaul of the foster-care system, which in many cities is on the verge of collapse. All too often, children are separated from siblings and shuttled from group homes to relatives to foster families, with no sense of the safety, security or stability they need to succeed in school and elsewhere. "If we don't have money for adequate care," says Ruth Massinga, a member of the National Commission on Children, "removing children from their homes is just another devastation."

Failure to make treatment available to drug addicts who seek it will ensure yet another generation of addicted babies and battered kids. In Los Angeles the number of drug-exposed babies entering the foster-care system rose 453% between 1984 and 1987. A survey of states found that drugs are involved in more than 2 out of 3 child abuse and neglect cases. Children born into a family of addicts are left with impossible choices: a life with the abusers they know, or a life at the mercy of a system filled with strangers—lawyers, judges, social workers, foster parents.

It is a common mistake to assume that all abuse is physical. The scars of other forms of abuse—like unrelenting verbal cruelty—can be just as apparent when children grow older, unloved and self-hating. "You can tell kids you love 'em, says April, a runaway in Hollywood. "But that's not the same as showing them. Broken promises is really what tears your heart apart." For April there is not much difference between insult and injury. "Beating kids will hurt kids. Sexual abuse will hurt a kid. But verbal abuse is the worst. I've had all three. If you're not strong enough as a person, and they've been telling you this all your life, that you can never amount to anything, you are going to believe it."

There have always been children who are survivors, who overcome the odds and find some adult—a teacher, a grandparent, a priest—who can provide the anchors the family could not. Touré Diggs, 18, grew up in a rough neighborhood of New Haven, Conn., and is now enrolled at Fairleigh Dickinson University. Since his parents separated three years ago, Touré has tried to help raise his brother Landis, who is 7. In the end Touré knows he is competing with the lure of the street for Landis' soul. "You got to start so young," Touré says. "It's like a game. Whoever gets to the kids first, that's how they are going to turn out."

Schools in particular have come to take that role very seriously, which accounts for the debate over how to teach values and self-discipline to a generation whose boundaries have been loosely drawn. But other institutions are slowly waking up to the implications of writing off an entire generation. The business community, in particular, wonders where it will find a trained, literate, motivated work force in the 21st century. The Business Roundtable, with representatives from the largest 200 companies, has made support for education its highest priority in the '90s. In Dallas, Texas Instruments helps fund the local Head Start program. Eventually, more and more companies may make parental leave a standard benefit, regardless of the messages coming from Washington.

In Des Moines business leaders are sponsoring a program called Smoother Sailing, which sends counselors like "Sunburst Lady" Toni Johansen into the city's elementary schools. National studies have shown that such support helps improve confidence, discipline and attitudes about school. With the extra funding, the city has been able to provide one guidance counselor for every 250 students, in contrast to a national average of one for 850.

But there will be no real progress, no genuine hope for America's children until the sense of urgency forces a reconsideration of values in every home, up to and including the White House. Polls suggest the will is there: 60% of Americans believe the situation for children has worsened over the past five years; 67% say they would be more likely to vote for a candidate who supported increased spending for children's programs even if it meant a tax increase.

When adults lament the absence of "values," it is worth recalling that children are an honest conscience, the perfect mirror of a society's priorities and principles. A society whose values are entirely material is not likely to breed a generation of poets; anti-intellectualism and indifference to education do not inspire rocket scientists. With each passing day these arguments become more apparent, the needs more pressing. Where is the leader who will seize the opportunity to do what is both smart and worthy, and begin retuning policy to focus on children and intercept trouble before it breeds?

—Reported by Julie Johnson/Des Moines, Melissa Ludtke/Boston and Michael Riley/Washington

(Article continues)

Struggling for Sanity

Mental and emotional distress are taking an alarming toll of the young

ANASTASIA TOUFEXIS

The dozen telephone lines at the cramped office of Talkline/Kids Line in Elk Grove Village, Ill., ring softly every few minutes. Some of the youthful callers seem at first to be vulgar pranksters, out to make mischief with inane jokes and naughty language. But soon the voices on the line—by turns wistful, angry, sad, desperate—start to spill a stream of distress. Some divulge their struggles with alcohol or crack and their worries about school and sex. Others tell of their feelings of boredom and loneliness. Some talk of suicide. What connects them all, says Nancy Helmick, director of the two hot lines, is a sense of "disconnectedness."

Such calls attest to the intense psychological and emotional turmoil many American children are experiencing. It is a problem that was not even recognized until just a decade ago. Says Dr. Lewis Judd, director of the National Institute of Mental Health: "There had been a myth that childhood is a happy time and kids are happy go lucky, but no age range is immune from experiencing mental disorders." A report prepared last year by the Institute of Medicine estimates that as many as 7.5 million children—12% of those below the age of 18—suffer from some form of psychological illness. A federal survey shows that after remaining constant for 10 years, hospitalizations of youngsters with psychiatric disorders jumped from 81,500 to about 112,000 between 1980 and 1986. Suicides among those ages 15 to 19 have almost tripled since 1960, to 1,901 deaths in 1987. Moreover, the age at which children are exhibiting mental problems is dropping: studies suggest that as many as 30% of infants 18 months old and younger are having difficulties ranging from emotional withdrawal to anxiety attacks.

What is causing so much mental anguish? The sad truth is that a growing number of American youngsters have home lives that are hostile to healthy emotional growth. Psyches are extremely fragile and must be nourished from birth. Everyone starts out life with a basic anxiety about survival. An attentive parent contains that stress by making the youngster feel secure and loved.

Neglect and indifference at such a crucial stage can have devastating consequences. Consider the case of Sid. (Names of the children in this story have been changed). When he was three months old, his parents left him with the maid while they took a five-week trip. Upon their return, his mother noticed that Sid was withdrawn, but she did not do anything about it. When Sid was nine months old, his mother left him again for four weeks while she visited a weight-loss clinic. By age three, Sid had still not started talking. He was wrongly labeled feebleminded and borderline autistic before he received appropriate treatment.

As children mature within the shelter of the family, they develop what psychologists call a sense of self. They acquire sensitivities and skills that lead them to believe they can cope independently. "People develop through a chain," observes Dr. Carol West, a child psychotherapist in Beverly Hills. "There has to be stability, a consistent idea of who you are."

The instability that is becoming the hallmark of today's families breeds in children insecurity rather than pride, doubts instead of confidence. Many

> **As many as 7.5 million children—12% of those below the age of 18—suffer from some form of psychological illness**

youngsters feel guilty about broken marriages, torn between parents and households, and worried about family finances. Remarriage can intensify the strains. Children may feel abandoned and excluded as they plunge into rivalries with stepparents and stepsiblings or are forced to adjust to new homes and new schools. Children from troubled homes used to be able to find a psychological anchor in societal institutions. But no longer. The churches, schools and neighborhoods that provided emotional stability by transmitting shared traditions and values have collapsed along with the family.

Such disarray hurts children from all classes; wealth may in fact make it harder for some children to cope. Says Hal Klor, a guidance counselor at Chicago's Lincoln Park High School: "The kids born into a project, they handle it. But the middle-class kids. All of a sudden—a divorce, loss of job, status. Boom. Depression."

Jennifer shuttled by car service across New York City's Central Park between her divorced parents' apartments and traveled by chartered bus to a prep school where kids rated one another according to their family cars. "In the eighth grade I had panic attacks," says Jennifer, now 18. "That's when your stomach goes up and you can't leave the bathroom and you get sweaty and you get headaches and the world closes in on you." Her world eventually narrowed so far that for several weeks she could not set foot outside her home.

The children who suffer the severest problems are those who are physically or sexually abused. Many lose all self-esteem and trust. Michele, 15, who is a manic-depressive and an alcoholic, is the child of an alcoholic father who left when she was two and a mother who took out her rage by beating Michele's younger sister. When Michele was 12, her mother remarried. Michele's new stepbrother promptly began molesting her. "So I molested my younger brother," confesses Michele. "I also hit him a lot. He was four. I was lost; I didn't know how to deal with things."

At the same time, family and society are expecting more from kids than ever before. Parental pressure to make good grades, get into college and qualify for the team can be daunting. Moreover, kids are increasingly functioning as junior adults in many homes, taking on the responsibility of caring for younger siblings or ailing grandparents. And youngsters' own desires—to be accepted and popular with their peers, especially—only add to the strain.

Children express the panic and anxiety they feel in myriad ways: in massive weight gains or losses, in nightmares and disturbed sleep, in fatigue or listlessness, in poor grades or truancy, in continual arguing or fighting, in drinking or drug abuse, in reckless driving or sexual promiscuity, in stealing and mugging. A fairly typical history among disturbed kids, says Dr. L. David Zinn, co-director of Northwestern Memorial Hospital's Adolescent Program, includes difficulty in school at age eight or nine, withdrawal from friends and family and persistent misbehavior at 10 or 11 and skipping school by 15. But the most serious indication of despair—and the most devastating—is suicide attempts. According to a report issued in June by a commission formed by the American Medical Association and the National Association of State Boards of Education, about 10% of teenage boys and 18% of girls try to kill themselves at least once.

Despite the urgency of the problems, only 1 in 5 children who need therapy receives it; poor and minority youngsters get the least care. Treatment is expensive, and even those with money and insurance find it hard to afford. But another reason is that too often the signals of distress are missed or put down to normal mischief.

Treatment relies on therapeutic drugs, reward and punishment, and especially counseling—not just of the youngster but of the entire family. The goal is to instill in the children a feeling of self-worth and to teach them discipline and responsibility. Parents, meanwhile, are taught how to provide emotional support, assert authority and set limits.

One of the most ambitious efforts to reconstruct family life is at Logos School, a private academy outside St. Louis that was founded two decades ago for troubled teens. Strict rules governing both school and extracurricular life are laid out for parents in a 158-page manual. Families are required to have dinner together every night, and parents are expected to keep their children out of establishments or events, say local hangouts or rock concerts, where drugs are known to be sold.

Parents must also impose punishments when curfews and other rules are broken. Says Lynn, whose daughter Sara enrolled at Logos: "My first reaction when I read the parents' manual was that there wasn't a thing there that I didn't firmly believe in, but I'd been too afraid to do it on my own. It sounds like such a cop-out, but we wanted Sara to be happy."

As necessary and beneficial as treatment may be, it makes better sense to prevent emotional turmoil among youngsters by improving the environment they live in. Most important, parents must spend more time with sons and daughters and give them the attention and love they need. To do less will guarantee that ever more children will be struggling for sanity. —*Reported by Kathleen Brady/New York, Elizabeth Taylor/Chicago and James Willwerth/Los Angeles*

THE GENE DREAM

Scientists are mapping our complete genetic code, a venture that will revolutionize medicine—and ethics.

Natalie Angier

Natalie Angier, *a New York City–based science writer, is the author of* Natural Obsessions: The Search for the Oncogene.

At first glance, the Petersons* of Utah seem like a dream family, the kind you see only on television. They're devout, traditional and very, very loving. Bob Peterson works at a hospital near home to support the family while he finishes up a master's program in electrical engineering. Diane, who studied home economics at Brigham Young University, is a full-time wife and mother. And her time is certainly full: The Petersons have five sons and two daughters, ranging in age from two to 13. (As Mormons, the parents don't practice birth control.)

The children are towheaded, saucer-eyed and subject to infectious fits of laughter. During the summer months, the backyard pool is as cheerily deafening as the local Y. Says Diane, "Our kids really like just spending time together."

Yet for all the intimacy and joy, the Petersons' story is threaded with tragedy. One of the daughters has cerebral palsy, a nerve- and muscle-cell disorder. The malady isn't fatal, but the girl walks with great difficulty, and she's slightly retarded.

*Not their real name.

Three of the other children suffer from cystic fibrosis, a devastating genetic disease in which the lungs become clogged with mucus, the pancreas fails, malnutrition sets in, and breathing becomes ever more labored. Thus far, their children's symptoms have been relatively mild, but Bob and Diane know the awful truth: Although a person with cystic fibrosis may live to be 20 or even 30, the disease is inevitably fatal.

"Right now, the kids don't act sick," says Bob. "They go on thinking, 'I have a normal life.' " But, he admits softly, " We know it won't last forever. If they do get bad, then we won't have a choice. We'll have to put them in a hospital."

The Petersons realize their children's ailments aren't likely to be cured in the immediate future, but they're battling back the best way possible. Bob, Diane, and their seven children, as well as the three surviving grandparents, have all donated blood samples to biologist Ray White and his team at the University of Utah in Salt Lake City. Scientists are combing through the DNA in the blood, checking for the distinctive chemical patterns present only in cystic fibrosis patients.

Their work is part of a vast biomedical venture recently launched by the government to understand all the genes that either cause us harm or keep us healthy. It's medicine's grandest dream: By comprehending the genome—the complete set of genetic information that makes us who we are—in minute detail, scientists hope to answer the most enigmatic puzzles of human nature. The effort is so immense in its scale and goals that some have called it biology's equivalent of the Apollo moonshot, or the atom bomb's Manhattan project.

In fact, it's the most ambitious scientific project ever undertaken; it will cost a whopping $3 billion and take at least 15 years to complete. By the time researchers are through, they will have deciphered the complete genome. They'll have drawn up a detailed genetic "map," with the size, position and role of all 100,000 human genes clearly marked. And they'll have figured out each gene's particular sequence of chemical components, called nucleotides.

Though there are only four types of nucleotides, represented by the letters A, T, C and G, spelling out all the combinations that make up our total genetic heritage will fill the equivalent of one million pages of text. "What we'll have," says Dr. Leroy Hood, a biologist at the California Institute of Technology in Pasadena, "is a fabulous 500-volume 'encyclopedia' of how to construct a human being." Nobel laureate Walter Gilbert goes so far as to describe the human genome as "the Holy Grail of biology."

 From *American Health*, March 1989, pp. 103-106, 108. Copyright © by American Health Partners and the author.

HUMAN GENE MAPS

The latest maps for chromosomes one through six show the location of genes associated with hereditary disorders.

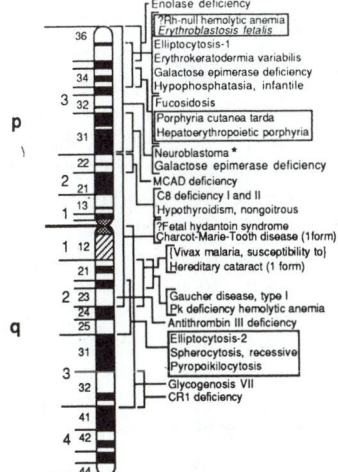

Enolase deficiency
?Rh-null hemolytic anemia
Erythroblastosis fetalis
Elliptocytosis-1
Erythrokeratodermia variabilis
Galactose epimerase deficiency
Hypophosphatasia, infantile
Fucosidosis
Porphyria cutanea tarda
Hepatoerythropoietic porphyria
Neuroblastoma *
Galactose epimerase deficiency
MCAD deficiency
C8 deficiency I and II
Hypothyroidism, nongoitrous
?Fetal hydantoin syndrome
Charcot-Marie-Tooth disease (1form)
[Vivax malaria, susceptibility to]
Hereditary cataract (1 form)
Gaucher disease, type I
Pk deficiency hemolytic anemia
Antithrombin III deficiency
Elliptocytosis-2
Spherocytosis, recessive
Pyropoikilocytosis
Glycogenosis VII
CR1 deficiency

Factor V deficiency

1

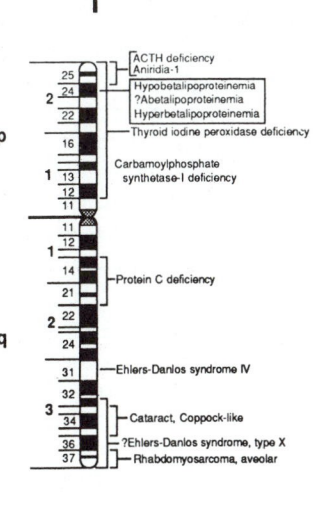

ACTH deficiency
Aniridia-1
Hypobetalipoproteinemia
?Abetalipoproteinemia
Hyperbetalipoproteinemia
Thyroid iodine peroxidase deficiency
Carbamoylphosphate synthetase-I deficiency
Protein C deficiency
Ehlers-Danlos syndrome IV
Cataract, Coppock-like
?Ehlers-Danlos syndrome, type X
Rhabdomyosarcoma, aveolar

2

☐   Allelic disorders (due to different mutations in the same gene)
[ ]   Nondisease
·   Cancers
■   Malformation syndrome
{ }   Specific infections with a single-gene basis for susceptibility
italics   Maternofetal incompatibility

Adapted from gene maps provided by Dr. Victor A. McKusick

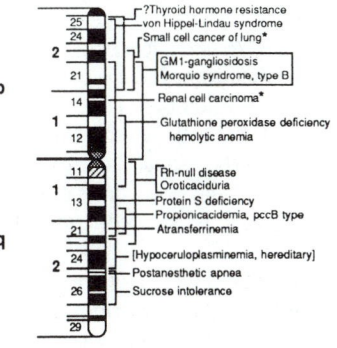

?Thyroid hormone resistance
von Hippel-Lindau syndrome
Small cell cancer of lung *
GM1-gangliosidosis
Morquio syndrome, type B
Renal cell carcinoma*
Glutathione peroxidase deficiency hemolytic anemia
Rh-null disease
Oroticaciduria
Protein S deficiency
Propionicacidemia, pccB type
Atransferrinemia
[Hypoceruloplasminemia, hereditary]
Postanesthetic apnea
Sucrose intolerance

3

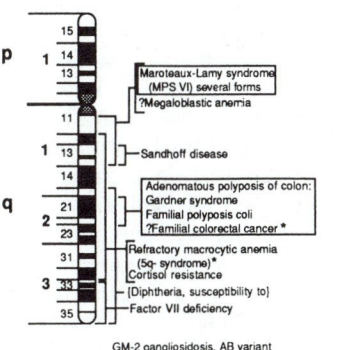

Huntington disease
PKU due to dihydropteridine reductase deficiency
Juvenile periodontitis
[Dysalbuminemic hyperzincemia]
[Dysalbuminemic hyperthyroxinemia]
Analbuminemia
[Hereditary persistence of alpha-fetoprotein]
Dentinogenesis imperfecta-1
?Acute lymphocytic leukemia
Mucolipidosis II
Mucolipidosis III
C3b inactivator deficiency
Rieger syndrome *
Dysfibrinogenesis, alpha, beta, gamma types
Sclerotylosis
Anterior segment mesenchymal dysgensis
Hepatocellular carcinoma *
Aspartylglucosaminuria

Pseudohypoaldosteronism

4

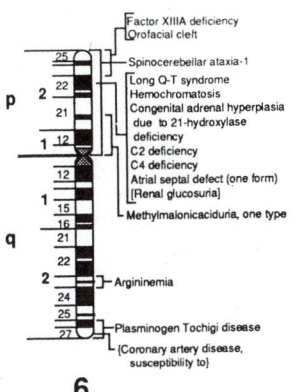

Maroteaux-Lamy syndrome (MPS VI) several forms
?Megaloblastic anemia
Sandhoff disease
Adenomatous polyposis of colon:
Gardner syndrome
Familial polyposis coli
?Familial colorectal cancer *
Refractory macrocytic anemia (5q- syndrome)*
Cortisol resistance
[Diphtheria, susceptibility to]
Factor VII deficiency

GM-2 gangliosidosis, AB variant

5

Factor XIIIA deficiency
Orofacial cleft
Spinocerebellar ataxia-1
Long Q-T syndrome
Hemochromatosis
Congenital adrenal hyperplasia due to 21-hydroxylase deficiency
C2 deficiency
C4 deficiency
Atrial septal defect (one form)
[Renal glucosuria]
Methylmalonicaciduria, one type
Argininemia
Plasminogen Tochigi disease
[Coronary artery disease, susceptibility to]

6

Some scientists, however, think their colleagues are chasing a will-o'-the-wisp. Current genetic engineering techniques, say critics, are too embryonic to attempt anything as massive as sequencing the entire genome. Dr. Robert Weinberg of the Whitehead Institute in Cambridge, MA, calls the whole project "misguided" and doubts that scientists will gain major insights even if they can sequence it.

Still, researchers involved in the Human Genome Initiative insist the knowledge will revolutionize the fields of medicine, biology, health, psychology and sociology, and offer a bounty of applications. Using advanced recombinant DNA techniques, scientists will pluck out the genes that cause the 4,000 known hereditary diseases, including childhood brain cancer, familial colon cancer, manic depression, Huntington's disease—the neurological disorder that killed folk singer Woody Guthrie—and neurofibromatosis, or Elephant Man's disease. Beyond analyzing rare inherited disorders, researchers will glean fresh insights into the more common and complicated human plagues, such as heart disease, hypertension, Alzheimer's, schizophrenia, and lung and breast cancer. Those studies will enable scientists to develop new drugs to combat human disease.

But the Genome Initiative is not restricted to the study of sickness. As biologists decode the complete "text" of our genetic legacy, they'll be asking some profound questions: Are there genes for happiness, anger, the capacity to fall in love? Why are some people able to gorge themselves and still stay slim, while others have trouble losing weight no matter how hard they diet? What genetic advantages turn certain individuals into math prodigies, or Olympic athletes? "The information will be fundamental to us *forever*," says Hood, "because that's what we are."

The most imaginative scientists foresee a day when a physician will be able to send a patient's DNA to a lab for scanning to detect any genetic mutations that might jeopardize the patient's health. Nobel laureate Paul Berg, a biochemistry professor at Stanford, paints a scenario in which we'll each have a genome "credit card" with all our genetic liabilities listed on it. We'll go to a doctor and insert the card into a machine. Instantly reading the medical record, the computer will help the doctor to put together a diagnosis, prognosis and treatment course. Says Caltech's Hood, "It's going to be a brave new world."

Coping with that new world will demand some bravery of our own. Once our genetic heritage has been analyzed in painstaking detail, we'll have to make hard choices about who is entitled to that information, and how the knowledge should be used. This technology is proceeding at an incredible rate, and we have to be sure that it doesn't lead to discrimination in jobs, health insurance or even basic rights, says Dr. Jonathan Beckwith, a geneticist at Harvard Medical School. "We don't want a rerun of eugenics, where certain people were assumed to be genetically inferior, or born criminals."

For better or worse, politicians are convinced that the knowledge is worth seeking. This year, Congress has earmarked almost $50 million for genome studies and, if current trends continue, by 1992 the government should be spending about $200 million annually. Opponents worry the price tag could leave other worthy biomedical projects in the lurch.

Even at that level of funding, the genome project could be beyond the resources of any single country. That's why research teams from Europe, Asia, North America and New Zealand have joined to form the Human Genome Organization. Among other goals, the newly created consortium plans to distribute money for worthwhile projects worldwide. Meanwhile, the Paris-based Center for the Study of Human Polymorphism distributes cell samples to researchers and shares their findings through an international data bank.

In this country, Nobel laureate James Watson, the co-discoverer of the molecular structure of DNA, is in charge of human genome research at the National Institutes of Health. And Dr. Charles Cantor, a highly respected geneticist from New York's Columbia University, has accepted the top spot at the Department of Energy's Human Genome Center.

THE GENETIC HAYSTACK

The Genome Initiative is sure to af-

fect everybody. Doctors estimate that each of us carries an average of four to five severe genetic defects in our DNA. The majority of those mutations are silent: They don't affect you. However, if you were to marry someone who carries the same defect, you could have a child who inherits both bad genes and is stricken with the disease.

Most genetic flaws are so rare that your chances of encountering another silent carrier are slim—let alone marrying and conceiving a child with such a person. But some defects are widespread. For example, five out of 100 people harbor the mutant cystic fibrosis gene; seven out of 100 blacks carry the trait for sickle cell anemia. Bob and Diane Peterson are both cystic fibrosis carriers—but they didn't realize their predicament until they gave birth to afflicted children.

For all the improvements of the last 10 years, prenatal diagnosis techniques remain limited. Doctors can screen fetuses for evidence of about 220 genetic disorders, but most of the tests are so time-consuming and expensive they won't be done unless family history suggests the child may have a disease.

One reason it's difficult to screen for birth defects is that most genes are devilishly hard to find. The 50,000 to 100,000 genes packed into every cell of your body are arrayed on 23 pairs of tiny, sausage-shaped chromosomes, which means that each chromosome holds a higgledy-piggledy collection of up to 4,400 genes. Scientists cannot look under a microscope to see the individual genes for cystic fibrosis, Down's syndrome or any other birth defect; instead, they must do elaborate chemical operations to distinguish one human gene from another. So daunting is the task of identifying individual genes that scientists have determined the chromosomal "address" of only about 2% of all human genes. "It's like finding a needle in a haystack," says Utah's Ray White.

Scientists must first chop up the 23 pairs of human chromosomes into identifiable pieces of genetic material and then study each fragment separately. To make the cuts, they use restriction enzymes—chemicals that break the bonds between particular sequences of nucleotides, the chemical components of genes.

Normally, restriction enzymes snip genetic material at predictable points, as precisely as a good seamstress cuts a swatch of fabric. But scientists have found that the enzymes also cut some fragments at unexpected places, yielding snippets that are longer than normal. It turns out that these variations are inherited, and many have been linked to certain genetic abnormalities. The fragments even serve as reference points for map-making efforts. The DNA segments produced by this technique are nicknamed "riff-lips," for restriction fragment length polymorphisms (RFLPs).

In the past three years, DNA sleuths have used the technique to isolate the genes for Duchenne muscular dystrophy, one of the most common genetic diseases; a grizzly childhood eye cancer; and a hereditary white-blood-cell disease commonly called CGD. But the technique remains labor-intensive and in some ways old-fashioned. Armies of graduate students and postdoctoral fellows do the bulk of the work, using tedious, error-prone methods.

Scientists everywhere are racing to build superfast computers to sort through chromosome samples and analyze RFLP patterns. Until they're devised, researchers are learning to make do. At White's lab, for instance, researchers have jerry-rigged a device that automatically dispenses exceedingly small samples of DNA into rows of test tubes. "It can do in two days what used to take a researcher two weeks," says a technician.

THE HAPGOODS BECOME IMMORTAL

Despite all the technology, the genome project remains deeply human—even folksy. That's because the people donating their blood and genes are from ordinary families who happen to have something extraordinary to offer. They're families like the Petersons, whose DNA may contain clues to cystic fibrosis.

Or they're families like the Hapgoods, whose greatest claim to fame may be their ability to live long and multiply. Brenda and Sam Hapgood,* a Mormon couple in their early 50s, are plump and boisterous, and love to be surrounded by people. That may explain why, although they have five

* not their real name.

girls, four boys, three sons-in-law, two daughters-in-law and five grandchildren, they wouldn't mind having a few more kids around. Says Brenda, "I almost wish I hadn't stopped at nine!"

The Hapgoods are one of 40 Utah families helping White construct a so-called linkage map of human DNA. He's trying to find chemical markers in the genome that are "linked" with certain genes. The markers will serve as bright signposts, dividing the snarl of genes into identifiable neighborhoods—just as road signs allow a traveler to pin down his location. Finding those markers is a crucial first step toward identifying the genes themselves, and for providing researchers with a decent chart of the terrain.

That's where the Hapgoods come in. To detect those tiny patches in the DNA that stand out from the background of surrounding genetic material, White must be able to compare the genomes of many related people over several generations. Mormon families are large, and they don't tend to move around much, so it's easy for White to get blood samples from many generations of a given family.

"The researchers told us there are lots of big families around," says Brenda. "What made us special was that all the grandparents were still with us."

In 1984, Brenda, Sam, their parents and nine children all donated blood to White's researchers. Lab technicians then used a special process to keep the blood cells alive and dividing forever—ensuring an infinite supply of Hapgood DNA for study. "Our linkage families are becoming more and more important as we go to the next stage of mapping," says Mark Leppert, one of White's colleagues. "Hundreds of researchers from all over will be using the information from their DNA."

"We're going to go down in medical history!" Brenda says excitedly. "But you know what I'm really worried about?" one son-in-law teases her. "They might decide to clone you!"

Another reason the Hapgoods were chosen for the linkage study is because, in contrast to the Petersons, they didn't seem to have any major hereditary diseases. White wanted his general-purpose map to be a chart of normal human DNA. Ironically, however, two years after the Hapgoods first donated blood, one of the daugh-

ters gave birth to a son with a serious genetic defect known as Menkes' disease, a copper deficiency.

The child is two years old but looks like a deformed six-month-old. He has 100 or more seizures a day. Half his brain and most of his immune system have been destroyed. Cradled in his mother Carol's arms, he moans steadily and sadly. "This is as big as he'll get," says Carol. "He'll only live to be four at the very most."

Carol and Brenda hope that the genome project will someday bring relief for Menkes victims. "We originally volunteered for the study to help the scientists out, to help their research," says Brenda. "But now we see that it could be important for people like us."

THE BIG PAYOFF

"You don't need to have the whole project done before you start learning something," says Dr. Daniel Nathans, a Nobel laureate and professor of molecular biology and genetics at Johns Hopkins University in Baltimore. "There are things to be learned every step of the way." The first spin-offs are likely to be new tests for hereditary diseases. Within one to three years, biologists hope to have cheap and accurate probes to detect illnesses known to be caused by defects in a single gene, such as susceptibility to certain kinds of cancers.

Another inherited ailment that could quickly yield to genome research is manic depression, which is also thought to be caused by an error in any one of several genes. The psychiatric disorder afflicts 1% of the population—2.5 million people in the U.S. alone—yet it's often difficult to diagnose. With the gene isolated, experts will be better able to distinguish between the disease and other mood disorders, explains Dr. Helen Donis-Keller, a professor of genetics at Washington University in St. Louis.

Of even greater relevance to the public, the Genome Initiative will give investigators their first handle on widespread disorders such as cancer, high blood pressure and heart disease. Researchers are reasonably certain that multiple DNA mutations share much of the blame for these adult plagues, but as yet they don't know which genes are involved. Only when biologists have an itemized map of the

genome will they be able to detect complex DNA patterns that signal trouble in many genes simultaneously.

As the quest proceeds, surprises are sure to follow. "There are probably hundreds or thousands of important hormones yet to be isolated," says Dr. David Kingsbury, a molecular biologist at George Washington University. Among them, he believes, are novel proteins that help nerve cells grow, or *stop* growing. Such hormones could be made into new cancer drugs that target tumors while leaving the rest of the body unscathed.

"I have an intuitive feeling that this is going to open up all sorts of things we couldn't have anticipated," says Donis-Keller. "Even mundane things like obesity and baldness—imagine the implications of having new therapies for them!"

The human genome also holds keys to personality and the emotions. Department of Energy gene chief Charles Cantor says it's estimated that half of our 100,000 genes are believed to be active only in brain cells, indicating that much of our DNA evolved to orchestrate the subtle dance of thought, feeling, memory and desire. "There are genes that are very important in determining our personality, how we think, how we act, what we feel," says Cantor. "I'd like to know how these genes work." Donis-Keller is also curious. "Is panic disorder inherited? Is autism?" she wonders. "These are controversial questions we can start to clarify."

Like the first Apollo rocket, the Human Genome Initiative has cleared the launch pad in a noisy flame of promise. Its crew is international, and so too will be the fruits of exploration. When the human genome is sequenced from tip to tail, the DNA of many people is likely to be represented—perhaps that of the Hapgoods and the Petersons, perhaps that of a Venezuelan peasant family. "It's going to be a genetic composite," predicts Yale professor of genetics Frank Ruddle. "The Indians will work on their genomes, the Russians on theirs, the Europeans on theirs. We'll pool the data and have one great patchwork quilt.

"I get a lot of pleasure out of thinking of this as a world project. No one single person will be immortalized by the research. But it will immortalize us all."

A New Genetic Code

The ABCs of DNA are changing radically. And that can bring tragedy.

SHARON BEGLEY

Puttering about the abbey garden 130 years ago, Gregor Mendel wasn't content to leave the birds and the bees to the birds and the bees. The Austrian monk carefully sprinkled pollen from a purple-flowered plant onto a white-flowered plant. He brushed pollen from a plant that grew wrinkled peas onto one that made smooth peas. He crossed whites with whites and purples with purples, smooth with smooth and wrinkled with wrinkled. Besides harvesting enough peas to turn the monks green and the abbey into allergen heaven, Mendel also discovered the rules of biological inheritance. His lessons were simple and, in their modern version, seemingly infallible. Babies inherit 23 chromosomes from each parent. Some genes (for blue eyes, say) are recessive and others (brown eyes) dominant; an offspring shows the recessive trait only if he inherits two copies of that gene and one of the dominant one. So went the rule book.

Well, even Newton had his Einstein, and now genetics revolutionaries are showing that Mendel's laws can be broken. Genes, it turns out, act so perversely they would have shocked the monk into a vow of perpetual silence. Mutant genes grow from one generation to the next like a sci-fi escapee, so that Grandma's tiny and innocuous mutation becomes Grandson's tragic birth defect. Genes costume themselves so that one inherited from Mom has a markedly different effect from the exact same gene inherited from Dad. "It's the sort of stuff that's just not supposed to happen," says geneticist and pediatrician Judith Hall of the University of British Columbia. "But it does."

The violations of Mendel's laws represent a true paradigm shift for genetics. They also have sobering clinical implications. Prenatal testing and genetic counseling both rely on Mendel's rules. Because Mendel wasn't 100 percent right, neither are they. Scientists don't know how often the rules fail "because we pick it up only when it leads to disease," says Hall. But the rules being violated are many:

■ **The Gertrude Stein rule.** A gene is a gene is a gene, says Mendelian genetics. But that was before researchers stumbled over "imprinted" genes a couple of years ago. It seems that some bits of DNA—genes strung along the chromosomes like beads on a string—can be marked, with the molecular equivalent of a pink or blue ribbon, as having come from a particular parent (diagram). For these genes, says Hall, "it makes a difference whether they are inherited from the mother or the father." (New molecular techniques can trace any gene in an individual to one or the other parent.) If the father's chromosome 15 is missing some DNA, for instance, his child will have the rare Prader-Willi syndrome, which is marked by mental retardation and growth abnormalities; if the mother is missing the same bit, the child will have Angelman syndrome, marked by more severe retardation, excess laughing and unusual movement. In other cases a paternal gene leaves the child healthy, but the identical maternal gene produces a birth defect. Psoriasis, diabetes and some forms of mental retardation all manifest themselves differently depending which parent they are inherited from. "It isn't nice and clean like it used to be," says Hall.

Even cancer may have a "parent of origin" effect. In some cases of a neck tumor called paraganglioma, patients inherited a bit of DNA on the chromosome 11 inherited from the father. Inheriting the identical bit from the mother doesn't cause tumors. Say a boy and girl, call them Dick and Jane, inherit the defective gene on chromosome 11 from their father; both develop the neck tumor. Jane passes the same gene she inherited from her father to her own children, but they don't develop the tumor: the gene came from a mother. But when Dick passes the DNA to his daughters, they do develop the tumor—the gene came from Dad. His daughters' children don't get the tumor.

How the sperm or egg gets tagged with these pink or blue bows remains a mystery. For eggs, at least, it happens when the child's mother is in the womb. That's when eggs form. A grandmother's exposure to chemicals, radiation or disease during her pregnancy, which affects her fetus's eggs, can affect her grandchildren's health.

■ **The stability rule.** Genes can mutate. But mutations are not supposed to grow like a loaf of bread with too much yeast. Yet consider Martha (not her real name), who has 50 copies of a particular snippet of DNA on her X chromosome (two X's make a girl a girl). Her daughter, Zoe, has 100 copies but is still healthy. Zoe's child has 1,000 copies—and is mentally retarded. Somehow, when the X was passing down through the generations, the dangerous bit grew like Topsy. In growing, it knocked out healthy genes; the more it grew the more healthy genes it toppled. "The same mutation, depending what gene it knocks out, can cause very different problems," says Dr. Haig Kazazian of Johns Hopkins medical school. "They could include manic depression, schizophrenia, coronary-artery disease and learning disabilities." So much for the conclusion of classical genetics that one mutation causes one specific defect.

■ **Federalism.** A cell supposedly has a strong central government. Its seat is the cell nucleus, and the laws are writ in the chromosomes within. But now geneticists find a rogue government in the hinterlands. The rebels are mitochondria, little bodies inside cells that generate energy to make muscles move, heart tissue contract, lungs expand. Each cell has hundreds of mitochondria. Each mitochondrion contains its own genes, which sometimes mutate. Mitochondria with mutant genes do not generate as much energy as normal mitochondria.

The trouble starts when the mutation hits a cell that is dividing to form, say, eggs. By chance, one egg may get the lion's share of mutant mitochondria. If it goes on to develop into a fetus, the child could grow up to have a disease of the heart, brain, muscle or other energy-guzzling organ. But that baby's sister, if born of an egg that happened to get very few mutant mitochondria, would be perfectly healthy. "Mendel's rules say that a single mutation should cause a single change and thus a single medical effect," says Douglas Wallace of Emory University. "But a mutation in mitochondria can have many different clinical effects, depending on what [percentage] of mutant mitochondria an individual inherits."

The effect also depends on what organs the mutants wind up in. When a fertilized egg divides and multiplies, the mutant mitochondria randomly go into one or another embryonic organ-to-be. If the nascent heart cells get a lot of mutants, for instance, the child will get heart disease. But if, in that child's brother, the mutants happen to go to the brain, the brother would have epilepsy. "Mitochondrial genetics defies everything you've ever learned about genetics," says Wallace. Among the diseases traced to mitochondrial mutations: adult-onset diabetes and blindness.

■ **Sexual equality.** According to the rules, children get their 23 pairs of chromosomes equally from Mom and Dad: one of each pair comes from Mom, the other from Dad. Now it turns out that both chromosomes of a pair

Mendel's Mistakes

The Sexual Equality Rule: Textbooks say each parent gives us one of each member of a pair of chromosomes. Turns out you can get two from mom and none from dad, and thus inherit a recessive disease like cystic fibrosis.

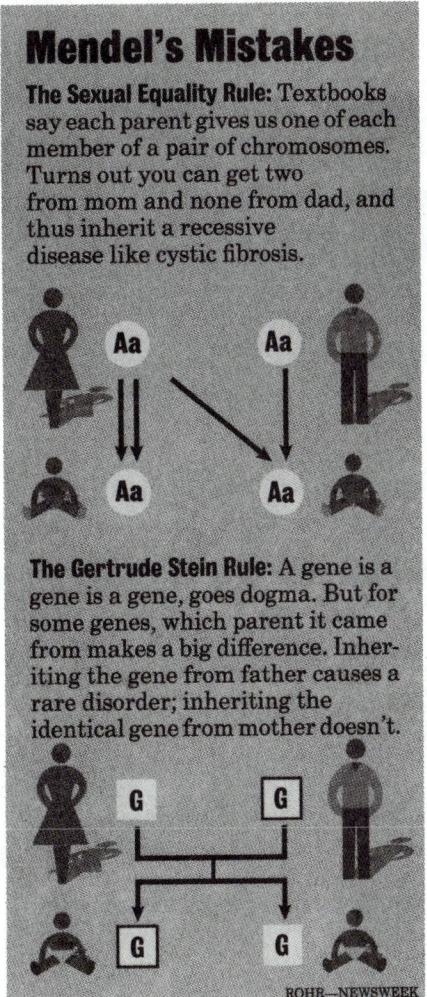

The Gertrude Stein Rule: A gene is a gene is a gene, goes dogma. But for some genes, which parent it came from makes a big difference. Inheriting the gene from father causes a rare disorder; inheriting the identical gene from mother doesn't.

ROHR—NEWSWEEK

can come from the same parent (diagram). Eggs and sperm are supposed to have just half of a human's requisite DNA per cell; when they fuse, the fetus has the right allotment. But sometimes an egg, or a sperm, has all the needed DNA; when it meets its mate, the embryo has too much DNA. Usually such an embryo aborts. But sometimes it survives, by shedding the extra DNA. If it's the DNA from the sperm that gets jettisoned, then the fetus grows with a double dose of maternal DNA.

And that can make genetic counselors look no wiser than palm readers. Say a couple is tested for cystic fibrosis. Joe doesn't have the gene; Carol has one CF gene and one normal gene. Since the normal gene masks the CF gene, she doesn't have CF. (As Mendel found, someone can show a recessive trait only if she has two of the recessive genes.) The counselor tells the couple that their child cannot inherit CF. But say the child inherits both chromosomes from Carol and, by chance, two copies of her disease gene. There is no healthy gene from Joe to defeat the CF gene. The child will have cystic fibrosis. At least five babies who "couldn't" inherit CF have recently been born with it.

Exceptions to Mendel's rules, and the heartbreak they cause, are probably rare. But then it took scientists more than a century after Mendel harvested his bumper crop of genetic laws to see that people are more complicated than peas. So far this genetics revolution has hit the lab more than the doctor's or counselor's office; researchers say practitioners hardly know what to make of it all. They should figure it out quickly.

MAPPING THE
BRAIN

With powerful new devices that peer through the skull and see the brain at work, neuroscientists seek the wellsprings of thoughts and emotions, the genesis of intelligence and language. They hope, in short, to read your mind.

If you have one of 1,000 test copies of this magazine, sometime while you read this article a specially embedded microchip will give you a mild electric shock. If you have an ordinary copy, there is no danger.

Deep inside your brain, a little knob-shaped organ no bigger than a chickpea is going like gangbusters right now (at least if you're the gullible type). The organ is called the amygdala, and when neuroscientists gave volunteers a version of this warning—that sometime during an experiment they might receive an electric shock—the nerve cells in the volunteers' amygdalae lit up like telephone lines during the World Series earthquake. How did the scientists know? They were reading their volunteers' minds—by mapping their brains.

It seems only fitting that, with 1492 in the air, one of the greatest uncharted territories in science is finally attracting its own cartographers. The terrain is the gelatinous three-pound world called the Brain, and the map makers' sextants are devices that stare right through the solid wall of the skull. The maps they are slowly piecing together will carry labels even more provocative than the 15th century's "Disappointment Islands." They will show, with the precision of the best atlas, the islands of emotion and the seas of semantics, the land of forethought and the peninsula of musical appreciation. They will show, in short, exactly where in the brain cognition, feelings, language and everything else that makes us human comes from.

It's called a functional map of the brain, and it is one of the grandest goals of what Congress and President George Bush have declared the "Decade of the Brain." The neuroscientists might actually achieve it, thanks to the technologies that open windows on the mind. With 100 billion cells—neurons—each sprouting about 1,000 sylphlike fingers to reach out and touch another, it's quite a view. "The brain is the last and greatest biological frontier," says James Watson, codiscoverer of the double helix that is DNA. In a book from the National Academy of Sciences released last month entitled "Discovering the Brain," Watson calls it "the most complex thing we have yet discovered in our universe."

To make sense of the jungle of neurons and swamps of gray matter, it won't be enough to take snapshots with, say, a CAT scanner. Computer-assisted tomography produces lovely pictures of brain structure, but can't distinguish between a live brain and a dead one. The challenge for brain cartography is to move beyond structure—all the cranial continents have been identified—to create a detailed diagram of which parts do what. For that, the map makers rely on an alphabet soup of technologies, from PETs to SQUIDs (page 20), that pinpoint neural activity in all its electrical, magnetic and chemical glory.

Each technique adds a different piece to the neural puzzle. Some magnetic imaging, for instance, is so spatially precise it can distinguish structures as small as a millimeter, but is much too slow to reveal the sequence in which different clumps of neurons blink on during a thought. But together, the technologies are yielding a map as detailed as that expected to be drawn for human DNA—though much more interesting. For instance, neuroscientists thought that the cerebellum was the patron saint of the clumsy, the region that controls balance and coordination and so keeps people from stumbling. New studies suggest that the cerebellum may also house the memory of rote movements: touch-typing or violin fingering may originate in the same place as the command not to trip over your own two feet. "Perhaps the brain can package a task very efficiently, even take it out of the conscious world [of the cortex] and just run the program unconsciously," speculates neurologist John Mazziotta of the University of California, Los Angeles. The mapping expeditions have also perked up philosophy. Once again, eminent thinkers are dueling over whether the mind is anything more than the brain.

The lofty abilities of the brain reside in the cortex, the quarter-inch-thick cap of grooved tissue that runs from the eyebrows to the ears. The cortex consists of two hemispheres, a left and a right, each composed of four distinct lobes (diagram, next page) and connected by a highway of fibers called the corpus callosum. Studies of patients with brain lesions, as well as electrical stimulation of conscious patients during brain surgery, have pinpointed scores of regions that seem to specialize in particular jobs. Some make sense of what the eyes see. Others distinguish irregular from regular verbs. But research on brain-damaged people always runs the risk that they aren't representative. The power of the new imaging techniques is that they peer inside the minds of the healthy. "They allow us to study how the living brain performs sophisticated mental functions," says neuroscientist Eric Kandel of Columbia University. "With them, we can address the most complicated questions in all science."

Some of the maps confirm what studies of brain-damaged patients had already shown. Last November, for instance, research-

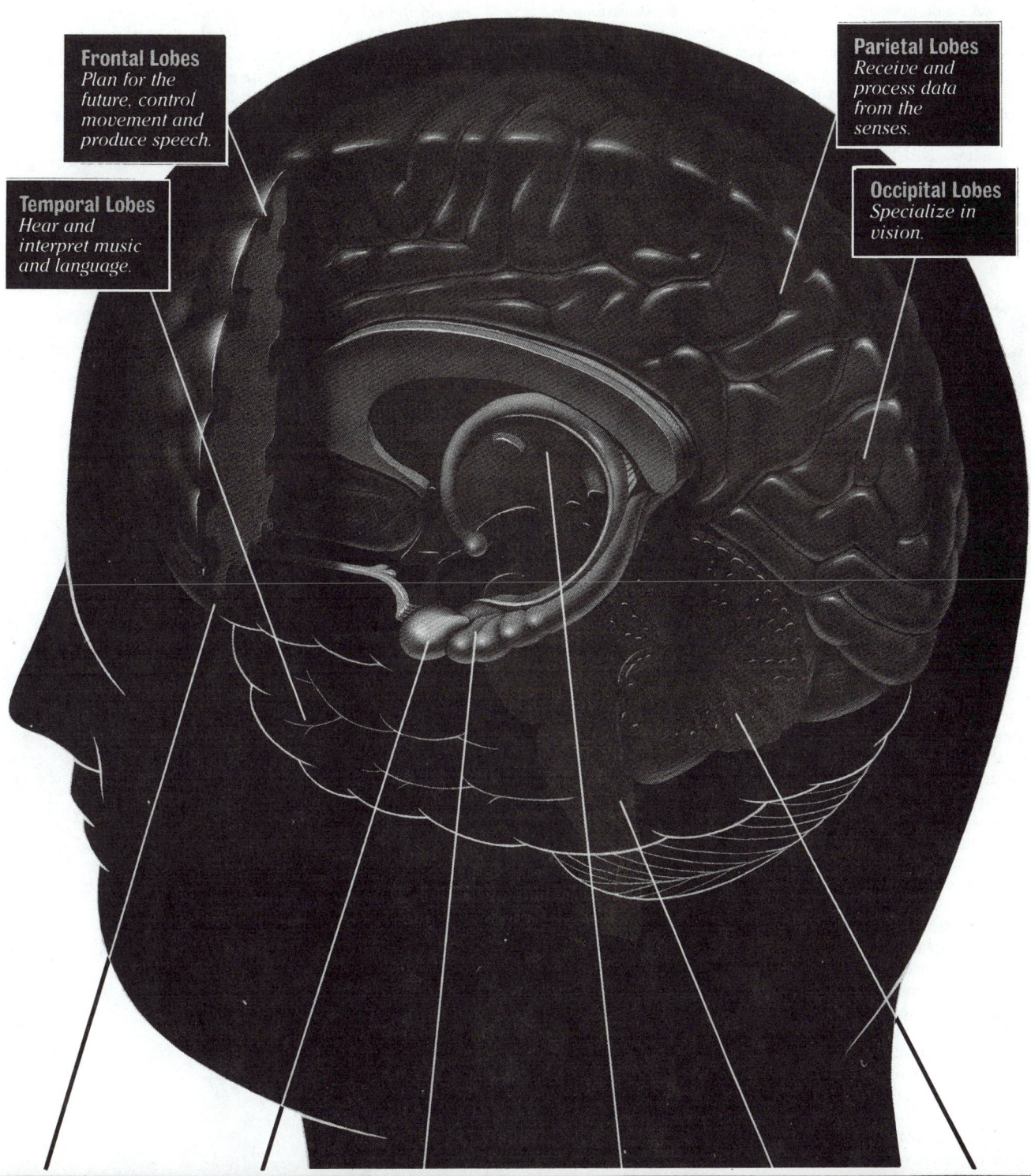

Frontal Lobes
Plan for the future, control movement and produce speech.

Temporal Lobes
Hear and interpret music and language.

Parietal Lobes
Receive and process data from the senses.

Occipital Lobes
Specialize in vision.

Cerebral Cortex
Covers the four lobes that make up the left and right hemispheres of the brain. It is just a few millimeters thick.

Amygdala
Generates emotions from perceptions and thoughts.

Hippocampus
Consolidates recently acquired information, somehow turning short-term memory into long term.

Thalamus
Takes sensory information and relays it to the cortex.

Brainstem
Controls automatic body functions like breathing. It is the junction between the brain and the spine.

Cerebellum
Governs muscle coordination and the learning of rote movements.

ers reported on a PET (positron emission tomography) study confirming that the hippocampus, a little sea-horse-shaped structure deep inside the brain, is necessary for forming and retrieving memories of facts and events (NEWSWEEK, Nov. 25, 1991). That's just what studies of amnesiacs had found. But while confirmation of old notions is nice, what the brain mappers really want is to stumble upon a Northwest Passage, connections that were totally unexpected, symphonies of neurons that had gone completely unheard. PET may do that. For a PET scan, volunteers are injected with radioactive glucose. Glucose, the body's fuel, mixes with the blood and wends its way to the brain. The more active a part of the brain is, the more glucose it uses. PET sensors arrayed around the head of a volunteer, who sits in a modified dentist's chair with his head behind black felt to keep out distractions, pinpoint the source of the radioactivity, and hence the heightened activity. They send the data to computers that produce two-dimensional drawings showing the neural hot spots.

PET is hardly the only technique to discover that the brain is organized in weird ways. Take music—as a team at New York University did. It has pioneered the use of the SQUID (superconducting quantum interference device), which senses tiny changes in magnetic fields. (When neurons fire, they create an electric current; electric fields induce magnetic fields, so magnetic changes indicate neural activity.) The device looks like a hair dryer from hell. When the NYU scientists aimed a SQUID at a brain listening to various notes, they found an eerie reflection of the black and white keys on a piano. NYU physicist Samuel Williamson and psychologist Lloyd Kaufman saw not only that the brain hears loud sounds in a totally different place from quieter sounds, but also that the areas that hear tones are laid out like a keyboard. "The distance between brain areas that hear low C and middle C is the same as the distance between areas that hear middle C and high C—just like on a piano," says Williamson.

In another unexpected find, brain systems that learn and remember faces turn out to reside in a completely different neighborhood from those that learn and recall man-made objects. The memory of a face activates a region in the right part of the brain that specializes in spatial configurations. The memory of a kitchen spatula, in contrast, activates areas that govern movement and touch. "What counts is how the brain acquires the knowledge," says neuroscientist Antonio Damasio of the University of Iowa College of Medicine. "The brain lays down knowledge in the very same systems that are engaged with the interactions"—in the case of a spatula, the memory resides in that part of the cortex that originally processed how the spatula felt and how the hands moved it.

Imagine four squares and form them into an "L." Now imagine two squares side by side. Fit the pieces into a smooth rectangle.

An area near the left side of the back of your head snapped to attention, especially if you're doing this without pencil and paper. It's one of the brain's centers for spatial reasoning—no surprise there. The astonishing thing is how hard it works. At the Brain Imaging Center at UC, Irvine, Richard Haier had volunteers play the computer game Tetris while in a PET scanner. In Tetris, players move and rotate squares, in various configurations such as an "I" or an "L," to create a solid block. This year, Haier found that people used lots of mental energy while learning Tetris, but after practicing for several weeks their brains burned much less energy—even though their scores had improved 700 percent. "Watching someone play Tetris at an advanced level, you might think, 'That person's brain must really be active'," says Haier. However, "[their] brains were actually not working as hard as when they played for the first time." Even more intriguing, the greater a volunteer's drop in the energy his brain used, the higher his IQ.

Intelligence, then, may be a matter of efficiency—neural efficiency. Smart brains may get away with less work because they use fewer neurons or circuits, or both. Conversely, when a less smart brain thinks, lots of extraneous or inefficient neural circuits crackle. Intelligence, in this model, is a function not of effort but of efficiency. Intelligence "may involve learning what brain areas *not* to use," says Haier.

One key to intelligence may be "pruning." At birth, a baby's brain is a rat's nest of jumbled neurons. It uses up more and more glucose until the child is about 5, when it is roughly twice as active as an adult's. Then glucose use and the number of circuits plummet until the early teen years. This is called neural pruning, and Haier speculates it's the key to neural efficiency. More intelligent people may get that way by more pruning, which leaves remaining circuits much more efficient. Might pruning explain the link between genius and madness? "Overpruning may result in the high intelligence often associated with creativity, but hyperpruning may result in psychopathology," suggests Haier. No one has a clue as to why some brains prune their circuits like prize bonsai and others let them proliferate

WINDOWS ON THE MIND?

Each scanning device has strengths and weaknesses. PET accurately tracks brain function, but can't resolve structures less than .5 inch apart. MRI can't detect function, but can distinguish structures even .05 inch apart.

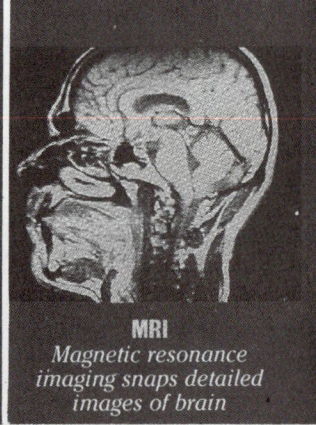

MRI
Magnetic resonance imaging snaps detailed images of brain

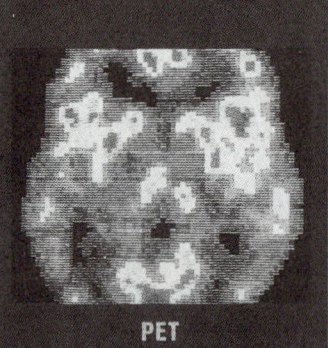

PET
Positron emission tomography tracks blood flow, a proxy for brain activity

SQUID
Superconducting quantum interference device picks up magnetic fields, a mark of brain action

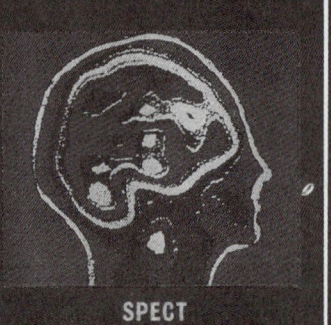

SPECT
Single-photon emission computerized tomography tracks blood flow, a sign of activity

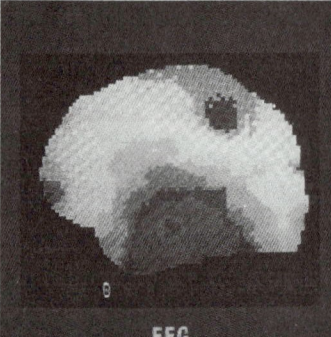

EEG
Electroencephalogram, an early brain-monitoring technique, detects electrical activity

like out-of-control wisteria. Edward Scissorhands, call Dr. Frankenstein.

Decide whether any words in this sentence rhyme. Now name an animal with a very long neck.

Your vision center, at the back of your head right behind your eyes, has been buzzing with activity as you read. That's to be expected. But until recently, scientists thought that all language skills—reading, writing and rhyming—were contained within a single brain circuit. They were wrong. Naming and reading are governed from two different places. You can thank several clusters of neurons scattered across the cortex for coming up with "giraffe"; that's where naming comes from. But these clusters are not necessarily involved in reading. Similarly, regions that process spoken language, midway back on the left side of your head, told you that no words in the sentence rhymed. That spot had been basically dormant until then: contrary to psych texts, words do not have to be pronounced in the mind's ear in order for the brain to assign them a meaning. In the new model, the brain processes

words by sight *or* sound. The result goes to the left frontal lobe, which imparts meaning to information received by either sense.

That finding undercuts psychologists' certainty that language is processed like a football play. Scholars had thought that to speak aloud a written word, the printed word had to pass from the visual cortex that saw it to the area that decoded it. From there, it was lateraled to the area in the frontal lobe that pronounces it. Touchdown! "The surprise is that when you see a word, and say it, it doesn't pass through the auditory part of the brain at all," says neuroscientist and PET pioneer Marcus Raichle of Washington University in St. Louis. "The old idea was that before you could say a word, the brain must change a visual code into a sound code. We don't see that at all." In fact, auditory areas of the brain are not active when one speaks, says Raichle: "You don't listen to what you say in the same way that you hear what others say."

Board. Tweal. Nlpfz.

Your visual cortex is still on the job, seeing words. But so are areas way outside the vision centers. To get at the great questions of language, Raichle and colleagues started small—with single words. As words flashed by on a computer screen, one per second, the PET volunteers' visual cortex lit up, as expected. But so did dime-size clusters of neurons way outside the vision centers, on the left side of the brain. Perhaps they hold the meanings of words. Call it Semantic Central. These same areas lit up when the volunteers saw nonwords that nevertheless obeyed rules of English— "tweal"—as if the brain were scrambling to assign a meaning to something that by all rights should have one. These semantic areas stayed dark when the volunteers saw consonant letter strings—*nlpfz*. Since babies aren't born knowing which letters form words and which don't, the brain has apparently learned what conforms to rules of English spelling and what does not. And it has carved out special zones that do nothing but analyze these rule-obeying strings of letters.

Supply a verb for each noun: pencil, oven, broom. And tell which animals in this list are dangerous: tapir, lion, lamb.

Two clusters in your cerebral cortex lit up. One, in the left frontal lobe, kicks in when the brain deals with meanings. But it gets bored easily. If you were asked to supply verbs for the same nouns, or analyze the same animals, over and over, the region wouldn't lift a neuron: it seems to play a role only "in the acquisition of a new skill, in this case linguistic," says Raichle. Then it bows out. The brain can still provide "write" for "pencil," but seems to do so on automatic pilot. In addition, to focus on the word problems, the "anterior cingulate gyrus" turns on, as it does whenever "subjects are told to pay attention," says Raichle. It also shines with activity when researchers ask volunteers to read words for colors—red, orange, yellow—written in the "wrong" color ink, such as "red" written in blue. Some neural arbiter must choose which processing center, that for reading "red" or naming blue, to activate. As the brain tries to resolve the conflict, the front of something called the cingulate cortex, located an inch or so beneath the center line of the front of the scalp, positively glows.

PETTING THE BRAIN

44.4
39.8
35.5
31.0
26.6
22.2
17.7
13.3
8.9
4.4
0.0
μmol/100gm/min

LEARNING
The brain of a novice computer-game player (left) is very active; with practice, the brain uses less energy

61.8
54.9
48.1
41.2
34.3
27.5
20.6
13.7
6.9
0.0
μmol/100gm/min

MENTAL RETARDATION
The brain of a retarded patient (left) is much more active than that of a normal volunteer

36.6
33.2
29.8
26.4
23.0
19.6
16.2
12.8
9.4

DEPRESSION
The brain of a clinically depressed person shows less activity (right) than that of a healthy person

Scans make it clear that the brain is a society of specialists. Different grape-size regions process proper but not common nouns, for instance. Not only that, separate zones also harbor tiny fragments of a larger idea, says Antonio Damasio. It can be an idea as lofty as Truth or as mundane as silver candlesticks. The Ph.D.s haven't figured out Truth yet, but they think they have a pretty good idea how your mind's eye sees the candlestick. PET scans show that these fragments come together in time but not in space, thanks to an as-yet-undiscovered maestro that takes the disparate tones and melds them into perfect harmony.

1. GENETIC AND PRENATAL INFLUENCES

Fragments of knowledge are scattered around the brain, especially in the back of the cortex. Areas closer to the front contain what Damasio calls "combinatorial codes," which assemble information from the rear. Damasio has christened these "convergence zones"; their location varies from one person to the next. A convergence zone recalls where in the back office the different attributes of the candlestick are stored. When it's time to reconstruct the silver candlestick, the convergence zone activates all the relevant storage sites simultaneously. One bundle of nerves sends in a pulse that means "silver," another shoots out "cylinder shaped," another offers "burns." "Our sensory experiences happen in different places," says Damasio. "There must be an area where the facts converge."

PETs have seen clues to convergence zones in people who, because of brain lesions, cannot name famous faces. They register a flicker of recognition, but deny they know whose face it is. The knowledge exists, says Damasio, but is "unavailable to consciousness." The lesion has apparently disrupted the links between the memories for various parts of a face—the shapes of its features, the tone of its skin—tucked away in the right part of the cortex and the memory of the name in another back office. The fragments remain, but the convergence zone cannot bring them together.

Sing "Row, Row, Row Your Boat." Lift your finger when you come to a four-letter word.

If you're female, tiny spots on both sides of your brain light up. If you're male, only one side does. That's the kind of map Cecile Naylor of the Bowman Gray School of Medicine saw when she scanned brains of people who had been marked with a radioactive tracer that homes in on active areas. In one task, they listened to words and raised a finger when they heard one four letters long. Women's mental acrobatics were all over the brain; men's were compartmentalized. In women but not in men, some areas associated with vision lit up. "You wonder if females are using more of a visual strategy than males," says Naylor. Perhaps they see the spelled word in their mind's eye and then count letters.

New windows into the brain are ready to open. Robert Turner of the National Institutes of Health recalls "the awe-inspiring experience" of lying inside a colossal MRI (magnetic resonance imaging) magnet as images flashed on and off before his eyes. The machine recorded changes in his brain that came 50 milliseconds apart. "You can see different areas light up at different times," marvels Turner. NYU uses five SQUIDs to spy on the brain; the Japanese are hard at work on a 200-SQUID array. At Massachusetts General Hospital, researchers are putting the finishing touches on "ecoplanar MRI," which snaps a picture of the brain in just 45 milliseconds. The brain's cartographers are poised to glimpse thoughts, feelings and memories as they spring from one tiny clump of cells, ignite others and blossom into an idea or a passion, a creative leap or a unique insight. When they do, science may truly have read the mind.

SHARON BEGLEY *in St. Louis with* LYNDA WRIGHT *in Los Angeles,* VERNON CHURCH *in New York and* MARY HAGER *in Washington*

NATURE OR NURTURE?

■

Old chestnut, new thoughts

Few questions of human behaviour are more controversial than this: are people programmed by their genes, or by their upbringing? There is no simple answer, but the academic world is starting to hear a lot more from the genes brigade—on both sides of the political spectrum

ARE criminals born or made? Is homosexuality a preference or a predisposition? Do IQ tests measure innate abilities or acquired skills?

For the past 50 years, respectable academic opinion, whenever it has deigned to deal with such layman's questions, has come down firmly for nurture over nature. Nazism discredited even the mildest attempts to produce genetic explanations of human affairs. And economic growth after the second world war encouraged most western governments to imagine that they could eliminate social problems by a mixture of enlightened planning and generous spending—that, in effect, they could steer (even change) human nature.

In this atmosphere, the social sciences flourished as never before. Sociologists made lucrative careers producing "nurture" explanations of everything from school failure to schizophrenia. Geneticists stuck to safe subjects such as fruit flies and honey bees, rather than risk being accused of a fondness for jackboots and martial music.

The fashion is beginning to change. The failure of liberal reforms to deliver the Great Society has cast doubt on the proposition that better nurture can deliver better nature. The failure of sociologists to find even a few of the purported (Freudian or social) causes of schizophrenia, homosexuality, sex differences in criminal tendencies and the like has undermined their credibility. And a better understanding of how genes work has made it possible for liberals who still believe in the perfectibility of man to accept genetic explanations. In at least one case—homosexuality—it is now the liberals who espouse nature and their opponents who point to nurture.

The pro-nature people are still a minority in universities. But they are a productive and increasingly vocal minority—and one which is beginning to increase its influence in the media. Open the American newspapers and you can read left-inclined pundits like Micky Kaus arguing that income inequality is partly the result of genetic differences. Turn on the television and you can see intelligent, unbigoted people claiming that male homosexuals have a different brain structure from heterosexual men.

This is only the beginning. Richard Herrnstein, a professor of psychology at Harvard University, and Charles Murray, a controversial critic of the welfare state, are collaborating on a study of the implications of biological differences for public policy. The book will highlight the tension between America's egalitarian philosophy and the unequal distribution of innate abilities.

The reaction of orthodox opinion has been scathing. America's National Institutes of Health provoked such an angry response to its decision to finance a conference on genetics and crime that it decided to withdraw the money. Mr Murray lost the patronage of the Manhattan Institute, a New York-based think-tank, when he decided to study individual differences and social policy.

Even in these days of politically correct fetishes, on no other subject is the gulf between academics and ordinary people so wide. Even the most hopeful of parents know that the sentiment "all men are created equal" is a pious dream rather than a statement of fact. They know full well that, say, one of their sons is brighter, or more musical or more athletic than another; they see, despite their best attentions, that girls turn every toy into a doll and boys turn every toy into a weapon; they rarely persist in believing that each and all of these differences is the result of early encouragement or training. They know that even if full equality of opportunity could be guaranteed, equality of outcome could not. Ability is not evenly distributed.

But parents' opinions are unscientific. Not until 1979 did a few academics begin to catch up. In that year the Minnesota Centre for Twin and Adoption Research began to contact more than 100 sets of twins and triplets who had been separated at birth and reared apart, mostly in the United States and Britain.

The centre subjected each pair to thorough psychological and physiological tests. If two twins are identical (or "monozygotic"), any differences between them are due to the environment they were reared in; so a measure of heritability can be attached to various mental features. The study concluded that about 70% of the variance in IQ was explained by genetic factors. It also found that on a large number of measures of personality and temperament—notably personal interests and social attitudes—identical twins reared apart are about as similar as identical twins reared together.

The Minnesota study represents the respectable end of an academic spectrum that stretches all the way through to outright racists. If IQ is 70% inherited, then perhaps much of the IQ difference between races is also inherited. The logic does not necessarily follow, since the differences could all lie in the 30% that is nurture; but still it is a hypothesis worth testing—at least for those prepared to risk being called politically incorrect.

Unfortunately, because there are no black-white pairs of identical twins, nobody has yet found a way to test whether racial differences in IQ are genetic. It would require getting 100 pairs of black parents and 100 pairs of white parents to rear their children on identical incomes in an identical suburb and send the children of 50 of each to the same good school and 50 of each to a bad one. Impossible.

This means that racial differences in IQ tend to attract scientists with dubious motives and methods. With increasing enthusiasm over the past decade, some psychologists have disinterred a technique already consigned to the attic by their Victorian predecessors: using physiological data to measure intellectual skill.

Arthur Jensen, a professor of educational psychology at the University of California, Berkeley, has assembled a large body of results purportedly demonstrating that IQ is closely correlated with speed of reaction, a theory abandoned around 1900. He claims that intelligence is correlated with the rate at which glucose is consumed in the brain, the speed of neural transmission and a large number of anatomical variables such as height, brain size and even head size.

Jean Philippe Rushton, a professor of psychology at the University of Western Ontario, Canada, has revived craniometry, the Victorian attempt to correlate head size with brain power. (In "The Adventure of the Blue Carbuncle", one of Arthur Conan Doyle's most ingenious Christmas stories, Sherlock Holmes deduces that a man is an intellectual from the size of his hat: "It is a question of cubic capacity . . . a man with so large a brain must have something in it.")

Mr Rushton has studied data on the head sizes of thousands of American servicemen, gathered to make sure that army helmets fit. Adjusting the raw data for variables such as body size, he argues that men have bigger craniums than women, that the well-educated have bigger craniums than the less educated, and that orientals have bigger craniums than whites, who have bigger craniums than blacks.

Mr Rushton has done wonders for the protest industry. David Peterson, a former premier of Ontario, called for his dismissal. Protesters likened him to the Nazis and the Ku Klux Klan. The Ontario Provincial police even launched an investigation into his work. An embarrassed university establishment required Mr Rushton to give his lectures on videotape.

Even if you could conclude that blacks have lower IQs than whites after the same education, it is not clear what the policy prescription would be. Presumably, it would only add weight to the argument for positive discrimination in favour of blacks, so as to redress an innate inferiority with a better education. The "entitlement liberalism" that prevails in American social policy and finds its expression in employment quotas and affirmative-action programmes already assumes that blacks need preferential rather than equal treatment. Indeed, to this way of thinking, merit is less important than eliminating group differences and promoting social integration.

The gene of Cain

Compared with the study of racial differences, the study of the genetics of criminality is only slightly more respectable. Harvard's Mr Herrnstein teamed up in the early 1980s with James Wilson, a political scientist, to teach a class on crime. The result was "Crime and Human Nature" (1985), a bulky book which argues that the best explanation for a lot of predatory criminal behaviour—particularly assault and arson—may be biological rather than sociological.

Certainly, a Danish study of the children of criminals adopted into normal households lends some support to the idea that a recidivist criminal's son is more likely to be a criminal than other sons brought up in the same household. But Mr Herrnstein and Mr Wilson then spoil their case with another Victorian throwback to "criminal types"—people with low verbal intelligence and "mesomorphic" (short and muscular) bodies who, they believe, are more likely to be criminal.

One reason such work strikes horror into sociologists is that it suggests an obvious remedy: selective breeding. Mr Herrnstein has suggested that the greater fertility of stupid people means that the wrong kind of selective breeding is already at work and may be responsible for falling academic standards. "We ought to bear in mind", Mr Herrnstein ruminates gloomily about America, "that in not too many generations differential fertility could swamp the effects of anything else we may do about our economic standing in the world." Luckily for Mr Herrnstein, studies reveal that, despite teenage parents in the inner cities, people of high social status are still outbreeding those of low social status. Rich men have more surviving children—not least because they tend to have more wives—than poor men.

In one sense, it is plain that criminality is innate: men resort to it far more than women. Martin Daly and Margo Wilson, of McMaster University in Canada, have compared the homicide statistics of England and Wales with those of Chicago. In both cases, the graphs are identical in shape, with young men 30 times as likely as women of all ages to commit homicide. It is perverse to deny the connection between testosterone and innate male aggressiveness. But it is equally perverse to ignore the fact that the scales of the two graphs are utterly different: young men in Chicago are 30 times as likely to kill as young men in England and Wales—which has nothing to do with nature and much to do with nurture. The sexual difference is nature; the national difference is nurture.

The most successful assault on the nurturist orthodoxy, however, has come not over race, or intelligence, or crime, but over sex. In the 1970s the nurturists vigorously repulsed an attack on their cherished beliefs by the then fledgling discipline of sociobiology. Sociobiology is the study of how animal behaviour evolves to fit function in the same way that anatomy does.

When sociobiologists started to apply the same ideas to human beings, principally through Edward Wilson of Harvard University, a furore broke out. Most of them retreated, as geneticists had done, to study animals again. Anthropologists insisted that their subject, mankind, was basically different from animals because it was not born with its behaviour but learnt it.

In the past few years, however, a new assault from scientists calling themselves Darwinian psychologists has largely refuted that argument. Through a series of experiments and analyses, they have asserted that (a) much sophisticated behaviour is not taught, but develops autonomously; and (b) learning is not the opposite of instinct, but is itself a highly directed instinct.

The best example of this is language. In 1957 Noam Chomsky of the Massachusetts Institute of Technology (MIT) argued that all human languages bear a striking underlying similarity. He called this "deep structure", and argued it was innate and not learnt. In recent years Steven Pinker of MIT and Paul Bloom of the University of Arizona have taken this idea further. They argue that human beings have a "language organ", specially designed for learning grammatical language. It includes a series of highly specific inbuilt assumptions that enable them to learn grammar from examples, without ever being taught.

Hence the tendency to learn grammatical language is human nature. But a child reared in isolation does not start to speak Hebrew unaided. Vocabulary, and accent, are obviously 100% nurture. In this combination of nature and nurture, argue the Darwinian psychologists, language is typical of most human traits. Learning is not the opposite of instinct; people have innate instincts to learn certain things and not others.

This is heresy to sociologists and anthropologists, who have been reared since Emile Durkheim to believe the human mind is a *tabula rasa*—a blank slate upon which any culture can be written. To this, John Tooby and Leda Cosmides of the University of California at Santa Barbara, two leading thinkers on the subject, have replied: "The assertion that 'culture' explains human variation will be taken seriously when there are reports of women war parties raiding villages to capture men as husbands."

Nor will the Darwinian psychologists concede that to believe in nature is to be a Hobbesian fatalist and that to believe in nurture is to be a Rousseau-ist believer in the perfectibility of man. Many totalitarians are actually nurturists: they believe that rearing people to worship Stalin works. History suggests otherwise.

The making of macho
Physiologists have also begun to add weight to the nature side of the scale with their discovery of how the brain develops. The brain of a fetus is altered by the child's genes, by its and its mother's hormones and, after birth, by its learning. Many of the changes are permanent; so as far as the adult is concerned, they are all "nature", though many are not genetic. For example, the human brain is feminine unless acted upon by male hormones during two bursts—one in the womb and another at puberty. The hormone is nurture, in the sense that it can be altered by

injections or drugs taken by the mother. But it is nature in the sense that it is a product of the body's biology.

This discovery has gradually altered the views of many psychologists about sex and education. An increasing number recognise that the competitiveness, roughness, mathematical ability and spatial skills of boys are the product of their biology (genes and hormones) not their family, and that the character-reading, verbal, linguistic and emotional interest and skills of girls are also biological. Hence girls get a better early education when kept away from boys. This conclusion, anathema to most practising educational psychologists, is increasingly common among those who actually do research on it.

Indeed, radical feminism is increasingly having to recognize the biological theme that underlies its claims. Feminists demand equality of opportunity, but they also routinely argue that women bring different qualities to the world: consensus-seeking, uncompetitive, caring, gentle qualities that inherently domineering men lack. Women, they argue, should be in Parliament or Congress in representative numbers to "represent the woman's point of view", which assumes that men cannot.

Many homosexuals have already crossed the bridge to nature. When sociobiologists first suggested that homosexuality might be biological, they were called

Nazis and worse. But in the past few years things have turned around completely. The discovery that the identical twin of a homosexual man has an odds-on chance of being homosexual too, whereas a non-identical twin has only a one-in-five chance, implies that there are some influential genes involved. And the discovery that those parts of the brain that are measurably different in women and men are also different in heterosexuals and homosexuals adds further weight to the idea that homosexuality is as natural as left-handedness. That is anathema to pro-family-value conservatives, who believe that homosexuality is a (misguided) personal choice.

Assuming that the new hereditarians are right and that many human features can be related to genes (or, more likely, groups of genes), it might one day be possible to equip each member of the species with a compact disc telling him which version of each of the 50,000-100,000 human genes he has. He might then read whether he was likely to have a weight problem, or be any good at music, whether there was a risk of schizophrenia or a chance of genius, whether he might go manic-depressive or be devoutly religious. But he could never be sure. For beside every gene would be an asterisk referring to a footnote that read thus: "This prediction is only valid if you are brought up by two Protestant, middle-class, white parents in Peoria, Illinois."

Making Babies

More than a million couples seek treatment for infertility each year. Now some remarkable insights into the mating dance of sperm and egg are bringing answers to their prayers.

PHILIP ELMER-DEWITT

Couched in a halo of nutrient cells, an egg smaller than the dot on an *i* drifts slowly down a Fallopian tube, one of a pair of narrow passages that lead from a woman's ovaries to her womb. Like a beacon guiding ships at night, the egg sends forth a calling signal. A convoy of sperm—the remnants of an armada that was once a couple of hundred million strong—sails into view, their long tails thrashing vigorously. Lured by the chemical signal, several hundred of the most energetic swimmers close in on the egg, their narrow tips unleashing a carefully timed sequence of biochemical salvos. One substance dissolves the jelly-like veil surrounding the egg. Another softens the egg's tough outer shell, preparing it for penetration. In the last moments before conception, a few dozen sperm race to break through the final barricade.

One and only one succeeds. The instant it tunnels its way past the egg's outer layer, an electric charge fires across the membrane and a signal from the sperm causes the eggshell to snap shut, blocking entry to any remaining contenders. The successful seed then releases its tightly coiled package of DNA, which fuses with the egg's own DNA and sets in motion a series of genetic events that culminate, nine months later, in the birth of a new human being.

That is how it is supposed to work. And for hundreds of thousands of years, without anyone knowing quite how or why, it *has* worked—well enough to perpetuate the species, populate the planet and bring the joy and responsibility of children to countless generations of parents.

But what if it doesn't work? What if egg meets sperm and nothing happens? Human sexual reproduction, as couples even before Sarah and Abraham have known, can be a heartbreakingly unreliable process. Even under the best of circumstances—a fertile couple having intercourse at the optimum moment in the woman's cycle—it fails 3 times out of 4. When conditions are less than ideal—when the woman is over 35, for example, or the man's sperm is defective or in short supply—the odds lengthen dramatically.

America today is in the midst of an infertility epidemic, the unforeseen consequence of a variety of historical and socioeconomic trends. The advent of the Pill, the women's movement and an economy that pushes women into the workplace during their most fertile years have led many members of the baby-boom generation to wait so long to have children that they are in danger of waiting forever. This same generation was also party to the sexual revolution, and that too has taken a toll. With exposure to more sex partners came a sharp rise in sexually transmitted diseases and other infections that can impair fertility. In addition, tens of thousands of women now in their 30s and 40s were born with malformed reproductive systems as a result of their mothers' use of the drug DES (diethylstilbestrol), which was widely prescribed in the 1940s and '50s to prevent miscarriage.

Taken together, more than 1 in 12 U.S. couples has difficulty conceiving—a number that is as high as 1 in 7 for couples in the thirtysomething years. And given the size of that age group, there have never been as

GLOSSARY

Artificial insemination: procedure in which a doctor deposits semen directly into the vagina or uterus.

In vitro (in glass) fertilization: procedure in which egg and sperm are combined in a Petri dish.

Gamete: a biologist's term for egg and sperm, the cells that carry the genetic information required for reproduction.

GIFT (gamete intra-Fallopian transfer): variation on in vitro procedure in which sperm and unfertilized eggs are inserted into Fallopian tube.

ZIFT (zygote intra-Fallopian transfer): variation on GIFT that combines sperm and egg in a Petri dish. Resulting pre-embryos (zygotes) are placed in Fallopian tube.

Microinjection: fertilization method using thin needle to insert single sperm through egg's outer membrane.

Zona drilling: fertilization technique that removes part of the outer layer (zona pellucida) of an unfertilized egg before mixing with sperm.

Embryo: developing baby from conception to second month of pregnancy. From then until birth, called a fetus.

many people looking for help. The number of doctor visits for fertility problems nearly tripled between 1968 and 1984. Last year more than a million new patients sought treatment, six times as many people as were treated for lung cancer and 10 times the number of reported cases of AIDS.

The sad fact is that half the people who seek assistance never overcome their infertility. But there is real hope for even the most difficult cases. Through a series of remarkable advances, scientists have opened a new window on the mysteries of fertilization that shows for the first time not only how the process works but also what can be done when it doesn't. Doctors today can manipulate virtually every aspect of the reproductive cycle, from artificially ripening eggs in the ovary to inserting individual sperm directly into the egg's inner membrane. Now researchers at several U.S. clinics are pushing the scientific envelope even further, screening embryos for genetic defects in the lab before placing them in their mothers' wombs.

The result is a reproductive revolution: an explosion of new techniques for overcoming infertility and an unprecedented rush by would-be parents to take advantage of them. Thirteen years after the birth of the first test-tube baby, Louise Brown, in England, in vitro fertilization (IVF) has not only reset the biological clock for thousands of patients—and produced some 10,000 babies in the U.S. alone—but spawned a host of new procedures, like GIFT, ZIFT, microinjection and zona drilling, that offer even greater promise. Today, using the new technology, an infertile couple in their mid-30s has as good a chance of getting pregnant artificially as a pair of fertile teenagers having unprotected sex at any random moment the old-fashioned way.

Families can be pieced together with borrowed sperm, borrowed eggs and borrowed wombs. Women are having babies long after their prime childbearing year—even after menopause. In yet another twist, Arlette Schweitzer, 42, of Aberdeen, S. Dak., is expected to give birth to her own twin grandchildren next month, having served as a surrogate for her daughter Christa, who was born without a uterus. "Next to Christa, I'm the happiest woman in the world," says Schweitzer. "We feel so blessed."

The brave new technologies stir up conflicting feelings, breeding hope and despair where once there was resignation. The high price of in vitro treatments (ranging from $6,000 to more than $50,000 per live birth) means that only the rich and well-insured can afford them. Patients who have undergone round after round say it is like riding an emotional roller coaster; you never know when you are going to run into a brick wall and have your heart broken.

The new techniques have also given birth to once unimaginable ethical dilemmas. Do sperm and egg donors have a claim on their biological offspring, and vice versa? Do embryos, frozen or thawed, have a constitutional right to life? How much manipulation of genetic material will society be willing to permit? "Technology makes us look at our most cherished conceptions of who we are and what we want to be," says Dr. Kenneth Ryan, a professor of reproductive biology at Harvard Medical School. "People have to decide what kind of society they want to live in."

But all these issues pale before the newly revealed miracle of fertilization, an event so dizzyingly complex that researchers say the more they know, the more they wonder that it works as often as it does. The actual merger of egg and sperm turns out to be one of the most straightforward steps in the process—and the easiest to duplicate in a test tube. The events that occur before and after that union, scientists say, are where the real troubles lie.

The long road to conception actually begins seven months before a woman is born, when microscopic eggs start to form in the buds that will become her ovaries. Unlike the testicles of a man, which continuously churn out sperm at the prodigious rate of 1,000 per sec. (30 billion a year), the ovaries never produce any new eggs. The eggs a woman is born with—usually about 2 million—are all she will ever have. By puberty, normal degeneration will have reduced that number to about 400,000. When the woman exhausts the supply, her ovaries will virtually shut down, an event she experiences as menopause.

The limited supply of eggs is believed to be a chief reason that fertility decreases with age. Each month, starting at puberty, hundreds of eggs begin the maturation process. One of them, growing in a fluid-filled sac called the follicle, quickly establishes itself as the first among equals. In a normal cycle, only that single egg will be released to the Fallopian tubes for possible fertilization. About 1,000 more will wither away and disappear. So although a woman may have 400,000 eggs to start with, the number she can effectively use is closer to 400.

To make matters worse for the aging female, the eggs that remain in her ovaries get older and less fertile with each passing year. Recent studies of egg donation provide strong evidence that it is the age of the eggs, and not the age of the reproductive system, that causes fertility to decline sharply after age 40: older women who receive eggs from younger women get pregnant at rates comparable to the age of the egg donor, not the age of the recipient.

None of this is to say that men do not play a role in infertility. On the contrary, the sperm of the human male is notoriously prone to defects. A typical sample is riddled with "pinheaded" sperm, which lack a full complement of DNA, two-headed freaks, and sperm that cannot swim a straight line. Urologists estimate that when a couple experiences infertility, so-called male factors are just as likely to be responsible as female ones. But because of the way sperm are manufactured, assembly-line fashion in the factory of the testes, not much can be done to change either their quality or rate of production (although scientists have developed some extraordinary new procedures to help deficient sperm accomplish their mission). Even the varicocelectomy, a widely prescribed operation that enhances sperm production by removing a varicose vein in the scrotum, seems from recent studies to have little effect on a couple's ability to conceive.

The sequence of events by which eggs mature and ovulate, by contrast, lends itself to all kinds of tinkering. Every step in that process is controlled by hormones, and much of the infertility work done in the '60s and '70s involved finding which hormones were out of balance and how to adjust them. A woman whose ovaries do not release their eggs properly, for example, might be given human chorionic gonadotropin, which triggers ovulation. A woman who tends to miscarry may be given progesterone, which helps soften the uterine lining to make it more receptive.

A widely used drug called Pergonal (menotropin), which for years was derived from the urine of postmenopausal Italian nuns, is rich in the hormone that stimulates eggs to develop and form follicles. This follicle-stimulating hormone usually allows only one egg to reach full maturity, but when administered in huge doses it can trick the ovaries into producing more than a dozen mature eggs in a single cycle. This abundance of eggs is key to most assisted-reproduction techniques. By fertilizing large numbers of eggs and selecting the healthiest embryos, fertility specialists maximize the odds of achieving a successful pregnancy.

Hormone treatments can cover a multiple of symptoms. But there are any number of problems that don't respond to hormone therapy. A woman's Fallopian tubes may be blocked or rendered inoperative by scarring from pelvic infections, sexually transmitted diseases or bits of tissue leaking out of the uterus, a condition called endometriosis. A man may have too few sperm that can make the long journey, or his sperm may lack specific enzymes needed to clear the passage to the egg. Some couples learn late in the game that they are incompatible at a cellular level. A woman can be allergic to her husband's sperm; her antibodies may destroy her partner's seeds before they get a chance to be sown.

There are treatments for each of these conditions. Blocked Fallopian tubes can be freed or cleared of obstructions by a variety of operations, ranging from laser-beam surgery to inflating a tiny balloon within the clogged passage. Men with extremely low sperm counts can be helped toward fatherhood by artificial insemination, which puts what sperm they have directly into the cervix, or by microinjection, which puts a single sperm right into the egg. And for couples with sperm-allergy problems, a procedure known as sperm washing strips the sperm of some of the chemical antigens that trigger the allergic reaction.

But most of these treatments have been supplanted by the family of techniques known as in vitro fertilization. The beauty and power of IVF are that it allows doctors to take many key events in reproduction out of the body, where they are subject to the vagaries of human biology, and perform them in vitro, "in glass." By removing mature eggs from the ovaries, mixing them with sperm in a Petri dish and reintroducing the resulting embryos directly into the uterus, doctors can bypass most of the important barriers to fertility, from low sperm counts to nonfunctioning Fallopian tubes.

The status of IVF has undergone a striking transformation in the past decade. It used to be considered an option of last resort; with success rates running below 5%, most doctors put couples through the full gamut of conventional therapies before turning to IVF. Today a couple in their 30s with undiagnosed infertility is likely to be told to skip invasive tests and exploratory surgeries and go straight to in vitro or related technologies. Streamlined procedures and lowered costs are part of the reason. But it was the development of two variations on the basic IVF procedure —GIFT and ZIFT—and the impressive success rates they have produced that have made believers of most doctors.

The major sticking point of the original procedure, it turned out, was that the embryos just wouldn't stick. Helped by hormone treatments, a woman might produce dozens of eggs each cycle. Her husband's sperm might fertilize 10 of them. But for reasons that remained mysterious, the embryos simply refused to take root—or implant—on the walls of the uterus. Even the best-run clinics were getting success rates not much higher than 15% to 20% just five years ago.

Scientists now know that implantation is one of the most difficult hurdles in the human reproductive system. It is estimated that even among perfectly fertile couples, as many as one-third of all pregnancies are lost, before anyone knows they have begun, because the embryos fail to implant in the uterus wall. Only in the past few years have researchers begun to understand why this is so.

A key breakthrough came in the mid-1980s at Dr. Ricardo Asch's laboratory at the University of Texas at San Antonio. Asch was trying to find a simpler way to do IVF, one that would not require the

skills of an embryologist, when he hit upon the procedure he called gamete intra-Fallopian transfer, or GIFT. Rather than attempting fertilization in a Petri dish, he simply loaded the sperm and eggs (known to biologists as gametes) into a fine pipette and inserted them into the Fallopian tube, where he hoped they would take care of business by themselves. Not only did they fertilize, but they implanted as well—at a much higher rate than he expected.

Scientists attribute the implantation rates of GIFT to the way in which the fertilized embryo enters the uterus. In IVF the embryo is squirted, rather violently, into a reproductive tract that has been pretty roughly treated, first by various hormone treatments, then by the egg-retrieval procedure. In GIFT, by contrast, the embryo drifts quietly into the uterus, much as it would naturally. To further improve the success rates, Asch's researchers tried fertilizing the egg in a lab dish and then placing the pre-embryo, or zygote, directly into the Fallopian tube—a procedure known as ZIFT (zygote intra-Fallopian transfer).

The results were startling. Using GIFT and ZIFT, clinics were soon reporting implantation rates two to three times as high as those achieved in their own IVF facilities. Among couples for whom sperm quality is not a factor, a single cycle of GIFT or ZIFT at Asch's clinic can result in pregnancy 40% to 50% of the time. A healthy, fertile couple trying to conceive naturally in any given month has about a 25% success rate.

The latest clue in the mystery of implantation was hit upon by scientists working on a completely different problem: lazy sperm. Some sperm lack the ability to penetrate the egg's outer membrane, or zona pellucida, often as a result of old testicular injuries or early exposure to toxic chemicals. Several methods have been devised to give these sperm a boost, including microinjection (the sperm is inserted directly into the egg by means of a microscopic needle) and partial zona drilling (a tiny hole is made in the egg's protective shell).

It was while working with patients with severe sperm deficiencies that researchers noticed something surprising. Eggs whose shells had been poked open were doing a much better job of sticking to the uterus wall. In a trial performed by Dr. Jacques Cohen, one of the scientists who developed the PZD procedure, embryos successfully lodged in the womb at a rate more than five times the national average for IVF. "I was so excited I couldn't sleep at night," says Cohen. Apparently eggs with a hole in their outer membrane somehow benefit from that hole. Cohen theorizes that embryos that don't implant may be having trouble "hatching" through the shell that housed the original egg. The tiny

hole Cohen makes to help the sperm get in may be helping the embryo get out—and may suggest a method for helping increase implantation rates across the board.

In April scientists from Israel and the U.S. reported a new finding that may offer yet another way to help infertile couples. It had long been assumed that there was no communication between egg and sperm until they collided in the Fallopian tube. But by closely watching the behavior of sperm in test tubes containing the fluid from an egg's follicular sac, an interesting effect was observed. A small number of sperm seemed to change their swimming patterns in response to chemicals secreted by the egg or cells around the egg.

It was not a dramatic effect, and not all eggs emitted even this weak chemical signal. But when the researchers correlated the results, they discovered a startling pattern: only eggs that emitted the "come hither" message were successfully fertilized. "This indicated to us that attraction may indeed be a key process in fertilization," says Michael Eisenbach at Israel's Weizmann Institute of Science. Now Eisenbach is trying to find out whether this phenomenon could be exploited to help treat the most stubborn infertility cases.

Scientists in South Korea are on the verge of a breakthrough in a procedure doctors have been dreaming about for some time: the freezing and storage of unfertilized eggs. Sperm and embryos are regularly frozen for later use, but not eggs, which quickly lose their viability when manipulated outside the body. But Dr. Kwang Yul Cha, an endocrinologist at Cha Women's Hospital in Seoul, reports that his team has produced two pregnancies from eggs matured not in an ovary but in a Petri dish—a major step in the eventual perfection of egg freezing. Many scientists expect that the procedure will be available within the next few years.

That could be a godsend for a young woman facing surgery or chemotherapy that would destroy the functioning of her ovaries. Such a woman would have the option of putting her healthy eggs on ice for future use. That option might also appeal to, say, a professional woman inclined to postpone childbearing. Theoretically, at least, she could store her best, grade-A eggs during her most fertile years and pull them out of the deep freezer at a later age should she run into trouble conceiving. Not everyone, though, would approve this use of an expensive technology.

Even more provocative is a new area of research that combines the techniques of in vitro fertilization with the latest advances in genetic screening. Abnormalities like sickle-cell anemia or cystic fibrosis are present in the genetic code from the moment of conception. Since embryos in their earliest stages are fairly forgiving—they can lose a cell or two without impairing their subsequent development—it is theoretically possible to remove a cell from, say, a 16-cell embryo, test it for a suspected defect, and get the answer before that embryo is inserted into the uterus for implantation.

Embryologists at several U.S. labs are doing just that. Doctors at Chicago's Illinois Masonic Medical Center have screened embryos from 15 couples who have a known risk of carrying such diseases as Tay-Sachs, a rare, crippling condition that often results in death by age four. Last week doctors at Cornell Medical Center began clinical studies on embryos at risk for cystic fibrosis.

These experiments are sure to arouse protests. Today most in vitro clinics are very careful never to purposely destroy viable embryos. Even when couples agree to freeze embryos, they are required to sign an agreement specifying what will happen to any embryos they don't need: they can be donated to couples that can't produce their own or donated to research. But the premise of pre-embryotic genetic testing is that defective embryos will be destroyed. If the problem is a debilitating disease like Tay-Sachs, this may be justifiable. But what if couples choose to reject embryos whose only offense is that they are of the wrong sex? "You're dealing with human tissues from a human body," says Lynne Lawrence, at the American Fertility Society. "Like sex, it tends to cut near and dear to people's hearts and raises a red flag."

Society has just begun to wrestle with the financial burden of assisted reproduction. "It takes courage and cash," says Dr. Georgeanna Jones, whose work with her husband, Dr. Howard Jones, in Norfolk, Va., produced the first IVF baby in the U.S. A single in vitro cycle can cost $6,000 to $8,000, a burden most medical plans are not eager to share. Nine states have passed laws requiring insurance companies to cover the cost of infertility treatments, but resistance in the remaining states is strong. The question, says Leroy Walters, at Georgetown University's Kennedy Institute of Ethics, is "to what extent society has a responsibility to assist couples that are infertile." In Walters' opinion, so-

ciety should pay for the diagnosis of the problem, "but beyond that, given the cost, I'd place the financial responsibility on the couples themselves." It may, for instance, be more in society's interest to encourage intractably infertile couples to adopt.

The Federal Government has tried to steer clear of infertility issues. Under pressure from right-to-life lobbies, it quietly cut funds for in vitro research in 1980, despite a Health Department study that called such a ban "neither justifiable nor wise." Last fall Congress appropriated $3 million for three contraceptive centers and five infertility centers. But because of the government's ban on funding IVF research, the scientists haven't been able to begin their work. "Britain and Australia are surpassing us in research because of the restraints we face in this country," says Harvard's Ryan. "The U.S. government has created a moral vacuum."

And where there is a moral vacuum, there are lawsuits. Around the country, a number of bizarre court cases have cropped up as a result of ambiguities in the rules governing the new technologies. In one peculiar case, a wealthy couple died in a plane accident, leaving two frozen embryos as their only direct heirs; a court decided that the embryos could not inherit the estate. In a case that is still pending, a divorced Tennessee couple are battling over whether the woman has the right to make use of frozen embryos created while the couple were still married.

Making matters more confusing for consumers is the fact that success rates among the nation's 225 IVF centers vary wildly—from zero for new ones to 40% and better at some of the top clinics. And infertility specialists are not always what they claim to be. Some obstetricians print INFERTILITY on their business cards on the strength of three-month residency training programs. "They pick up infertility because it's easier than delivering babies at 3 a.m.," scoffs Dr. Richard Marrs, who headed the ethics committee of the American Fertility Society.

Horror stories abound. It is not unusual for a poorly trained physician to schedule advanced infertility treatments—even surgery—on a woman without first checking her partner's sperm count. A lawsuit is pending against a physician in Torrance,

Calif., who is accused of duping patients into believing he was performing in vitro fertilization when he wasn't even collecting eggs. Consumers are advised to seek guidance from either the American Fertility Society, based in Birmingham, or Resolve, a national infertility organization with headquarters in Somerville, Mass. "You need to be a careful consumer," warns Dr. Arthur Wisot, a Redondo Beach, Calif., infertility specialist. "If you're going to invest all your life's hopes and dreams, you should at least check out the qualifications of the medical group."

Pamela and Jonathan Loew know about investing all their hopes and dreams in achieving pregnancy. The Los Angeles couple went through a five-year effort that included hormone treatment, artificial insemination, an ectopic pregnancy, sperm washing and finally GIFT. "Intellectually you know it's a medical problem," says Pamela, "but emotionally you can't get it out of your mind that you're not like a normal woman."

When Pamela and Jonathan learned during a Las Vegas vacation that their first GIFT procedure had failed, they sat together in a rental car and cried. "It was pretty devastating," recalls Pam. When Jonathan got a call telling him that their second GIFT attempt was successful and that his wife was at long last pregnant, he was incredulous: "I couldn't believe that after five years we had finally hit the jackpot."

Today the passage of time has dulled the pain. Little Alexandra is 17 months old, and her parents are thinking about having a second child. They still have 12 frozen embryos saved from their second GIFT procedure, and during the next few months those embryos will be thawed and inserted, a few at a time. But whether it works or not is of much less moment to Pamela and Jonathan now than it would have been two years earlier. As baby Alex sits in the living room, engrossed in a music video playing on the VCR, they know full well that they are already ahead of the game.

—Reported by Ann Blackman/ Washington, Barbara Dolan/Norfolk and Jeanne McDowell/Los Angeles

SPERM UNDER SIEGE

MORE THAN WE EVER GUESSED, HAVING A HEALTHY BABY MAY DEPEND ON DAD

Anne Merewood

IT DIDN'T MAKE SENSE. Kate Malone's* first pregnancy had gone so smoothly. Yet when she and her husband Paul* tried to have a second child, their efforts were plagued by disaster. For two years, Kate couldn't become pregnant. Then she suffered an ectopic pregnancy, in which the embryo began to grow in one of her fallopian tubes and had to be surgically removed. Her next pregnancy heralded more heartache—it ended in miscarriage at four months and tests revealed that the fetus was genetically abnormal. Within months, she became pregnant and miscarried yet again. By this point, some four years after their troubles began, the couple had adopted a son; baffled and demoralized by the string of apparent bad luck, they gave up trying to have another child. "We had been to the top doctors in the country and no one could find a reason for the infertility or the miscarriages," says Kate.

Soon, however, thanks to a newspaper article she read, Kate uncovered what she now considers the likely cause of the couple's reproductive woes. When it all started, Paul had just been hired by a manufacturing company that used a chemical called paradichlorobenzene, which derives from benzene, a known carcinogen. The article discussed the potential effects of exposure to chemicals, including benzene, on a man's sperm. Kate remembered hearing that two other men in Paul's small office were also suffering from inexplicable infertility. Both of their wives had gone through three miscarriages as well. Kate had always considered their similar misfortunes to be a tragic coincidence. Now she became convinced that the chemical (which has not yet been studied for its effects on reproduction) had blighted the three men's sperm.

Paul had found a new job in a chemical-free workplace, so the couple decided to try once more to have a baby. Kate conceived immediately—and last August gave birth to a healthy boy. The Malones are now arranging for the National Institute for Occupational Safety and Health (NIOSH), the

*These names have been changed.

federal agency that assesses work-related health hazards for the public, to inspect Paul's former job site. "Our aim isn't to sue the company, but to help people who are still there," says Kate.

The Malones' suspicions about sperm damage echo the concerns of an increasing number of researchers. These scientists are challenging the double standard that leads women to overhaul their lives before a pregnancy—avoiding stress, cigarettes and champagne—while men are left confident that their lifestyle has little bearing on their fertility or their future child's health. Growing evidence suggests that sperm is both more fragile and potentially more dangerous than previously thought. "There seems to have been both a scientific resistance, and a resistance based on cultural preconceptions, to accepting these new ideas," says Gladys Friedler, Ph.D, an associate professor of psychiatry and pharmacology at Boston University School of Medicine.

But as more and more research is completed, sperm may finally be stripped of its macho image. For example, in one startling review of data on nearly 15,000 newborns, scientists at the University of North Carolina in Chapel Hill concluded that a father's drinking and smoking habits, and even his age, can increase his child's risk of birth defects—ranging from cleft palates to *hydrocephalus,* an abnormal accumulation of spinal fluid in the brain. Other new and equally worrisome studies have linked higher-than-normal rates of stillbirth, premature delivery and low birthweight (which predisposes a baby to medical and developmental problems) to fathers who faced on-the-job exposure to certain chemicals. In fact, one study found that a baby was more likely to be harmed if the father rather than the mother worked in an unsafe environment in the months before conception.

The surprising news of sperm's delicate nature may shift the balance of responsibility for a newborn's wellbeing. The research may also have social and economic implications far beyond the concerns of couples planning a family. In recent years a growing number of companies have sought to ban women of childbearing age from jobs that entail exposure to hazardous substances. The idea is to protect the women's future children from defects—and the companies themselves from lawsuits. Already, the "fetal protection policy" of one Milwaukee-based company has prompted female employees to file a sex discrimination suit that is now before the U.S. Supreme Court. Conversely, if the new research on sperm is borne out, men whose future plans include fatherhood may go to court to *insist* on protection from hazards. Faced with potential lawsuits from so many individuals, companies may be forced to ensure that workplaces are safe for *all* employees.

SPERM UND DRANG

At the center of all this controversy are the microscopic products of the male reproductive system. Sperm (officially, spermatozoa) are manufactured by *spermatagonia,* special cells in the testes that are constantly stimulated by the male hormone testosterone. Once formed, a sperm continues to mature as it travels for some 80 days through the *epididymis* (a microscopic network of tubes behind the testicle) to the "waiting area" around the prostate gland, where it is expelled in the next ejaculation.

A normal sperm contains 23 chromosomes—the threadlike strands that house DNA, the molecular foundation of genetic material. While a woman is born with all the eggs she will ever produce, a man creates millions of sperm every day from puberty onwards. This awesome productivity is also what makes sperm so fragile. If a single sperm's DNA is damaged, the result may be a mutation that distorts the genetic information it carries. "Because of the constant turnover of sperm, mutations caused by the environment can arise more frequently in men than in women," says David A. Savitz, Ph.D., an associate professor of epidemiology and chief researcher of the North Carolina review.

If a damaged sperm fertilizes the egg, the consequences can be devastating. "Such sperm can lead to spontaneous abortions, malformations, and functional or behavioral abnormalities," says Marvin Legator, Ph.D., director of environmental toxicology at the department of preventative medicine at the University of Texas in Galveston. And in some cases, sperm may be too badly harmed even to penetrate an egg, leading to mysterious infertility.

Though the findings on sperm's vulnerability are certainly dramatic, researchers emphasize that they are also preliminary. "We have only a very vague notion of how exposure might affect fetal development, and the whole area of research is at a very early stage of investigation," says Savitz. Indeed, questions still far outnumber answers. For starters, there is no hard evidence that a chemical damages an infant by adversely affecting the father's sperm. A man who comes in contact with dangerous substances might harm the baby by exposing his partner indirectly—for example, through contaminated clothing. Another theory holds that the harmful pollutants may be carried in the seminal fluid that buoys sperm. But more researchers are becoming convinced that chemicals can inflict their silent damage directly on the sperm itself.

THE CHEMICAL CONNECTION

The most well-known—and most controversial—evidence that chemicals can harm sperm comes from research on U.S. veterans of the Vietnam war who were exposed to the herbicide Agent Orange (dioxin), used by the U.S. military to destroy foliage that hid enemy forces. A number of veterans believe the chemical is responsible for birth defects in their children. The latest study on the issue, published last year by the Harvard School of Public Health, found that Vietnam vets had almost twice the risk of other men of fathering infants with one or more major malformations. But a number of previous studies found conflicting results, and because so little is known about how paternal exposure could translate into birth defects, the veterans have been unsuccessful in their lawsuits against the government.

Scientific uncertainty also dogs investigations into other potentially hazardous chemicals and contaminants. "There seem to be windows of vulnerability for sperm: Certain chemicals may be harmful only at a certain period during sperm production," explains Donald Mattison, M.D., dean of the School of Public Health at the University of Pittsburgh. There isn't enough specific data to make definitive lists of "danger chemicals." Still, a quick scan of the research shows that particular substances often crop up as likely troublemakers. Chief among them: lead, benzene, paint solvents, vinyl chloride, carbon disulphide, the pesticide DBCP, anesthetic gases and radiation. Not surprisingly, occupations that involve contact with these substances also figure heavily in studies of sperm damage. For example, men employed in the paper, wood, chemical, drug and paint industries may have a greater chance of siring stillborn children. And increased leukemia rates have been detected among children whose fathers are medical workers, aircraft or auto mechanics, or who are exposed regularly to paint or radiation. In fact, a study of workers at Britain's Sellafield nuclear power plant in West Cambria found a sixfold leukemia risk among children whose fathers were exposed to the plant's highest radiation levels (about 9 percent of all employees).

Workers in "high-risk" industries should not panic, says Savitz. "The credibility of the studies is limited because we have no firm evidence that certain exposures cause certain birth defects." Yet it makes sense to be watchful for warning signs. For example, if pollution levels are high enough to cause skin irritations, thyroid trouble, or breathing problems, the reproductive system might also be at risk. Another danger signal is a clustered outbreak of male infertility or of a particular disease: It was local concern about high levels of childhood leukemia, for instance, that sparked the investigation at the Sellafield nuclear plant.

The rise in industrial "fetal protection policies" is

adding even more controversy to the issue of occupational hazards to sperm. In 1984, employees brought a class-action suit against Milwaukee-based Johnson Controls, the nation's largest manufacturer of car batteries, after the company restricted women "capable of bearing children" from holding jobs in factory areas where lead exceeded a specific level. The suit—which the Supreme Court is scheduled to rule on this spring—focuses on the obstacles the policy creates for women's career advancement. Johnson Controls defends its regulation by pointing to "overwhelming" evidence that a mother's exposure to lead can harm the fetus.

In effect, the company's rule may be a case of reverse discrimination against men. Males continue to work in areas banned to women despite growing evidence that lead may not be safe for sperm either. In several studies over the past 10 years, paternal exposure to lead (and radiation) has been connected to Wilms' tumor, a type of kidney cancer in children. In another recent study, University of Maryland toxicologist Ellen Silbergeld, Ph.D., exposed male rats to lead amounts equivalent to levels below the current occupational safety standards for humans. The rats were then mated with females who had not been exposed at all. Result: The offspring showed clear defects in brain development.

Johnson Controls claims that evidence linking fetal problems to a father's contact with lead is insufficient. But further research into chemicals' effects on sperm may eventually force companies to reduce pollution levels, since *both* sexes can hardly be banned from the factory floor. Says Mattison: "The workplace should be safe for everyone who wants to work there, men and women alike!"

FATHER TIME

Whatever his occupation, a man's age may play an unexpected role in his reproductive health. When researchers at the University of Calgary and the Alberta Children's Hospital in Canada examined sperm samples taken from 30 healthy men aged 20 to 52, they found that the older men had a higher percentage of sperm with structurally abnormal chromosomes. Specifically, only 2 to 3 percent of the sperm from men between ages 20 and 34 were genetically abnormal, while the figure jumped to 7 percent in men 35 to 44 and to almost 14 percent in those 45 and over. "The findings are logical," says Renée Martin, Ph.D., the professor of pediatrics who led the study. "The cells that create sperm are constantly dividing from puberty onwards, and every time they divide they are subject to error."

Such mistakes are more likely to result in miscarriages than in unhealthy babies. "When part of a chromosome is missing or broken, the embryo is more likely to abort as a miscarriage [than to carry to term]," Martin says. Yet her findings may help explain why Savitz's North Carolina study noted a doubled rate of birth defects like cleft palate and hydrocephalus in children whose fathers were over 35 at the time of conception, no matter what the mothers' age.

Currently, there are no tests available to pre-identify sperm likely to cause genetic defects. "Unfortunately there's nothing offered, because [the research] is all so new," says Martin. But tests such as amniocentesis, alpha fetoprotein (AFP) and chorionic villi sampling (CVS) can ferret out some fetal genetic defects that are linked to Mom *or* Dad. Amniocentesis, for example, is routinely recommended for all pregnant women over 35 because with age a woman increases her risk of producing a Down's syndrome baby, characterized by mental retardation and physical abnormalities.

With respect to Down's syndrome, Martin's study provided some good news for older men: It confirmed previous findings that a man's risk of fathering a child afflicted with the syndrome actually drops with age. Some popular textbooks still warn that men over 55 have a high chance of fathering Down's syndrome babies. "That information is outdated," Martin insists. "We now know that for certain."

THE SINS OF THE FATHERS?

For all the hidden dangers facing a man's reproductive system, the most common hazards may be the ones most under his control.

Smoking. Tobacco addicts take note: Smoke gets in your sperm. Cigarettes can reduce fertility by lowering sperm count—the number of individual sperm released in a single ejaculation. "More than half a pack a day can cause sperm density to drop by 20 percent," says Machelle Seibel, M.D., director of the Faulkner Centre for Reproductive Medicine in Boston. One Danish study found that for each pack of cigarettes a father tended to smoke daily (assuming the mother didn't smoke at all), his infant's birthweight fell 4.2 ounces below average. Savitz has found that male smokers double their chances of fathering infants with abnormalities like hydrocephalus, *Bell's palsy* (paralysis of the facial nerve), and mouth cysts. In Savitz's most recent study, children whose fathers smoked around the time of conception were 20 percent more likely to develop brain cancer, lymphoma and leukemia than were children whose fathers did not smoke (the results still held regardless of whether the mother had a tobacco habit).

This is scary news—and not particularly helpful: Savitz's studies didn't record how frequently the fathers lit up, and no research at all suggests why the links appeared. Researchers can't even say for sure that defective sperm was to blame. The babies may instead have been victims of passive smoking—affected by Dad's tobacco while in the womb or shortly after birth.

Drinking. Mothers-to-be are routinely cautioned against sipping any alcohol while pregnant. Now studies suggest that the father's drinking habits just before conception may also pose a danger. So far, research hasn't discovered why alcohol has an adverse effect on sperm, but it does suggest that further investigation is needed. For starters, one study of laboratory rats linked heavy alcohol use with infertility because the liquor lowered testosterone levels. Another study, from the University of Washington in Seattle, discovered that newborn babies whose fathers drank at least two glasses of wine or two bottles of beer per day weighed an average of 3 ounces less than babies whose fathers were only occasional sippers—even when all other factors were considered.

Illicit Drugs. Many experts believe that a man's frequent use of substances such as marijuana and cocaine may also result in an unhealthy fetus, but studies that could document such findings have yet to be conducted. However, preliminary research has linked marijuana to infertility. And recent tests at the Yale Infertility Clinic found that long-term cocaine use led to both very low sperm counts and a greater number of sperm with motion problems.

WHAT A DAD CAN DO

The best news about sperm troubles is that many of the risk factors can be easily prevented. Because the body overhauls sperm supplies every 90 days, it only takes a season to get a fresh start on creating a healthy baby. Most experts advise that men wait for three months after quitting smoking, cutting out drug use or abstaining from alcohol before trying to sire a child.

Men who fear they are exposed to work chemicals that may compromise the health of future children can contact NIOSH. (Write to the Division of Standards Development and Technology Transfer, Technical Information Branch, 4676 Columbia Parkway, Mailstop C-19, Cincinnati, OH 45226. Or call [800] 356-4674.) NIOSH keeps files on hazardous chemicals and their effects, and can arrange for a local inspection of the workplace. Because it is primarily a research institution, NIOSH is most useful for investigating chemicals that haven't been studied previously for sperm effects (which is why

the Malones approached NIOSH with their concerns about paradichlorobenzene). For better-known pollutants, it's best to ask the federal Occupational Safety and Health Administration (OSHA) to inspect the job site (OSHA has regional offices in most U.S. cities).

There is also advice for men who are concerned over exposure to radiation during medical treatment. Direct radiation to the area around the testes can spur infertility by halting sperm production for more than three years. According to a recent study, it can also triple the number of abnormal sperm the testes produce. Men who know they will be exposed to testicular radiation for medical reasons should consider "banking" sperm before the treatment, for later use in artificial insemination. Most hospitals use lead shields during radiation therapy, but for routine X-rays, even dental X-rays, protection might not be offered automatically. If it's not offered, patients should be sure to request it. "The risks are really, really low, but to be absolutely safe, patients—male or female—should *always* ask for a lead apron to protect their reproductive organs," stresses Martin.

Though the study of sperm health is still in its infancy, it is already clear that a man's reproductive system needs to be treated with respect and caution. Women do not carry the full responsibility for bearing a healthy infant. "The focus should be on both parents—not on 'blaming' either the mother or the father, but on accepting that each plays a role," says Friedler.

Mattison agrees: "Until recently, when a woman had a miscarriage, she would be told it was because she had a 'blighted ovum' [egg]. We never heard anything about a 'blighted sperm.' This new data suggests that both may be responsible. That is not unreasonable," he concludes, "given that it takes both an egg and a sperm to create a baby!"

WHAT CRACK DOES TO BABIES

BY JANICE HUTCHINSON

Janice Hutchinson is a pediatrician and former senior scientist for the American Medical Association. She is now the medical director of the Child and Youth Services Administration of the District of Columbia Department of Mental Health.

INQUIRING TEACHERS want to know: Who are these kids and how did they get this way? The question refers to the unprecedented numbers of children—estimates range as high as one-half to one million—who are entering the classroom having suffered inutero exposure to cocaine.

Crack, the cooked form of cocaine, became widely available in 1985; the children of the first crack addicts are now in school. Teachers have described them as a new breed, unlike other children with histories of drug exposure. They are often in constant motion, disorganized, and very sensitive to stimuli. Crawling, standing, and walking take longer to develop. They are irritable and hard to please. It is hard for them to make friends. They respond less to the environment. Internal stability is poor. Learning is more difficult. Smiling and eye contact are infrequent. They do not seem to know how to play with toys or with others. And nothing you do for them seems to matter or help.

If teachers are to meet the challenges that these children bring, they may find it helpful to understand the bio-neuro-physiological effects of cocaine on the developing fetus. Scientists are just beginning to understand these effects; research in the area is incomplete and at times conflicting. Thus what we know and what we can speculate about, some of which is summarized below, is just the tip of a rather unknown iceberg. There are surely many more effects—and more complicated avenues of effect—than those so far identified. Nonetheless, there are findings—mainly from research sponsored by the National Institutes of Health and the National Institute on Drug Abuse—that allow us to begin to make some sense of what is happening to the behaviors and learning styles of these children.

IMAGINE THAT a crack molecule has entered the body. It enters into the mucous membranes of the mouth. From there it enters the lungs, where it is absorbed into the bloodstream, and through which it then passes to the heart and, very quickly, to the brain. The immediate effect is an increase in breathing, blood pressure, and heart rate.

Upon arriving in the brain, crack acts at several sites along what is known as the brain's "pleasure pathway"—a collection of sites in the brain that seem in some ways to relate and affect each other. At one point on the pleasure pathway is the limbic system, which is the seat of strong emotional responses, including the very primitive urges to feed, flee, fight, and reproduce. At another point along the pathway is the motor cortex of the brain, which directs the body's movement. Between the limbic system and the motor cortex lies the nucleus accumbens. This is the "attraction center" of the brain; it is what pulls you toward pleasurable activity.

The crack is very active here in the nucleus accumbens; a ripple effect then seems to carry the destruction around to other points along the pleasure pathway. Within the nucleus accumbens, as elsewhere in the brain, are numerous nerve cells; the space between each nerve cell ending is known as the synaptic space. Each of these nerve cells communicates with the others across the synaptic space by sending a variety of neurotransmitters back and forth.

One such neurotransmitter is dopamine. Under normal biological conditions, dopamine, like other neurotransmitters, is continually moving across the synaptic space. In a constantly recurring pattern, the dopamine leaves its home cell, crosses the synaptic space, and reaches receptors on the receiving cell, an action that sends an electrical signal through the receiver cell. The dopamine then disattaches from the receptor cell and returns to its cell of origin where it will be recycled.

But if crack has been ingested, this normal cycle will be disrupted. Crack, upon entering the brain and then the pleasure pathway, seems to settle into the synaptic space between the neurotransmitters. It then acts to pre-

Reprinted with permission from *American Educator,* Spring 1991, pp. 31-32. *American Educator,* the quarterly journal of the American Federation of Teachers.

vent the dopamine from returning to its home cell. Unable to return home, the dopamine continues to stimulate the receiver cell until the crack has spent itself and dissipated. It is probably this constant stimulation of the receiver cell that causes the euphoric feeling associated with the first few minutes of cocaine ingestion. But the crack high lasts only a few minutes, after which the user will either replenish his intake or experience an often devastating "low." The constant resupply soon leads to a physical addiction, the breaking of which is accompanied by extremely painful withdrawal symptoms.

WHILE THE crack is acting on the mother's brain, what is happening to the fetus? The crack crosses the placental barrier and heads for the inutero brain. The exact effect of the crack on the fetus will depend on the age of the fetus, the dosage of the crack, and probably on other variables that we have not yet identified. But it seems likely that in general a number of things happen. First, the crack probably acts on the fetal nucleus accumbens in the same way that it acts on the user's, leading the fetus to become highly stimulated and, often, addicted. As it stimulates the nucleus accumbens, and surely in other ways as well, the crack damages fetal brain cells and thus causes neurological damage all along the pleasure pathway and in other nearby parts of the brain.

Damage to brain cells in the limbic system, the nucleus accumbens, and elsewhere along the pleasure pathway would likely impair or alter a wide range of the child's normal emotional responses, including, for example, the ability to respond to pleasurable experiences, to form emotional attachments, or to make certain kinds of judgments. Perhaps this explains in part why the crack baby is often unable to proceed through the normal phases of separation-individuation described by child psychiatrist Margaret Mahler; crack babies appear to experience much greater anxiety and difficulty in leaving their mothers when it is time for school.

In addition, the brain's motor cortex may be damaged, which might explain such effects as the slow development of crawling, standing, and walking. The brain location for speech is also nearby, and damage to it may account for the speech impairments suffered by many crack babies. In turn, the speech impairment inhibits the child's ability to communicate, which may, in turn, account for some of the difficulty these children have in forming relationships.

In addition, crack, like nicotine, constricts the adult and fetal arteries, thus slowing the blood—and therefore the oxygen flow—to the fetus and around it. This condition of low oxygenation—known as hypoxia—can also produce brain damage, and it can bring on low birthweight. Low birthweight is, in turn, associated with a wide range of disabling symptoms, including intellectual disabilities.

Reading, mathematics, spelling, handwriting, and the arts are often difficult tasks for low-birthweight babies. Speech and language problems are prominent. Temperamental problems, such as low adaptability, low persistence, and arrhythmicity (for example, the failure to sleep and wake at normal, regular times) may be part of their behavioral style. They typically cry when separated from the mother, have trouble expressing themselves, speak only in short phrases, are very active, and clumsy.

Findings to date suggest that temperament influences both behavior and cognition.

These low birthweight children tend to perform poorly on the Mullen Scale of Early Learning. This test, which consists of four scales, suggests the range of learning abilities that seem to be impaired in the children exposed inutero to crack. The Visual Receptive Organization (VRO) scale assesses visual discrimination, short-term memory, visual organization and sequencing, and visual spatial awareness, including position, size, shape, left/right, and detail. The Visual Expressive Organization (VEO) assesses bilateral and unilateral manipulation, writing, visual discrimination, and visual-motor plan and control. The language receptive organization (LRO) scale assesses auditory comprehension, short- and long-term auditory memory, integration of ideas and visual spatial cues, auditory sequencing, and verbal spatial concepts. The language expressive organization (LEO) scale assesses spontaneous and formal verbal ability, language formulation, auditory comprehension, and short- and long-term memory.

What all of this means ultimately is that these low-birthweight crack children experience the world around them in a very different way from other children. Adults, including teachers, are often unaware that these children see and hear their environment in a completely different manner from adults or even other children. What the teacher often does not realize is that this difficult-to-teach, hard-to manage child is processing information in an unusual way that the child does not determine. Hence, conflict and frustration can arise between teacher and student (and also at home between parent and child).

The combined effects of prenatal drug exposure with a home environment that provides little or no nurturance, understanding, or support for the child create a terrible challenge to teachers. But initial experimental programs suggest that these children can benefit greatly from placement in highly structured, highly tailored educational day care settings beginning in early infancy. In four Washington, D.C.-area therapeutic nurseries that provide such care, two-thirds of the children seem so far to have been successfully mainstreamed into first grade.

Among the characteristics that seem to make such programs successful are early identification of the infants and very low student-teacher ratios. The establishment of an emotionally supportive atmosphere and structure is necessary. Teaching must be intense and focal. Tasks should initially be simple and singular. Too many tasks or activities overstimulate these children, and they cannot respond. Teachers must also provide emotional support and form bonds with the children. Success also depends on aggressively approaching and engaging parents in the psychotherapeutic progress. Consultation with mental health professionals may assist teachers, parents, and students. Intellectually limited students may still require individual tutoring; some students will eventually require special education; and very emotionally disturbed students may require a mental health-based psychotherapy program.

But it does seem clear that with early, appropriate interventions many of these children can improve their behavior and academic performance. Like most childhood problems, the time to act is now; later is too late.

WAR BABIES

What happens when mothers-to-be become the victims of starvation? Now three generations after World War II, we are still learning the disturbing answers.

Jared Diamond

Contributing editor Jared Diamond is a professor of physiology at the UCLA School of Medicine. In June he wrote about the search for eternal youth [for Discover*].*

I*t is easy to write now that each person got 400 calories a day. In practice it was quite another thing. . . . People sought food everywhere in the streets and the surrounding countryside. Anything edible was picked up in this way, and they were lucky who found a potato or two or a handful of greens. . . . People dropped from exhaustion in the streets and many died there. Often people were so fatigued that they were unable to return home, before curfew; so they hid in barns or else-where to sleep and there died. . . . Older people, who lacked the strength to go searching for food, stayed at home in bed and died.*
—Famine and Human Development: The Dutch Hunger
Winter of 1944–1945

Among the homey images I recall from my wife's pregnancy are the bigger-than-usual milk cartons in the refrigerator and her vitamin bottles on the kitchen counter. To our generation the value of good nutrition for pregnant women seems obvious. But what makes us so sure? After all, we can't run experiments on people to prove it. Starving hundreds of pregnant women and then comparing their kids with well-nourished cousins would be absolutely unthinkable.

Yet such an inhuman experiment was indeed once conducted. By imposing a famine on part of the population of the Netherlands during the last seven months of World War II, the Nazis effectively reduced 40,000 pregnant women to starvation. These cruel circumstances resulted in a study of the effects of prenatal nutrition that was grimly well-designed, complete with a control group: while these women were starving, other mothers-to-be in the same society were eating comparatively healthy rations.

Years later, when the babies who survived had grown into adults, epidemiologists could distinguish the different effects of prenatal and postnatal nutrition; they could even discern the effects of malnutrition at different stages of pregnancy, for at the time the famine took hold, some women were further along in their pregnancy than others. Even now we are still learning what toll was exacted by the events of 45 years ago. Only recently have researchers learned that the famine's effects reached far beyond its immediate victims: now that girls born to the starved Dutch women have grown up and had children of their own, it's become apparent that some of these children too are marked by the deprivations suffered years earlier by their grandmothers!

Today we accept without question that proper nutrition is important for maintaining our health as adults and even more important for the development of our children. The evidence seems most persuasive when we look at the malnourished Third World and see shorter life spans, lowered resistance to disease, and high infant mortalities. But even in the industrialized world we can readily see the positive effects of a good diet. For one thing, today's adults tend to be taller than their parents; the difference approaches six inches in Japan. On average, too, people who are poor, with comparatively limited access to food, are shorter and less healthy than their wealthier countrymen. Moreover, it is not just physical health that seems to be at risk. Many tests of mental function suggest that poor nutrition in childhood may affect learning ability throughout life.

One might speculate that if we are so susceptible to the effects of poor nutrition as children, we must be especially sensitive to those effects while we're still in the womb, when our brain and body are forming. And, indeed, many studies have shown an association between poor nutrition, low weight at birth, and poor physical and mental performance later on. Yet it's not easy to prove that inadequate prenatal nutrition itself is the culprit. Sadly, babies poorly nourished in the womb are likely to be poorly nourished after birth as well. Furthermore, diet may not be the only thing influencing their health. Access to medical care, schooling, and stimulation outside school may play a part.

Figuring out just how big a role prenatal malnutrition plays in this miserable chain of events, then, is difficult at best. But the starvation in the Nazi-occupied Netherlands nearly half a century ago offers some thought-provoking answers.

The Dutch tragedy was the result of one of the most controversial decisions of World War II. After the Allied forces invaded Normandy and liberated France in the summer of 1944, our generals debated two strategies for completing Germany's defeat: to advance northeastward from France into Germany's Ruhr industrial region or to push eastward into the Saar. Had all our resources been concentrated on a single strategy, either might have succeeded. In fact both advances were attempted at once, and both ground to a standstill.

The northern advance hinged on the famous Battle of Arnhem, which inspired the film *A Bridge Too Far*. On September 17, 1944, British paratroops were dropped on the Dutch city of Arnhem to take command of a crucial bridge over the Rhine; other Allied forces, meanwhile, tried to join them from the south. Dutch railroad workers courageously called a general strike to impede the Nazis' efforts to bring up reinforcements. But stiff Nazi resistance forced the Allies to retreat, on September 25, after heavy losses. The Allies then shifted their military effort away from the Netherlands, most of which remained under German occupation until May 1945.

In retaliation for the Dutch strike an embargo on transport in the Netherlands, including transport of food, was ordered by the notorious Nazi Reichskommissar Seyss-Inquart, later tried and hanged at Nuremberg. The predictable result of the embargo, which began in October 1944, was a famine that became progressively worse as stored food supplies were exhausted and that was not lifted until the Netherlands was liberated the following spring. Because an unusually severe winter hampered relief efforts, the famine became known as the Dutch Hunger Winter.

Intake dropped as low as 400 calories a day, down from an already-reduced daily ration of 1,500 calories. Still, some people were better off than others. The hunger was milder in the farming regions of the north and south; it was most severe in the large industrial cities of the west, such as Amsterdam, Rotterdam, and The Hague. Those people with enough strength went to the countryside to seek food, including tulip bulbs, in the fields. The hunger was also somewhat selective by social class: people of higher socioeconomic status were able to use money, property, and influence to obtain additional food.

Altogether 10,000 people starved to death, and malnutrition contributed to the deaths of countless others. Adults in the famine cities who survived lost, on average, 15 to 20 percent of their body weight. Some women weighed less at the end of their pregnancy than at its inception.

When the Allies finally liberated the Netherlands in early May 1945, they rushed in food, and conditions quickly improved. But by then 40,000 fetuses had been subjected to the hardships of famine. Depending on their date of conception, these babies were exposed at various stages of gestation, for periods as long as seven months. For example, babies conceived in April 1944 and born in early January 1945 were exposed to the starvation just in the last trimester of pregnancy; those conceived in February 1945 and born in November 1945 were exposed only in the first trimester. Babies unlucky enough to be conceived in August 1944 and born in May 1945 spent their entire second and third trimesters inside increasingly malnourished mothers.

In the late 1960s four researchers at Columbia University School of Public Health—Zena Stein, Mervyn Susser, Gerhart Saenger, and Francis Marolla, all of whom had studied malnutrition in urban ghettos—realized that much might be learned from the now-grown babies of the Dutch Hunger Winter. The outcomes of pregnancies in the stricken cities of the west could be compared with those in towns to the north or south, outside the worst-hit area. In addition, the results of pregnancies during the famine could be compared with those that occurred before and after it.

Hospital records and birth registries yielded statistics on the health of the wartime mothers and their newborns. And at least for the boys, follow-up information on those same children as young adults could be extracted from the records of the Dutch military draft system. Virtually all boys at age 19 were called up for an exam that recorded their height and weight, medical history, results of mental-performance tests, level of schooling completed, and father's occupation; the latter served as a rough indicator of socioeconomic status.

A starving mother was forced to unconsciously "choose" whether to devote the few available calories to her own body or to her fetus.

These studies provided some important insights, the first of which concerned the famine's effect on fertility. During the winter of 1944 conceptions quickly declined to one-third the normal level. This suggests that the women's fertility became impaired as their fat reserves, already depleted due to reduced wartime rations, were rapidly used up. The decline was more pronounced for wives of manual workers than of nonmanual workers, presumably because the former had less means to buy their way out of starvation.

The Dutch results agree with other evidence that body weight affects our reproductive physiology. Women in German concentration camps often ceased to menstruate (while low sperm counts and impotence were common among male inmates). Moreover, studies have shown that girls begin menstruating earlier in well-fed industrialized nations than in underfed Third World countries. The same trend applies to the present generation of American women compared with their less well nourished grandmothers. All these pieces of evidence suggest that a woman's fertility is dependent on having sufficient body weight to support conception.

Among the famine babies themselves, the most obvious effects were seen in those who were exposed during the last trimester, which is normally the period when a fetus undergoes its most rapid weight gain: these babies had markedly lower average birth weights (6 pounds 10 ounces) than those born before the famine began (7 pounds 6 ounces). Starvation during the third trimester also resulted in babies who were born slightly shorter and with smaller head circumferences, indicating slightly slower than normal growth of the bones and brain. But the main impact was to retard the growth of muscle and fat.

The prefamine pregnancies had taken place while wartime rations still hovered around 1,500 daily calories—meager for a pregnant woman, who normally requires 2,500 calories a day. Medical records showed that these expectant mothers lost weight themselves but were able to maintain a normal birth weight for their babies. Once rations dropped below 1,500 calories, however, babies began to share the impact. And eventually, as the famine wore on and severe starvation struck, all further weight loss was suffered by the baby rather than the mother. Birth weight recovered quickly when food supplies improved, though: babies born three months after the famine's end had normal weights.

Both during and right after the Hunger Winter there was a sharp rise in infant deaths in the Netherlands' hard-hit cities. For babies exposed to famine only in the first trimester, the rate of stillbirth nearly doubled. Those babies had been conceived just three months before the famine's end, and so they in fact completed most of their gestation inside mothers who were relatively well nourished. Yet malnutrition during those first three months had evidently planted a slow-fuse time bomb that went off at birth.

Still greater, however, was the effect on babies exposed during the second, and especially the third, trimesters. Those babies had a higher-than-normal death rate in their first week of life, and the rate continued to climb until they were at least three months old. Some of these babies died of malnutrition itself, others succumbed to normal childhood infections to which they had lowered resistance. Fortunately, once the famine babies reached the age of one year, their increased risk of death disappeared.

L et's now see how the babies who survived the perils of birth and early infancy were faring 19 years later, when the boys were called up for the draft. In many respects these young men were similar to any others their age. Their height, for example, showed

all the usual effects of socioeconomic factors, including family size and diet: sons of manual workers averaged nearly an inch shorter than sons of wealthier fathers, children from families with many mouths to feed were shorter than only children, and later-born sons were shorter than first-born sons. The common thread is that children who have access to less food end up shorter. But postnatal, rather than prenatal, nutrition was the culprit here. If you picked any given group—say, sons of manual workers—the young men whose mothers were starved during pregnancy were no shorter than their peers.

Records from the Dutch draft exams also allowed the Columbia researchers to see if poor nutrition in pregnancy might cause lasting mental deficits as well as physical ones. Experiments with rats had shown that offspring of mothers that are starved in pregnancy end up with fewer-than-normal brain cells and learning disabilities. So when the researchers compared the grown-up famine babies' performance on tests of mental proficiency with the performance of those who had received better prenatal nourishment, they expected to find poorer scores for those who had been starved during gestation.

No such result was forthcoming. The draft exam, which included tests of verbal, arithmetic, clerical, and mechanical skills, clearly showed the effects of social environment, which were parallel to the physical effects already mentioned—thus, sons of manual laborers, sons from large families, and sons born late into a family of several children tended to score below other young men. But no effect whatsoever could be attributed to prenatal starvation. One possible explanation is that our brain has enough extra cells to preserve mental function even if some of our cells are lost. At any rate, whatever effects can be attributed to nutrition must be due to nutrition after birth, not before it.

The genetic interests of the fetus are served by saving itself. Hence we evolve as fetuses to be parasites commandeering our mother's nutrients.

This, then, was the good news, such as it was. Those starved children who made it to adulthood were no worse off than their better-nourished counterparts. However, the medical records of the male famine babies who never made it to a draft physical did reveal one consequence of prenatal starvation—and it was sobering. Fetuses exposed to famine during their first three months in the womb were twice as likely as others to have defects of the central nervous system, such as spina bifida (in which the spine fails to close properly) and hydrocephalus (a related condition, characterized by fluid accumulating in the brain). The birth defects, it now appears, almost certainly arose from starvation during the first trimester, when the nervous system was being laid down.

Just how did a lack of food have such a dire result? Animal experiments have raised the suspicion that such defects can arise from a deficiency of the B vitamin folic acid early in pregnancy. A year ago this finding was confirmed for humans in a study of 22,776 pregnant women in Boston. Babies born to mothers who took multivitamins including folic acid during the first six weeks of pregnancy had a nearly fourfold lower frequency of central nervous system defects than did babies born to women who did not take such supplements. Brands of multivitamins that lacked folic acid, or multivitamins taken only after the seventh week of pregnancy, offered no protection.

All the results from the Dutch famine studies that I've discussed so far describe the effects of starvation on mothers and their children. But recent findings have raised disturbing questions about the famine's effect on a third generation. By now the famine babies are 45 or 46, and most of the girls have long since had children of their own; the "girls" themselves are women at the end of their reproductive careers. More than 100 of these women happened to have had their babies in the same Amsterdam hospital in which they themselves were born, which makes for an easy comparison of birth records. An examination of those records has revealed something very odd: it turns out that those women who were themselves fetuses in their first and second trimester during the Dutch Hunger Winter gave birth to underweight babies. That is, the babies were somehow affected by the starvation of their grandmothers many decades earlier.

This result might have been easier to understand if the mothers themselves had been underweight at birth or were small as adults. Neither was true. Recall that starvation in the first or second trimester produced babies with normal birth weights. Only third-trimester starvation led to small babies. Yet, paradoxically, when these small babies later became mothers, they gave birth to normal-size babies. It was the women who were themselves normal size at birth who became mothers of underweight infants.

Somehow the grandmothers' suffering programmed their children in utero so that the grandchildren would be affected. This astonishing result will undoubtedly inspire experiments aimed at identifying the still-unknown cellular mechanism. But what is indisputable is that the Dutch famine left its harsh imprint on at least three generations.

From the perspective of evolutionary biology, the famine posed to the bodies of pregnant mothers an agonizing dilemma. What would you do in a situation threatening both your life and your child's life if anything you did to help one would hurt the other? Think quickly: If you see a car about to crash head-on into your car, do you throw yourself in front of your child sitting strapped in the seat beside you or do you try to protect yourself instead? Now let's make the choice more agonizing: What if your child's subsequent survival hinges on your own? You've all heard the airlines' standard safety announcement that in the event of a loss of cabin pressure, place the oxygen mask on yourself first, *then* place the mask on your child. In that situation, you have to help yourself first, because you'll be in no state to help your child if you are unconscious.

Similarly a mother starving in the Netherlands in 1944 was forced to unconsciously "choose" whether to devote the few available calories to her own body or to her fetus. This is a classic example of a conflict between two genetically related individuals. Natural selection favors the individual who passes on his or her genes to the most descendants. The genetic interests of the fetus are served by saving itself, and hence we evolve as fetuses to be parasites on our mother, commandeering her nutrients as efficiently as possible. But the mother's genetic interests are served by passing her genes to offspring. She gains nothing if her nutritional sacrifices kill not only herself but her child. Perhaps she would be best off, from an evolutionary point of view, if she sacrificed that fetus and tried again later. Yet there is no certainty that she will have another chance later.

The outcome of the Dutch famine indicates that natural selection struck a compromise. When the famine began, a mother's body at first accepted the full brunt, losing weight while preserving the weight of the fetus. In the next stage of famine both the fetus and the mother shared the hardship. In the last stage all weight loss came at the expense of the fetus, because any more weight loss by the mother would have threatened the mother's survival and thereby the survival of her child.

These pregnant women had no say in how their body allocated its precious resources, of course. Natural selection proceeded along its inexorable journey oblivious to any human agony or ethical dilemma. To ask whether the decisions it made were wise, whether they were somehow the "right" decisions, is irrelevant. The choices were arrived at in accordance with the cold logic of evolution and nothing more.

But what about the decisions that created such cruel conditions in the first place? What about the reasoning that even today, in the guise of wartime expediency, can compel one group of people to consciously impose starvation on another and thus scar the lives of unborn generations? For that matter, what about the reduction of social programs in our own society that might subject untold numbers of children, both before and after birth, to the dangers of malnutrition simply by failing to ensure proper nourishment for them and their mothers? The lessons of the Dutch Hunger Winter are there for the learning. We can ignore them only at our children's, and our grandchildren's, expense.

Development During Infancy and Early Childhood

No period in human development has received more attention during the past quarter century than infancy. Much of this research has been stimulated by Jean Piaget, the Swiss developmental theorist, who argued that the many abilities of infants evolve slowly over their first two years as a product of the combined forces of maturation and experience. A major portion of research has focused on infants' perceptual skills and cognitive abilities. These studies have made it quite apparent that infants are far from the passive, unknowing beings they were once thought to be. In fact, many of these abilities appear so early that Piaget's views are now being strongly challenged. In "A New Perspective on Cognitive Development," a leading researcher, Jean Mandler, advances a competing view that the perceptual and cognitive abilities of the infant are more a part of the basic endowment of the child than a product of learning and practice.

Perhaps modern-day opinions on child rearing merely reflect the ebb and flow of advice that has been brought forth over the ages. This is expanded in "The Child Yesterday, Today, and Tomorrow."

The many skills of the newborn multiply dramatically over the first several years of life, transforming the physically helpless infant into a child who, by age three or even earlier, is capable of thinking, communicating, and skillfully solving problems. Knowledge of the readiness to learn that is now so evident in infants and toddlers has brought with it questions about the best ways to nurture early intellectual and social development. One point of view, supported by many parents eager to give their young children a head start toward academic success, places emphasis on a relatively narrow band of school-related skills. In "Preschool: Head Start or Hard Push?" Philip R. Piccigallo argues that this view is a dangerously narrow one that fails to recognize the importance of everyday experience in creating meaningful learning opportunities for the young child. Many early childhood experts caution that structured learning experiences bring with them the risk of placing too much pressure on the child; they argue that such pressures can, in turn, stunt creativity and turn learning into drudgery rather than a spontaneous process of discovery.

"How Three Key Countries Shape Their Children" is an illuminating look at the ways in which preschools in Japan, China, and the United States are designed to instill distinctly different values. U.S. preschools stress experiences that promote individuality, while those of Japan and China place far greater emphasis on inculcating a sense of community spirit and responsibility.

Cultures also differ widely in their definition of appropriate roles for the two sexes. For more than a century, scientists have been debating the source of gender differences. As gender research has become more sophisticated, it has also become more controversial. However, most scientists agree that the sexes are more alike than different, with greater variation within each sex than between the sexes. Are boys really better at math and girls more verbal? Are girls really kinder and gentler and boys more aggressive? "Sizing Up the Sexes" examines recent research on this topic and puts forth the argument that hormonal differences and brain structure play a far more important role in gender differences than has been assumed in the past.

"The Day Care Generation" considers a critical problem in the United States: the lack of quality supplemental child care facilities for children. Over 50 percent of working mothers have children under the age of six. This statistic underlines the magnitude of the problem and the urgent need for effective solutions. Parents must choose among various day care options without the aid of any industry-wide standards, knowing that day care centers are operated with practically no federal or state regulations or guidelines to ensure quality. The article identifies a number of key factors to consider in evaluating day care arrangements, and reviews some of the studies that have played an important role in the national debate over early child care.

Looking Ahead: Challenge Questions

Discuss the pros and cons of beginning as early as possible to teach young children skills such as reading and math. Explain why you agree or disagree with these principles.

How have scientist's views about the competencies of the infant changed in the past several decades?

What effect does work have on the development of attachment relationships between mother and infant, or on the effectiveness of discipline in school-age children? Does society have a responsibility to provide supplementary care for children of working mothers? Does industry have this responsibility?

Why has so much effort been devoted to the study of sex differences in the past several decades? How would you summarize the general feelings of this body of research in brief?

Unit 2

A New Perspective on Cognitive Development in Infancy

Jean M. Mandler

Jean Mandler received her Ph.D. from Harvard in 1956. She is currently professor of psychology and cognitive science at the University of California, San Diego. Her interests are cognition and cognitive development, with emphasis on the representation of knowledge. She has done research on how our knowledge of stories, events, and scenes is organized and the way in which such organization affects remembering. In recent years her research has concentrated on conceptual development in infancy and early childhood. Preparation of this article was supported by an NSF grant. Address: Department of Cognitive Science D-015, University of California, San Diego, La Jolla, CA 92093.

Over the past decade something of a revolution has been taking place in our understanding of cognitive development during infancy. For many years one theory dominated the field—that of the Swiss psychologist Jean Piaget. Piaget's views on infancy were so widely known and respected that to many psychologists at least one aspect of development seemed certain: human infants go through a protracted period during which they cannot yet think. They can learn to recognize things and to smile at them, to crawl and to manipulate objects, but they do not yet have concepts or ideas. This period, which Piaget called the sensorimotor stage of development, was said to last until one-and-a-half to two years of age. Only near the end of this stage do infants learn how to represent the world in a symbolic, conceptual manner, and thus advance from infancy into early childhood.

Piaget formulated this view of infancy primarily by observing the development of his own three children—few laboratory techniques were available at the time. More recently, experimental methods have been devised to study infants, and a large body of research has been accumulating. Much of the new work suggests that the theory of a sensori-motor stage of development will have to be substantially modified or perhaps even abandoned (Fig. 1). The present article provides a brief overview of Piaget's theory of sensorimotor development, a summary of recent data that are difficult to reconcile with that theory, and an outline of an alternative view of early mental development.

In Piaget's (1951, 1952, 1954) theory, the first stage of development is said to consist of sensorimotor (perceptual and motor) functioning in an

Recent research suggests that infants have the ability to conceptualize much earlier than we thought

organism that has not yet acquired a representational (conceptual) capacity. The only knowledge infants have is what things look and sound like and how to move themselves around and manipulate objects. This kind of sensorimotor knowledge is often termed procedural or implicit knowledge, and is contrasted with explicit, factual (conceptual) knowledge (e.g., Cohen and Squire 1980; Schacter 1987; Mandler 1988). Factual knowledge is the kind of knowledge one can think about or recall; it is usually considered to be symbolic and propositional. Some factual information may be stored in the form of images, but these are also symbolic, in the sense that they are constructed from both propositional and spatial knowledge. Sensorimotor knowledge, on the other hand, is subsymbolic knowledge; it is knowing *how* to recognize something or use a motor skill, but it does not require explicitly knowing *that* something is the case. It is the kind of knowledge we build into robots in order to make them recognize and manipulate objects in their environment, and it is also the kind of knowledge we ascribe to lower organisms, which function quite well without the ability to conceptualize facts. It is the kind of knowledge that tends to remain undisturbed in amnesic patients, even when their memory for facts and their personal past is severely impaired.

In the case of babies, the restriction of functioning to sensorimotor processing implies that they can neither think about absent objects nor recall the past. According to Piaget, they lack the capacity even to form an image of things they have seen before; a fortiori, they have no capacity to imagine what will happen tomorrow. Thus, the absence of a symbolic capacity does not mean just that infants cannot understand language or reason; it means that they cannot remember what they did this morning or imagine their mother if she is not present. It is, in short, a most un-Proustian life, not thought about, only lived (Mandler 1983).

According to Piaget, to be able to think about the world requires first that perceptual-motor schemas of objects and relations among them be formed. Then, symbols must be created to stand for these schemas. Several aspects of Piaget's formulation account for the slow course of both these developments. First, on the basis of his observations Piaget assumed that the sensory modalities are unconnected at birth, each delivering separate types of information. Thus, he thought that one of the major tasks of the first half of the sensorimotor stage is to construct schemas integrating the information from initially disconnected sights, sounds, and touches. Until this integration is

From *American Scientist*, Vol. 78, No. 3, May/June 1990, pp. 236-243. Reprinted by permission of *American Scientist*, journal of Sigma Xi, The Scientific Research Society.

accomplished, stable sensorimotor schemas of three-dimensional, solid, sound-producing, textured objects cannot be formed and hence cannot be thought about.

In addition, babies must learn about the causal interrelatedness of objects and the fact that objects continue to exist when not being perceived. Piaget thought that these notions were among the major accomplishments of the second half of the sensorimotor stage. He suggested that they derive from manual activity—for example, repeated covering and uncovering, poking, pushing, and dropping objects while observ-

represent bottles in their absence.

All the anticipatory behavior that Piaget observed throughout the first 18 months was accounted for in similar terms. Signs of anticipation of future events became more wide-ranging and complex but did not seem to require the use of images or other symbols to represent what was about to happen. Rather, Piaget assumed that an established sensorimotor schema set up a kind of image-less expectation of the next event, followed by recognition when the event took place. He used strict criteria for the presence of imagery—for example, verbal recall of the past

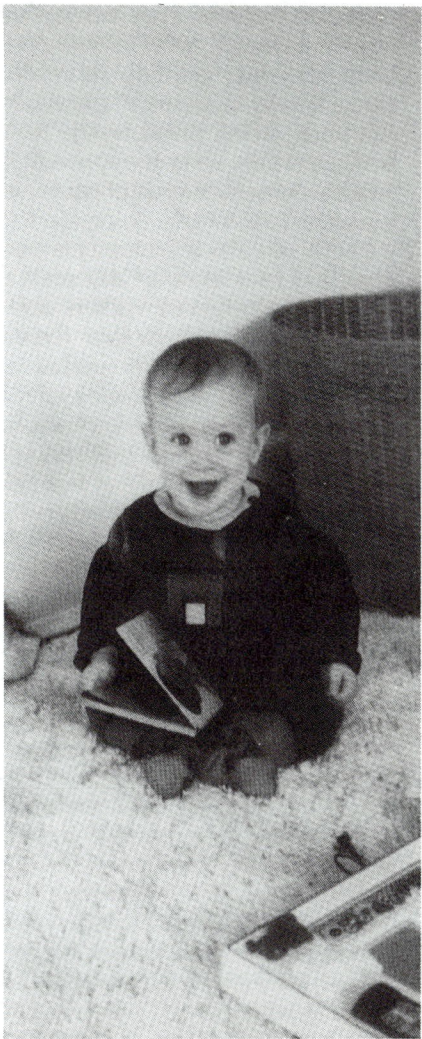

William James described the perceptual world of the infant as a ''blooming, buzzing confusion''

ing the results. Handling objects leads to understanding them; it allows the integration of perceptual and motor information that gives objects substantiality, permanence, and unique identities separate from the self. Since motor control over the hands is slow to develop, to the extent that conceptual understanding requires physical interaction with objects, it is necessarily a late development. Much of the first year of life, then, is spent accomplishing the co-ordination of the various sources of perceptual and motor information required to form the sensorimotor object schemas that will then be available to be conceptualized.

According to Piaget, the development of the symbolic function is itself a protracted process. In addition to constructing sensorimotor schemas of objects and relations, which form the basic content or meaning of what is to be thought about, symbols to refer to these meanings must be formed. Piaget assumed that the latter development has its precursors in the expectancies involved in conditioning. For example, the sight of a bottle can serve as a signal that milk will follow, and babies soon learn to make anticipatory sucking movements. This process, essentially the same as that involved in Pavlovian conditioning, does not imply a symbolic function; there is no indication that the baby can use such signals to

(which implies the ability to represent absent events to oneself) or rapid problem-solving without trial and error. Neither of these can be ascribed merely to running off a practiced sensorimotor schema, but they require instead some representation of information not perceptually present.

Piaget did not observe recall or covert problem-solving until the end of the sensorimotor period. One might think that the fact that infants begin to acquire language during the latter part of the first year would be difficult to reconcile with a lack of symbolic capacity. However, Piaget characterized early words as imitative schemas, no different in kind from other motor schemas displayed in the presence of familiar situations.

Imitation, in fact, plays an important role in this account, because it provides the source of the development of imagery. Piaget assumed that images are not formed merely from looking at or hearing something, but arise only when what is being perceived is also analyzed. The attempt to imitate the actions of others provides the stimulus for such analysis to take place. Although infants begin to imitate early, it was not until near the end of the first year or beyond that Piaget found his children able to imitate novel actions or actions involving parts of their bodies they could not see themselves, such as blinking or sticking out their

Figure 1. According to the Swiss psychologist Jean Piaget, babies like the author's 8-month-old grandson shown here have learned to recognize people, and their smile is a sign of that recognition. However, Piaget believed that babies have not yet learned to think at such an early age and thus cannot recall even the most familiar people in their lives when those people are not present. Recent research suggests that this view may be mistaken and that babies such as this one are already forming concepts about people and things in their environment.

tongues. He took this difficulty as evidence that they could not form an image of something complex or unobserved until detailed analysis of it had taken place; it is presumably during this analysis that imagery is constructed. Piaget's study of imitation suggested that such analysis, and therefore the formation of imagery, was a late development in infancy. To complete the process of symbol formation, then, the anticipatory mechanisms of sensorimotor schemas become speeded up and appear as images of what will occur, thus allowing genuine representation. Finally, by some mechanism left unspecified, these newly created images can be used to represent the world independent of ongoing sensorimotor activity.

All these developments—constructing sensorimotor schemas, establishing a coherent world of objects and events suitable to form the content of ideas, learning to imitate and to form images that can be used to stand for things—are completed in the second half of the second year, and result in the child's at last being able to develop a conceptual system of ideas. Images can now be used to recall the past and to imagine the future, and even perceptually present objects can begin to be interpreted conceptually as well as by means of motor interactions with them. With the onset of thought, an infant is well on the way to becoming fully human.

This theory of the sensorimotor foundations of thought has come under attack from two sources. One is experimental work suggesting that a stable and differentiated perceptual world is established much earlier in infancy than Piaget realized. The other is recent work suggesting that recall and other forms of symbolic activity (presumably mediated by imagery) occur by at least the second half of the first year. I will discuss each of these findings in turn.

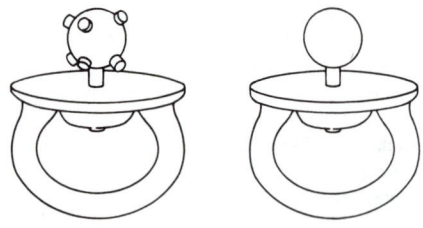

Figure 2. The old idea that the senses are unconnected at birth and are gradually integrated through experience is contradicted by an experiment using bumpy and smooth pacifiers to study the visual recognition of an object that has been experienced only tactilely. A one-month-old infant is habituated to one of the two kinds of pacifiers in its mouth without being allowed to see it. The pacifier is then removed, and the infant is shown both kinds of pacifiers. Infants look longer at the nipple they felt in their mouth. (After Meltzoff and Borton 1979.)

Perceptual development

The notion that the senses are unconnected at birth and that they become integrated only through experience is an old idea that was popularized by William James's (1890) description of the perceptual world of the infant as a "blooming, buzzing confusion." Recent work, however, suggests that either the senses are interrelated at birth or the learning involved in their integration is extremely rapid. There is evidence for integration of auditory and visual information as well as of vision and touch in the first months of life. What follows is a small sample of the research findings.

From birth, infants turn their heads to look at the source of a sound (Wertheimer 1961; Mendelson and Haith 1976). This does not mean that they have any particular expectations of what they will see when they hear a given sound, but it does indicate a mechanism that would enable rapid learning. By four months, if one presents two films of complex events not seen before and accompanied by a single sound track, infants prefer to look at the film that matches the sound (Spelke 1979). Perhaps even more surprising, when infants are presented with two films, each showing only a speaker's face, they will choose the correct film, even when the synchrony between both films and the soundtrack is identical (Kuhl and Meltzoff 1988). In addition, one-month-olds can recognize visually presented objects that they have only felt in their mouths (Fig. 2; Meltzoff and Borton 1979; Walker-Andrews and Gibson 1986). Such data suggest either that the output of each sensory transducer consists in part of the same amodal pattern of information or that some central processing of two similar patterns of information is accomplished. In either case, the data strongly support the view that there is more order and coherence in early perceptual experience than Piaget or James realized.

In addition to sensory coordination, a good deal of information about the nature of objects is provided by the visual system alone, information to which young infants have been shown to be sensitive. For example, it used to be thought that infants have difficulty separating objects from a background, but it ap-

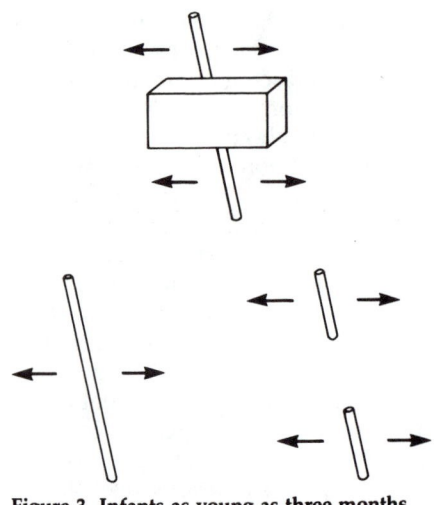

Figure 3. Infants as young as three months can use the perception of relative movement to determine object boundaries. They are habituated to the display shown at the top, which represents a rod moving back and forth behind a block of wood. Then they are tested with the two displays on the bottom: the rod moving as it did before, but with no block in front, or the two pieces of the rod that were visible behind the block, also moving as they did before. Infants tend to continue to habituate to the whole moving rod—that is, they cease to look at it, indicating that it is familiar to them. They prefer to look at the broken rod, indicating that they consider it something new. If the same experiment is done with a stationary rod behind a block, infants exhibit no preference when presented with a whole stationary rod or a broken stationary rod. (After Kellman and Spelke 1983.)

pears that such confusion is a rare event, not the norm. Infants may not "see" that a cup is separable from a saucer without picking it up, but in general they do not have difficulty determining the boundaries of objects. They use information from motion to parse objects from the perceptual surround long before they are able to manipulate them manually. At an age as young as three months, they can use the relative motion of objects against both stationary and moving backgrounds to determine the objects' boundaries (Fig. 3; Kellman and Spelke 1983; Spelke 1988). Even stationary objects are seen as separate if they are spatially separated, whether in a plane or in depth. Infants also use motion to determine object identity, treating an object that moves behind a screen and then reappears as one object rather than two (Spelke and Kestenbaum 1986).

Other work by Spelke and by

Baillargeon (Baillargeon et al. 1985; Baillargeon 1987a; Spelke 1988) shows that infants as young as four months expect objects to be substantial, in the sense that the objects cannot move through other objects nor other objects through them (Fig. 4), and permanent, in the sense that the objects are assumed to continue to exist when hidden. Finally, there is evidence that by six months infants perceive causal relations among moving objects (Leslie 1988) in a fashion that seems to be qualitatively the same as that of adults (Michotte 1963).

From this extensive research program, we can conclude that objects are seen as bounded, unitary, solid, and separate from the background, perhaps from birth but certainly by three to four months of age. Such young infants obviously still have a great deal to learn about objects, but the world must appear both stable and orderly to them, and thus capable of being conceptualized.

Conceptual development

It is easier to study what infants see than what they are thinking about. Nevertheless, there are a few ways to assess whether or not infants are thinking. One way is to look for symbolic activity, such as using a gesture to refer to something else. Piaget (1952) himself called attention to a phenomenon he called motor recognition. For example, he observed his six-month-old daughter make a gesture on catching sight of a familiar toy in a new location. She was accustomed to kicking at the toy in her crib, and when she saw it across the room she made a brief, abbreviated kicking motion. Piaget did not consider this true symbolic activity, because it was a motor movement, not a purely mental act; nevertheless, he suggested that his daughter was referring to, or classifying, the toy by means of her action. In a similar vein, infants whose parents use sign language have been observed to begin to use conventional signs at around six to seven months (Prinz and Prinz 1979; Bonvillian et al. 1983; see Mandler 1988 for discussion).

Another type of evidence of conceptual functioning is recall of absent objects or events. Indeed, Piaget accepted recall as irrefutable evidence

of conceptual representation, since there is no way to account for recreating information that is not perceptually present by means of sensorimotor schemas alone; imagery or other symbolic means of representation must be involved. Typically we associate recall with verbal recreation of the past, and this, as Piaget observed, is not usually found until 18 months or older. But recall need not be verbal—and indeed is usually not when we think about past events—so that in principle it is possible in preverbal infants.

One needs to see a baby do something like find a hidden object after a delay or imitate a previously observed event. Until recently, only diary studies provided evidence of recall in the second half of the first year—for example, finding an object hidden in an unfamiliar location after

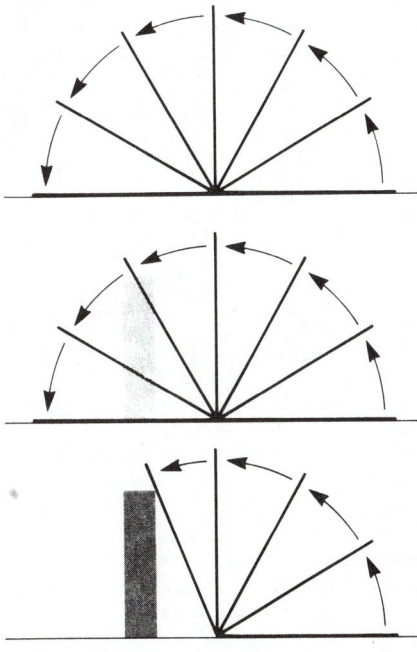

Figure 4. Shown here is a procedure used to demonstrate four- and five-month-olds' memory for the location of a hidden object. At the top is a screen moving through a 180° rotation, to which infants viewing from the right are habituated by repetition. Following habituation, a box is placed behind the screen, and the infants see two test events: an impossible *(middle)* and a possible event *(bottom)*. In the impossible event, the screen continues to rotate 180°, moving "magically" through the hidden box (which the experimenter has surreptitiously removed). In the possible event, the screen rotates only to the point where it would hit the box. The infants' surprise at the impossible event demonstrates that they remember an object they cannot see. (After Baillargeon 1987a.)

a 24-hour delay (Ashmead and Perlmutter 1980). Now, however, similar phenomena are beginning to be demonstrated in the laboratory. Meltzoff (1988) showed that nine-month-olds could imitate actions that they had seen performed 24 hours earlier. Each action consisted of an unusual gesture with a novel object—for example, pushing a recessed button in a box (which produced a beeping sound)—and the infants were limited to watching the experimenter carry it out; thus, when they later imitated the action, they could not be merely running off a practiced motor schema in response to seeing the object again. Control subjects, who had been shown the objects but not the actions performed on them, made the correct responses much less frequently. We have replicated this phenomenon with 11-month-olds (McDonough and Mandler 1989).

Because of the difficulties that young infants have manipulating objects, it is not obvious that this technique can be used with infants younger than about eight months. One suspects, however, that if nine-month-olds can recall several novel events after a 24-hour delay, somewhat younger infants can probably recall similar events after shorter delays.

There is a small amount of data from a procedure that does not require a motor response and that, although using quite short delays, suggests recall-like processes. Baillargeon's experiments on object permanence, mentioned earlier, use a technique that requires infants to remember that an object is hidden behind a screen. For example, she has shown that infants are surprised when a screen appears to move backward through an object they have just seen hidden behind it (see Fig. 4). In her experiments with four- and five-month-olds, the infants had to remember for only about 8 to 12 seconds that there was an object behind the screen (Baillargeon et al. 1985; Baillargeon 1987a). However, in more recent work with eight-month-olds, Baillargeon and her colleagues have been successful with a delay of 70 seconds (Fig. 5; Baillargeon et al. 1989). This kind of performance seems to require a representational capacity not attributable to sensorimotor schemas. Not only is an absent

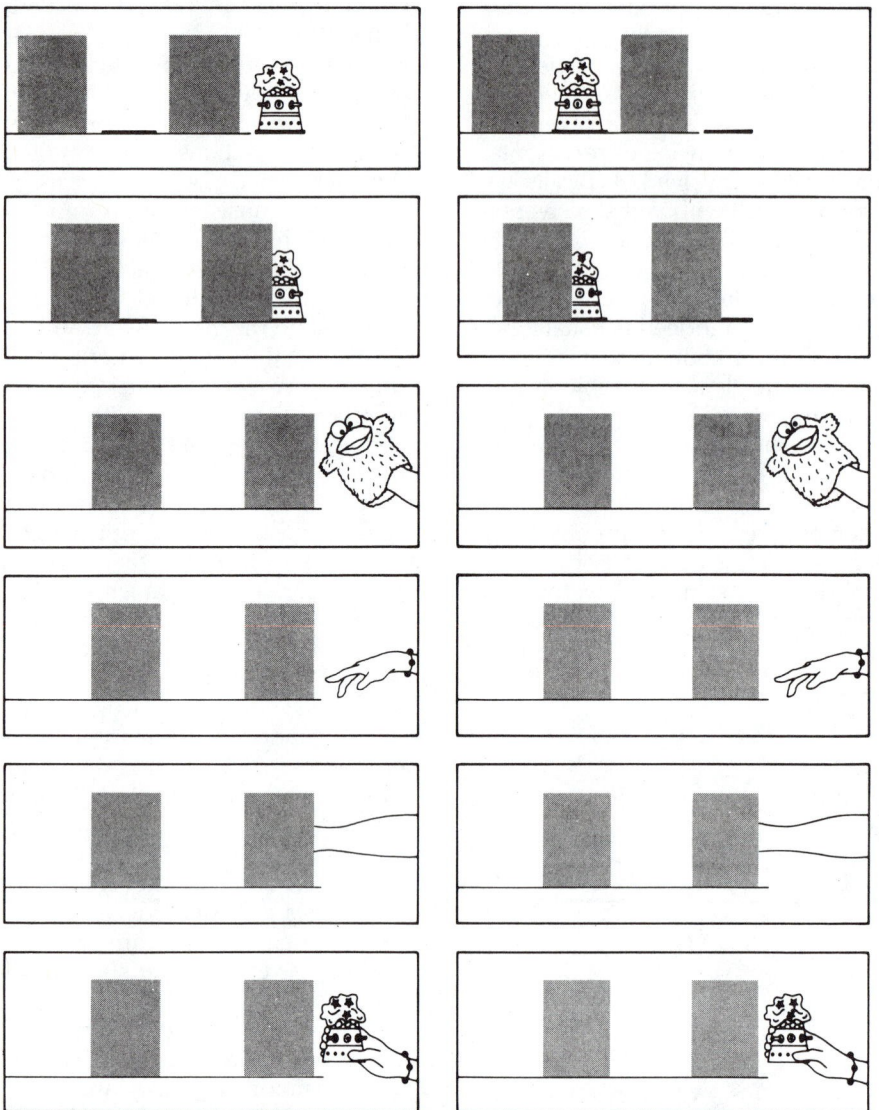

Figure 5. Another procedure involving possible *(left)* and impossible events *(right)* elicits meaningful responses from eight-month-old infants after a delay of 70 seconds. Moving from top to bottom, an object is hidden respectively behind the right or left of two screens; puppets and hand tiptoes are used to keep infants attentive during the delay period; the experimenter reaches behind the right screen and brings the hidden object into view from behind it. (The object was placed there surreptitiously as part of the impossible event.) Surprise at the impossible event indicates memory of the place where the object was hidden. The apparent recall suggests a kind of conceptual functioning that goes beyond the sensorimotor functioning described by Piaget. (After Baillargeon et al. 1989.)

object being represented, but the information is rather precise—for example, Baillargeon (1987b) found that infants remembered not only that an object was hidden but where it was located and how tall it was.

Where do concepts come from?

The data described above indicate that the theory of an exclusively sensorimotor stage of development, in which babies cannot yet represent the world conceptually, is in need of considerable revision. There does not appear to be a protracted period during which infants have no conception of objects or events and cannot represent them in their absence. A great deal of information is available to and used by infants from an early age, even before they have developed the motor coordination enabling manual exploration that Piaget thought was crucial to conceptual development.

Indeed, a good deal of evidence suggests that we have tended to confuse infants' motor incompetence with conceptual incompetence. Piaget was particularly influenced in his theorizing by the difficulties that children as old as a year have finding a hidden object, especially when it is hidden in more than one location a number of times in succession. The phenomena he demonstrated have been replicated many times, but it now appears that much of the difficulty infants have in such situations is due not to a lack of understanding of object permanence but to other factors. For example, repeatedly hiding an object in different locations can be confusing and leads to perseverative responding to the same place (see Diamond 1985; Mandler 1988, in press).

If a conceptual system of knowledge has begun to be formed by at least six months and perhaps earlier, where does it come from? Piaget's theory of a transformation of well-developed action schemas into conceptual thought cannot account for conceptual knowledge occurring before the action schemas themselves have developed. On the other hand, perceptual schemas about objects and events develop early. What is needed, then, is some mechanism for transforming these schemas into concepts, or ideas, about what is being perceived, preferably a mechanism that can operate as soon as perceptual schemas are formed.

Little has been written about this problem. One approach is to assume that even young infants are capable of redescribing perceptual information in a conceptual format. I have suggested a mechanism that might accomplish this (Mandler 1988): perceptual analysis, a process by which one perception is actively compared to another and similarities or differences between them are noted. (Such analysis, like other sorts of concept formation, requires some kind of vocabulary; this aspect, still little understood, is discussed below.) The simplest case of perceptual analysis occurs when two simultaneously presented objects are compared, or a single object is compared to an already established representation (i.e., one notes similarities or differences between what one is looking at and what one recalls about it). It is the process by which we discover that sugar bowls have two handles and teacups only one, or that a friend wears glasses. Unless we have engaged in this kind of analysis (or someone has told us), the information will not be accessible for us to think about. Much of the time, of course, we do not make such comparisons, which is why we often can recall few details of even recent experiences.

Although it is analytic, perceptual analysis consists primarily of simplification. Our perceptual system regularly processes vast amounts of information that never become accessible to thought. For example, we make use of a great deal of complex information every time we recognize a face: proportions, contours, subtle shading, relationships among various facial features, and so on. Yet little of this information is available to our thought processes. Few people are aware of the proportions of the human face—it is not something they have ever conceptualized. Even fewer know how they determine whether a face is male or female (this categorization depends on subtle differences in proportions). For the most part we do not even have words to describe the nuances that our perceptual apparatus uses instantly and effortlessly to make such a perceptual categorization.

For us to be able to think about such matters, the information must be reduced and simplified into a conceptual format. One way this redescription is done is via language; someone (perhaps an artist who has already carried out the relevant analytic process) conceptualizes aspects of a face for us. The other way is to look at a face and analyze it ourselves, such as noting that the ears are at the same level as the eyes. The analysis is often couched in linguistic form, but it need not be. Images can be used, but these, in spite of having spatial properties, have a major conceptual component (e.g., Kosslyn 1983).

An infant, of course, does not have the benefit of language, the means by which older people acquire much of their factual knowledge. So if infants are to transform perceptual schemas into thoughts, they must be able to analyze the perceptual information they receive. The perceptual system itself cannot decide that only animate creatures move by themselves or that containers must have bottoms if they are to hold things, and so forth. These are facts visually observed, but they are highly simpli-

Infants whose parents use sign language have been observed to begin to use conventional signs at around six to seven months

fied versions of the information available to be conceptualized.

The notion of perceptual analysis is similar to the process that Piaget theorized as being responsible for the creation of images. He thought that this kind of analysis does not even begin until around eight or nine months and does not result in imagery until later still. However, he had no evidence that image formation is such a late-developing process, and his own description of his children's imitative performance as early as three or four months strongly suggests that the process of perceptual analysis had begun. For example, he observed imitation of clapping hands at that time, a performance that would seem to require a good deal of analysis, considering the difference between what infants see and what they must do. In many places in his account of early imitation, Piaget

noted that the infants watched him carefully, studying both their own and his actions. Other developmental psychologists have commented on the same phenomenon. For example, Werner and Kaplan (1963) noted that infants begin "contemplating" objects at between three and five months. Ruff (1986) has documented intense examination of objects at six months (the earliest age she studied).

To investigate contemplation or analysis of objects experimentally is not easy. A possible measure is the number of times an infant looks back and forth between two objects that are presented simultaneously. Janowsky (1985), for example, showed that this measure increased significantly between four and eight months. At four months infants tend to look first at one object and then the other; at eight months they switch back and forth between the two a

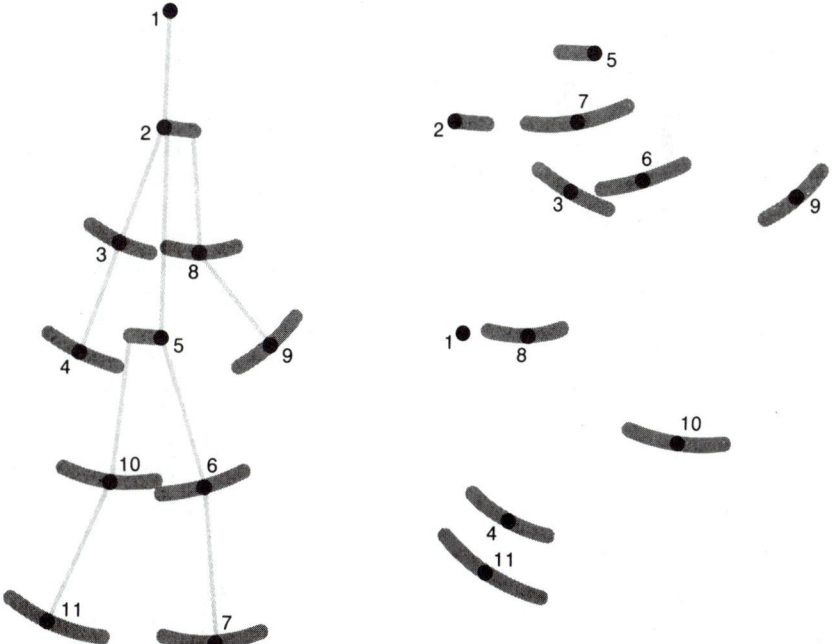

Figure 6. An equally subtle ability is involved in this demonstration of three-month-olds' responses to biological as opposed to nonbiological motion. The infants watch videotapes of computer-generated displays. On the left is a display of 11 point-lights moving as if attached to the head and major joints of a person walking. The motion vectors drawn through each point represent the perceived motions of the display; the lines connecting points, like the numbers and vectors, are not visible to the infants. The display on the right is identical to the normal walker except that the relative locations of the point-lights are scrambled. Correspondingly numbered points in the two displays undergo identical motions. Infants show greater interest in the scrambled display, indicating that they consider it novel. (After Bertenthal et al. 1987.)

good many times. Fox and his colleagues (1979) have reported a similar phenomenon. Interestingly, Janowsky found that the differences in looking back and forth are not associated with differences in total looking time, the rate at which infants habituate to objects (cease to look at them), or accuracy of recognition. So the looking back and forth must serve some other function. I would suggest that it is a comparison process, by which one object is being contrasted with the other.

A vocabulary for concepts

Assuming that perceptual analysis can lead to concept formation, it is still necessary to formulate the vocabulary in which the resulting concepts are couched. But here we face one of the major stumbling blocks in psychological theory: the problem of specifying conceptual primitives (see Smith and Medin 1981). Perhaps because of its difficulty, it has been largely ignored by developmental psychologists, in spite of the fact that any theory of conceptual development must resolve the issue of what the earliest concepts are like, no matter when they may first be formed. Leslie (1988) has offered an analysis of the primitives involved in early causal concepts, and people working on language acquisition have speculated about semantic primitives. For example, Slobin (1985) points out that children must already have concepts of objects and events, as well as relational notions about them, in order for language to be acquired. Since language comprehension begins at around nine to ten months (and perhaps earlier for sign language), some kind of conceptual system must be well established by that time. But we have almost no information as to its character.

Help may come from recent studies by cognitive linguists (e.g., Fauconnier 1985; Johnson 1987; Lakoff 1987). Although the primary goal of these theorists is to understand how language works, their analyses of the root concepts expressed in language may be of use in our search for babies' earliest concepts. For example, Lakoff and Johnson have proposed that image schemas—notions derived from spatial structure, such

as trajectory, up-down, container, part-whole, end-of-path, and link— form the foundation of the conceptualizing capacity. These authors suggest that image schemas are derived from preconceptual perceptual structures, forming the core of many of our concepts of objects and events and of their metaphorical extensions to abstract realms. They demonstrate in great detail how many of our most complex concepts are grounded in such primitive notions. I would characterize image schemas as simplified redescriptions of sensorimotor schemas, noting that they seem to be reasonably within the capacity of infant conceptualization.

The potential usefulness of image schemas as conceptual primitives can be illustrated by the example of the container schema. According to Johnson and Lakoff, the structural elements of this image schema are "interior," "boundary," and "exterior." It has a bodily basis likely to be appreciated by quite young infants, and a perceptual basis that seems to require minimal redescription of the object schemas described earlier. It also has a simple binary logic—either in or not-in; if A is in B and B is in C, then A is in C—that may or may not be the sensorimotor basis of the Boolean logic of classes, as Lakoff suggests, but is certainly a characteristic of concepts as opposed to percepts. (The conceptual system tends to reduce the continuous information delivered by the perceptual system to a small number of discrete values.)

The use of such an image schema might be responsible for the better performance nine-month-old infants show on hiding tasks when a container is used rather than cloths or screens (Freeman et al. 1980). Current work by Baillargeon (pers. com.) suggests that at approximately the same age infants are surprised when containers without bottoms appear to hold things. Of course, these are only fragments of the kind of information needed to document the development of the idea of a container, but

they indicate how we might go about tracking the early establishment of simple concepts.

A more complex concept that may also be acquired relatively early in infancy is that of animacy. Consider some possible sources for such a concept. We know that infants differentiate biological from nonbiological motion as early as three months (Fig. 6; Bertenthal et al. 1987). This perceptual differentiation, although an excellent source of information, does not constitute a concept by itself; it is an accomplishment similar to categorizing male and female faces, which infants have learned to do by six months (Fagan and Singer 1979). As discussed earlier, such perceptual categorization is not accessible for purposes of conceptual thought unless it has been redescribed in conceptual terms. An infant needs to conceptualize some differences between categories of moving objects, such as noting that one type starts up on its own and (sometimes) responds to the infant's signals, whereas the other type does not. An image schema of a notion such as beginning-of-path could be used to redescribe the perceptual information involved in initiation of motion. A link schema (whose elements are two entities and some kind of path between them) could be used to describe the observation of responsivity to self. From such simple foundations might arise a primitive concept of animal, a concept that we have reason to believe is present in some form by at least the end of the first year of life (Golinkoff and Halperin 1983; Mandler and Bauer 1988).

These are some examples of how a conceptual system might emerge from a combination of perceptual input and some relatively simple redescriptions of that input. I have suggested that a mechanism of perceptual analysis could enable such redescription, with the terms of the redescription being derived from spatial structure. The mechanism would not require an extended period of

---

A good deal of evidence suggests that we have tended to confuse infants' motor incompetence with conceptual incompetence

exclusively sensorimotor functioning but would allow conceptualization of the world to begin early in infancy. The data I have summarized indicate that babies do indeed begin to think earlier than we thought. Therefore, it seems safe to assume that they either are born with or acquire early in life the capacity to form concepts, rather than to assume that conceptual functioning can occur only as an outcome of a lengthy sensorimotor stage.

References

Ashmead, D. H., and M. Perlmutter. 1980. Infant memory in everyday life. In *New Directions for Child Development: Children's Memory*, vol. 10, ed. M. Perlmutter, pp. 1–16. Jossey-Bass.

Baillargeon, R. 1987a. Object permanence in 3.5- and 4.5-month-old infants. *Devel. Psychol.* 23:655–64.

———. 1987b. Young infants' reasoning about the physical and spatial properties of a hidden object. *Cognitive Devel.* 2:179–200.

Baillargeon, R., J. De Vos, and M. Graber. 1989. Location memory in 8-month-old infants in a nonsearch AB task: Further evidence. *Cognitive Devel.* 4:345–67.

Baillargeon, R., E. S. Spelke, and S. Wasserman. 1985. Object permanence in five-month-old infants. *Cognition* 20:191–208.

Bertenthal, B. I., D. R. Proffitt, S. J. Kramer, and N. B. Spetner. 1987. Infants' encoding of kinetic displays varying in relative coherence. *Devel. Psychol.* 23:171–78.

Bonvillian, J. D., M. D. Orlansky, and L. L. Novack. 1983. Developmental milestones: Sign language and motor development. *Child Devel.* 54:1435–45.

Cohen, N. J., and L. R. Squire. 1980. Preserved learning and retention of pattern-analyzing skills in amnesia: Dissociation of knowing how and knowing that. *Science* 210:207–10.

Diamond, A. 1985. The development of the ability to use recall to guide action, as indicated by infants' performance on AB. *Child Devel.* 56:868–83.

Fagan, J. F., III, and L. T. Singer. 1979. The role of simple feature differences in infant recognition of faces. *Infant Behav. Devel.* 2:39–46.

Fauconnier, G. 1985. *Mental Spaces*. MIT Press.

Fox, N., J. Kagan, and S. Weiskopf. 1979. The growth of memory during infancy. *Genetic Psychol. Mono.* 99:91–130.

Freeman, N. H., S. Lloyd, and C. G. Sinha. 1980. Infant search tasks reveal early concepts of containment and canonical usage of objects. *Cognition* 8:243–62.

Golinkoff, R. M., and M. S. Halperin. 1983. The concept of animal: One infant's view. *Infant Behav. Devel.* 6:229–33.

James, W. 1890. *The Principles of Psychology*. Holt.

Janowsky, J. S. 1985. Cognitive development and reorganization after early brain injury. Ph.D. diss., Cornell Univ.

Johnson, M. 1987. *The Body in the Mind: The Bodily Basis of Meaning, Imagination, and Reason*. Univ. of Chicago Press.

Kellman, P. J., and E. S. Spelke. 1983. Perception of partly occluded objects in infancy. *Cognitive Psychol.* 15:483–524.

Kosslyn, S. M. 1983. *Ghosts in the Mind's Machine: Creating and Using Images in the Brain*. Norton.

Kuhl, P. K., and A. N. Meltzoff. 1988. Speech as an intermodal object of perception. In *Perceptual Development in Infancy: The Minnesota Symposia on Child Psychology*, vol. 20, ed. A. Yonas, pp. 235–66. Erlbaum.

Lakoff, G. 1987. *Women, Fire, and Dangerous Things: What Categories Reveal about the Mind*. Univ. of Chicago Press.

Leslie, A. 1988. The necessity of illusion: Perception and thought in infancy. In *Thought without Language*, ed. L. Weiskrantz, pp. 185–210. Clarendon Press.

Mandler, J. M. 1983. Representation. In *Cognitive Development*, ed. J. H. Flavell and E. M. Markman, pp. 420–94. Vol. 3 of *Manual of Child Psychology*, ed. P. Mussen. Wiley.

———. 1988. How to build a baby: On the development of an accessible representational system. *Cognitive Devel.* 3:113–36.

———. In press. Recall of events by preverbal children. In *The Development and Neural Bases of Higher Cognitive Functions*, ed. A. Diamond. New York Academy of Sciences Press.

Mandler, J. M., and P. J. Bauer. 1988. The cradle of categorization: Is the basic level basic? *Cognitive Devel.* 3:247–64.

McDonough, L., and J. M. Mandler. 1989. Immediate and deferred imitation with 11-month-olds: A comparison between familiar and novel actions. Poster presented at meeting of the Society for Research in Child Development, Kansas City.

Meltzoff, A. N. 1988. Infant imitation and memory: Nine-month-olds in immediate and deferred tests. *Child Devel.* 59:217–25.

Meltzoff, A. N., and R. W. Borton. 1979. Intermodal matching by human neonates. *Nature* 282:403–04.

Mendelson, M. J., and M. M. Haith. 1976. The relation between audition and vision in the newborn. *Monographs of the Society for Research in Child Development*, no. 41, serial no. 167.

Michotte, A. 1963. *The Perception of Causality*. Methuen.

Piaget, J. 1951. *Play, Dreams and Imitation in Childhood*, trans. C. Gattegno and F. M. Hodgson. Norton.

———. 1952. *The Origins of Intelligence in Children*, trans. M. Cook. International Universities Press.

———. 1954. *The Construction of Reality in the Child*, trans. M. Cook. Basic Books.

Prinz, P. M., and E. A. Prinz. 1979. Simultaneous acquisition of ASL and spoken English (in a hearing child of a deaf mother and hearing father). Phase I: Early lexical development. *Sign Lang. Stud.* 25:283–96.

Ruff, H. A. 1986. Components of attention during infants' manipulative exploration. *Child Devel.* 57:105–14.

Schacter, D. L. 1987. Implicit memory: History and current status. *J. Exper. Psychol.: Learning, Memory, Cognition* 13:501–18.

Slobin, D. I. 1985. Crosslinguistic evidence for the language-making capacity. In *The Crosslinguistic Study of Language Acquisition*, vol. 2, ed. D. I. Slobin, pp. 1157–1256. Erlbaum.

Smith, E. E., and D. L. Medin. 1981. *Categories and Concepts*. Harvard Univ. Press.

Spelke, E. S. 1979. Perceiving bimodally specified events in infancy. *Devel. Psychol.* 15:626–36.

———. 1988. The origins of physical knowledge. In *Thought without Language*, ed. L. Weiskrantz, pp. 168–84. Clarendon Press.

Spelke, E. S., and R. Kestenbaum. 1986. Les origines du concept d'objet. *Psychologie française* 31:67–72.

Walker-Andrews, A. S., and E. J. Gibson. 1986. What develops in bimodal perception? In *Advances in Infancy Research*, vol. 4, ed. L. P. Lipsitt and C. Rovee-Collier, pp. 171–81. Ablex.

Werner, H., and B. Kaplan. 1963. *Symbol Formation*. Wiley.

Wertheimer, M. 1961. Psychomotor coordination of auditory and visual space at birth. *Science* 134:1692.

The Child Yesterday, Today, and Tomorrow

David Elkind

The child is a gift of nature, the image of the child is man's creation. It is the image of the child, rather than nature's gift, that determines educational practice in any historical epoch. And the image of the child, man's creation, is as often wrong as it is correct. Wrong images are more powerful and more easily grasped than true ones. In the present as in the past, our task as educators of young children is not simply to be true to nature's gift, but also to fight against the false images that, in any age, threaten the healthy education of young children.

Images of the past

The image of the child in antiquity was that of young citizen who had to be educated by the laws and culture of society. The children of Babylon went to school at age 6 and even poor children learned to read and write except that their books were bricks and their writing tools

This article is, with a few minor changes, the address Dr. Elkind gave at NAEYC's November 1986 Annual Conference at the Opening General Session, Washington Hilton Hotel. **David Elkind** *is NAEYC's President.*

a reed and damp clay. Children in ancient Greece played with go-carts and dolls, and at the age of 7 boys went to school. In ancient Rome, women had a more equal place and both boys and girls went to school where the discipline was strict and where they learned to write with a stylus and wax tablet.

During the Middle Ages, children fared less well and the prevailing image of the child was that of chattel, or piece of property consistent with the ideology of serfdom. The medieval castle was no place for a child, built as it was for defense rather than for comfort. The children of serfs worked and lived with the animals. Discipline was strict and punishment harsh. In England, there was a brief, golden era for children during the reign of Good Queen Bess. And during this era, the faithful nanny begins to appear in folklore and literature.

Toward the end of the 17th Century, the struggle between Cavaliers and Puritans was reflected in their quite dissimilar images of children. The Cavaliers held a mixed image of the child as part nuisance, part plaything. In contrast, the Puritans constructed an image of the child as one tainted with original sin. "Your child," wrote James Janeway, "is never too young to go to hell."

In this country the images of children changed with our rapidly changing society. In colonial times children were seen as financial

assets who could help work the farm or be apprenticed out of the home at an early age. The children of slaves were an extreme example of this, but they were not the only children who labored from dawn to dark. With the industrial revolution, children, especially the children of immigrants and the poor, came to be seen as cheap factory workers until the cruelty of child labor was made public. The ensuing social reform movement transformed the image of the child from one of cheap factory labor to one of apprentice to factory work. Instead of being sent to the factory, children were sent to school to prepare them to work in factories. School bells, like factory whistles, signaled the beginning and the end of the school day. And children, like their parents, carried lunch pails to be opened at the noon whistle.

As we see, there have been many different images of children, some of which were more beneficial to child health, welfare, and education than others. And there have always been those who, at any given point in history, have been critical of the image of the child current at that time. Often this criticism took the form of an attack on parents and upon parenting, but in fact it was an attack upon the then "accepted" image of the child. A review of these attacks upon the images of the child that were raised in earlier times is instructive. It tells us that the image of the child at any point in history never goes unchallenged and that the challengers in the past, as today, often come from the ranks of early childhood educators.

The criticism of prevailing images of the child has a long history. For his ideal Republic, Plato wanted children to be raised by professional child caretakers, and St. Augustine proclaimed, "Give me other mothers and I will give you other worlds." Rousseau's opening statement in *Emile* to the effect that everything is good as it comes from the hand of the Maker and deteriorates in the hands of man, is an indictment of the image of the child as a young savage who had to be socialized.

Pestalozzi and Froebel did not criticize parents directly, but did believe that parents needed to be given a truer image of the child that would result in more healthy child-rearing practices. Parent education was an important component of early childhood education practiced by Pestalozzi and Froebel. Pestalozzi's book, *How Gertrude Teaches Her Children*, which is subtitled *An Attempt To Help Mothers Teach Their Own Children*, reflects this emphasis upon training parents. The same theme was repeated in Froebel's *The Education of Man* and in his *Songs for Mothers and Nursery Songs*.

Their successor Maria Montessori never criticized parents either, but she had less faith in parent education than her predecessors. Like Plato she wanted children reared by professionals, not by parents. For her, childrearing was too important a task to be left to untrained parents whose image of the child gave too little credit to their budding intellecual powers.

In the past, the prevailing image of the child that dictated child-rearing and education was determined by a complex of social, economic, and cultural factors that may have had little or nothing to do with the natural child. And since early times, there have been critics

of the prevailing conception of the child. These critics fought to replace the false image of the child with a truer one that would provide for a healthier, happier, and more productive child life.

Images of the present

Historically, predominant images of the child were derived from the prevailing political, social, or religious ethos. What is remarkable about modern images of the child is that they are, or are said to be, scientific in origin. Unfortunately, their scientific origin has not rendered them any more valid than those that had social, political, or religious derivations. In some ways, the scientific origin of some of the contemporary images of the child makes them even more difficult to combat than previous images. I want now to usurp the role of critic and review and comment upon three modern images of the child that have contributed to what I call miseducation, namely putting children at risk for no purpose.

The sensual child

The advent of Freudian psychology gave rise to the image of the sensual child. In this view, the child was "polymorphous perverse" in the sense of having the whole gamut of sexual instincts and proclivities that were once reserved to adults. In Freudian terms, children whose sexual instincts were unduly repressed were destined to become neurotic. The childrearing and educational implications of this image of the sensual child were straightforward. Children had to be allowed to express themselves, and play was the natural medium of self-expression. With adequate self-expression at home and at school, children would develop healthy personalities and their intelligence would take care of itself.

Like so many images of the child, this idea contains a partial truth. Freud made it clear that a certain amount of repression was healthy,

indeed necessary, for people to live in a society. It was *excessive* repression, not repression, that produced neuroses. But that point was sometimes lost on those who fought for expression at all costs.

The malleable child

Another image of the child that has dominated contemporary thought has come from the anthropologists who were concerned with the conflict between generations. The leading writers of this genre were Kingsley Davis, Ruth Benedict, and Margaret Mead. Although they differed in detail, they were all making the same point, namely, when it comes to adapting to social change, children are plastic and adaptable whereas adults are rigid and unadaptable. Children, they argued, are better suited to social change than are adults.

Davis, for example, argued that adults are locked into the orientation they received as children and this makes it difficult, if not impossible, for them to appreciate the changed circumstances of their offspring, hence the generational conflict. Benedict said that adults are independent and children are dependent, and that it was the adult's inability to deal with the child's growing independence that was the cause of the generational conflict. And Margaret Mead argued that in a rapidly changing culture, children, who are free of ingrained habits of thought, are much better able to adapt to new and changing technologies than adults.

This image of child malleability in contrast to adult rigidity is sometimes misinterpreted. Anthropologists are talking about change in the overall society, *not* about changes within the immediate family. When a family moves, the children have more trouble with the change than adults. And, while divorce may be hard on adults, it is certainly much harder on children. Children thrive on consistency, stability, and security, while it is adults

Courtesy U.S. Department of Labor

who seek new experience and adventure. Children adapt less easily to change within the family than adults do, but the reverse image fostered by a misapplication of social scientists' ideas about change in society persists and contributes to miseducation.

The introduction of computers into early childhood education, and the teaching of programming to young children, is a direct offshoot of this malleability conception. It is simply a fact of technological development that as technology develops it requires more, rather than less, intellectual maturity. A child can use a shovel but not a power shovel; a child can use a hand saw or hand drill, but not a power saw or power drill; a child can ride a horse, but cannot drive an automobile and certainly cannot fly an airplane. The more advanced the technology, the more advanced the intelligence required to use it. Modern warfare is another example. Modern weapons require college

graduates if they are to be used properly. The modern army has no place for a Sergeant York trained with a hunting rifle. And even when a technology is easy to use, such as television, it can still be dangerous to young children.

Yet the idea that children should be programming and running computers persists despite the fact that the complexity and technological sophistication of computers is far beyond what a young child can really comprehend and master. To be used by young children, computers have to be converted into teaching machines presenting programmed learning. And programmed learning is simply boring. Exposing young children to computers in this way runs the risk that they will get turned off to computers before they have a chance to see what they can really do. It is a good example of miseducation, of putting children at risk for no purpose.

In the same way, I am often asked

about programs to inform young children about the threats of nuclear war. Presumably, children have to be exposed to this idea at an early age so they will be better prepared for a nuclear holocaust when it comes. Even if one accepts this shaky premise, it has to be recognized that the concept of nuclear war is completely foreign to young children, who do not even have a conception of biological death, much less of millions of people and the power of nuclear weapons to destroy them. Recent suggestions that young children be taught about AIDS also stem from this wrong-headed image of child malleability.

To be sure, children are fresh learners to the extent that they are not handicapped by previous ideas and concepts. But this does not mean that they are ready to learn everything and anything—far from it. Their openness to learning is limited and we need to recognize these limitations. There is a time and a place for everything and early childhood education is not the time nor the place to teach children computer programming, the threat of nuclear war, or for that matter, the dangers of AIDS.

The competent infant

Perhaps the most pervasive and most pernicious contemporary image of the child is one that has been promoted by psychologists writing in the 60s. Responding to the Civil Rights Movement, to the War on Poverty, and to the inadequacies of the educational system, many writers gave voice to a vision of childhood that would undo these wrongs and undo them at an early age. All these wrongs, it was said, could be righted if we only got to children early enough. The result was a new image of infants and young children as having much more capacity to learn academic skills than children, regardless of background, actually have. It is true that all young children have intellectual abilities and that their thinking should be encouraged but within the context of their psychological stage of development. This 60s image of the child as consumer of skills has come to haunt us in the 80s.

In his book *The Process of Education,* Jerome Bruner voiced his now famous hypothesis that you can "teach any child, any subject matter at any age in an intellectually responsible way." Bruner was really speaking to curriculum writers and probably did not fully appreciate the extent to which his hypothesis would be accepted, not as a hypothesis, but rather as a fact by the public at large. And it has also become the motto of entrepreneurs hawking flash cards to parents with the proclamation that you can teach a young child "anything."

But is it true? It is only true if you either redefine the child or redefine the subject matter. The curriculum writers of the 60s, academicians such as Max Beberman at the University of Illinois or Robert Karplus at Berkeley knew their subject matter but not young children. The curricula they designed in effect redefined the competence of children without recourse to children's actual abilities or limitations. For example, variable base arithmetic was said to be easier for children to learn than base ten arithmetic. But even parents had trouble with variable base arithmetic! It was also claimed that children would learn math better if it were introduced as a language. Instead of answering what is the sum of $2 + 2$, children were asked to "Make this sentence true."

The error here came from confusing what is simple to an expert in a subject with what is simple for the novice. Simplicity is the end result of learning a skill or a discipline, not its starting point. Reading is simple once you know how, but is far from simple when you first start out. Understanding multiple base arithmetic may be simple once you know base ten, but not if you don't. Understanding the relation of language to mathematics is simple if you have a firm grasp of language and mathematics, but not if you don't. We have to always be aware of the danger of assuming that the end point for us as adults should be the starting point for children.

The other side of Bruner's hypothesis requires redefining the subject matter. When an infant who responds to flash cards is said to be "reading" or doing "math," these subject matters have been drastically redefined. Suppose, for example, that I tell you that I can balance 100 pounds on my finger. You would not believe me. But suppose I take out a 3×5 card and write *100 pounds* on it. Now I put the card on my finger, and voilà, I am holding 100 pounds on my finger. Claiming to teach infants to read and do math is the same; it is a sleight-of-hand trick accomplished by redefining what is usually meant by reading and by math.

Yet people are taken in by this trickery and really believe that they are teaching their children these subjects. And this trickery has another negative fallout effect. Redefining the subject matter makes it much easier to acquire. Parents then believe that their child who is "reading" flash cards at age 2 is a budding genius. But they will be disappointed in the end. Unfortunately, making a task easier does not make children brighter.

Another contribution to the image of the competent infant came from educational psychologist Benjamin Bloom who argued from statistical summaries of IQ data that 4-year-olds had attained half of their intellectual ability and that it was incumbent upon us to impose formal learning on young children because otherwise we might lose out on this period of phenomenal mental growth. This idea that you must teach as much as possible to young children because their minds are growing so rapidly has become part of the contemporary folk wisdom and is deeply ingrained in our contemporary image of the child.

But is it true? Bloom was talking about mental test data, not about mental growth. Because infants and young children are not good test takers, their intelligence test performance is not a good index of their later test performance. By the age of 4, however, the child is sufficiently verbal and has sufficient ability to concentrate attention, and her or his test performance is a better index of true ability. From the test score a child attains at the age of 4 you can predict with some 50% accuracy what that child's test score will be at age 17. And that is all that a child attaining half of her or his mental ability at age 4 means.

It does not mean that at age 4 the child has half of all the knowledge, skills, and values she or he will ever have. It does not mean that if a child attains an IQ of 100 at age 4 she or he will attain an IQ score of 200 at age 17. It does not mean that a child at age 4 is a better learner than she or he will be at age 17. Even if we grant that mental growth is rapid during the early years of life, it does not follow as dawn follows the night, that this calls for formal, teacher-directed learning. During periods of rapid mental growth, children seek out the stimuli to nourish themselves mentally. We serve them best by providing an environment rich in materials to observe, explore, manipulate, talk, write, and think about. You do not prune during the growing season.

Still a third writer who has contributed to the contemporary image of the competent infants is J. McV. Hunt. In his book *Intelligence and Experience* he surveyed a great deal of evidence and concluded that intelligence was malleable and not fixed, the view he attributed to professionals of the time. But no reputable psychologist ever claimed that intelligence was fixed. In 1954, in a chapter of the *Handbook of Child Psychology,* Florence Goodenough made it clear that all

Courtesy U.S. Department of Labor

the evidence supported the view that the environmental factors accounted for between 20 and 40% of an individual's IQ.

Up until the 60s, however, psychologists were mainly concerned with middle-class children who, presumably, had maximized their environmental potential. It was only when attention was turned to low-income children who had less than optimal environmental input that the significance of environmental input became a matter of concern. Consider the following analogy. Suppose you place a group of undernourished children on a full calorie, well-balanced diet. Surely such children will make significant gains in both height and weight, but similar gains will not be made by children who are already on a full calorie, well-balanced diet. The potential benefits of an improved program are always relative to the quality of the previous environment.

This idea of intellectual malleability has become common cur-

rency among parents who are being told that with the proper program of stimulation they can have a "brighter child" or that they can raise their child's IQ. Yet there is no evidence that children growing up in an environment where they are talked to, played with, and read to, and which is rich in things to look at, listen to, and explore, will derive additional benefit from prescribed exercises and symbolic materials. If anything, most middle-class children today are over- rather than understimulated.

The last contributor to the image of the competent child is not a psychologist but a historian. In his book *Centuries of Childhood,* Phillip Aries argues that childhood is a social invention and that there was no such conception in the Middle Ages when children were depicted and treated much as adults. The implication is that for the last couple of hundred years we have been coddling children and infantalizing them and ignoring their true com-

petence and abilities. This thesis fit in neatly with the other ideas about infant competence and gave it a historical dimension.

More recent historians of childhood, like Pollack, have shown Aries was wrong. Even in the times Aries was writing, diaries of parents show quite clearly that adults appreciated that children were different from adults and had to be treated differently. Sir Francis Bacon, writing in the 16th Century, even talked about the value of "allowances" and the negative effects of not giving a child a sufficient allowance, and suggested that "The proof is best when men keep their authority towards their children, but not their purse."

These four ideas, then, that a child can be taught any subject at any age, that children have half their intellectual ability at age 4 when mental growth is more rapid, that the IQ is malleable, and that childhood is an invention, all emerged in the 1960s to form a new image of child competence. Although this new image may have corrected a previous image that played down child competence, it went to the other extreme. Ideas meant to improve the conditions of low-income children have been taken over by middle-class parents and have become the rationale for much of the miseducation of young children today.

As in the past, we have not only to assert the values of child-centered early childhood education, but we must also struggle to reveal the concepts of early childhood malleability and competence for what they are, namely distortions of how young children really grow and learn.

Images of the future

Given the brief history I have just outlined, it seems reasonable to predict that the false images of children today will be replaced by equally false images tomorrow. I have no crystal ball, only a belief that history is prologue and that the image of the child at any point in history always fills the predominant parent needs and defenses of that developmental epoch. We have to ask then what the needs of future parents will be and how these will be reflected in a new image of the child.

Our society is already a service and information society with more than 70% of our population in these occupations. I believe that we will eventually get high quality child care for all those youngsters who need it and that those who care for infants and young children will have positions of respect and will be paid well. We may even have parent professionals to care for and rear other people's children. This will not happen immediately and without a great deal of hard work and pain, but I do believe we will get there.

What then? What new image will emerge when the image of the malleable competent child has run its course? What sort of image of the child will be most in keeping with the needs of tomorrow's parents? If present trends continue, it appears that parents will spend less time than ever parenting. Once parents no longer feel guilty or uncomfort-

able about this, the need for the image of child intellectual competence will diminish. In its place will emerge a new image of child social sophistication and self-sufficiency. In an information and service society these are the requisite skills. We already see hints of this in the current emphasis upon social cognition. Psychologists are eager to point out that Piaget was wrong and that infants and young children are much more socially skilled than we gave them credit for being.

And while it may be true that children are more socially proficient and self-sufficient than we may have recognized, they will not be as socially proficient as the image of social sophistication will have us believe. And the cycle will once again repeat itself, the next generation of early childhood educators will have to challenge the new image of the child as, to use the computer term that may well become the catchword of this new image, *an expert system* with respect to social interaction. The next generation will once again have to reassert the values of sound early childhood education.

Our task as early childhood educators then is never ending. Each

generation presents a new challenge and a new battle. And it is a battle that we can never really win, because each new generation is prone to the same mistakes. Yet if we do not fight it is a battle we can most assuredly lose. For those of us in early childhood education it is a battle well worth fighting and, even if we fall before our time, we can take comfort in the knowledge that there will always be others, sufficiently committed to the well-being of young children, to carry on the fight.

Bibliography

Aries, P. (1962). *Centuries of childhood.* New York: Knopf.

Benedict, R. (1938). Continuities and discontinuities in cultural conditioning. *Psychiatry, 1,* 161–167.

Bloom, B. (1964). *Stability and change in human behavior.* New York: Wiley.

Bruner, J. (1962). *The process of education.* Cambridge, MA: Harvard University Press.

Davis, K. (1940). The sociology of parent-youth conflict. *American Sociological Review, 5,* 523–525.

Freud, S. (1905). *Three essays on sexuality.* New York: Basic.

Hunt, J. McV. (1961). *Intelligence and experience.* New York: Ronald.

Mead, M. (1970). *Culture and commitment.* New York: Natural History Press/Doubleday.

Pollack, L. (1983). *Forgotten children.* Cambridge: Cambridge University Press.

Preschool: Head Start or Hard Push?

Philip R. Piccigallo

PHILIP R. PICCIGALLO, a public affairs consultant, formerly was assistant to the president of the American Federation of Teachers.

Not long ago an old friend called to congratulate my wife and me on the birth of our son. During the catch-up conversation, he asked about my then three-year-old daughter's progress. Was she taking gymnastics, ballet, or swimming? Was she enrolled in reading, math, and computer classes? Had I succeeded in placing her name on preliminary lists for testing and admission to selective preschools and private kindergartens? "One can never start too early," he assured. "Oh, and how has she done on early tests?"

Though presumably well intentioned, his matter-of-fact advocacy of a child-development approach that has been seriously questioned by a considerable number of national experts troubled me. Controversial ideas about early childhood education are not new, of course. Since the 1960s debates have raged over whether out-of-home learning programs for young children are harmful or beneficial. My friend's views, however, are reflective of a steadily widening contemporary phenomenon: the near singleminded determination of many baby boomer and other new or prospective parents to "fast track" or "position" their children into high achievement careers through early participation in formal programs of academic instruction. In preschools and kindergartens across America, young children are being "taught" to read, do math, interface with computers, play the violin, compete with peers, and "outsmart" tests.

Yet a substantial body of professional evidence suggests that such an approach may be misguided. According to such research, imposing undue pressure to learn on young children may generate anxieties or even neuroses that impair long-term educational and psychological development. While moderate exposure to rigorous intellectual stimuli may be helpful, the possibility of exposing children to early failure by asking more than they are capable of giving poses substantial risk to future achievement. Finally, a series of national education reports conducted in the 1980s spell out a distinct role for early childhood education—one which fundamentally differs from that sought after by many success-driven parents.

Despite such contrary evidence, many parents are impelled by the notion of propelling Jason/Jennifer on an unbroken path from preschool to Harvard. Consumed by their own competitiveness and fueled by books bearing such titles as *How To Have A Smarter Baby, Teach Your Baby Math,* and *Raising Brighter Children,* growing numbers of parents scramble madly for the earliest and optimal advantages.

The search now precedes kindergarten. Consider, for example, the extensive application and admission procedures for the most elite, achievement-oriented preschools in the Washington, D.C., and New York City areas. As described by *The Washington Post,* parents must submit an application form, visit the school, and then arrange a child's visit. Parents are asked to provide previous, if any, school recommendation forms. Children are then scheduled for a group visit with other applicants, and are tested by a series of games played while under observation. Many parents interviewed worried that they lacked the "right connections or enough money to make a large bequest and influence the decision." The costliest of such schools start at about $6,500 annually.[1]

In a feature entitled, "Fast Lane Kids," *The New York Times* similarly depicted the efforts of "many hard-driving parents" who anxiously seek admission to elite preschools, and "load up" their children with exhausting academic, music, dance, sports, and crafts programs. Rejection often means broken dreams, jettisoned expectations. Both stories, for example, cited parents "devastated" by their eighteen-month-old's failure to win admission to an elite school.[2]

Significantly, this increasingly growing phenomenon is not restricted to any geographical region or to exclusive

> **Imposing undue pressure to learn on young children may generate anxieties or even neuroses.**

> **"Everyone wants to raise the smartest kid in America rather than the best adjusted, happiest kid."**

schools. According to David Elkind, a child psychologist and author of *Miseducation: Preschoolers At Risk,* the proliferation of private and public academic programs for young people "has become a societal norm." Books, lecturers, and the media, he contends, have helped to propagate the idea that only "adultified" or "superkids" can succeed in a highly competitive future America.[3]

This sense that children must academically leapfrog ahead of their peers early to ensure later success has been heightened by demographic changes. Hundreds of school districts across America closed schools in the 1970s and early 1980s as the baby boom ebbed. Now many elementary schools overflow as the children of that postwar generation enroll in increasing numbers.

Kindergartens have been particularly affected. There nationwide enrollment in public schools swelled to 3,310,000 in 1986 from 2,687,000 in 1981, or 23 percent, according to the U.S. Department of Education. Baby boomers are having fewer, not more children than their parents. Nevertheless, their large numbers alone are creating the squeeze. High population growth areas, such as Florida, California, and the Rocky Mountain states, are especially pressed.[4]

Societal stress often filters downward. The incidence of highly pressured parents imposing high-pressure learning situations on their children, observes Elaine Bennett, an instructor of pediatrics at Georgetown University and wife of former U.S. Education Secretary William Bennett, has "really gotten out of hand. . . . It's not good for the children, the parents or the schools." Dina Bray, director of Columbia Grammar School in Manhattan, believes that such parents are "forcing their children into an experience that is the antithesis of childhood. . . . Rather than just letting their kids be

kids, it's as if these parents are asking the children, 'How many points did you get today?'"[5]

THE ONGOING DEBATE
But what are the consequences, if any, of imposing high-pressure learning methods and expectations on young children?

There are different schools of thought on the subject. Proponents are best represented, as one would imagine, by the authors of the best-selling "smart baby" books. Siegfried and Therese Englemann, authors of *Give Your Child A Superior Mind,* for instance, propose a step-by-step instructional program for parents to increase their children's intelligence. "Lessons, examples, experiments, and guidelines" for ages birth through five are offered to teach children "the basic rules of language, the alphabet, geometric shapes, telling time, counting, reading, math, algebra, equations, and more."[6]

Glen Doman, founder of the Better Baby Institute, suggests that a child who has not learned to read early may be irreversibly disadvantaged. "A four-year-old learns reading quicker than a five," he says, "a three-year-old quicker than a four, and I dare say a less-than-one-year-old learns quicker than a one-year-old." His book, *How To Teach Your Baby To Read,* has sold two million copies worldwide.[7]

Yet parents should be aware of counterarguments. An impressive body of professionals contend that the pressures of inducing formal, instruction on young children may actually constitute, in Dr. Elkind's phrase, "miseducation." Consequently, they can "invoke internal conflicts and can set the groundwork" for serious psychological problems.[8]

Child psychologists and educators stress children's enjoyment in learning; also their sense of fulfillment in meeting parents' expectations. But gratification derived from growth and learning can turn sour, observes Francis Roberts, superintendent of the Cold Spring Harbor Schools in New York, "when early learning is pressured" and goals exceed yet undeveloped capabilities.[9] A "child pushed too hard" too early, "both before they begin the primary grades and after their formal schooling is already underway," can be "turned off from any zest for learning," cau-

tion educational psychologists Julius and Zelda Seigal.[10]

The human infant, it is true, can be "taught" to recite numbers at two, read by three, and cope with early expectations. The important question, according to T. Berry Brazelton, pediatrician and author of *Toddlers and Parents*, is at what price? "Everyone wants to raise the smartest kid in America rather than the best adjusted, happiest kid," he adds.[11]

Virtually all experts, even proponents of preschool academic programs like the Englemanns, agree that "the biggest possible harm that could come from early reading is early failure."[12] If young children "can be saved from the experience of early failure," believe child psychologists David and Barbara Bjorklund, "they quite possibly can be saved from later failure and the accompanying feelings of low self-esteem and poor self-confidence."[13] Nor is reading at an early age necessarily of undiluted benefit. Many children who learned to read early often developed more reading problems than those who started later, concludes Dr. Benjamin Spock and others. The national Commission on Reading recommends, above all, that any systematic reading instructions should be "free from undue pressure" so as not to "turn our kindergartens, and even nursery schools and day-care centers, into boot camps."[14] Perhaps Elkind put the entire matter most assertively: "No authority in the field of child psychology, pediatrics, or child psychiatry advocates the formal instruction, in any domain, of infants and young children."

Similarly, most educators prefer that young children be educated under a "developmental curriculum" rather than a formal one. Based primarily on the research of David Weikart, of the High Scope Foundation in Michigan, developmental curriculum emphasizes experiential, play-oriented, self-driven learning that supports a young child's cognitive processes.[15]

The national education reports, again, embraced the notion of enriched childhood education. But typically their principal accent was on "any well-designed, professionally supervised program to stimulate and socialize" culturally disadvantaged three- and four-year-olds. The U.S. Department of Education advocates preschool educational activities. But, sig-

> Notions of "genius building" and intimidating, high-powered preschools appear more suited to serving parents' rather than children's needs.

nificantly, in its straightforward booklet, "What Works: Research About Teaching and Learning," it omits reference to formal preschooling altogether. Instead, it urges reliance on informal practices—creating an enriched "curriculum of the home" featuring books, supplies, and a special place for studying, closer parent-teacher-student interaction, increased parental attention to school matters, and disciplined study habits, for example, to help children of all socioeconomic backgrounds learn.[16]

EARLY CHILDHOOD EDUCATION AND REFORM

The current public interest in and support for school improvement stems from a series of studies conducted between 1983 and 1988 by a Presidential Commission on Excellence in Education, the Carnegie Corporation of New York, the Twentieth Century Fund, the Committee for Economic Development (CED), and other public-private organizations. These reports variously reported serious deficiencies in our educational system, and offered proposals for rectifying them.

Many of the reports highly praised and recommended enriched childhood education, as well as early investment in prenatal health care. They drew heavily upon the fruitful experience of the federal government's Head Start program, the successful Perry Preschool program in Ypsilanti, Michigan, and the New York University preschool study in Harlem, New York. Investment in such enterprises, they concluded, will produce multifold dividends for society—via savings in remedial education, health services, and less crime—over future years.[17]

To Barbara Finberg, vice president for programs at the Carnegie Corporation, which helped finance several of the projects, the studies reinforced "the idea that early childhood education, at least for disadvantaged youngsters, really does give them a boost toward better educational achievement. . . . It suggests that as children gain a sense of self-worth and confidence in their ability to learn, that in turn leads teachers to believe they can learn.[18]

The essential point is that the reports uniformly recommended early childhood education programs for a distinct group of youngsters, specifically those deemed to be "at risk." As defined by the CED, such "educationally disadvantaged" children are those who "cannot take advantage of available educational opportunities," or those where the "educational resources available to them are inherently unequal." In short, children who, due to poverty, broken homes, disability, or other environmental deprivation *need* additional and reinforced academic stimulation and instruction just to keep up with sufficiently engaged children.[19] As Mortimer Adler put it in *The Paideia Proposal* in 1982, "preschool" tutelage must be provided for those who do not get such preparation from favorable environments."[20]

This is not to say that sufficiently prepared children do not, or should not, benefit from preschool programs. All evidence suggests otherwise. In fact, in 1985 two-thirds of four-year-olds and 54 percent of three-year-olds in families with incomes of $35,000 or more attended preschool programs. In contrast, fewer than 33 percent of four-year-olds and 17 percent of three-year-olds in families with annual incomes of less than $10,000 were enrolled in such programs in 1985. And Head Start reaches only 18 percent of the 2.5 million children who need its services.[21]

Two salient points thus emerge: 1) not nearly enough of those children who most need early enriched intellectual instruction and stimulation presently receive it; and 2) the overwhelming majority of middle- and upper-income parents who heatedly pursue enhanced academic learning for their children may be administering an unnecessary remedy, one which may carry negative consequences.

THE JAPANESE "EDUCATIONAL MIRACLE"

And what about the "Japanese educational challenge"? Aren't they well along in launching young children on rapid academic and high-tech tracks? Yes. But as the leading American authority on the subject, sociologist Merry White, cautions, while learning from the Japanese we should not view their educational system "as a model to be emulated."[22]

Their system functions within a tightly knit, homogeneous society, one that places great importance on uniquely Japanese values such as conformity and consensus. Japanese teachers, in fact, discourage individual competition. Instead, they emphasize group effort and achievement. Such practice would prove unsuitable to Americans, steeped in individualism and pluralism.

Also, it would be difficult to imagine American mothers adopting the role of their Japanese counterparts in their children's education. Japanese mothers—"the best Jewish mothers in the world," says White—study alongside of and are held directly accountable for students' academic achievements or failures. At a time when more than 50 percent of new mothers remain in the American workforce, such behavior seems impracticable. Furthermore, adds White, Japan's intensely competitive, test-driven educational system has been the source of serious psychological strains on students of all ages. It has been widely said that Japanese youngsters have no childhood to speak of.[23]

"RESPECT THE CHILD"

Educational reform currently heads the national agenda. Educators, business leaders, governmental representatives, and parents now urge more rigorous school assignments, upgraded and enforceable standards, professionalized teaching, and expanded accountability.

Early childhood education too has been targeted for reform. Public efforts include lowering the age at which children start formal schooling. "Now that kindergarten for five-year-olds has become virtually universal in the nation's schools," observes Edward B. Fiske, educational editor of *The New York Times,* "demand is rising to make formal instruction available to all four-year-olds."[24] As noted, prekindergarten programs with heavy emphasis on academic instruction and testing for three- and four-year-olds are increasing.

Many experts are concerned that too much societal emphasis— by schools and parents, and now reformers—is being placed on the formal instruction of young children. The Early Childhood Literacy Development Committee of the International Reading Association, comprised of national organizations involved in elementary and early childhood education, expressed misgivings in 1986. Too many pre-first-graders, noted the committee, were then exposed to the excessive pressures of accelerated academic and formal pre-reading programs. Consequently, many participating children tend to avoid experimentation and risk-taking. They are easily frustrated. Many grow to dislike reading.

Such programs, said the committee, offer little attention to individual development and individual learning needs. Also, by overly stressing isolated skill development, such programs focus insufficient attention on the comprehensive reading process, which entails the integration of verbal language, writing, and listening with reading. As a result of such practices, warned the committee, otherwise adequately prepared children could become "at risk."[25]

Recent findings by the National Assessment of Educational Progress, administered by the Educational Testing Service, too are not encouraging. According to NAEP, the youngest children in a class are more likely to repeat a grade than their older classmates, a disadvantage that continues through the eighth grade.[26]

From the moment of birth children possess the ability and desire to learn. Educators and child psychologists agree that parents should nurture this inclination by reading to their children regularly, finding time for nature exploration, museum and library visits, and a generous diet of interesting, two-way conversation. Creative interest in the child's domestic and external activities is essential. Moreover, enriched socialization and play programs outside the home can be highly beneficial, not only to children's awakening to the world around them, but

to two-worker households.

The present trend toward inducing stressful, often unachievable, academic performance expectations from young children, however, seems excessive. Notions of "genius building" and intimidating, high-powered preschools, featuring instruction even test-driven curriculums, appear more suited to serving parents' rather than children's needs.

Preschool should be a stressless, stimulating, and socializing experience. Tests or measurements beyond prekindergarten assessments of a child's understanding of basic concepts—big and small, light and heavy, less and more, counting, for example—should be suspect. Peer competition and pressures to excel should be discouraged. Parents and social policymakers intent on priming youngsters for future academic careers must bear in mind, as early childhood educators know, that the "principal source of development in the early years is play."[27]

Children have a lifetime to cope with the struggles of educational and career success. "The secret of Education lies in respecting the pupil," wrote Emerson. "It is not for you to choose what he shall know, what he shall do. . . . [O]nly he holds the key to his own secret. Wait and see the new product of Nature. Respect the child. Be not too much the parent."[28]

NOTES

[1]*The Washington Post* (April 26, 1988), pp. 1, 10.

[2]Anita Shreve, "Fast-Lane Kids," *The New York Times Magazine*, Special Supplement, The Business World (June 12, 1988), p. 55.

[3]David Elkind, *Miseducation: Preschoolers at Risk* (New York: Alfred Knopf, 1987), pp. 3-4.

[4]As reported in *The New York Times* (April 29, 1988), p. B1.

[5]Quoted in *The Washington Post* (April 26, 1988), p. 10, and in Shreve, p. 55.

[6]Siegfried and Therese Engelmann, *Give Your Child a Superior Mind* (New York: Simon & Schuster, 1981), quoted in Robin Marantz Henig, "Should Baby Read?" *The New York Times Magazine* (May 22, 1988), p. 37.

[7]Ibid.

[8]Elkind, p. xiv.

[9]Francis Roberts, "School Days," *Parents* (March 1988), p. 46.

[10]Julius and Zelda Seigal, *Growing Up Smart and Happy* (New York: McGraw-Hill, 1985), p. 71.

[11]Quoted in Ibid., and *New Age Journal* (January 1985), p. 54.

[12]Engelmann, p. 28.

[13]David and Barbara Bjorklund, "Is Your Child Ready for School?" *Parents* (June 1988), p. 112.

[14]C. Anderson et al., *Becoming a Nation of Readers: The Report of the Commission on Reading* (Washington, D.C.: National Institute of Education, 1985), pp. 29-30.

[15]See, Madeline Drexler, "The Kindergarten Game: Is Your Child Ready to Play?" *Bostonia* (Jan./Feb. 1988), p. 32; *Changed Lives: The Effects of the Perry Preschool Program on Youths Through Age 19* (Ypsilanti: High/Scope Educational Research Foundation, 1984).

[16]*What Works: Research about Teaching and Learning*, 2nd edition (Washington, D.C.: U.S. Department of Education, 1986), p. 53.

[17]See, "The Payoffs for Preschooling," *The Chicago Tribune* (Dec. 25, 1984); Ann Crittenden, "A Head Start Pays Off in the End," *The Wall Street Journal* (Nov. 29, 1984); Larry Rohter, "Study Stresses Preschool Benefits," *The New York Times*, (April 9, 1985); and the Committee for Economic Development, *Children in Need: Investment Strategies for the Educationally Disadvantaged* (New York: CED, 1987), chapter 1.

[18]Quoted in *The New York Times* (April 9, 1985), p. C1.

[19]CED, pp. 5-9.

[20]Mortimer J. Adler, *The Paideia Proposal: An Educational Manifesto* (New York: Collier, 1982), p. 38.

[21]Children's Defense Fund, *A Call for Action to Make Our Nation Safe for Children* (Washington, D.C.: CDF, 1988), p. 7.

[22]Merry White, *The Japanese Educational Challenge: A Commitment to Children* (New York: Free Press, 1987), p. 191; "Japanese Education: How Do They Do It?" *In the Public Interest* (Summer 1984).

[23]White, pp. 33, 115, 187-88; "Mothers with Babies and Jobs," *The New York Times* (June 19, 1988).

[24]Edward B. Fiske, "Early School Is Now the Rage," *The New York Times* (April 13, 1986), pp. 24-30.

[25]Early Childhood Literacy Development Committee of the International Reading Association, "Literacy Development and Pre-First Grade," *Young Children* (1986), pp. 10-11.

[26]Cited in Drexler, p. 31.

[27]Joan Moyer, Harriet Egerston, and Joan Isenberg, "The Child-Centered Kindergarten," *Childhood Education* (April 1987), p. 238.

[28]Ralph Waldo Emerson, "Education," in *The Complete Writings of Ralph Waldo Emerson* (New York: Wise and Co., 1929), p. 993.

HOW THREE KEY COUNTRIES SHAPE THEIR CHILDREN

Spending a day with four-year-olds in China, Japan, and the US shows that these cultures have distinctively different aims—and some common goals—as they turn to preschools to preserve values in a time of change.

- **VIDEO SHOT, CHINA:** At 7:45 on a brisk Monday morning in early spring parents pull up to the Dong-feng Kindergarten's front gate on bicycles, each carrying a brightly dressed child riding on the back. In the courtyard, two middle-aged nurses, dressed in white, examine the arriving children, one by one...
- **VIDEO SHOT, JAPAN:** At 9:30 the "clean-up" song is played over loudspeakers audible throughout the Komatsudani preschool. As the children put away toys, balls, and tricycles, the music changes to the equally lively exercise song...
- **VIDEO SHOT, UNITED STATES:** At 7:30 a compact car pulls into the parking lot of St. Timothy's Child Center, and a father and his three-year-old son get out and walk hand in hand across the playground and into one of the classrooms. While Steve Cooper signs in on the attendance sheet, his son, Mark, puts his He-Man lunch box away in his cubby...

Joseph J. Tobin, David Y. H. Wu, and Dana H. Davidson

Joseph J. Tobin, a human development specialist at the University of Hawaii, will soon join the Family Studies faculty at the University of New Hampshire.

Cultural anthropologist David Y. H. Wu is a research associate at the East-West Center in Honolulu.

Dana H. Davidson is an associate professor in Family Resources at the University of Hawaii, Manoa.

N CHINA, JAPAN, AND THE UNITED STATES preschool is an increasingly common way to provide care, education, and group experience for children between infancy and the start of formal schooling. In all three societies, the rise of the preschool is viewed, for better or worse, as a radical departure from traditional modes of caring for young children—who, in previous eras, were raised in their homes by full-time mothers, taken to the fields by parents who farmed, or cared for by hired country girls, mother's helpers, maiden aunts, grandmothers, or older brothers or sisters.

Yet several years of study lead us to view preschools as agents more of cultural conservation than of change. Using videotapes, interviews, questionnaires, and other means of research, we have found that preschools both reflect and moderate social change in these three cultures.

For example, in China preschools are expected to provide an antidote to the spoiling that Chinese fear is inevitable in an era of governmentally decreed single-child families. Chinese parents, preschool educators, and child-development experts are very worried about the problem they call the "4-2-1 syndrome": four grandparents and two parents lavishing attention on one child.

Japanese parents believe that preschools offer their children their best chance of learning to function in a large group and of becoming, in Japanese terms, truly human. The need for such experience arises from an increasing nuclearization and gentrification of the family brought on by a shrinking birthrate, an ongoing migration of young people from big households in the country to single-family apartments in large cities, and the rise of the middle-class *sarariman* (salaried employee) life style.

In the United States, preschools are being asked to respond to changing patterns of men's and women's work, a high divorce rate, and a growing concern for the needs of single-parent families.

As perceptions of work, marriage, and the family change in all three societies, they look to preschools to provide stability, richness, and guidance to children's lives. We have set out not to rate the preschools in the three cultures but to find out what they are meant to do and to be.

Why, for instance, do nonworking Japanese mothers work so hard to make the perfect school lunch? Why do they take pains to dress up so early in the morning just to meet other mothers?

An American woman living in Kyoto with a son in a local preschool explained the burden of lunch making:

"In America I just make a peanut butter sandwich and put in some chips and a piece of fruit and some carrot sticks. But here it is an entirely different story. One day my son came home crying and told me that the Japanese kids had laughed at his sandwich. The next day I made him a Japanese lunch, a *bentō*. But he came home from school again unhappy, again about his lunch. I said, 'Now what's wrong? I made you a Japanese lunch.' He said, in tears, 'But you didn't cut the apple slices so they look like bunny rabbits like the other mothers do.'"

For these nonemployed Japanese mothers, preparing their children for school is their most important work; their children's education is the center of their interests. And meeting other mothers before and after school is, other than shopping, their only daily personal contact with the outside world. The point is not that Japanese society as a whole is more limiting and restrictive for women than is Chinese or American society but rather that Japanese preschools play a more central role in defining mothers' identities and role demands than do preschools in the United States or China.

Today more than 95% of Japanese children attend preschool before they begin first grade. Japanese mothers today, like those of a century ago, remain the chief caretakers of infants and toddlers and thus the chief source of training in one-to-one relationships. What has changed is that the teaching of social skills and the fostering of an identity as a member of a group have become primarily the responsibility of preschools.

The nonpunitive attitude toward a "bad boy" in the Japanese school we videotaped would not necessarily be the same as that in all Japanese preschools. But it illustrates concern for the group. The teachers are careful not to isolate a disruptive child by singling him out for punishment or censure or excluding him from a group activity. They think their most powerful source of influence over children is their being viewed unambivalently as benevolent figures. They seek to maintain order—without intervening directly in children's disputes and misbehavior—by encouraging in various ways other children to deal with their classmates' troubles and misdeeds.

Isn't the bad boy's disruptiveness hard on the other children? "No," said the school director, laughing, "he makes things interesting." "No," said the assistant principal, "by having to learn how to deal with a child like [the bad boy], they learn to be more complete human beings."

By contrast, most of our Chinese informants told us unapologetically that they see the role of the preschool as teaching children to behave properly and instilling in them an appreciation for the values of self-control, discipline, social harmony, and responsibility. At the school we videotaped, even going to the bathroom was regimented, all 26 children being taken to a single large room at the same time.

"Of course, if a child cannot wait, he is allowed to go to the bathroom when he needs to," said one of our Chinese informants.

"But, as a matter of routine, it's good for children to learn to regulate their bodies and attune their rhythms to those of their classmates."

The word used most frequently in China to refer to teachers' control and regimentation of children is *guan*—literally, "to govern." When Ms. Xiang, as we shall see in a day at her school, tells the children to eat their lunch in silence and finish every bite, that is *guan*. When Ms. Wang criticizes one child for squirming and smiling while praising another for sitting straight with her hands behind her back and serious expression on her face, that, too, is *guan*. Instead of waiting to act until minor indiscretions grow into large ones, a good Chinese preschool teacher intervenes aggressively at the beginning.

At the American school we videotaped, the children talked animatedly as they ate—one sign of the relative freedom at the school, though an erring boy had to take a "time out" alone on a chair until he was ready to correct his behavior. When our questionnaire asked, "What is the most important reason for a society to have preschools?" our American respondents gave as their top answer: "to make young children more independent and self-reliant."

With this much of a hint of the differences and similarities we found, please join us in visiting preschools in Japan, China, and the US by means of transcripts condensed from our videotapes.

 ## A Day at Komatsudani.

Komatsudani Hoikuen, a Buddhist preschool located on the grounds of a 300-year-old temple on a hill on the east side of Kyoto, has 120 students. Twelve of these children are infants, under 18 months, who are cared for in a nursery by four teachers. Another 20 Komatsudani children are toddlers, under three years of age, who are cared for in two groups of 10 by three teachers

and an aide. The rest of the children are divided into three-year-old, four-year-old, and five-year-old classes, each with 25 to 30 students and one teacher. Each class has its own homeroom within the rambling old temple.

The school opens each morning at 7 a.m., and soon after, children begin to arrive, brought to school by a parent or grandparent on foot, by bicycle, or, less commonly, by car. By 9 a.m. most of the children have arrived, put their lunch boxes and knapsacks away in the cubby holes in their homerooms, and begun playing with their friends in the classrooms, corridors, or playground. Some of the older children stop by the nursery to play with the babies or to take toddlers for a walk on the playground.

At 9:30 the "clean-up" song is played over loudspeakers audible throughout the entire school area. As the children put away toys, balls, and tricycles, the music changes from the clean-up song to the equally lively exercise song.

Then, with their teachers' encouragement, the children form a large circle on the playground and go through 10 minutes of stretching, jumping, hopping, and running together in a group.

Taiso (morning exercise) complete, the "end-of-exercise-go-to-your-room" song comes over the loudspeakers, and the children, led by their teachers, run in a line into the school building, class by class, each child removing his or her shoes in the entranceway.

Inside, the 28 four-year-olds of *Momogumi* (Peach Class) enter their homeroom, which is identified by pictures of peaches on the door and the word *momogumi* written in *hiragana* (the phonetic alphabet). The Momogumi room has four child-sized tables, each with eight chairs that are covered with gaily embroidered seat covers the children have brought from home.

The *Momogumi-san-tachi* (Peach Class children) come in and stand behind their chairs while their teacher, Fukui-sensei, a 23-year-old university graduate, plays the morning song on a small organ and the two *toban* (daily monitors) lead the class in singing...

After attendance is taken by roll call, a counting song is sung to the tune of "Ten Little Indians" to determine how many children are in school that day...

The housekeeping chores and morning ceremonies completed, the children begin a workbook project which lasts about 30 minutes. Throughout this session there is much laughing, talking, and even a bit of playful fighting among tablemates. Fukui-sensei makes no attempt to stop them but forges ahead with the task at hand...

After they turn in their workbooks, the children begin to play loud chasing games, *janken* (paper-rock-scissors), and to engage in mock karate and sword fights. After 20 minutes or so of this free and raucous play and trips to the bathroom, the children, heeding their teacher, grab their *bentō*

(box lunch) from their cubbies and take their place at the table, arranging their lunch and cups and placemats in front of them. The food from home is supplemented by one warm course provided by the school and by a small bottle of milk. All the children sing in unison, under the direction of the daily *toban* and to the accompaniment of the organ:

> As I sit here with my lunch
> I think of Mom
> I bet it's delicious
> I wonder what she's made?

After the song the children stand, bow their heads, put their hands together, and recite: "Buddha, thank you. Honorable father, honorable mother, we humbly thank you."

Lunch itself is loud and lively, each child eating at his or her own pace, which varies from less than 10 minutes for some to 45 minutes or more for others. Fukui-sensei sits with the children at one of the four tables each day (the children keep careful track of whose turn it is), talking quietly to the children near her and occasionally using her chopsticks to help a child snare a hard-to-pick-up morsel from his *bentō*.

Some girls ask Fukui-sensei for help in properly tying up their lunch things in the large cloth *furoshiki* they have brought from home.

On the narrow covered porch adjoining their classroom four girls stand in a cluster, talking and laughing. Several boys are singing songs from television cartoon shows, engaging in more mock-fighting, and playing a game with flash cards meant to teach the *hiragana* syllabary.

One especially energetic boy, Hiroki, who has been much the noisiest and most unruly child in the class throughout the day (though it must be said that no one has tried very hard to control or quiet him), becomes increasingly raucous in his play. Midori runs inside to tell the teacher of Hiroki's misconduct and is encouraged by Fukui-sensei with a "go get 'em" sort of pat on the back to return to the balcony and deal with the problem herself.

Eventually the fighting ceases, the cards are cleaned up (with Fukui-sensei's help), and the children settle in at their desks, where they sing the after-lunch song ("Thank you. It was delicious...") and then rest with their heads on the table for five minutes or so while Fukui-sensei plays a soothing tune on the organ.

Rest time over, a major origami project begins, the children led by their teacher through a 20-step process resulting in the production by each child of an inflatable ball. ("Can you make a triangle? Good, now take these two ends of the triangle and make a smaller triangle, as I'm doing...") Soon the children, paper balls in hand, run laughing and screaming from the classroom to the playground for an extended period of outdoor play.

Back inside, Fukui-sensei reads a story to the class, using not a book but a *kami shibai*, a series of a dozen or so large cards, each with a picture on one side and the narrative to be read by the teacher on the back. A song and a snack round out the schedule. After singing the good-bye song ("Teacher, good-bye, everyone, good-bye..."), the children go outside to the playground once more to play until their parents come for them between 4:30 and 6 p.m.

A Day at Dong-feng.

Dong-feng (East Wind) Kindergarten is a preschool run by a city in southwest China for the children of municipal employees. Occupying the grounds of an old estate, the six red brick one- and two-story buildings provide space for 270 three- to six-year-old children and 60 staff members. Three-quarters of Dong-feng's children are day (ri tuo) students who attend school from about 8 a.m. to 6 p.m. Monday through Saturday. The other quarter are boarding (guan tuo—literally, "whole care") students who go home only on Wednesday evenings and weekends.

At 7:45 on a brisk Monday morning in early spring parents pull up to the front gate on bicycles, each carrying a brightly dressed child riding on the back. In the front courtyard, two middle-aged nurses *(bao jian yuan)*, dressed in white, examine the arriving children one by one.

When four-year-old Li Aimei finishes her health check, her father, Li Chou, takes her by the hand and leads her down a corridor to the four-year-old boarding students' classroom and dormitory. Martial music, played over loudspeakers, fills the courtyard.

A dozen children are already inside, eating steamed buns. Aimei's grip on her father's hand tightens as one of her teachers, Ms. Xiang, approaches, saying good morning. Aimei whispers earnestly to her father: "Don't forget to come and pick me up on Wednesday evening. Keep that thought in your mind, Dad!" After a minute or two, Mr. Li, with a final good-bye and pat on the back, literally hands Aimei over to her teacher.

Mr. Li, by now outside the room, furtively sticks his head back in. Seeing his daughter involved with a steamed bun, neither crying nor searching for him, Mr. Li smiles and strides across the courtyard.

Two columns of desks, each with an attached bench large enough to seat two students, run down the middle of the classroom. Above a blackboard is a mural of children playing in a field with forest animals.

While 40-year-old Ms. Xiang and her coteacher, 25-year-old Ms. Wang, arrange the children in a circle for morning exercise, their assistant *(bao yu yuan)*, 24-year-old Ms. Chen, takes the breakfast bowls and glasses away to the central kitchen to be washed. With Ms. Wang playing an up-tempo song on a small organ, Ms. Xiang leads the children in

calisthenics. All of them participate with enthusiasm and surprising grace.

Ms. Wang announces, "Let's do the 'Little Train Friendship Song.' " The children smile and clap. Ms. Wang begins to dance and sing: "I'm a little train looking for some friends. Who will come and ride on me?" Eventually, all the children are hooked up, snake-dancing around the room, singing along with their teacher.

After singing another song (about ducklings), the children are told to sit down at their desks. The teachers distribute wooden parquetry blocks to each child. Ms. Xiang says:

"We all know how to build with blocks, right? Just pay attention to the picture of the building and build it. When we play games like this, we must use our minds, right? Begin. Do your best. Build according to order."

The children begin to work in silence. Those who are working in a non-orderly way are corrected: A child whose box is placed askew on her desk has it placed squarely in the desk's upper right-hand corner by Ms. Xiang. Ms. Wang says: "Keep still! There is no need to talk while you are working."

It is now 10 o'clock, time for the children to go the bathroom. Following Ms. Wang, the 26 children walk in single file across the courtyard to a small cement building. Inside there is only a long ditch running along three walls. Leaving the toilet, again in single file, the children line up in front of a pump, where two daily monitors are kept busy filling and refilling a bucket with water the children use to wash their hands. Several boys in the back of the line indulge in some mock kung fu while other children talk and laugh. After washing their hands the children line up for a game of tag.

At 10:45 it is bath time for the boarding students. Three or four at a time, the children bathe in large tubs. Most of them are able to dry off and get dressed with minimal help from their teachers.

The children return to the classroom and take their seats. Ms. Wang drills them in addition and subtraction. As she pins hand-painted paper apples onto a large piece of cardboard, the children count out loud in unison. The students participate enthusiastically, each correctly answering at least one problem...

Lunch is delivered from the central kitchen in buckets. Again, the children march outside and wash their hands at the pump. By the time they return, a bowl of soybeans, vegetables, and shredded pork, a steamed bun, and a cup of water that has been boiled have been placed on each desk. Ms. Xiang reminds the children to eat in silence and not to waste any food: "Concentrate on your eating as much as you do on your studying. That's the correct way to eat."

The monitors collect the empty bowls and cups and place them in a bin to be returned to the kitchen. Other children wipe off the desk tops. Ms. Xiang then announces "Naptime." There are 26 beds in the dormitory room, each covered with a brightly colored, embroidered quilt. The children take their cups, scoop water from the bucket on a table, gargle loudly, spit into a spittoon on the floor, and wipe their faces with their washcloths. The children place their shoes neatly under their beds, remove their pants and jackets and place them on a corner of the bed, and crawl under their quilts dressed in T-shirts and underpants.

Naptime lasts from noon to 2:30, although most of the children do not sleep the whole time. While they rest, the teachers catch up on paperwork, eat, and relax in the classroom next door.

After nap, Ms. Chen once again takes the children to the bathroom and then to the pump to wash. Next comes a snack of cookies and reconstituted powdered milk.

Returning to their classroom, the children are taught to recite a patriotic story in unison. After the story, the children move outside for some relay races. Ms. Xiang says:

"Today we are going to play the 'Traffic Rules Game.' When I hold up this green card, you can run as fast as you can. Pretend you are bicycles flying down the street. When I hold up this red card, you must stop. If you don't stop, I will make you go back to the start and your team will fall behind. Cheer for your teammates to help them do their best. Don't let your team down."

At 5 p.m., following another group visit to the toilet, the children sit down at tables for supper. Ms. Xiang says, "Let's do the Puppet Song." Following their teachers' stiff movements, the children imitate marionettes as they recite loudly in unison, "We are wooden puppets. We can neither speak nor move." As they finish the verse they freeze...The children are served their evening meal of meat cooked with vegetables and rice.

It is now 6 p.m.. In the courtyard children can be heard calling out to their parents, who have arrived to pick them up. Inside, the children of the boarding class listen to records. They again rinse out their mouths, wipe off their faces, and struggle out of their clothes, some needing the assistance of a teacher. By 7:45 the children are all in bed under their warm quilts, and by 8 all are quiet and appear to be asleep.

 ### A Day at St. Timothy's.

St. Timothy's Child Center operates a set of programs including full-day and half-day care for children two through five years old, a kindergarten for five- and six-year-olds, and after-school care for elementary school children. The center, a nonprofit institution affiliated with St. Timothy's Episcopal Church of Honolulu, is located on the church grounds in a neighborhood of mixed single-family homes, condominiums, and shopping centers. The preschool program, which serves 95 children, is housed in five large classrooms bordering a central playground.

Linda Rios and Pat McNair, two of St. Timothy's 10 teachers, arrive a few minutes after 7 a.m. to open the school. At 7:30 a compact car pulls into the parking lot and a father and his three-year-old son get out and walk hand in hand to one of the classrooms. While Steve Cooper signs in on the attendance sheet, his son, Mark, puts his He-Man lunch box away in his cubby.

Steve says,"Here you go, Mark; you can help Pat feed Pinky [a rabbit] and clean his cage." Pat says, "Yeah, come on, Marky. We could use your help." Steve gives Mark a pat on the back and says, "Have a good day, Champ," but Mark spins around and grabs his father's arm.

Steve: "I'll stay just a minute, and then I have to go."

Mark: "How long's a minute? Stay millions of minutes."

Pat (picking up Mark in her arms): "Let's walk your father to the gate and say good-bye there."

Steve: "See you later, Buddy. Thanks, Pat."

With a final wave, Steve drives off. As soon as the car is out of sight, Mark stops crying. Mark and Pat walk hand in hand over to Pinky's cage, Pat talking animatedly about how Pinky should be fed.

At 9 a.m. the school day formally begins. Cheryl Takashige calls the children in her class to come inside and sit in a circle on the rug in the middle of the room. Once the 18 four-year-olds are seated, Cheryl (32 years old) and her assistant teacher, Linda Rios (46), say good morning to the children.

Cheryl asks if anyone has anything to "show and tell" to the class today. Three hands go up. Lance, with Cheryl's prompting, relates a weekend family trip to see an active volcano. Next Rose shows the class her newest Care Bear, describing the difficulty she had choosing it over a My Little Pony. Mike proudly exhibits a wooden boat he made with his father.

Cheryl then leads the class in an activity involving a felt board and cutout flannel shapes. Linda prepares a large tray with a book, a paintbrush, a block, a puzzle piece, a toy frying pan, and a small brass ring. While Cheryl puts away the felt and flannel, Linda leads the children in singing a song. After finishing the song, Linda holds out the tray and says: "Look. Here are the [learning] centers for this morning...."

In the housekeeping corner—which includes a small table and chairs, a toy stove, sink, refrigerator, and shelves stocked with empty food boxes, plastic pots and pans, and miscellaneous dress-up clothes—Lisa decides that she will be the mother and Rose the auntie. Derek refuses to play the role Lisa assigns him as the baby, opting instead to be the family dog.

In the story corner, sitting on a big stuffed pillow, Linda reads to Kelly and Suzy, who are leaning against her. Across the room, Pete works at unscrewing parts from an old radio (donated to the school by a parent).

Cheryl finds a pile of unattended Legos. She looks around the room and, spotting Kerry in a corner with a puzzle, calls in his direction. Kerry doesn't budge. Cheryl walks over and puts her face directly in front of Kerry's:

"Kerry, listen to me. Look at me while I'm talking to you. I want you to go over there and clean up the Legos you dumped out before someone steps on them and gets hurt....You have nothing to say? Then you can sit over there on the time-out chair and think about it until you are ready to clean up."

Kerry walks over to the chair and sits with his head in his hands. After a minute or so, Cheryl calls to him, "Are you ready to clean up now? Good. You can get up now and clean up the Legos."

During the 45-minute learning-center period, the children shift from activity to activity according to their interests. At 10:15 Cheryl flicks the lights to announce clean-up time. Once all the toys have been put away, Linda leads the children to the boys' and girls' bathrooms, after which they run onto the playground for free outdoor play....

Snack time. Children line up for a cup of grape juice and a graham cracker and sit on the grass to eat.

The children return to their classrooms for a second round of learning centers. This time there are four new activities: washing baby dolls in a small basin, playing with Play-Doh (an ersatz clay made from flour, oil, water, and food coloring), stringing beads, and cooking. Cheryl explains about making potato soup:

"What's this? A potato, right? What color is it? Brown....We have to be very careful because we will be cutting and using fire."

Working with dull plastic knives, the children, in shifts of six, laboriously cut up the potatoes and carrots. Cheryl adds the vegetables to a pot and each child takes a turn stirring.

Cheryl flicks the lights to signal clean-up time, and the children put away their toys and then come to sit in their assigned places in a circle. Cheryl sits on the floor beside Kerry and puts her arm around his shoulders. Linda leads them in a song:

One gray elephant went out to play
He went out on a sunny day
He had such enormous fun
He called another elephant: COME!

On the word "Come" a child standing in the center of the circle reaches out for the hand of a child sitting down and pulls him into the middle. The song continues until all the children are standing and singing. Sitting down again, the children are served the soup they helped make. Cheryl reminds them of how the soup was made and explains what makes it nutritious.

When the children finish their soup, they throw away their Styrofoam cups and spoons, grab their lunch boxes (decorated with cartoon and television characters), and go outside to sit around the low table to eat lunch. The children talk animatedly while eating.

At 12:45 the teachers announce naptime. The children go the bathroom to brush their teeth and then return to the classroom, where they unroll the mats they keep in their cubbies and find a spot to stretch out.

Cheryl and Linda walk quietly around the room occasionally whispering to children to keep quiet or rubbing the backs of those having trouble falling asleep. By 1:15 all the children are asleep, and the teachers have about an hour to relax and prepare for afternoon activities.

The afternoon schedule is less structured than the morning. Following a snack of fruit and juice, the children play outside with balls, listen to the record player, look at picture books, and draw and cut and paste. From 4 o'clock on children begin to be picked up by their mothers or fathers.

At 5:55 Nicole's mother, Sandy, finally arrives. Cheryl calls out, "Nicole, your mom's here," and Nicole runs over to give her mother a hug. After sending Nicole inside to get her lunch box, Sandy engages Cheryl in conversation:

Sandy: "Sorry, Cheryl. Am I very late? What time is it, anyway?"

What are the most important things for children to learn in preschool?

300 Japanese, 240 Chinese, and 210 American preschool teachers, administrators, parents, and child-development specialists were asked this question. Here are their first choices.

	CHINA	JAPAN	US
Perseverance	13%	2%	3%
Cooperation and how to be a member of a group	37%	30%	32%
Sympathy/empathy/concern for others	4%	31%	5%
Creativity	17%	9%	6%
Beginning reading and math skills	6%	0%	1%
Self-reliance/self-confidence	6%	11%	34%
Art/music/dance	1%	.3%	1%
Communication skills	4%	1%	8%
Physical skills	1%	.3%	1%
Good health, hygiene, and grooming habits	11%	14%	1%
Gentleness	0%	0%	0%

Graphic by Dave Herring

2. INFANCY AND EARLY CHILDHOOD

Cheryl: "No, that's okay, you made it."
Sandy: "How'd Nicole do today?"
Cheryl: "Fine, I think...."

AFTERWORD. The emphasis on variety and choice we found at St. Timothy's does seem to be far more characteristic of American than Chinese or Japanese preschools. And Americans tend to view independence as a characteristically Western trait and dependence as characteristically Asian.

Yet our interviews and questionnaires suggest that Chinese view the most important mission of the preschool as making spoiled, overdependent single children less spoiled, more self-reliant, and less dependent on their parents. Japanese children, in classrooms with ratios of 30 students to one teacher, are by both necessity and design more independent of adult supervision than are their peers in American preschool classrooms with much smaller teacher/student ratios. The promotion of self-reliance and independence in young children is therefore American but not uniquely American.

In China and Japan as well as in the United States, helping children develop language skills is believed to be central to the mission of the preschool. But the three systems have very different notions of the power and purpose of words.

In China the emphasis is on enunciation, diction, memorization, and self-confidence in speaking and performing. American and Japanese visitors to Chinese preschools are invariably impressed by the self-possession and command of language of Chinese children who flawlessly deliver long, rehearsed speeches and belt out multiversed songs.

Language in Japan, both in and out of preschools, is divided into formal and informal systems of discourse. Children in preschools are allowed to speak freely, loudly, even vulgarly to each other during much of the day. But this unrestrained use of language alternates with periods of polite, formal, teacher-directed group recitation of expressions of greeting, thanks, blessing and farewell. Language in Japan—at least the kind of language teachers teach children—is viewed less as a tool for self-expression than as a medium for expressing group solidarity and shared social purpose.

Americans, in contrast, view words as the key to promoting individuality, autonomy, problem solving, friendship, and cognitive development in children. In American preschools children are taught the rules and conventions of self-expression and free speech.

In China citizenship is more widely viewed as something important to teach than it is in Japan and the United States. We see concern for citizenship as part of the more encompassing concern that young children be taught to identify with something larger than themselves and their families. This is perhaps *the* single most important function of preschools in China, Japan, and the United States, since in all three cultures it is the lesson hardest for parents to teach at home.

In Japan the child is taken to preschool to learn to enjoy ties to peers, to learn to transfer some of the warmth of parent-child relations to other relationships, to learn to balance the spontaneity enjoyed at home with formality, emotion with control, and family with society, to learn to become, in other words, truly Japanese.

In China children belong to parents *and* to society. As parents, Chinese naturally have a great desire to cherish and protect their children. But, as citizens, Chinese want to see their children grow up identified with their nation and its struggles, not just with narrower individual and familial concerns. Chinese preschools, and the ongoing debate surrounding them, reflect this search for balance.

American folklore celebrates the loner and the self-made man and looks with scorn on the "ant-colony mentality" seen as characteristic of group-oriented cultures. But some Americans worry that in the celebration of individualism the threads that bind people to one another have been stretched too thin. They are looking to government, church, and community organizations—including preschools —for direction and for a sense of shared purpose and identity.

In all three cultures children enter preschool belonging to their parents and leave with more diffuse, more complex ties to a world still centered on, but now much larger than, their families.

The Day Care Generation

PAT WINGERT
AND BARBARA KANTROWITZ

Meryl Frank is an expert on child care. For five years she ran a Yale University program that studied parental leave. But after she became a new mother two years ago, Frank discovered that even though she knew about such esoteric topics as staff-child ratios and turnover rates, she was a novice when it came to finding someone to watch her own child. Frank went back to work part time when her son, Isaac, was 5 months old, and in the two years since then she has changed child-care arrangements *nine* times.

Her travails began with a well-regarded day-care center near her suburban New Jersey home. On the surface, it was great. One staff member for every three babies, a sensitive administrator, clean facilities. "But when I went in," Frank recalls, "I saw this line of cribs and all these babies with their arms out crying, wanting to be picked up. I felt like crying myself." She walked out without signing Isaac up and went through a succession of other unsatisfactory situations—a babysitter who couldn't speak English, a woman who cared for 10 children in her home at once—before settling on a neighborhood woman who took Isaac into her home. "She was fabulous," Frank recalls wistfully. Three weeks after that babysitter started, she got sick and had to quit. Frank advertised for help in the newspaper and got 30 inquiries but no qualified babysitter. (When Frank asked one prospective nanny about her philosophy of discipline, the woman replied: "If he touched the stove, I'd punch him.") A few weeks later she finally hired her 10th babysitter. "She's a very nice young woman," Frank says. "Unfortunately, she has to leave in May. And I just found out I'm pregnant again and due in June."

That's what happens when a *pro* tries to get help. For other parents, the situation can be even worse. Child-care tales of woe are a common bond for the current generation of parents. Given the haphazard state of day care in this country, finding the right situation is often just a matter of luck. There's no guarantee that a good thing will last. And always, there's the disturbing question that lurks in the back of every working parent's mind: *what is this doing to my kids?*

The simple and unsettling answer is, nobody really knows for sure. Experts say they're just beginning to understand the ramifications of raising a generation of youngsters outside the home while their parents work. Mothers in this country have always had jobs, but it is only in the past few years that a majority have gone back to the office while their children are still in diapers. In the past, most mothers worked out of necessity. That's still true for the majority today, but they have also been joined by mothers of all economic classes. Some researchers think we won't know all the answers until the 21st century, when the children of today's working mothers are parents themselves. In the meantime, results gathered so far are troubling.

Some of the first studies of day care in the 1970s indicated that there were no ill effects from high-quality child care. There was even evidence that children who were out of the home at an early age were more independent and made friends more easily. Those results received wide attention and reassured many parents. Unfortunately, they don't tell the whole story. "The problem is that much of the day care available

> **Child care has immediate problems. But what about the long-term effect it will have on kids?**
> ———

in this country is not high quality," says Deborah Lowe Vandell, professor of educational psychology at the University of Wisconsin. The first research was often done in university-sponsored centers where the child-care workers were frequently students preparing for careers as teachers. Most children in day care don't get such dedicated attention.

Since the days of these early studies, child care has burgeoned into a $15 billion-a-year industry in this country. Day-care centers get most of the attention because they are the fastest-growing segment, but they account for only a small percentage of child-care arrangements. According to 1986 Census Bureau figures, more than half of the kids under 5 with working mothers were cared for by nonrelatives: 14.7 percent in day-care centers and 23.8 percent in family day care, usually a neighborhood home where one caretaker watches several youngsters. Most of the rest were in nursery school or preschool.

Despite years of lobbying by children's advocates, there are still no federal regulations covering the care of young children. The government offers consumers more guidance choosing breakfast cereal than child care. Each state makes its own rules, and they vary from virtually no governmental supervision to strict enforcement of complicated licensing procedures for day-care centers. Many child-development experts recommend that each caregiver be responsible for no more than three infants under the age of 1. Yet only three states—Kansas, Maryland and Massachusetts—require that ratio. Other states are far more lax. Idaho, for example, allows one caregiver to look after as many as 12 children of any age (including babies). And in 14 states there are absolutely no training requirements before starting a job as a child-care worker.

Day-care centers are the easiest to supervise and inspect because they usually operate openly. Family day care, on the other hand, poses big problems for regulatory agencies. Many times, these are informal arrangements that are hard to track down. Some child-care providers even say that regulation would make matters worse by imposing confusing rules that would keep some potential caregivers out of business and intensify the shortage of good day care.

No wonder working parents sometimes feel like pioneers wandering in the wilderness. The signposts point every which way. One set of researchers argues that babies who spend more than 20 hours a week in child care may grow up maladjusted. Other experts say the high turnover rate among poorly paid and undertrained child-care workers has created an unstable environment for youngsters who need dependability and consistency. And still others are worried about health issues—the wisdom of putting a lot of small children with limited immunities in such close quarters. Here's a synopsis of the current debate in three major areas of concern.

There's no question that the care of the very youngest children is by far the most controversial area of research. The topic so divides the child-development community that a scholarly journal, Early Childhood Research Quarterly, recently devoted two entire issues to the subject. Nobody is saying that mothers ought to stay home until their kids are ready for college. Besides that, it would be economically impossible; two thirds of all working women are the sole support of their families or are married to men who earn less than $15,000 a year. But as the demographics have changed, psychologists are taking a second look at what happens to babies. In 1987, 52 percent of mothers of children under the age of 1 were working, compared with 32 percent 10 years earlier. Many experts believe that day-care arrangements that might be fine for 3- and 4-year-olds may be damaging to infants.

Much of the dispute centers on the work of Pennsylvania State University psychologist Jay Belsky. He says mounting research indicates that babies less than 1 year old who receive nonmaternal care for more than 20 hours a week are at a greater risk of developing insecure relationships with their mothers; they're also at increased risk of emotional and behavioral problems in later childhood. Youngsters who have weak emotional ties to their mothers are more likely to be aggressive and disobedient as they grow older, Belsky says. Of course, kids whose mothers are home all day can have these problems, too. But Belsky says that mothers who aren't with their kids all day long don't get to know their babies as well as mothers who work part time or not at all. Therefore, working mothers may not be as sensitive to a baby's first attempts at communication. In general, he says, mothers are more attentive to these crucial signals than babysitters. Placing a baby in outside care increases the chance that an infant's needs won't be met, Belsky says. He also argues that working parents have so much stress in their lives that they have little energy left over for their children. It's hard to find the strength for "quality time" with the kids after a 10- or 12-hour day at the office. (It is interesting to note that not many people are promoting the concept of quality time these days.)

Work by other researchers has added weight to Belsky's theories. Wisconsin's Vandell studied the day-care histories of 236 Texas third graders and found that youngsters who had more than 30 hours a week of child care during infancy had poorer peer relationships, were harder to discipline and had poorer work habits than children who had been in part-time child care or exclusive maternal care. The children most at risk were from the lowest and highest socioeconomic classes, Vandell says, probably because poor youngsters usually get the worst child care and rich parents tend to have high-stress jobs that require long hours away from home. Vandell emphasizes that her results in the Texas study may be more negative than those for the country as a whole because Texas has minimal child-care regulation. Nonetheless, she thinks there's a "serious problem" in infant care.

Other experts say there isn't enough information yet to form any definitive conclusions about the long-term effects of infant

Who's Minding the Children?

Even with the sharp rise in working mothers, most children are still cared for at home—their own or someone else's.

Percent of Mothers Working

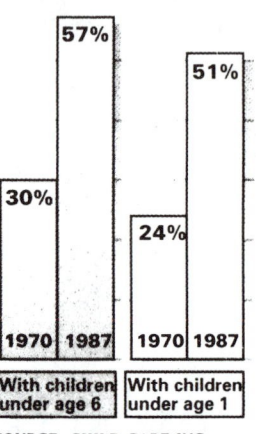

30% (1970)	57% (1987)
24% (1970)	51% (1987)

With children under age 6 / With children under age 1

SOURCE: CHILD CARE INC.

Day Care
WHO LOOKS AFTER CHILDREN UNDER AGE 5 WHILE THEIR MOTHERS WORK

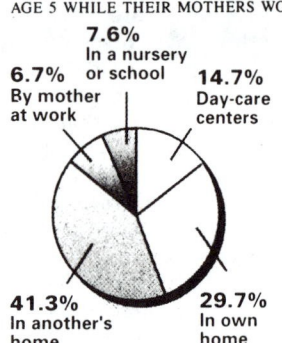

- 7.6% In a nursery or school
- 6.7% By mother at work
- 14.7% Day-care centers
- 41.3% In another's home
- 29.7% In own home

SOURCE: U.S. CENSUS BUREAU

Day care that might be fine for 3- or 4-year-olds may be damaging to infants

care. "There is no clear evidence that day care places infants at risk," says Alison Clarke-Stewart, a professor of social ecology at the University of California, Irvine. Clarke-Stewart says that the difference between the emotional attachments of children of working and of nonworking mothers is not as large as Belsky's research indicates. She says parents should be concerned but shouldn't overreact. Instead of pulling kids out of any form of day care, parents might consider choosing part-time work when their children are very young, she says.

For all the controversy over infant care, there's little dispute over the damaging effects of the high turnover rate among caregivers. In all forms of child care, consistency is essential to a child's healthy development. But only the lucky few get it. "Turnover among child-care workers is second only to parking-lot and gas-station attendants," says Marcy Whitebook, director of the National Child Care Staffing Study. "To give you an idea of how bad it is, during our study, we had tiny children coming up to our researchers and asking them, 'Are you my teacher?'"

The just-released study, funded by a consortium of not-for-profit groups, included classroom observations, child assessments and interviews with staff at 227 child-care centers in five cities. The researchers concluded that 41 percent of all child-care workers quit each year, many to seek better-paying jobs. In the past decade, the average day-care-center enrollment has nearly doubled, while the average salaries for child-care workers have decreased 20 percent. Typical annual wages are very low: $9,931 for full-time, year-round employment ($600 less than the 1988 poverty threshold for a family of three). Few child-care workers receive any benefits.

Parents who use other forms of day care should be concerned as well, warns UCLA psychologist Carollee Howes. Paying top dollar for au pairs, nannies and other in-home caregivers doesn't guarantee that they'll stay. Howes conducted two studies of 18- to 24-month-old children who had been cared for in their own homes or in family day-care homes and found that most had already experienced two or three changes in caregivers and some had had as many as six. In her research, Howes found that the more changes children had, the more trouble they had adjusting to first grade.

The solution, most experts agree, is a drastic change in the status, pay and training of child-care workers. Major professional organizations, such as the National Association for the Education of Young Children, have recommended standard accreditation procedures to make child care more of an established profession, for everyone from workers in large for-profit centers to women who only look after youngsters in their neighborhood. But so far, only a small fraction of the country's child-care providers are accredited. Until wide-scale changes take place, Whitebook predicts that "qualified teachers will continue to leave for jobs that offer a living wage." The victims are the millions of children left behind.

When their toddlers come home from day care with a bad case of the sniffles, parents often joke that it's "schoolitis"—the virus that seems to invade classrooms from September until June. But there's more and more evidence that child care may be hazardous to a youngster's health.

A recent report from the Centers for Disease Control found that children who are cared for outside their homes are at increased risk for both minor and major ailments because they are exposed to so many other kids at such a young age. Youngsters who spend their days in group settings are more likely to get colds and flu as well as strep throat, infectious hepatitis and spinal meningitis, among other diseases.

Here again, the state and federal governments aren't doing much to help. A survey released this fall by the American Academy of Pediatrics and the American Public Health Association found that even such basic health standards as immunization and hand washing were not required in child-care facilities in half the states. Inspection was another problem. Without adequate staff, states with health regulations often have difficulty enforcing them, especially in family day-care centers.

Some experts think that even with strict regulation, there would still be health problems in child-care centers, especially among infants. "The problem is that caretakers are changing the diapers of several kids, and it's difficult for them to wash their hands frequently enough [after each diaper]," says Earline Kendall, associate dean of graduate studies in education at Belmont College in Nashville, Tenn. Kendall, who has operated four day-care centers herself, says that very young babies have the most limited immunities and are the most vulnerable to the diseases that can be spread through such contact. The best solution, she thinks, would be more generous leave time so that parents can stay home until their kids are a little older.

Despite the compelling evidence about the dark side of day care, many experts say there's a great reluctance to discuss these problems publicly. "People think if you say anything against day care, you're saying young parents shouldn't work, or if they do work, they're bad parents," says Meryl Frank, who is now a consultant on family and work issues. "For a lot of parents, that's just too scary to think about. But we have to be realistic. We have to acknowledge that good day care may be good for kids, but bad day care is bad for kids."

There is a political battle as well. Belsky, who has become a lightning rod for controversy among child-development professionals, says "people don't want working mothers to feel guilty" because "they're afraid the right wing will use this to say that only mothers can care for babies, so women should stay home." But, he says, parents should use these problems as evidence to press for such changes as paid parental leave, more part-time jobs and higher-quality child care. The guilt and anxiety that seem to be part of every working parent's psyche aren't necessarily bad, Belsky says. Parents who worry are also probably alert to potential problems—and likely to look for solutions.

Child-Care Checklist

Questions to ask at day-care centers:

■ **What are the educational and training backgrounds of staff members?**

■ **What is the child-staff ratio for each age?** Most experts say it should be no more than 4:1 for infants, 5:1 for 18 months to 2 years, 8:1 for 2 to 3 years, 10:1 for 3 to 4 years and 15:1 for 5 to 6 years.

■ **What are the disciplinary policies?**

■ **Are parents free to visit at any time?**

■ **Are the center's facilities clean and well maintained?**

■ **Are child-safety precautions observed?** Such as heat covers on radiators, childproof safety seals on all electrical outlets?

■ **Are staff members careful about hygiene?** It's important to wash hands between diaper changes in order to avoid spreading diseases.

■ **Are there facilities and staff for taking care of sick children?**

■ **Is there adequate space, indoors and out, for children to play?**

■ **Most important of all, do the children look happy and cared for?** Trust your instincts.

Sizing Up The Sexes

Scientists are discovering that gender differences have as much to do with the biology of the brain as with the way we are raised

CHRISTINE GORMAN

What are little boys made of?
What are little boys made of?
Frogs and snails
And puppy dogs' tails,
That's what little boys are made of.

What are little girls made of?
What are little girls made of?
Sugar and spice
And all that's nice,
That's what little girls are made of.
— Anonymous

Many scientists rely on elaborately complex and costly equipment to probe the mysteries confronting humankind. Not Melissa Hines. The UCLA behavioral scientist is hoping to solve one of life's oldest riddles with a toybox full of police cars, Lincoln Logs and Barbie dolls. For the past two years, Hines and her colleagues have tried to determine the origins of gender differences by capturing on videotape the squeals of delight, furrows of concentration and myriad decisions that children from 2 1/2 to 8 make while playing. Although both sexes play with all the toys available in Hines' laboratory, her work confirms what most parents (and more than a few aunts, uncles and nursery-school teachers) already know. As a group, the boys favor sports cars, fire trucks and Lincoln Logs, while the girls are drawn more often to dolls and kitchen toys.

But one batch of girls defies expectations and consistently prefers the boy toys. These youngsters have a rare genetic ab-

normality that caused them to produce elevated levels of testosterone, among other hormones, during their embryonic development. On average, they play with the same toys as the boys in the same ways and just as often. Could it be that the high levels of testosterone present in their bodies before birth have left a permanent imprint on their brains, affecting their later behavior? Or did their parents, knowing of their disorder, somehow subtly influence their choices? If the first explanation is true and

biology determines the choice, Hines wonders, "Why would you evolve to want to play with a truck?"

Not so long ago, any career-minded researcher would have hesitated to ask such questions. During the feminist revolution of the 1970s, talk of inborn differences in the behavior of men and women was distinctly unfashionable, even taboo. Men dominated fields like architecture and engineering, it was argued, because of social, not hormonal, pressures. Women did the vast majority

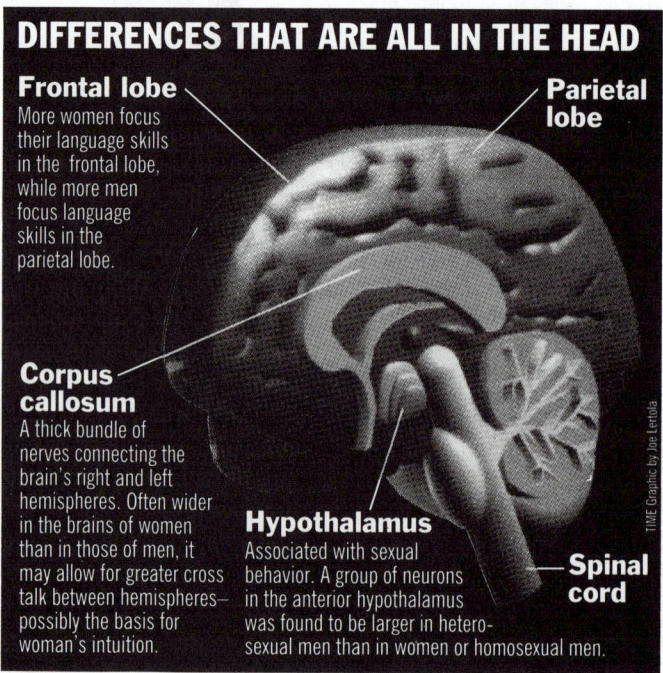

DIFFERENCES THAT ARE ALL IN THE HEAD

Frontal lobe
More women focus their language skills in the frontal lobe, while more men focus language skills in the parietal lobe.

Parietal lobe

Corpus callosum
A thick bundle of nerves connecting the brain's right and left hemispheres. Often wider in the brains of women than in those of men, it may allow for greater cross talk between hemispheres—possibly the basis for woman's intuition.

Hypothalamus
Associated with sexual behavior. A group of neurons in the anterior hypothalamus was found to be larger in heterosexual men than in women or homosexual men.

Spinal cord

TIME Graphic by Joe Lertola

of society's child rearing because few other options were available to them. Once sexism was abolished, so the argument ran, the world would become a perfectly equitable, androgynous place, aside from a few anatomical details.

But biology has a funny way of confounding expectations. Rather than disappear, the evidence for innate sexual differences only began to mount. In medicine, researchers documented that heart disease strikes men at a younger age than it does women and that women have a more moderate physiological response to stress. Researchers found subtle neurological differences between the sexes both in the brain's structure and in its functioning. In addition, another generation of parents discovered that, despite their best efforts to give baseballs to their daughters and sewing kits to their sons, girls still flocked to dollhouses while boys clambered into tree forts. Perhaps nature is more important than nurture after all.

Even professional skeptics have been converted. "When I was younger, I believed that 100% of sex differences were due to the environment," says Jerre Levy, professor of psychology at the University of Chicago. Her own toddler toppled that utopian notion. "My daughter was 15 months old, and I had just dressed her in her teeny little nightie. Some guests arrived, and she came into the room, knowing full well that she looked adorable. She came in with this saucy little walk, cocking her head, blinking her eyes, especially at the men. You never saw such flirtation in your life." After 20 years spent studying the brain, Levy is convinced: "I'm sure there are biologically based differences in our behavior."

Now that it is O.K. to admit the possibility, the search for sexual differences has expanded into nearly every branch of the life sciences. Anthropologists have debunked Margaret Mead's work on the extreme variability of gender roles in New Guinea. Psychologists are untangling the complex interplay between hormones and aggression. But the most provocative, if as yet inconclusive, discoveries of all stem from the pioneering exploration of a tiny 3-lb. universe: the human brain. In fact, some researchers predict that the confirmation of innate differences in behavior could lead to an unprecedented understanding of the mind.

Some of the findings seem merely curious. For example, more men than women are lefthanded, reflecting the dominance of the brain's right hemisphere. By contrast, more women listen equally with both ears while men favor the right one.

Other revelations are bound to provoke more controversy. Psychology tests, for instance, consistently support the notion that men and women perceive the world in subtly different ways. Males excel

EMOTIONS

FEMALE INTUITION: THERE MAY BE SOMETHING TO IT

Do women really possess an ability to read other people's hidden motives and meanings? To some degree, they do. When shown pictures of actors portraying various feelings, women outscore men in identifying the correct emotion. They also surpass men in determining the emotional content of taped conversation in which the words have been garbled. This ability may result from society's emphasis on raising girls to be sensitive. But some researchers speculate that it has arisen to give women greater skill in interpreting the cues of toddlers before they are able to speak.

MALE INSENSITIVITY: IT'S A CULTURAL RELIC

If men seem less adept at deciphering emotions, it is a "trained incompetence," says Harvard psychologist Ronald Levant. Young boys are told to ignore pain and not to cry. Some anthropologists argue that this psychic wound is inflicted to separate boys from their mothers and prepare them for warfare. Many men, says Levant, can recognize their emotions only as a physical buzz or tightness in the throat—a situation that can be reversed, he insists, with training.

at rotating three-dimensional objects in their head. Females prove better at reading emotions of people in photographs. A growing number of scientists believe the discrepancies reflect functional differences in the brains of men and women. If true, then some misunderstandings between the sexes may have more to do with crossed wiring than cross-purposes.

Most of the gender differences that have been uncovered so far are, statistically speaking, quite small. "Even the largest differences in cognitive function are not as large as the difference in male and female height," Hines notes. "You still see a lot of overlap." Otherwise, women could never read maps and men would always be lefthanded. That kind of flexibility within the sexes reveals just how complex a puzzle gender actually is, requiring pieces from biology, sociology and culture.

Ironically, researchers are not entirely sure how or even why humans produce two sexes in the first place. (Why not just one—or even three—as in some species?)

What is clear is that the two sexes originate with two distinct chromosomes. Women bear a double dose of the large X chromosome, while men usually possess a single X and a short, stumpy Y chromosome. In 1990 British scientists reported they had identified a single gene on the Y chromosome that determines maleness. Like some kind of biomolecular Paul Revere, this master gene rouses a host of its compatriots to the complex task of turning a fetus into a boy. Without such a signal, all human embryos would develop into girls. "I have all the genes for being male except this one, and my husband has all the genes for being female," marvels evolutionary psychologist Leda Cosmides, of the University of California at Santa Barbara. "The only difference is which genes got turned on."

Yet even this snippet of DNA is not enough to ensure a masculine result. An elevated level of the hormone testosterone is also required during the pregnancy. Where does it come from? The fetus' own undescended testes. In those rare cases in which the tiny body does not respond to the hormone, a genetically male fetus develops sex organs that look like a clitoris and vagina rather than a penis. Such people look and act female. The majority marry and adopt children.

The influence of the sex hormones extends into the nervous system. Both males and females produce androgens, such as testosterone, and estrogens—although in different amounts. (Men and women who make no testosterone generally lack a libido.) Researchers suspect that an excess of testosterone before birth enables the right hemisphere to dominate the brain, resulting in lefthandedness. Since testosterone levels are higher in boys than in girls, that would explain why more boys are southpaws.

Subtle sex-linked preferences have been detected as early as 52 hours after birth. In studies of 72 newborns, University of Chicago psychologist Martha McClintock and her students found that a toe-fanning reflex was stronger in the left foot for 60% of the males, while all the females favored their right. However, apart from such reflexes in the hands, legs and feet, the team could find no other differences in the babies' responses.

One obvious place to look for gender differences is in the hypothalamus, a lusty little organ perched over the brain stem that, when sufficiently provoked, consumes a person with rage, thirst, hunger or desire. In animals, a region at the front of the organ controls sexual function and is somewhat larger in males than in females. But its size need not remain constant. Studies of tropical fish by Stanford University neurobiologist Russell Fernald reveal that certain cells in this tiny region of the brain swell markedly in an individual male whenever he comes to dominate a school. Unfortunately for the piscine pasha, the cells will also shrink if he loses control of his harem to another male.

Many researchers suspect that, in humans too, sexual preferences are controlled by the hypothalamus. Based on a study of 41 autopsied brains, Simon LeVay of the Salk Institute for Biological Studies announced last summer that he had found a region in the hypothalamus that was on average twice as large in heterosexual men as in either women or homosexual men. LeVay's findings support the idea that varying hormone levels before birth may immutably stamp the developing brain in one erotic direction or another.

These prenatal fluctuations may also steer boys toward more rambunctious behavior than girls. June Reinisch, director of the Kinsey Institute for Research in Sex, Gender and Reproduction at Indiana University, in a pioneering study of eight pairs of brothers and 17 pairs of sisters ages 6 to 18 uncovered a complex interplay between hormones and aggression. As a group, the young males gave more belligerent answers than did the females on a multiple-choice test in which they had to imagine their response to stressful situations. But siblings who had been exposed in utero to synthetic antimiscarriage hormones that mimic testosterone were the most combative of all. The affected boys proved significantly more aggressive than their unaffected brothers, and the drug-exposed girls were much more contentious than their unexposed sisters. Reinisch could not determine, however, whether this childhood aggression would translate into greater ambition or competitiveness in the adult world.

PERCEPTION

HE CAN READ A MAP BLINDFOLDED, BUT CAN HE FIND HIS SOCKS?

It's a classic scene of marital discord on the road. Husband: "Do I turn right?" Wife, madly rotating the map: "I'm not sure where we are." Whether men read maps better is unclear, but they do excel at thinking in three dimensions. This may be due to ancient evolutionary pressures related to hunting, which requires orienting oneself while pursuing prey.

IF LOST IN A FOREST, WOMEN WILL NOTICE THE TREES

Such prehistoric pursuits may have conferred a comparable advantage on women. In experiments in mock offices, women proved 70% better than men at remembering the location of items found on a desktop—perhaps reflecting evolutionary pressure on generations of women who foraged for their food. Foragers must recall complex patterns formed of apparently unconnected items.

While most of the gender differences uncovered so far seem to fall under the purview of the hypothalamus, researchers have begun noting discrepancies in other parts of the brain as well. For the past nine years, neuroscientists have debated whether the corpus callosum, a thick bundle of nerves that allows the right half of the brain to communicate with the left, is

larger in women than in men. If it is, and if size corresponds to function, then the greater crosstalk between the hemispheres might explain enigmatic phenomena like female intuition, which is supposed to accord women greater ability to read emotional clues.

These conjectures about the corpus callosum have been hard to prove because the structure's girth varies dramatically with both age and health. Studies of autopsied material are of little use because brain tissue undergoes such dramatic changes in the hours after death. Neuroanatomist Laura Allen and neuroendocrinologist Roger Gorski of UCLA decided to try to circumvent some of these problems by obtaining brain scans from live, apparently healthy people. In their investigation of 146 subjects, published in April, they confirmed that parts of the corpus callosum were up to 23% wider in women than in men. They also measured thicker connections between the two hemispheres in other parts of women's brains.

Encouraged by the discovery of such structural differences, many researchers have begun looking for dichotomies of function as well. At the Bowman Gray Medical School in Winston-Salem, N.C., Cecile Naylor has determined that men and women enlist widely varying parts of their brain when asked to spell words. By monitoring increases in blood flow, the neuropsychologist found that women use both sides of their head when spelling while men use primarily their left side. Because the area activated on the right side is used in understanding emotions, the women apparently tap a wider range of experience for their task. Intriguingly, the effect

LANGUAGE

IN CHOOSING HER WORDS, A WOMAN REALLY USES HER HEAD

For both sexes, the principal language centers of the brain are usually concentrated in the left hemisphere. But preliminary neurological studies show that women make use of both sides of their brain during even the simplest verbal tasks, like spelling. As a result, a woman's appreciation of everyday speech appears to be enhanced by input from various cerebral regions, including those that control vision and feelings. This greater access to the brain's imagery and depth may help explain why girls often begin speaking earlier than boys, enunciate more clearly as tots and develop a larger vocabulary.

IF JOHNNY CAN'T READ, IS IT BECAUSE HE IS A BOY?

Visit a typical remedial-reading class, and you'll find that the boys outnumber the girls 3 to 1. Stuttering affects four times as many boys as girls. Many researchers have used these and other lopsided ratios to support the argument that males, on average, are less verbally fluent than females. However, the discrepancy could also reflect less effort by teachers or parents to find reading-impaired girls. Whatever the case, boys often catch up with their female peers in high school. In the past few years, boys have even begun outscoring girls on the verbal portion of the Scholastic Aptitude Test.

occurred only with spelling and not during a memory test.

Researchers speculate that the greater communication between the two sides of the brain could impair a woman's performance of certain highly specialized visual-spatial tasks. For example, the ability to tell directions on a map without physically having to rotate it appears stronger in those individuals whose brains restrict the process to the right hemisphere. Any crosstalk between the two sides apparently distracts the brain from its job. Sure enough, several studies have shown that this mental-rotation skill is indeed more tightly focused in men's brains than in women's.

But how did it get to be that way? So far, none of the gender scientists have figured out whether nature or nurture is more important. "Nothing is ever equal, even in the beginning," observes Janice Juraska, a biopsychologist at the University of Illinois at Urbana-Champaign. She points out, for instance, that mother rats lick their male offspring more frequently than they do their daughters. However, Juraska has demonstrated that it is possible to reverse some inequities by manipulating environmental factors. Female rats have fewer nerve connections than males into the hippocampus, a brain region associated with spatial relations and memory. But when Juraska "enriched" the cages of the females with stimulating toys, the females developed more of these neuronal connections. "Hormones do affect these things—it's crazy to deny that," says the researcher. "But there's no telling which way sex differences might go if we completely changed the environment." For humans, educational enrichment could perhaps enhance a woman's ability to work in three dimensions and a man's ability to interpret emotions. Says Juraska: "There's nothing about human brains that is so stuck that a different way of doing things couldn't change it enormously."

Nowhere is this complex interaction between nature and nurture more apparent than in the unique human abilities of speaking, reading and writing. No one is born knowing French, for example; it must be learned, changing the brain forever. Even so, language skills are linked to specific cerebral centers. In a remarkable series of experiments, neurosurgeon George Ojemann of the University of Washington has produced scores of detailed maps of people's individual language centers.

First, Ojemann tested his patients' verbal intelligence using a written exam. Then, during neurosurgery—which was performed under a local anesthetic—he asked them to name aloud a series of objects found in a steady stream of black-and-white photos. Periodically, he touched different parts of the brain with an electrode that temporarily blocked the activity of that region. (This does not hurt because the brain has no sense of pain.) By noting when his patients made mistakes, the surgeon was able to determine which sites were essential to naming.

Several complex sexual differences emerged. Men with lower verbal IQs were more likely to have their language skills located toward the back of the brain. In a number of women, regardless of IQ, the naming ability was restricted to the frontal lobe. This disparity could help explain why strokes that affect the rear of the brain seem to be more devastating to men than to women.

Intriguingly, the sexual differences are far less significant in people with higher verbal IQs. Their language skills developed in a more intermediate part of the brain. And yet, no two patterns were ever identical. "That to me is the most important finding," Ojemann says. "Instead of these sites being laid down more or less the same in everyone, they're laid down in subtly different places." Language is scattered randomly across these cerebral centers, he hypothesizes, because the skills evolved so recently.

What no one knows for sure is just how hardwired the brain is. How far and at what stage can the brain's extraordinary flexibility be pushed? Several studies suggest that the junior high years are key. Girls show the same aptitudes for math as boys until about the seventh grade, when more and more girls develop math phobia. Coincidentally, that is the age at which boys start to shine and catch up to girls in reading.

By one account, the gap between men and women for at least some mental skills has actually started to shrink. By looking at 25 years' worth of data from academic tests, Janet Hyde, professor of psychology and women's studies at the University of Wisconsin at Madison, discovered that overall gender differences for verbal and mathematical skills dramatically decreased after 1974. One possible explanation, Hyde notes, is that "Americans have changed their socialization and educational patterns over the past few decades. They are treating males and females with greater similarity."

Even so, women still have not caught up with men on the mental-rotation test. Fascinated by the persistence of that gap, psychologists Irwin Silverman and Marion Eals of York University in Ontario wondered if there were any spatial tasks at which women outperformed men. Looking at it from the point of view of human evolution, Silverman and Eals reasoned that while men may have developed strong spatial skills in response to evolutionary pressures to be successful hunters, women would have needed other types of visual skills to excel as gatherers and foragers of food.

The psychologists therefore designed a test focused on the ability to discern and later recall the location of objects in a complex, random pattern. In series of tests, student volunteers were given a minute to study a drawing that contained such unrelated objects as an elephant, a guitar and a cat. Then Silverman and Eals presented their subjects with a second drawing containing additional objects and told them to cross out those items that had been added and circle any that had moved. Sure enough, the women consistently surpassed the men in giving correct answers.

What made the psychologists really sit up and take notice, however, was the fact that the women scored much better on the mental-rotation test while they were menstruating. Specifically, they improved their scores by 50% to 100% whenever their estrogen levels were at their lowest. It is not clear why this should be. However, Silverman and Eals are trying to find out if women exhibit a similar hormonal effect for any other visual tasks.

Oddly enough, men may possess a similar hormonal response, according to new research reported in November by Doreen Kimura, a psychologist at the University of Western Ontario. In her study of 138 adults, Kimura found that males perform better on mental-rotation tests in the spring, when their testosterone levels are low, rather than in the fall, when they are higher. Men are also subject to a daily cycle, with testosterone levels lowest around 8 p.m. and peaking around 4 a.m. Thus, says June Reinisch of the Kinsey Institute: "When people say women can't be trusted because they cycle every month, my response is that men cycle every day, so they should only be allowed to negotiate peace treaties in the evening."

Far from strengthening stereotypes about who women and men truly are or how they should behave, research into innate sexual differences only underscores humanity's awesome adaptability. "Gender is really a complex business," says Reinisch. "There's no question that hormones have an effect. But what does that have to do with the fact that I like to wear pink ribbons and you like to wear baseball gloves? Probably something, but we don't know what."

Even the concept of what an innate difference represents is changing. The physical and chemical differences between the brains of the two sexes may be malleable and subject to change by experience: certainly an event or act of learning can directly affect the brain's biochemistry and physiology. And so, in the final analysis, it may be impossible to say where nature ends and nurture begins because the two are so intimately linked.

—Reported by
J. Madeleine Nash/Los Angeles

Development During Childhood

- **Social and Emotional Development (Articles 16–18)**
- **Cognitive and Language Development (Articles 19–21)**
- **Developmental Problems (Articles 22 and 23)**

The transition to childhood brings many new and difficult challenges to parents in promoting healthy social and emotional growth in their children while encouraging and supporting effective cognitive and language development. The subsection *Social and Emotional Development* begins with a review of perspectives on the factors that promote an effective sense of right and wrong and the self-discipline to function in accordance with the dictates of society. "The Good, the Bad and the Difference" reviews several competing contemporary accounts. Though they differ in important respects, all agree that parents *do* play a major role in inculcating moral standards in their children.

The next selection, "Your Loving Touch," examines the importance of touch in human development. Americans are not an especially touch-oriented culture, often refraining from physical contact. However, many child specialists stress the benefits of affectionate physical contact at all age levels.

All life transitions create some degree of stress. Although some children react to stress by striking out against the perceived source of the stress, and others respond to it by withdrawing and attempting to isolate themselves, some children seem to take stress-producing situations in stride. These "invulnerable" or "resilient" children, as pointed out in "The Miracle of Resiliency,"

have developmental histories that may include extreme poverty or chronic family stress. Most people would consider both factors to be potentially damaging to the development of personal and social competence skills. Yet these hardy children do not become victims; instead, they develop effective interpersonal skills. Without question, studies of these children will contribute important knowledge to our understanding of personality development and child-rearing practices.

The articles in the *Cognitive and Language Development* subsection focus on developmental changes or learning patterns in cognitive processing and on the acquisition of language. During the past two decades, the study of cognitive development was dominated by Jean Piaget's theory. Although this theory provides a rich description of what a child can and cannot do during a particular stage of development, it is less adequate for explaining how a child acquires various cognitive skills. Thus, many developmentalists have turned to information-processing models in an effort to integrate cognitive psychology with cognitive developmental theory. Information-processing research has directed attention to individual differences in skill acquisition, challenging traditional concepts of intelligence.

Young children learn best when they can touch, explore, and move about. Knowing what is best and actually implementing these findings into the classroom are two different matters. In the "back to basics" movement of the 1980s, homework, drills, and discipline were emphasized. However, children at the age of 6 are not physically ready to sit for sustained periods; they think concretely rather than abstractly. The article "How Kids Learn" points out that young children should be taught by different methods than those used for older children, and it illustrates teaching methods especially suitable for younger pupils.

Head Start is one of the few federally funded programs dating back to the "Great Society" initiatives of the 1960s that has wide support in both major political parties. The selection "A Head Start Does Not Last" evaluates this early childhood program for children from poor families. The main message is that educational intervention must continue for many years beyond the preschool period for the achievement of long-term educational gains.

Most children begin talking at sometime between 10 and 14 months of age. The article "Now We're Talking!" encourages parents to make language fun for their children. This can be accomplished by talking, reading, and playing with the child, as well as also listening to the child. Parents are cautioned not to cross the barrier from being a parent to being a teacher.

The *Developmental Problems* subsection addresses issues relating to the socialization and education of children who are handicapped as a result of drug use by their mothers during pregnancy, genetic anomalies, or severe physical disabilities such as cerebral palsy. "Clipped Wings" describes the effects of prenatal exposure to drugs, alcohol, and smoking by the mother. Exposure to any of these can result in low birth weight. As babies, they are more likely to be inattentive, socially withdrawn, and hyperactive. When they reach school age, they are at a higher risk for failure. However, early intervention can greatly improve the intellectual functioning of these children and their ability to cope with the demands of structured school settings.

Children with varying degrees of mental or physical disabilities—some quite severe—are learning to communicate via computers. For some children, as pointed out in "Tykes and Bytes," this is not only the first medium they have had for communicating their needs and feelings, but also the first opportunity they have had to play. The ability of multiple handicapped children to express themselves through this medium is both impressive and heartwarming.

Looking Ahead: Challenge Questions

Children who are described as resilient are an enigma. How would you explain such strength of personality in the face of so many potentially disruptive influences in their lives? What coping mechanisms seem to provide resilient children with such strength of character?

What role should parents play in instilling moral values in their children?

To what extent are parents responsible for the pace of language growth in their young children?

Why do you think Head Start has commanded such wide respect when so many other "social engineering" initiatives have met with failure?

Sentiment is growing for restructuring the primary grades to reflect the ways in which young children learn. How high a priority would you place on efforts to bring about these changes?

The Good, The Bad And The DIFFERENCE

BARBARA KANTROWITZ

Like many children, Sara Newland loves animals. But unlike most youngsters, she has turned that love into activism. Five years ago, during a trip to the zoo, the New York City girl learned about the plight of endangered species, and decided to help. With the aid of her mother, Sara—then about 4 years old—baked cakes and cookies and sold them on the sidewalk near her apartment building. She felt triumphant when she raised $35, which she promptly sent in to the World Wildlife Fund.

A few weeks later, triumph turned into tears when the fund wrote Sara asking for more money. "She was devastated because she thought she had taken care of that problem," says Polly Newland, who then patiently told her daughter that there are lots of big problems that require continual help from lots of people. That explanation worked. Sara, now 9, has expanded her causes. Through her school, she helps out at an inner-city child-care center; she also regularly brings meals to homeless people in her neighborhood.

A sensitive parent can make all the difference in encouraging—or discouraging—a child's developing sense of morality and values. Psychologists say that not only are parents important as role models, they also have to be aware of a child's perception of the world at different ages and respond appropriately to children's concerns. "I think the capacity for goodness is there from the start," says Thomas Lickona, a professor of education at the State University of New York at Cortland and author of "Raising Good Children." But, he says, parents must nurture those instincts just as they help their children become good readers or athletes or musicians.

That's not an easy task these days. In the past, schools and churches played a key role in fostering moral development. Now, with religious influence in decline and schools wavering over

the way to teach values, parents are pretty much on their own. Other recent social trends have complicated the transmission of values. "We're raising a generation that is still groping for a good future direction," says psychologist William Damon, head of Brown University's education department. Many of today's parents were raised in the '60s, the age of permissiveness. Their children were born in the age of affluence, the '80s, when materialism was rampant. "It's an unholy combination," says Damon.

These problems may make parents feel they have no effect on how their children turn out. But many studies show that parents are still the single most important influence on their children. Lickona says that the adolescents most likely to follow their consciences rather than give in to peer pressure are those who grew up in "authoritative" homes, where rules are firm but clearly explained and justified—as opposed to "authoritarian" homes (where rules are laid down without explanation) or "permissive" homes.

The way a parent explains rules depends, of course, on the age of the child. Many adults assume that kids see right and wrong in grown-up terms. But what may be seen as "bad" behavior by an adult may not be bad in the child's eyes. For example, a young child may not know the difference between a fanciful tale and a lie, while older kids—past the age of 5—do know.

Many psychologists think that in children, the seeds of moral values are emotional, not intellectual. Such traits as empathy and guilt—observable in the very young—represent the beginning of what will later be a conscience. Even newborns respond to signs of distress in others. In a hospital nursery, for example, a bout of crying by one infant will trigger wailing all around. Research on children's attachment to their mothers shows that babies who are most secure (and those whose mothers are most responsive to their needs) later turn out to be leaders in

> **A sensitive parent is crucial in encouraging a child's sense of morality and values**

school: self-directed and eager to learn. They are also most likely to absorb parental values.

The first modern researcher to describe the stages of a child's moral development was Swiss psychologist Jean Piaget. In his groundbreaking 1932 book, "The Moral Judgment of the Child," he described three overlapping phases of childhood, from 5 to 12. The first is the "morality of constraint" stage: children accept adult rules as absolutes. Then comes the "morality of cooperation," in which youngsters think of morality as equal treatment. Parents of siblings will recognize this as the "If he got a new Ninja Turtle, I want one, too," stage. In the third, kids can see complexity in moral situations. They can understand extenuating circumstances in which strict equality might not necessarily mean fairness ("He got a new Ninja Turtle, but I got to go to the ball game, so it's OK.")

Although Piaget's conclusions have been expanded by subsequent researchers, his work forms the basis for most current theories of moral development. In a study begun in the 1950s, Lawrence Kohlberg, a Harvard professor, used "moral dilemmas" to define six phases. He began with 50 boys who were 10, 13 and 16. Over the next 20 years, he asked them their reactions to carefully constructed dilemmas. The most famous concerns a man named Heinz, whose wife was dying of cancer. The boys were told, in part, that a drug that might save her was a form of radium discovered by the town pharmacist. But the pharmacist was charging 10 times the cost of manufacture for the drug and Heinz could not afford it—although he tried to borrow money from everyone he knew. Heinz begged the pharmacist to sell it more cheaply, but he refused. So Heinz, in desperation, broke into the store and stole the drug. Kohlberg asked his subjects: Did Heinz do the right thing? Why?

Kohlberg and others found that at the first stage, children base their answers simply on the likelihood of getting caught. As they get older, their reasons for doing the right thing become more complex. For example, Lickona says typical 5-year-olds want to stay out of trouble. Kids from 6 to 9 characteristically act out of self-interest; most 10- to 13-year-olds crave social approval. Many 15- to 19-year-olds have moved on to thinking about maintaining the social system and being responsible.

Over the years, educators have used these theories to establish new curricula at schools around the country that emphasize moral development. The Lab School, a private preschool in Houston, was designed by Rheta DeVries, a student of Kohlberg's. The teacher is a "companion/guide," not an absolute authority figure. The object of the curriculum is to get kids to think about why they take certain actions and to think about consequences. For example, if two children are playing a game and one wants to change the rules, the teacher would ask the other child if that was all right. "Moral development occurs best when children live in an environment where fairness and justice is a way of life," says DeVries.

Not everyone agrees with the concept of moral development as a series of definable stages. Other researchers say that the stage theories downplay the role of emotion, empathy and faith. In "The Moral Life of Children," Harvard child psychiatrist Robert Coles tells the story of a 6-year-old black girl named Ruby, who braved vicious racist crowds to integrate her New Orleans school—and then prayed for her tormentors each night before she went to bed. Clearly, Coles says, she did not easily fall into any of Kohlberg's or Piaget's stages. Another criticism of stage theorists comes from feminist psychologists, including Carol Gilligan, author of "In a Different Voice." Gilligan says that the stages represent only *male* development with the emphasis on the concepts of justice and rights, not female development, which, she says, is more concerned with responsibility and caring.

But many psychologists say parents can use the stage theories to gain insight into their children's development. At each phase, parents should help their children make the right decisions about their behavior. In his book, Lickona describes a typical situation involving a 5-year-old who has hit a friend over the head with a toy while playing at the friend's house. Lickona suggests that the parents, instead of simply punishing their son, talk to him about why he hit his friend (the boy played with a toy instead of with him) and about what he could do next time instead of hitting. The parents, Lickona says, should also discuss how the friend might have felt about being hit. By the end of the discussion, the child should realize that there are consequences to his behavior. In Lickona's example, the child decides to call his friend and apologize—a positive ending.

For older children, Lickona suggests family "fairness meetings" to alleviate tension. If, for example, a brother and sister are constantly fighting, the parents could talk to both of them about what seem to be persistent sources of irritation. Then, youngsters can think of ways to bring about a truce—or at least a cease-fire.

Children who learn these lessons can become role models for other youngsters—and for adults as well. Sara Newland tells her friends not to be scared of homeless people (most of them rush by without even a quick glance, she says). "Some people think, 'Why should I give to them?'" she says. "But I feel that you should give. If everyone gave food, they would all have decent meals." One recent evening, she and her mother fixed up three plates of beef stew to give out. They handed the first to the homeless man who's always on their corner. Then, Sara says, they noticed two "rough-looking guys" down the block. Sara's mother, a little scared, walked quickly past them. Then, she changed her mind and asked them if they'd like some dinner. "They said, 'Yes, God bless you',", Sara recalls. "At that moment, they weren't the same people who were looking through a garbage can for beer bottles a little while before. It brought out a part of them that they didn't know they had."

With TESSA NAMUTH *in New York and* KAREN SPRINGEN *in Chicago*

Your Loving Touch

The hugs, cuddles, and kisses you give your children will benefit them throughout their lives.

Janice T. Gibson, Ed.D.

Janice T. Gibson, Ed.D., is a contributing editor of *Parents* Magazine.

Like most mothers, I remember vividly the births of my two children, Robin and Mark. Each time I cuddled my newborn children in my arms—snuggling them gently against my skin and caressing them with my hands and lips—I felt peace and an extraordinarily personal happiness. For each child, born four years apart, it took only an instant for me to fall in love! My joy made me want to continue cuddling and, in the process, strengthened a learned need to hug. Years later, when Mark was in fourth grade, I would hide behind the kitchen door and nab him for a hug when he came home from school. (He always put up with me, except in front of his friends.) And when Robin dressed for the prom, I zipped her gown, patted her on the shoulders, and wrapped my arms around her before she left with her date.

The power of touch.

Affectionate physical contact is meaningful at all age levels. Everyone needs affection, especially when frightened, insecure, or overtired. But particularly for children who cannot yet talk or understand words, cuddling and other forms of affectionate touch convey strong nonverbal messages and serve as important means of communication. When your baby is tired and snuggles in your arms, the gentle body-to-body contact relaxes him and communicates, "You're special. I love you."

Cuddling teaches infants about their environment and the people in it. They explore by touching with their fingers and tongue. Since touching is a reciprocal act, by cuddling your child you teach him to cuddle back. And by responding to his actions, you teach your baby to feel good about himself.

As your child grows older and snuggles with you after a frightening experience, a gentle hug that says "You are safe" will relieve him of his anxiety and help him to feel secure. If during a tantrum he lets you pick him up and hold him on your lap, he will be able to calm down and gain control of his emotions. Furthermore, your affectionate touch can help if your child misbehaves. If he hits his baby brother, for example, you can hold him on your lap as you tell him, "Hitting your brother is not okay." These words, together with the affectionate actions, tell him that although his behavior is not acceptable, you still love him. And when your child exhibits positive behavior, by praising him with a hug and a kiss or an enthusiastic high five, you will convey the message "I'm proud of you."

Why touch is so important.

Physical affection is crucial to a child's development. First of all, parents form strong affectional ties to their children by cuddling and touching them. Gary Johnson, of Delavan, Wisconsin, recalls how he felt after the birth of his first child, Jake: "I got to hold him in my arms for the first twenty minutes of his life. From those first moments together, I never felt strange with him. He was this little helpless creature who needed to be held, cuddled, and protected."

Whether an attachment such as the one Gary describes occurs immediately or over time, it increases the probability that parents will respond to their children's needs. Later, this strong attachment increases the child's psychological well-being.

For babies whose parents don't respond to their signals for close bodily contact, the result is what Mary Ainsworth, Ph.D., professor of psychology emeritus at the University of Virginia, in Charlottesville, has termed "anxious avoidance attachment." She and her colleagues found that babies whose mothers seldom pick them up to comfort them, and who rebuff their attempts to snuggle and cuddle, eventually learn to mask their emotions. When these babies are anxious and upset and most want their mother, they will avoid her so as not to risk being rejected again. "These babies often become adults who don't trust people and find it difficult to form close attachments," remarks Ainsworth. Thus the cycle becomes vicious and self-perpetuating.

The results of a recently completed 36-year study further demonstrate that the effects of parental affection are lifelong. In 1951 a team of psychologists from Harvard University, in Cambridge, Massachusetts, studied 379 five-year-olds in Boston. They asked the children's mothers about their own and their husband's child-rearing practices, including how the mothers responded when their child cried and whether they played with him; whether the father hugged and kissed the child when he came home from work; and whether he spent free time with the child. The researchers found that kindergartners whose parents were warm and affectionate and cuddled them frequently were happier, played better, and had fewer feeding, behavior, and bed-wetting problems than did their peers raised by colder and more reserved parents.

In a 1987 follow-up study involving 76 of the original subjects, researchers found that as adults, those who were raised by warm, nurturing parents tended to have longer, happier marriages and better relationships with close friends than did adult peers whose early child rearing was not so warm. According to psychologist Carol Franz, Ph.D., one of the study's researchers, "Affectionate touching was always associated with a lot of warmth. The more warmth parents exhibited, the more socially adjusted their child was at midlife."

Cuddling barriers.

Most parents provide what their babies need and want. Holding, carrying, rocking, and caressing are part of child rearing in most societies. Infant massage, in which babies are systematically touched and stroked in caring ways, is practiced throughout the world. In some countries, such as India, mothers massage with scented oils. And in China, moms not only massage their youngsters but also use acupuncture to relax them.

But in contrast with people from other countries, Americans, in general, aren't "touchy." In my own cross-cultural studies of child rearing, I've found that although mothers and fathers in the United States are basically as affectionate as other parents, they tend to refrain from physical expressions of love. Although a baby's need for constant physical attention is obvious, the need is less obvious for older children and adults. Consequently, as U.S. children grow older, touching becomes less a part of parent-child interaction.

Some parents are uncomfortable behaving affectionately because they are afraid that it will spoil their children. Far from spoiling children, however, it teaches them to trust you and to view the world as a safe place to explore. Youngsters whose parents pick them up and hug them when they are hurt, frightened, or insecure develop feelings of security that make it easier for them to do things on their own.

Although there has been a lot of talk about how much more involved dads are today, many fathers still have a problem touching their children affectionately. Ronald Levant, Ed.D., former director of Boston University's Fatherhood Project and coauthor of *Between Father and Child* (Penguin), explains that today's generation of men have been raised to be like their fathers, who were the family breadwinners, and as a result they have grown up to be stoic. "As boys, they did not learn the basic psychological skills that girls did—such as self-awareness and empathy—which are necessary to nurture and care for children."

Furthermore, when dads do give their children affection, they tend to give more hugs and kisses to their daughters than to their sons. Why? Some fathers think that cuddling is not masculine and that too much physical affection will turn boys into "sissies." One dad admitted that when his wife was pregnant with their first child, he secretly hoped for a girl. "My father was not a very tactile person. We mostly shook hands. So I was concerned that if I had a son, I'd be too reserved. I was afraid to touch a son." Levant assures, however, that boys who are cuddled by their dads will not become "sissies" but will learn to be nurturing themselves. And more good news: The fathers of this generation are recognizing that they missed affection from their dads and, says Levant, are "breaking the old molds" of masculine reserve.

Some women also feel uncomfortable kissing and hugging their children because their parents weren't comfortable showing affection. One mother says that on the surface, her parents were warm and loving and she was well taken care of, "but I was rarely touched, hugged, or kissed." She wasn't comfortable cuddling with her children until she went into therapy and talked about her feelings. Now, she says, "I don't even think about it anymore. Hugging comes very naturally."

The high rate of divorce today, and the large number of single-parent homes in which the head of the household must work outside the home, also make it more difficult for some parents to provide the physical affection that their children may want or need at any given time. The recent concern raised by the specter of child abuse hasn't made it easier either. Highly publicized cases of purported sexual abuse of children by caregivers or estranged parents make some adults afraid that cuddling and touching may be construed as sexual and harmful. So what can be done? Although it is critical to protect children from sexual abuse, it is equally important to show all children that they are loved and needed. Children need healthy affection, and parents need to find ways to provide it.

Some parents are uncomfortable behaving affectionately with their children because they are afraid it will spoil them. On the contrary, it will help them develop feelings of security.

There are 1,001 ways to demonstrate affection, and not everyone needs to do it the same way. Parents who aren't comfortable giving their children big hugs and kisses shouldn't feel obliged to do so. Patting on the hand or back—or giving a squeeze—plus some loving words, can convey affection if it is done in a meaningful way.

Cuddling comfort.

Like some parents, some children are uncomfortable about being held closely, not because they don't want affection, but because they are uncomfortable feeling physically constrained. For such children, you can stroke their shoulders or back gently, give them lots of kisses, or tickle them gently so that they don't feel entrapped. Eventually they may even like to be cuddled. Gary Johnson's four-year-old daughter, Hallie, and one-year-old son, Nate, weren't as cuddly from the beginning with their father as was their older brother, Jake. But now Hallie is "Daddy's little girl and a permanent fixture on my lap." And Nate has just recently started to want Gary to cuddle him. "It's a real thrill to me to have him reach out for a hug from Dad," he says.

If you work outside the home and are away for most of the day, be sure that your caregiver supplies all the physical love your child needs. The Johnsons were concerned about leaving their kids in somebody else's care. "Becky and I believe that kids need plenty of physical love and affection, and we were afraid that someone else might not give them enough," says Gary. So they searched carefully. "We were fortunate to find a warm, loving, and wonderful caregiver. We can tell the kids are happy."

When peers become important to your child, he may start to shun your affections, particularly if his friends are present. Statements of rejection, such as "Yuck, Mom, don't kiss me" and "Leave my hair alone," do sting, but they signal that your child is growing up and striving for independence. Because he still needs your affection, you might try hugging him at bedtime when his friends aren't around.

As boys and girls reach puberty, touching becomes charged with sexual meaning, making it hard for many adolescents even to acknowledge the desire to touch or be touched in non-sexual ways. Parents should respect their teens' discomfort. When a hug may be too threatening, you can still express your love with a squeeze of the hand or a pat on the back.

If you are divorced, your child needs love from both you and your ex-spouse, even more than before the separation. So, if possible, work together with your ex-spouse to help your child to understand that both of you care. Sometimes boys raised in fatherless households, interpreting the loss of their father as making them the "man of the house," decide that permitting their mother to hug or kiss them makes them less manly. Mothers should respect these feelings but should not stop showing affection: A hug at bedtime or a lingering pat on the arm while going over homework will do wonders.

A recent experience underscored the message for me that even in adulthood, we still need, and benefit from, touch. It was while my now adult children and I were mourning their father's death. We stood silently for some minutes in a circle, our arms around one another, holding on tightly. The feel of our bodies touching consoled us and gave us strength. It convinced us, in a very concrete way, that we would be able to get on with our lives.

the
MIRACLE
OF RESILIENCY

DAVID GELMAN

There are sharp differences in the way children bear up under stress

A prominent child psychiatrist, E. James Anthony, once proposed this analogy: there are three dolls, one made of glass, the second of plastic, the third of steel. Struck with a hammer, the glass doll shatters; the plastic doll is scarred. But the steel doll proves invulnerable, reacting only with a metallic ping.

In life, no one is unbreakable. But child-health specialists know there are sharp differences in the way children bear up under stress. In the aftermath of divorce or physical abuse, for instance, some are apt to become nervous and withdrawn; some may be illness-prone and slow to develop. But there are also so-called resilient children who shrug off the hammer blows and go on to highly productive lives. The same small miracle of resiliency has been found under even the most harrowing conditions—in Cambodian refugee camps, in crack-ridden Chicago housing projects. Doctors repeatedly encounter the phenomenon: the one child in a large, benighted brood of five or six who seems able to take adversity in stride. "There are kids in families from very adverse situations who really do beautifully, and seem to rise to the top of their potential, even with everything else working against them," says Dr. W. Thomas Boyce, director of the division of behavioral and developmental pediatrics at the University of California, San Francisco. "Nothing touches them; they thrive no matter what."

Something, clearly, has gone right with these children, but what? Researchers habitually have come at the issue the other way around. The preponderance of the literature has to do with why children fail, fall ill, turn delinquent. Only

recently, doctors realized they were neglecting the equally important question of why some children *don't* get sick. Instead of working backward from failure, they decided, there might be as much or more to be learned from studying the secrets of success. In the course of looking at such "risk factors" as poverty, physical impairment or abusive parents, they gradually became aware that there were also "protective factors" that served as buffers against the risks. If those could be identified, the reasoning went, they might help develop interventions that could change the destiny of more vulnerable children.

At the same time, the recognition that many children have these built-in defenses has plunged resiliency research into political controversy. "There is a danger among certain groups who advocate nonfederal involvement in assistance to children," says Duke University professor Neil Boothby, a child psychologist who has studied children in war zones. "They use it to blame people who don't move out of poverty. Internationally, the whole notion of resiliency has been used as an excuse not to do anything."

The quest to identify protective factors has produced an eager burst of studies in the past 10 or 15 years, with new publications tumbling off the presses every month. Although the studies so far offer no startling insights, they are providing fresh perspectives on how nature and nurture intertwine in childhood development. One of the prime protective factors, for example, is a matter of genetic luck of the draw: a child born with an easygoing disposition invariably handles stress better than one with a nervous, overreactive temperament. But even highly reactive children can acquire resilience if they have a consistent, stabilizing element in their young lives—something like an attentive parent or mentor.

The most dramatic evidence on that score comes not from humans but from their more researchable cousins, the apes. In one five-year-long study, primate researcher Stephen Suomi has shown that by putting infant monkeys in the care of supportive mothers, he could virtually turn their lives around. Suomi, who heads the Laboratory of Comparative Ethology at the National Institute of Child Health and Human Development, has been comparing "vulnerable" and "invulnerable" monkeys to see if there are useful nurturing approaches to be learned. Differences of temperament can be spotted in monkeys before they're a week old. Like their human counterparts, vulnerable monkey infants show measurable increases in heart rate and stress-hormone production in response to threat situations. "You see a fairly consistent pattern of physiological arousal, and also major behavioral differences," says Suomi. "Parallel patterns have been found in human-developmental labs, so we feel we're looking at the same phenomena."

Left alone in a regular troop, these high-strung infants grow up to be marginal figures in their troops. But by putting them in the care of particularly loving, attentive foster mothers within their first four days of life, Suomi turns the timid monkeys into social lions. Within two months, they become bold and outgoing. Males in the species Suomi has been working with normally leave their native troop at puberty and eventually work their way into a new troop. The nervous, vulnerable individuals usually are the last to leave home. But after being "cross-fostered" to loving mothers, they develop enough confidence so that they're first to leave.

Once on their own, monkeys have complicated (but somehow familiar) patterns of alliances. Their status often depends on whom they know and to whom they're related. In squabbles, they quickly generate support among friends and family members. The cross-fostered monkeys grow very adept at recruiting that kind of support. It's a knack they somehow get through interaction with their foster mothers, in which they evidently pick up coping styles as well as information. "It's essentially a social-learning phenomenon," says Suomi. "I would argue that's what's going on at the human level, too. Evidently, you can learn styles in addition to specific information."

In the long run, the vulnerable infants not only were turned around to normality, they often rose to the top of their hierarchies; they became community leaders. Boyce notes there are significant "commonalities" between Suomi's findings and studies of vulnerable children. "The implications are that vulnerable children, if placed in the right social environment, might become extraordinarily productive and competent adult individuals," he says.

Children, of course, can't be fostered off to new parents or social conditions as readily as monkeys. Most resiliency research is based on children who have not had such interventions in their lives. Nevertheless, some of the findings are revealing. One of the definitive studies was conducted by Emmy E. Werner, a professor of human development at the University of California, Davis, and Ruth S. Smith, a clinical psychologist on the Hawaiian island of Kauai. Together,

they followed 698 children, all descendants of Kauaiian plantation workers, from their birth (in 1955) up to their early 30s. About half the children grew up in poverty; one in six had physical or intellectual handicaps diagnosed between birth and age 2. Of the 225 designated as high risk, two thirds had developed serious learning or behavior problems within their first decade of life. By 18 they had delinquency records, mental-health problems or teenage pregnancies. "Yet one out of three," Werner and Smith noted, "grew into competent young adults who loved well, worked well, played well and expected well."

Some of the protective factors the two psychologists identified underscore the nature-nurture connection. Like other researchers, they found that children who started out with robust, sunny personalities were often twice lucky: not only were they better equipped to cope with life to begin with, but their winning ways made them immediately lovable. In effect, the "nicer" the children, the more readily they won affection—both nature and nurture smiled upon them. There were also other important resiliency factors, including self-esteem and a strong sense of identity. Boyce says he encounters some children who even at 2 or 3 have a sense of "presence" and independence that seem to prefigure success. "It's as if these kids have had the 'Who am I' questions answered for them," he says.

One of the more intriguing findings of the Kauai research was that resilient children were likely to have characteristics of both sexes. Boys and girls in the study tended to be outgoing and autonomous, in the male fashion, but also nurturant and emotionally sensitive, like females. "It's a little similar to what we find in creative children," observes Werner. Some other key factors were inherent in the children's surroundings rather than their personalities. It helped to have a readily available support network of grandparents, neighbors or relatives. Others note that for children anywhere, it doesn't hurt at all to be born to well-off parents. "The advantage of middle-class life is there's a safety net," says Arnold Sameroff, a developmental psychologist at Brown University's Bradley Hospital. "If you screw up, there's someone to bail you out."

In most cases, resilient children have "clusters" of protective factors, not just one or two. But the sine qua non, according to Werner, is a "basic, trusting relationship" with an adult. In all the clusters in the Kauai study, "there is not one that didn't include that one good relationship, whether with a parent, grandparent, older sibling, teacher or mentor—someone consistent enough in that person's life to say, 'You count,' and that sort of begins to radiate other support in their lives." Even children of abusive or schizophrenic parents may prove resilient if they have had at least one caring adult looking out for them—someone, as Tom Boyce says, "who serves as a kind of beacon presence in their lives."

Such relationships do the most good when they are lasting. There is no lasting guarantee for resiliency itself, which is subject to change, de-

Researchers can spot differences of temperament in monkeys before they're a week old

pending on what sort of ups and downs people encounter. Children's ability to cope often improves naturally as they develop and gain experience, although it may decline after a setback in school or at home. Werner notes that around half the vulnerable children in the Kauai study had shaken off their previous problems by the time they reached their late 20s or early 30s. "In the long-term view, more people come through in spite of circumstances. There is an amazing amount of recovery, if you don't focus on one particular time when things are falling apart."

Ironically, this "self-righting" tendency has made the resiliency issue something of a political football. Conservatives have seized on the research to bolster their case against further social spending. "It's the politics of 'It's all within the kid'," says Lisbeth Schorr, a lecturer in social medicine at Harvard Medical School whose book, "Within Our Reach: Breaking the Cycle of Disadvantage," has had a wide impact in the field. "The conservative argument against interventions like Operation Head Start and family-support programs is that if these inner-city kids and families just showed a little grit they would pull themselves up by their own bootstraps. But people working on resilience are aware that when it comes to environments like the inner city, it really doesn't make a lot of sense to talk about what's intrinsic to the kids, because the environment is so overwhelming."

So overwhelming, indeed, that some researchers voice serious doubts over how much change can be brought about in multiple-risk children. Brown's Sameroff, who has been dealing with poor inner-city black and white families in Rochester, N.Y., says the experience has left him "more realistic" about what is possible. "Interventions are important if we can target one or two things wrong with a child. So you provide psychotherapy or extra help in the classroom, then there's a lot better chance." But the children he deals with usually have much more than that going against them—not only poverty but large families, absent fathers, drug-ridden neighborhoods and so on. "We find the more risk factors the worse the outcome," says Sameroff. "With eight or nine, *nobody* does well. For the majority of these children, it's going to involve changing the whole circumstance in which they are raised."

Others are expressing their own reservations, as the first rush of enthusiasm in resiliency research cools somewhat. "A lot of the early intervention procedures that don't follow through have been oversold," says Emmy Werner. "Not every-

There are kids from adverse situations who do beautifully and seem to rise to their potential

one benefited equally from such programs as Head Start." Yet, according to child-development specialists, only a third of high-risk children are able to pull through relatively unaided by such interventions. Says Werner: "At least the high-risk children should be guaranteed basic health and social programs."

Interestingly, when Suomi separates his vulnerable monkeys from their foster mothers at 7 months—around the same time that mothers in the wild go off to breed, leaving their young behind—the genes reassert themselves, and the monkeys revert to fearful behavior. According to Suomi, they do recover again when the mothers return and their new coping skills seem to stay with them. Yet their experience underscores the frailty of change. Boyce, an admirer of Suomi's work, acknowledges that the question of how lasting the effects of early interventions are remains open. But, he adds, programs like Head Start continue to reverberate as much as 15 years later, with reportedly higher school-completion rates and lower rates of delinquency and teen pregnancies.

Boyce recalls that years ago, when he was at the University of North Carolina, he dealt with an 8-year-old child from an impoverished, rural black family, who had been abandoned by his mother. The boy also had "prune-belly syndrome," an anomaly of the abdominal musculature that left him with significant kidney and urinary problems, requiring extensive surgery. But he also had two doting grandparents who had raised him from infancy. They showered him with love and unfailingly accompanied him on his hospital visits. Despite his physical problems and loss of a mother, the boy managed to perform "superbly" in school. By the age of 10, when Boyce last saw him, he was "thriving."

Children may not be as manageable or resilient as laboratory monkeys. If anything, they are more susceptible in the early years. But with the right help at the right time, they can overcome almost anything. "Extreme adversity can have devastating effects on development," says psychologist Ann Masten, who did some of the groundbreaking work in the resiliency field with her University of Minnesota colleague Norman Garmezy. "But our species has an enormous capacity for recovery. Children living in a hostile caregiving environment have great difficulty, but a lot of ability to recover to better functioning if they're given a chance. That's a very important message from the resiliency literature." Unfortunately, the message may not be getting through to the people who can provide that chance.

How Kids Learn

Ages 5 through 8 are wonder years. That's when children begin learning to study, to reason, to cooperate. We can put them in desks and drill them all day. Or we can keep them moving, touching, exploring. The experts favor a hands-on approach, but changing the way schools teach isn't easy. The stakes are high and parents can help.

BARBARA KANTROWITZ & PAT WINGERT

With Howard Manly in Atlanta and bureau reports

It's time for number games in Janet Gill's kindergarten class at the Greenbrook School in South Brunswick, N.J. With hardly any prodding from their teacher, 23 five- and six-year-olds pull out geometric puzzles, playing cards and counting equipment from the shelves lining the room. At one round table, a group of youngsters fits together brightly colored wooden shapes. One little girl forms a hexagon out of triangles. The others, obviously impressed, gather round to count up how many parts are needed to make the whole.

After about half an hour, the children get ready for story time. They pack up their counting equipment and settle in a circle around Gill. She holds up a giant book about a zany character called Mrs. Wishy-washy who insists on giving farm animals a bath. The children recite the whimsical lines along with Gill, obviously enjoying one of their favorite tales. (The hallway is lined with drawings depicting the children's own interpretation of the book; they've taken a few literary liberties, like substituting unicorns and dinosaurs for cows and pigs.) After the first reading, Gill asks for volunteers to act out the various parts in the book. Lots of hands shoot up. Gill picks out four children and

they play their parts enthusiastically. There isn't a bored face in the room.

This isn't reading, writing and arithmetic the way most people remember it. Like a growing number of public- and private-school educators, the principals and teachers in South Brunswick believe that children between the ages of 5 and 8 have to be taught differently from older children. They recognize that young children learn best through active, hands-on teaching methods like games and dramatic play. They know that children in this age group develop at varying rates and schools have to allow for these differences. They also believe that youngsters' social growth is as essential as their academic achievement. Says Joan Warren, a teacher consultant in South Brunswick: "Our programs are designed to fit the child instead of making the child fit the school."

Educators call this kind of teaching "developmentally appropriate practice"—a curriculum based on what scientists know about how young children learn. These ideas have been slowly emerging through research conducted over the last century, particularly in the past 30 years. Some of the tenets have appeared

The Lives and Times of Children

Each youngster proceeds at his own pace, but the learning curve of a child is fairly predictable. Their drive to learn is awesome, and careful adults can nourish it. The biggest mistake is pushing a child too hard, too soon.

● Infants and Toddlers
They're born to learn. The first important lesson is trust, and they learn that from their relationships with their parents or other caring adults. Later, babies will begin to explore the world around them and experiment with independence. As they mature, infants slowly develop gross motor (sitting, crawling, walking) and fine motor (picking up tiny objects) skills. Generally, they remain egocentric and are unable to share or wait their turn. New skills are perfected through repetition, such as the babbling that leads to speaking.

■ 18 months to 3 years
Usually toilet training becomes the prime learning activity. Children tend to concentrate on language development and large-muscle control through activities like climbing on jungle gyms. Attention spans lengthen enough to listen to uncomplicated stories and carry on conversations. Vocabulary expands to about 200 words. They enjoy playing with one other child, or a small group, for short periods, and learn that others have feelings too. They continue to look to parents for encouragement and protection, while beginning to accept limits on their behavior.

▲ 3-year-olds
Generally, they're interested in doing things for themselves and trying to keep up with older children. Their ability to quietly listen to stories and music remains limited. They begin telling stories and jokes. Physical growth slows, but large-muscle development continues as children run, jump and ride tricycles. They begin to deal with cause and effect; it's time to plant seeds and watch them grow.

● 4-year-olds
They develop better small motor skills, such as cutting with scissors, painting, working with puzzles and building things.
They can master colors, sizes and shapes. They should be read to and should be encouraged to watch others write; let them scribble on paper but try to keep them away from walls.

■ 5-year-olds
They begin to understand counting as a one-to-one correlation. Improved memories make it easier for them to recognize meaningful words, and with sharper fine motor skills, some children will be able to write their own names.

▲ Both 4s and 5s
Both groups learn best by interacting with people and concrete objects and by trying to solve real problems. They can learn from stories and books, but only in ways that relate to their own experience. Socially, these children are increasingly interested in activities outside their immediate family. They can play in groups for longer periods, learning lessons in cooperation and negotiation. Physically, large-muscle development continues, and skills such as balancing emerge.

● 6-year-olds
Interest in their peers continues to increase, and they become acutely aware of comparisons between themselves and others. It's a taste of adolescence: does the group accept them? Speech is usually well developed, and children are able to joke and tease. They have a strong sense of true and false and are eager for clear rules and definitions. However, they have a difficult time differentiating between minor and major infractions. Generally, children this age are more mature mentally than physically and unable to sit still for long periods. They learn better by firsthand experiences. Learning by doing also encourages children's "disposition" to use the knowledge and skills they're acquiring.

■ 7- to 8-year-olds
During this period, children begin developing the ability to think about and solve problems in their heads, but some will continue to rely on fingers and toes to help them find the right answer. Not until they're 11 are most kids capable of thinking purely symbolically; they still use real objects to give the symbols—such as numbers—meaning. At this stage they listen better and engage in give and take. Generally, physical growth continues to slow, while athletic abilities improve—children are able to hit a softball, skip rope or balance on a beam. Sitting for long periods is still more tiring than running and jumping.

---

under other names—progressivism in the 1920s, open education in the 1970s. But they've never been the norm. Now, educators say that may be about to change. "The entire early-childhood profession has amassed itself in unison behind these principles," says Yale education professor Sharon Lynn Kagan. In the last few years, many of the major education organizations in the country—including the National Association for the Education of Young Children and the National Association of State Boards of Education—have endorsed remarkably similar plans for revamping kindergarten through third grade.

Bolstered by opinions from the experts, individual states are beginning to take action. Both California and New York have appointed task forces to recommend changes for the earliest grades. And scores of individual school districts like South Brunswick, figuring that young minds are a terrible thing to waste, are pushing ahead on their own.

The evidence gathered from research in child development is so compelling that even groups like the Council for Basic Education, for years a major supporter of the traditional format, have revised their thinking. "The idea of putting small children in front of workbooks and asking them to sit at their desks all day is a nightmare vision," says Patte Barth, associate editor of Basic Education, the council's newsletter.

At this point, there's no way of knowing how soon change will come or how widespread it will be. However, there's a growing recognition of the importance of the early grades. For the past few years, most of the public's attention has focused on older children, especially teenagers. "That's a Band-Aid kind of approach," says Anne Dillman, a member of the New Jersey State Board of Education. "When the product doesn't come out right, you try and fix it at the end. But we really have to start at the beginning." Demographics have contributed to the sense of urgency. The baby boomlet has replaced the baby-bust generation of the 1970s. More kids in elementary school means more parents asking if there's a better way to teach. And researchers say there is a better way. "We've made remarkable breakthroughs in understanding the development of children, the development of learning and the climate that enhances that," says Ernest Boyer of The Carnegie Foundation for the Advancement of Teaching. But, he adds, too often, "what we know in theory and what we're doing in the classroom are very different."

The early grades pose special challenges because that's when children's attitudes toward school and learning are shaped, says Tufts University psychologist David Elkind. As youngsters move from home or preschool into the larger, more competitive world of elementary school, they begin to make judgments about their own abilities. If they feel inadequate, they may give up. Intellectually, they're also in transition, moving from the intensely physical exploration habits of infancy and toddlerhood to more abstract reasoning. Children are born wanting to learn. A baby can spend hours studying his hands; a toddler is fascinated by watching sand pour through a sieve. What looks like play to an adult is actually the work of childhood, developing an understanding of the world. Studies show that the most effective way to teach young kids is to capitalize on their natural inclination to learn through play.

But in the 1980s, many schools have tried to do just the opposite, pressure instead of challenge. The "back to basics" movement meant that teaching methods intended for high school students were imposed on first graders. The lesson of the day was more: more homework, more tests, more discipline. Children should be behind their desks, not roaming around the room. Teachers should be at the head of the classrooms, drilling knowledge into their charges. Much of this was a reaction against the trend toward open education in the '70s. Based on the British system, it allowed children to develop at their own pace within a highly structured classroom. But too many teachers and principals who tried open education thought that it meant simply tearing down classroom walls and letting children do whatever they wanted. The results were often disastrous. "Because it was done wrong, there was a backlash against it," says Sue Bredekamp of the National Association for the Education of Young Children.

At the same time, parents, too, were demanding more from their elementary schools. By the mid-1980s, the majority of 3- and 4-year-olds were attending some form of pre-school. And their parents expected these classroom veterans to be reading by the second semester of kindergarten. But the truth is that many 5-year-olds aren't ready for reading—or most of the other academic tasks that come easily to older children—no matter how many years of school they've completed. "We're confusing the numbers of years children have been in school with brain development," says Martha Denckla, a professor of neurology and pediatrics at Johns Hopkins University. "Just because a child goes to day care at age 3 doesn't mean the human brain mutates into an older brain. A 5-year-old's brain is still a 5-year-old's brain."

As part of the return to basics, parents and districts demanded hard evidence that their children were learning. And some communities took extreme measures. In 1985 Georgia became the first state to require 6-year-olds to pass a standardized test before entering first grade. More than two dozen other states proposed similar legislation. In the beginning Georgia's move was hailed as a "pioneering" effort to get kids off to a good start. Instead, concedes state school superintendent Werner Rogers, "We got off on the wrong foot." Five-year-olds who used to spend their days finger-painting or singing were hunched over ditto sheets, preparing for the big exam. "We would have to spend a month just teaching kids how to take the test," says Beth Hunnings, a kindergarten teacher in suburban Atlanta. This year Georgia altered the tests in favor of a more flexible evaluation; other states have changed their minds as well.

The intense, early pressure has taken an early toll. Kindergartners are struggling with homework. First graders are taking spelling tests before they even understand how to read. Second graders feel like failures. "During this critical period," says David Elkind in his book "Miseducation," "the child's bud-

In Japan, First Grade Isn't a Boot Camp

Japanese students have the highest math and science test scores in the world. More than 90 percent graduate from high school. Illiteracy is virtually nonexistent in Japan. Most Americans attribute this success to a rigid system that sets youngsters on a lock-step march from cradle to college. In fact, the early years of Japanese schooling are anything but a boot camp; the atmosphere is warm and nurturing. From kindergarten through third grade, the goal is not only academic but also social—teaching kids to be part of a group so they can be good citizens as well as good students. "Getting along with others is not just a means for keeping the peace in the classroom but something which is a valued end in itself," says American researcher Merry White, author of "The Japanese Educational Challenge."

Lessons in living and working together grow naturally out of the Japanese culture. Starting in kindergarten, youngsters learn to work in teams, with brighter students often helping slower ones. All children are told they can succeed if they persist and work hard. Japanese teachers are expected to be extremely patient with young children. They go over lessons step by step and repeat instructions as often as necessary. "The key is not to scold [children] for small mistakes," says Yukio Ueda, principal of Mita Elementary School in Tokyo. Instead, he says, teachers concentrate on praising and encouraging their young charges.

As a result, the classrooms are relaxed and cheerful, even when they're filled with rows of desks. On one recent afternoon a class of second graders at Ueda's school was working on an art project. Their assignment was to build a roof with poles made of rolled-up newspapers. The children worked in small groups, occasionally asking their teacher for help. The room was filled with the sound of eager youngsters chatting about how to get the job done. In another second-grade class, the subject was math. Maniko Inoue, the teacher, suggested a number game to practice multiplication. After a few minutes of playing it, one boy stood up and proposed changing the rules just a bit to make it more fun. Inoue listened carefully and then asked if the other students agreed. They cheered, "Yes, yes," and the game continued according to the new rules.

Academics are far from neglected in the early grades. The Education Ministry sets curriculum standards and goals for each school year. For example, third graders by the end of the year are supposed to be able to read and write 508 characters (out of some 2,000 considered essential to basic literacy). Teachers have time for play and lessons: Japanese children attend school for 240 days, compared with about 180 in the United States.

Mothers' role: Not all the teaching goes on in the classroom. Parents, especially mothers, play a key role in education. Although most kindergartens do not teach writing or numbers in any systematic way, more than 80 percent of Japanese children learn to read or write to some extent before they enter school. "It is as if mothers had their own built-in curriculum," says Shigefumi Nagano, a director of the National Institute for Educational Research. "The first game they teach is to count numbers up to 10."

For all their success in the early grades, the Japanese are worried they're not doing well enough. After a recent national curriculum review, officials were alarmed by what Education Minister Takeo Nishioka described as excessive "bullying and misconduct" among children—the result, according to some Japanese, of too much emphasis on material values. So three years from now, first and second graders will no longer be studying social studies and science. Instead, children will spend more time learning how to be good citizens. That's "back to basics"—Japanese style.

BARBARA KANTROWITZ *with* HIDEKO TAKAYAMA *in Tokyo*

ding sense of competence is frequently under attack, not only from inappropriate instructional practices . . . but also from the hundred and one feelings of hurt, frustration and rejection that mark a child's entrance into the world of schooling, competition and peer-group involvement." Adults under similar stress can rationalize setbacks or put them in perspective based on previous experiences; young children have none of these defenses. Schools that demand too much too soon are setting kids off on the road to failure.

It doesn't have to be this way. Most experts on child development and early-childhood education believe that young children learn much more readily if the teaching methods meet their special needs:

Differences in thinking: The most important ingredient of the nontraditional approach is hands-on learning. Research begun by Swiss psychologist Jean Piaget indicates that somewhere between the ages of 6 and 9, children begin to think abstractly instead of concretely. Younger children learn much more by touching and seeing and smelling and tasting than by just listening. In other words, 6-year-olds can easily understand addition and subtraction if they have actual objects to count instead of a series of numbers written on a blackboard. Lectures don't help. Kids learn to reason and communicate by engaging in conversation. Yet most teachers still talk at, not with, their pupils.

Physical activity: When they get to be 10 or 11, children can sit still for sustained periods. But until they are physically ready for long periods of inactivity, they need to be active in the classroom. "A young child has to make a conscious effort to sit still," says Denckla. "A large chunk of children can't do it for very long. It's a very energy-consuming activity for them." Small children actually get more tired if they have to sit still and listen to a teacher talk than if they're allowed to move around in the classroom. The frontal lobe, the part of the brain that applies the brakes to children's natural energy and curiosity, is still immature in 6- to 9-year-olds, Denckla says. As the lobe develops, so does what Denckla describes as "boredom tolerance." Simply put, learning by doing is much less boring to young children.

Language development: In this age group, experts say language development should not be broken down into isolated skills—reading, writing and speaking. Children first learn to reason and to express themselves by talking. They can dictate stories to a teacher before they actually read or write. Later, their first attempts at composition do not need to be letter perfect; the important thing is that they learn to communicate ideas. But in many classrooms, grammar and spelling have become more important than content. While mastering the technical aspects of writing is essential as a child gets older, educators warn against emphasizing form over content in the early grades. Books should also be interesting to kids—not just words strung together solely for the purpose of pedagogy. Psychologist Katherine Nelson of the City University of New York says that her extensive laboratory and observational work indicates that kids can learn language—speaking, writing or reading—only if it is presented in a way that makes sense to them. But many teachers still use texts that are so boring they'd put anybody to sleep.

Socialization: A youngster's social development has a profound effect on his academic progress. Kids who have trouble getting along with their classmates can end up behind academically as well and have a higher incidence of dropping out. In the early grades especially, experts say youngsters should be encouraged to work in groups rather than individually so that teachers can spot children who may be having problems making friends. "When children work on a project," says University of Illinois education professor Lillian Katz, "they learn to work together, to disagree, to speculate, to take turns and de-escalate tensions. These skills can't be learned through lecture. We all know people who have wonderful technical skills but don't have any social skills. Relationships should be the first 'R'."

Feelings of competence and self-esteem: At this age, children are also learning to judge themselves in relation to others. For most children, school marks the first time that their goals are not set by an internal clock but by the outside world. Just as the 1-year-old struggles to walk, 6-year-olds are struggling to meet adult expectations. Young kids don't know how to distinguish between effort and ability, says Tynette Hills, coordinator of early-childhood education for the state of New Jersey. If they try hard to do something and fail, they may conclude that they will never be able to accomplish a particular task. The effects of obvious methods of comparison, such as posting grades, can be serious. Says Hills: "A child who has had his confidence really damaged needs a rescue operation."

Rates of growth: Between the ages of 5 and 9, there's a wide range of development for children of normal

intelligence. "What's appropriate for one child may not be appropriate for another," says Dr. Perry Dyke, a member of the California State Board of Education. "We've got to have the teachers and the staff reach children at whatever level they may be at . . . That takes very sophisticated teaching." A child's pace is almost impossible to predict beforehand. Some kids learn to read on their own by kindergarten; others are still struggling to decode words two or three years later. But by the beginning of the fourth grade, children with very different histories often read on the same level. Sometimes, there's a sudden "spurt" of learning, much like a growth spurt, and a child who has been behind all year will catch up in just a few weeks. Ernest Boyer and others think that multigrade classrooms, where two or three grades are mixed, are a good solution to this problem—and a way to avoid the "tracking" that can hurt a child's self-esteem. In an ungraded classroom, for example, an older child who is having problems in a particular area can practice by tutoring younger kids.

Putting these principles into practice has never been easy. Forty years ago Milwaukee abolished report cards and started sending home ungraded evaluations for kindergarten through third grade. "If anything was developmentally appropriate, those ungraded classes were," says Millie Hoffman, a curriculum specialist with the Milwaukee schools. When the back-to-basics movement geared up nationally in the early 1980s, the city bowed to pressure. Parents started demanding letter grades on report cards. A traditional, direct-teaching approach was introduced into the school system after some students began getting low scores on standardized tests. The school board ordered basal readers with controlled vocabularies and contrived stories. Milwaukee kindergarten teachers were so up-

---

A Primer for Parents

When visiting a school, trust your eyes. What you see is what your child is going to get.

● Teachers should talk to small groups of children or individual youngsters; they shouldn't just lecture.

■ Children should be working on projects, active experiments and play; they shouldn't be at their desks all day filling in workbooks.

▲ Children should be dictating and writing their own stories or reading real books.

● The classroom layout should have reading and art areas and space for children to work in groups.

■ Children should create freehand artwork, not just color or paste together adult drawings.

▲ Most importantly, watch the children's faces. Are they intellectually engaged, eager and happy? If they look bored or scared, they probably are.

set by these changes that they convinced the board that their students didn't need most of the standardized tests and the workbooks that go along with the readers.

Some schools have been able to keep the progressive format. Olive School in Arlington Heights, Ill., has had a nontraditional curriculum for 22 years. "We've been able to do it because parents are involved, the teachers really care and the children do well," says principal Mary Stitt. "We feel confident that we know what's best for kids." Teachers say they spend a lot of time educating parents about the teaching methods. "Parents always think school should be the way it was for them," says first-grade teacher Cathy Sauer. "As if everything else can change and progress but education is supposed to stay the same. I find that parents want their children to like school, to get along with other children and to be good thinkers. When they see that happening, they become convinced."

Parental involvement is especially important when schools switch from a traditional to a new format. Four years ago, Anne Norford, principal of the Brownsville Elementary School in Albemarle County, Va., began to convert her school. Parents volunteer regularly and that helps. But the transition has not been completely smooth. Several teachers refused to switch over to the more active format. Most of them have since left the school, Norford says. There's no question that some teachers have trouble implementing the developmentally appropriate approach. "Our teachers are not all trained for it," says Yale's Kagan. "It takes a lot of savvy and skill." A successful child-centered classroom seems to function effortlessly as youngsters move from activity to activity. But there's a lot of planning behind it—and that's the responsibility of the individual teacher. "One of the biggest problems," says Norford, "is trying to come up with a program that every teacher can do—not just the cadre of single people who are willing to work 90 hours a week." Teachers also have to participate actively in classroom activities and give up the automatic mantle of authority that comes from standing at the blackboard.

Teachers do better when they're involved in the planning and decision making. When the South Brunswick, N.J., schools decided in the early 1980s to change to a new format, the district spent several years studying a variety of curricula. Teachers participated in that research. A laboratory school was set up in the summer so that teachers could test materials. "We had the support of the teachers because teachers were part of the process," says teacher consultant Joan Warren.

One residue of the back-to-basics movement is the demand for accountability. Children who are taught in nontraditional classrooms can score slightly lower on commonly used standardized tests. That's because most current tests are geared to the old ways. Children are usually quizzed on specific skills, such as vocabulary or addition, not on the concepts behind those skills. "The standardized tests usually call for one-word answers," says Carolyn Topping, principal of Mesa Elementary School in Boulder, Colo. "There may be three words in a row, two of which are misspelled and the child is asked to circle the correctly spelled word. But the tests never ask, 'Does the child know how to write a paragraph?' "

Even if the tests were revised to reflect different kinds of knowledge, there are serious questions about the reliability of tests on young children. The results can vary widely, depending on many factors—a child's mood, his ability to manipulate a pencil (a difficult skill for many kids), his reaction to the person administering the test. "I'm appalled at all the testing we're doing of small children," says Vanderbilt University professor Chester Finn, a former assistant secretary of education under the Reagan administration. He favors regular informal reviews and teacher evaluations to make sure a student understands an idea before moving on to the next level of difficulty.

Tests are the simplest method of judging the effectiveness of a classroom—if not always the most accurate. But there are other ways to tell if children are learning. If youngsters are excited by what they are doing, they're probably laughing and talking to one another and to their teacher. That communication is part of the learning process. "People think that school has to be either free play or all worksheets," says Illinois professor Katz. "The truth is that neither is enough. There has to be a balance between spontaneous play and teacher-directed work." And, she adds, "you have to have the other component. Your class has to have intellectual life."

Katz, author of "Engaging Children's Minds," describes two different elementary-school classes she visited recently. In one, children spent the entire morning making identical pictures of traffic lights. There was no attempt to relate the pictures to anything else the class was doing. In the other class, youngsters were investigating a school bus. They wrote to the district and asked if they could have a bus parked in their lot for a few days. They studied it, figured out what all the parts were for and talked about traffic rules. Then, in the classroom, they built their own bus out of cardboard. They had fun, but they also practiced writing, problem solving, even a little arithmetic. Says Katz: "When the class had their parents' night, the teacher was ready with reports on how each child was doing. But all the parents wanted to see was the bus because their children had been coming home and talking about it for weeks." That's the kind of education kids deserve. Anything less should get an "F."

A Head Start Does Not Last

A new study finds that poor kids need intensive help long after they leave nursery school

Head Start is virtually the only antipoverty program backed by liberals and conservatives, parents and early-childhood experts. Even in the midst of the recession the federal government doled out $2.2 billion this academic year for programs in all 50 states, guaranteeing up to two years of preschool for 600,000 3- to 5-year-olds. This week, President Bush is expected to announce that he is asking for a record increase in Head Start funding in the fiscal 1993 budget. Much of the support for Head Start is based on the belief that it levels the playing field for poor kids, giving them, as Bush put it in his 1988 campaign, "an equal place at the starting line." But now, a new long-term study suggests that underprivileged youngsters need a much bigger boost if they are going to finish the race.

J. S. Fuerst of Chicago's Loyola University School of Social Work studied the lives of 684 children who attended six special, publicly funded schools in Chicago between 1967 and 1977. Most had not only two years of preschool but also from two to seven additional years in an intensive elementary-school program that Fuerst describes as "Head Start to the fourth power." The six child-parent centers set up in the city's worst neighborhoods encouraged parents to help out at school and gave kids a heavy dose of academics, with an emphasis on language development.

All of the children were black, and a majority were raised in single-parent families. Sixty percent were on welfare. Classes had no more than 20 students and in many cases children had the same team of teachers and aides for a number of years. Students spent all of their school hours—half days for preschoolers, full days for primary pupils—at the centers. There were different instructional programs, but all were academically oriented. After they finished the program, most went on to regular public schools; others transferred to parochial schools.

In 1974, when he first looked at reading- and math-test scores of center graduates, Fuerst found that they outranked their neighborhood peers and even exceeded national norms. Most of the kids he studied were then 13 or under. Their high scores were especially remarkable because Chicago had a rapidly deteriorating public-school system that former education secretary William Bennett later classified as America's worst. A decade later, when Fuerst and his wife, Dorothy, began gathering data for a much larger study tracking center kids through their high-school years, he found that many of those early gains had been lost. Only 62 percent graduated from high school. That was better than the 49 percent graduation rate among a control group of 676 non-Center kids from the same backgrounds, but well under the national

average of about 80 percent for 19-year-olds. Even more alarming, there were stark differences between boys and girls. A total of 74 percent of the girls finished school, but only 49 percent of the boys got diplomas. It was a dramatic reversal of his 1974 finding that boys' and girls' test scores were almost identical when they left the centers.

Some hope: At first glance, these seem like extremely discouraging results. But Fuerst says that when he studied the numbers more closely, he found some hope. At one of the six centers, children received an extraordinary amount of special instruction: seven to nine years. In that group the gains in high-school graduation were dramatic: 70 percent of the boys and 85 percent of the girls finished. Fuerst thinks his study shows that girls should get four to six years of extra help, while boys—who appear to be much more susceptible to peer pressures—need seven to nine years of intensive academics. "Nobody wants to knock the one ray of light warming a sea of darkness," says Fuerst. "But overestimating Head Start isn't fair to these kids."

Fuerst's study adds considerable weight to a growing sentiment among early-childhood educators that inner-city kids need much more than a year or two of preschool. "The best program in the world for a very short time at age 4 is not going to help children survive the onslaught" of neighborhoods devastated by crime and drugs, says Barbara Willer, public-affairs director of the National Association for the Education of Young Children. "If you view it as an inoculation, you're in for a surprise."

Head Start's long-term effectiveness was just a theory at its conception in 1965. Initially, Head Start's creators envisioned it as a six- to eight-week summer program. "We thought that very minimal intervention would give us very big payoffs," says Edward Zigler, a psychology professor at Yale who helped develop Head Start and was one of its first directors. Zigler says the founders soon realized that kids needed at least a year or two of Head Start. Early studies of Head Start and similar programs confirmed that this preparation did indeed help kids in their first years of grammar school.

In the public mind, however, Head Start's benefits got a tremendous boost in the past decade from a widely publicized study of the Perry Preschool Project in Ypsilanti, Mich. That research indicated that early intervention could lower delinquency, joblessness and teen-pregnancy rates. Some early-childhood experts say these results have been misinterpreted: the Ypsilanti project was not a Head Start program and was more rigorous than typical Head Start classes.

In the last few years, educators have been looking for effective ways to sustain Head Start's gains. The search has become more urgent, with so many children in single-parent homes. They are the most likely to grow up in poverty and have

---

Nursery Tales

About one third of the nation's 3- and 4-year-olds go to preschool classes.

Twice as many students attend private preschools as public.

The odds against failing in school, researchers say, rest on a litany of factors. Poor children are the most at risk. Their chances get worse if they have a single parent who didn't finish school or has limited English skills.

In this academic year, Washington doled out $2.2 billion for Head Start programs in all 50 states, guaranteeing up to two years of pre-school for 600,000 3- to 5-year-olds.

SOURCES: NATIONAL CENTER FOR EDUCATIONAL STATISTICS; HEAD START

---

problems in school. Zigler says he favors a three-year "transition" project in the early elementary grades that would emphasize parental involvement. At Johns Hopkins University in Baltimore, Robert Slavin and his colleagues at the Center for Research on Effective Schooling for Disadvantaged Students have developed the "Success for All" program for preschool through third grade. It emphasizes extra help in reading, family support and teacher training. So far, the results are encouraging: most third graders are reading at grade level, and many are over.

Helping parents: Wade Horn, the federal Head Start administrator, says Washington is also looking for new approaches. Getting parents involved in school is generally recognized as a key ingredient, and Horn says that part of the Head Start budget is going toward what he calls a "two-generation model." By the end of this year, he says, there will be adult-literacy programs in every Head Start center, and there are ongoing efforts to include job-training and substance-abuse projects. Head Start has also given out $20 million in research grants to experimental transition-to-school programs.

The Chicago programs Fuerst studied have survived in greatly modified form. Now they're mostly for preschoolers; many of the auxiliary staffers, such as social workers and full-time nurses, have been laid off. But Claretta Edwards still has fond memories of the Cole Child Parent Center. In 1967 she was one of the first 4-year-olds in the program. "We were pushed to do our best," she says. After high school Edwards earned a bachelor's degree in nursing, and she now works in a hospital emergency room. Her 4-year-old daughter, Kiah, attends preschool at Cole, where some of the same teachers who inspired Edwards now help her daughter. Those teachers also get a lot of support on the home front. For Christmas, Edwards gave her daughter a gift with clear long-term benefits: 30 books.

BARBARA KANTROWITZ *with* JOHN MCCORMICK *in Chicago*

Now We're Talking!

Bernard Ohanian and Greta Vollmer

Bernard Ohanian wrote about circumcision in the June/July issue of Parenting Magazine. *Greta Vollmer is a language-development specialist at the International Studies Academy in San Francisco.*

AS MARY STEINBERG OF STORRS, Connecticut, remembers, it happened in the kitchen, when a little voice suddenly burst forth from the high chair with "cat." For Judy Henry of Potsdam, New York, it came when months of her daughter's not-quite-intelligible babbling suddenly melted into one clear "bye-bye." Time to dash to the baby book and record the hour and place; it's Baby's First Word, a milestone in our children's lives—and in ours.

With this first of what linguists call "one-word utterances," your child has entered into the kingdom of words, where genius and beauty, evil and banality have lived for centuries. And now that the first "bye-bye" has emerged, can the plaintive "Daddy, will you buy me this?" the mortified "Mom, how could you?" or the tentative "Can I borrow the car tonight?" be far behind?

Well, yes, actually. In the meantime, there's lots for your child to learn about language, and the learning process is sure to provide you with plenty of stories that—first-time parents be warned—will inevitably be funnier and cuter to you than to your friends and coworkers. It also is sure to give you lots to worry about: Is my kid talking early enough? clearly enough? correctly enough? Does she know enough words? What can I do to help?

The first thing you can do is relax. Linguists will tell you that almost all children are born with an innate ability to learn language, and while parents can certainly enrich that learning experience, there's very little they can do that will get in the way. The second thing you can do is have fun, and marvel at a process that even leading child-language specialists will admit remains a mystery. Experts in the field don't know exactly how it happens, but by about age five your child will know some 8,000 words. Moreover, she will have grasped a basic grammatical system that, no matter what the language, is as complex as some of the most sophisticated theorems taught in university-level mathematics courses.

YOUR CHILD MAY HAVE just entered the kingdom of words, but she has been living in the realm of language for some time. In fact, whether you realize it or not, you've been teaching her language skills since the day she was born. By responding to her post-feeding burps with an approving "That's a good baby!" for instance, you've been introducing her to conversational patterns: One person "says" something, another person responds. You've been teaching her intonation patterns as well, albeit higher-pitched, more singsong versions than adults and older children use. She, meanwhile, has communicated by gesturing, grabbing, and, of course, crying.

In the weeks leading up to your baby's first word, she will start to understand specific words and will begin to practice a kind of preverbal speech: using varied intonations, gestures, and sounds that approximate what she hears. This is the stage at which an older sibling is likely to say with frustration, "My baby brother is talking; he's just not saying anything!"

Then, finally, it comes: the word, a seemingly simple feat perhaps, but one that requires the human brain to operate at its synchronic best. The basic meaning of a word bubbles up from one part of the brain's left hemisphere, the Wernicke's area, and is fired off to another part of the brain known as the Broca's area. Once there, it is processed for speech and sent to the brain's motor cortex, which controls muscles in the mouth, lips, tongue, and voice box. Receiving their signals from the cortex, these muscles contract simultaneously, and in less than a millisecond—the time it takes the idea to travel from the recesses of the brain to the tip of the tongue—your child has become a talker.

For most kids, this neurological wizardry first takes place sometime between the ages of 10 and 14 months, but bear in mind that as with any childhood development, there is a great range of what is normal. Parents don't necessarily need to worry if their child doesn't follow this timetable. Girls will generally talk sooner than boys, and both first-born children and children born at least four years after their closest sibling will talk sooner than other kids. Even though, as Harvard University linguist Catherine Snow says, "our culture's notion of intelligence is tied up with talking," there is absolutely no evidence that early talkers are any smarter than later talkers. Nor will the process necessarily be a linear one: A child may learn a word, forget it for a while, and come back to it. "The first stage of language learning is not easy," says Snow, "Parents don't realize how hard those first ten words are for kids."

YOU CAN'T HELP A CHILD LEARN LANGUAGE ANY FASTER OR EARLIER, BUT YOU CAN HELP HER LEARN TO LOVE WORDS

Parents also may not realize how different those first ten words may be from child to child. In recent studies of English-speaking children in the United States, Katherine Nelson, a psychology professor at City University of New York, has identified two types of language learners: referential and expressive. "The first words of referential kids usually will be the names of objects," she explains, "while expressive children will often first use socially useful phrases like 'I want,' 'stop it,' or 'all gone.' " She emphasizes, however, that most kids who are

learning to talk are part referential and part expressive—with varying degrees of each—and that it's not clear whether these differences reflect other personality tendencies.

What is clear is that the referential-versus-expressive model of language acquisition is not universal. Bambi Schieffelin, an anthropologist at New York University who studied child language acquisition in Papua New Guinea, says, "In other cultures children might first learn people's names, kin terms, how to greet and tease people, and how to ask for things correctly." Schieffelin points out, however, that children in New Guinea follow more or less the same time frame as children here: They too will master their language by the time they are five. Children in different cultures, she says, share a common neurological denominator; but once set in motion, neurology takes a back seat to social influences.

WHEN CHILDREN BEGIN TO TALK, they suddenly seem more human to us. And so great is our desire to communicate with our new conversationalists that we repeat back to them what we think they're saying, a practice linguists call modeling or shaping. We also simplify our language to make it easier for children to understand, using what specialists call motherese or child-directed speech and what the rest of us call baby talk.

And here, perhaps, is the greatest controversy about the language-acquisition process. Ask ten parents whether baby talk is healthy or harmful, and you'll get ten different answers; linguists

---

TAKING IT TO THE PROFESSIONALS

While their pronunciation, grammar, and choice of words may occasionally be so goofy that we can't help but laugh, most children do get the hang of their native language pretty quickly. A small minority, however, develop one or more of a variety of language problems and will need the help of a speech pathologist.

"Most parents I work with are afraid they've done something wrong," says Sandy Friel-Patti, an associate professor of communication disorders at the University of Texas at Dallas. "But it's important that parents understand that they are not to blame for their child's speech disorder." That's not to say that linguists necessarily know what *is* causing the problem. "We don't know what causes language impairment in children, except in cases where they've suffered neurological traumas or head injuries," says Friel-Patti.

What Makes a Speech Problem?
Speech and language problems are difficult to pin down because they differ depending on a child's age. "A child who is unintelligible at the age of two is not a problem," says speech pathologist Joan Kaderavek of Perrysburg, Ohio. "But a three-

year-old who is unintelligible could be." Parents shouldn't be alarmed, Kaderavek says, if their child is a little later in talking than her playmates or siblings, but "if a child is not using words at 18 months, then the parent should check with a specialist."

Another reason to see a specialist may be if your child stutters, but again, a child's age will determine whether the stuttering warrants professional attention or not. Many children between the ages of two-and-a-half and four pass through periods of stuttering or nonfluency, and as Kaderavek points out, there are both normal and abnormal patterns of nonfluency. "If your child says 'Mommy, Mommy, Mommy, I want to go outside,' and she's completing all of her words, there shouldn't be any cause for concern," Kaderavek says. "If she seems frustrated by her inability to complete words, or changes her choice of words to consistently avoid a certain sound, it might be more than just a period of nonfluency."

Other children have developmental articulation disorders—that is, they have problems with certain sounds. Some youngsters, says Kaderavek, can't pronounce *r* sounds until they are about seven years old. But if your three-year-old

still can't pronounce the basic consonant sounds—*b, p, m, t, w, d*—you might want to make an appointment with a speech pathologist.

Speech Specialists: What They Do
When you bring your child to a speech pathologist, he will probably run her through standard tests for hearing, comprehension, and the complexity of her grammar and vocabulary, as well as conduct a physical exam of her articulation mechanism. The pathologist will also watch your child at play, to see how communicative and cooperative she is. Based on his findings, he may recommend speech games or exercises to do at home or speech therapy with a specialist.

Kaderavek, whose own five-year-old son has a speech disorder, counsels patience to parents. "People say to me, 'You're a speech pathologist. Why can't you fix your son?' But all I can do is what I do with any child who has speech problems, which is to try to create an environment that encourages his language growth," she says.

If you suspect your child has a language problem, you can call the American Speech-Language-Hearing Association in Rockville, Maryland, for a recommendation to a certified speech pathologist in your area: (800) 638-8255.

are somewhat divided as well, although current thinking leans toward the belief that child-directed speech is not only good but is also, in our culture at least, almost unavoidable. For linguists, child-directed speech isn't simply a matter of truncating our words and pitching our voice an octave higher. Rather, it involves adjusting adult speech down to a child's level so that it can be understood, and then constantly revising the level upward as the child learns more and more words.

Specialists believe that most parents, if they talk and listen to their children, will do this almost automatically. But a problem can arise when parents are too slow to raise their level of speech. We all know such parents, those slightly embarrassing folks who still call a rabbit a "bunny-wunny" when talking to a four-year-old. Sandy Friel-Patti, an associate professor of communication disorders at the University of Texas at Dallas, says baby talk is linguistically appropriate at certain stages, "but sometimes parents hang on to it beyond when it's appropriate."

These parents may give baby talk a bad name, but they're probably in the minority. In fact, says Joan Kaderavek, a Perrysburg, Ohio, speech pathologist who favors simplified language but opposes the use of exaggerated baby talk, the main problem in the achievement-oriented eighties is not that parents use baby talk too often, but that they "use language with kids that's too adult."

Snow, who falls into the there's-nothing-wrong-with-baby-talk school, agrees. "Too many parents claim, 'My kid is so verbal, and it's because I didn't talk baby talk to him.'" Snow says that's a false assumption. The most important part of language acquisition, to her, is that kids can express what they feel and think and can understand others. That may mean parents' using baby talk, she says, because "it's not crazy to use words that kids have some hope of replicating."

So if you and your 18-month-old are playing with a toy truck and she can say "truck" but is not yet stringing several words together, Kaderavek says, "don't bombard her with 'Look at the fast truck racing around the track. Isn't it a nice red truck?' You are better off saying 'See the truck? Red truck. Truck can go. Truck can go fast.'"

Besides, you'll be able to pull out your long sentences about fast red trucks racing around tracks soon enough. Somewhere between 18 and 21 months, your child will advance to the two-word-utterance stage—although just as some children skip crawling altogether, later talkers may bypass the one-word stage and start directly with two- and three-word phrases. Now the child is generally commenting on the world, often on the absence or presence of someone or something: "water gone," "Daddy back," or "doggie big."

Then comes the explosion. "At 18 months a parent could probably tell you every word in her kid's vocabulary," says Friel-Patti. "At 30 months there's no way she could." During this rapid expansion, children start out learning 30 to 60 words per month and wind up with a vocabulary of 250 words or so by the end of the second year.

It is during this period that parents will think, fleetingly at least, that their child is a genius. "It's pretty amazing," says Snow, "when your kid uses some word that you don't remember having taught her." But hold your nominations for Baby Nobels; while it's true

that some children are in fact more verbal than others, it's also true that the neighbor's three-year-old is probably learning language just as quickly as yours.

GIVEN THE DAZZLING SPEED with which children learn language, parents of suddenly eloquent preschoolers can't help but wonder whether there is something they can do to enhance the process even further. Within limits, there is. While you can't do anything to speed up the pace by which your child learns words, you can enrich her understanding of language—and more important, convey to her a delight in using language to communicate.

The best thing to do, linguists say, is also the most obvious: Talk to your child as much as you can. Talking directly to her is much more effective than trying to expose her to language indirectly by, say, plopping her down in front of the television or just talking with your spouse in front of her; according to Snow, two-year-olds absorb very little language from what they overhear. Nor do they pick up language from other kids. "It's a misconception that children learn to talk in a play group or daycare center," says Friel-Patti. "That may be where they learn to use their language socially, but they learn to talk from one-on-one conversations with adults."

As part of talking, of course, parents should listen carefully to their kids. "You should try to make guesses at what your children are attempting to say," says Eve Clark, a professor of linguistics at Stanford University. "The more you let them know that you understand, the more they'll produce. Don't dismiss what they're saying as meaningless; instead, try to supply the context they need verbally." And try to talk about what the child is interested in at that moment. As Kaderavek says, "You don't want to talk to her about her blocks if she's playing with an eggbeater."

Reading to children also enriches their language skills by teaching them words in an imaginative context and by developing their sense of narrative. Parents should take care, however, to choose books that will captivate their children's imagination. "Kids learn what makes sense to them," says Nelson. "They're not going to learn if you read them the encyclopedia." The experience will also be less fruitful if a parent turns a story into a test, flipping the pages and pointing to pictures while asking the child to name the objects in them. "Asking children to label," says Kaderavek, "is not teaching language."

"Children don't learn 15 words a day just by having them recited to them," says Snow. "They have to hear the words in context. So don't simply show your child a picture of a window; ask her to open the window."

While expanding their vocabulary, young children are also busy increasing their understanding of grammar. In fact, once children begin to figure out grammatical rules, they become more systematic about language than the language is itself. Many of a child's grammatical mistakes, for instance, stem from the expectation that language will be more regular than it really is: hence made-up words like "plantman" for gardener or "fixman" for mechanic; plurals like "tooths," "foots," and "mans"; and verb forms like "he goed."

As linguists point out, although parents may think a child's language is slipping backward if she switches from saying "he

Word by Word

The chart below indicates, by age, the age progression of language development in children. Don't panic if your child doesn't follow this schedule exactly. Many kids will fall outside of the normal timetable at one stage or another. Girls and first-born children, for instance, can be expected to reach a new stage a bit sooner than boys and younger siblings, and there can be other perfectly acceptable individual differences as well.

0–3 months
- Smiles, responds to voices
- Coos, makes vowel-like sounds

4–6 months
- Chuckles, giggles, babbles

6–9 months
- Tries to imitate sounds
- Engages in speechlike babbling
- Uses consonant sounds

10–12 months
- May say first word
- Uses intonation patterns that sound like sentences

12–18 months
- Uses one-word utterances to express a thought: "cat," "cookie," "bye-bye"

18–21 months
- Begins two-word utterances: "red truck," "mommy sick"
- Uses verbs
- Vocabulary explosion begins: May know 50 words

24–27 months
- Regularly uses two- and three-word utterances: "No go outside," "Kitty come back"
- Begins using pronouns, although not always correctly: "Me no want"
- Vocabulary explosion continues: May know 250 words

30–33 months
- Vocabulary explosion is in full swing
- Uses three- to four-word sentences
- Word order and phrase structures approximate adult speech much of the time

3 years and up
- Uses well-formed sentences that follow grammatical rules
- Speaks with approximately 90 percent comprehensibility; makes most sounds correctly, with possible exceptions of r, l, s, and th

went" to "he goed," it's actually a sign of progress, because she has begun to grasp an important tenet of English grammar: To form the past tense, tack on -d or -ed to the infinitive verb. "When children first use a word like *went*," says Stanford's Clark, "it's not at all clear to them that it's part of the verb *to go.*" But because children are, in Clark's words, "great pattern-makers," once they start to understand English's verb-conjugation system, they may say "wents," "wenting," and "goed." Then when they learn that there are some exceptions to the way

we form the past tense, they'll settle back on *went* and discard *goed*—but usually only after a period of using the two interchangeably.

Tempting as it may be, parents shouldn't bother correcting their children when they make grammatical mistakes. Parents who do will soon learn what a futile exercise it is. "Kids under the age of five won't accept a change unless it belongs in their system. They'll say the word the way you want one time to please you, but the next time they'll go back to their way," says Friel-Patti. This back-and-forth is likely to continue until the child figures out how the correct version fits into her sense of the way language works, a discovery she will make at her own pace. Constant correction "tells children that you're more focused on how they're talking than on what they're telling you," Friel-Patti points out. "If that message comes across too strongly, they'll quit talking."

BY TALKING TO KIDS, listening to them, reading to them, and of course playing with them, parents can help them learn to love language in all its power and mystery. But linguists caution against trying to do too much: "Parents should be parents," advises Friel-Patti. "They shouldn't be teachers. Using flash cards and teaching two-year-olds to read is highly inappropriate."

Still, it's natural to worry about how our kids are going to do in school, and to wonder what language skills will serve them best. Snow says you may be able to help prepare your kids for school by having extended conversations with them on single topics, by discussing events that are taking place beyond their immediate and present world, and by asking them to recount things that happened when you weren't around. And she adds an important caveat for parents whose native language is not English: "Parents need to be talking to kids in a language they speak very, very well," she says. "A child is better prepared for school if you speak good Polish at home rather than bad English. She'll learn English quickly enough at school."

What a child needs most, then, is a sense that communicating is fun, that language is a great source of creativity. Your child may not talk as much as other kids, but as Friel-Patti says, "not all adults are blabby adults, and not all kids are blabby kids." If your child focuses more on expressive language than referential language, it may lead to concern on your part that she's not analytical enough. Don't worry, says Nelson: "The world doesn't necessarily belong to the analytical types. We need children who tell stories, as well as children who solve math problems." We need Faulkners as well as Einsteins, and Woolfs as well as Curies.

And we need children who are relaxed enough with language, and curious enough about language, that they will enjoy the fullest range of expression. So encourage your little genius to talk, to make up stories and poems, and to play with words in ways that you've forgotten how to. Talk with her about what you're doing and what you've done, and realize that when she says "My feets hurt," she's actually outsmarting the language. We often forget what a breathtaking place this kingdom of words is; with the help of our children, we can discover its magic all over again.

CLIPPED WINGS

The Fullest Look Yet at How
Prenatal Exposure to Drugs, Alcohol, and Nicotine
Hobbles Children's Learning

LUCILE F. NEWMAN AND STEPHEN L. BUKA

Lucile F. Newman is a professor of community health and anthropology at Brown University and the director of the Preventable Causes of Learning Impairment Project. Stephen L. Buka is an epidemiologist and instructor at the Harvard Medical School and School of Public Health.

SOME FORTY thousand children a year are born with learning impairments related to their mother's alcohol use. Drug abuse during pregnancy affects 11 percent of newborns each year—more than 425,000 infants in 1988. Some 260,000 children each year are born at below normal weights—often because they were prenatally exposed to nicotine, alcohol, or illegal drugs.

What learning problems are being visited upon these children? The existing evidence has heretofore been scattered in many different fields of research—in pediatric medicine, epidemiology, public health, child development, and drug and alcohol abuse. Neither educators, health professionals, nor policy makers could go to one single place to receive a full picture of how widespread or severe were these preventable causes of learning impairment.

In our report for the Education Commission of the States, excerpts of which follow, we combed these various fields to collect and synthesize the major studies that relate prenatal exposure to nicotine, alcohol, and illegal drugs* with various indexes of students' school performance.

The state of current research in this area is not always as full and satisfying as we would wish. Most of what

*The full report for the ECS also addressed the effect on children's learning of fetal malnutrition, pre- and postnatal exposure to lead, and child abuse and neglect.

exists is statistical and epidemiological data, which document the frequency of certain high-risk behaviors and correlate those behaviors to student performance. Such data are very interesting and useful, as they allow teachers and policy makers to calculate the probability that a student with a certain family history will experience school failure. But such data often cannot control for the effects of other risk factors, many of which tend to cluster in similar populations. In other words, the same mother who drinks during her pregnancy may also use drugs, suffer from malnutrition, be uneducated, a teenager, or poor—all factors that might ultimately affect her child's school performance. An epidemiological study generally can't tell you how much of a child's poor school performance is due exclusively to a single risk factor.

Moreover, the cumulative damage wrought by several different postnatal exposures may be greater than the damage caused by a single one operating in isolation. And many of the learning problems that are caused by prenatal exposure to drugs can be compounded by such social factors as poverty and parental disinterest and, conversely, overcome if the child lives in a high-quality postnatal environment.

All of these facts make it difficult to isolate and interpret the level and character of the damage that is caused by a single factor. Further, until recently, there was little interest among researchers in the effects of prenatal alcohol exposure because there was little awareness that it was affecting a substantial number of children. The large cohort of children affected by crack is just now entering the schools, so research on their school performance hasn't been extensive.

What does clearly emerge from the collected data is that our classrooms now include many students whose ability to pay attention, sit still, or fully develop their visual, auditory, and language skills was impaired even before they walked through our schoolhouse doors. On the

From *American Educator,* Spring 1991, pp. 27-33, 42. Adapted from "Every Child a Learner: Reducing Risks of Learning Impairment During Pregnancy and Infancy," supported by the Exxon Educational Foundation, published by the Education Commission of the States.

brighter side, the evidence that many of these impairments can be overcome by improved environmental conditions suggests that postnatal treatment is possible; promising experiments in treatment are, in fact, under way and are outlined at the end of this article.

1. Low Birthweight

The collection of graphs begins with a set on low birthweight, which is strongly associated with lowered I.Q. and poor school performance. While low birthweight can be brought on by other factors, including maternal malnutrition and teenage pregnancy, significant causes are maternal smoking, drinking, and drug use.

Around 6.9 percent of babies born in the United States weigh less than 5.5 pounds (2,500 grams) at birth and are considered "low-birthweight" babies. In 1987, this accounted for some 269,100 infants. Low birthweight may result when babies are born prematurely (born too early) or from intrauterine growth retardation (born too small) as a result of maternal malnutrition or actions that restrict blood flow to the fetus, such as smoking or drug use.

In 1987, about 48,750 babies were born at very low birthweights (under 3.25 lbs. or 1,500 grams). Research estimates that 6 to 8 percent of these babies experience major handicaps such as severe mental retardation or cerebral palsy (Eilers et al., 1986; Hack and Breslau, 1986). Another 25 to 26 percent have borderline I.Q. scores, problems in understanding and expressing language, or other deficits (Hack and Breslau, 1986; Lefebvre et al., 1988; Nickel et al., 1982; Vohr et al., 1988). Although these children may enter the public school system, many of them show intellectual disabilities and require special educational assistance. Reading, spelling, handwriting, arts, crafts, and mathematics are difficult school subjects for them. Many are late in developing

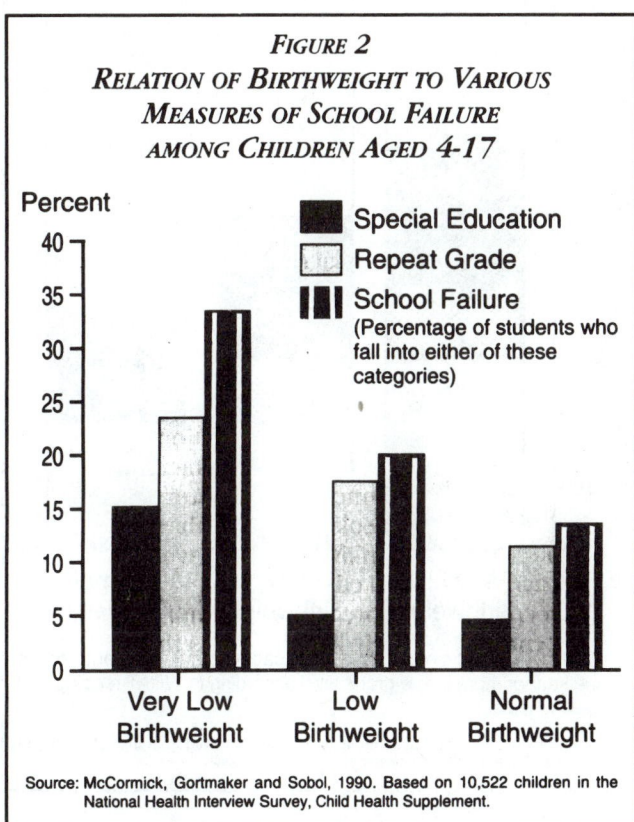

FIGURE 2
RELATION OF BIRTHWEIGHT TO VARIOUS MEASURES OF SCHOOL FAILURE AMONG CHILDREN AGED 4-17

Source: McCormick, Gortmaker and Sobol, 1990. Based on 10,522 children in the National Health Interview Survey, Child Health Supplement.

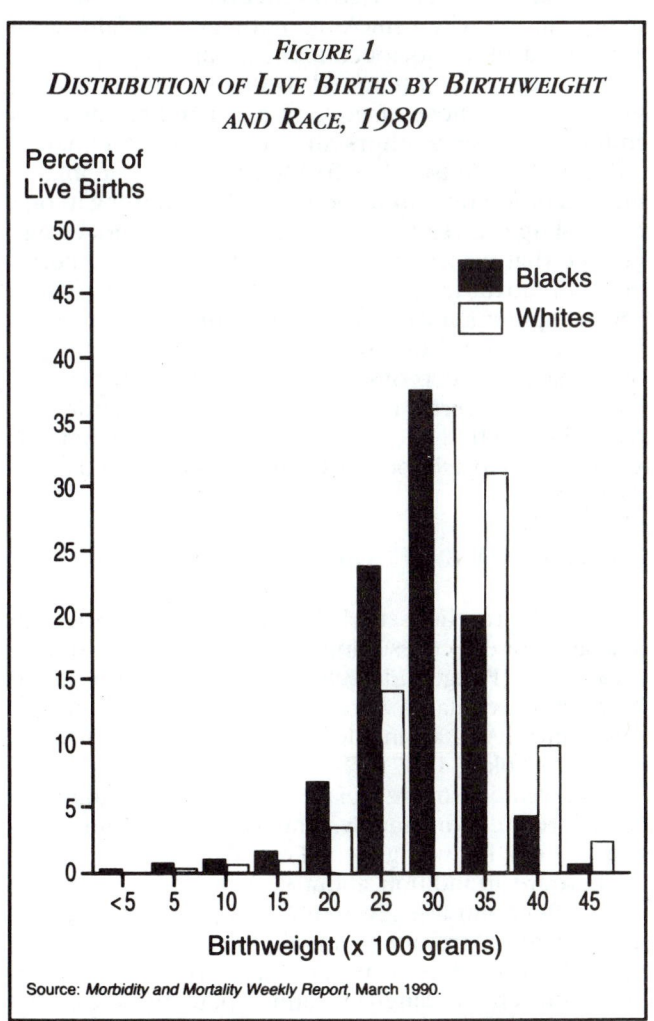

FIGURE 1
DISTRIBUTION OF LIVE BIRTHS BY BIRTHWEIGHT AND RACE, 1980

Source: *Morbidity and Mortality Weekly Report*, March 1990.

their speech and language. Children born at very low birthweights are more likely than those born at normal weights to be inattentive, hyperactive, depressed, socially withdrawn, or aggressive (Breslau et al., 1988).

New technologies and the spread of neonatal intensive care over the past decade have improved survival rates of babies born at weights ranging from 3.25 pounds to 5.5 pounds. But, as Figures 2 and 3 show, those born at low birthweight still are at increased risk of school failure. The increased risk, however, is very much tied to the child's postnatal environment. When the data on which Figure 2 is based are controlled to account for socioeconomic circumstances, very low-birthweight babies are approximately twice, not three times, as likely to repeat a grade.

3. CHILDHOOD: Developmental Problems

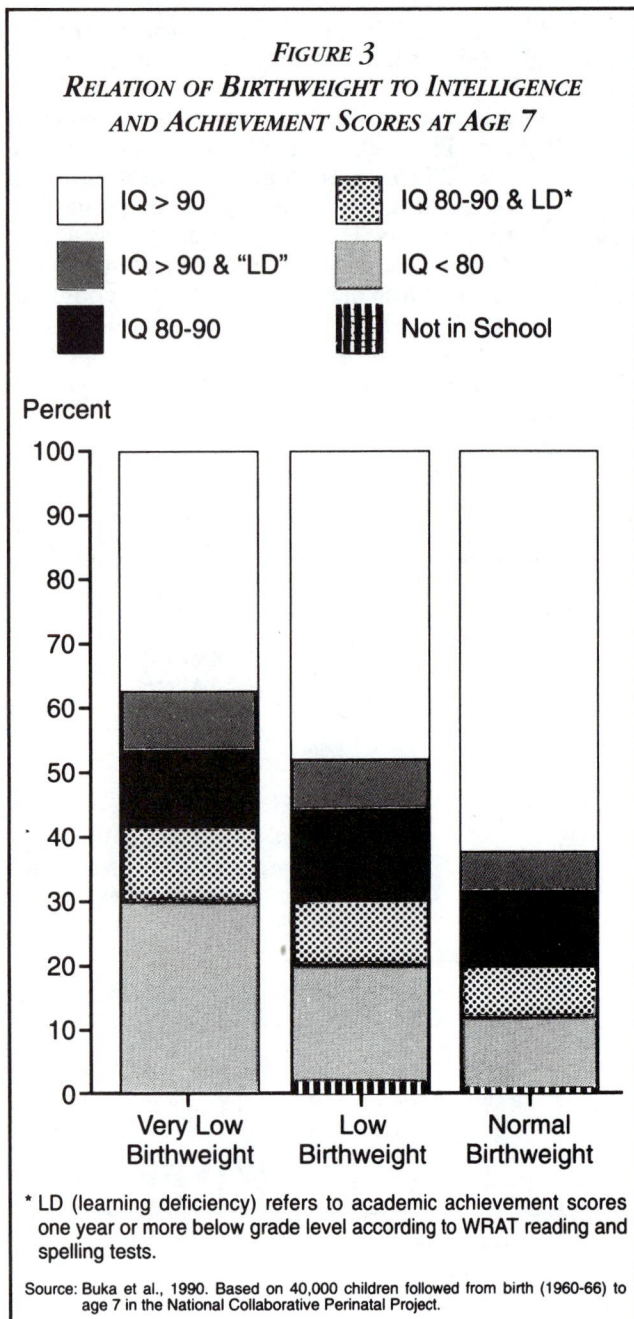

FIGURE 3

RELATION OF BIRTHWEIGHT TO INTELLIGENCE AND ACHIEVEMENT SCORES AT AGE 7

- ☐ IQ > 90
- ▨ IQ 80-90 & LD*
- ▨ IQ > 90 & "LD"
- ▨ IQ < 80
- ■ IQ 80-90
- ▥ Not in School

Percent

Very Low Birthweight / Low Birthweight / Normal Birthweight

* LD (learning deficiency) refers to academic achievement scores one year or more below grade level according to WRAT reading and spelling tests.

Source: Buka et al., 1990. Based on 40,000 children followed from birth (1960-66) to age 7 in the National Collaborative Perinatal Project.

Indeed, follow-up studies of low-birthweight infants at school age have concluded that "the influence of the environment far outweighs most effects of nonoptimal prenatal or perinatal factors on outcome" (Aylward et al., 1989). This finding suggests that early assistance can improve the intellectual functioning of children at risk for learning delay or impairment (Richmond, 1990).

2. Maternal Smoking

Maternal smoking during pregnancy has long been known to be related to low birthweight (Abel, 1980), an increased risk for cancer in the offspring (Stjernfeldt et al., 1986), and early and persistent asthma, which leads to, among other problems, frequent hospitalization and school absence (Streissguth, 1986). A growing number of new studies has shown that children of smokers are smaller in stature and lag behind other children in cognitive development and educational achievement. These children are particularly subject to hyperactivity and inattention (Rush and Callahan, 1989).

Data from the National Collaborative Perinatal Project on births from 1960 to 1966 measured, among other things, the amount pregnant women smoked at each prenatal visit and how their children functioned in school at age seven. Compared to offspring of nonsmokers, children of heavy smokers (more than two packs per day) were nearly twice as likely to experience school failure by age seven (see Figure 4). The impact of heavy smoking is apparently greater the earlier it occurs during pregnancy. Children of women who smoked heavily during the first trimester of pregnancy were more than twice as likely to fail than children whose mothers did not smoke during the first trimester. During the second and third trimesters, these risks decreased. In all of these analyses, it is difficult to differentiate the effects of exposure to smoking before birth and from either parent after birth; to distinguish between learning problems caused by low birthweight and those caused by other damaging effects of smoking; or, to disentangle the effects of smoke from the socioeconomic setting of the smoker. But it is worth noting that Figure 4 is based on children born in the early sixties, an era when smoking mothers were fairly well distributed across socioeconomic groups.

One study that attempted to divorce the effects of smoking from those of poverty examined middle-class children whose mothers smoked during pregnancy (Fried and Watkinson, 1990) and found that the infants showed differences in responsiveness beginning at one week of age. Later tests at 1, 2, 3, and 4 years of age showed that on verbal tests "the children of the heavy smokers had mean test scores that were lower than those born to lighter smokers, who in turn did not perform as well as those born to nonsmokers." The study also indicated that the effects of smoke exposure, whether in the womb or after birth, may not be identifiable until later ages when a child needs to perform complex cognitive functions, such as problem solving or reading and interpretation.

3. Prenatal Alcohol Exposure

Around forty thousand babies per year are born with fetal alcohol effect resulting from alcohol abuse during pregnancy (Fitzgerald, 1988). In 1984, an estimated 7,024 of these infants were diagnosed with fetal alcohol syndrome (FAS), an incidence of 2.2 per 1,000 births (Abel and Sokol, 1987). The three main features of FAS in its extreme form are facial malformation, intrauterine growth retardation, and dysfunctions of the central nervous system, including mental retardation.

There are, in addition, about 33,000 children each year who suffer from less-severe effects of maternal alcohol use. The more prominent among these learning impairments are problems in attention (attention-deficit disorders), speech and language, and hyperactivity. General school failure also is connected to a history of fetal alcohol exposure (Abel and Sokol, 1987; Ernhart et al., 1985). Figure 5 shows the drinking habits of women of child-bearing age by race and education.

When consumed in pregnancy, alcohol easily crosses the placenta, but exactly how it affects the fetus is not well known. The effects of alcohol vary according to how far along in the pregnancy the drinking occurs. The first trimester of pregnancy is a period of brain growth and organ and limb formation. The embryo is most susceptible to alcohol from week two to week eight of development, a point at which a woman may not even know she is pregnant (Hoyseth and Jones, 1989). Researchers have yet to determine how much alcohol it takes to cause problems in development and how alcohol affects each critical gestational period. It appears that the more alcohol consumed during pregnancy, the worse the effect.

And many of the effects do not appear until ages four to seven, when children enter school.

Nearly one in four (23 percent) white women, eighteen to twenty-nine, reported "binge" drinking (five

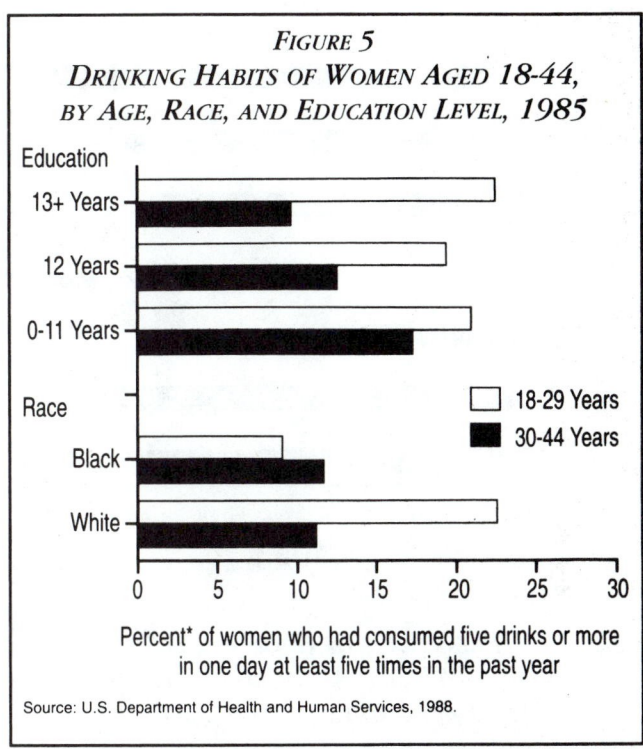

FIGURE 5
DRINKING HABITS OF WOMEN AGED 18-44, BY AGE, RACE, AND EDUCATION LEVEL, 1985

Percent* of women who had consumed five drinks or more in one day at least five times in the past year

Source: U.S. Department of Health and Human Services, 1988.

drinks or more a day at least five times in the past year). This was nearly three times the rate for black women of that age (about 8 percent). Fewer women (around 3 percent for both black and white) reported steady alcohol use (two drinks or more per day in the past two weeks).

4. Fetal Drug Exposure

The abuse of drugs of all kinds—marijuana, cocaine, crack, heroin, or amphetamines—by pregnant women affected about 11 percent of newborns in 1988—about 425,000 babies (Weston et al., 1989).

Cocaine and crack use during pregnancy are consistently associated with lower birthweight, premature birth, and smaller head circumference in comparison with babies whose mothers were free of these drugs (Chasnoff et al., 1989; Cherukuri et al., 1988; Doberczak et al., 1987; Keith et al., 1989; Zuckerman et al., 1989). In a study of 1,226 women attending a prenatal clinic, 27 percent tested positive for marijuana and 18 percent for cocaine. Infants of those who had used marijuana weighed an average of 2.8 ounces (79 grams) less at birth and were half a centimeter shorter in length. Infants of mothers who had used cocaine averaged 3.3 ounces (93 grams) less in weight and .7 of a centimeter less in length and also had a smaller head circumference than babies of nonusers (Zuckerman et al., 1989). The study concluded that "marijuana use and cocaine use during pregnancy are each independently associated with impaired fetal growth" (Zuckerman et al., 1989).

In addition, women who use these substances are like-

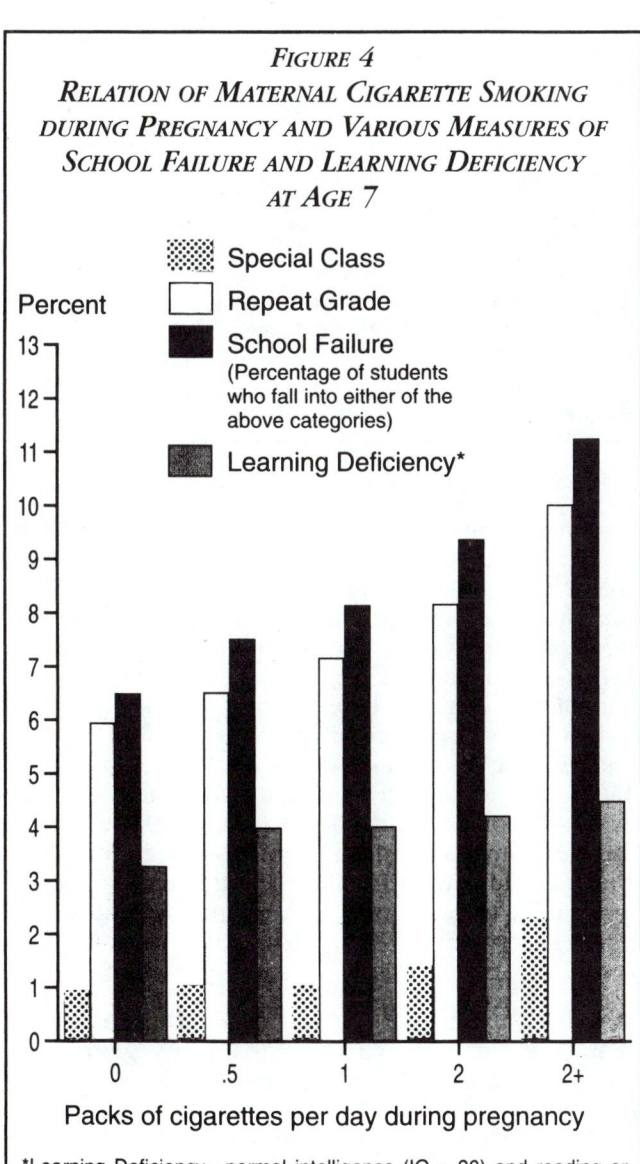

FIGURE 4
RELATION OF MATERNAL CIGARETTE SMOKING DURING PREGNANCY AND VARIOUS MEASURES OF SCHOOL FAILURE AND LEARNING DEFICIENCY AT AGE 7

Special Class

Repeat Grade

School Failure
(Percentage of students who fall into either of the above categories)

Learning Deficiency*

Percent

Packs of cigarettes per day during pregnancy

*Learning Deficiency= normal intelligence (IQ > 90) and reading or spelling scores one year or more below grade level on the WRAT.

Source: Buka et al., 1990. Based on 40,000 pregnancies with infants followed to age 7 in the National Collaborative Perinatal Project.

3. CHILDHOOD: Developmental Problems

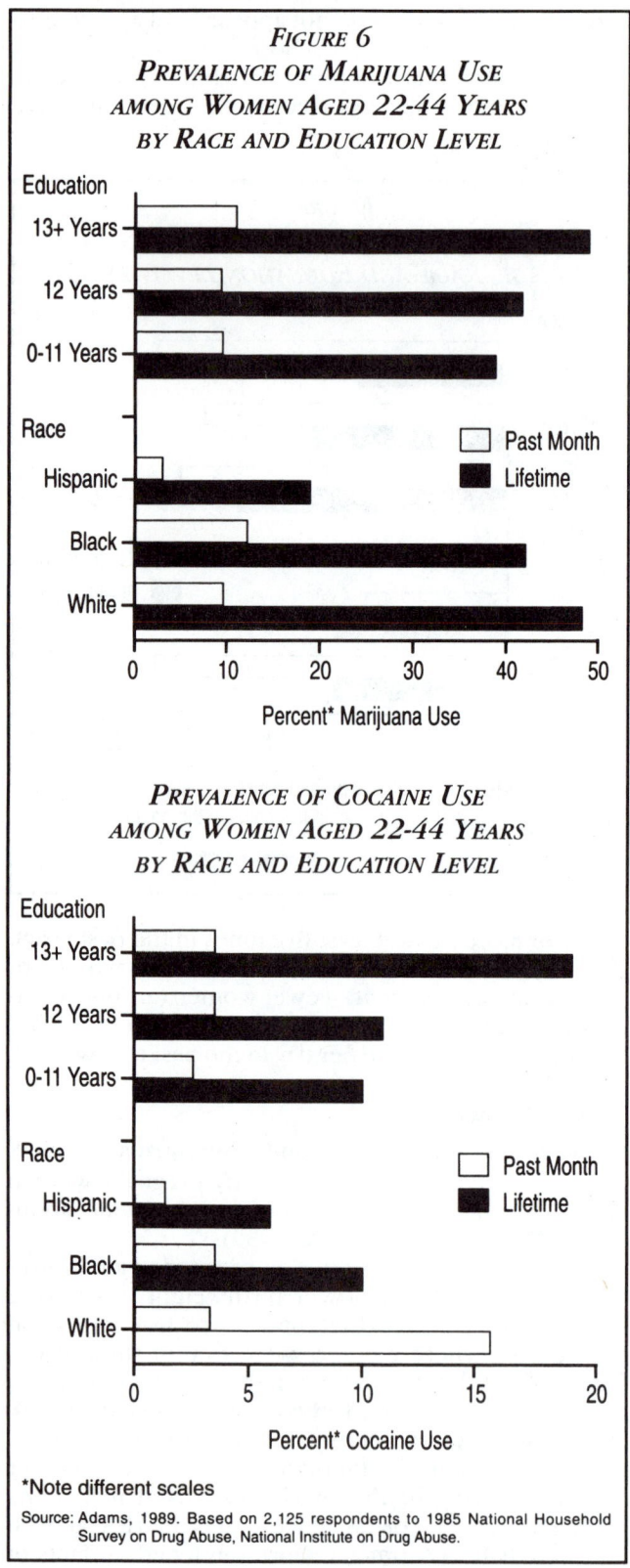

FIGURE 6
PREVALENCE OF MARIJUANA USE
AMONG WOMEN AGED 22-44 YEARS
BY RACE AND EDUCATION LEVEL

Percent* Marijuana Use

PREVALENCE OF COCAINE USE
AMONG WOMEN AGED 22-44 YEARS
BY RACE AND EDUCATION LEVEL

Percent* Cocaine Use

*Note different scales

Source: Adams, 1989. Based on 2,125 respondents to 1985 National Household Survey on Drug Abuse, National Institute on Drug Abuse.

aged nearly a pound (14.6 ounces or 416 grams) smaller than those born to women who had normal weight gain and did not use cigarettes, marijuana, and cocaine (see Table 1). The effect of these substances on size is more than the sum of the risk factors combined.

Like alcohol use, drug use has different effects at different points in fetal development. Use in very early pregnancy is more likely to cause birth defects affecting organ formation and the central nervous systems. Later use may

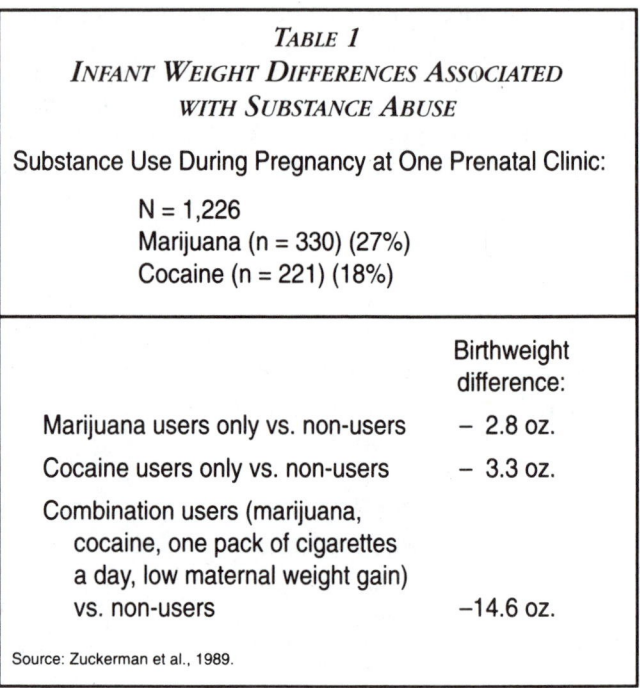

TABLE 1
INFANT WEIGHT DIFFERENCES ASSOCIATED
WITH SUBSTANCE ABUSE

Substance Use During Pregnancy at One Prenatal Clinic:

N = 1,226
Marijuana (n = 330) (27%)
Cocaine (n = 221) (18%)

	Birthweight difference:
Marijuana users only vs. non-users	− 2.8 oz.
Cocaine users only vs. non-users	− 3.3 oz.
Combination users (marijuana, cocaine, one pack of cigarettes a day, low maternal weight gain) vs. non-users	−14.6 oz.

Source: Zuckerman et al., 1989.

result in low birthweight due to either preterm birth or intrauterine growth retardation (Kaye et al., 1989; MacGregor et al., 1987; Petitti and Coleman, 1990). While some symptoms may be immediately visible, others may not be apparent until later childhood (Weston et al., 1989; Gray and Yaffe, 1986; Frank et al., 1988).

In infancy, damaged babies can experience problems in such taken-for-granted functions as sleeping and waking, resulting in exhaustion and poor development. In childhood, problems are found in vision, motor control, and in social interaction (Weston et al., 1989). Such problems may be caused not only by fetal drug exposure but also by insufficient prenatal care for the mother or by an unstimulating or difficult home environment for the infant (Lifschitz et al., 1985).

WHAT CAN be done to ameliorate the condition of children born with such damage? Quite a bit, based on the success of supportive prenatal care and the results of model projects that have provided intensive assistance to both baby and mother from the time of birth. These projects have successfully raised the I.Q. of low- and very-low birthweight babies an average of ten points or more—an increase that may lift a child with below-average intelligence into a higher I.Q. cate-

ly to smoke and to gain less weight during pregnancy, two factors associated with low birthweight. The cumulative effect of these risk factors is demonstrated by the finding that infants born to women who gained little weight, who had smoked one pack of cigarettes a day, and who tested positive for marijuana and cocaine aver-

gory (i.e., from retarded to low average or from low average to average). Generally known as either educational day care or infant day care, these programs provide a developmentally stimulating environment to high-risk babies and/or intensive parent support to prepare the parent to help her child.

In one such program based at the University of California/Los Angeles, weekly meetings were held among staff, parents, and infants over a period of four years. By the project's end, the low-birthweight babies had caught up in mental function to the control group of normal birthweight children (Rauh et al., 1988). The Infant Health and Development Project, which was conducted in eight cities and provided low-birthweight babies with pediatric follow-up and an educational curriculum with family support, on average increased their I.Q. scores by thirteen points and the scores of very-low birthweight children by more than six points. Another project tar-

geted poor single teenage mothers whose infants were at high risk for intellectual impairment (Martin, Ramey and Ramey, 1990). One group of children was enrolled in educational day care from six and one-half weeks of age to four and one-half years for five days a week, fifty weeks a year. By four and one-half years, the children's I.Q. scores were in the normal range and ten points higher than a control group. In addition, by the time their children were four and one-half, mothers in the experimental group were more likely to have graduated from high school and be self-supporting than were mothers in the control group.

These studies indicate that some disadvantages of poverty and low birthweight can be mitigated and intellectual impairment avoided. The key is attention to the cognitive development of young children, in conjunction with social support of their families.

Tykes and Bytes

With a Boost From Computers, Kids With Disabilities Find the World's Filled With Possibilities

Bettijane Levine

Times Staff Writer

The first thing to know about the bright-eyed toddlers who zoom, lurch, plop, play, sing and go potty at UCLA's Intervention Program is that they are the advance guard of an army yet to mobilize.

Mostly, they act just like toddlers everywhere—but they're not.

With varying degrees of disability due to cerebral palsy, Down's syndrome and an array of what program director Dr. Judy Howard calls "fancy diagnoses," they are among the world's youngest computer whizzes.

Sure, some have poor motor skills and muscle tone, little or no speech, minimal vision—all sorts of knotty physical or mental problems. But at ages 18 months to 3 years, these toddler technocrats are already equipped with PC's, power pads, switches, speech synthesizers and other electronic gear designed to even the playing field between them and so-called normal children.

They are part of the first toddler generation whose disabilities can be mitigated by technology, who can be judged by their potential rather than by their limitations. They are the first to prepare from babyhood for a life that will be computer-friendly in the extreme, and, as a result, productive.

Jay Horrell, 2, has used his computer since he was 18 months old. "I don't know where we'd be without it," says his father, Michael, who explains that some Down's syndrome children, such as his son, are "able to receive a lot more information than they can give back. They know the answers and they know what's going on, but can't respond" as they'd like to.

The computer allows Jay to display and improve various skills. It talks to him and waits patiently for answers; it puts him on more even footing with classmates at the Intervention Program and with his brother in their North Hollywood home, where Jay's setup includes an Apple PC, an electronic touch pad (in place of a keyboard), a speech synthesizer that gives voice to the letters and pictures he calls up on screen—and as many software programs as his parents can find.

Jay will attend a regular preschool in September. Down the line, Horrell adds, "I believe the computer will allow him to be a productive member of society."

Gabriela Cellini was 17 months old, had cerebral palsy and lacked certain motor skills when her parents took her to the Computer Access Center in Santa Monica. There, a staff member explained what the toddler could do with a computer and special accessories suited to her needs.

"Gabriela took one look and was riveted to the screen," her mother, Harriet, recalls. "Her muscle tone increased. She was so motivated to play with it that she sat up straight all by herself for about a half-hour. She quickly understood the cause-and-effect principle of hitting the switch and activating games."

Now 2 1/2 and a student at the UCLA Intervention Program, Gabriela uses computers at her Pacific Palisades home and in class. "It's delightful to watch," her mother says. "This strange computer voice says 'Gabriela, stack the blocks.' Or 'Gabriela, build a face.' Or she shoots airplanes off a carrier, increasing her speed each time she scores a hit." Gabriela still needs some assistance in other areas, Cellini says, but she's her own person in front of the computer.

UCLA's Howard, a pediatrician who has headed the Intervention Program since 1974, began teaming disabled toddlers with computers in 1981. She found children of that age are "automat-ically computer friendly, which immediately sets up a positive response in adults. Suddenly, you see they have abilities, and you start to set expectations for them that you weren't able to set before. When you have children who cannot talk, who are visually handicapped, who for any reason cannot pick up a crayon and draw or play with dolls, puzzles and toys to show you what they can do," it is difficult to know what they are capable of, she explains.

The first step is to find a way for each child to access the computer. In the early 1980s, there were few devices commercially available to provide that access. Now there are dozens: large switches, oversized alternative keyboards, touch windows with built-in sensors that attach with Velcro to a computer screen. And there is growing body of knowledge about how to rig the devices so a child can work the computer by using whatever part of his body he controls best. Says Howard: "Every child can work one, even if he can only use one finger, his head or a toe. With appropriate software, they can solve puzzles, build with blocks, dress dolls. They can even play all the traditional favorite toddler games—two kids at the computer together—so they learn sharing, success and winning.

"Toddlers soon start to visually track on the screen because they're so highly motivated. They hold their little heads up and you see all the things that eventually lead to reading. That's the purpose of all this."

Kit Kehr, executive director of the UCLA program, says: "The younger you help these children, the better they'll do down the road. A kid who can't build with blocks or push cars around the way other kids can is missing essential play experiences." He also falls behind in language development and social skills, she says.

Rev Korman, a computer consultant in special education for the Los Angeles

Unified school district, remembers such a child, named Kim. "She'd had a stroke before she was born. It affected her vocal cords, so she had no speech and the doctors told her parents she'd always be a vegetable. She was 3 when they rolled her into my office in her wheelchair. I set up a communication board, a speech synthesizer and the computer, so that it would speak for her. She took about 10 minutes to learn to push the pictures that communicated her needs and wants. 'I don't want to go to bed. I want a red balloon.'

"We then moved to a 24-picture board, which she mastered quickly. By using this setup, she was able to communicate for the first time in her life so that people could hear her. She spent the next 45 minutes using the Muppet keyboard, and by the end of her visit she was teaching herself the alphabet.

"Kim's parents went right out and bought the computer, the speech synthesizer, the electronic board. Now she's reading and the whole bit."

(Computer setups for children like Kim cost about $2,000, Korman says.)

Dr. Phillip Callison, head of special education for the Los Angeles Unified School District, has participated in the UCLA project from its beginning, and is credited with providing assistance and inspiration. He says he believes in computers for all children, especially those with disabilities. Right now, the school district can provide such equipment for severely handicapped students, he says.

(Six hundred toddlers with a variety of disabilities are using computers in 45 United Cerebral Palsy Assn. nursery school programs across the country. The projects are run by a coalition of the association, UCLA and Apple Computers.)

Many adults still know little about home computers and next to nothing about the rest of the exotic equipment needed to adapt it for use by children with disabilities. In fact, UCLA's Kehr says that even the salespeople in most computer stores "won't know what you're talking about" if you walk in and ask for a power pad, a speech synthesizer and a special switch to help you adapt a PC for your child.

Jackie and Steve Brand of Albany, Calif., found little help in 1983, when they realized their 6-year-old daughter, Shoshana, "needed technology in her life." Shoshana has multiple disabilities, including cerebral palsy and poor vision. "The standard teaching tools just weren't working," Jackie Brand says. Her husband took a one-year sabbatical from his teaching job, went to computer school and eventually put together a

system Shoshana could use. It had a touch-sensitive keyboard with large keys and a synthesizer that gave voice to whatever she typed, so she could hear what she was doing rather than having to see it on the monitor.

"My daughter played for the first time in her life," when she got her computer, Brand says. "By that time she was 9, and we realized we needed to establish a program so others don't have to sacrifice years of their kids' lives."

The couple started the Alliance for Technology Access, which now has 43 chapters in 32 states. Each is a resource center where anyone with any disability—or parents of disabled children—can learn in informal, friendly surroundings what technology is available and how to customize it for their needs.

Nothing is sold at the centers, but they house an array of computers, access devices and information on companies that manufacture accessories not available in local stores but essential for those with special needs. The goal, Brand says, is simply to show people what they can do for themselves or their children, without making them go through "the usual hoops."

"Typically, you go to a doctor, evaluation center or clinic where they do an extensive evaluation of a child and prescribe what they think the right technology might be. In some situations that's needed." But doctors and clinics are not always on target when it comes to decisions about recreation and education for kids with handicaps, she says.

Sometimes they tell parents a child won't benefit from technology, Brand says. "But the bottom line is that each family knows their child's potential. They need to find out what their options are and try out different hardware and software to see what works best for the child. They need to be empowered to make their own decisions. That is what the Alliance helps them do.

"To people who say we must have realistic expectations for our children, I say I hope every family [of a handicapped child] has *unrealistic* expectations. That's the only way you will find your child's potential, so that your child can show you who he is and what he can do."

Brand's daughter will go into ninth grade in a regular public school in the fall. She uses a wheelchair, a computer for writing and a tape recorder with special levers for recording her notes, which she listens to at night. "This is a kid who nobody would have thought could function in a regular school program, and without technology, she couldn't. Yet she is doing phenomenally

well. And she's not unique, she is typical," Brand says.

The Computer Access Center, which rents space from the John Adams Middle School in Santa Monica, is one of three Southern California chapters of the Alliance. The volunteer staff helps each visitor (by appointment) to understand how life for a disabled person can be enhanced through the magic of technology. And they are very up-to-date.

Last week, for example, the staff arranged a demonstration by Daniel Fortune and John Ortiz of Zofcom, a Palo Alto–based firm.

The two men have designed a device called the TongueTouch Keypad, which looks like an ordinary orthodontic retainer worn by most kids after their braces are off.

But this retainer is a wireless transmitter with built-in sensors. By touching different sensors with one's tongue, a user unable to move any other part of his body can gain almost total control of his environment.

To the astonishment of onlookers, Fortune answered the phone when it rang without seeming to move a muscle. He turned on and off the VCR, the TV, the fan. He used the computer and explained that there is an almost "unlimited array" of equipment that can be operated (including a page-turner) with the new device, which will probably be marketed at the end of the year.

Mary Ann Glicksman, a staff member at the center, was intrigued. Her son, John Duganne, just graduated from Santa Monica High School and starts college in the fall. He intends to make animated films and already works part time, creating computer graphics for a software firm.

Duganne drives his power wheelchair with his chin, she says, but that's about the extent of what his body can do. (He has cerebral palsy.) To work the computer on which he does his schoolwork and art, he uses a headset with an ultrasonic device and a bite switch in his mouth. If the TongueTouch could work for him, it would be an improvement, she said. The designers cautioned that it is meant primarily for people with spinal cord injuries, and that those with cerebral palsy might not have enough tongue control. But with optimism typical of Alliance members, Glicksman said she'd rather give her son a chance to find out if it works than take the inventor's word that it won't.

Two other Southern California branches of the Alliance for Technology Access, funded by Apple Computers, are: The Special Awareness Computer Center in Simi Valley and Team of Advocates for Special Kids in Anaheim.

Family, School, and Cultural Influences on Development

- **Parenting (Articles 24–27)**
- **Stress and Maltreatment (Articles 28–30)**
- **Cultural Influences (Articles 31–34)**
- **Education (Articles 35 and 36)**

The articles in the *Parenting* subsection touch upon a number of the formidable issues that today's parents face. As we approach the middle of the last decade of the twentieth century, parents as well as children are perhaps subject to more sources of psychological stress than at any time in the recent past. Some of the chief sources of parental stress stem from single parenting, the decline of intergenerational families, and the increase in teenage mothers and fathers. These factors and others have strained the support services available for families in our society. Families that are stressed may turn to expedient rearing techniques even when they are aware of "expert" opinion. One such expediency is the use of physical punishment in order to "discipline" children. However, physical punishment is an ineffective form of discipline that teaches lack of self-control and promotes the use of aggression in order to control someone else's behavior. Today, child-rearing advice seems to have struck a middle road between strict and permissive approaches. Parents are encouraged to cuddle their infants, to provide their children with ample love, to use reason as the major disciplinary technique, and to encourage verbal interaction—all in an environment where rules are clearly spelled out and enforced. Suggestion, persuasion, and explanation have become the preferred techniques of rule enforcement, rather than spanking or withdrawal of love.

"Same Family, Different Lives" by Bruce Bower offers an attempt to disentangle the effects of environment versus genetics. In other words, the article examines the nature-nurture controversy. However, Bower concludes that no two children will have exactly the same perceptions of the same family.

"Putting Children First" focuses primarily on changes in the family, particularly negative changes, but it also alludes to other societal changes that are not positive for American children.

Part of parenting is spending time with your kids. However, as "Can Your Career Hurt Your Kids?" points out, with the decreasing number of mothers who stay home and the increasing number of single-parent families, parents are spending less time with their kids. Many of these children are in day care, especially the younger ones, but as they get older, a large number become latchkey children. This article looks at the advantages and disadvantages of day care, examines possible effects of leaving adolescents on their own, and considers the consequences on family relationships of parents coming home too tired to interact with their children.

In all walks of life, fathers are disappearing in ever-increasing numbers. Are they necessary for effective child rearing? "Life Without Father" explores some of the social and emotional effects of father absence on each member of the family, including fathers themselves.

The *Stress and Maltreatment* subsection points out that, taken to extremes, severe disciplinary techniques can spill over into physical abuse. What are the long-term consequences of physical, psychological, and sexual abuse? We often assume that abused children become maladjusted and abusing parents. However, as discussed in "The Lasting Effects of Child Maltreatment," the story is not that simple. Many, perhaps most, abused children become well-adjusted adults. Similarly, most abusing adults were not targets of abuse as children. Other factors, such as poverty, play a major role in determining the outcome of earlier experiences.

"Children of Violence" points out that children who grow up with violence all around them may become desensitized as their exposure to violence increases. Many of these children suffer posttraumatic stress disorder and may exhibit a number of different symptoms such as aggression, indifference, or inability to concentrate. However, some proportion of children reared under highly negative conditions show an amazing resiliency in their ability to survive. Experts believe that early intervention can be crucial in helping children recover from incidents of violence in which they have been an observer or a participant.

Divorce is one of the more common major sources of stress. Regardless of who wins custody, children do not have an easy time adjusting to the separation of their parents. Suggestions for helping children to cope often require a level of parental cooperation that may be unrealistic. The results of a longitudinal study of the effects of divorce on children, presented in "Children After Divorce," indicate that the psychological effects many be longer lasting than previously thought. In spite of forces threatening to tear families apart, however, the influence of the family on the life of an individual remains strong and pervasive.

The articles in the *Cultural Influences* subsection profile two key influences on development—gender and ethnicity. In "Biology, Destiny, and All That," Paul Chance

Unit 4

reviews evidence for sex differences and concludes that many differences between the sexes are differences in how characteristics are expressed rather than absolute differences.

Americans are both mystified and impressed by the educational achievements of Japanese children. How do they do it? "Why Japanese Kids Are Smarter (or Are They?)" looks at the many influences in Japanese culture, including the home environment and the school, that contribute to academic excellence. But, as the article points out, the stellar performance of Japanese children has its emotional and intellectual drawbacks as well. The article concludes that, while we can learn much of value from the Japanese approach to education, there is also much they can learn from us.

School expands a child's social network beyond the neighborhood peer group and often presents new social adjustment problems. In "Alienation and the Four Worlds of Childhood," Urie Bronfenbrenner draws attention to the increase in disorganized families and environment, which contribute to alienation from family, friends, school, and work.

The final article in this subsection is a summary of a symposium discussion that took place at the 1990 meeting of the Society for Research in Child Development, a key organization for child research specialists. The participants stressed the need for more careful and more systematic consideration of ethnicity and cultural factors in conducting research on development.

In the *Education* subsection, the article "Tracked to Fail" notes that among those who are at risk to fail are children who acquire negative labels at a very early age based on criteria such as reading ability or developmental test scores. The article shows how labels tend to stick all through school, regardless of the child's ability. All too often, slow-track children are expected to do poorly, are given "watered-down education," and suffer lasting effects on self-esteem.

An additional aspect of contemporary education is addressed in the final selection. In "Why We Need to Understand Science," renown astronomer Carl Sagan argues that an appreciation of science is essential so that citizens can make informed decisions about policy matters pertaining to science and technology.

Looking Ahead: Challenge Questions

It is relatively easy to blame teen pregnancy and teen substance abuse on the disorganization of the American family. It is far more difficult to suggest effective solutions to the problems. What changes do you believe should be instituted to resolve such problems as divorce, child abuse, teen pregnancy, racism, sexism, and substance abuse?

It is abundantly clear that parents can cross the line between discipline and abuse. Is it also possible for parents to cross the line in the other direction—by providing too well for their children?

Will you raise your children the way your parents raised you? If not, how would you do it differently and why?

The financial implications of single parenting are pretty obvious. What are some of the frequent social and emotional consequences for the child of a single parent?

What are some of the things you like and dislike about the Japanese approach to child rearing and education?

There are some obvious advantages to early identification and tracking of children who have exceptional abilities as well as those who seem destined to fail. Do you think the advantages outweigh the disadvantages or vice versa?

Why is it important for the American public to be scientifically literate? What are the probable consequences of a public that does not understand or appreciate science?

Same Family, Different Lives

Family experiences may make siblings different, not similar

BRUCE BOWER

Psychologists uncovered a curious feature of military morale during World War II. Those in branches of the service handing out the most promotions complained the most about their rank. The investigators cited "relative deprivation" as an explanation for the trend — it's not what you have, but what you have compared with others in the same situation.

Relative deprivation achieves a more profound influence through the daily battles and negotiations that constitute life in the nuclear family, maintain researchers in human behavioral genetics. Each child in a family harbors an exquisite sensitivity to his or her standing with parents, brothers and sisters, and thus essentially grows up in a unique psychological environment, according to these investigators. The result: Two children in the same family grow to differ from one another in attitudes, intelligence and personality as much as two youngsters randomly plucked from the population at large.

While one-of-a-kind experiences and perceptions of family life combine with each child's genetic heritage to create pervasive sibling differences, shared genes — which account for half the genes possessed by all siblings save for identical twins — foster whatever similarities they display, argue scientists who apply behavioral genetics to child development.

The emphasis on children's diverse experiences cultivating sibling differences seems ironic coming from scientists dedicated to estimating the genetic contribution to individual development. Yet behavioral genetic data provide a compelling antidote to the increasingly influential notion among psychiatrists that defective genes and broken brains primarily cause mental disorders, asserts psychologist Robert Plomin of Pennsylvania State University in University Park, a leading researcher in human behavioral genetics. Ongoing studies also challenge the assumption of many developmental psychologists that important family features, such as parental education, child-rearing styles and the quality of the marital relationship, affect all siblings similarly, Plomin adds.

"What runs in families is DNA, not shared experiences," Plomin contends. "Significant environmental effects are specific to each child rather than common to the entire family."

In a further challenge to child development researchers, Plomin and psychologist Cindy S. Bergeman of the University of Notre Dame (Ind.) contend that genetic influences substantially affect common environment measures, such as self-reports or experimenter observations of family warmth and maternal affection. "Labeling a measure environmental does not make it environmental," they conclude in the September BEHAVIORAL AND BRAIN SCIENCES. "We need measures ... that can capture the individual's active selection, modification and creation of environments."

Not surprisingly, the trumpeting of "non-shared" sibling environments and the questioning of traditional measures of the family milieu have drawn heated rebukes from some psychologists. In particular, critics claim that behavioral genetics studies rely on statistical techniques that inappropriately divvy up separate genetic and environmental effects on individual traits, rather than examining more important interactions between genes and environment.

Human behavioral genetics use family, adoption and twins studies to estimate the importance of genes and environment to individual development. Family studies assess the similarity among genetically related family members on measures of intelligence, extroversion, verbal ability, mental disturbances and other psychological traits. Adoption studies obtain psychological measures from genetically related individuals adopted by different families, their biological parents, and their adoptive parents and siblings. Researchers assume that similar scores between adoptees and biological parents reflect a greater genetic contribution, while adoptees showing similarity to adoptive parents and their children illuminate environmental effects. Twin studies compare the resemblance of identical twins on various measures to the resemblance of fraternal twins on the same measures. If heredity shapes a particular trait, identical twins display more similarity for it than fraternal twins, behavioral geneticists maintain.

Psychologist John C. Loehlin of the University of Texas at Austin directed a twin study published in 1976 that greatly influenced human behavioral genetics. Averaging across a broad range of personality measures obtained from 514 identical and 336 fraternal pairs of twins culled from a national sample of high school seniors, Loehlin's group found a correlation of 0.50 for identical twins and 0.28 for fraternal twins.

Correlations numerically express associations between two or more variables. The closer to 1.0 a correlation figure reaches, the more one variable resembles another — say, one twin's IQ and the corresponding twin's IQ. A correlation of zero between twin IQs would signify a complete lack of resemblance, with twin pairs as different in intelligence scores as randomly selected pairs of youngsters.

The Texas researchers doubled the difference between identical and fraternal twin correlations to obtain a "heritability estimate" of 0.44, or 44 percent, an estimate of how much genes contribute to individual differences. This means that genes accounted for just under half of the individual personality differences observed in the sample of twins. Thus, environment accounted for slightly more than half of the twin's personality variations.

A further finding intrigued the scientists. The correlation on personality measures for identical twins only reached 0.50, suggesting the environment orchestrated one-half of their personality differences. Since these twins carried matching sets of genes and grew up in the same families, only "non-shared" family experiences could account for such differences, Loehlin's group argued.

Subsequent twin and adoption studies carried out in Colorado, Minnesota, Sweden and England confirmed the importance of the non-shared environment for most aspects of personality, as well as intelligence and mental disorders such as schizophrenia, Plomin asserts. He and psychologist Denise Daniels of Stanford University reviewed much of this data in the March 1987 BEHAVIORAL AND BRAIN SCIENCES, followed by a book on the subject written with Penn State psychologist Judy Dunn titled *Separate Lives: Why Siblings Are So Different* (1990, Basic Books).

All the correlations and heritability estimates boil down to a simple point, Plomin maintains: Allegedly shared family influences, such as parent's emotional warmth or disciplinary practices, get filtered through each child's unique perceptions and produce siblings with strikingly diverse personalities. For example, a shy 9-year-old who gets picked on by schoolmates will react differently to an emotional, permissive mother than a gregarious 7-year-old sibling who attracts friends easily.

Many factors divide sibling's perceptions of family life, Plomin says, including age spacing, peer and school experiences, accidents, illnesses, random events and — to a lesser extent — birth order and sex differences.

Each sibling's temperament and behavior also generate specific perceptions and responses from parents that further shape non-shared environments, he argues.

As researchers in molecular genetics vigilantly pursue genes that predispose people to a variety of mental disorders, psychiatrists should not neglect the importance of the environment specific to each child in a family, contends Plomin and two colleagues — psychiatrist David Reiss of George Washington University in Washington, D.C., and psychologist E. Mavis Hetherington of the University of Virginia in Charlottesville — in the March AMERICAN JOURNAL OF PSYCHIATRY.

The three researchers bluntly warn psychiatrists enamored of the new genetic techniques that biology alone cannot explain the development of serious mental disorders. For example, a large, ongoing study in Sweden — conducted by Plomin and several other researchers — has found that when one identical twin develops schizophrenia, the other twin contracts the disorder about one-third of the time. Heredity shoulders considerable responsibility for fomenting schizophrenia, Plomin acknowledges, but an individual's experience of family life, peers and chance events plays at least as strong a role in triggering the devastating fragmentation of thought and emotion that characterizes the disorder.

Research directed by George Washington's Reiss, and described in his article with Plomin and Hetherington, suggests non-shared experiences protect some siblings, but not others, from alcoholism when one or both parents drink alcohol uncontrollably. Family members often shield the protected child from alcoholic behavior during that child's most cherished family practices, such as Christmas celebrations, Reiss' team finds. In this way, the protected sibling gradually learns to minimize brushes with the corrosive effects of alcoholism within and outside the family, the investigators observe. Upon reaching adolescence and adulthood, the protected sibling maintains limited family contacts to avoid the influence of an alcoholic parent and often marries a non-alcoholic person.

Given the importance of non-shared environments, developmental researchers need to study more than one child per family and devise better measures of children's perceptions of family experiences, Plomin contends. He and Bergeman find that several self-report tests currently used to assess the home environment largely ignore unique individual experiences within the family and rely on measures that show substantial genetic influence. In one case they cite,

unpublished data from a study of 179 reared-apart twin pairs (both identical and fraternal) and 207 reared-together twin pairs indicate that genes account for one-quarter of the individual differences plumbed by the widely used Family Environment Scales, which is generally regarded to measure environmental influences. These scales include ratings of emotional warmth, conflict, cohesion and cultural pursuits within the family.

Even the time children spend watching television — a seemingly vacuum-sealed environmental measure employed in many studies — significantly stems from genetically influenced characteristics, Plomin and his colleagues argue in the November 1990 PSYCHOLOGICAL SCIENCE. Parental restrictions do not exert strong effects on children's television viewing, since about 70 percent of parents put no limits on how much time their offspring can spend watching the tube, they state.

Plomin's team tested 220 adopted children three times, at 3, 4 and 5 years of age, as well as their biological and adoptive parents, younger adopted and non-adopted siblings, and control families with no adopted children. Biological parents and their children adopted by others spent a surprisingly similar amount of time watching television, indicating an important genetic influence on the behavior, Plomin's team asserted. Shared home environment, such as the television viewing habits of parents, also influenced children's television time, but to a lesser extent.

The results do not imply that some people follow a genetic imperative to sit glassy-eyed in front of the television for hours, day after day. "We can turn the television on or off as we please, but turning it off or leaving it on pleases individuals differently, in part due to genetic factors," the investigators conclude.

Some scientists who have long labored to understand family influences on psychological development take no pleasure in the conclusions of behavioral genetics researchers. Psychologist Lois W. Hoffman of the University of Michigan in Ann Arbor offers a critique of research highlighting sibling differences in the September PSYCHOLOGICAL BULLETIN.

Behavioral genetics tends to overestimate sibling differences because it concentrates on self-reports of personality traits, rather than on observations of coping skills and social behavior typically relied upon by developmental psychologists, Hoffman holds. A child may exaggerate differences from siblings on self-reports, whereas behavioral observations by experimenters may turn up sibling similarities in aggression or other attributes, she maintains.

Even in behavioral genetics research, significant sibling similarities apparently due to shared family environment turn up in political and religious beliefs and in general interests such as music, Hoffman adds.

Some family environments may more easily produce similarities among siblings than others, she argues. When both parents share the same values, attitudes and child-rearing styles, the chances increase that their pattern of behavior will rub off on all their children, in Hoffman's opinion.

Behavioral genetics researchers also incorrectly assume that only strong correlations between the personalities of adoptive parents and their adopted children reflect an environmental influence, the Michigan psychologist contends. Parental influences can weaken parent-child correlations on all sorts of personality measures, she points out. For instance, domineering, powerful parents may produce an anxious child, and an extremely self-assured, professionally successful parent may make a child feel inadequate.

Behavioral genetics comes under additional fire for its reliance on statistics that treat genetic and environmental influences on personality separately. This approach simply lacks the statistical power to pick up the interactions between genes and environment that primarily direct physical and psychological development, rendering current research in human behavioral genetics meaningless, argues Canadian psychologist Douglas Wahlsten of the University of Alberta in Edmonton. Much larger samples might begin to pick up such interactions, he adds.

Behavioral geneticists rely on statistics derived from a technique known as analysis of variance (ANOVA). This method is used throughout psychology to calculate whether a significant relationship, or correlation, exists between experimental variables by comparing variations in individual scores from a group's average value. Statisticians developed ANOVA in the 1920s as a way to estimate whether different types and amounts of fertilizer substantially increased the yield of various agricultural crops.

When applied to human personality and behavior, an ANOVA-based approach treats heredity and environment as mutually exclusive influences on personality, Wahlsten argues. Psychologists possess no conclusive test of interactions between genes and environments. But evidence of their interplay — as in the widely accepted theory that specific genes combine with particular family experiences to produce a psychotic disorder — may begin to emerge in behavioral genetics studies employing samples of 600 or more individuals, Wahlsten maintains. Mathematical formulas used in conjunction with ANOVA stand a better chance of ferreting out gene-environment interactions in extremely large samples, Wahlsten concludes in the March 1990 BEHAVIORAL AND BRAIN SCIENCES.

Psychologist Daniel Bullock of Boston University takes a bleaker view of ANOVA, citing its neglect of the intertwined forces guiding personality development. "The special status of ANOVA in psychology is an utter anachronism," he contends. "Many past claims by behavioral geneticists are unreliable."

Plomin rejects such charges. "To say that genetic and environmental effects interact and therefore cannot be disentangled is wrong," he states.

Twin and adoption studies consistently find strong separate effects of genes and non-shared environments on personality and other developmental measures, even when researchers painstakingly seek out possible interactions of nature and nurture, Plomin points out. Investigators may devise more sensitive statistical tests to illuminate cooperative ventures between genes and family experiences, but that will not invalidate the insights of behavioral genetics, he maintains.

That includes the discovery that what parents do similarly to two children does not importantly influence personality or problem behavior in the long run; rather, each child's perceptions of what goes on in the family prove critical. Appreciating the differences of offspring based on their individual qualities, with minimal preferential treatment of one child over another, seems a good general rule for concerned parents, Plomin says. Parents should recognize that siblings as well as "only children" harbor a keen sensitivity to their standing within the family, he adds.

"If we are reasonable, loving, but not perfect parents, the children will grow up to be themselves — all different but okay," says psychologist Sandra Scarr of the University of Virginia, a behavioral genetics researcher. "Children experience us as different parents, depending on their own characteristics, and we simply cannot make them alike or easily spoil their chances to be normal adults."

PUTTING CHILDREN FIRST

WILLIAM A. GALSTON

William A. Galston, the author most recently of Liberal Purposes: Goods, Virtues, and Diversity in the Liberal State *(Cambridge University Press), teaches at the University of Maryland, College Park. He is an advisor to the Washington, D.C.-based Progressive Policy Institute and a co-editor of* The Responsive Community, *a new journal that seeks a better balance between rights and responsibilities. This article is an expanded version of an essay that appeared in the December 2, 1991, issue of* The New Republic, *with material drawn from* Putting Children First: A Progressive Family Policy for the 1990s *by Elaine Ciulla Kamarck and William A. Galston, published by the Progressive Policy Institute.*

THE AMERICAN family has changed dramatically in the past generation, and it is children who have paid the price. From Ozzie and Harriet to the Simpsons, from one breadwinner to two, from child-centered nuclear families that stayed together for the sake of the children to the struggling one-parent families of today; the revolution in the American family has affected us all. Divorce rates have surged, and child poverty has risen alarmingly. The signs are everywhere around us that America's children are suffering—economically, educationally, and emotionally. Although this fact is obvious, indeed increasingly obtrusive, it has hardly been discussed by intellectuals and policy elites until quite recently. Several broad forces—racial conflict, feminism, the culture of individual rights—help explain this odd silence.

The story begins in 1965, with the publication of Daniel Patrick Moynihan's *The Negro Family: The Case for National Action,* which identified the breakdown of the black family as a growing obstacle to racial progress. Although intended as the analytical backdrop to major federal initiatives, it was received as a call for quietism, even as a subtle relegitimation of racism. Black civil rights leaders and white liberal scholars argued that the emphasis on family structure would inevitably divert attention from economic inequalities and would justify "blaming the victims" for the consequences of discrimination. As William Julius Wilson has argued, this enraged response had the consequence of suppressing public debate over, and serious scholarly inquiry into, the relation between black family structure and the problems of the ghetto poor—suppressing it for an entire generation.

Feminism also contributed to the silence. The postwar American women's movement began as a criticism of the 1950s family. "Liberation" meant leaving the domestic sphere for the world of work outside the home. It also meant denying traditional theories of gender difference that seemed to legitimate inequalities of resources, power, and self-respect. To be equal was to be the same: to compete on the same terms as men, with the same focus on individual separateness and independence. As Sylvia Ann Hewlett argues, the unquestionable moral force of the feminist movement muted the voices of those who, though dubious about its denial of gender differences and deeply concerned about its consequences for the well-being of children, did not wish to be accused of a disguised effort to ratify the patriarchal or chauvinist status quo.

Then there was the cultural upheaval of the 1960s, which yielded an ethic of self-realization through incessant personal experimentation, the triumph of what has been termed "expressive individualism." An increasingly influential therapeutic vocabulary emphasized the constraints that relations could impose on personal growth and encouraged adults to turn inward toward the self's struggles for sovereignty, to view commitments as temporary or endlessly renegotiable—to behave, in effect, like adolescents. This vocabulary was anything but hospitable to the discourse of parental continuity, commitment, and self-sacrifice.

A related legacy of the generation just past has been an impoverishment of moral vocabulary. What some regard as a descent into relativism is more accurately characterized as the relentless expansion of morality understood as the articulation of the rights of individuals. This development is not alien to the American experience, and it is not wholly to be deplored. Rights, after all, do support self-respect and offer protection against evils. Still, we now know that there is a difficulty: Although systems of rights can guide some spheres of life tolerably well, they can obscure and distort others. In particular, the effort to understand family relations as the mutual exercise of rights led to a legal and emotional cul-de-sac.

IN RECENT years, however, the climate has changed. Debates within the black community, and among social democrats as well as conservatives, have helped to relegitimate the discussion of the links between family structure and a range of social ills. To acknowledge such links, it is not necessary to sever the causal connections between structural inequalities at the political and economic level and disintegration at the family level, or to focus exclusively on the "culture of poverty." The point is, rather, that the cultural effects of past discrimination can take on a life of their own, that they can persist even in the face of changing opportunity structures.

The women's movement is changing, too. In place of equality understood as sameness, feminists such as Sara Ruddick, Carol Gilligan, and Jean Bethke Elshtain have embraced categories of difference, nurturance, and care. Martha Albertson Fineman insists that public policy "recognize and accommodate the positive and lasting nature of mothers' ties to their children." Surely this style of feminist argument will prove far more compatible with traditional understandings of the family than anyone could have predicted a decade ago.

And even broader cultural changes are under way, provoked by demographic shifts. Baby boomers who delayed marriage until their thirties have discovered that the moral universe of their young adulthood is not a suitable place for parents with young children. Others have discovered that the casting off of binding relationships is not necessarily the path to liberation and happiness. A generation that once devoted itself to the proliferation of rights and the expression of individuality has begun haltingly to explore counterbalancing notions of responsibility and community; several polls have documented rapid shifts during the past two years in public attitudes toward a range of family issues.

The most important shift is a welcome expansion of concern beyond narrow bounds of race and class. For too long, worries about children and families focused on such issues as teenage pregnancy, dire deprivation, and collapsing marriage rates. These are serious problems, but they are disproportionately characteristic of the ghetto poor. Such measurements, in other words, enabled the American middle class, scholars as well as citizens, to believe that families and children were someone else's problem. But with increased attention to the clash between work and family, to parental time deficits, and to the impact of divorce, the middle class can no longer sustain such an illusion. The decay of the family is its problem, too. The children of the middle class are also at risk; and its choices can be just as shortsighted, self-

There is growing recognition that we must place the family at the center of our thinking about social issues and children at the center of our thinking about the family.

indulgent, and harmful to the young as any ever contemplated in the culture of poverty.

THESE RECENT trends are at last producing important changes at the level of national politics. For decades, the revolution in the American family evoked a polarized reaction: Liberals talked about structural economic pressures facing families and avoided issues of personal conduct, and conservatives did just the reverse. Liberals habitually reached for bureaucratic responses, even when they were counter-productive, and conservatives reflexively rejected government programs even when they would work.

Both are wrong. Traditional conservatives' support for families is largely rhetorical; their disregard for new economic realities engenders a policy of unresponsive neglect—expressed for example, in President Bush's misguided veto of the Family Leave Act. Conversely, traditional liberals' unwillingness to acknowledge that intact two-parent families are the most effective units for raising children has led them into a series of policy cul-de-sacs.

Recently, however, this clash of conflicting worldviews has begun to give way to a new spirit of accommodation. As E.J. Dionne Jr. has observed, recent proposals for pro-family tax reform reflect the realization that both values and dollars count. Many younger conservatives are addressing social problems long neglected by their movement. Many younger Democrats, meanwhile, are looking for new forms of nonbureaucratic, choice-based public activism as a supplement to the frequently cumbersome and intrusive institutions of the welfare state. There is growing recognition that we must place the family at the center of our thinking about social issues and children at the center of our thinking about the family. We need policies that support and compensate families as they carry out their critical social role—providing for the economic and moral well-being of children. As we will see, a large body of evidence supports the conclusion that in the aggregate, the intact two-parent family is best suited to this task. Making this premise our point of departure takes us toward policies that *reinforce* families and away from bureaucratic approaches that seek to *replace* family functions.

To avoid misunderstanding, I want to make it clear that a general preference for the intact two-parent family does not mean that this is the best option in every case. Nor does it mean that all single-parent families are somehow dysfunctional; that proposition would diminish the achievements of millions of single parents who are struggling successfully against the odds to provide good homes for their children. Rather, the point is that at the level of statistical aggregates and society-wide phenomena, significant differences do emerge between one-parent and two-parent families, differences that can and should shape our understanding of social policy.

I DO NOT mean to suggest that the renewed emphasis on the family is solely the product of cultural and ideological change. Equally important is a broad process of social learning—a growing (and increasingly painful) awareness of the consequences of the choices that we already have made, individually and collectively, over the past generation.

The economic facts are distressing. As Hewlett summarizes the data: Among all children eighteen years and under, one in five is poor, nearly twice the poverty rate for the elderly; among children younger than six, the rate is almost one in four; among children in families headed by adults younger than thirty, one in three; among black children, almost one in two. And noneconomic trends are no less stark. In the past quarter-century, the amount of time that parents spend with their children has dropped by 40 percent, from thirty hours a week to just seventeen; and there is no evidence that these remaining shreds of parental availability represent "quality time." On the contrary: As social historian Barbara Whitehead reports, "Increasingly, family schedules are intricate applications of time-motion principles."

These stress-filled lives reflect changes in the economy that have prompted momentous shifts in the labor force in this country. Since 1973, under the pressure of declining productivity and mounting international competition, family incomes have stagnated while the relative costs of a middle-class existence—in particular, of homeownership, health care, and higher education—have soared. Wage prospects have grown increasingly dismal, especially for young people with no more than a high school education. The surge of women into the work force may have begun three decades ago as a cultural revolt against household roles experienced as stifling, but it has been sustained by increasingly urgent economic necessity. Today two-thirds of all mothers with children younger than eighteen do at least some work outside the home, as do more than one-half of all mothers with children under five.

For tens of millions of American families, the second income means the difference between keeping and losing a tenuously maintained middle-class way of life. To be sure, some adjustments at the margin are possible: Young families can live in smaller houses and stop eating at restaurants. Still, the hope of many moral traditionalists that the 1950s family can somehow be restored flies in the face of contemporary market forces. The tension between remunerative work and family time will not be overcome in the foreseeable future—unless increased income from nonmarket sources allows parents with young children to do less work outside the home. Many thoughtful conservatives are coming to the realization that they must choose between their vision of a well-ordered family and their desire for smaller, less costly government.

THESE TENSIONS and others have clearly taken their toll. Test scores are down, and not just the much-discussed SATs. At BellSouth in Atlanta, for example, only about 10 percent of job applicants can pass exams that test basic learning ability, versus 20 percent a decade ago. Theft, violence, and the use of illicit drugs are far more prevalent among teenagers than they were thirty years ago; and the rate of suicide among teenagers has tripled.

It is tempting to dismiss these data as one sided, or to interpret them as mere cyclical variations within longer-term stability. After all, virtually every generation in every culture has complained of a decline of the family. But this is an alibi. We must face the fact that the conditions we take for granted are the product of a social revolution that has rapidly unfolded over just the past three decades. And at the heart of this revolution lie changes in family structure.

In thirty years, the percentage of children born outside of marriage has quintupled, and now stands at 18 percent for whites and 63 percent for blacks. In this same period, the divorce rate has tripled, as has the percentage of children living with only one parent. Of white children born in the early 1950s, 81 percent lived continuously until the age of seventeen with their two biological parents; the projected rate for children born in the early 1980s is 30 percent. The corresponding rate for black children has fallen from 52 percent in the 1950s to only 6 percent today.

These structural shifts are responsible for a substantial portion of child poverty. As David Ellwood has observed, "[t]he vast majority of children who are raised entirely in a two-parent home will never be poor during childhood. By contrast, the vast majority of children who spend time in a single-parent home will experience poverty." As Ellwood showed in *Poor Support,* in any given year, fully 50 percent of children in one-parent families will experience poverty, versus 15 percent for those in two-parent families; 73 percent of children from one-parent families will experience poverty at some point during their childhood, versus 20 percent for children from two-parent families; 22 percent of children from one-parent families will experience persistent poverty (seven years or more), versus only 2 percent from two-parent families.

These data suggest that the best anti-poverty program for children is a stable, intact family. And this conclusion holds even for families headed by younger parents with very modest levels of educational attainment. For married high school graduates with children, the 1987 poverty rate was 9 percent, versus more than 47 percent for families headed by female high school graduates. Even for married high school dropouts with children, the poverty rate was 25 percent, versus more than 81 percent for families headed by female high school dropouts. Overall, Frank Furstenberg Jr. and Andrew Cherlin conclude, the differences in family structure go "a long way toward accounting for the enormous racial disparity in poverty rates. Within family types, black families are still poorer than white families; but the racial gap in poverty shrinks considerably when the marital status of the household head is taken into account."

'The vast majority of children who are raised entirely in a two-parent home will never be poor during childhood. By contrast, the vast majority of children who spend time in a single-parent home will experience poverty.'

TO BE SURE, the causal arrow could point in the opposite direction: differences in family structure might be thought to reflect differences in economic status. Wilson offered an influential statement of this counterthesis in *The Truly Disadvantaged:* Reduced black marriage rates reflect dramatically higher rates of black male unemployment, which reduces the "male marriageable pool"—under the assumption that "to be marriageable a man needs to be employed." But the most recent research offers only modest support for this hypothesis. Robert Mare and Christopher Winship find that changes in employment rates among young black males account for only 20 percent of the decline in their marriage rates since 1960; they speculate that the various family disruptions of the past three decades may be self-reinforcing.[1] Though Wilson continues to defend the validity of his thesis for the hard-hit central cities of the Northeast and Midwest, he is now willing to say that "the decline in marriage among inner-city blacks is not simply a function of the proportion of jobless men . . . it is reasonable to consider the effects of weaker social structures against out-of-wedlock births."

Along with family non-formation, family breakup is a potent source of poverty, especially among children. According to a recently released Census Bureau study by Susan Bianchi, who identified and tracked twenty thousand households, it turns out that after their parents separate or divorce, children are almost twice as likely to be living in poverty as they were before the split. The gross income of the children and their custodial parent (usually the mother) dropped by 37 percent immediately after the family breakup (26 percent after adjustment for the decline in family size) and recovered only slightly after sixteen months. These findings support the arguments of scholars who have long contended that divorce under current law spells economic hardship for most custodial parents and their minor children.

As Furstenberg and Cherlin show in their admirably balanced survey of current research, there are at least three sets of reasons for this outcome: Many women bargain away support payments in return for sole custody of their children or to eliminate the need to deal with their former spouses; when awarded, child support payments are on average pitifully inadequate; and many fathers cough up only a portion (at best) of their required payments. A Census Bureau report from the mid-1980s showed that of mothers with court-ordered support payments, only half received all of what they were owed, a quarter received partial payments, and the remaining quarter got nothing at all.

IF THE economic effects of family breakdown are clear, the psychological effects are just now coming into focus. As Karl Zinsmeister summarizes an emerging consensus, "There is a mountain of scientific evidence showing that when families disintegrate children often end up with intellectual, physical, and emotional scars that persist for life. . . . We talk about the drug crisis, the education crisis, and the problems of teen pregnancy and juvenile crime. But all these ills trace back predominantly to one source: broken families."

As more and more children are reared in one-parent families, it becomes clear that the economic consequences of a parent's absence (usually the father) may pale beside the psychological consequences—which include higher than average levels of youth suicide, low intellectual and educational performance, and higher than average rates of mental illness, violence, and drug use.

Nowhere is this more evident than in the longstanding and strong relationship between crime and one-parent families. In a recent study, Douglas Smith and G. Roger Jarjoura found that "neighborhoods with larger percentages of youth (those aged 12 to 20) and areas with higher percentages of single-parent households also have higher rates of violent crime."[2] The relationship is so strong that controlling for family configuration erases the relationship between race and crime and between low income and crime. This conclusion shows up time and time again in the literature; poverty is far from the sole determinant of crime.

While the scarcity of intact families in the ghetto is largely a function of the failure of families to form in the first place, in the larger society the central problem is family disintegration, caused primarily by divorce. This pervasive phenomenon has effects that are independent of economics. It is to these studies that we now turn.

In 1981, John Guidubaldi, then president of the National Association of School Psychologists, picked a team of 144 psychologists in thirty-eight states, who gathered long-term data on seven hundred children, half from intact families, the other half children of divorce. Preliminary results published in 1986 showed that the effects of divorce on children persisted over time and that the psychological consequences were significant even after correcting for income differences.[3]

The problems engendered by divorce extend well beyond vanishing role models. Children need authoritative rules and stable schedules, which harried single parents often have a hard time supplying. As Guidubaldi puts it, "One of the things we found is that children who had regular bedtimes, less TV, hobbies and after-school activities—children who are in households that are orderly and predictable—do better than children who [did] not. I don't think we can escape the conclusion that children need structure, and oftentimes the divorce household is a chaotic scene."

The results of the Guidubaldi study have been confirmed and deepened by Judith Wallerstein's ten-year study of sixty middle-class divorced families. Among her key findings:

• Divorce is almost always more devastating for children than for their parents.

• The effects of divorce are often long lasting. Children are especially affected because divorce occurs during their formative years. What they see and experience becomes a part of their inner world, their view of themselves, and their view of society.

• Almost half the children entered adulthood as worried, underachieving, self-deprecating, and sometimes angry young men and women.

• Adolescence is a period of grave risk for children in divorced families; those who entered adolescence in the immediate wake of their parents' divorces had a particularly bad time. The young people told us time and again how much they needed a family structure, how much they wanted to be protected, and how much they yearned for clear guidelines for moral behavior.[4]

Furstenberg and Cherlin offer a nuanced, but ultimately troubling, account of the noneconomic consequences of divorce. For most children, it comes as an "unwelcome shock," even when the parents are openly quarreling. In the short-term, boys seem to have a harder time coping than girls, in part because of an "escalating cycle of misbehavior and harsh response between mothers and sons." Girls more typically respond with internalized disruption rather than external behavior—with heightened levels of anxiety, withdrawal, and depression that may become apparent only years later. These differences reflect the fact that divorce almost always means disrupted relations with the father. It is difficult to overstate the extent of the disruption that typically occurs. Even in the period relatively soon after divorce, only one-sixth of all children will see their fathers as often as once a week, and close to one-half will not see them at all. After ten years, almost two-thirds will have no contact.

These findings are less than self-interpreting, Furstenberg and Cherlin point out, because they must be compared with the effects on children of intact but troubled families. On the one hand, various studies indicate that the children of divorce do no worse than children in families in which parents fight continuously. On the other hand, a relatively small percentage of divorces result from, and terminate, such clearly pathological situations. There are many more cases in which there is little open conflict, but one or both partners feels unfulfilled, bored, or constrained. Indeed, the onset of divorce in these families can intensify conflict, particularly as experienced by children. As Nicholas Zill observes, "Divorces tend to generate their own problems."

Given the profound psychological effects of divorce, it is hardly surprising to discover what teachers and administrators have known for some time: One of the major reasons for America's declining educational achievement is the disintegrating American family. And if we continue to neglect the crisis of the American family, we will have undercut current efforts at educational reform.

Untangling just what it is about family structure that makes for high or low educational achievement is a dif-ficult task. Clearly the economics of the family have a great deal to do with achievement; children from poor families consistently do less well than do children from non-poor or well-to-do families. Nevertheless, income is clearly not the whole story. When studies control for income, significant differences in educational achievement appear between children from single-parent families and children from intact families.

For example, a study conducted under the auspices of the National Association of Elementary School Principals and the Institute for Development of Educational Activities shows that family background has an important effect on educational achievement above and beyond income level—especially for boys. Lower-income girls with two parents, for instance, score higher on achievement tests than do higher-income boys with one parent. At the very bottom of the achievement scale are lower-income boys with one parent.[5]

WHAT SHOULD be our response to these developments? The recent literature suggests three broad possibilities. First, we may applaud, with Judith Stacey, the demise of the traditional (rigid, patriarchal) family and the rise of "postmodern" (flexible, variegated, female-centered) arrangements, which are allegedly far more consistent with egalitarian democracy. Second, we may accept Jan Dizard and Howard Gadlin's suggestion that moral change (in the direction of autonomy) and economic change (in the direction of a two-earner, postindustrial economy) have rendered obsolete the older model of the private family; in its place, they advocate a dramatically expanded public sphere on the Swedish model that assumes many of the private family's functions. And third, there is the response, neither postmodern nor socialist, that might be called neotraditional.

It goes something like this. A primary purpose of the family is to raise children well, and for this purpose stably married parents are best. Sharply rising rates of divorce, unwed mothers, and runaway fathers do not represent "alternative lifestyles." They are, instead, most truly characterized as patterns of adult behavior with profoundly negative consequences for children. Families have primary responsibility for instilling traits such as discipline, ambition, respect for the law, and regard for others; and it is a responsibility that cannot be discharged as effectively by auxiliary social institutions such as public schools. This responsibility entails a sphere of legitimate parental authority that should be bolstered—not undermined—by society. It requires personal sacrifice and the delay of certain forms of gratification on the part of parents. It means that government should devote substantial resources to stabilizing families and to enhancing their child-rearing capacity. But at the same time it must minimize bureaucratic cost, complexity, and intrusiveness, working instead to broaden family choice, opportunity, and responsibility.

The willingness to join the languages of economics and morals, and to consider new approaches to old goals, is increasingly characteristic of public discussion of the family. As Barbara Whitehead notes, this approach suffuses the recent report of the National Commission on Children. The volume edited by David Blankenhorn, Steven Bayme, and Jean Bethke Elshtain is particularly strong along the moral dimension. To be sure, it is easy for this stance to give the appearance of ineffectual exhortation. The editors of *The New York Times* assert that the commission's final report "swims in platitudes." Still, there are eminently practical ways of embedding moral concerns in policies and institutions. Richard Louv argues for moral change focused on the community as much as the individual. He urges us to reweave the tattered "web" of social relationships—parent-school ties, neighborhoods, communal child care arrangements, and the like—that provide a supportive environment for families and help nurture children. Although Louv emphasizes the importance of civil society, he does not imagine that the web can be adequately repaired without major changes in public policy.

Here Louv joins an emerging consensus that differs over details but not over essentials. The point is not to be driven to make a false choice between moral and economic concerns, but rather to combine them in a relation of mutual support. It might well be argued, for example, that the government has a responsibility not to tax away the money that families need to raise children. Four decades ago, the United States had a disguised family allowance: In 1948 the personal exemption was $600 (42 percent of per-capita personal income), while today's personal exemption is only 11 percent of per-capita income. This meant that a married couple at the median income with two minor dependents paid only 0.3 percent of their 1948 income in federal income taxes, compared to today's 9.1 percent. The 1948 couple's total tax bill (federal, state, and Social Security) was 2 percent of personal income. Today that total comes to about 30 percent.

Thus, one proposal now gaining support is to raise the personal exemption from the current $2,050 to at least $4,000, and perhaps eventually to $7,500. To make this more affordable, the bulk of the increase could be targeted to young children, and the increase could be phased out for upper-income taxpayers. Another approach, endorsed by the National Commission on Children, would create a $1,000 tax credit for each child; low-income families that owe no taxes would receive a cash payment for the amount of the credit. (To avoid potentially perverse incentives, this proposal should be coupled with a broader program of welfare reform.)

Reducing the tension between work and family will take changes in the private as well as the public sector. Hewlett, Louv, and many others argue for a "family-oriented workplace" with far more adaptable schedules: more flexible hours, greater opportunities for working at home and communicating by computer, for part-time employment, and for job sharing. Resistance to these changes reflects primarily the ignorance or the obduracy of middle-aged male managers, not negative impact on corporate balance sheets. Much the same is true of unpaid leave for parents following the birth of a child. Studies at the state level indicate that the costs and disruptive effects of such leaves, even when legally mandatory, are minimal. President Bush's opposition to federal family leave legislation is increasingly indefensible.

Adequate reward for labor force participation represents another important link between morals and public policy. If we believe that the presence of a parent who works outside the home furnishes a crucial moral example for his or her children, then surely the community has a responsibility to ensure that full-time work by a parent provides a nonpoverty family income. As Robert Shapiro of the Progressive Policy Institute has argued, the most efficient way to accomplish this goal would be to expand the Earned Income Tax Credit and tie it to family size.

This emphasis on the use of the tax code to promote family opportunity and responsibility is characteristic of a political outlook that has been called "neoprogressive." This is not to suggest that traditional liberal approaches are in every case misguided. Some of them—prenatal care, WIC (the nutrition program for poor women, infants, and children), childhood immunization, and Head Start—efficiently promote the well-being of children and families, and the political consensus supporting their expansion now stretches from KidsPac (a liberal, children-oriented political action committee) and the Children's Defense Fund to the Bush administration and the corporate-based Committee for Economic Development. And yet the neoprogressives are more willing than the traditional liberals to re-examine the programs of the past and to distinguish between what works and what doesn't.

IF THE PRIVATE and public sectors must assume greater responsibility for the well-being of families with children, so must parents. In particular, the moral obligation to help support one's biological children persists regardless of one's legal relationship to them, and the law is fully justified in enforcing this obligation. The 1988 Family Support Act requires states to collect the Social Security numbers of both parents (married or unmarried) at birth, to increase efforts to establish contested paternity, to use (as at least rebuttable presumptions) their guidelines concerning appropriate levels of child support, and to move toward collecting all new support awards through automatic payroll deductions.

These are steps in the right direction, but they don't go far enough. Mary Ann Glendon has argued powerfully that a "children first" principle should govern our spousal support and marital property law:

> The judges' main task would be to piece together, from property and income and inkind personal care, the best possible package to meet the needs of children and their physical guardian. Until the welfare of the children had been adequately secured in this way, there would be no question of, or debate about, "marital property." All assets, no matter when or how acquired, would be subject to the duty to provide for the children.[6]

Moreover, the state-level reforms mentioned above do nothing to address what is in many cases the chief impediment to support collection: fathers moving from state to state to slow or avoid apprehension. Conflicting state laws and a morass of administrative complexity discourage mothers from pursuing their claims across jurisdictions. Ellwood and others have called for the federalization of the system, with payroll deductions remitted to, and support payments drawn from, a centralized national fund. The U.S. Commission on Interstate Child Support, created by Congress to develop a blueprint for reform, is considering this idea.

Even when child support is collected regularly from absent parents who can afford to provide it, payments are typically set too low to avoid tremendous disruption in the lives of custodial mothers and their children. Writing from very different perspectives, Lenore Weitzman, Martha Albertson Fineman, and Furstenberg and Cherlin converge on the conclusion that the laws and the practices of many states leave men in a far more favorable situation after divorce. Furstenberg and Cherlin cite approvingly a proposal to require noncustodial fathers to pay a fixed proportion of their income, 17 percent to 34 percent, depending on the number of minor children; the adoption of this standard nationwide would raise total child support due by roughly two-thirds. Fineman advocates a need-based approach that would (she argues) yield better results for women and children than would ostensibly egalitarian standards.

During the past generation, the presumption in favor of awarding mothers custody of their children has been replaced in many cases by the presumption of equal claims. This development has generated a rising number of joint custody arrangements that do not, on average, work out very well. It has also worsened the post-divorce economic status of custodial mothers and their children: Because women tend to view custody as a paramount issue, they often compromise on economic matters to avoid the custody battle made possible by the new, supposedly more egalitarian, legal framework. And here, too, scholars from various points on the ideological spectrum are converging on the conclusion that the traditional arrangement had much to recommend it. They propose a "primary caretaker" standard: judges should be instructed to award custody of young children to the parent who has (in the words of a leading advocate) "performed a substantial majority of the [direct] caregiving tasks for the child."

THESE AND similar proposals will help custodial mothers and their children pick up the pieces after divorce, but they will do little to reduce the incidence of divorce. For Furstenberg and Cherlin, this is all that can be done: "We are inclined to accept the irreversibility of high levels of divorce as our starting point for thinking about changes in public policy." Hewlett is more disposed to grasp the nettle. While rejecting a return to the fault-based system of the past, she believes that the current system makes divorce too easy and too automatic.

Government should send a clearer moral signal that families with children are worth preserving. In this spirit, she suggests that parents of minor children seeking divorce undergo an eighteen-month waiting period, during which they would be obliged to seek counseling and to reach a binding agreement that truly safeguards their children's future.

The generation that installed the extremes of self-expression and self-indulgence at the heart of American culture must now learn some hard old lessons about commitment, self-sacrifice, the deferral of gratification, and simple endurance. It will not be easy. But other sorts of gratifications may be their reward. Perhaps the old morality was not wrong to suggest that a deeper kind of satisfaction awaits those who accept and fulfill their essential human responsibilities.

REFERENCES

[1]Mare, Robert D. and Winship, Christopher, "Socio-economic Change and the Decline of Marriage for Blacks and Whites." In *The Urban Underclass,* edited by Christopher Jencks and Paul Peterson. Washington, D.C.: The Brookings Institute, 1991.

[2]Smith, Douglas A., Jarjoura, G. Roger, "Social Structure and Criminal Victimization." In *Journal of Research in Crime and Delinquency,* Vol. 25, No. 1, February 1988.

[3]Guidubaldi, J., Cleminshaw, H.K., Perry, J.D., Nastasi, B.K., and Lightel, J., "The Role of Selected Family Environment Factors in Children's Post-Divorce Adjustment." In *Family Relations,* Vol. 35, 1986.

[4]Wallerstein, Judith S., and Blakeslee, Sandra, *Second Chances: Men, Women, and Children a Decade after Divorce.* New York: Ticknor and Fields, 1989.

[5]Sally Banks Zakariya, "Another Look at the Children of Divorce," *Principal Magazine,* September 1982, p. 35. See also, R.B. Zajonc, "Family Configuration and Intelligence," *Science,* Vol. 192, April 16, 1976, pp. 227-236. In a later and more methodologically sophisticated study, the authors try to define more completely what it is about two-parent families that make them better at preparing students for educational success. Income clearly stands out as the most important variable; but the close relationship between one-parent status, lower income, and lack of time for things like homework help and attendance at parent teacher conferences—to name a few of the variables considered—led the authors to say that "the negative effects of living in a one-parent family work primarily through other variables in our model." Ann M. Milne, David E. Myers, Alvin S. Rosenthal, and Alan Ginsburg, "Single Parents, Working Mothers, and the Educational Achievement of School Children," *Sociology of Education,* 1986, Vol. 59 (July), p. 132.

[6]Glendon, Mary Ann, *Abortion and Divorce in Western Law.* Cambridge, MA: Harvard University Press, 1987 (pp. 93-95).

CAN YOUR CAREER HURT YOUR KIDS?

Mommy often gets home from work too tired to talk. Daddy's almost never around. Says one expert: "We can only guess at the damage being done to the very young."

Kenneth Labich

BECAUSE CHILDREN are the future, America could be headed for bad bumps down the road. Some of the symptoms are familiar—rising teenage suicides and juvenile arrest rates, average SAT scores lower than 30 years ago. But what is the disease festering beneath that disturbing surface? Says Alice A. White, a clinical social worker who has been counseling troubled children in Chicago's prosperous North Shore suburbs for nearly two decades: "I'm seeing a lot more emptiness, a lack of ability to attach, no sense of real pleasure. I'm not sure a lot of these kids are going to be effective adults."

Not all children, or even most of them, are suffering from such a crisis of the spirit. In fact, some trends are headed in a promising direction. For example, drug use among young people has fallen sharply since the 1970s. But a certain malaise does seem to be spreading. Far more and far earlier than ever before, kids are pressured to take drugs, have sex, deal with violence. In a world ever more competitive and complex, the path to social and economic success was never more obscure.

And fewer traditional pathfinders are there to show the way. Divorce has robbed millions of kids of at least one full-time parent. With more and more women joining the work force, and many workaholic parents of both sexes, children are increasingly left in the care of others or allowed to fend for themselves. According to a University of Maryland study, in 1985 American parents spent on average just 17 hours a week with their children.

This parental neglect would be less damaging if better alternatives were widely available, but that is decidedly not the case. Families that can afford individual child care often get good value, but the luxury of

REPORTER ASSOCIATE *Jung Ah Pak*

a compassionate, full-time, $250-a-week nanny to watch over their pride and joy is beyond the reach of most American parents. They confront a patchwork system of informal home arrangements and more structured day care centers. In far too many cases, parents with infants or toddlers cannot feel secure about the care their children get. Says Edward Zigler, a professor of child development at Yale, who has spent much of his career fighting the abuses of child care: "We are cannibalizing children. Children are dying in this system, never mind achieving optimum development."

For older children with no parental overseer, the prospects can be equally bleak. Studies are beginning to show that preteens and teenagers left alone after school, so-called latchkey children, may be far more prone than other kids to get involved with alcohol and illegal drugs.

For some experts in the field, the answer to all this is to roll back the clock to an idyllic past. Mom, dressed in a frilly apron, is merrily stirring the stew when Dad gets home from work. Junior, an Eagle Scout, and Sally—they call her Muffin—greet him with radiant smiles. Everybody sits down for dinner to talk about schoolwork and Mom's canasta party.

For others more in touch with the economic temper of the times—especially the financial realities behind the rising number of working mothers—the solution lies in improving the choices available to parents. Government initiatives to provide some financial relief may help, but corporations could make an even greater difference by focusing on the needs of employees who happen to be parents. Such big companies as IBM and Johnson & Johnson have taken the lead in dealing with employee child care problems, and many progressive corporations are discovering the benefits of greater

flexibility with regard to family issues. At the same time, an array of professional child care organizations has sprung up to help big corporations meet their employees' demands.

Without doubt, helping improve child care is in the best interest of business—today's children, after all, are tomorrow's labor pool. Says Sandra Kessler Hamburg, director of education studies at the Committee for Economic Development, a New York research group that funnels corporate funds into education projects: "We can only guess at the damage being done to very young children right now. From the perspective of American business, that is very, very disturbing. As jobs get more and more technical, the U.S. work force is less and less prepared to handle them."

The state of America's children is a political mine field, and threading through the research entails a lot of gingerly probing as well as the occasional explosion. Much work in the field is contradictory, and many additional longer-range studies need to be done before anyone can say precisely what is happening.

Moreover, any researcher who dwells on the problems of child care—of infants in particular—risks being labeled antiprogressive by the liberal academic establishment. If the researcher happens to be male, his motives may seem suspect. If he says babies are at risk in some child care settings, he may be accused of harboring the wish that women leave the work force and return to the kitchen. Much valid research may be totally ignored because it has been deemed politically incorrect.

For example: Jay Belsky, a Penn State professor specializing in child development, set off a firestorm in 1986 with an article in *Zero to Three*, an influential journal that summarizes existing academic research. His conclusions point to possible risks for very small children in day care outside the home. Though he scrupulously threw in a slew of caveats and even went so far as to confess a possible bias because his own wife stayed home with their two children, Belsky came under heavy attack. Feminist researchers called his scholarship into question. Says Belsky: "I was flabbergasted by the response. I felt like the messenger who got shot."

Belsky's critics charged, among other things, that he had ignored studies that document some more positive results from infant day care. Since then, for example, a study conducted by researchers at the University of Illinois and Trinity College in Hartford, Connecticut, found that a child's intellectual development may actually be helped during the second and third years of life if the mother works. The study, which tracked a nationwide sample of 874 children from ages 3 to 4, determined that the mental skills of infants in child care outside the home were lower than those of kids watched over by their mothers during the first year, but then picked up enough at ages 2 and 3 to balance out.

Whatever the merits of his critics' assault, Belsky presents a disturbing picture of the effects on infants of nonparental child care outside the home. In a 1980 study he cited in the article, involving low-income women in the Minneapolis-St. Paul area, infants in day care were disproportionately likely to avoid looking at or approaching their mothers after being separated from them for a brief period.

ANOTHER STUDY, conducted in 1974, concluded that 1-year-olds in day care cried more when separated from their mothers than those reared at home; still another, in 1981, found that day care infants threw more temper tantrums. To at least some extent, the observations seem to apply across socioeconomic boundaries. A 1985 University of Illinois study of infants from affluent Chicago families showed that babies in the care of full-time nannies avoided any sort of contact with their mothers more often than those raised by moms during their first year.

An infant's attachment, or lack of it, to the mother is especially crucial because it can portend later developmental problems. In the Minnesota study, toddlers who had been in day care early on displayed less enthusiasm when confronted with a challenging task. They were less likely to follow their mothers' instructions and less persistent in dealing with a difficult problem. Another study, which took a look at virtually all 2-year-olds on the island of Bermuda, found more poorly adjusted children among the early day care group regardless of race, IQ, or socioeconomic status.

Researchers in Connecticut investigating 8- to 10-year-old children in 1981 found higher levels of misbehavior and greater withdrawal from the company of others among those who had been in day care as infants, no matter what the educational level of their parents. In a study of kindergarten and first-grade children in North Carolina, the early day care kids were found more likely than others to hit, kick, push, threaten, curse, and argue with their peers.

What we should take away from the research, says an unrepentant Belsky, is this: "There is an accumulating body of evidence that children who were cared for by people other than their parents for 20 or more hours per week during their first year are at increased risk of having an insecure relationship with their parents at age 1—and at increased risk of being more aggressive and disobedient by age 3 to 8."

Belsky adds several "absolutely necessary caveats": First, the results of all these studies must be viewed in light of the added stress that many families experience when both parents work and of the fact that affordable high-quality day care is not always available. Belsky agrees with some of his academic opponents that the quality of day care matters. His second warning: The results of these studies are generalizations and do not apply to every single child. Third, he says, nobody really knows what causes underlie the findings.

Research on older children who spend at least part of the day on their own is far less controversial, though no less disturbing. A recent study by the American Academy of Pediatrics focused on substance abuse by nearly 5,000 eighth-graders around Los Angeles and San Diego. The sample cut across a wide range of ethnic and economic backgrounds and was split about half and half between boys and girls. The researchers concluded that 12- and 13-year-olds who were latchkey kids, taking care of themselves for 11 or more hours a week, were about twice as likely as supervised children to smoke, drink alcohol, and use marijuana. About 31% of the latchkey kids have two or more drinks at a time; only about 17% of the others do. Asked whether they expected to get drunk in the future, 27% of the latchkey kids and 15% of the others said yes.

Increasingly, isolation from parents is a problem even when the family is physically together. Beginning in infancy, children are highly attuned to their parents' moods. And when parents have little left to give to their offspring at the end of a stressful day, the kids' disappointment can be crushing. Says Eleanor Szanton, executive director of the National Center for Clinical Infant Programs, a nonprofit resource center in Virginia: "What happens between parents and children during the first hour they are reunited is as important as anything that happens all day. If the mother is too exhausted to be a mother, you've got a problem."

When children become adolescents and begin to test their wings by defying their parents' authority, stressed-out families may break down completely because no strong relationship between parents and children has developed over the years. In high-achiever families, says Chicago social worker Alice White, family life can become an ordeal where children must prove their worth to their parents in the limited time available. Conversation can be a series of "didjas"—Didja ace that test, win the election, score the touchdown? What's missing is the easygoing chatter, the long, relaxed conversations that allow parents and children to know each other.

White says that many of today's kids don't understand how the world works because they haven't spent enough time with their parents to understand how decisions are made, careers are pursued, personal relationships are formed. She finds herself spending more and more time acting as a surrogate mother for the seemingly privileged kids she counsels, advising them on everything from sexual issues to recipes for a small dinner party. Says White: "The parents serve as a model of success, but the kids are afraid they won't get there because nobody has shown them how."

JUST ABOUT EVERYONE in the child-development field agrees that all this adds up to a discouraging picture, but opinions vary wildly as to what ought to be done about it—and by whom. For a growing band of conservative social thinkers, the answer is simple: Mothers ought to stay home. These activists, working at private foundations and conservative college faculties, rail against what they see as the permissiveness of recent decades. They save their most lethal venom for organized child care, blaming it for everything from restraining kids' free will to contributing to major outbreaks of untold diseases. One conservative researcher, Bryce Christensen of the Rockford Institute in Illinois, has likened day care to the drug Thalidomide. Day care, he writes, is "a new threat to children that not only imperils the body, but also distorts and withers the spirit."

Gary L. Bauer, president of a conservative Washington research outfit called the Family Research Council, is among the most visible of these social activists. Bauer, a domestic-policy adviser in the Reagan White House, believes strongly that the entry of great numbers of women into the work force has harmed America's children. He says the importance of bonding between a mother and her children became clear to him and his wife one morning several years ago when they were dropping their 2-year-old daughter at a babysitter's home. The child went immediately to the sitter, calling her "Mommy." That was something of an epiphany for Bauer's wife, Carol: She quit her job as a government employment counselor soon after and has since stayed home to raise the couple's three children.

Still, the dual-career trend continues. No

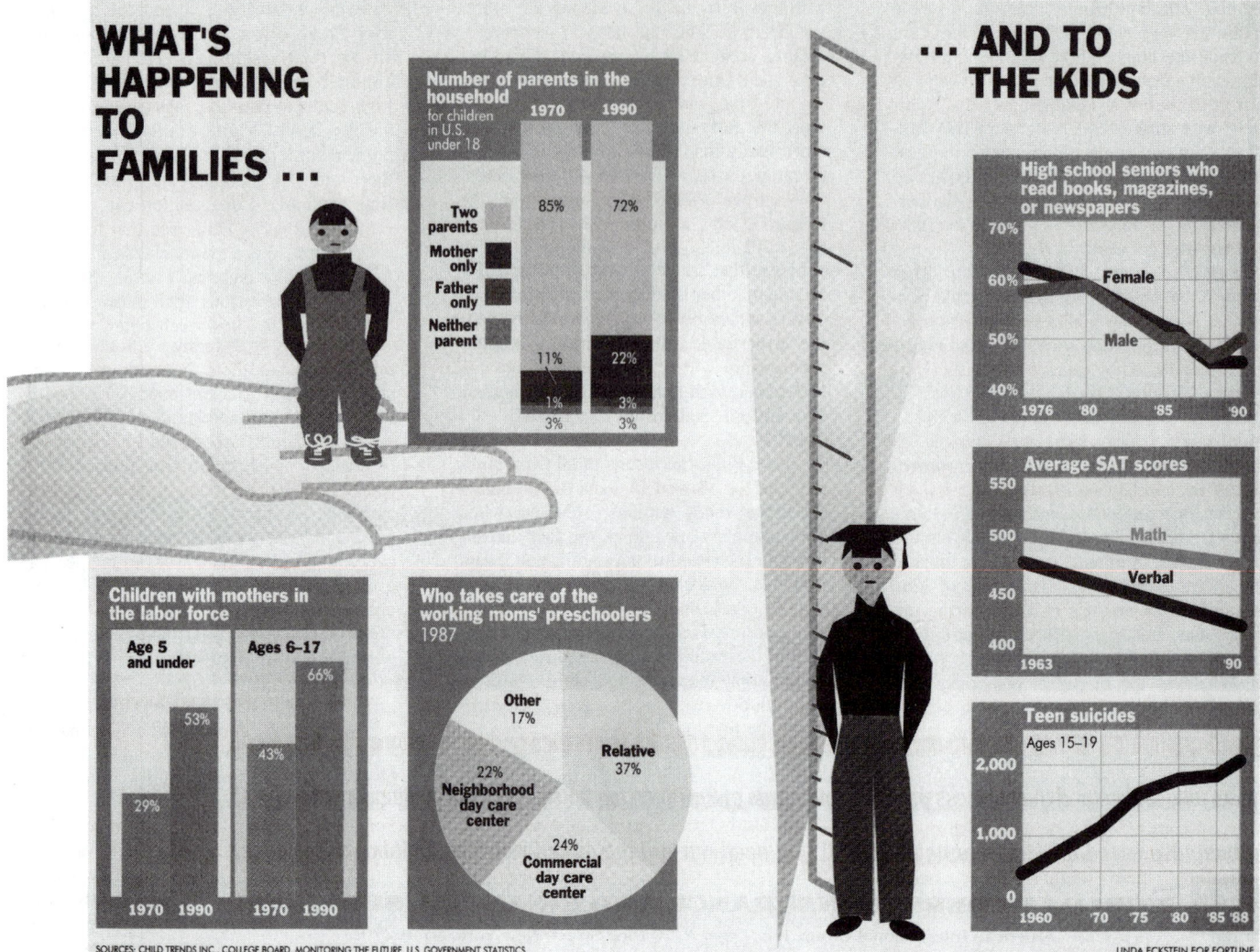

WHAT'S HAPPENING TO FAMILIES ...

... AND TO THE KIDS

Number of parents in the household
for children in U.S. under 18

	1970	1990
Two parents	85%	72%
Mother only	11%	22%
Father only	1%	3%
Neither parent	3%	3%

Children with mothers in the labor force

Age 5 and under: 1970 — 29%, 1990 — 53%
Ages 6–17: 1970 — 43%, 1990 — 66%

Who takes care of the working moms' preschoolers
1987

- Other 17%
- Relative 37%
- Neighborhood day care center 22%
- Commercial day care center 24%

High school seniors who read books, magazines, or newspapers
Female, Male — 1976, '80, '85, '90

Average SAT scores
Math, Verbal — 1963, '90

Teen suicides
Ages 15–19 — 1960, '70, '75, '80, '85, '88

SOURCES: CHILD TRENDS INC., COLLEGE BOARD, MONITORING THE FUTURE, U.S. GOVERNMENT STATISTICS

LINDA ECKSTEIN FOR FORTUNE

wonder. Most American families could not afford to forfeit a second income, a fact that renders the conservatives' yearning for a simpler past quixotic at best. Real weekly earnings for workers declined 13% from 1973 to 1990. So in most cases two paychecks are a necessity. Also, about a quarter of American children—and about half of black children—live in single-parent homes. Those parents are nearly all women. Though some receive child support or other income, their wages are usually their financial lifeblood. About half the mothers who have been awarded child support by the courts do not get full payments regularly.

From the standpoint of the national economy, a mass exodus of women from the work force would be a disaster: There simply won't be enough available males in the future. Women now make up over 45% of the labor force, and they are expected to fill about 60% of new jobs between now and the year 2000.

EVEN IF a child's welfare were the only consideration, in many cases full-time motherhood might not be the best answer. Children whose mothers are frustrated and angry about staying home might be better off in a high-quality day care center. And many kids may well benefit from the socializing and group activities available in day care. A mother and child alone together all day isn't necessarily a rich environment for the child.

In the end, the short supply of high-quality day care is the greatest obstacle to better prospects for America's children. Experts agree on what constitutes quality in child care—a well-paid and well-trained staff, a high staff-child ratio, a safe and suitable physical environment. They also generally concur that if those criteria are met, most children will not just muddle through but prosper. Says Barbara Reisman, executive director of the Child Care Action Campaign, a nonprofit educational and advocacy organization in New York: "Despite all the questions that have been raised, the bottom line is that if the quality is there, and the parents are comfortable with the situation, the kids are going to be fine."

But even tracking, much less improving, child care quality is a monumental task. Something like 60% of the approximately 11 million preschool kids whose mothers work are taken care of in private homes. That can be a wonderful experience: Grandma or a warm-hearted neighbor spends the day with the wee ones baking cookies and imparting folk wisdom. Or it can be hellish. Yale's Edward Zigler speaks in horror of the home where 54 kids in the care of a 16-year-old were found strapped into car seats all day. Low pay and the lack of status associated with organized day care centers make it tough to recruit and retain qualified workers. A study by a research group called the Child Care Employee Project in Oakland revealed an alarming 41% annual turnover rate at day care operations across the U.S. One big reason: an average hourly salary of $5.35. Says Zigler: "We pay these people less than we do zoo keepers—and then we expect them to do wonders."

The experts have floated various schemes to make more money available. The Bush Administration has offered $732 million in block grants to the states for child care and has also proposed increasing the modest tax credits (current maximum: $1,440) for lower-income parents using most kinds of day care. Another current idea: increase the personal exemption. If it had kept pace with inflation since 1950, it would be about $7,000 instead of $2,050. Zigler has proposed that couples be allowed to dip into their Social Security accounts for a short while when their children are young. Under his plan families would be limited to tapping the accounts for up to three years per child, and their retirement benefits would be reduced or delayed proportionately. Zigler would also limit the amount of money withdrawn to some reasonable maximum.

Under all these proposals, parents—especially women—could more easily afford to pay for high-quality day care, scale back their work hours, or even stay at home longer with a newborn if they wished. A 1989 Cornell University study found that about two-thirds of mothers who work full time would cut their hours if they didn't need the extra income. In other surveys, even greater percentages of working mothers with infants say they would reduce their hours or stay home if money were no problem.

In his recent book, *Child Care Choices*, Zigler presents some innovative notions about improving care for older children. He would start organized classes in the public school system beginning at age 3, and keep schools open in the afternoon and early evening for the use of kids with working parents. School libraries, gyms, music rooms, and art rooms would be available. Says Zigler: "All you need is a traffic cop." The city of Los Angeles and the entire state of Hawaii have begun after-school programs along these lines.

BUSINESS has a crucial role to play in helping employees who are parents cope with their responsibilities. The U.S. Congress is currently considering legislation that would guarantee 12 weeks of unpaid leave in the event of a family illness or the birth of a child. According to a study conducted by economics professors at Cornell University and the University of Connecticut, the costs of allowing such leaves for most workers is less than letting them quit and hiring permanent replacements. Companies can provide big-time relief with smaller gestures as well: making a telephone available to assembly-line workers so they can check up on their latchkey kids, say, or letting office workers slip out for a parent-teacher conference without a hassle.

As the competition for good workers heats up, many companies will be forced to grapple with the problems working parents face, or risk losing desirable employees. Says Douglas Besharov, a resident scholar at the American Enterprise Institute in Washington: "If you need workers, you will do what has to be done."

Many corporations have already taken the plunge. IBM, among other companies, offers employees a free child-care referral service; IBM uses 250 different organizations. The company has also pledged $22 million over five years to improve the quality of day care available in the towns and cities where most of its employees live. Johnson & Johnson provides an array of goodies: one-year unpaid family care leaves, an extensive referral network, dependent care reimbursement accounts so that employees can pay child care expenses with pretax dollars, and up to $2,000 toward the cost of adoption.

J&J also supports an on-site day care center at its headquarters in New Brunswick, New Jersey. The company subsidizes part of the cost, but employees using the center still pay $110 to $130 a week depending on the age of the child. Depending on the region, average charges for a preschooler range from $67 to $115 a week. Infant care can cost up to $230 a week, and the affluent few with a full-time nanny pay $200 to $600.

Some smaller companies are paying attention as well. American Bankers Insurance Group, based in Miami, maintains a day care center for employees' children ages 6 weeks to 5 years. After that the child can attend a company-run private school for an additional three years. The school takes care of the child from 8 A.M. to 6:15 P.M. and keeps its doors open during school holidays and summer vacations.

The child care business is growing rapidly. Approximately 77,000 licensed child care centers now serve about four million children daily. Financially troubled Kinder-Care Learning Centers of Montgomery, Alabama, is the industry giant, with 1,257 centers around the country and revenues of $396 million a year. The runner-up is a Kansas City, Missouri, outfit called La Petite Academy Inc. It operates about 750 centers and did $201 million worth of business in 1990.

ServiceMaster, the widely diversified management company based near Chicago, jumped into the field last year and now runs three centers in suburban office parks, with four more under construction. The beauty part of the business is that ServiceMaster typically gets some form of financial help from a landlord or corporate client—reduced rent or lower occupancy costs—and then charges market rates for its services.

Parents working at companies such as Sears, Abbott Laboratories, Ameritech, and Mobil pay about $140 to $150 a week for infants and about $95 a week for 3- to 5-year-olds. ServiceMaster executives consider this a business with splendid growth prospects: They plan to open another half-dozen centers by the end of 1991 and then begin expanding beyond the Chicago area.

Child-development experts admire a relatively new and growing company, Bright Horizons Children's Centers of Cambridge,

Massachusetts, for the innovative on-site day care it provides for major corporations including IBM, Prudential, and Dun & Bradstreet. Founded in 1986 by Linda Mason and her husband, Roger Brown, both former economic development workers in Africa, Bright Horizons now operates 38 centers up and down the East Coast. In most cases the corporate client donates space for child care in or near its office building, providing Bright Horizons with a handsome cost advantage. Fees can be steep—up to $225 per week for infants—but companies often subsidize the payments for employees low on the wage scale.

Because the centers are close to the workplace, parents are encouraged to drop in throughout the day. Bright Horizons' teaching staff members earn up to $20,000 per year, far more than most day care centers pay, plus a full benefits package. They can pursue a defined career track and move into management ranks if they qualify. As a result, turnover runs at a relatively low 16% to 24%.

Brown and Mason concede that many children might be damaged by second-rate child care, but they contend that parents rarely have anything to fear from the kind of high-quality attention their centers provide. Says Mason: "It's very much like health care. If you can afford to pay for it, you can receive the best child care in the world in this country."

For business, helping employees find their way through the child care thicket makes increasing sense—and not only as a method of keeping today's work force happy. More and more companies with an eye on the future recognize the importance of early childhood development, and many are alarmed by the discouraging signals they see in the upcoming generation of workers. At BellSouth in Atlanta, for instance, only about one job applicant in ten passes a battery of exams that test learning ability; ten years ago, twice as many did. Even those who make it through the tests often require extensive training and carry heavy personal baggage: A startling 70% of BellSouth's unmarried employees support at least one child.

More companies are finding that they have to help employees cope not just with their children but also with the gamut of life's vicissitudes. Says Roy Howard, BellSouth's senior vice president for corporate human resources: "Business used to feel that you ought to leave your personal problems at home. We can no longer afford to take that view." The psychic welfare of workers—and of their children—is increasingly a legitimate management concern, and companies that ignore it risk their employees' future as well as their own.

LIFE WITHOUT FATHER

AS MORE AND MORE AMERICAN MEN DISCONNECT FROM FAMILY LIFE, SOCIETY SUFFERS THE CONSEQUENCES

Nina J. Easton

Staff writer Nina J. Easton's last story for this magazine was on the career frustrations of college graduates.

There's a warrant out for David Bell's arrest. A fitting tribute to the ineptitude of the nation's child-support system, the warrant will sit for eight weeks on a desk at the Glendale Police Department. A judge issued it after Bell pulled a no-show at a court hearing concerning $1,500 he owes for the care of his 9-year-old son.

It's not as if Bell is hard to find. Hours after the warrant comes down, he answers the telephone at the office of his small phone-installation company in Pasadena. And during the next two months he'll continue going to work, going home, going about his daily routine until the police plow through an inches-thick pile of warrants for armed robbers and drug dealers and embezzlers to reach the paperwork on David Bell, errant father.

I talk to Bell the same day the judge orders his arrest. The story he tells about his child-support payments sounds well-rehearsed. He says he has been sending checks to the county-appointed trustee, who must have lost them. He even reads me the address and recounts the runaround he gets each time he calls to find out what happened to the money. (A deposition signed by the deputy district attorney assigned to the case tells a different story.) I've heard explanations like this from other men who fall behind in child support, and by now economists are familiar with the consequences: It's one reason that one in three households headed by women live below the poverty line.

But, by themselves, these stories don't capture the full picture of fatherless families. I'm more curious about something else. I've met Bell's son—let's call him Jason. The kid is irresistible. He inherited his mom's dimples and his dad's dirty-blond hair. He displays that combination of innocent candor and unbridled enthusiasm that makes young boys so endearing. Lori Thompson, an office administrator who looks much younger than her 30 years, has been more than willing to let Bell be a part of her son's life. Jason lives a 15-minute drive away from his dad, yet rarely sees him. Why?

That's a question Bell isn't prepared for. "I don't know, it's difficult," he starts. Then he tries to explain. "Because of the money. Every time I want to see my son, we have to discuss money," he says, referring to his ex-wife. "These things are always hanging over my head. It's hard to be part of someone's life like that."

Last year, guilt pangs nudged Bell back into his son's life after a six-year absence. There were the visits to Little League games, the afternoons at the movies, the weekend of water-skiing in Arizona. Then came the broken promises: the science-fair project never built together, the Fast Traks set that arrived a week too late for Christmas, and the time Bell promised a night out bowling—and even called to say he was on his way. Jason ran to the window every time he heard a car. His dad never showed.

"That's true," Bells responds when I ask him about the bowling incident. "Things happen. It usually revolves around money. Lori will want this or that. . . ."

"It's difficult," he repeats.

Like a mantra come these vague feelings from absent fathers all across the country: *"I don't know." "Things happen." "It's difficult."*

The failure of men like David Bell to help support their children has moved toward the center of the national debate about poverty and gender equality. Feminist and child-advocate groups call for more generous support awards and stricter enforcement. Local district attorneys organize "deadbeat dad" roundups, knowing they'll get a free hit of favorable publicity. Reporters recount story after story about women thrown into poverty—and onto taxpayer-financed welfare rolls—because fathers refuse to make their support payments. Child support has even become a high-profile issue in the presidential campaign, with Bill Clinton proposing to use the IRS to crack down on non-paying fathers.

But Bell's delinquent checks are only one part of the equation. A growing body of research says that society should be equally worried about the emotional void left in the lives of children like Jason when their fathers check out. "There is this clichéd image out there of the deadbeat dad," says David Blankenhorn, president of the Institute for American Values, a New York think tank that studies family issues. "And there are equally clichéd solutions. The story we tell ourselves is a curiously old-fashioned story, that fatherhood equals economic support. But fatherhood is more than sending checks. And the consequences of fatherlessness are deep and profound and long-lasting."

Researchers now are attempting to measure the full range of those consequences. Consider two of our nation's most serious problems—crime and teen-age pregnancy. Studies show that the most reliable predictor of these behaviors is not income. Nor race. It is family structure: Pregnant girls and criminal boys tend to come from fatherless families. An astonishing 70% of imprisoned U.S. minors have spent at least part of their lives without fathers. Gangs feed on fatherless sons. Father Greg Boyle of Dolores Mission Church in East Los Angeles once listed the names of the first 100 gang members that came to mind and then jotted a family history next to each. All but five were no longer living with their biological fathers—if they ever had.

As the smoke clears after the riots in Los Angeles, debates over urban problems are once again in vogue—with Great Society-style liberals calling for more government aid and Reagan-era conservatives blaming the nation's welfare programs for creating a "culture of dependency." Both sides of that debate may miss the point. "People who do not talk about the family are waltzing themselves down a tried-and-true path of nothing getting better," says Elaine Ciulla Kamarck, a senior fellow at Washington's Progressive Policy Institute who has written about family issues. "Really random and serious violence—that's what's correlated to fatherless families."

The White House attempted to make that point after the riots, but botched it by sending out exactly the wrong messenger. Vice President Dan Quayle's attack on sitcom character Murphy Brown for "mocking the importance of fathers by bearing a child alone" was construed as a condemnation of struggling single mothers. Afterward, President Bush ran for political cover, while much of the media played the remark as another in a long line of Quayle gaffes.

We meticulously talk in gender-neutral terms about "single-parent households" and "parenthood." But discussion about the particular importance of fathers is rare. In this feminist age, Blankenhorn contends, there's an assumption that women can do just fine by themselves, thank you. They survive as independent women, as single mothers (Murphy Brown was not the

'HERE'S MY KID. I CREATED HIM. BUT THE MONEY I'M GOING TO SPEND ON HIM I COULD HAVE SPENT ON A LAMBORGHINI.'

first prime-time woman to have a baby on her own) and even as welfare recipients (such social critics as Barbara Ehrenreich have argued that it's perfectly rational for poor women to find welfare checks more reliable and less troublesome than men). Even the nation's social-services system focuses its financial and counseling assistance on mothers—often to the exclusion of fathers, critics contend.

But many researchers now single out fathers as providing a form of child-rearing distinct from that of mothers—and just as essential to a child's development. Whether they are roughhousing with a 5-year-old or scaring the bejesus out of a delinquent teen, fathers bring a different style to parenting, says Kyle Pruett, psychiatry professor at the Yale Child Study Center and author of "The Nurturing Father."

Social thinkers across the political spectrum are beginning to emphasize the role of fathers in building safe communities. Conservative sociologist James Q. Wilson contends that while "neighborhood standards [are] set by mothers, they are enforced by fathers. . . . The absence of fathers deprives the community of those little platoons that effectively control boys on the street." Likewise, New Jersey legislator Wayne R. Bryant, a liberal African-American, describes the difference between the boy who throws a bottle on the ground in a stable suburb and one who does the same in an almost-fatherless housing project. The first boy picks it up when challenged by the man next door; the second responds to a female neighbor's request with a menacing "Don't you tell me what to do." Without men around as role models, adolescent boys create their own rites of passage: perhaps getting a girl pregnant or dealing drugs or murdering a rival.

Throughout history, men have been torn from their families by war, disease and death. But in '90s America, men are choosing to disconnect from family life on a massive scale, and at far higher rates than other industrialized countries. "Men are drifting away from family life," says Blankenhorn. "We are in danger of becoming a fatherless society."

That is especially true in minority communities, where poverty rates are the highest. In nearly two-thirds of black households and in one-third of Latino households, only one parent—usually the mother—is present. Divorce rates, though still high, have reached a plateau. The most important factor behind the increase in fatherless households is the seemingly unstoppable rise in out-of-wedlock births. In 1989, a startling 66% of black children and 36% of Latino children were born to unwed parents.

But fathers are harder to find in white suburbia as well. Nearly a quarter of white homes are headed by one parent, and the percentage of white children born to unwed parents has nearly doubled over the last decade, to almost 20%—a much faster growth rate than that found in black communities. Lest white America become too complacent: Blankenhorn has crunched Census Bureau figures to show that white families now experience breakups at the same pace as black families did in 1965, when President Johnson called "the breakdown of the Negro family structure" one of the most pressing issues of the era.

All across America tonight, one-third of the nation's children will go to bed without their biological fathers in the next room. And most of them won't see their fathers the next day, either. According to studies by Frank F. Furstenberg Jr., a University of Pennsylvania sociologist, about 40% of the children who live in fatherless households haven't seen their fathers in at least a year; for many others, contact is sporadic. In any month, only one in five of these children sleeps even one night in their father's home. "It's a minority of [absent] fathers that have at least once-a-week contact," says Furstenberg.

Researchers are quick to note that plenty of single mothers raise well-adjusted children, and that children are better off not living with emotionally or physically abusive fathers. But, they add, the odds are stacked against fatherless children—particularly those who live in poverty. Children with fathers tend to do better in school, are less prone to depression and are more successful in relationships. "It shows up on cognitive achievement, on social achievement, everywhere," says San Diego psychiatrist Martin Greenberg, author of "The Birth of a Father." Greenberg describes the fatherless young criminals he counsels as brimming with rage over being "abandoned." And fatherless girls, Greenberg and other researchers note, often experience low self-esteem and rocky romantic relationships as they search for the ideal father substitute. Most of the time, stepfathers can't begin to fill the void.

That vulnerability is evident in the comments of Lori Thompson and mothers like her, who worry about the periods of depression they see in their children. Ask the normally buoyant Jason about his father, and his mood darkens. Little-boy fingers drop to his lap and tug at each other fitfully. A tiny tear surfaces,

> ALL ACROSS AMERICA TONIGHT, ONE-THIRD OF THE NATION'S CHILDREN WILL GO TO BED WITHOUT THEIR FATHERS IN THE NEXT ROOM.

and he swats away the unwelcome drop. "He's OK," Jason says. Then comes a halting, deep breath. "I don't know when he's telling the truth or when he's actually going to show up."

Another mother, an aspiring producer abandoned by her boyfriend, says that no matter how much she tries to bolster her 9-year-old son, his self-esteem remains fragile. Outwardly, he appears to be a cheerful, well-adjusted child thoroughly at ease in the company of adults. But his mother confesses that he has frightened her with talk about wanting to kill himself. "Issues of potential loss affect him deeply," she says. "I've been dating a guy for one week, and he already wants me to marry him and make him his daddy."

Even before the L.A. riots, a handful of national leaders were beginning to talk about the toll that fatherless homes take on children and society. Health and Human Services Secretary Louis W. Sullivan says that when he came into office and examined the department's programs, it dawned on him that the social welfare system is primarily designed to compensate for family disruption. "The net result is not as good as having an intact family," he says.

Now Sullivan is selling his message of "male responsibility" around the country. "Most of our national dialogue on family issues . . . has focused exclusively on the mother," he says. "However, it is not women who are abandoning or neglecting their children."

Democratic contender Clinton has woven a similar message into his oft-repeated theme of personal responsibility. During a March 29 debate in New York, he presented this prescription for the woes of the urban poor: "You've got to emphasize requirements for responsible behavior in return for [government] benefits. You've got to change the internal culture. You have to change the ways these families operate by going in and teaching the parents."

All this talk of family values is a political hot button. Witness the firestorm that erupted last month over Quayle's comments. Much of the political Establishment continues to shrink from the debate over "values" (the term *out of wedlock*, for example, is politically incorrect in many circles because it smacks of judging others' lifestyles). But even some liberals are becoming convinced that child support is only one part of a cultural agenda that should address such concerns as fleeing fathers and out-of-wedlock births.

Conservatives traditionally are more comfortable talking about values. But they have their own Achilles' heel: How can you ask fathers to be fathers without providing the training and jobs to enable them to become breadwinners? Or without footing the bill for the added cost of paying welfare to men—as well as women and children—in the home?

Since 1973, real earnings of men between 25 and 29 have declined more than 20%, leading some researchers to conclude that men flee family life—or are pushed out by women—because they are not reliable breadwinners. Sullivan says he sees a role for government funding of both parenting programs and job training, but stops short of saying that government should be responsible for generating better-paying jobs. The Administration's post-riot urban aid plan allocates $683 million to job training, but critics say the problem requires a bolder and more comprehensive approach.

Neither political party seems capable of untangling the Gordian knot of poverty and crime. If they looked beyond their ideological blinders, the nation's leaders might see that two strings of that knot are a creaky child-support system and a social culture that encourages fathers to flee. Values and economics, inextricably wound together.

To get the full picture of what policymakers are up against, it's instructive to visit the offices of family-law attorneys like Jeffrey Marckese, where fathers come to fight paternity battles, resist child support and, on this spring afternoon, offer their thoughts about fatherhood.

Mark looks like a guy who belongs on the living room couch, Budweiser in hand, watching the NBA playoffs. (Although Mark is only 22, the Buds appear to have a head start on his waistline.) But today, the young man, who works as a messenger, has agreed to sit on his lawyer's couch and talk about a topic that, he says, only occasionally crosses his mind—his young son. "I think he's 3. . . . He was born in December, '88."

Mark started having sex when he was 16. His luck, he says, ran out when he was 19 and he got his girlfriend pregnant. She wanted to have the baby. He wasn't so sure, but he stuck by her until she was a month away from delivery. Then they had a fight, and he split. When his son was about 6 months old, Mark returned for some quality time.

"It was overwhelming. I picked up this baby and thought, 'Here's my kid. I created him. But you know what?' " he asks, dead serious. " 'The money I'm going to spend on him I could have spent on a Lamborghini.' "

On that note, a deep-throated chuckle builds inside

Marckese's Wilshire-corridor office. It spreads from Mark in the middle of the couch to Ben "The Procreator" on his right (Marckese invented the nickname—Ben has seven children by four women), to the gray-bearded James on his left, who has seen his 12-year-old daughter only once. They laugh with knowing abandon, these three men who were strangers until only a few minutes before. Then they catch themselves—there's a female reporter present. They throw sheepish looks my way, and the laughter subsides.

The experts have their own terminology for Mark's way of thinking. Blankenhorn of the Institute for American Values calls it "expressive individualism," our culture's overweening emphasis on personal fulfillment and freedom at the expense of commitment to family and community. This "me-firstism," he argues, dovetails with today's tendency to discount the role of fathers, to turn them into superfluous check-writers.

The caseworkers at the county district attorney's office on the front lines of the child-support battle know what Blankenhorn is talking about. They spend their days tracking down errant fathers, garnishing their wages and, on occasion, putting them in jail—all in an effort to force compliance with court orders issued at the time of a divorce or when an unwed mother establishes paternity. They also hear some stories that make Mark look like Cliff Huxtable.

There was, for example, the father who said he couldn't pay his child support because he needed the money to board his two pure-bred Doberman pinschers. Another was furious because prosecutors seized his Rolls-Royce to partly cover $200,000 in back child and spousal support. (There was also the man who claimed he was no longer the father because he had had a sex-change operation, but that's a different story.)

Mothers know what Blankenhorn is talking about, too. But they look at it a different way. I interviewed several mothers of fatherless children who believe that these men relish the image of fatherhood but not the reality, not the chaos and clutter of child-rearing—particularly when it impinges on their careers or lifestyles. In other words, men are spoiled and irresponsible. "This man was not cut out to be a parent," says a woman whose attorney husband of 15 years left behind three kids, only to see them at restaurant outings with his girlfriend. "He couldn't cope with the noise. His career was the most important thing in his life."

Furstenberg of the University of Pennsylvania and Judith Wallerstein, author of several books on divorce, are more generous toward absent fathers. They note that men regard marriage and relationships as "a kind of package deal," as Furstenberg puts it. Divorcing the wife means divorcing the children. Moreover, most men move on to invest their emotions and money in another marriage or relationship, so there's not much left over. "It's hard when they also want to close the door on that first marriage," says Wallerstein.

But as I sit listening in Marckese's office, none of these explanations seems to fully explain Mark's self-imposed exile. Then I remember the words of my friend Beth, whose son has never seen his father. "You want to hear my theory?" she asked one day over lunch. "Once you break up, once you divorce, men have lost control of the situation, so they don't want any part of it at all."

As Mark and the others tell their stories, the issue of

control comes up again and again, though none of them use that word. Each wants control over how his child-support checks are spent. "Can't they make her show receipts?" asks Mark. (In fact, challenging his ex's spending habits would require that Mark actually see his child. Then he could argue before a judge that his son is not being adequately cared for.)

These three men also want control over the upbringing of their children—even as they insist that they are not the fathers. Like the others, Mark still won't believe the blood test that showed a 99.91% probability of his paternity. But when Marckese refuses to indulge Mark's doubts, his client suddenly changes his tune. If he is the biological father, Mark says, he intends to "go after the kid" in a custody battle.

"Huh?" I ask, startled, though half-remembering that Beth's ex-boyfriend fought paternity and demanded custody at the same time.

"Is this for revenge?" Marckese asks his client.

"Partly." Pause. "She owes me an immense amount of time with this child [because of the payments]. And I think I could do a much better job as a parent. She's collecting welfare, she comes from a welfare family. . . . Either way, I have to pay for the kid. The Lamborghini is gone. It's already down the freeway."

James tells a more complicated story. Like Mark, he initially wanted nothing to do with being a father. And some part of him still doesn't want to believe he is one. "You ever read a blood test? It's an algebraic nightmare," he says, handing me the results. Maybe so, but one line is pretty clear. It states that the statistical probability of his fathering the child is 99.91%.

James, who declines to give his age but appears to be in his late 40s, was seeing a woman in Los Angeles, got her pregnant ("She insisted she was safe," he says) but wasn't interested in becoming a parent. "I didn't want responsibility, any kids or family," he says. When I press him, James makes veiled reference to a troubled upbringing and adds, "Family life scared me."

After James' daughter was born 12 years ago, his girlfriend moved to Florida, where her family could help support her. Since then, James has seen his child once, when she and her mother came here on a vacation and he took her to the beach to fly kites. James, unemployed and vague about his work history, insists he hasn't visited the child because he couldn't afford the air fare. Why not pick up the phone? At that, he starts to say he didn't know where they were living. He finally admits, "I didn't have an interest in seeing the kid."

Now, however, James says, his spiritual life has changed; he recently turned to Christianity. He's older and more mature. And he's ready to be a father to his child. But he's worried about how she will react to a father who initially denied paternity. "That's a deep cut," James says. "This is the guy who denied you in court."

As he turns toward me, the look in his eyes is distinctly out of place amid the male ribaldry and banter: James is terrified. "Let me ask you something," he says to me, a stranger. "What do you think I should say now? How should I say it?"

From Homer on, there have been those who contend that fatherhood, unlike motherhood, is a learned role, not a natural one. If that's true, it could explain why so many absent fathers feel awkward in their relationships with their children, and avoid them rather than learn to cope. An absent father's "repertoire of skills to directly relate to the child is limited," says Furstenberg. "Fathers play at most a co-pilot role even during the marriage. So after the marriage, that is not an easy relationship."

It is especially hard for men like James, who were never married to the mother and never experienced being a parent. What do you do with a 3-year-old on visiting day? How do you discipline when you're not part of a child's daily life? How do you react when a teen-ager won't talk to you? And, for James, how do you ask a child's forgiveness? "To be a visiting parent is hell," says Wallerstein, who teaches many of her clients "visiting skills." "You're damned if you do and damned if you don't."

And mothers—who are typically hostile to their ex-husbands and boyfriends—cannot be counted on to smooth the way. Many mothers openly admit to sharing their hostility with the children. How can an absent father compete with that? Even mothers with more balanced attitudes aren't likely to help an absent father develop or renew a close relationship with his child. One mother has watched the father of her little girl, now 5, come by the house every six weeks to take the child out to dinner, even when she was a toddler. Wouldn't it be more appropriate for him to play with her at the park or his house? "I used to make those kinds of suggestions," responds the mother, a child-development specialist. Now she feels it would be more honest to allow the child to see her real father, without trying to make him appear any better—or worse—than he is.

Ben, our father of seven, loves children and bristles at the label "absent father." He has a 13-year-old daughter and an 11-year-old son from his only marriage. He also has two 7-year-olds (by different women), a 5-year-old, a 4-year-old and, now, an infant of 4 months. He pays regular child support to his first six children and hired Marckese because he refused to pay support on his seventh child until blood tests proved he was the father.

He considers himself a good dad to this brood and is puzzled by my assertion that he seems to take procreation casually. "I don't know what you mean by that," he says, indignant that a role he takes so seriously could be questioned.

Ben's attitude is not so surprising. Out-of-wedlock births, particularly in some minority communities, have become so common that many unwed young people don't give a second thought to having children. Much has been written about the reasons teen-age girls and young women have children without the emotional and financial commitment of marriage: peer pressure, the need for love, the apparent absence of other alternatives. Only recently has attention begun to focus on unwed fathers, with such influential commentators as William Julius Wilson, author of "The Truly Disadvantaged," citing joblessness and low pay as one reason many men don't marry, and others placing more emphasis on a society-wide breakdown in values.

For Ben, a machinist who shells out $1,000 a month in child support, money is not the issue. He explains his burgeoning family as the logical consequence of playing the field. The art of contraception is obviously no secret to this 34-year-old man. But he laughingly talks of how the mind shuts down "and other things take over" in the heat of romance.

He refuses to call any of his children accidents, nor does he blame the mothers for getting pregnant. But at one point he complains that women "set you up. They know the type of person you are, and they know I'm a good dad and I make money."

Has he ever considered marrying the mother of one of these children? Not since his divorce more than a decade ago, he says. "I play around. I play around a lot. But my kids always come first anyways."

Ben's attitude toward marriage and fatherhood may have something to do with his own fatherless childhood. But it may also reflect his definitions of manhood. During our session in Marckese's office, Ben is so stunned by James' spiritually guided decision to forgo premarital sex that he comes back to the issue again and again. At one point, Ben even wonders if the older man has trouble relating to his daughter because he isn't having sex.

It's not hard today to find men much younger than Ben who want to become fathers, children making children, even if they have no intention of staying with the mother, nor any means of supporting their children. That was apparent when I interviewed four East L.A. gang members, all unwed fathers, all under 19. I asked each of them why they had fathered children. And, to a man, they said they did it because they wanted to; they weren't coerced or tricked or pressured. I gave them every out I could think of: "No contraceptives around?" "Maybe your girlfriend pressured you?" They wouldn't budge.

George, 18, recently out of a juvenile facility, was inspired by the sight of another homeboy playing with his kids in the park. Afterward, though, reality set in. Of his second child that was on the way, he mumbled, "More trouble, more trouble." Titi, head shaved and body covered with tattoos, described the joy of hanging out on the corner with homies until late at night, his infant in his arms. Curly, an 18-year-old with a warm and open face, insisted that he will always be there for his 2-year-old son, even though his girlfriend was now with someone else.

Researchers have concluded that having children has become a sign of manhood in commu-

nities where there are no role models left to point to other ways. The scent of death among these gang members—Father Boyle insists that most of them don't expect to live past age 25—probably accelerates that process. Once they have children, these young men aren't exactly considered prize catches as husbands: Without high-school diplomas, their economic prospects are bleak. And, so far, their girlfriends have managed to survive on their own and support their children by collecting welfare benefits.

But there's also the breakdown of traditional values to consider. In many communities, fathering children without assuming full responsibility for their care has become commonplace, and often spans two or three generations within one family. Researchers say that men like George and Titi no longer face social rebuke for their actions. Even the economic-minded William Julius Wilson raises concerns about "weaker social strictures against out-of-wedlock births."

Often, the parents of both these gang members and their girlfriends even condone the baby-making, hoping—as one gang member put it—that fatherhood will force them to "straighten out." Oddly enough, those having the babies tend to be the "good girls"—not those with loose reputations. "It's no accident who these [young men] pick to have their children," says Father Boyle.

So Ben is not the bleakest side of the statistics. He may contest paternity, but once he is proved the father, he will pay his child support. And every weekend, he says, he brings all his children to his house (though he concedes that his girlfriend is the primary babysitter during these stays).

What is more worrisome to society are the fathers who don't stick around long enough to see their kids out of the hospital, let alone off to kindergarten. "There's a certain lawlessness that runs through these unmarried relationships. There's no code of conduct," says Betty Nordwind, director of L.A.'s Harriett Buhai Center for Family Law. Nordwind, who helps clients collect child support from fathers, blames the rising out-of-wedlock birthrate for her mounting frustrations on the job.

"You ask, 'Where are the men?' " she says. "From what I can see, they're onto the next relationship, they've rolled into the next bed."

Government cannot force men to be good fathers. California's Supreme Court stated as much in 1981, when it ruled against a mother who wanted to force the father of her infant daughter to visit. But that is not stopping social engineers around the country from using government money and public policy in their efforts to revive fatherhood.

On secluded church grounds in the heart of San Antonio, low-income Latino men gather for a retreat, participating in traditional American Indian ceremonies and taking vows of nonviolence and responsible fatherhood. These "rites of manhood" are a central component of the fatherhood program at Avance (Get Ahead), a government- and corporate-funded parenting school aimed at San Antonio's barrio, where role models are in short supply.

Avance founder Gloria Rodriquez originally taught only women. But she quickly sensed that their newfound skills and confidence threatened their husbands and boyfriends. Rather than risk breaking up families, Avance opened its doors to men, who attend regular classes on child development and parenting techniques.

Program Supervisor Isaac Cardenas concedes that some men—forced into the classes by the courts—drop out or refuse to change their ways. But he prefers to dwell on the success stories like George Gomez, whose drinking and violence nearly caused his family's break-up. Two years after he was arrested for beating his wife and neglecting his children, this 25-year-old sign maker's preferred topic of conversation is his strategy for potty-training his toddler. "Everyone is surprised how much I've changed," he says.

Inside New Jersey's state Capitol building in Trenton, a no-nonsense Democratic legislator has pushed through a plan to reform the state's welfare system by promoting family unity. In Wayne Bryant's opinion, it's sheer lunacy to think that the nation's largest welfare program—created 57 years ago to support widowed women and their children—would work in the modern world.

Aid to Families With Dependent Children has taught three or four generations of men that "if you want your children to do well, you've got to leave," says Bryant. He is referring to AFDC rules that prevent a woman from receiving full benefits if the father at home has an employment record or works more than 100 hours a month. Although research is spotty, many policy-makers agree with Bryant's contention that AFDC's conditions discourage family formation.

Signed into law along with his more controversial proposal to withhold extra benefits if a woman has additional children once she's on welfare, Bryant's legislation eliminates the bias against households with fathers. Wisconsin has adopted similar reforms that would increase benefits to women who marry, provided they and their husbands attend job training and parenting classes.

In Portland, Ore., Memphis, Tenn., and eight other American cities, 3,000 low-income men are beginning to stream into job-training and peer-support sessions designed to lure them back to their families as breadwinners. This is the experimental Parents' Fair Share demonstration program, run by New York's nonprofit Manpower Demonstration Research Corp. and funded with state, federal and corporate money.

These men have plenty of excuses for abandoning their families or failing to pay child support. A few told MDRC researchers that their ex-partners didn't want them around because they were broke. "If you don't got money, they don't want to deal with you," said one man. Some complained that their girlfriends wasted their money on drugs. Others said they had been replaced by a new boyfriend. Yet during focus groups, these same men displayed flashes of strong emotion about the meaning of fatherhood, about "doin' right," and how "a dog can make a baby, but a man can take care of it." As part of the lesson plan, the fathers are being asked to write obituaries for themselves—as their children would write them.

The most serious obstacle between these men and their families was a lack of stable employment at livable wages, the program designers concluded. Many fathers couldn't find jobs, while others were working two marginal jobs and still felt they couldn't afford child support. Even the criminals, one researcher noted, didn't seem to be making much money. So the program's founders decided to target their efforts at job training. "Contrary to popular impressions, a lot of these men do have an interest in their children," says the MDRC's Gordon Berlin.

In addition to these kinds of programs, policy-makers are debating more sweeping government action to support families. A massive overhaul of the support-collection system would raise more children out of poverty and could make money a less valid excuse for not coming around to the house. If David Bell's paycheck were automatically debited for child support each month, would money issues be hanging over his head every time he thought of visiting Jason? Eliminating AFDC and replacing it with a welfare system to support families—rather than just women with children—is another idea gaining attention. But it's unlikely that budget-conscious Washington will soon foot the bill.

In the end, though, all of this policy-wonking may be as effective as changing the spark plugs on a dead engine. Bryant concedes that his welfare changes are not likely to alter behavior patterns for another 10 years—and even then he only expects a 25% drop in single-parent births. And what about that broad swath of middle-class fathers beyond the reach of welfare reform and parenting programs, who dutifully pay their child support but rarely see their children?

Blankenhorn argues that before fathers will come home, society as a whole—from MTV video jocks and politicians to mechanics and lawyers—must decide that fatherhood is a cultural ideal worth defending. "In the end," he says, "Madonna lyrics matter more than who gets elected President."

Change could come sooner than we think. An analogy I heard more than once equated errant fathers with cigarette smokers. Twenty years ago, few people would have seriously considered restricting their freedom. Then, boom! First we relegated them to separate sections; then we kicked them out of office buildings and airplanes. In a few years, smokers fell into disgrace.

What if society treated errant fathers the same way?

THE LASTING EFFECTS OF CHILD MALTREATMENT

Raymond H. Starr, Jr.

Raymond H. Starr, Jr., is a developmental psychologist on the faculty of the University of Maryland, Baltimore County. He has been conducting research with maltreated children and their families for more than sixteen years and was also a founder and first president of the National Down Syndrome Congress.

Every day, the media contain examples of increasingly extreme cases of child abuse and neglect and their consequences. The cases have a blurring sameness. Take, for example, the fourteen-year-old crack addict who lives on the streets by selling his body. A reporter befriends him and writes a vivid account of the beatings the boy received from his father. There is the pedophile who is on death row for mutilating and murdering a four-year-old girl. His record shows a sixth-grade teacher threatened to rape and kill him if he told anyone what the teacher had done to him. There is the fifteen-year-old girl who felt that her parents didn't love her. So she found love on the streets and had a baby she later abandoned in a trash barrel. And here are the prostitutes on a talk show who tell how the men their mothers had trusted sexually abused them as children. These and hundreds more examples assault us and lead us to believe that abused children become problem adolescents and adults.

Are these incidents the whole story? Case examples are dramatic, but have you ever wondered how such maltreatment changes the course of a child's life? In this sound-bite era, most of us rarely stop to think about this important question. We seldom ask why trauma should play such an important role in shaping the course of a child's life.

To examine these questions, we need to understand what psychologists know about the course of lives and how they study them—the subject of the field of life-span developmental psychology.

LIFE-SPAN DEVELOPMENT

*U*nderstanding why people behave the way they do is a complex topic that has puzzled philosophers, theologians, and scientists. The course of life is so complex that we tend to focus on critical incidents and key events. Most of us can remember a teacher who played an important role in our own development, but we have to consider that other teachers may have been important. If his seventh-grade civics teacher, Ms. Jones, is the person Bill says showed him the drama of the law, leading him to become a lawyer, does this mean that his sixth-grade English teacher, Ms. Hazelton, played no role in his career choice? An outside observer might say that Ms. Hazelton was the key person because she had a debate club and Bill was the most able debater in his class.

Case descriptions fascinate us, but it is hard to divine the reasons for life courses from such examples. It is for this reason that scientists studying human behavior prefer to use prospective studies. By following people from a certain age, we can obtain direct evidence about the life course and factors that influence it. However, most of our information comes from retrospective studies in which people are asked what has happened to them in the past and how it relates to their present functioning.

Life-span developmental theory seeks to explain the way life events have influenced individual development. Of necessity, such explanations are complex; lives themselves are complex. They are built on a biological foundation, shaped by genetic characteristics, structured by immediate events, and indirectly influenced by happenings that are external to the family. As if this were not complex enough, contemporary theory holds that our interpretation of each event is dependent on the prior interactions of all these factors.

Hank's reaction to the loss of his wife to cancer will differ from George's reaction to his wife's death from a similar cancer. Many factors can contribute to these differing reactions. Hank may have grown up with two parents who were loving and attentive, while George may never have known his father. He may have had a mother who was so depressed that from the time he was two, he had lived in a series of foster homes, never knowing a secure, loving, consistent parent.

MALTREATED CHILDREN AS ADULTS

*R*esearch has shown that there is a direct relation between a child's exposure to negative emotional, social, and environmental events and the presence of problems during adulthood. Psychiatrist Michael Rutter compared young women who were removed from strife-filled homes and who later came back to live with their parents to women from more harmonious homes.[1] The women from discordant homes were more likely to become pregnant as teens, were less skilled in parenting their children, and had unhappy marriages to men who also had psychological and social problems. Adversity begat adversity.

Do the above examples and theoretical views mean that abused and neglected children will, with great certainty, become adults with problems? Research on this issue has focused on three questions: First, do maltreated children grow up to

tween 25 percent and 35 percent.[2] Thus, it is far from certain that an abused child will grow up to be an abusive parent. Physical abuse should be seen as a risk factor for becoming an abusive adult, not as a certainty. Many abusive adults were never abused when they were children.

Researchers have also taken a broader approach by examining the cycle of family violence. Sociologist Murray Straus surveyed a randomly selected national sample of families about the extent of violence between family members.[3] Members of the

as a training ground for later child abuse.

To summarize, this evidence suggests that maltreatment during childhood is but one of many factors that lead to a person's becoming an abusive parent. Being abused as a child is a risk marker for later parenting problems and not a cause of such difficulties. It accounts for, at most, less than a third of all cases of physical abuse. Research suggests that a number of other factors, such as stress and social isolation, also play a role as causes of child abuse.[4]

Research has shown that there is a direct relation between a child's exposure to negative emotional, social, and environmental events and the presence of problems during adulthood.

---

maltreat their children? Second, are yesterday's maltreated children today's criminals? Third, are there more general effects of abuse and neglect on later psychological and social functioning? A number of research studies have examined these questions.

The cycle of maltreatment. It makes logical sense that we tend to raise our own children as we ourselves were raised. Different theoretical views of personality development suggest that this should be the case. Psychoanalytic theorists think that intergenerational transmission of parenting styles is unconscious. Others, such as learning theorists, agree that transmission occurs but differ about the mechanism. Learning parenting skills from our parents is the key mode by which childrearing practices are transmitted from one generation to the next, according to members of the latter group of theorists.

Research suggests that the correspondence between being maltreated as a child and becoming a maltreating adult is far from the one-to-one relationship that has been proposed. Studies have focused on physical abuse; data are not available for either sexual abuse or neglect. In one recent review, the authors conclude that the rate of intergenerational transmission of physical abuse is be-

surveyed families were asked about experiences of violence when they were children and how much husband-wife and parent-child violence there had been in the family in the prior year.

Straus concluded that slightly fewer than 20 percent of parents whose mothers had been violent toward them more than once a year during childhood were abusive toward their own child. The child abuse rate for parents with less violent mothers was less than 12 percent. Having or not having a violent father was less strongly related to whether or not fathers grew up to be abusive toward their own children. Interestingly, the amount of intergenerational transmission was higher if a parent was physically punished by his or her opposite-sex parent.

Straus also found that the abusive adults in his study did not have to have been abused in childhood to become abusive adults. A violent home environment can lead a nonabused child to become an abusive adult. Boys who saw their fathers hit their mothers were 38 percent more likely to grow up to be abusive than were boys who never saw their father hit their mother (13.3 vs. 9.7 percent). Similarly, mothers who saw their mothers hit their fathers were 42 percent more likely to become abusive mothers (24.4 vs. 17.2 percent). Straus views seeing parents fight

Maltreatment and later criminality. Later criminal behavior is one of the most commonly discussed consequences of child abuse. Research on this subject has examined the consequences of both physical abuse and sexual abuse. Maltreatment has been linked to both juvenile delinquency and adult criminality.

It is difficult to do research on this topic. Furthermore, the results of studies must be carefully interpreted to avoid overstating the connection between maltreatment and criminality. For example, researchers often combine samples of abused and neglected children, making it hard to determine the exact effects of specific forms of maltreatment.

Two types of study have typically been done. Retrospective studies examine the family backgrounds of criminals and find the extent to which they were maltreated as children. It is obvious that the validity of the results of such studies may be compromised by the criminals' distortion of or lack of memory concerning childhood experiences. Prospective studies, in which a sample of children is selected and followed through childhood and into adolescence or adulthood, are generally seen as a more valid research strategy. Such studies are expensive and time-consuming to do.

One review of nine studies concluded that from 8 to 26 percent of delinquent youths studied retrospectively had been abused as children.[5] The rate for prospective studies was always found to be less than 20 percent. In one of the best studies, Joan McCord analyzed case records for more than 250 boys, almost 50 percent of whom had been abused by a parent.[6] Data were also collected when the men were in middle age. McCord found that 39 percent of the abused boys had been convicted of a crime as juveniles, adults, or at both ages, compared to 23 percent of a sample of 101 men who, as boys, had been classified as loved by their parents. The crime rate for both sets of boys is higher than would be expected because McCord's sample lived in deteriorated, urban areas where both crime and abuse are common.

Researchers have also examined the relationship between abuse and later violent criminality. Research results suggest that there is a weak relationship between abuse and later violence. For example, in one study, 16 percent of a group of abused children were later arrested —but not necessarily convicted—as suspects in violent criminal cases.[7] This was twice the arrest rate for nonabused adolescents and adults. Neglected children were also more likely to experience such arrests. These data are higher than would be the case in the general population because the samples contained a disproportionately high percentage of subjects from low-income backgrounds.

The connection between childhood sexual abuse and the commission of sex crimes in adolescence and adulthood is less clear. Most of the small number of studies that have been done have relied upon self-reports of childhood molestation made by convicted perpetrators. Their results show considerable variation in the frequency with which childhood victimization is reported. Incidence figures range from a low of 19 percent to a high of 57 percent. However, we should look at such data with suspicion. In an interesting study, perpetrators of sex crimes against children were much less likely to report that they had been sexually abused during their own childhood when they knew that the truthfulness of their answers would be validated by a polygraph examination and that lies were likely to result in being sent to jail.[8] Thus, people arrested for child sexual abuse commonly lie, claiming that they were abusing children because they themselves had been victims of sexual abuse as children.

To summarize, there is a link between childhood abuse and later criminality. Although some studies lead to a conclusion that this relationship is simple, others suggest that it is really quite complex. The latter view is probably correct.

The case of neglect is an example of this complexity. Widom, in her study discussed above, found that 12 percent of adolescents and adults arrested for violent offenses were neglected as children and 7 percent experienced both abuse and neglect (compared to 8 percent of her nonmaltreated control adolescents and adults).

These data raise an interesting question: Why is neglect, typically considered to be a nonviolent offense, linked to later criminality? Poverty seems to be the mediating factor. Neglect is more common among impoverished families. Poor families experience high levels of frustration, known to be a common cause of aggression. Similarly, we know that lower-class families are, in general, more violent.[9] For these reasons, all the forms of maltreatment we have considered make it somewhat more likely that a maltreated child will grow up to commit criminal acts.

Maltreatment in context. Research suggests that maltreatment during childhood has far-reaching consequences. These are best seen as the results of a failure to meet the emotional needs of the developing child. Indeed, in many cases, the trust the child places in the parent is betrayed by the parent.

This betrayal has been linked to many and varied consequences. The greatest amount of research has focused on the long-term effects of sexual abuse. Studies have looked at samples that are representative of the normal population and also at groups of adults who are seeking psychotherapy because of emotional problems. The most valid findings come from the former type of study. One review of research concluded that almost 90 percent of studies found some lasting effect of sexual abuse.[10]

Sexual abuse has been linked to

Psychoanalytic theorists think that intergenerational transmission of parenting styles is unconscious.

a wide variety of psychological disturbances. These include depression, low self-esteem, psychosis, anxiety, sleep problems, alcohol and drug abuse, and sexual dysfunction (including a predisposition to revictimization during adulthood). As was true for the research reviewed in the preceding two sections of this article, any particular problem is present in only a minority of adult survivors of childhood sexual victimization.

We know less about the long-term effects of physical abuse. Most of the limited amount of available research has used data obtained from clinical samples. Such studies have two problems. First, they rely on retrospective adult reports concerning events that happened during childhood. Second, the use of such samples results in an overestimate of the extent to which physical abuse has long-term consequences. Compared with a random sample of the general population, clinical samples contain individuals who are already identified as having emotional difficulties, regardless of whether or not they have been abused.

Researchers in one study found that more than 40 percent of inpatients being treated in a psychiatric hospital had been sexually or physically abused as children, usually by a family member.[11] Also, the abuse was typically chronic rather than a onetime occurrence. The abused patients were almost 50 percent more likely to have tried to commit suicide, were 25 percent more likely to have been violent toward others, and were 15 percent more likely to have had some involvement with the criminal justice system than were other patients at the same hospital who had not experienced childhood maltreatment.

Much research remains to be done in this area. We know little about the long-term consequences of particular forms of abuse. The best that we can say is that many victims of physical and sexual abuse experience psychological trauma lasting into adulthood.

The lack of universal consequences. The above analysis suggests that many victims of childhood maltreatment do *not* have significant problems functioning as adults. Researchers are only beginning to ask why many adult victims apparently have escaped unsullied. Factors that mediate and soften the influence of abuse and neglect are called buffers.

The search for buffers is a difficult one. Many of the negative outcomes that have been discussed in the preceding sections may be the result of a number of factors other than maltreatment itself. For example, abused children commonly have behavior problems that are similar to those that have been reported in children raised by drug addicts or adults suffering from major psychological disturbances. Abused children do not exhibit any problems that can be attributed only to abuse. A given behavior problem can have many causes.

One view of the way in which buffers act to limit the extent to which physical abuse is perpetuated across succeeding generations has been proposed by David Wolfe.[12] He believes that there is a three-part process involving the parent, the child, and the relationships between

ating factors that work at this level include normal developmental changes in child behavior, parental attendance at child management classes, and the development of parental ability to cope with the child's escalating annoying actions. Finally, additional compensatory factors work to limit the ongoing use of aggression as a solution to parenting problems.

One study compared parents who broke the cycle of abuse to those who did not.[13] Mothers who were not abusive had larger, more supportive social networks. Support included help with child care and financial assistance during times of crisis. Mothers who did not continue the abusive cycle also were more in touch with their own abuse as children and expressed

The amount of intergenerational transmission was higher if a parent was physically punished by his or her opposite-sex parent.

Parents may realize that researchers are indeed correct when they say that physical punishment is an ineffective way of changing child behavior. In addition, children may respond positively to parental use of nonaggressive disciplinary procedures and, at a broader level, society or individuals in the parents' circle of friends may inhibit the use of physical punishment by making their disapproval known. Parents who were abused as children are therefore less likely to abuse their own children if any or all of these mediating factors are present.

Research suggests that the factors

doubts about their parenting ability. This awareness made them more able to relive and discuss their own negative childhood experiences.

To summarize, investigators have gone beyond just looking at the negative consequences of childhood maltreatment. They are devoting increasing attention to determining what factors in a child's environment may inoculate the child against the effects of maltreatment. While research is starting to provide us with information concerning some of these mediating influences, much more work needs to be done before we can specify the most important mediators and know how they exert their influences.

Physical abuse should be seen as a risk factor for becoming an abusive adult, not as a certainty.

CONCLUSIONS

We know much about the intergenerational transmission of childhood physical and sexual abuse. Research suggests that abused children are (1) at an increased risk of either repeating the acts they experienced with their own children or, in the case of sexual abuse, with both their own and with unrelated children; (2) more likely to be involved with the criminal justice system as adolescents or adults; and (3) likely to suffer long lasting emotional effects of abuse even if they do not abuse their own children or commit criminal acts.

This does not mean that abused chil

the two. In the first stage, factors predisposing a parent to child abuse (including stress and a willingness to be aggressive toward the child) are buffered by such factors as social support and an income adequate for the purchase of child-care services. Next, Wolfe notes that children often do things that annoy parents and create crises that may lead to abuse because the parent is unprepared to handle the child's provocative behavior. Amelior-

mentioned by Wolfe and other influences all can work to buffer the adult effects of childhood maltreatment. These include knowing a nurturing, loving adult who provides social support, intellectually restructuring the maltreatment so that it is not seen so negatively, being altruistic and giving to others what one did not get as a child, having good skills for coping with stressful events, and getting psychotherapy.

People arrested for child sexual abuse commonly lie, claiming that they were abusing children because they themselves had been victims of sexual abuse as children.

dren invariably grow up to be adults with problems. Many adults escape the negative legacy of abuse. They grow up to be normal, contributing members of society. Their escape from maltreatment is usually related to the presence of factors that buffer the effects of the physical blows and verbal barbs.

The knowledge base underlying these conclusions is of varied quality. We know more about the relationship of physical and sexual abuse to adult abusiveness and criminality, less about long-term psychological problems and buffering factors, and almost nothing about the relationship of neglect to any of these outcomes. Almost no research has been done on neglect, a situation leading to a discussion of the reasons behind our "neglect of neglect."[14] Our ignorance is all the more surprising when we consider that neglect is the most common form of reported maltreatment.

The issues involved are complex. We can no longer see the development of children from a view examining such simple cause-effect relationships as exemplified by the proposal that abused children grow up to be abusive adults. Contemporary de-velopmental psychology recognizes that many interacting forces work together to shape development. Children exist in a context that contains their own status as biological beings, their parents and the background they bring to the task of child-rearing, the many and varied environments such as work and school that exert both direct and indirect influences on family members, and the overall societal acceptance of violence.

Advances in research methods allow us to evaluate the interrelationships of all the above factors to arrive at a coherent view of the course of development. Appropriate studies are difficult to plan and expensive to conduct. Without such research, the best that we can do is to continue performing small studies that give us glimpses of particular elements of the picture that we call the life course.

Research is necessary if we are to develop and evaluate the effectiveness of child maltreatment prevention and treatment programs. Our existing knowledge base provides hints that are used by program planners and psychotherapists to find families where there is a high risk of maltreatment and to intervene early. But when such hints are all we have to guide us in working to break the cycle of maltreatment, there continues to be risk of intergenerational perpetuation.

1. Michael Rutter, "Intergenerational Continuities and Discontinuities in Serious Parenting Difficulties," in *Child Maltreatment: Theory and Research on the Causes and Consequences of Child Abuse and Neglect*, ed., Dante Cicchetti and Vicki Carlson (New York: Cambridge University Press, 1989), 317–348.

2. Joan Kaufman and Edward Zigler, "Do Abused Children Become Abusive Adults?" *American Journal of Orthopsychiatry* 57 (April 1987): 186–192.

3. Murray A. Straus, "Family Patterns and Child Abuse in a Nationally Representative American Sample," *Child Abuse and Neglect* 3 (1979): 213–225.

4. Raymond H. Starr, Jr., "Physical Abuse of Children," in *Handbook of Family Violence* ed. Vincent B. Van Hasselt, et al. (New York: Plenum Press, 1988): 119–155.

5. Cathy Spatz Widom, "Does Violence Beget Violence? A Critical Examination of the Literature," *Psychological Bulletin* 106 (1989): 3–28.

6. Joan McCord, "A Forty-year Perspective on Effects of Child Abuse and Neglect," *Child Abuse and Neglect* 7 (1983): 265–270. Joan McCord, "Parental Aggressiveness and Physical Punishment in Long-term Perspective," in *Family Abuse and Its Consequences*, ed. Gerald T. Hotaling, et al. (Newbury Park, Calif.: Sage Publishing, 1988): 91–98.

7. Cathy Spatz Widom, "The Cycle of Violence," *Science*, 14 April 1989.

8. Jan Hindman, "Research Disputes Assumptions about Child Molesters," *National District Attorneys' Association Bulletin* 7 (July/August 1988): 1.

9. Murray A. Straus, Richard J. Gelles, and Suzanne K. Steinmetz, *Behind Closed Doors: Violence in the American Family* (New York: Anchor Press, 1980).

10. David Finkelhor and Angela Browne, "Assessing the Long-term Impact of Child Sexual Abuse: A Review and Conceptualization," in *Family Abuse and Its Consequences*, ed. Gerald T. Hotaling, et al.: 270–284.

11. Elaine (Hilberman) Carmen, Patricia Perri Rieker, and Trudy Mills, "Victims of Violence and Psychiatric Illness," *American Journal of Psychiatry* 141 (March 1984): 378–383.

12. David A. Wolfe, *Child Abuse: Implications for Child Development and Psychopathology* (Newbury Park, Calif.: Sage Publishing, 1987).

13. Rosemary S. Hunter and Nancy Kilstrom, "Breaking the Cycle in Abusive Families," 136 (1979): 1320–22.

14. Isabel Wolock and Bernard Horowitz, "Child Maltreatment as a Social Problem: The Neglect of Neglect," *American Journal of Orthopsychiatry* 54 (1984); 530–543.

CHILDREN
of
VIOLENCE

What Happens to Kids Who Learn as Babies to Dodge Bullets and Step Over Corpses on the Way to School?

LOIS TIMNICK

Lois Timnick is a Times staff writer. Lilia Beebe contributed to this report.

THE morning after a 19-year-old gang member was gunned down at a phone box at 103rd and Grape streets in Watts, his lifeless body lay in a pool of blood on the sidewalk as hundreds of children walked by, lunch boxes and school bags in hand, on their way to the 102nd Street Elementary School. A few months later, during recess, kindergartners at the school dropped to the ground as five shots were fired rapidly nearby, claiming another victim. On still another occasion, an outdoor school assembly was disrupted by the crackle of gunshots and wailing sirens as students watched a neighborhood man scuffle with police officers.

Terrifying occurrences such as these have brought together six youngsters, ages 6 through 11, who sit in a circle around a box of Kleenex in a colorful classroom. The children are a bit fidgety and shy at first, as a psychiatric social worker asks if anyone would like to share a recent event that made them sad. With hesitation, then with the words spilling out, each tells his story—pausing frequently to grab a tissue to wipe away the tears.

"They shoot somebody every day," begins Lester Ford, who is 9 and lives with his mother and brother in the vast Jordan Downs housing project across from the school. When he's playing outside and hears gunshots, the solemn child says softly, "I go in and get under the bed and come out after the shooting stops."

He says he has lost seven relatives. "My daddy got knifed when he got out of jail," Lester explains, and suddenly tears begin streaming down his face. "My uncle got shot in a fight—there was a bucket of his blood. And I had two aunties killed—one of them was pushed off the freeway and there were maggots on her."

Sitting next to Lester, 11-year-old Trevor Dixon, whose mother and father died of natural causes, puts a comforting arm around his friend. "We don't come outside a lot now," he says of himself and his twin sister. "It's like the violence is coming down a little closer."

When it's her turn, 8-year-old Danielle Glover peers through thick glasses and says matter-of-factly: "Just three people [in my family] died." At night their ghosts haunt her, she says. "I been seein' two of them."

This is grief class at the 102nd Street Elementary School, and it is one of the front lines in the battle against violence in South-Central Los Angeles and other urban war zones.

Experts and mental health professionals are just beginning to learn what happens to children like Lester, Trevor and Danielle as they grow into adulthood: **Even if these children of violence survive the drugs, the gangs and the shootings, they might not survive the psychological effects of the constant barrage.**

Though therapists are finding encouraging signs of resiliency, they believe that no child who is victimized, witnesses violent crime or simply grows up in its maelstrom escapes unscathed. Despite a fragmented and sometimes underfunded approach, these researchers are developing therapies to address the problem.

Two years ago, 102nd Street school principal Melba Coleman, the school guidance counselor and the school psychologist had seen some children regress to bed-wetting, others become overly withdrawn or hostile and good students struggle to concentrate. They called on the Los Angeles Unified School District's mental health center, and social worker Deborah Johnson, to develop a way to help the kids overcome their experiences.

So far, 30 children have participated in the weekly hour-long class, which is thought to be the first regular grief and loss program for elementary school students in the nation. They are encouraged to talk about life, death and ways to keep safe in an unsafe world. The hope is that, by sharing their thoughts and emotions with others, the children will come to terms with their feelings of loss, anger and confusion before long-term, irreversible problems develop. And it seems to be working.

Says Kentral Brim, 10, whose two older brothers were killed and who barely escaped injury himself during a gang fight that broke out at Martin Luther King Jr./Drew Medical Center: "I was getting mad and fighting." With the group's help, the neatly dressed, polite young boy says, "I settled down."

SETTLING DOWN IS hard in South-Central Los Angeles, in the shadow of the famous Watts Towers and within a few blocks of four squalid public housing projects. Sleepless nights are punctuated by gunshots, sirens and hovering police helicopters. Liquor stores are routinely robbed. Children as young as 6 are recruited as drug-runners. Some babies' first words and gestures are the names and hand signs of their parents' gangs. The color of a T-shirt can determine whether someone lives or dies, and the most important lesson of childhood is that survival depends on hitting the ground when the inevitable shooting starts. Some families are so fearful that whenever gang warfare flares up, they live behind closed curtains with the lights off, sleeping and eating on the floor to avoid stray bullets.

The scope of violence in South-Central Los Angeles is horrifying. In the first seven months of this year, there have been 237 homicides, 413 rapes, 5,864 robberies and 9,068 aggravated assaults in one of the most turbulent areas of the city. Thirty-five of the homicide victims were under 18. A study headed last year by Dr. Gary Ordog at King/Drew Medical Center found that 34 children under 10 years old were treated there for gunshot wounds between 1980 and 1987. Records showed none in earlier years.

Perhaps most telling of all is the fact that 90% of children taken to the psychiatric clinic at the hospital have witnessed some act of violence, a recent UCLA survey found.

"How can children see all that [violence] and *not* be affected?" asks Gwen Bozart, a third-grade teacher at Compton Avenue Elementary School. Especially when such violence takes place against a landscape of deprivation and failure. Standardized school test scores in South-Central Los Angeles are far below the average for the rest of the city and state. The dropout rate in some high schools is nearly twice that of the rest of the district. More than half the adult population is unemployed. And mental health professionals say depression and suicide attempts are disproportionately high among a despairing population that is barely surviving.

"There's just so much stress that an individual can take before he is completely overwhelmed," notes UCLA child psychiatrist Gloria Johnson Powell, who grew up in the tough Roxbury section of Boston and this fall will establish a center at Harvard University to focus on the special needs of minority children. Often, Powell points out, inner-city children witness violence at home as well as at school and in the streets. They frequently endure abusive family relationships and watch endless hours of romanticized TV violence. "[Many of] these children have daily stress from the time they wake up until they go to bed," she says.

Researchers have found that youngsters growing up in a war-zone environment such as South-Central Los Angeles are likely to become anxious or depressed. Youngsters who have been direct victims or who have witnessed, say, the brutal murder of a parent, are most likely to suffer post-traumatic stress disorder, today's term for a cluster of symptoms recognized in soldiers and others for many years but given labels such as "shellshock" or "combat neurosis."

In children, post-traumatic stress disorder takes the form of reliving the violent experience repeatedly in play, nightmares and sudden memories that intrude during class or other activities. Kids with the disorder can be easily startled, apathetic, hopeless or possessed by a fear of death. Many children regress to early childhood behaviors such as clinginess, become extremely irritable and develop stomachaches and headaches that have no organic cause.

They play differently, too, going beyond the roughhousing that is part of normal child development. Such traumatized children tend to be more aggressive and more willing to take risks—wrestling to hurt companions, for example, or jumping from high places. Others can become inhibited, forsaking sports they used to enjoy; still others might re-enact a gruesome event in play. (The popular childhood game of ring-around-the-rosy with its "ashes, ashes, all fall down" is thought to have originated as a response to the bubonic plague, when children watched people die and saw streets filled with corpses.) A psychiatrist tells of a child who, after having witnessed the stabbing of her mother, painted her hands red with her paintbrush.

Most devastating perhaps for school-age children, post-traumatic stress disorder reduces the ability to concentrate and remember, resulting in poor school performance. But it doesn't stop there. Principal Coleman says the teachers at the 102nd Street school identified about 10% of the school's more than 1,200 youngsters as showing "high risk" behaviors and notes that these children also interfere with the others' ability to learn. "High risk" behaviors, which include repeatedly cursing at and hitting adults, are thought to be early signs that a child could become a social misfit.

Older children sometimes cope by affecting an indifference to the violence around them, experts say. They exhibit an emotional denial that can cripple all of their relationships. The seeming indifference is evident in random conversations with South-Central Los Angeles children over the last year. One group spoke dispassionately of finding a murdered woman's mutilated body—"Her eyeball was in her shoe," a child said. Another group, when told about a fatal shooting, appeared less interested in the victim than in the details of his shiny new truck and its equipment. And, when asked for class field-trip ideas, an 11-year-old boy suggested, "How about the cemetery?"

Other conversations reveal further emotional distancing: Several 8-year-olds discussing whether the murder of a lifeguard was justified because he had ordered someone to get out of the pool agreed that, as one child explained, "Yeah, he [the killer] shudda done it." To them, killing seemed a reasonable response to a perceived insult. A 16-year-old girl at Jordan High School, ticking off the

'The more kids are exposed to violence, the more desensitized they become.'

names of at least nine people who had been shot recently, put it this way: "The ones [bodies] I see in the street that are killed, that don't mean nothin' to me anymore."

Such callous talk among children alerts mental health professionals to underlying emotional difficulties. "You're not going to be very trusting [as an adult] if you observe or have close to you violent behavior," says Santa Monica therapist Ruth Bettelheim, a former consultant to Head Start and daughter of noted child psychologist Bruno Bettelheim. "You tend to keep your distance psychologically—making close and intimate relationships difficult. And that isolation fuels depression, which is already there because of previous losses."

But, Bettelheim says, some children are able to overcome these problems if the adults and children around them can offer support. "It's old psychology wisdom that the same fire that melts butter hardens steel," she adds, so the very violence that spells destruction for one child might make a strong survivor out of another.

Psychiatrist William Arroyo, acting director of the Los Angeles County/USC child-adolescent psychiatric clinic, has studied refugee children from Central America and children from inner-city areas as well. He acknowledges that supportive parents, schools and neighborhoods can serve as buffers against stressful environments, then shakes his head sadly at the fact that South-Central Los Angeles offers so little: Many households are chaotic and headed by uneducated welfare mothers, nutrition and prenatal care are poor, mental health programs are scarce, and Watts doesn't even have a YMCA, where kids can participate in structured activities instead of hanging out and getting into trouble.

"The more they are exposed to violence, the more desensitized they become until it's no longer horrifying but merely an occurrence in daily living," Arroyo says. "We are *very* concerned about those who already have psychiatric disorders and those who have poor impulse control, who then witness violence either in real life or on television. If youngsters learn that the way of succeeding in everyday tasks includes maiming or killing community members, stealing and generally engaging in sorts of behavior that larger society calls criminal, we'll see a larger population of these types."

T HE CALENDAR SAYS it happened more than five years ago. But Ana Anaya Gonzalez, now nearly 16, still pictures it clearly. Even when she tries to forget, her scarred body and recurring nightmares have been constant reminders.

It was a winter Friday afternoon in South-Central Los Angeles, just as children were being dismissed from the 49th Street Elementary School. A deranged neighborhood resident fired 57 times at the playground from his second-story window across the street, killing two people and injuring 13 others.

Ana, a fifth-grader at the time, remembers that she was playing on the monkey bars while her sister, Rosa, went back inside to get her sweater.

"I thought it sounded like gunfire, but a friend said, 'No, it's firecrackers.' Then a bullet hit the ground near me, and everybody dropped. I fell on my knees. I couldn't feel my legs, but I didn't know I was hit."

Inside the school, Rosa's teacher pushed her to the floor and fell on top of her to protect her. A passing jogger spotted the sniper, shouted to him to stop and, seeing that Ana was moving, threw himself over her. He was hit by the next round of gunfire and died two months later.

"I was wearing a pink dress," Ana says, "and when I saw it was full of blood, I tried to scream to a teacher in the doorway to help me. He looked at me and then turned around and closed the door."

Ana spent five months in the hospital. She lost a kidney, still suffers leg pain, cannot bend backward and experiences stomach discomfort when she eats. A single bullet wound scars her back; surgical incisions mark her abdomen.

She also suffers from post-traumatic stress disorder, according to Dr. Quinton C. James, the psychiatrist who treated her and several others injured in the sniper attack. "Whether you're talking about violence in Belfast, Beirut or South-Central Los Angeles, I think it all has an impact, although you never know how it will manifest itself in a particular child. Up to a point, one child may adapt with no [apparent] impairment, while for another it may impair [his] ability to function adequately, socially and academically," says James, the former chief of child/adolescent services at the Augustus Hawkins Mental Health Center (a part of King/Drew Medical Center) who now works with the School Mental Health Center and the Centinela Child Guidance Clinic in Inglewood.

Immediately after the attack, mental health professionals from the school district, the Los Angeles County Mental

Art Therapy: Drawing From Experience

EVEN WHEN children can't verbalize the effect that violence has on them, they sometimes express it by drawing pictures full of blood, guns and knives, says Dr. Spencer Eth, acting chief of psychiatry of the West Los Angeles Veteran's Administration Medical Center and medical director of a trauma unit associated with Cedars-Sinai Medical Center.

Eth worked with the crisis team that responded to the shooting at the 49th Street Elementary School. He says that when children too traumatized to talk are told, "Just draw about anything you want," their pictures reveal much about what's on their minds. This enables therapists to ask children to tell a story, which usually has some connection with the trauma they have suffered.

For example, after a boy threatened to jump off the roof at an elementary school as his horrified classmates watched, children spontaneously made drawings that depicted the incident and the hospital where they imagined the boy was taken.

Says Eth: "Drawing is one of the most effective techniques we have for getting a child to open up and confront difficult feelings—the first step in healing." —*L.T.*

Pictures from several schools, clockwise from top, depict a classmate's suicide; a man killing his baby; the "cemetery where baby is"; sadness about a classmate who drowned.

Health Department, County-USC and UCLA medical centers and the Cedars-Sinai Psychological Trauma Center and various university and private consultants volunteered to help students, as well as parents and teachers. Over the next several weeks, using art therapy (see box above) and in-depth discussions of the shooting, the experts helped those who had witnessed the attack deal with its shattering effects. Social workers continued to work with the children several days a week for the next year.

A month after the shooting, a team headed by Dr. Robert Pynoos, an associate professor of psychiatry at the UCLA School of Medicine, returned to see how the children were doing. Those most severely affected reported feeling stressed, upset and afraid just from thinking about the shooting, and fearful that it might happen again. They complained of jumpiness, nightmares, loss of interest in activities, difficulty paying attention in school and other disturbances. Those who had experienced other violence, an unexpected death or physical injury during the preceding year described having renewed thoughts and images of that event—even if they were not directly exposed to the playground shooting. Many were depressed or grieving a year later, the team found.

"You can cope with it," James says he told Ana at the start of her psychotherapy. "There are things that happen in life, but you don't have to be defeated by them. You'll have physical scars, emotional scars, but you have to accept that it happened and that we don't know why. . . . The thing is you're still alive . . . and there is something you can do. We'll find out together; I'll help you, and so will your family and other relatives, people at school and other agencies."

With her determination and the help of intense psychotherapy, Ana's condition improved. After seeing James every day for the first month she was hospitalized and five days a week for the next four months, she was able to return to finish sixth grade at the 49th Street school, although she never again ventured onto the playground.

Ana continues to progress, but memories of the shooting plague her, James says. As recently as last February—on the anniversary of the incident—she told James: "I still feel the same way. I get scared about things. . . . I get nervous and start crying about the past."

Though she knows the sniper killed himself, Ana occasionally feels as if he is stalking her. She is sometimes afraid to be alone and sleeps in a bed with Rosa. Until recently, she has had a recurring nightmare: A man is chasing her and shoots her. "I wake up when he shoots me and can't go back to sleep."

Formerly an excellent student, Ana has had trouble concentrating, has required a tutor and is working at about average academic level—although her grades are improving at Jefferson High School, where she is now a junior.

Other members of Ana's family are dealing with the shooting as well. Rosa, now 14, appears withdrawn and more traumatized than Ana, perhaps because she has received less therapy, James says. She was reluctant to return to school, avoids discussing the attack and remains fearful and anxious.

Their mother, Esperanza "Blanca" Gonzalez, a waitress who has four other children, suffered a nervous breakdown and had to be hospitalized briefly.

"I feel sick for Ana," Gonzalez says. "She's very nervous and restless in the classroom. She's lost a lot of her spirit." Gonzalez knows that her daughter "cries every night . . . and is sad much of the time," but she says the family cannot afford psychotherapy.

The Gonzalezes live in the same neighborhood, still frightened by the gunshots they hear in the night. "I still get scared," Ana says. "When I hear the shots outside, sometimes I feel like they are shooting at me."

Ana's mother says she remains bitter about the police department's failure to respond to previous complaints about the sniper's brandishing and firing guns. "Until we see blood, we can't do anything about him," she says officers told neighbors.

On the outside, Ana is a pretty, dark-haired teen-ager who appears bubbly, caught up in plans with her girlfriends for her upcoming Sweet 16 birthday party. She landed a summer job selling theater tickets and says she goes to dances and parties as much as possible.

She is talkative—but not about the shooting. "It's not going to change anything to talk about it," she says, then adds, "but I would like to go back to therapy because I like to draw the pictures about what happened. I get too nervous now, and I think talking with the doctor helps."

James adds that Ana is one of the lucky ones, a child whose outlook is much brighter for having a "very supportive network." Without caring family, friends and school person-

nel, she might have become another trauma victim unable to envision a future. But Ana has career hopes, "like maybe becoming a doctor. I liked how they worked when I was in the hospital."

WHILE EDUCATORS and mental health professionals work closely with youngsters in the classroom, researchers continue studying—and in some cases, debating—how violence affects the young.

The first attempts to evaluate scientifically the phenomenon investigated children during wartime. Studies by Anna Freud and others after World War II suggested that children are minimally affected by war and sometimes find it exciting. This work has now been largely debunked. After studying the survivors of Belfast, Cambodia and Beirut, most experts contend instead that the effects of trauma can be masked, delayed or minimized—but never eliminated.

Some experts such as UCLA's Pynoos have found that exposure to violence can cause physiological changes in a child's developing brain stem, altering the brain's chemistry and causing personality changes—such as reduced impulse control, an attraction to danger or a debilitating sense of fear.

But whatever the theory, almost all the experts speak with awe of the emotional strength children possess, even those youngsters from the bleakest backgrounds.

One of the few studies exploring the roots of resilience in young children followed nearly 700 Hawaiian children over a 30-year period, ending in 1985. The study, conducted by Emmy Werner, a child psychologist at the University of California, Davis, found that one out of every four children classified as "high risk" infants had developed into a competent, confident and caring young adult. Some seemed to have a natural strength, but for others, the scales tipped from vulnerability to resilience because the children found strong emotional support at home, school, work or church.

Raiford Woods, manager of the Jordan High Student Health Clinic, sees examples of resiliency every day in the heart of Los Angeles' most violent neighborhood. With or without outside support, some of "these kids are marvelous and have the psychological strength to survive," he says. "You compare a kid from Watts to one from Orange County or Westwood; he can handle twice as much pressure."

Studies and observations like this form the basis for the widely held belief among experts that early intervention is essential—that anti-gang programs must begin in junior high, that grade-school children need support to get them off to a good start and make them less vulnerable, that "drug babies" and preschoolers need special care. And a growing number of programs seek to apply this premise in young lives.

"Some [older children] are lost causes," psychiatrist James says. "We have to focus our attention on those coming along. I met with some youngsters who all told me they'd already been in jail. 'Doc, you're wasting your time with us,' one said. 'You work with our little brothers and sisters.' "

A few Los Angeles programs focus on prevention, others with helping youngsters cope after the damage has been done. The Los Angeles Unified School District, for instance, offers a kindergarten intervention project in which children who are identified as having social problems often stemming from exposure to violence, are assigned a volunteer "special friend" to act as a companion and confidant.

Preschoolers known to have been prenatally exposed to drugs are the focus of a new program at the Salvin Special Education Center, where early childhood specialists try to interrupt behaviors, often violent, that are forerunners of school failure.

At Jordan High School, alone in the district, all ninth-graders are required to take a violence prevention course. Among other things, the course stresses how to avoid fights, how to be manly without being macho and how to deal positively with anger.

UCLA's Program in Trauma, Violence and Sudden Bereavement responds to requests for assistance from cities across the United States where extreme acts of violence—such as sniper attacks, hostage-taking and shootings—have occurred. The Cleveland Elementary School in Stockton asked for assistance after the mass shooting in January. (While these incidents are obviously traumatic, experts say, they differ significantly from the chronic violence experienced in the inner city.) The program also trains mental health professionals, provides counseling and studies children who have witnessed violence in the home or community. Likewise, the Psychological Trauma Center affiliated with Cedars-Sinai Medical Center provides psychological assistance to schools where tragedy has struck.

'These children have stress from the time they wake up until they go to bed.'

Effective ways of coping with a reality that can't be erased are not likely to lie with any single approach, the experts say. Nor can therapy ignore the web of problems that make dealing with violence even worse. Success lies in the cooperative efforts of the police, mental health and health services, schools, churches and concerned parents, and in solutions that address violence as well as drug abuse, poverty and single-parent homes.

Early-prevention programs are important, such as camp programs that give children an opportunity to see the world outside their everyday existence and television. Parents, especially mothers, need exposure to alternatives, with programs that give them a break from the draining responsibility of caring for several children around the clock, on limited resources and without male support. And ways to bring fathers into the system also need to be found.

For two years, the 102nd Street school program has focused mainly on grief and loss. Run by the school staff, the class is based on the theory that, with the support of their peers, troubled children can learn to deal with feelings they might otherwise suppress or act out at school or at home.

The program's pilot group began with social worker Johnson reading a story about a young boy who flew kites with his uncle. The uncle dies—"and there was not a dry eye in the room," Johnson remembers—but at the end, the boy goes out alone with his kite and remembers the good times they had shared. "That set the stage for the rest," she says.

"Our focus is on recognizing and expressing feelings, getting them to come to grips with the fact that they've experienced a loss and leading toward an acceptance that loss is something we all experience," says Johnson, who has spent most of the past 15 years working with disadvantaged children and their families and responding to violent crises at various schools.

Activities in the grief class include using a "feeling board," on which children draw or write whatever they want. Children play a game in which they make faces in a mirror to reflect different feelings, and they perform relaxation exercises such as deep breathing and stretching. They also listen to soft music while they visualize a place that makes them feel good. And they plant small gardens, which helps instill in them a sense of responsibility while symbolizing the beginning, growth and end of all life.

The program has not been scientifically evaluated. Some participants remain deeply troubled and have required referrals for outside counseling, and a few families have moved in hopes that memories will fade faster in a new setting. But teachers say the attitude, behavior and academic performance of most of the youngsters have improved markedly.

It is those little ones who are maturing and progressing amid daily bloodshed who give hope to Johnson and her colleagues.

"Even though all these horrible things are happening, there is a resilience there. These children and their families do respond to interventions. They have strengths even though life circumstances don't allow them to live outside this war zone," she says. "They've seen a lot, but for some some reason they're still children, still trying to walk the tightrope between the craziness of the adult world and a carefree kind of kid world."

CHILDREN AFTER DIVORCE

WOUNDS THAT DON'T HEAL

Judith S. Wallerstein

Judith S. Wallerstein is a psychologist and author of "Second Chances: Men, Women & Children a Decade After Divorce," published by Ticknor & Fields. This article, adapted from the book, was written with the book's co-author, Sandra Blakeslee, who is a regular contributor to The New York Times.

As recently as the 1970's, when the American divorce rate began to soar, divorce was thought to be a brief crisis that soon resolved itself. Young children might have difficulty falling asleep and older children might have trouble at school. Men and women might become depressed or frenetic, throwing themselves into sexual affairs or immersing themselves in work.

But after a year or two, it was expected, most would get their lives back on track, at least outwardly. Parents and children would get on with new routines, new friends and new schools, taking full opportunity of the second chances that divorce brings in its wake.

These views, I have come to realize, were wishful thinking. In 1971, working with a small group of colleagues and with funding from San Francisco's Zellerback Family Fund, I began a study of the effects of divorce on middle-class people who continue to function despite the stress of a marriage breakup.

That is, we chose families in which, despite the failing marriage, the children were doing well at school and the parents were not in clinical treatment for psychiatric disorders. Half of the families attended church or synagogue. Most of the parents were college educated. This was, in other words, divorce under the best circumstances.

Our study, which would become the first ever made over an extended period of time, eventually tracked 60 families, most of them white, with a total of 131 children, for 10, and in some cases 15, years after divorce. We found that although some divorces work well—some adults are happier in the long run, and some children do better than they would have been expected to in an unhappy intact family—more often

than not divorce is a wrenching, long-lasting experience for at least one of the former partners. Perhaps most important, we found that for virtually all the children, it exerts powerful and wholly unanticipated effects.

Our study began with modest aspirations. With a colleague, Joan Berlin Kelly—who headed a community mental-health program in the San Francisco area—I planned to examine the short-term effects of divorce on these middle-class families.

We spent many hours with each member of each of our 60 families—hearing their first-hand reports from the battleground of divorce. At the core of our research was the case study, which has been the main source of the fundamental insights of clinical psychology and of psychoanalysis. Many important changes, especially in the long run, would be neither directly observable nor easily measured. They would become accessible only through case studies: by examining the way each of these people processed, responded to and integrated the events and relationships that divorce brings in its wake.

We planned to interview families at the time of decisive separation and filing for divorce, and again 12 to 18 months later, expecting to chart recoveries among men and women and to look at how the children were mastering troubling family events.

We were stunned when, at the second series of visits, we found family after family still in crisis, their wounds wide open. Turmoil and distress had not noticeably subsided. Many adults were angry, and felt humiliated and rejected, and most had not gotten their lives back together. An unexpectedly large number of children were on a downward course. Their symptoms were worse than they had been immediately after the divorce. Our findings were absolutely contradictory to our expectations.

Dismayed, we asked the Zellerbach Fund to support a follow-up study in the fifth year after divorce. To our surprise, interviewing 56 of the 60 families in our original study, we found that although half the men and two-thirds of the women (even many of those suffering economically) said they were more content with their lives, only 34 percent of the children were clearly doing well.

Another 37 percent were depressed, could not concentrate in school, had trouble making friends and suffered a wide range of other behavior problems. While able to function on a daily basis, these children were not recovering, as everyone thought they would. Indeed most of them were on a downward course. This is a powerful statistic, considering that these were children who were functioning well five years before. It would be hard to find any other group of children—except, perhaps, the victims of a natural disaster—who suffered such a rate of sudden serious psychological problems.

The remaining children showed a mixed picture of good achievement in some areas and faltering achievement in others; it was hard to know which way they would eventually tilt.

The psychological condition of these children and adolescents, we found, was related in large part to the overall quality of life in the post-divorce family, to what the adults had been able to build in place of the failed marriage. Children tended to do well if their mothers and fathers, whether or not they remarried, resumed their parenting roles, managed to put their differences aside, and allowed the children a continuing relationship with both parents. Only a handful of kids had all these advantages.

We went back to these families again in 1980 and 1981 to conduct a 10-year follow-up. Many of those we had first interviewed as children were now adults. Overall, 45 percent were doing well; they had emerged as competent, compassionate and courageous people. But 41 percent were doing poorly; they were entering adulthood as worried, underachieving, self-deprecating and sometimes angry young men and women. The rest were strikingly uneven in how they adjusted to the world; it is too soon to say how they will turn out.

At around this time, I founded the Center for the Family in Transition, in Marin County, near San Francisco, which provides counseling to people who are separating, divorcing or remarrying. Over the years, my colleagues and I have seen more than 2,000 families—an experience that has amplified my concern about divorce. Through our work at the center and in the study, we have come to see divorce not as a single circumscribed event but as a continuum of changing family relationships—as a process that begins during the failing marriage and extends over many years. Things are not getting better, and divorce is not getting easier. It's too soon to call our conclusions definitive, but they point to an urgent need to learn more.

It was only at the 10-year point that two of our most unexpected findings became apparent. The first of these is something we call the sleeper effect.

A divorce-prone society is producing its first generation of young adults, men and women so anxious about attachment and love that their ability to create enduring families is imperiled.

The first youngster in our study to be interviewed at the 10-year mark was one who had always been a favorite of mine. As I waited for her to arrive for this interview, I remembered her innocence at age 16, when we had last met. It was she who alerted us to the fact that many young women experience a delayed effect of divorce.

As she entered my office, she greeted me warmly. With a flourishing sweep of one arm, she said, "You called me at just the right time. I just turned 21!" Then she startled me by turning immediately serious. She was in pain, she said.

She was the one child in our study who we all thought was a prime candidate for full recovery. She had denied some of her feelings at the time of divorce, I felt, but she had much going for her, including high intelligence, many friends, supportive parents, plenty of money.

As she told her story, I found myself drawn into unexpected intricacies of her life. Her trouble began, typically, in her late teens. After graduating from high school with honors, she was admitted to a respected university and did very well her freshman year. Then she fell apart. As she told it, "I met my first true love."

The young man, her age, so captivated her that she decided it was time to have a fully committed love affair. But on her way to spend summer vacation with him, her courage failed. "I went to New York instead. I hitchhiked across the country. I didn't know what I was looking for. I thought I was just passing time. I didn't stop and ponder. I just kept going, recklessly, all the time waiting for some word from my parents. I guess I was testing them. But no one—not my dad, not my mom—ever asked me what I was doing there on the road alone."

She also revealed that her weight dropped to 94 pounds from 128 and that she had not menstruated for a year and a half.

"I began to get angry," she said. "I'm angry at my parents for not facing up to the emotions, to the feelings in their lives, and for not helping me face up to the feelings in mine. I have a hard time forgiving them."

I asked if I should have pushed her to express her anger earlier.

She smiled patiently and said, "I don't think so. That was exactly the point. All those years I denied feelings. I thought I could live without love, without sorrow, without anger, without pain. That's how I coped with the unhappiness in my parents' marriage. Only when I met my boyfriend did I become aware of how much feeling I was sitting on all those years. I'm afraid I'll lose him."

It was no coincidence that her acute depression and anorexia occurred just as she was on her way to consummate her first love affair, as she was entering the kind of relationship in which her parents failed. For the first time, she confronted the fears, anxieties, guilt and concerns that she had suppressed over the years.

Sometimes with the sleeper effect the fear is of betrayal rather than commitment. I was shocked when another young woman—at the age of 24, sophisticated, warm and friendly—told me she worried if her boyfriend was even 30 minutes late, wondering who he was with and if he was having an affair with another woman. This fear of betrayal occurs at a frequency that far exceeds what one might expect from a group of people randomly selected from the population. They suffer minute to minute, even though their partners may be faithful.

In these two girls we saw a pattern that we documented in 66 percent of the young women in our study between the ages of 19 and 23; half of them were seriously derailed by it. The sleeper effect occurs at a time when these young women are making decisions with long-term implications for their lives. Faced with issues of commitment, love and sex in an adult context, they are aware that the game is serious. If they tie in with the wrong man, have children too soon, or choose harmful life-styles, the effects can be tragic. Overcome by fears and anxieties, they begin to make connections between these feelings and their parents' divorce:

"I'm so afraid I'll marry someone like my dad."

"How can you believe in commitment when anyone can change his mind anytime?"

"I am in awe of people who stay together."

We can no longer say—as most experts have held in recent years—that girls are generally less troubled by the divorce experience than boys. Our study strongly indicates, for the first time, that girls experience serious effects of divorce at the time they are entering young adulthood. Perhaps the risk for girls and boys is equalized over the long term.

When a marriage breaks down, men and women alike often experience a diminished capacity to parent. They may give less time, provide less discipline and be less sensitive to their children, since they are themselves caught up in the maelstrom of divorce and its aftermath. Many researchers and clinicians find that parents are temporarily unable to separate their children's needs from their own.

In a second major unexpected finding of our 10-year study, we found that fully a quarter of the mothers and a fifth of the fathers had not gotten their lives back on track a decade after divorce. The diminished parenting continued, permanently disrupting the child-rearing

functions of the family. These parents were chronically disorganized and, unable to meet the challenges of being a parent, often leaned heavily on their children. The child's role became one of warding off the serious depression that threatened the parents' psychological functioning. The divorce itself may not be solely to blame but, rather, may aggravate emotional difficulties that had been masked in the marriage. Some studies have found that emotionally disturbed parents within a marriage produce similar kinds of problems in children.

These new roles played by the children of divorce are complex and unfamiliar. They are not simple role reversals, as some have claimed, because the child's role becomes one of holding the parent together psychologically. It is more than a caretaking role. This phenomenon merits our careful attention, for it affected 15 percent of the children in our study, which means many youngsters in our society. I propose that we identify as a distinct psychological syndrome the "overburdened child," in the hope that people will begin to recognize the problems and take steps to help these children, just as they help battered and abused children.

One of our subjects, in whom we saw this syndrome, was a sweet 5-year-old girl who clearly felt that she was her father's favorite. Indeed, she was the only person in the family he never hit. Preoccupied with being good and helping to calm both parents, she opposed the divorce because she knew it would take her father away from her. As it turned out, she also lost her mother who, soon after the divorce, turned to liquor and sex, a combination that left little time for mothering.

A year after the divorce, at the age of 6, she was getting herself dressed, making her own meals and putting herself to bed. A teacher noticed the dark circles under her eyes, and asked why she looked so tired. "We have a new baby at home," the girl explained. The teacher, worried, visited the house and discovered there was no baby. The girl's story was designed to explain her fatigue but also enabled her to fantasize endlessly about a caring loving mother.

Shortly after this episode, her father moved to another state. He wrote to her once or twice a year, and when we saw her at the five-year follow-up she pulled out a packet of letters from him. She explained how worried she was that he might get into trouble, as if she were the parent and he the child who had left home.

"I always knew he was O.K. if he drew pictures on the letters," she said. "The last two really worried me because he stopped drawing."

Now 15, she has taken care of her mother for the past 10 years. "I felt it was my responsibility to make sure that Mom was O.K.," she says. "I stayed home with her instead of playing or going to school. When she got mad, I'd let her take it out on me."

I asked what her mother would do when she was angry.

"She'd hit me or scream. It scared me more when she screamed. I'd rather be hit. She always seemed so much bigger when she screamed. Once Mom got drunk and passed out on the street. I called my brothers, but they hung up. So I did it. I've done a lot of things I've never told anyone. There were many times she was so upset I was sure she would take her own life. Sometimes I held both her hands and talked to her for hours I was so afraid."

In truth, few children can rescue a troubled parent. Many become angry at being trapped by the parents' demands, at being robbed of their separate identity and denied their childhood. And they are saddened, sometimes beyond repair, at seeing so few of their own needs gratified.

Since this is a newly identified condition that is just being described, we cannot know its true incidence. I suspect that the number of overburdened children runs much higher than the 15 percent we saw in our study, and that we will begin to see rising reports in the next few years—just as the reported incidence of child abuse has risen since it was first identified as a syndrome in 1962.

The sleeper effect and the overburdened-child syndrome were but two of many findings in our study. Perhaps most important, overall, was our finding that divorce has a lasting psychological effect on many children, one that, in fact, may turn out to be permanent.

Children of divorce have vivid memories about their parents' separation. The details are etched firmly in their minds, more so than those of any other experiences in their lives. They refer to themselves as children of divorce, as if they share an experience that sets them apart from all others. Although many have come to agree that their parents were wise to part company, they nevertheless feel that they suffered from their parents' mistakes. In many instances, conditions in the post-divorce family were more stressful and less supportive to the child than conditions in the failing marriage.

If the finding that 66 percent of the 19- to 23-year-old young women experienced the sleeper effect was most unexpected, others were no less dramatic. Boys, too, were found to suffer unforeseen long-lasting effects. Forty percent of the 19- to 23-year-old young men in our study, 10 years after divorce, still had no set goals, a limited education and a sense of having little control over their lives.

In comparing the post-divorce lives of former husbands and wives, we saw that 50 percent of the women and 30 percent of the men were still intensely angry at their former spouses a decade after divorce. For women over 40 at divorce, life was lonely throughout the decade; not one in our study remarried or sustained a loving relationship. Half the men over 40 had the same problem.

In the decade after divorce, three in five children felt rejected by one of their parents, usually the father—whether or not it was true. The frequency and duration of visiting made no difference. Children longed for their fathers, and the need increased during adolescence. Thirty-four percent of the youngsters went to live with their fathers during adolescence for at least a year. Half returned to the mother's home disappointed with what they had found. Only one in seven saw both mother and father happily remarried after 10 years. One in two saw their mother or their father undergo a second divorce. One in four suffered a severe and enduring drop in the family's standard of living and went on to observe a lasting discrepancy between their parents' standards of living.

We found that the children who were best adjusted 10 years later were those who showed the most distress at the time of the divorce—the youngest. In general, pre-schoolers are the most frightened and show the most dramatic symptoms when marriages break up. Many are afraid that they will be abandoned by both parents and they have trouble sleeping or staying by themselves. It is therefore surprising to find that the same children 10 years later seem better adjusted than their older siblings. Now in early and mid-adolescence, they were rated better on a wide range of psychological dimensions than the older children. Sixty-eight percent were doing well, compared with less than 40 percent of older children. But whether having been young at the time of divorce will continue to protect them as they enter young adulthood is an open question.

Our study shows that adolescence is a period of particularly grave risk for children in divorced families. Through rigorous analysis, statistical and otherwise, we were able to see clearly that we weren't dealing simply with the routine angst of young people going through transition but rather that, for most of them, divorce was the single most important cause of enduring pain and anomie in their lives. The young people told us time and again how much they needed a family structure, how much they wanted to be protected, and how much they yearned for clear guidelines for moral behavior. An alarming number of teenagers felt abandoned, physically and emotionally.

For children, divorce occurs during the formative years. What they see and experience becomes a part of their inner world, influencing their own relationships 10 and 15 years later, especially when they have witnessed violence between the parents. It is then, as these young men and women face the developmental task of establishing love and intimacy, that they most feel the lack of a template for a loving relationship between a man and a woman. It is here that their anxiety threatens their ability to create new, enduring families of their own.

As these anxieties peak in the children of divorce throughout our society, the full legacy of the rising divorce rate is beginning to hit home. The new families being formed today by these children as they reach adulthood appear particularly vulnerable.

Because our study was such an early inquiry, we did not set out to compare children of divorce with children from intact families. Lacking fundamental knowledge about life after the breakup of a marriage, we could not know on what basis to build a comparison or control group. Was the central issue one of economics, age, sex, a happy intact marriage—or would any intact marriage do? We began, therefore, with a question— What is the nature of the divorce experience?—and in answering it we would generate hypotheses that could be tested in subsequent studies.

This has indeed been the case. Numerous studies have been conducted in different regions of the country, using control groups, that have further explored and validated our findings as they have emerged over the years. For example, one national study of 699 elementary school children carefully compared children six years after their parents' divorce with children from intact families. It found—as we did—that elementary-age boys from divorced families show marked discrepancies in peer relationships, school achievement and social adjustment. Girls in this group, as expected, were hardly distinguishable based on the experience of divorce, but, as we later found out, this would not always hold up. Moreover, our findings are supported by a litany of modern-day statistics. Although one in three children are from divorced families, they account for an inordinately high proportion of children in mental-health treatment, in special-education classes, or referred by teachers to school psychologists. Children of divorce make up an estimated 60 percent of child patients in clinical treatment and 80 percent—in some cases, 100 percent—of adolescents in inpatient mental hospital settings. While no one would claim that a cause and effect relationship has been established in all of these cases, no one would deny that the role of divorce is so persuasively suggested that it is time to sound the alarm.

All studies have limitations in what they can accomplish. Longitudinal studies, designed to establish the impact of a major event or series of events on the course of a subsequent life, must always allow for the influence of many interrelated factors. They must deal with chance and the uncontrolled factors that so often modify the sequences being followed. This is particularly true of children, whose lives are influenced by developmental changes, only some of which are predictable, and by the problem of individual differences, about which we know so little.

Our sample, besides being quite small, was also drawn from a particular population slice—predominately white, middle class and relatively privileged suburbanites.

Despite these limitations, our data have generated working hypotheses about the effects of divorce that can now be tested with more precise methods, including appropriate control groups. Future research should be aimed at testing, correcting or modifying our initial findings, with larger and more diverse segments of the population. For example, we found that children—especially boys and young men—continued to need their fathers after divorce and suffered feelings of rejection even when they were visited regularly. I would like to see a study comparing boys and girls in sole and joint custody, spanning different developmental stages, to see if greater access to both parents counteracts these feelings of rejection. Or, does joint custody lead to a different sense of rejection—of feeling peripheral in both homes?

It is time to take a long, hard look at divorce in America. Divorce is not an event that stands alone in childrens' or adults' experience. It is a continuum that begins in the unhappy marriage and extends through the separation, divorce and any remarriages and second divorces. Divorce is not necessarily the sole culprit. It may be no more than one of the many experiences that occur in this broad continuum.

Profound changes in the family can only mean profound changes in society as a whole. All children in today's world feel less protected. They sense that the institution of the family is weaker than it has ever been before. Even those children raised in happy, intact families worry that their families may come undone. The task for society in its true and proper perspective is to strengthen the family—all families.

A biblical phrase I have not thought of for many years has recently kept running through my head: "Watchman, what of the night?" We are not I'm afraid, doing very well on our watch—at least for our children. We are allowing them to bear the psychological, economic and moral brunt of divorce.

And they recognize the burdens. When one 6-year-old boy came to our center shortly after his parents' divorce, he would not answer questions; he played games instead. First he hunted all over the playroom for the sturdy Swedish-designed dolls that we use in therapy. When he found a good number of them, he stood the baby dolls firmly on their feet and placed the miniature tables, chairs, beds and, eventually, all the playhouse furniture on top of them. He looked at me, satisfied. The babies were supporting a great deal. Then, wordlessly, he placed all the mother and father dolls in precarious positions on the steep roof of the doll house. As a father doll slid off the roof, the boy caught him and, looking up at me, said, "He might die." Soon, all the mother and father dolls began sliding off the roof. He caught them gently, one by one.

"The babies are holding up the world," he said.

Although our overall findings are troubling and serious, we should not point the finger of blame at divorce per se. Indeed, divorce is often the only rational solution to a bad marriage. When people ask whether they should stay married for the sake of the children, I have to say, "Of course not." All our evidence shows that children exposed to open conflict, where parents terrorize or strike one another, turn out less well-adjusted than do children from divorced families. And although we lack systematic studies comparing children in divorced families with those in unhappy intact families, I am convinced that it is not useful to provide children with a model of adult behavior that avoids problem-solving and that stresses martyrdom, violence or apathy. A divorce undertaken thoughtfully and realistically can teach children how to confront serious life problems with compassion, wisdom and appropriate action.

Our findings do not support those who would turn back the clock. As family issues are flung to the center of our political arena, nostalgic voices from the right argue for a return to a time when divorce was more difficult to obtain. But they do not offer solutions to the wretchedness and humiliation within many marriages.

Still we need to understand that divorce has consequences—we need to go into the experience with our eyes open. We need to know that many children will suffer for many years. As a society, we need to take steps to preserve for the children as much as possible of the social, economic and emotional security that existed while their parents' marriage was intact.

Like it or not, we are witnessing family changes which are an integral part of the wider changes in our society. We are on a wholly new course, one that gives us unprecedented opportunities for creating better relationships and stronger families—but one that also brings unprecedented dangers for society, especially for our children.

BIOLOGY, DESTINY, AND ALL THAT

Grabbing hold of a tar baby
of research findings, our writer
tries to pull apart truth from myth
in ideas about the differences
between the sexes.

Paul Chance

Paul Chance is a psychologist, writer, and contributing editor of *Psychology Today*.

In the 1880s, scholars warned against the hazards of educating women. Some experts of the day believed that too much schooling could endanger a woman's health, interfere with her reproductive ability, and cause her brain to deteriorate. In the 1980s we laugh at such absurd ideas, but have we (men and women alike) really given up the ancient idea that a woman is fundamentally an inferior sort of man? It seems not.

It's hard to find evidence these days of gross discrimination against women as a company policy. Successful lawsuits have made that sort of prejudice expensive. Yet evidence of more subtle forms of bias abound. The sociologist Beth Ghiloni conducted a study while she was a student at the University of California, Santa Cruz, that shows that some corporations are meeting the demands of affirmative action by putting women into public relations posts. Public relations is important but distant from the activities that generate revenue, so PR assignments effectively keep women out of jobs that include any real corporate power. Thus, women increasingly complain of facing a "glass ceiling" through which they can see, but cannot reach, high level corporate positions.

It seems likely that such discrimination reflects some very old ideas about what men and women are like. Men, the stereotype has it, are aggressive and self-confident. They think analytically, and are cool under fire. They enjoy jobs that offer responsibility and challenge. They are, in other words, ideally suited for important,

high-level positions. Put them on the track that may one day lead to corporate vice president.

Women, the thinking goes, are passive and filled with self-doubt. They think intuitively, and are inclined to become emotionally distraught under pressure. They therefore enjoy jobs that involve working with people. Give them the lower-rung jobs in the personnel department, or send them to public affairs.

Figuring out how truth and myth intertwine in these stereotypes is difficult. The research literature on sex differences is a tar baby made of numbers, case studies, and anecdotal impressions. To paraphrase one researcher, "If you like ambiguity, you're gonna love sex-difference research." Nevertheless, let us be brave and take the stereotypes apart piece by piece.

Aggression

On this there is no argument: Everyone agrees that men are more aggressive than women. In a classic review of the literature, the psychologists Eleanor Maccoby of Stanford University and Carol Jacklin of the University of Southern California found that boys are more aggressive than girls both physically and verbally, and the difference begins to show up by the age of 3. Boys are more inclined to rough-and-tumble play; girls have tea parties and play with dolls.

The difference in aggressiveness is most clearly seen in criminal activity. There are far more delinquent boys than girls, and prisons are built primarily to contain men. The most aggressive crimes, such as murder and assault, are especially dominated by men.

It seems hardly likely that male aggressiveness, as it is documented by the research, would win favor among personnel directors and corporate headhunters. Yet aggressiveness is considered not only a virtue but an essential trait for many jobs. Vice President George Bush learned the value of aggressiveness when he managed to put aside his wimp image by verbally attacking the CBS news anchorman Dan Rather on national television. The assumption seems to be that the same underlying trait that makes for murderers, rapists, and strong-arm bandits also, in more moderate degree or under proper guidance, makes people more competitive and motivated to achieve great things.

But the research suggests that women may be just as aggressive in this more civilized sense as men. For instance, most studies of competitiveness find no differences between the sexes, according to the psychologists Veronica Nieva and Barbara Gutek, co-authors of *Women and Work*. And many studies of achievement motivation suggest that women are just as eager to get things done as men.

Self-confidence

Men are supposed to be self-confident, women full of self-doubt. Again there is some evidence for the stereotype, but it isn't particularly complimentary to males. Various studies show that males overestimate their abilities, while females underestimate theirs. Researchers have found, for instance, that given the option of choosing tasks varying in difficulty, boys erred by choosing those that were too difficult for them, while girls tended to select tasks that were too easy.

Other research shows that women are not only less confident of their ability to do a job, when they succeed at it they don't give themselves credit. Ask them why they did well and they'll tell you it was an easy task or that they got lucky. Ask men the same thing and they'll tell you they did well because of their ability and hard work.

It is perhaps this difference in self-confidence that makes women better risks for auto insurance, and it may have something to do with the fact that almost from the day they can walk, males are more likely to be involved in pedestrian accidents.

Rational Thinking

A great many studies have found that men do better than women on tests of mathematical reasoning. Julian Stanley, a psychologist at Johns Hopkins University, has been using the mathematics portion of the Scholastic Aptitude Test to identify mathematically gifted youths. He and his colleagues have consistently found that a majority of the high scoring students are boys. Stanley reports that "mathematically gifted boys outnumber gifted girls by a ratio of about 13 to 1." Moreover, the very best scores almost inevitably come from boys.

But while some findings show that men are better at mathematical reasoning, there is no evidence that they are more analytical or logical in general. In fact, the superiority of men at mathematical problem solving seems not to reflect superior analytical thinking but a special talent men have for visualizing objects in space. Women are every bit the match of men at other kinds of problems such as drawing logical conclusions from written text. Indeed, girls have an advantage over boys in verbal skills until at least adolescence.

As for the idea that women are more intuitive, forget it. Numerous studies have shown that women are better at reading body language, and it is probably this skill (born, perhaps, of the need to avoid enraging the more aggressive sex) that gives rise to the myth of women's intuition. In reality, women and men think alike.

Emotionality

In Victorian England, to judge by the novels of the day, a woman was no woman at all if she didn't feel faint or burst into tears at least once a week. The idea that women are more emotional than men, that they feel things more deeply and react accordingly, persists. Is it true?

No. Carol Tavris and Carole Wade, psychologists and co-authors of *The Longest War: Sex Differences in Perspective*, write that the sexes are equally likely to feel anxious in new situations, to get angry when insulted, to be hurt when a loved one leaves them, and to feel embarrassed when they make mistakes in public.

The sexes are equally emotional, but there are important differences in how willing men and women are to express emotions, which emotions they choose to express, and the ways in which they express them. If you ask men and women in an emotional situation what they are feeling, women are likely to admit that they are affected, while men are likely to deny it. Yet studies show that when you look at the psychological correlates of emotion—heartbeat, blood pressure, and the like—you find that those strong silent men are churning inside every bit as much as the women.

Men are particularly eager to conceal feelings such as fear, sorrow, and loneliness, according to Tavris and Wade. Men often bottle these "feminine" feelings even with those they hold most dear.

Another difference comes in how emotions are expressed. Women behave differently depending upon what they feel. They may cry if sad, curse if angry, pout if their pride is hurt. Men tend to respond to such situations in a more or less uniform way. Whether they have been jilted, frightened, or snubbed, they become aggressive. (Men, you will recall, are very good at aggression.) As for the notion that keeping one's head is characteristic of men, well, don't get sore fellows, but it ain't necessarily so.

"It's unlikely that male aggressiveness, as documented by research, would win favor among personnel directors."

Men's math superiority reflects a special talent for visualizing objects in space.

Job Interests

If you ask men and women what they like about their work, you will get different answers. In 1957, Frederick Herzberg published a study of what made work enjoyable to employees. Men, he concluded, enjoyed work that offered responsibility and challenge. For women, on the other hand, the environment was the thing. They wanted an attractive work area, and some pleasant people to talk to while they did whatever needed to be done. Give your secretary an office with some nice wallpaper, put a flower on her desk once in a while, and she'll be happy.

Experts now agree, however, that such differences probably reflect differences in the jobs held by the people studied. You may get such findings, suggest *Women and Work* co-authors Nieva and Gutek, if you compare female file clerks and male engineers—but not if you compare female and male engineers. In a study of workers in various jobs, Daphne Bugental, a psychologist at the University of California, Santa Barbara, and the late Richard Centers found no consistent differences in the way men and women ranked "intrinsic" job characteristics such as responsibility and challenge and "extrinsic" characteristics such as pleasant surroundings and friendly co-workers. In other words, the dif-

ferences in what men and women find interesting about work reflect differences in the kinds of work men and women characteristically do. People in relatively high level jobs enjoy the responsibility and challenge it offers; people in low level jobs that offer little responsibility and challenge look elsewhere for satisfaction.

Where Do the Differences Come From?

So, what differences separate the boys from the girls? Men are reported to be more aggressive than women in a combative sense, but they are not necessarily more competitive. Men are more confident, perhaps recklessly so, and women may be too cautious. Men are not more likely to be cool under fire, but they are more likely to become aggressive regardless of what upsets them. Men are not more analytic in their thinking, nor women more intuitive, but men are better at solving mathematical problems, probably because they are better at spatial relationships. Finally, women are less interested in the responsibility and challenge of work, but only because they usually have jobs that offer little responsibility and challenge.

While this seems to be the gist of the matter, it leaves open the question of whether the differences are due to biology or to environment. Are

THE DEVELOPMENT OF THE "WEAKER SEX"
(AND THE DEMORALIZATION OF THE DUDE).

VASSAR GRADUATE.—"These are the dumb-bells I used last term in our gymnasium; won't one of you gentleman just put them up? It's awfully easy."

"All-male groups may be better at brainstorming, while all-female groups may be better at finding a solution."

men more aggressive because they are born that way or because of lessons that begin in the cradle? Are women less confident than men because different hormones course through their blood, or because for years people have told them that they can't expect much from themselves?

The research on the nature-nurture question is a candy store in which people of varying biases can quickly find something to their liking. Beryl Lieff Benderly, an anthropologist and journalist, critiqued the physiological research for her new book, *The Myth of Two Minds*. The title tells the story. She even challenges the notion that men are stronger than women. "The plain fact is that we have no idea whether men are 'naturally' stronger than women," she writes. Short of conducting an experiment along the lines of *Lord of the Flies*, we are unlikely to unravel the influences of nature and nurture to everyone's satisfaction. Nevertheless, research does offer hints about the ways that biology and environment affect stereotypical behavior. Take the case of aggression. There are any number of studies linking aggression to biological factors. Testosterone, a hormone found in much higher levels in men than in women, has been found in even larger quantities in criminally aggressive males. Castration, which decreases the level of testosterone, has been used for centuries to produce docile men and animals. And girls who have had prenatal exposure to high levels of testosterone are more tomboyish than other girls.

Yet biology is not quite destiny. In her famous *Six Cultures* study, the anthropologist Beatrice Whiting and her colleagues at Harvard University found that in each of the societies studied, boys were more aggressive than girls. But the researchers also found such wide cultural differences that the girls in a highly aggressive society were often more aggressive than the boys in another, less aggressive society.

The same mix of forces applies wherever we look. Biology may bend the twig in one direction, but the environment may bend it in another. But whether biology or environment ultimately wins the hearts and minds of researchers is less important than how the differences, wherever they come from, affect behavior in the workplace. If someone explodes in anger (or breaks down in tears) in the midst of delicate contract negotiations, it matters little to the stockholders whether the lost business can, in the end, be blamed on testosterone or bad toilet training. The more important question is, what are the implications of sex difference research for business?

What Difference Do the Differences Make?

The research on sex differences suggest three points that people in business can usefully con-

sider. First, the differences between the sexes are small. Researchers look for "statistically significant" differences. But statistically significant differences are not necessarily practically significant. There is a great deal of overlap between the sexes on most characteristics and especially on the characteristics we have been considering. Men are, on average, better at solving mathematical problems, but there are many women who are far above the average man in this area. Women are, on average, less confident than men. But there are many men who doubt themselves far more than the average woman. A study of aggressiveness is illustrative. The psychologist D. Anthony Butterfield and the management expert Gary N. Powell had college students rate the ideal U.S. President on various characteristics, including aggressiveness. Then they had them rate people who were running for President and Vice President at the time: Ronald Reagan, Walter Mondale, George Bush, and Geraldine Ferraro. Researchers found that the ideal president was, among other things, aggressive. They also found that Geraldine Ferraro was judged more aggressive than the male candidates. The point is that it is impossible to predict individual qualities from group differences.

Indeed, Carol Jacklin suggests that differences in averages may give a quite distorted view of both sexes. She notes that while, on average, boys play more aggressively than girls, her research shows that the difference is due to a small number of very aggressive boys. Most of the boys are, in fact, very much like the girls. "I'd be willing to bet," Jacklin says, "that much of the difference in aggressiveness between men and women is due to a small number of extremely aggressive men—many of whom are in prison—and that the remaining men are no more aggressive than most women."

Second, different doesn't necessarily mean inferior. It is quite possible that feminine traits (in men or women) are assets in certain situations, while masculine traits may be advantageous in other situations. The psychologist Carol Gilligan, author of *In a Different Voice*, says that women are more comfortable with human relationships than men are, and this may sometimes give them an edge. For instance, Roderick Gilkey and Leonard Greenhalgh, psychologists at Dartmouth University, had business students simulate negotiations over the purchase of a used car and television advertising time. The women appeared better suited to the task than the men. They were more flexible, more willing to compromise, and less deceptive. "Women can usually come to an agreement on friendly terms," says Greenhalgh. "They're better at avoiding impasses."

In another study, the psychologist Wendy Wood of Texas A&M University asked college students to work on problems in groups of three.

"Biology may bend the twig in one direction, but the environment may bend it in another."

Some groups consisted only of men, others of women. The groups tried to solve problems such as identifying the features to consider in buying a house. The men, it turns out, came up with more ideas, while the women zeroed in on one good idea and developed it. Wood concluded that all-male groups might be better for brainstorming, while all-female groups might be better for finding the best solution to a problem.

Third, sometimes people lack the characteristics needed for a job until they are in the job. Jobs that offer responsibility and challenge, for example, tend to create a desire for more responsibility and challenge. While there are research studies to support this statement, an anecdote from the sociologist Rosabeth Moss Kanter is more telling. Linda, a secretary for 17 years in a large corporation, had no interest in being anything but a secretary, and when she was offered a promotion through an affirmative action program, she hesitated. Her boss persuaded her to take the job and she became a successful manager and loved the additional responsibility and challenge. She even set her sights on a vice president position. As a secretary, Linda would no doubt have scored near the female stereotype. But when she became a manager, she became more like the stereotypical male.

Kanter told that story a dozen years ago, but we are still struggling to learn its lesson. A discrimination case against Sears, Roebuck and Company recently made news. The Equal Employment Opportunity Commission (EEOC) argued that Sears discriminated against women because nearly all of the employees in the company who sell on commission are men. Sears presented evidence that women expressed little interest in commission-sales work, preferring the less risky jobs in salaried sales. In the original decision favoring Sears, the U.S. District Court had found that "noncommission saleswomen were generally happier with their present jobs at Sears, and were much less likely than their male counterparts to be interested in other positions, such as commission sales. . . ." But in the U.S. Court of Appeals, Appellate Judge Cudahy, who dissented in part from the majority, wrote that this reasoning is "of a piece with the proposition that women are by nature happier cooking, doing the laundry, and chauffeuring the children to softball games than arguing appeals or selling stocks."

The point is not that employees must be made to accept more responsible positions for their own good, even if it is against their will. The point is that business should abandon the stereotypes that lock men and women into different, and often unequal, kinds of work. If it finally does, it will discover the necessity—and value—of finding ways of enticing men and women into jobs for which, according to the stereotypes, they are not suited. If business doesn't do that, it may discover that differences between men and women really do separate the sexes.

WHY JAPANESE KIDS ARE SMARTER

(or Are They?)

Japanese education envy has hit America en masse and puzzled parents are scrambling for the answers to its school success. But hold on to your calculators—the solution may just surprise you!

Stephanie Wood

Akiko Ogasawara* will never forget her native Japan. Like many immigrants, she wants to stay connected to her heritage—and she wants her children to be familiar with the culture of the homeland they will know only through excursions across the Pacific. She often holds a traditional tea ceremony in the Japanese garden that she has cultivated in her suburban backyard in Darien, Connecticut, so that Tomoko, 8, and Akito, 5, will come to appreciate its meditative benefits. Ogasawara also prefers to feed her family a good-for-you Japanese diet of seafood, rice, and vegetables so their bodies will stay as sharp and lean as their minds, unlike many of their American peers.

But when it comes to education Ogasawara rates the U.S. school system higher. Surprised? You're not the only one. American parents and educators have been searching for the secrets to Japanese academic success for decades, but the truth is, those good grades aren't all due to intellect—and may not carry over to contemporary lifestyle. "In Japanese schools, group harmony is emphasized; they don't want the

children to stick out," explains Ogasawara, who recalls getting into trouble as a youngster because she didn't want to go to the bathroom with the other kids at the appointed time. "Educators should teach children independence, confidence, and self-respect, but the Japanese don't see it that way. Instead, they teach conformity, and that won't give children the skills they need to get along in the non-Japanese world."

For a while now, America has been fascinated with Japan—and all things Japanese. We've replaced our long, smooth American automobiles of yesteryear with efficient little Toyotas and Hondas. We listen to high-tech hi-fi systems brought to us by Sony, Sanyo, Hitachi, and JVC. And above all, the par-

ents among us are practically obsessed with the academic prowess of Japanese students. They continually outperform, outscore, and outright embarrass us, both in international education comparisons and in our own classrooms on these shores. According to the International Association for the Evaluation of Educational Achievement, during the past two decades the performance of American children in science has slipped from seventh to 14th place (out of 17 countries tested), while Japan and Hungary have juggled the number one and two positions between them. Other studies show that as early as first grade, Japanese children score 20 percent higher in math than their U.S. counterparts.

Even the Ozzie-and-Harriet-type parenting of the 1950s doesn't make the grade when it comes to mothering Japanese-style.

*These people's names have been changed at their request.

"How do they do it?" ambitious parents with similar aspirations for their offspring wonder not-so-silently in suburbs like Chevy Chase, Evanston, and Scarsdale. While many American educators quickly counter the implied criticism by pointing to Japan's notoriously rigorous rote-study routine, stringent discipline and performance pressure, and the sheer hours devoted to homework and after-school cram classes, other experts see a deeper influence. "It's in their character," says Bruce Feiler, author of the just-published *Learning to Bow*, an account of his recent years as an American teacher in the Japanese school system. "The Japanese create an educational environment in which discovery is valued. To them, learning is an attitude, a state of mind. And learning encompasses everything from pouring tea to riding a bike. All that is necessary for life is taught in school."

Which may explain why Japanese children attend school 60 more days a year than American children. But there is indeed something else happening here, and increasingly research reveals that it's occurring in the Japanese home—a place where children are raised practically from birth to conform, cooperate, and succeed. And from what we've seen so far, succeed they do indeed.

Will the Real Supermother Please Stand Up?

Once upon a time, most American mothers stayed home with their children. In fact, many women today are deciding to downshift from the contemporary pressures of the career track and return to full-time mothering, at least temporarily while their children are young. But even the Ozzie-and-Harriet-type parenting this trend evokes doesn't make the grade when it comes to mothering Japanese-style. Japanese mothers not only don't work, they don't use babysitters, and they seldom stray far from their children—studies show that mothers usually sleep next to the child in the same room until he reaches school age, and will often actually hold an infant while he sleeps. In fact, Japanese mothers interviewed in a study by Marguerite Stevenson Barratt, Ph.D., a child and family studies professor at the University of Wisconsin in Madison, "simply cannot

imagine a mother leaving her infant so far away that she must depend on an electronic device to hear the baby."

Since even the most successful of Japanese families usually dwell in modest-size urban apartments, privacy certainly goes out the window along with the need for baby monitors. Still, the mother-child bond goes much deeper than a cramped lifestyle might dictate. "In Japan, more focus is given to the emotional side of childrearing," emphasizes Jushichiro Naito, M.D., the Dr. Spock of his nation and author of more than 30 parenting books, including *Childcare: Nurturing the Heart*, soon to be published in the U.S. "Japanese mothers offer a selfless love to their not-yet-walking infants."

This love includes a constant togetherness that not only is impossible by American standards, it cultivates a personality trait that's undesirable in our society: dependence. "The mother does her very best to satisfy the infant's basic needs so as to 'convince' the child to rely on her," notes Dr. Barratt.

A linchpin attitude of Japanese childrearing, this "full care," called *amae*, results in the child feeling "few frustrations and peace of mind," according to Dr. Naito. And who wouldn't, if his mom was at his beck and call 24 hours a day?

In spite of what sounds to Westerners like excessive doting and spoiling, Japanese mothers do have ways of controlling their children's behavior. In a 12-year comparison study of Japanese and American families, Robert Hess, Ph.D., a professor of human development at Stanford University in Palo Alto, California, and Hiroshi Azuma, Ph.D., a colleague at the University of Tokyo, found that Japanese mothers are more likely to appeal to the child's feelings or impress upon him the consequences of his behavior in order to gain cooperation. American mothers, however, most often take an authoritative approach to discipline, coaxing, demanding, even threatening a child who acts up. For example, when asked how she would respond if her child drew on the wall with crayons, one mother in the U.S. said that she'd tell him, "You know better than that. We're going to put the crayons away until you know how to play with them—and clean the wall!" A Japanese mother, however,

replied that she'd tell her mischievous child: "The wall is crying."

But how does this intense nurturing result in high test scores? According to a breakthrough study conducted in the 1960s by the late William Caudill, Ph.D., of the University of Chicago, Japanese mothers spend more than twice as much time rocking their infant children, and substantially more time holding them (24.6 percent versus 17.4) than American mothers. All of this early physical contact, researchers have concluded, produces a mental environment conducive to right-brain development, which enhances the child's spatial intelligence as well as logical and mathematical reasoning skills. And Drs. Hess and Azuma also found in their study that "the close bonding between the Japanese mother and child is at least as important as the extra study hours put in by the children."

Adding Up the Education Equation

Once Japanese children reach the classroom, the teacher takes over not merely as an academic guide, but also as an emotional, social, and disciplinary leader. "When I first came here and saw American schools, the biggest surprise was to see the schoolteachers wearing high heels!" says Yumiko Uchida, a Fort Lee, New Jersey, mother of Mamiko, 10, and Yoshitaka, 6. "In Japan, the teachers go out to play with the students on the field, so it's impossible to be concerned with high fashion."

Indeed, Japanese teachers do everything with their homeroom class, or **kumi**. Teacher and students eat lunch together, play together during recess, and clean the classroom together after the school day ends. "One of the most striking differences in their system is the sense of community created in homeroom," notes Feiler. "A sense of belonging to a group and the propriety within that group are critical to the Japanese self-concept. And it's just a short jump from this early sense of community and service to company loyalty later in life. It's a very deliberate government policy."

This same sort of commitment is also applied to academics. Japanese teachers drill their students relentlessly on math problems, scientific formulas, and historical data—then the kids go home and practice some more. According to the Institute for Social Research at the University of Michigan in Ann Arbor, the average grade-schooler in Japan spends 8.3 hours per week on homework, compared to 1.8 hours for his American peers." The Japanese do a supe-

Trading Places

If American and Japanese parents traded childrearing skills as frequently as their countries exchange dollars and yen, the combined characteristics of the next generation would ensure success on all fronts.

WHAT WE CAN LEARN FROM THE JAPANESE:

- Getting back to basics (math, science, geography) in school.
- A stronger work ethic.
- Loyalty to others and the sense of belonging that comes from feeling attached to a group or team.
- The critical need for parental support in the education process.
- The value of strong mother-infant bonding and a return to an appreciation of mothering as a full-time job.
- The importance of good citizenship and patriotism.

WHAT THE JAPANESE CAN LEARN FROM US:

- How to communicate better verbally.
- The emotional fulfillment that comes from creative expression.
- An appreciation of kids' individual talents and learning styles.
- How to nurture a child's self-concept.
- How to become independent without losing touch with family.
- The importance of the father's role in childrearing, which is sadly nonexistent in Japanese society.

rior job in the detail-oriented areas of math and science," notes Feiler. "Their monologue-style lectures work well in these subjects. The give-and-take dialogue of American teachers, however, is superior in conceptual areas such as literature, philosophy, and art."

A few years into elementary school, Japanese students add yet another activity to their academic agendas: *juku* school, private tutoring agencies where children starting at about age 8 go after school each weekday and often on Saturday, to cram for their government-mandated high school and university entrance exams. Jukus have become so common in Japan that many are beginning to crop up in Japanese communities in the U.S. so that students who move here temporarily can keep up with competition at home.

"It's a stupid system, but a fact of life in Japan," says Uchida. "The entrance exams are so hard to pass that from fourth or fifth grade, children have to go to juku. A lot of Japanese parents believe that going to a good university is everything." And indeed it is in Japan, where employers hire recent graduates solely on the basis of the university degree they hold. In fact, notes Feiler, a student's grades aren't nearly as important to employers as the fact that he got into the prestigious university.

Although it may seem that the Japanese mother's role diminishes once the child is caught up in this study cycle, the reality is exactly the opposite. "Educating children has become the 'work' of Japanese mothers," explains Ogasawara. "It becomes a competition between them to see whose child can land the best university acceptance and then the best job."

This practice of applying maternal academic pressure has become so prevalent in Japan that it's become a sort of cult with its own name: *kyoiku mamas*, which translates as "education mothers." "It is not a desirable thing to have kyoiku mamas," notes Dr. Naito. "The pressure is too intense and it becomes difficult to raise a child to have a rich and plentiful heart." Nevertheless, Dr. Naito, like his countrymen, passes off this "unhealthy trend" as a way of life. "There is a tendency in Japan for a person to be evaluated not by the kind of work she does, but by what university she graduated from. Therefore, all efforts are poured into passing the entrance exams," he says.

Students in Japan seem to hold up well in the face of the pressure that results from their society's enormous expectations, however. "The message of defying authority has never caught on in Japan as it has in the West," Feiler notes. Statistics support

this. While Japan did have a high youth suicide rate after World War II, when much of the population was depressed about the country's future, those numbers have dropped off in recent years so that they're about equal to U.S. statistics.

It's another story though for those Japanese-American youths who are trying to fit into a different cultural norm. Tales of Japanese teenagers in this country who rebel against their parents—sometimes with physical force—abound, and morbid statistics sketch a picture of alienation and confusion. Suicide rates among Asian-American youths ages 15 to 24 have tripled in the past two decades, according to the Department of Health and Human Services in Washington, DC. For Japanese in particular, the rate is 54 percent higher than for same-age Americans.

The Cultural Exchange

One of the biggest ironies then may well be that while American educators have been trying to figure out how to combine higher-level performance with creative, student-centered classroom pursuits intended to make learning pleasurable on these shores, the forward-thinking parents of the Pacific Rim are trying to be more like us. Even as President Bush and Education Secretary Lamar Alexander call for a controversial national test to rate student performance that is fairly similar to the stringent exam system of Japan, the pupils of that nation are rebelling against strict dress codes by spiking or tinting their hair, young women are refusing to marry and give up their chances at careers, and government officials are throwing up their hands in dismay over a generation that seems to be too selfish to be concerned with the nation's "social welfare."

"The older generation of Japanese recalls the devastation of World War II and still subscribes to the idea that the people, as a group, are the strongest resource of Japan," says Feiler. "Those in their 20s and 30s, however, don't remember the need for poverty and mass perseverance. They recognize instead the need for individual development, and that they must become 'good citizens of the world' to learn to work with other nations."

One way the Japanese are pursuing that goal is in promoting greater verbal acuity, and knowledge of the English language in

One of the most striking differences between our school system and theirs is the sense of community created in the Japanese classroom.

particular. Dr. Caudill's earlier studies revealed that the physically attentive mothering style of the Japanese, which relies on instinct and emotions, actually discourages verbal development, a skill that American mothers promote in their infant interactions. The result is that as adults, their communicative abilities are substantially more limited than their spatial abilities.

"One of the greatest things about the school system here is the English as a Second Language program," says Uchida. "My children wouldn't get this kind of English instruction at home. The main things I want them to learn while they're here are to speak well and to express their opinions in front of others. Japanese children are often too shy to do so."

Another Americanism Uchida considers worth adopting is the ability to enjoy life, American-style. "The Japanese work too hard. It's important to admire someone who does a good job, but you have to have time for your family, too," she says.

Since the Uchidas will be transferred back to their Yokohama home within a couple of years, daughter Mamiko has chosen to go to a Japanese school. "She had a difficult time in public school at first, but is much happier now that she is with other children like herself," her mother notes, a not unfamiliar occurrence among U.S.-based Japanese, who are sometimes subjected to not-a-little resentment from equally achievement-oriented American families.

Western moms and dads might, in fact, take a lesson from the Japanese about parental expectations, which, for the latter culture, often translates to a self-fulfilling prophecy. According to research from the University of Michigan in Ann Arbor, Japanese mothers ranked effort as the most important factor in their children's success. Their American counterparts, however, felt innate ability was the primary influence on achievement, leading researchers to conclude that parents in the U.S. are less likely to stress hard work.

In spite of the tendency on the part of both cultures to focus on scores and performance ratings, experts on each side of the fence are beginning to recognize that we just may be trying to mix apples and oranges. "Comparing averages is not an accurate portrayal of Japanese and American students," emphasizes Michael Boyle, Ph.D., a school psychologist at Chicago-based Loyola University who conducted a recent study comparing thinking styles of Japanese and American students. "The Japanese education system does not account for individual differences in children." The end result: Those children who are less bright, or whose intelligence and talents take a nontraditional turn (toward art or music, for instance), are weeded out at the university exam level and subjected to lives as supporting players in the blue-collar or agricultural world.

Certainly the opposing values of our peoples—conformity, dependence, and group loyalty in Japan; assertiveness, independence, and individual success in the U.S.—make it hard to believe that we could adopt each other's ways. But we can certainly learn from each other, and work together in the spirit of acceptance. Even the "God of Childcare," as Dr. Naito has been dubbed by his people, admits that "the way in which an American child becomes independent from her parents is a wonderful thing, as is the fact that American parents accept their children's independence."

Wonderful indeed. "Being different is a *good* thing," emphasizes Ogasawara. "All children have abilities and interests and, with the right education, can develop the confidence to be successful at them. We have to quit looking at the things they *can't* do." And that, dear parents, is the new international language of education.

ALIENATION

AND THE FOUR WORLDS OF CHILDHOOD

The forces that produce youthful alienation are growing in strength and scope, says Mr. Bronfenbrenner. And the best way to counteract alienation is through the creation of connections or links throughout our culture. The schools can build such links.

Urie Bronfenbrenner

Urie Bronfenbrenner is Jacob Gould Shurman Professor of Human Development and Family Studies and of Psychology at Cornell University, Ithaca, N.Y.

To be alienated is to lack a sense of belonging, to feel cut off from family, friends, school, or work—the four worlds of childhood.

At some point in the process of growing up, many of us have probably felt cut off from one or another of these worlds, but usually not for long and not from more than one world at a time. If things weren't going well in school, we usually still had family, friends, or some activity to turn to. But if, over an extended period, a young person feels unwanted or insecure in several of these worlds simultaneously or if the worlds are at war with one another, trouble may lie ahead.

What makes a young person feel that he or she doesn't belong? Individual differences in personality can certainly be one cause, but, especially in recent years, scientists who study human behavior and development have identified an equal (if not even more powerful) factor: the circumstances in which a young person lives.

Many readers may feel that they recognize the families depicted in the vignettes that are to follow. This is so because they reflect the way we tend to look at families today: namely, that we see parents as being good or not-so-good without fully taking into account the circumstances in their lives.

Take Charles and Philip, for example. Both are seventh-graders who live in a middle-class suburb of a large U.S. city. In many ways their surroundings seem similar; yet, in terms of the risk of alienation, they live in rather different worlds. See if you can spot the important differences.

CHARLES

The oldest of three children, Charles is amiable, outgoing, and responsible. Both of his parents have full-time jobs outside the home. They've been able to arrange their working hours, however, so that at least one of them is at home when the children return from school. If for some reason they can't be home, they have an arrangement with a neighbor, an elderly woman who lives alone. They can phone her and ask her to look after the children until they arrive. The children have grown so fond of this woman that she is like another grandparent—a nice situation for them, since their real grandparents live far away.

Homework time is one of the most important parts of the day for Charles and his younger brother and sister. Charles's parents help the children with their homework if they need it, but most of the time they just make sure that the children have a period of peace and quiet—without TV—in which to do their work. The children are allowed to watch television one hour each night—but only after they have completed their homework. Since Charles is doing well in school, homework isn't much of an issue, however.

Sometimes Charles helps his mother or father prepare dinner, a job that everyone in the family shares and enjoys. Those family members who don't cook on a given evening are responsible for cleaning up.

Charles also shares his butterfly collection with his family. He started the collection when he first began learning about butterflies during a fourth-grade science project. The whole family enjoys picnicking and hunting butterflies together, and Charles occasionally asks his father to help him mount and catalogue his trophies.

Charles is a bit of a loner. He's not a very good athlete, and this makes him somewhat self-conscious. But he does have one very close friend, a boy in his class who lives just down the block. The two boys have been good friends for years.

Charles is a good-looking, warm, happy young man. Now that he's beginning to be interested in girls, he's gratified to find that the interest is returned.

PHILIP

Philip is 12 and lives with his mother, father, and 6-year-old brother. Both of his parents work in the city, commuting more than an hour each way. Pandemonium strikes every weekday morning as

From *Phi Delta Kappan*, February 1986, pp. 430-436. Reprinted by permission of the author and Phi Delta Kappan.

153

the entire family prepares to leave for school and work.

Philip is on his own from the time school is dismissed until just before dinner, when his parents return after stopping to pick up his little brother at a nearby day-care home. At one time, Philip took care of his little brother after school, but he resented having to do so. That arrangement ended one day when Philip took his brother out to play and the little boy wandered off and got lost. Philip didn't even notice for several hours that his brother was missing. He felt guilty at first about not having done a better job. But not having to mind his brother freed him to hang out with his friends or to watch television, his two major after-school activities.

The pace of their life is so demanding that Philip's parents spend their weekends just trying to relax. Their favorite weekend schedule calls for watching a ball game on television and then having a cookout in the back yard. Philip's mother resigned herself long ago to a messy house; pizza, TV dinners, or fast foods are all she can manage in the way of meals on most nights. Philip's father has made it clear that she can do whatever she wants in managing the house, as long as she doesn't try to involve him in the effort. After a hard day's work, he's too tired to be interested in housekeeping.

Philip knows that getting a good education is important; his parents have stressed that. But he just can't seem to concentrate in school. He'd much rather fool around with his friends. The thing that he and his friends like to do best is to ride the bus downtown and go to a movie, where they can show off, make noise, and make one another laugh.

Sometimes they smoke a little marijuana during the movie. One young man in Philip's social group was arrested once for having marijuana in his jacket pocket. He was trying to sell it on the street so that he could buy food. Philip thinks his friend was stupid to get caught. If you're smart, he believes, you don't let that happen. He's glad that his parents never found out about the incident.

Once, he brought two of his friends home during the weekend. His parents told him later that they didn't like the kind of people he was hanging around with. Now Philip goes out of his way to keep his friends and his parents apart.

THE FAMILY UNDER PRESSURE

In many ways the worlds of both

> **I**nstitutions that play important roles in human development are rapidly being eroded, mainly through benign neglect.

teenagers are similar, even typical. Both live in families that have been significantly affected by one of the most important developments in American family life in the postwar years: the employment of both parents outside the home. Their mothers share this status with 64% of all married women in the U.S. who have school-age children. Fifty percent of mothers of preschool children and 46% of mothers with infants under the age of 3 work outside the home. For single-parent families, the rates are even higher: 53% of all mothers in single-parent households who have infants under age 3 work outside the home, as do 69% of all single mothers who have school-age children.[1]

These statistics have profound implications for families — sometimes for better, sometimes for worse. The determining factor is how well a given family can cope with the "havoc in the home" that two jobs can create. For, unlike most other industrialized nations, the U.S. has yet to introduce the kinds of policies and practices that make work life and family life compatible.

It is all too easy for family life in the U.S. to become hectic and stressful, as both parents try to coordinate the disparate demands of family and jobs in a world in which everyone has to be transported at least twice a day in a variety of directions. Under these circumstances, meal preparation, child care, shopping, and cleaning — the most basic tasks in a family — become major challenges. Dealing with these challenges may sometimes take precedence over the family's equally important child-rearing, educational, and nurturing roles.

But that is not the main danger. What

threatens the well-being of children and young people the most is that the external havoc can become internal, first for parents and then for their children. And that is exactly the sequence in which the psychological havoc of families under stress usually moves.

Recent studies indicate that conditions at work constitute one of the major sources of stress for American families.[2] Stress at work carries over to the home, where it affects first the relationship of parents to each other. Marital conflict then disturbs the parent/child relationship. Indeed, as long as tensions at work do not impair the relationship between the parents, the children are not likely to be affected. In other words, the influence of parental employment on children is indirect, operating through its effect on the parents.

That this influence is indirect does not make it any less potent, however. Once the parent/child relationship is seriously disturbed, children begin to feel insecure — and a door to the world of alienation has been opened. That door can open to children at any age, from preschool to high school and beyond.

My reference to the world of school is not accidental, for it is in that world that the next step toward alienation is likely to be taken. Children who feel rootless or caught in conflict at home find it difficult to pay attention in school. Once they begin to miss out on learning, they feel lost in the classroom, and they begin to seek acceptance elsewhere. Like Philip, they often find acceptance in a group of peers with similar histories who, having no welcoming place to go and nothing challenging to do, look for excitement on the streets.

OTHER INFLUENCES

In contemporary American society the growth of two-wage-earner families is not the only — or even the most serious — social change requiring accommodation through public policy and practice in order to avoid the risks of alienation. Other social changes include lengthy trips to and from work; the loss of the extended family, the close neighborhood, and other support systems previously available to families; and the omnipresent threat of television and other media to the family's traditional role as the primary transmitter of culture and values. Along with most families today, the families of Charles and Philip are experiencing the unraveling and disintegration of social institutions that in the past were central to the health and well-being of children and their parents.

Notice that both Charles and Philip come from two-parent, middle-class families. This is still the norm in the U.S. Thus neither family has to contend with two changes now taking place in U.S. society that have profound implications for the future of American families and the well-being of the next generation. The first of these changes is the increasing number of single-parent families. Although the divorce rate in the U.S. has been leveling off of late, this decrease has been more than compensated for by a rise in the number of unwed mothers, especially teenagers. Studies of the children brought up in single-parent families indicate that they are at greater risk of alienation than their counterparts from two-parent families. However, their vulnerability appears to have its roots not in the single-parent family structure as such, but in the treatment of single parents by U.S. society.[3]

In this nation, single parenthood is almost synonymous with poverty. And the growing gap between poor families and the rest of us is today the most powerful and destructive force producing alienation in the lives of millions of young people in America. In recent years, we have witnessed what the U.S. Census Bureau calls "the largest decline in family income in the post-World War II period." According to the latest Census, 25% of all children under age 6 now live in families whose incomes place them below the poverty line.

COUNTERING THE RISKS

Despite the similar stresses on their families, the risks of alienation for Charles and Philip are not the same. Clearly, Charles's parents have made a deliberate effort to create a variety of arrangements and practices that work against alienation. They have probably not done so as part of a deliberate program of "alienation prevention" — parents don't usually think in those terms. They're just being good parents. They spend time with their children and take an active interest in what their children are thinking, doing, and learning. They control their television set instead of letting it control them. They've found support systems to back them up when they're not available.

Without being aware of it, Charles's parents are employing a principle that the great Russian educator Makarenko employed in his extraordinarily success-

ful programs for the reform of wayward adolescents in the 1920s: "The maximum of support with the maximum of challenge."[4] Families that produce effective, competent children often follow this principle, whether they're aware of it or not. They neither maintain strict control nor allow their children total freedom. They're always opening doors — and then giving their children a gentle but firm shove to encourage them to move on and grow. This combination of support and challenge is essential, if children are to avoid alienation and develop into capable young adults.

From a longitudinal study of youthful alienation and delinquency that is now considered a classic, Finnish psychologist Lea Pulkkinen arrived at a conclusion strikingly similar to Makarenko's. She found "guidance" — a combination of love and direction — to be a critical predictor of healthy development in youngsters.[5]

No such pattern is apparent in Philip's family. Unlike Charles's parents, Philip's parents neither recognize nor respond to the challenges they face. They have dispensed with the simple amenities of family self-discipline in favor of whatever is easiest. They may not be indifferent to their children, but the demands of their jobs leave them with little energy to be actively involved in their children's lives. (Note that Charles's parents have work schedules that are flexible enough to allow one of them to be at home most afternoons. In this regard, Philip's family is much more the norm, however. One of the most constructive steps that employers could take to strengthen families would be to enact clear policies making such flexibility possible.)

But perhaps the clearest danger signal in Philip's life is his dependence on his peer group. Pulkkinen found heavy reliance on peers to be one of the strongest predictors of problem behavior in adolescence and young adulthood. From a developmental viewpoint, adolescence is a time of challenge — a period in which young people seek activities that will serve as outlets for their energy, imagination, and longings. If healthy and constructive challenges are not available to them, they will find their challenges in such peer-group-related behaviors as poor school performance, aggressiveness or social withdrawal (sometimes both), school absenteeism or dropping out, smoking, drinking, early and promiscuous sexual activity, teenage parenthood, drugs, and juvenile delinquency.

This pattern has now been identified in a number of modern industrial societies, including the U.S., England, West Germany, Finland, and Australia. The pattern is both predictable from the circumstances of a child's early family life and predictive of life experiences still to come, e.g., difficulties in establishing relationships with the opposite sex, marital discord, divorce, economic failure, criminality.

If the roots of alienation are to be found in disorganized families living in disorganized environments, its bitter fruits are to be seen in these patterns of disrupted development. This is not a harvest that our nation can easily afford. Is it a price that other modern societies are paying, as well?

A CROSS-NATIONAL PERSPECTIVE

The available answers to that question will not make Americans feel better about what is occurring in the U.S. In our society, the forces that produce youthful alienation are growing in strength and scope. Families, schools, and other institutions that play important roles in human development are rapidly being eroded, *mainly through benign neglect*. Unlike the citizens of other modern nations, we Americans have simply not been willing to make the necessary effort to forestall the alienation of our young people.

As part of a new experiment in higher education at Cornell University, I have been teaching a multidisciplinary course for the past few years titled "Human Development in Post-Industrial Societies." One of the things we have done in that course is to gather comparative data from several nations, including France, Canada, Japan, Australia, Germany, England, and the U.S. One student summarized our findings succinctly: "With respect to families, schools, children, and youth, such countries as France, Japan, Canada, and Australia have more in common with each other than the United States has with any of them." For example:

• The U.S. has by far the highest rate of teenage pregnancy of any industrialized nation — twice the rate of its nearest competitor, England.

• The U.S. divorce rate is the highest in the world — nearly double that of its nearest competitor, Sweden.

• The U.S. is the only industrialized society in which nearly one-fourth of all infants and preschool children live in families whose incomes fall below the poverty line. These children lack such basics as adequate health care.

• The U.S. has fewer support systems for individuals in all age groups, including adolescence. The U.S. also has the highest incidence of alcohol and drug abuse among adolescents of any country in the world.[6]

All these problems are part of the unraveling of the social fabric that has been going on since World War II. These problems are not unique to the U.S., but in many cases they are more pronounced here than elsewhere.

WHAT COMMUNITIES CAN DO

The more we learn about alienation and its effects in contemporary post-industrial societies, the stronger are the imperatives to counteract it. If the essence of alienation is disconnectedness, then the best way to counteract alienation is through the creation of connections or links.

For the well-being of children and adolescents, the most important links must be those between the home, the peer group, and the school. A recent study in West Germany effectively demonstrated how important this basic triangle can be. The study examined student achievement and social behavior in 20 schools. For all the schools, the researchers developed measures of the links between the home, the peer group, and the school. Controlling for social class and other variables, the researchers found that they were able to predict children's behavior from the number of such links they found. Students who had no links were alienated. They were not doing well in school, and they exhibited a variety of behavioral problems. By contrast, students who had such links were doing well and were growing up to be responsible citizens.[7]

In addition to creating links within the basic triangle of home, peer group, and school, we need to consider two other structures in today's society that affect the lives of young people: the world of work (for both parents and children) and the community, which provides an overarching context for all the other worlds of childhood.

Philip's family is one example of how the world of work can contribute to alienation. The U.S. lags far behind other industrialized nations in providing child-care services and other benefits designed to promote the well-being of children and their families. Among the most needed benefits are maternity and paternity leaves, flex-time, job-sharing

> ## Caring is surely an essential aspect of education in a free society; yet we have almost completely neglected it.

arrangements, and personal leaves for parents when their children are ill. These benefits are a matter of course in many of the nations with which the U.S. is generally compared.

In contemporary American society, however, the parents' world of work is not the only world that both policy and practice ought to be accommodating. There is also the children's world of work. According to the most recent figures available, 50% of all high school students now work part-time — sometimes as much as 40 to 50 hours per week. This fact poses a major problem for the schools. Under such circumstances, how can teachers assign homework with any expectation that it will be completed?

The problem is further complicated by the kind of work that most young people are doing. For many years, a number of social scientists — myself included — advocated more work opportunities for adolescents. We argued that such experiences would provide valuable contact with adult models and thereby further the development of responsibility and general maturity. However, from their studies of U.S. high school students who are employed, Ellen Greenberger and Lawrence Steinberg conclude that most of the jobs held by these youngsters are highly routinized and afford little opportunity for contact with adults. The largest employers of teenagers in the U.S. are fast-food restaurants. Greenberger and Steinberg argue that, instead of providing maturing experiences, such settings give adolescents even greater exposure to the values and lifestyles of their peer group. And the adolescent peer group tends to emphasize immediate gratification and consumerism.[8]

Finally, in order to counteract the

mounting forces of alienation in U.S. society, we must establish a working alliance between the private sector and the public one (at both the local level and the national level) to forge links between the major institutions in U.S. society and to re-create a sense of community. Examples from other countries abound:

• Switzerland has a law that no institution for the care of the elderly can be established unless it is adjacent to and shares facilities with a day-care center, a school, or some other kind of institution serving children.

• In many public places throughout Australia, the Department of Social Security has displayed a poster that states, in 16 languages: "If you need an interpreter, call this number." The department maintains a network of interpreters who are available 16 hours a day, seven days a week. They can help callers get in touch with a doctor, an ambulance, a fire brigade, or the police; they can also help callers with practical or personal problems.

• In the USSR, factories, offices, and places of business customarily "adopt" groups of children, e.g., a day-care center, a class of schoolchildren, or a children's ward in a hospital. The employees visit the children, take them on outings, and invite them to visit their place of work.

We Americans can offer a few good examples of alliances between the public and private sectors, as well. For example, in Flint, Michigan, some years ago, Mildred Smith developed a community program to improve school performance among low-income minority pupils. About a thousand children were involved. The program required no change in the regular school curriculum; its principal focus was on building links between home and school. This was accomplished in a variety of ways.

• A core group of low-income parents went from door to door, telling their neighbors that the school needed their help.

• Parents were asked to keep younger children out of the way so that the older children could complete their homework.

• Schoolchildren were given tags to wear at home that said, "May I read to you?"

• Students in the high school business program typed and duplicated teaching materials, thus freeing teachers to work directly with the children.

• Working parents visited school classrooms to talk about their jobs and about how their own schooling now helped them in their work.

WHAT SCHOOLS CAN DO

As the program in Flint demonstrates, the school is in the best position of all U.S. institutions to initiate and strengthen links that support children and adolescents. This is so for several reasons. First, one of the major — but often unrecognized — responsibilities of the school is to enable young people to move from the secluded and supportive environment of the home into responsible and productive citizenship. Yet, as the studies we conducted at Cornell revealed, most other modern nations are ahead of the U.S. in this area.

In these other nations, schools are not merely — or even primarily — places where the basics are taught. Both in purpose and in practice, they function instead as settings in which young people learn "citizenship": what it means to be a member of the society, how to behave toward others, what one's responsibilities are to the community and to the nation.

I do not mean to imply that such learnings do not occur in American schools. But when they occur, it is mostly by accident and not because of thoughtful planning and careful effort. What form might such an effort take? I will present here some ideas that are too new to have stood the test of time but that may be worth trying.

Creating an American classroom. This is a simple idea. Teachers could encourage their students to learn about schools (and, especially, about individual classrooms) in such modern industrialized societies as France, Japan, Canada, West Germany, the Soviet Union, and Australia. The children could acquire such information in a variety of ways: from reading, from films, from the firsthand reports of children and adults who have attended school abroad, from exchanging letters and materials with students and their teachers in other countries. Through such exposure, American students would become aware of how attending school in other countries is both similar to and different from attending school in the U.S.

But the main learning experience would come from asking students to consider what kinds of things *should* be happening — or not happening — in American classrooms, given our nation's values and ideals. For example, how should children relate to one another and to their teachers, if they are doing things in an *American* way? If a student's idea seems to make sense, the American tradition of pragmatism makes the next step obvious: try the idea to see if it works.

The curriculum for caring. This effort also has roots in our values as a nation. Its goal is to make caring an essential part of the school curriculum. However, students would not simply learn about caring; they would actually engage in it. Children would be asked to spend time with and to care for younger children, the elderly, the sick, and the lonely. Caring institutions, such as daycare centers, could be located adjacent to or even within the schools. But it would be important for young caregivers to learn about the environment in which their charges live and the other people with whom their charges interact each day. For example, older children who took responsibility for younger ones would become acquainted with the younger children's parents and living arrangements by escorting them home from school.

Just as many schools now train superb drum corps, they could also train "caring corps" — groups of young men and women who would be on call to handle a variety of emergencies. If a parent fell suddenly ill, these students could come into the home to care for the children, prepare meals, run errands, and serve as an effective source of support for their fellow human beings. Caring is surely an essential aspect of education in a free society; yet we have almost completely neglected it.

Mentors for the young. A mentor is someone with a skill that he or she wishes to teach to a younger person. To be a true mentor, the older person must be willing to take the time and to make the commitment that such teaching requires.

We don't make much use of mentors in U.S. society, and we don't give much recognition or encouragement to individuals who play this important role. As a result, many U.S. children have few significant and committed adults in their lives. Most often, their mentors are their own parents, perhaps a teacher or two, a coach, or — more rarely — a relative, a neighbor, or an older classmate. However, in a diverse society such as ours, with its strong tradition of volunteerism, potential mentors abound. The schools need to seek them out and match them with young people who will respond positively to their particular knowledge and skills.

The school is the institution best suited to take the initiative in this task, because the school is the only place in which all children gather every day. It is also the only institution that has the right (and the responsibility) to turn to the community for help in an activity that represents the noblest kind of education: the building of character in the young.

There is yet another reason why schools should take a leading role in rebuilding links among the four worlds of childhood: schools have the most to gain. In the recent reports bemoaning the state of American education, a recurring theme has been the anomie and chaos that pervade many U.S. schools, to the detriment of effective teaching and learning. Clearly, we are in danger of allowing our schools to become academies of alienation.

In taking the initiative to rebuild links among the four worlds of childhood, U.S. schools will be taking necessary action to combat the destructive forces of alienation — first, within their own walls, and thereafter, in the life experience and future development of new generations of Americans.

1. Urie Bronfenbrenner, "New Worlds for Families," paper presented at the Boston Children's Museum, 4 May 1984.

2. Urie Bronfenbrenner, "The Ecology of the Family as a Context for Human Development," *Developmental Psychology*, in press.

3. Mavis Heatherington, "Children of Divorce," in R. Henderson, ed., *Parent-Child Interaction* (New York: Academic Press, 1981).

4. A.S. Makarenko, *The Collective Family: A Handbook for Russian Parents* (New York: Doubleday, 1967).

5. Lea Pulkkinen, "Self-Control and Continuity from Childhood to Adolescence," in Paul Baltes and Orville G. Brim, eds., *Life-Span Development and Behavior*, Vol. 4 (New York: Academic Press, 1982), pp. 64-102.

6. S.B. Kamerman, *Parenting in an Unresponsive Society* (New York: Free Press, 1980); S.B. Kamerman and A.J. Kahn, *Social Services in International Perspective* (Washington, D.C.: U.S. Department of Health, Education, and Welfare, n.d.); and Lloyd Johnston, Jerald Bachman, and Patrick O'Malley, *Use of Licit and Illicit Drugs by America's High School Students — 1975-84* (Washington, D.C.: U.S. Government Printing Office, 1985).

7. Kurt Aurin, personal communication, 1985.

8. Ellen Greenberger and Lawrence Steinberg, *The Work of Growing Up* (New York: Basic Books, forthcoming).

Culture, race too often ignored in child studies

Tina Adler

Monitor staff

SEATTLE

Child development researchers have not paid enough attention to both the environmental conditions in which children grow up and their cultural and racial identities, researchers said at an ethics symposium at the biennial meeting of the Society for Research in Child Development (SRCD) here. As a result of these and other oversights, they said they fear the findings may not apply to a wide population or get at the core of what makes children tick.

Although research practices per se are not unethical, many researchers are not sufficiently informed about cultural and racial influences and that can cause them to develop faulty studies, the researchers suggested. And there are ethical implications when the studies' findings are applied that need to be examined, said psychologist Celia Fisher. Researchers at the symposium outlined their opinions of the problems with studies and how the problems evolved.

For example, the speakers said that studies too often do not include subjects from different cultural and racial backgrounds. As a result, these studies' findings don't apply to those different groups. And that means researchers are not able to design good interventions or help those children as well as they might.

Researchers identified other problems with child development studies. For instance, too many researchers

don't describe their subjects' racial or socioeconomic background in the studies. They often overlook the very powerful influence of the environment on children. Also, many studies are too short to find out if children could be helped by a specific intervention. More attention needs to be given to the special needs of high-risk children, who are increasingly the subjects of child development research.

Many child development researchers don't study minority infants who are not at a high risk for developmental problems, said Fisher, who is at Fordham University. As a result, little is known about healthy minority children. That may not violate any ethical code but is unjust because it makes it hard to design good interventions for them when needed, she said.

"At present, most data on low-risk infants cannot be generalized beyond the behaviors of white, middle-class families," she said.

In one recent review of infant studies in major child development journals, Fisher found that almost half of the 102 articles "did not report cultural background or ethnicity of their sample." Of those that did, seven studies looked only at minority subjects, 26 examined only whites and nine included mixed samples.

The studies were no better in their treatment of socioeconomic status, she said. Also, of the studies that do report race, many just look at whites.

In an interview, Fisher offered several possible explanations for these findings.

Researchers may be looking at mixed groups, but not reporting the

ethnic make-up of their subject pool because of a notion from the 1960s that it would be derogatory, she said. Researchers who look at whites only and neglect to say so may assume readers will think that if no race is specified, the subjects are white.

Others may not describe the racial or economic backgrounds of their subjects, or not use a varied subject pool, because "some people assume there are universal aspects of development and don't see any need to test cultural differences," she said.

Still other researchers may want to include a more varied pool than they can get access to. Some communities, such as the college campus or surrounding community where researchers get their subjects from, are populated primarily by one race. Also, researchers tend to get infant subjects by reading birth announcements and calling the parents, who are often middle-class, she said.

Funding plays a role as well in limiting the scope of research. Federal and state agencies tend to support projects that look at social problems. That results in more research on poor people, including lower class minorities, she said. As a result, normative data for healthy, middle-class minorities doesn't exist, she said.

These problems are being addressed "little by little," she said. "It's very slow, but the attendance at our [SRCD] symposium was indicative of the interest people have in this."

It is critical to look at children's socioeconomic and cultural background, because poverty is a much stronger predictor of how children will develop than all other factors combined, said Lewis P. Lipsitt, executive director for science at the American Psychological Association and a Brown University child research psychologist. Yet not enough research is being done on the environment's influence, he said at the conference.

Many people still think that tests are the best predictors of children's outcomes, he said.

"Our society is too test-happy. . . . We overlook the processes and mechanisms that got [the test taker] to that point in the first place," he said in an interview.

T. Berry Brazelton, a pediatrician at Harvard Medical School, agreed, saying that the trouble with most assessment scales is that the environment is the best predictor of outcome, particularly for high-risk children. Brazelton developed the scale named after him that measures very young infants' development.

The most exciting findings right now are coming from neuropsychological work, said Brazelton. Researchers are discovering that children's minds and bodies can bounce back from a variety of insults, such as the abuses of poverty, better than scientists had realized. This makes intervention even more important, he said.

Both federal and private agencies that fund research make poor decisions at times about what they will and won't fund. The reason for the poor decisions concerning behavioral science is, in part, "because there are natural human biases against studying human behavior," he said. For example, agencies are reluctant to fund surveys on people's sexual behavior. Also, behavioral science research proposals on crib death, the leading cause of death for babies, have been poorly funded.

In addition, review committees are at times closed-minded about the reasonableness of research proposals in general, and about the rights of researchers to do studies, Lipsitt said.

"Review committees act as though the mere act of research is an imposition on humans," he said. Instead, they need to operate from the viewpoint that "people have the right to benefit from research results, and thus from the research enterprise. We need data on human behavior in order to help people."

Psychologist Michael Lewis of the Robert Wood Johnson Medical School also decried the limitations put on researchers. Researchers are often forced to implement interventions with limited funds and to end them too soon. As a result, it appears that many interventions don't work, he said. That leads some policy makers to conclude that the people whom the interventions are designed for can't really be helped, he said.

As a result, researchers' work may inadvertently support what he calls a "conservative world view," which holds that change is relatively difficult.

Some policy-makers and researchers also fall prey to viewing interventions in general as cures that last forever, Lewis said. That is like thinking you can go to confession "once in 1962 and that should save your soul forever," Lewis said.

Interventions are too often falsely assumed by researchers and policy-makers to work equally well for all kids, such as shy and extroverted kids. Instead of looking at the aggregate results for all children and deciding if an intervention works, researchers should see which children it worked or did not work for, and then design another program for the latter group.

The goals of an intervention also have to be reconsidered, he said.

"We've decided that smarter is the most important outcome, but why didn't we choose happier?" Lewis said. Emotional outcomes need more attention, he believes. He pointed out that suicide is the third leading cause of death for children.

Asked in an interview where the money would come from for interventions with a limitless expense account, Lewis said if the United States has billions of dollars for the Persian Gulf war, it can find money for thorough interventions and evaluations.

Much of what he discussed is published in a chapter in *Ethics in Applied Developmental Psychology: Emerging Issues in an Emerging Field,* published in 1990 by Abelex Publishing Corporation and edited by Celia Fisher.

Researchers are becoming increasingly aware of ethical issues as they turn their focus to high-risk babies. In studying this group, researchers are faced with ethical dilemmas that are not part of the picture in studies of low-risk children, Fisher said. For example, researchers can't just study high-risk children and not help them. And the parents' desperate need for help may influence researchers' responses.

"When research enters the lives of vulnerable families, ethical concerns . . . play an increasingly central role in research design and implementation," Fisher said.

As part of the design and implementation of a study, researchers need to promote participants' welfare and their right to make decisions about their lives, she said. They also need to ensure that the knowledge gained from the study is applicable to a wide group by not just studying one racial or socio-economic group, for example. The study's finding should also be distributed widely, she wrote in a paper presented at the conference.

"Informed consent is seen by many as the major means of protecting the rights of research participants," she wrote. But for participants to be truly informed, the information needs to be tailored to their cognitive level, language ability, cultural background and to their societal expectations, she wrote.

Finally, she said, researchers may uncover a variety of developmental problems, psychological distress or maltreatment when studying high-risk children. Researchers need to make clear to the parents what of this information they will share with them and others during the course of the study.

Tracked to Fail

In today's schools, children who test poorly may lose the chance for a quality education. Permanently.

Sheila Tobias

Sheila Tobias is the author of Breaking the Science Barrier *(in preparation),* Succeed With Math *(1987) and* Overcoming Math Anxiety *(1978).*

No one who has ever read Aldous Huxley's anti-utopian novel, *Brave New World,* can forget the book's opening scene, a tour of the "Hatchery and Conditioning Centre." There human embryos in their first hours of existence are transformed into Alphas, Betas, Gammas, Deltas and Epsilons—the five social classes that collectively meet the economy's manpower needs. Arrested in their development, the Gamma, Delta and Epsilon embryos are programmed *in vitro* for a lower-class future. After "birth," whatever individuality remains with these pre-ordained proletarians will be conditioned out of each child, until there is no one in this brave new world who does not grow up accepting and even loving his bleak servitude.

Huxley's totalitarian embryology may seem fanciful to us, but his real message was political, not technological. Huxley understood, as he wrote in the foreword to the 1946 edition of *Brave New World,* that any "science of human differences" would enable the authorities to assess the relative capacities of each of us and then assign everybody his or her appropriate place in society. Huxley's vision of the modern state, with its desire for social control, implies that the discovery that ability can be measured will suggest that it *should* be. Similarly, the knowledge that people can be sorted by ability will lead irresistibly to the belief that they ought to be.

Today, many educators contend that a "science of human differences" does exist in the form of standardized tests for intelligence and ability. And, as Huxley foresaw, the pressures have grown to put these discriminating instruments to use. Education in this country is becoming a process of separating the "gifted" from the "average," the "intelligent" from the "slow"—one is tempted to say, the wheat from the chaff. From an early age, children are now ranked and sorted (a process known variably as tracking, ability grouping or screening) as they proceed through school. Those who test well are encour-aged and expected to succeed and offered the most challenging work. Those who do not, get a watered-down curriculum that reflects the system's minimal expectations of them.

All this is a far cry from the vision of schooling that America's founding educators had in mind. Horace Mann, the father of American public education and the influential first secretary of the Massachusetts board of education from 1837 to 1848, thought public education would be "the great equal-izer" in a nation of immigrants. For over a century now, Mann's egalitarian vision, translated into educational policy, has helped millions of immigrants to assimilate and to prosper here. But this vision is now threatened by a competing view of individual potential—and worth. We are becoming a society where test-taking skills are the prerequisites for a chance at getting a good education, and where hard work, hope and ambition are in danger of becoming nothing more than mean-ingless concepts.

A poor showing on tests was once a signal to all con-cerned—child, teacher, parents—that greater effort was needed to learn, or to teach, what was required. It didn't mean that a child *couldn't* learn. But the damaging assumption behind testing and tracking as they are now employed in many schools is that *only* those who test well are capable of learning what is needed to escape an adult life restricted to menial, dead-end jobs. This new message imparted by our schools is profoundly inegalitarian: that test-measured ability, not effort, is what counts. What many students are learning is that they are *not* equal to everybody else. Gammas, Deltas and Epsilons shouldn't even try to compete with Alphas. Alphas are better, *born* better, and it is impossible for others to catch up. What's tragic about this change is not just that it's unjust—but that it's untrue.

A Lifetime of Testing

In a private Los Angeles primary school, a 4-year-old is being taught to play a game-like test he is going to have to pass to show that he is ready for kindergarten. This is the first in an endless series of evaluations that will determine who he is, what he can learn and how far he will go in school. Just before the test begins, the counselor hands him the red plastic cube he will use. But he doesn't need her cube. He has taken this test so often, as his parents drag him around from his preschool admissions screenings, that when the time comes to play, he pulls his *own* bright red cube out of his pocket. Whether or not he is ready for this particular school, he is more than ready for the test.

Each year after this child's admission to kindergarten, he will take "norm-referenced tests" to show his overall achievement against those of his age group and "criterion-referenced tests," which examine the specific skills he is supposed to have learned in each grade. Even if he and his parents are not told his test scores (a practice that varies from school to school), ability-grouping in elementary school will soon let him know where he stands. "By the second or third grade," says Susan Harter, a psychology professor at the University of Denver who studies social development in children, "children know precisely where they stand on the 'smart or dumb' continuum, and since most children at this age want to succeed in school, this knowledge profoundly affects their self-esteem."

The point is that today "smart or dumb" determinations are made very early. "Those who come to school knowing how to read or who learn very quickly are pronounced bright," says Jeannie Oakes, author of *Keeping Track: How Schools Structure Inequality.* "Those for whom reading is still a puzzle at the end of the first grade are judged slow." And these early decisions stick. As children proceed through the elementary grades, more and more of their course work is grouped by ability. By ninth grade, 80% to 90% of students are in separate classes determined by whether they are judged to be "fast," "average" or "slow."

Magnifying Our Differences

Tracking in all its variants is rarely official policy, and the validity and fairness of standardized testing have long been under fire. Nevertheless, both tracking and testing are becoming more common. As a result, argues University of Cincinnati education professor Joel Spring (in unwitting resonance with Huxley), education in America has become a "sorting machine."

Moreover, the stunting effects of this machine may remain with students for a lifetime. "Adults can remember well into middle age whether they were 'sharks' or 'goldfish' in reading," says Bill Kelly, professor of education at Regis College in Denver. Students learn whether they have good verbal skills or mathematical ones. They learn whether or not they are musically or mechanically inclined, and so on. There are millions of adults who carry with them the conviction that they "can't do math" or play an instrument or write well. And it may all be the result of assessments made of them and internalized as children — long before they had any idea of what they wanted from life. Their sense of inadequacy may prevent them from exploring alternative careers or simply narrow their experiences.

Why are testing and tracking on the rise? Oakes, who has studied more than 13,000 junior- and senior-high-school students, their schools and their teachers, suggests that the answer has several components. They range from the focus on educational excellence during the last decade to widespread public confidence that testing is an accurate, appropriate way of gauging educational potential. Oakes also believes that testing and tracking comprise a not-so-subtle effort to resegregate desegregated schools. But they reflect as well a preference among teachers for "homogeneous groupings" of students, which are easier to teach than classes composed of students of varying abilities.

Whatever the motives, Oakes is convinced that the basic premise of the whole system is wrong. There is no way, she says, to determine accurately the potential of young or even older children by standardized tests. One key reason: Such examinations are always fine-tuned to point out differences, not similarities. They eliminate those items that everyone answers the same way — either right or wrong. Thus, small differences that may or may not measure ability in general are amplified to give the test makers what they want, namely ease of sorting. Test results, then, will make any group of individuals appear to be more different than they really are.

Benjamin Bloom, Distinguished Service Professor Emeritus of Education at the University of Chicago, agrees. "I find that many of the individual differences in school learning are man-made and accidental rather than fixed in the individual at the time of conception," he writes in his book *All Our Children Learning.* "When students are provided with unfavorable learning conditions, they become even more dissimilar." Bloom concedes that some longitudinal studies show that between grades 3 and 11, for example, children's rank in class remains virtually the same. But this is not because intelligence is fixed, he argues. It is the result of the unequal, unsupportive education the schools provide. So long as schools think there is little they can do about "learning ability," says Bloom, they will see their task as weeding out the poorer learners while encouraging the better learners to get as much education as they can.

Watered-Down Education

Research generated by Oakes and others supports Bloom, revealing that placement in a low track has a corroding impact on students' self esteem. Worse yet, because there are real differences not just in level but in the *content* of what is being taught, tracking may in fact contribute to academic failure.

Students in low-track courses are almost never exposed to what educators call "high-status knowledge," the kind that will be useful in colleges and universities. They do not read works of great literature in their English classes, Oakes's team found, and instead of critical-thinking skills and expository writing, low-track students are taught standard English usage and "functional literacy," which involves mainly filling out forms, job applications and the like. In mathematics, high-track students were exposed to numeration, computational systems, mathematical models, probability and statistics in high school. "In contrast," writes Oakes, "low-track classes focused grade after grade on basic computational skills and arithmetic facts" and sometimes on simple measurement skills and converting English to metric.

More generally, Oakes's team also found that high-track classes emphasize reasoning ability over simple memorization of disembodied facts. Low-track students, meanwhile, are taught by rote, with an emphasis on conformity. "Average" classes — the middle track — resembled those in the high track, but they are substantially "watered down."

Is this discriminatory system the only way to handle differences in ability among students? One innovative program is challenging that notion. Called "accelerated learning," it is the creation of Henry M. Levin, a professor of education and economics at Stanford University. Levin, an expert on worker-managed companies, decided to apply the principles of organizational psychology to an analysis of the crisis in education. He began with a two-year-study, during which he surveyed the literature on education and looked at hundreds of evaluations of at-risk students at elementary and middle schools. Fully one-third of all students, he estimated, were "educationally disadvantaged" in some way, were consigned to a low track and were falling farther and farther behind in one or more areas. These children needed remedial help, but that help, Levin writes, treated "such students and their educators as educational discards, marginal to mainstream education." For them, the pace of instruction was slowed to a crawl and progressed by endless repetition. The whole system seemed designed to demoralize and fail everyone who was a part of it. As Levin told one reporter, "As soon as you begin to talk about kids needing remediation, you're talking about damaged merchandise. And as soon as you have done that, you have lost the game."

To try to change the game, Levin designed and is helping to implement the Accelerated Schools Program. Now being tested in California, Utah, Missouri and (this fall) Illinois, the project accepts that elementary school children who are having academic problems *do* need special assistance, but it departs radically from traditional tracking in every other respect. First, Accelerated Schools are expected to have all their students learning at grade level by the time they reach the sixth grade. In other words, the remedial track exists only to get students off it. Collectively, the teachers and administrators at each school are allowed to design their own curricula, but they must create a clear set of measurable (and that means testable) goals for students to meet each year they are in the program. Finally, it is expected that the curriculum, whatever its specifics, will be challenging and fast-paced and will emphasize abstract reasoning skills and a sophisticated command of English.

Levin's program reflects the current administration's view that business practice has much to contribute to schooling. Levin wants schools to find a better way to produce what might be called their product — that is, children willing and able to get the quality education they will need in life. To do this, he recognizes that schools must offer better performance incentives to students, teachers and administrators. "Everyone benefits from the esprit de corps," explains Levin, "and the freedom to experiment with curriculum and technique — which we also encourage — is an incentive for teachers." By insisting upon school and teacher autonomy, the regular attainment of measurable goals and the development of innovative, engaging curricula, Accelerated Schools also hope to erase the stigma associated with teaching or needing remediation. The early results of this six-year test program are encouraging: The Hoover Elementary School in Redwood City, CA, one of the first schools to embark on the project, is reporting a 22 percentile increase in sixth-grade reading scores, actually outperforming state criteria. Both Levin and Ken Hill, the district superintendent, caution that these results are preliminary and the improved scores could be due to many factors other than the Accelerated Schools Program. But regardless of the program's measurable impact, Hill sees real changes in the school. "Teachers are now working with the kids on science projects and developing a literature-based reading program. There's a positive climate, and all the kids are learners."

Another alternative to tracking is what Bloom calls "mastery learning." He believes that it is the rate of learning, not the capacity to learn, that differentiates students with "high" or "low" abilities. This is a critical distinction, for we are rapidly approaching the day when all but the most menial jobs will require relatively complex reasoning and technical skills.

In a mastery class, children are given as much time as they need to become competent at a certain skill or knowledge level.

Teachers must take 10% to 15% more time with their classes and break the class down into small groups in which the fast learners help their peers along. In time, the slower students catch up both in the amount of knowledge acquired and in the rate at which they learn. Though slow students may start out as much as five times slower than their classmates, Bloom says, "in mastery classes, fast and slow students become equal in achievement and increasingly similar in their learning rates."

At present, fewer than 5% of the nation's schools are following either of these promising strategies, estimates Gary Fenstermacher, dean of the University of Arizona's College of Education. He is a firm believer that de-tracking in some form must be the educational wave of the future. "There are ethical and moral imperatives for us to do whatever we can to increase the equality of access to human knowledge and understanding," he says.

Second Class and Dropping Out

Until society responds to those ethical and moral imperatives, however, the educational system, with its testing, tracking and discriminatory labeling, will continue on its questionable course. Today, around 25% of America's teenagers — 40% to 60% in inner-city schools — do not graduate from high school, according to Jacqueline P. Danzberger of the Institute for Educational Leadership in Washington, DC. Most of the attrition occurs by the third year of high school, and many educators believe increased testing is a contributing factor.

Norman Gold, former director of research for the District of Columbia's public school system, says school dropouts are linked to the raising of standards (with no compensatory programs) in the late 1970s and the end of "social promotions" — the habit of routinely allowing failing students to move to a higher grade. "Studies show," he says, "that the risk of dropping out goes up 50% if a child fails one school year." Neil Shorthouse, executive director of Atlanta's Cities in Schools, which enrolls 750 teenagers on the point of dropping out, agrees. "Most of these kids quit school," he says of his students, "because they repeatedly get the message that they are bad students, 'unteachables.' "

Ending social promotions was long overdue. What purpose is served by graduating high-school students who can't read, write or do simple arithmetic? But schools have done little to help these failing students catch up. The present system is continuing to produce a whole class of people, particularly inner-city blacks and Hispanics, who have little economic role in our society. High school, Gold observes, has become an obstacle course that a significant number of young people are unable to negotiate. "We expect them to fail. We have to have greater expectations, and equally great support."

These failing students are missing what John Ogbu, an educational anthropologist at the University of California, Berkeley, calls "effort optimism," the faith that hard work will bring real rewards in life. Ogbu's ethnographic studies of black and Hispanic schoolchildren in Stockton, CA, suggest that one reason today's inner-city children do poorly in tests is that "they do not bring to the test situation serious attitudes and do not persevere to maximize their scores." The fault lies neither with their intelligence, Ogbu argues, nor with the absence of the "quasi-academic training" that middle-class children experience at home. Rather, it is **their lower caste status and the limited job prospects of their parents that lower their sights. Tracking formalizes this caste humiliation and leads to disillusionment about school and what school can do for their lives.**

What Parents Can Do

If you are worried that your own child is losing his or her enthusiasm for schoolwork as a result of being put in a lower, "dumber" track, Susan Harter of the University of Denver advises you to watch for the following signs of trouble:

Decline in intrinsic motivation, the kind of curiosity and involvement in school work that promises long-term academic success, and its replacement with *extrinsic* motivation, doing just enough to get by while depending too much on the teacher for direction and help.

Indifference to school and schoolwork; losing homework on the way to school, or homework assignments on the way back; delivering homework that is crumpled, dirty or incomplete.

Constant self-deprecation: "I'm no good." "I can't do long division."

Signs of helplessness: unwillingness to try a task, especially new ones; starting but not finishing work; difficulty in dealing with frustration.

Avoiding homework, or school, altogether. (The most frequent cause of truancy, says Olle Jane Sahler of the pediatrics department at the University of Rochester, is low self-esteem with regard to school subjects.)

Should parents whose kids have problems undertake compensatory home instruction? Sherry Ferguson and Lawrence E. Mazin, authors of *Parent Power: A Program to Help Your Child Succeed in School,* think so, not because parents can make their children "smart," but because they have the power to make their kids persistent, competitive and eager. Here are some specific steps parents can take at home to achieve this end, according to Abigail Lipson, Ph.D., a clinical psychologist at the Harvard University Bureau of Study Counsel:

Praise your child for effort, not just for achievement. Children learn about persistence from many contexts, not just academic ones, so praise your child for hard work at any task: developing a good hook shot, painting a picture, etc.

Ask your child to explain her homework, or the subjects she is studying at school, to you. Try to learn *from* your child, don't just instruct her.

Find a regular time when you and your child can work in the same space. When children are banished to their rooms to do homework, they are cut off from social interaction. It can be very lonely. Setting up a special study time together can help both (or all) of you focus on accomplishing difficult or onerous tasks. While your child is doing homework, you can balance your checkbook, pay bills, whatever.

Help your child find a learning activity he feels good about. If the subject is animals, go to a zoo. If it's cars, select some car books together from the library. Encourage him to pursue his natural interests.

Games of all kinds are good for teaching children about persistence and achievement. Competitive games emphasize strategies for competing effectively and fairly, while noncompetitive games provide children with a sense of accomplishment through perseverance.

— S.T.

Who Is "Smart"?
Who Will "Succeed"?

The consequences of increased testing and tracking are only now beginning to be felt. First there is personal trauma, both for students who do reasonably well but not as well as they would like, and for those who fail. "When a child is given to understand that his or her worth resides in what he or she achieves rather than in what he or she is, academic failure becomes a severe emotional trauma," David Elkind writes in *The Child and Society.*

But the most severe consequence may be what only dropouts are so far demonstrating—an overall decline in Ogbu's effort optimism. Its potential social effects extend well beyond the schoolroom. Intelligence and ability, says writer James Fallows, have become legally and socially acceptable grounds for discrimination, and both are measured by the testing and tracking system in our schools. Doing well in school has thus come to be the measure of who is intelligent and who has ability. Beyond that, Fallows writes, our culture increasingly accepts that "he who goes further in school will go further in life." Many of the best jobs and most prestigious professions are restricted to those with imposing academic and professional degrees, thus creating a monopoly on "positions of privilege."

At a time when our economy requires better-educated workers than ever before, can we afford to let abstract measures of ability curtail the educational aspirations and potential accomplishments of our children? Quite aside from questions of national prosperity, do we really want to become a culture whose fruits are not available to most of its citizens? Despite income disparities and more classism than many observers are willing to admit, there has always been the *belief* in America that success, the good life, is available to all who are willing to work for it. But with our current fixation on testing and tracking, and what Fallows calls credentialism, we may be abandoning that belief and, with it, the majority of our young people.

Why We Need To Understand Science

Ignorance of science threatens our economic well-being, national security and the democratic process. We must do better.

Carl Sagan

Carl Sagan teaches and does research at Cornell University. His Emmy and Peabody Award-winning TV science series COSMOS *has been seen in more than 60 countries by 400 million people. Videocassettes of all 13 episodes will be available in stores later this year from Turner Home Entertainment. The accompanying book, "Cosmos," is the best-selling science book ever published in the English language.*

As I got off the plane, he was waiting for me, holding up a sign with my name on it. I was on my way to a conference of scientists and TV broadcasters, and the organizers had kindly sent a driver.

"Do you mind if I ask you a question?" he said as we waited for my bag. "Isn't it confusing to have the same name as that science guy?"

It took me a moment to understand. Was he pulling my Leg? "I *am* that science guy," I said. He smiled. "Sorry. That's my problem. I thought it was yours too." He put out his hand. "My name is William F. Buckley." (Well, his name wasn't *exactly* William F. Buckley, but he did have the name of a contentious TV interviewer, for which he doubtless took a lot of good-natured ribbing.)

As we settled into the car for the long drive, he told me he was glad I was "that science guy"—he had so many questions to ask about science. Would I mind? And so we got to talking. But not about science. He wanted to discuss UFOs, "channeling" (a way to hear what's on the minds of dead people—not much it turns out), crystals, astrology. . . . He introduced each subject with real enthusiasm, and each time I had to disappoint him: "The evidence is crummy," I kept saying. "There's a much simpler explanation." As we drove on through the rain, I could see him getting glummer. I was attacking not just pseudoscience but also a facet of his inner life.

And yet there is so much in real science that's equally exciting, more mysterious, a greater intellectual challenge—as well as being a lot closer to the truth. Did he know about the molecular building blocks of life sitting out there in the cold, tenuous gas between the stars? Had he heard of the footprints of our ancestors found in 4-million-year-old volcanic ash? What about the raising of the Himalayas when India went crashing into Asia? Or how viruses subvert cells, or the radio search for extraterrestrial intelligence or the ancient civilization of Ebla? Mr. "Buckley"—well-spoken, intelligent, curious—had heard virtually nothing of modern science. He *wanted* to know about science. It's just that all the science got filtered out before it reached him. What the society permitted to trickle through was mainly pretense and confusion. And it had never taught him how to distinguish real science from the cheap imitation.

All over America there are smart, even gifted, people who have a built-in passion for science. But that passion is unrequited. A recent survey suggests that 94% of Americans are "scientifically illiterate."

A prescription for disaster. We live in a society exquisitely dependent on science and technology, in which hardly anyone knows anything about science and technology. This is a clear prescription for disaster. It's dangerous and stupid for us to remain ignorant about global warming, say, or ozone depletion, toxic and radioactive wastes, acid rain. Jobs and wages depend on science and technology. If the United States can't manufacture, at high quality and low price, products people want to buy, then industries will drift out of the United States and transfer a little prosperity to another part of the world. Because of the low birthrate in the '60s and '70s, the National Science Foundation projects a shortage of nearly a million professional scientists and engineers by 2010. Where will they come from? What about fusion, supercomputers, abortion, massive reductions in strategic weapons, addiction, high-resolution TV, airline and airport safety, food additives, animal rights, superconductivity, Midgetman vs. rail-garrison MX missiles, going to Mars, finding cures for AIDS and cancer? How can we decide national policy if we don't understand the underlying issues?

I know that science and technology are not just cornucopias pouring good deeds out into the world. Scientists not only conceived nuclear weapons; they also took political leaders by the lapels, arguing that *their* nation—whichever it happened to be—had to have one first. Then they arranged to manufacture 60,000 of them. Our technology has produced thalidomide, CFCs, Agent Orange, nerve gas and industries so powerful they can ruin the climate of the planet. There's a *reason* people are nervous about science and technology.

And so the image of the mad scientist haunts our world—from Dr. Faust to Dr. Frankenstein to Dr. Strangelove to the white-coated loonies of Saturday morning children's TV. (All this doesn't inspire budding scientists.) But there's no way back. We can't just conclude that science puts too much power into the hands of morally feeble technologists or corrupt, power-crazed politicians and decide to get rid of it. Advances in medicine and agriculture have saved more lives than have been lost in all the wars in history. Advances in transportation, communication and entertainment have transformed the world. The sword of science is double-edged. Rather, its awesome power forces on all of us, including politicians, a new responsibility—more attention to the long-term consequences of technology, a global and transgenerational perspective, an incentive to avoid easy appeals to nationalism and chauvinism. Mistakes are becoming too expensive.

Science is much more than a body of knowledge. It is a way of thinking. This is central to its success. Science invites us to let the facts in, even when they don't conform to our preconceptions. It counsels us to carry alternative hypotheses in our heads and see which best match the facts. It urges on us a fine balance between no-holds-barred openness to new ideas, however heretical, and the most rigorous skeptical scrutiny of everything— new ideas *and* established wisdom. We need wide appreciation of this kind of thinking. It works. It's an essential tool for a democracy in an age of change. Our task is not just to train more scientists but also to deepen public understanding of science.

How bad is it? Very bad. "It's Official," reads one newspaper headline: "We Stink in Science." Less than half of all Americans know that the Earth moves around the Sun and takes a year to do it—a fact established a few centuries ago. In tests of average 17-year-olds in many world regions, the U.S. ranked dead last in algebra. On identical tests, the U.S. kids averaged 43% and their Japanese counterparts 78%. In my book, 78% is pretty good—it corresponds to a C+, or maybe even a B−; 43% is an F. In a chemistry test, students in only two of 13 nations did worse than the U.S. Compared to us, Britain, Singapore and Hong Kong were so high they were almost off-scale, and 25% of Canadian 18-year-olds knew just as much chemistry as a select 1% of American high school seniors (in their second chemistry course, and most of them in "advanced" programs). The best of 20 fifth-grade classrooms in Minneapolis was outpaced by every one of 20 classrooms in Sendai, Japan, and 19 out of 20 in Taipei, Taiwan. South Korean students were far ahead of American students in all aspects of mathematics and science, and 13-year-olds in British Columbia (in Western Canada) outpaced their U.S. counterparts across the boards (in some areas they did better than the Koreans). Of the U.S. kids, 22% say they dislike school; only 8% of the Koreans do. Yet two-thirds of the Americans, but only a quarter of the Koreans, say they are "good at mathematics."

Why we're flunking. How do British Columbia, Japan, Britain and Korea manage so much better than we do?

During the Great Depression, teachers enjoyed job security, good salaries, respectability. Teaching was an admired profession, partly because learning was widely recognized as the road out of poverty. Little of that is true today. And so science (and other) teaching is too often incompetently or uninspiringly done, its practitioners, astonishingly, having little or no training in their subjects—sometimes themselves unable to distinguish science from pseudoscience. Those who do have the training often get higher-paying jobs elsewhere.

We need more money for teachers' training and salaries, and for laboratories—so kids will get hands-on experience rather than just reading what's in the book. But all across America, school-bond issues on the ballot are regularly defeated. U.S. parents are much more satisfied with what their children are learning in science and math than are, say, Japanese and Taiwanese parents—whose children are doing so much better. No one suggests that property taxes be used to provide for the military budget, or for agriculture, or for cleaning up toxic wastes. Why just education? Why not support it from general taxes on the local and state levels? What about a special education tax for those industries with special needs for technically trained workers?

American kids don't do enough schoolwork. The average high school student spends 3.5 hours a week on homework. The total time devoted to studies, in and out of the classroom, is about 20 hours a week. Japanese *fifth*-graders average 33 hours a week.

But most American kids aren't stupid. Part of the reason they don't study hard is that they've received few tangible benefits when they do. Competency (that is, actually knowing the stuff) in verbal skills, mathematics and science these days doesn't increase earnings for average young men in their first eight years out of high school—many of whom take service rather than industrial jobs.

In the productive sectors of the economy, though, the story is different. There are furniture factories, for example, in danger of going out of business because few entry-level workers can do simple arithmetic. A major electronic company reports that 80% of its job applicants can't pass a *fifth*-grade math test. The United States already is losing some $25 billion a year (mainly in lost productivity and the cost of remedial education) because workers, to too great a degree, can't read, write, count or think. Parents should know that their children's livelihoods may depend on how much math and science they know. Now, while the kids are in school, is the time for them to learn. Parents might encourage their schools to offer—and their kids to take—comprehensible, well-taught advanced science courses. They might also limit the amount of mind-numbing TV their children watch.

What we can do. Those in America with the most favorable view of science tend to be young, well-to-do, college-educated white males. But three-quarters of new American workers between now and 2001 will be women, nonwhites and immigrants. Discriminating against them isn't only unjust, it's also self-defeating. It deprives the American economy of desperately needed skilled workers.

Black and Hispanic students are doing better in standardized science tests now than in the late 1960s, but they're the only ones who are. The average math gap between white and black U.S. high school graduates is still huge—two to three grade levels; but the gap between white U.S. high school graduates and those in, say, Japan, Canada, Great Britain or Finland is more than *twice* as big. If you're poorly motivated and poorly educated, you won't know much—no mystery here. Suburban blacks with college-educated parents do just as well in college as suburban whites with college-educated parents. Enrolling a poor child in a Head Start program doubles his or her chances to be employed later in life; one who completes an Upward Bound program is four times as likely to get a college education. If we're serious, we know what to do.

What about college and university? There are obvious steps similar to what should be done in high schools: salaries for teachers that approach what they could get in industry; more scholarships, fellowships and laboratory equipment; laboratory science courses required of everyone to graduate; and special attention paid to those traditionally steered away from science. We should also provide the financial and moral encouragement for academic scientists to spend more time on public education—lectures, newspaper and magazine articles, TV appearances. This requires scientists to make themselves understandable and fun to listen to. To me, it seems strange that some scientists, who depend on public funding for their research, are reluctant to explain to the public what it is that they do. Fortunately, the number of scientists willing to speak to the public—and capably—has been increasing each year. But there are not yet nearly enough.

Virtually every newspaper in America has a daily astrology column. How many have a daily science column? When I was growing up, my father would bring home a daily paper and consume (often with great gusto) the baseball box scores. There they were, to me dry as dust, with obscure abbreviations (W, SS, SO, W-L, AB, RBI), but they spoke to him. Newspapers everywhere printed them. I figured maybe they weren't too hard for me. Eventually I too got caught up in the world of baseball statistics. (I know it helped me in learning decimals, and I still cringe a little when I hear that someone is "batting a thousand." But 1.000 is not 1,000. The lucky player is batting one.)

Or take a look at the financial pages. Any introductory material? Explanatory footnotes? Definition of abbreviations? None. It's sink or swim. Look at those acres of statistics! Yet people voluntarily read the stuff. It's not beyond their ability. It's only a matter of motivation. Why can't we do the same with math, science, and technology?

By far the most effective means of raising interest in science is television. There's lots of pseudoscience on TV, a fair amount of medicine and technology, but hardly any science—especially on the three big commercial networks, whose executives think science programming means ratings declines and lost profits, and nothing else matters. Why in all America is there no TV drama that has as its hero someone devoted to figuring out how the Universe works?

Stirring projects in science and technology attract and inspire youngsters. The number of science Ph.D.s peaked around the time of the Apollo program and declined thereafter. This is an important potential side-effect of such projects as sending humans to Mars, or the Superconducting Supercollider to explore the fine structure of matter, or the program to map all human genes.

Every now and then, I'm lucky enough to teach a class in kindergarten or the first grade. Many of these children are curious, intellectually vigorous, ask provocative and insightful questions and exhibit great enthusiasm for science. When I talk to high school students, I find something different. They memorize "facts." But, by and large, the joy of discovery, the life behind those facts, has gone out of them. They're worried about asking "dumb" questions; they're willing to accept inadequate answers; they don't pose follow-up questions; the room is awash with sidelong glances to judge, second-by-second, the approval of their peers. Something has happened between first and 12th grade, and it's not just puberty. I'd guess that it's partly peer pressure *not* to excel (except in sports); partly that the society teaches short-term gratification; partly the impression that science or math won't buy you a sports car; partly that so little is expected of students; and partly that there are so few role models for intelligent discussion of science and technology or for learning for its own sake.

But there's something else: Many adults are put off when youngsters pose scientific questions. Children ask why the Sun is yellow, or what a dream is, or how deep you can dig a hole, or when is the world's birthday or why we have toes. Too many teachers and parents answer with irritation or ridicule, or quickly move on to something else. Why adults should pretend to omniscience before a 5-year-old, I can't for the life of me understand. What's wrong with admitting that you don't know? Children soon recognize that somehow this kind of question annoys many adults. A

few more experiences like this, and another child has been lost to science.

There are many better responses. If we have an idea of the answer, we could try to explain. If we don't, we could go to the encyclopedia or the library. or we might say to the child: "I don't know the answer. Maybe no one knows. Maybe when you grow up, you'll be the first to find out."

But mere encouragement isn't enough. We must also give children the tools to winnow the wheat from the chaff. I'm haunted by the vision of a generation of Americans unable to distinguish reality from fantasy, hopefully clutching their crystals for comfort, unequipped even to frame the right questions or to recognize the answers. I want us to rescue Mr. "Buckley" and the millions like him. I also want us to stop turning out leaden, incurious, unimaginative high school seniors. I think America needs, and deserves, a citizenry with minds wide awake and a basic understanding of how the world works.

Public understanding of science is more central to our national security than half a dozen strategic weapons systems. The submediocre performance of American youngsters in science and math, and the widespread adult ignorance and apathy about science and math, should sound an urgent alarm.

Development During Adolescence and Early Adulthood

The onset of adolescence is marked by the emergence of secondary sex characteristics and the achievement of reproductive maturity. However, adolescence also brings substantive shifts in memory and problem-solving skills, in preferred activities, and in emotional behavior. "Those Gangly Years" presents the results of a study following a group of adolescents over a three-year period, highlighting early vs. late maturation differences in boys and girls.

The timing of puberty affects many events in the adolescent's life, including school achievement, moods, interaction with the opposite sex, and family relationships.

Teenagers today are faced with temptations such as drugs, sex, and mobility at an earlier age than their predecessors. At the same time, they are less likely to get the guidance they need from adults, due to such factors as the high rate of single-parent homes and working

Unit 5

mothers. As a consequence, teen-related problems such as drug and alcohol use, teen pregnancy, high school dropout rate, and suicide occur at distressingly high rates. These issues are examined in "A Much Riskier Passage."

In some cultures, a ritualistic ceremony marks the transition to adulthood—a transition that occurs quickly, smoothly, and with relatively few problems. The onset of adulthood is more difficult to distinguish in modern industrial societies. In American culture, the transition is vague. Does someone become an adult when he or she achieves the right to vote, the privilege of obtaining a driver's license, the ability to legally order an alcoholic drink in a bar, or the right to volunteer for the armed forces?

Adolescence has its ups and downs, but some researchers argue that much of the storm and stress attributed to adolescence is exaggerated. "The Myth About Teenagers" reveals that while adolescents are subject to mood-swings, most are basically well-adapted and happy. Focusing on the negative aspects of adolescent behavior may create a set of expectations that the adolescent strives to fulfill. However, for some adolescents the transition to adulthood is fraught with despair, loneliness, and interpersonal conflict. The pressures of peer group, school, and family may produce conformity or may lead to rebellion against or withdrawal from friends, parents, or society at large. These pressures may peak as the adolescent prepares to separate from the family and assume the independence and responsibilities of adulthood. Bruce Baldwin's analysis in "Puberty and Parents" suggests that adolescence spans a 20-year period, roughly between the ages of 10 and 30. Three separate periods can be identified: early adolescence (adhering to tribal loyalties), middle adolescence (testing adult realities), and late adolescence (joining up). Understanding adolescent attitudes and confronting emotional reactions to adolescents can promote parental growth and development as much as it promotes the development of the adolescent.

In "Girls' Self-Esteem Is Lost on Way to Adolescence, New Study Finds," Suzanne Daley presents the work of psychologist Carol Gilligan. Gilligan contends that girls enter their teen years with a healthy self-esteem and emerge with a poor self-image. The article reviews why this is the case.

Although much attention has been given to the problems of adolescence and the transition to adulthood, developmentalists have shown far less interest in the early years of adulthood. Yet, during early adulthood, many individuals experience significant changes in their lives. Marriage, parenthood, divorce, single parenting, employment, and the effects of sexism may be powerful influences on ego development, self-concept, and personality. Negative emotions such as jealousy and envy subvert efforts to establish effective interpersonal relationships, and often lead to hostility or isolation. In "Jealousy and Envy," Jon Queijo describes three strategies—self-reliance, selective ignoring, and self-bolstering—that individuals can use in their attempts to cope with negative emotions. Some individuals seem to grow stronger when confronted by the stresses of daily living, whereas others have great difficulty coping. The challenge for developmentalists is to discover the factors that contribute to one's ability to cope with stress and the natural crises of life with minimum disruption to the integrity of one's personality.

Looking Ahead: Challenge Questions

Why does adolescence seem to be fraught with so many difficulties, even for the well-adjusted? Do you think adolescence really continues into the late 20s?

What techniques do you use to deal with your emotional ups and downs? Which do you think are effective and which are ineffective? Do you see any signs of growth or change in yourself?

Why do you think so many adolescents and young adults find it easier to lose themselves in drugs or cults than to confront their problems and take steps to develop self-control and self-reliance? What kinds of parenting techniques might have given such individuals sufficient self-esteem and coping skills to combat their self-doubts and loneliness?

The Myth About Teen-Agers

Richard Flaste

Richard Flaste is Science and Health Editor of The New York Times.

A father I know tells of one unsettling moment when he was sure he would never understand the teen-age mind. The mind in question was that of his own teen-ager, a 15-year-old blonde possessed of considerable charm and an aggressive reticence. The pivotal moment was this effort at conversation:

"So, how was your day at school?"

"Good."

"Was it more than just good? I mean, did anything actually happen that was interesting?"

"No, it was just good."

"What about the bio test? Didn't you have a test?"

(The answer this time came with a gleam of irritation in her eyes.) "I told you, everything was *good*."

He backed away, feeling foolish, sorry he had tried, sorry he'd stirred her pique. What could possibly be going on in her mind? And he wondered about himself, too, as he slipped away into a friendlier room. Was he actually afraid of her?

Later, having thought about that scene many times, he concluded that he had in fact been frightened, but not so much of her — after all, they had their good times, and she did seem to love and respect him at least every now and then. Rather it was the condition of adolescence that scared him. On occasions like that abortive effort at conversation he wasn't just confronting a teen-ager who might or might not be in the mood to talk to him but also everything he had ever heard about adolescence, the Sturm, the Drang and the plain old orneriness of it. That flash of annoyance in her eyes was all that was necessary to evoke an image of those infamous raging hormones boiling inside a pubescent caldron.

The burden was a heavy one to take into a small inquiry about a person's day. It was an unnecessary burden, too. For, although most of us aren't aware of it, the concept of adolescence as a period of angry, dark turmoil has largely been overthrown, and along with it the idea that kids need to be tormented and perverse to make the storm-tossed transition to adulthood. That concept is being replaced by a new psychology of adolescence, a growing body of work that reflects a vigorous attempt to find out what life is genuinely like for normal teen-agers, and which reveals that delight plays as large a role among most adolescents as misery does.

A substantial number of psychotherapists and personality theorists still believe that adolescence is a trial by fire, as do many writers of juvenile fiction. But what is now the mainstream of psychological research dismisses this emphasis on turmoil as balderdash. It is a misguided emphasis, many researchers say, which grew out of the overwrought imaginations of romanticists ranging from the Freuds (mostly Anna) to Goethe (particularly, "The Sorrows of Young Werther").

In the 1970's, I wrote regularly about child-development issues for this newspaper, and I accepted the idea that any teen-ager was necessarily a little mad. To a large extent this notion was promoted by the psychoanalytic literature, but it was embraced by many of us as a handy way to explain hard times with our teen-agers. We could say that noxious behavior such as naked aggression was normal, and so we didn't have to worry. We reassured ourselves constantly, usually with a knowing laugh about the craziness of teen-agers. But I did not believe it completely. Why should only this age group carry the label of madness? Coming back to the question now, I am struck by how different the mood among many psychologists and psychiatrists is. By and large, they are more determined to draw an empirical and detailed picture of the varied and complex adolescent experience.

Some researchers have surveyed thousands of teen-agers to learn what they believe about themselves and their families. Others have given youngsters beepers to carry around, so that when they are signaled they will report their moods at that moment. And still others have worked with families, asking parents, teen-agers and their siblings to take batteries of tests.

Among the most influential of this cadre of researchers is Dr. Daniel Offer of the University of Chicago, a psychiatrist who believes that the widespread idea that the teen years are unavoidably insane has mischaracterized the lives of millions of people. Moreover, he contends that the emphasis on turmoil has created the expectation of Sturm and Drang for every teen-ager, thereby masking the serious emotional difficulties of a significant minority of adolescents who need professional help. Dr. Offer was moved to declare a "Defense of Adolescents" in The Journal of the American Medical Association, and he made a presentation along the same lines to the convention of the American Psychiatric Association last May.

Dr. Offer's team was among the earliest to plumb the day-to-day feelings of large numbers of teen-agers. Their first explorations, in the 1960's, began to reveal that, incredible as it might have seemed, most teen-agers were happy most of the time. After years of confirmatory work, he confidently told the psychiatrists' convention that "the vast majority of adolescents are well-adjusted, get along well with their peers and their parents, adjust well to the mores and values of their social environment and cope well with their internal and external worlds." Dr. Offer recalled in a recent interview that this message disturbed some of his colleagues, because they didn't believe that teen-agers' responses to questions could be trusted.

The work of Dr. Offer and his team has provided a starting point for many of the nation's researchers. By no means do they make adolescence out to be an easy time, any more than life as a whole is easy. Adolescence is a period of rapid and profound change in the body and mind. It is a time to find out who you are and to begin to move toward what you will become. Family bickering is bound to escalate during this period, but it usually centers on what one psychologist calls the "good-citizen topics," such as chores, dress and schoolwork. Most researchers feel that this conflict is useful, because it allows a teen-ager to assert his or her individuality over relatively minor issues.

There are several explanations for this rise in family quarreling. A widely cited cognitive explanation comes from the work of the Swiss psychologist Jean Piaget, who showed that children do not have the capacity for the abstract, analytical thinking he called "formal operations" until the teen years. The arrival of that tool is what enables them, in the view of some experts, to question their parents' thinking.

RESEARCH BY JUDITH G. SMETANA, AN ASSOCIATE PROfessor of education, psychology and pediatrics at the University of Rochester, has recently aroused much interest among psychologists. She contends that concentrating on the development of a child's ability to think logically isn't useful in elucidating family relationships. Instead, she focuses on the way parents and children conceptualize their experiences. According to her research, there are two fundamentally different world views at the core of family conflict: adolescents tend to see much of their behavior as a "personal" matter, affecting no one but themselves and therefore up to them entirely, while their parents tend to hold to what she calls "conventional thinking," which sees society's rules and expectations as primary. The dichotomy provides for commonplace clashes:

"Clean up your room. This family does not live in a hovel."

"It's my room and I like hovels."

In a recent paper Smetana charts the typical evolution from personal to conventional thinking in a teen-ager. A child of 12 or 13 generally has no use for conventions when it comes to family issues. Between 14 and 16 the teen-ager comes to recognize conventions as the way society regulates itself. Then comes a brief period in which conventions are rejected again, but more thoughtfully. Between 18 and 25 conventions are seen as playing an important and admirable role in facilitating the business of society.

As the teen-ager moves in fits and starts in the direction of his or her parents, the parents generally stick to their guns. Nevertheless, the adolescent has begun to reason like them, and so, by the age of 15 or 16, the quarreling usually subsides, at least for a while. It is replaced by a period in which members of the family are able to negotiate more successfully than in the past. The teen-ager learns how to "work on mom and dad" to achieve goals like staying out late at night or using the family car.

Indeed, "negotiation" has emerged as one of the key words in the new psychology of adolescence. Instead of talking about rebellion and a painful separation from the family, many psychologists now see adolescence as a time in which parents and children negotiate new relationships with one another. The teen-ager must gain more authority over his or her own life; the parents must come to see their child as more nearly an equal, with a right to differing opinions.

ANOTHER WAY OF LOOKING AT THIS PERIOD OF NEGOTIAtion has been formulated by psychologists Harold D. Grotevant at the University of Texas at Austin and Catherine R. Cooper at the University of California, Santa Cruz. They believe that typically there is an elaborate interplay between a teen-ager's striving to be an individual who is separate from the family and his attempts to maintain a close, caring relationship with his parents. In a recent study they found that teen-agers who had the strongest sense of themselves as individuals were raised in families where the parents offered guidance and comfort but also permitted their children to develop their own points of view.

For some families, this can be a terrible period. Parents who try to exert too much control over their children and find it impossible to yield in a conflict can be driven into a frenzy by the efforts of their teen-agers to establish their own identities. But most parents are more pliable, and find ways to compromise.

A neighbor of mine, unlucky enough to have a son who became a teen-ager when punk was hot, remembers how uncontrollably rattled she would get when she saw him dressed for school in the morning. "He would throw on any rag, this way and that," she recalls. She couldn't contain her exasperation and her fear that this monstrous style of dressing would somehow reflect on her. She imagined that others might pity her for her misfortune. After repeated failed confrontations, she decided not to come downstairs until her son was gone. It seems to her now that he dressed a little more sensibly if he knew she wouldn't be there to see it.

The influence of peers in everything from dress to sexual mores is undeniably strong during the teen-age years, although some experts downplay it because, like turmoil, it's been given more press than they think it's worth, and because they believe the emphasis on peers underestimates the importance of continuing attachments to the family. Parents may find it comforting to realize that this growing influence of friends is not the first assault on their authority. Throughout most of a child's life—not just in adolescence—parents share control with others: teachers, friends, siblings. After the earliest years parents are no longer in a position to know about whole segments of their children's lives, because so much takes place outside the home. Gerald R. Adams, a psychologist at Utah State University, making this point in a recent conversation, said, "If I interviewed your family, you'd be shocked at how little you know about the life of your child—school life, social life. Most parents don't really know the world of their children."

There are many things that children don't tell us because they know we won't approve, even if we are trying very hard to give them a measure of greater freedom. Who among us really wants to know everything about a child's sexual experimentation or moments of embarrassment?

But that isn't the only reason for reticence. Sometimes, teen-agers, like the rest of us, just don't feel like talking. The notorious moodiness of teen-agers is one of the most interesting areas of the latest psychological investigations. Dr. Offer says that he has found little tendency among normal teen-agers to plummet into deep and dark despair. (He points out that, although teen-age suicide is a deeply troubling phenomenon, the suicide rate for adolescents is lower than it is for people in their 20's and far lower than it is for people in their 70's.)

Reed Larson, a psychologist at the University of Illinois, has found a middle ground between coloring all of adolescence with dark moods or dismissing moodiness altogether. In studies carried out by giving kids beepers that signaled them when to report their feelings, he found that mood swings are a fact of teenage life. On average, adolescents feel more delight and more sadness at any given moment than adults and move from one mood to another more rapidly. For teen-agers, emotional states generally last no more than 15 minutes. Even the strongest feelings tend not to last more than a half-hour, while the same kinds of feelings may last for two hours or longer among adults. But Larson and his colleagues concluded that these mood swings are healthy and natural, a reasonable response to a time of life filled with fast-paced events. "The typical adolescent may be moody," they wrote in a recent paper, "but not in turmoil."

As word of the new insights into teen-age life gets out, parents are bound to benefit. They will learn to expect a certain amount of bickering in early adolescence, and they'll realize that it has a normal course to run. Parents might find it helpful to abandon the old vocabulary of rebellion and defiance. The words have been so widely misapplied that they are even used to characterize things like the piercing of ears against mother's wishes or staying out late. When self-assertion and self-indulgence are overdramatized by parents and viewed as rebellion or defiance, they take on the aura of criminal acts instead of being part of the fascinating interplay between parent and child in which the child eventually becomes an adult and the parent eventually accepts that.

In the case of the teen-ager who resists parental efforts at conversation, parents should realize that kids are sometimes out of sorts, or they may be too bewildered by the hectic events of their lives to find the words to describe them. Some teen-agers are more apt to engage in friendly conversation at dinner time, or just before they go to bed, than at times when the stresses of the day are still fresh. (Of course, when a teen-ager senses that his or her parents' attempts at conversation are prompted by their need to be in control, conversation will often be resisted on that ground alone.)

While a momentary rebuff or a bit of surliness should not be reason for deep concern, parents ought to worry about those moods that don't change. Teenagers who are depressed for long periods of time, relentlessly combative, friendless, reclusive or miserable in other ways are not going through a normal adolescence; they and their families need help, perhaps professional.

Implicit in much of the new work on adolescence is the belief that parents must take a strong grip on their own sense of themselves, their own worth, so that they are not so easily shaken by every normal challenge to their control, and so that they can hold on to their children while confidently letting out some line.

Parents should find life a little easier, in any event, if the bogeyman of necessary insanity in adolescence is finally vanquished. For many parents that will mean they no longer need to fear their children's adolescence but can relax and maybe even enjoy it.

Girls' Self-Esteem Is Lost on Way To Adolescence, New Study Finds

Suzanne Daley

Girls emerge from adolescence with a poor self-image, relatively low expectations from life and much less confidence in themselves and their abilities than boys, a study to be made public today has concluded.

Confirming earlier studies that were smaller and more anecdotal, this survey of 3,000 children found that at the age of 9 a majority of girls were confident, assertive and felt positive about themselves. But by the time they reached high school, less than a third felt that way.

The survey, commissioned by the American Association of University Women, found that boys, too, lost some sense of self-worth, but they ended up far ahead of the girls.

For example, when elementary school boys were asked how often they felt "happy the way I am," 67 percent answered "always." By high school, 46 percent still felt that way. But with girls, the figures dropped from 60 percent to 29 percent.

Race as a Factor

"It's really quite staggering to see that this is still going on," said Myra Sadker, a professor at American University in Washington, who has spent most of the last decade studying the way teachers treat girls in the classroom. "No one has taken such a large-scale look at self-esteem before, but we have known of this issue for years. And here you see that it is not going away."

Among the girls, race is apparently a factor in the retention of self-esteem, the survey found. Far more black girls surveyed were still self-confident in high school, compared with white and Hispanic girls, and white girls lost their self-assurance earlier than Hispanic girls.

The subject of girls' self-esteem has emerged relatively recently as a field of study, generating considerable controversy. Some academics say the psychological development process of women differs profoundly from that of men; others disagree.

Dr. Carol Gilligan, a professor of education at Harvard and a pioneer in studying the development of girls, said the survey's findings would force a series of more complex questions about what happens to girls' self-esteem during adolescence.

"This survey makes it impossible to say what happens to girls is simply a matter of hormones," said Dr. Gilligan, an adviser on the development of questions asked in the survey. "If that was it, then the loss of self-esteem would happen to all girls and at roughly the same time.

"This work raises all kinds of issues about cultural contributions," she added, "and it raises questions about the role of the schools, both in the drop of self-esteem and in the potential for intervention."

Sharon Schuster, president of the American Association of University Women, a research and advocacy group, said the association had commissioned the study to draw attention to the plight of girls at a time when education changes is a topic of widespread interest.

Are girls still shortchanged in the classroom?

"Generally, most people feel that girls are getting a good education," Ms. Schuster said. "I think this survey shows that the system has some shortfalls. We wanted to put some factual data behind our belief that girls are getting shortchanged in the classroom."

Based on an index of personal self-esteem created by the responses to such statements as "I like the way I look," "I like most things about myself" and "I wish I were somebody else," the study found that overall, boys had a higher sense of self-esteem than girls in elementary school and retained it better over the years.

The study, conducted by Greenberg-Lake Analysis Group Inc., surveyed 2,400 girls and 600 boys at 36 public schools in 12 communities throughout the country last fall. The children, in grades 4 through 10, were asked to answer written questions in the classroom.

The researchers said the margin of sampling error was plus or minus three percentage points for the girls and plus or minus five percentage points for the boys.

Enough girls were questioned for the researches to draw conclusions about race distinctions, but no such conclusions could be drawn about the boys because there were too few boys included in the survey.

The findings among the girls, combined with the answers that black girls gave regarding their relationships with teachers, prompted the researchers to conclude that black girls drew their apparent self-confidence from their families and communities rather than the school system.

Janie Victoria Ward, a Rockefeller fellow at the University of Pennsylvania who is studying the socialization of black families and was an adviser to the study, said one factor that might help black girls is that they are often surrounded by strong women they admire. Black women are more likely than others to have a full-time job and run a household.

Another factor, she said, may be that black parents often teach their children that there is nothing wrong with them, only with the way the world treats them.

"In order to maintain that high self-esteem they are disassociating from school," said Dr. Ward.

Linda Kerber, a professor of history at the University of Iowa, said she, too, found the results about black girls to be particularly interesting.

"This should encourage white people to look with admiration at the black community," Dr. Kerber said. "So often we look at the black family as a locus of problems, but here we can see that they are doing something right."

Dr. Gilligan of Harvard said that what appeared to be happening to black girls had both good and bad consequences. "The danger is that the black girls will miss the opportunity of school," she said. "You can't just romanticize this."

To some degree, the new study supports the work Dr. Gilligan has been doing in recent years. One of her studies looked intensively at about 100 girls enrolled at a private school outside of Cleveland, and fol-lowed their development closely for more than five years.

Dr. Gilligan also found that adolescence is the moment when girls begin to doubt themselves: while 11-year-olds tend to be full of self-confidence, she said, by 15 and 16 they start to say, " 'I don't know. I don't know. I don't know.' "

But Dr. Gilligan said her study was too small to draw broad-based conclusions about race. "We did see some of these things," she said. "But we could not make the kind of generalizations that this survey allows."

The American Association of University Women's survey also examined children's attitudes toward science and mathematics, finding that girls who did poorly in math tended to see their problems as "personal failures," while boys more often attributed their lack of success or interest in math to a sense that the subject "was not useful."

Indeed, young women who like math are more confident about their appearances than are young men, whether they like math or not, the study found.

Those Gangly Years

*NEW BODIES, NEW SCHOOLS AND NEW
EXPECTATIONS NOTWITHSTANDING,
MOST EARLY ADOLESCENTS WEATHER THE
EXPERIENCE SURPRISINGLY WELL.*

ANNE C. PETERSEN

*Anne C. Petersen, Ph.D., a develop-
mental psychologist, is a professor of
human development at Pennsylvania
State University, where she heads the
interdisciplinary department of individual and family studies.*

How can you stand studying adolescents? My daughter has just become one and she's impossible to live with. Her hormones may be raging, but so am I!" A colleague at a cocktail party was echoing the widespread view that the biological events of puberty necessarily change nice kids into moody, rebellious adolescents. The view has gained such a foothold that some parents with well-behaved teenagers worry that their kids aren't developing properly.

They needn't worry. My research, and that of many others, suggests that although the early teen years can be quite a challenge for normal youngsters and their families, they're usually not half as bad as they are reputed to be. And even though the biological changes of puberty do affect adolescents' behavior, attitudes and feelings in many important ways, other, often controllable, social and environmental forces are equally important.

One 14-year-old, for example, who tried to excuse his latest under-par report card by saying, "My problem is testosterone, not tests," only looked at part of the picture. He ignored, as many do, the fact that, because of a move and the shift to junior high school, he had been in three schools in as many years.

My colleagues and I at Pennsylvania State University looked at a three-year span in the lives of young adolescents to find out how a variety of biological and social factors affected their behavior and their feelings about themselves. A total of 335 young adolescents were randomly selected from two suburban school districts, primarily white and middle- to upper-middle-class. Two successive waves of these kids were monitored as they moved from the sixth through the eighth grade. Twice a year we interviewed them individually and gave them psychological tests in groups. When the youngsters were in the sixth and eighth grades, we also interviewed and assessed their parents. Just recently we again interviewed and assessed these young people and their

I DIDN'T LIKE BEING EARLY. BUT BY EIGHTH GRADE, EVERYONE WORE A BRA AND HAD THEIR PERIOD. I WAS NORMAL.

parents during the adolescents' last year of high school.

We followed the children's pubertal development by asking them to judge themselves every six months on such indicators as height, pubic hair and acne in both boys and girls; breast development and menstruation in girls; and voice change and facial-hair growth in boys. We also estimated the timing of puberty by finding out when each youngster's adolescent growth spurt in height peaked, so we could study the effects of early, on-time or late maturing.

Although we have not yet analyzed all the data, it's clear that puberty alone does not have the overwhelming psychological impact that earlier clinicians and researchers assumed it did (see "The Puzzle of Adolescence," this article). But it does have many effects on body image, moods and relationships with parents and members of the opposite sex.

Being an early or late maturer (one year earlier or later than average), for example, affected adolescents' satisfaction with their appearance and their body image—but only among seventh- and eighth-graders, not sixth-graders. We found that among students in the higher two grades, girls who were physically more mature were generally less satisfied with their weight and appearance than their less mature classmates.

A seventh-grade girl, pleased with being still childlike, said, "You can do more things—you don't have as much weight to carry around." A girl in the eighth grade, also glad to be a late maturer, commented, "If girls get fat, they have to worry about it." In contrast, an early-maturing girl subsequently commented, "I didn't like be-

ing early. A lot of my friends didn't understand." Another girl, as a high school senior, described the pain of maturing extremely early: "I tried to hide it. I was embarrassed and ashamed." However, her discomfort ended in the eighth grade, she said, because "by then everyone wore a bra and had their period. I was normal."

We found the reverse pattern among boys: Those who were physically more mature tended to be more satisfied with their weight and their overall appearance than their less mature peers. One already gangling seventh-grade boy, for example, said he liked being "a little taller and having more muscle development than other kids so you can beat them in races." He conceded that developing more slowly might help "if you're a jockey" but added, "Really, I can't think of why [developing] later would be an advantage." In reflecting back from the 12th grade, a boy who had matured early noted that at the time the experience "made me feel superior."

For seventh- and eighth-grade boys, physical maturity was related to mood. Boys who had reached puberty reported positive moods more often than their prepubertal male classmates did. Pubertal status was less clearly and consistently related to mood among girls, but puberty did affect how girls got along with their parents. As physical development advanced among sixth-grade girls, their relationships with their parents declined; girls who were developmentally advanced talked less to their parents and had less positive feelings about family relationships than did less developed girls. We found a similar pattern among eighth-grade girls, but it was less clear in the seventh grade, perhaps because of the many other changes occurring at that time, such as the change from elementary to secondary school format and its related effects on friendship and school achievement.

The timing of puberty affected both school achievement and moods. Early maturers tended to get higher grades than later maturers in the same class. We suspect that this may stem from the often documented tendency of teachers to give more positive ratings to larger pupils. Although early maturers had an edge academically, those who matured later were more likely to report positive moods.

As we have noted, among relatively physically mature adolescents, boys and girls had opposite feelings about their appearance: The boys were pleased, but the girls were not. We believe that, more generally, pubertal change is usually a positive experience for boys but a negative one for girls. While advancing maturity has some advantages for girls, including gaining some of the rights and privileges granted to maturing boys, it also brings increased limitations and restrictions related to their emerging womanhood. One sixth-grade girl stated emphatically, "I don't like the idea of getting older or any of that. If I had my choice, I'd rather stay 10." Or, as one seventh-grade boy graphically explained the gender differences, "Parents let them [boys] go out later than girls because they don't have to worry about getting raped or anything like that."

Differences in the timing of puberty also affect interactions with members of the opposite sex. But it takes two to tango, and in the sixth grade, although many girls have reached puberty and are ready to socialize with boys, most boys have not yet made that transition. Thus, as one girl plaintively summed up the sixth-grade social scene, "Girls think about boys more than boys think about girls."

In the seventh and eighth grades, the physically more mature boys and girls are likely to be pioneers in exploring social relations with members of the opposite sex, including talking with them on the phone, dating, having a boyfriend or girlfriend and "making out." We had the sense that once these young people began looking like teenagers, they wanted to act like them as well.

SHIFTING SCHOOLS EXPOSES TEENS TO NEW EXTRACURRICULAR ACTIVITIES—LICIT AND ILLICIT

But puberty affects the social and sexual activity of individual young adolescents both directly and indirectly; the pubertal status of some students can have consequences for the entire peer group of boys and girls. Although dating and other boy-girl interactions are linked to pubertal status, and girls usually reach puberty before boys do, we found no sex differences in the rates of dating throughout the early-adolescent period. When the early-maturing kids began socializing with members of the opposite sex, the pattern quickly spread throughout the entire peer group. Even prepubertal girls were susceptible to thinking and talking about boys if all their girlfriends were "boy crazy."

The physical changes brought on by puberty have far-reaching effects, but so do many other changes in the lives of adolescents. One we found to be particularly influential is the change in school structure between the sixth and eighth grades. Most young adolescents in our country shift from a relatively small neighborhood elementary school, in which most classes are taught by one teacher, to a much larger, more impersonal middle school or junior high school (usually farther from the child's home), in which students move from class to class and teacher to teacher for every subject. This shift in schools has many ramifications, including disrupting the old peer-group structure, exposing adolescents to different achievement expectations by teachers and providing opportunities for new extracurricular activities—licit and illicit.

Both the timing and number of school transitions are very important. In our study, for example, students who changed schools earlier than most of their peers, as well as those who changed schools twice (both experiences due to modifications of the school system), suffered an academic slump that continued through eighth grade. Therefore, early or double school transition seemed stressful, beyond the usual effects of moving to a junior high school.

Puberty and school change, which appear to be the primary and most pervasive changes occurring during early adolescence, are often linked to other important changes, such as altered family relations. Psychologist Laurence Steinberg of the University of Wisconsin has found that family re-

THE PUZZLE OF ADOLESCENCE

At the turn of the century, psychologist G. Stanley Hall dignified adolescence with his "storm and stress" theory, and Anna Freud subsequently argued influentially that such storm and stress is a normal part of adolescence. Ever since, clinicians and researchers have been trying—with only limited success—to develop a coherent theory of what makes adolescents tick.

Psychoanalytic theorist Peter Blos added in the late 1960s and 1970s that adolescents' uncontrolled sexual and aggressive impulses affect relationships with their parents. He suggested that both adolescents and their parents may need more distant relationships because of the unacceptable feelings stimulated by the adolescents' sexuality.

Research conducted in the 1960s showed that not all adolescents experience the storm and stress psychoanalytic theory predicts they should. Many studies, including those of Roy Grinker; Joseph Adelson and Elizabeth Douvan; Daniel Offer; and Albert Bandura, demonstrated that a significant proportion of adolescents make it through this period without appreciable turmoil. These findings suggest that pubertal change per se cannot account for the rocky time

some adolescents experience.

Other theories of adolescent development have also been linked to pubertal change. For example, in his theory of how children's cognitive capacities develop, Swiss psychologist Jean Piaget attributed the emergence of "formal operational thought," that is, the capacity to think abstractly, to the interaction of pubertal and environmental changes that occur during the same developmental period.

Some researchers have linked the biological events of puberty to possible changes in brain growth or functioning. Deborah Waber, a psychologist at Boston Children's Hospital, has shown that the timing of pubertal change is related to performance differences between the right- and left-brain hemispheres on certain tasks and to the typical adult pattern of gender-related cognitive abilities: Later maturers, including most men, have relatively better spatial abilities, and earlier maturers, including most women, have relatively better verbal abilities.

It has also been suggested that pubertal change affects adolescent behavior through the social consequences of altered appearance. Once young adolescents look like adults,

they are more likely to be treated as adults and to see themselves that way, too.

Coming also from a social psychological perspective, psychologist John Hill of Virginia Commonwealth University, together with former Cornell University doctoral student Mary Ellen Lynch, have proposed that pubertal change leads parents and peers to expect more traditional gender-role behavior from adolescents than from younger children; they suggest that both boys and girls become more aware of these gender stereotypes in early adolescence and exaggerate their gender-related behavior at this age.

Despite all these theories, most studies that look at how puberty affects adolescent development are finding that puberty per se is not as important as we once thought. Puberty does specifically affect such things as body image and social and sexual behavior, but it does not affect all adolescent behavior, and it affects some adolescents more strongly than others. In fact, many studies, like ours, are revealing that other changes in early adolescence, particularly social and environmental ones, are at least as important as biological ones.

lationships shift as boys and girls move through puberty. During mid puberty, he says, conflict in family discussions increases; when the conflict is resolved, boys usually become more dominant in conversations with their mothers. (Psychologist John Hill of Virginia Commonwealth University has found that family conflict increases only for boys.) Other research, however, suggests that adolescents wind up playing a more equal role relative to both parents.

In our study, the parents of early-maturing girls and late-maturing boys reported less positive feelings about their children in the sixth and eighth grades than did parents of boys and girls with other patterns of pubertal timing. (These effects were always stronger for fathers than for mothers.) The adolescents, however, reported that their feelings about their parents were unrelated to pubertal timing.

The feelings of affection and support that adolescents and their parents reported about one another usually declined from the sixth to the eighth grades, with the biggest decline in feelings between girls and their mothers. But importantly, the decline was from very positive to less positive—but still not negative—feelings.

Early adolescence is clearly an unusual transition in development because of the number of changes young people experience. But the impact of those changes is quite varied; changes that may challenge and stimulate some young people can become overwhelming and stressful to others. The outcome seems to depend on prior strengths and vulnerabilities—both of the individual adolescents and their families—as well as on the pattern, timing and intensity of changes.

Youngsters in our study who changed schools within six months of peak pubertal change reported more depression and anxiety than those whose school and biological transitions were more separated in time. Students who experienced an unusual and negative change at home—such as the death of a parent or divorce of parents—reported even greater difficulties, a finding that supports other research. Sociologists Roberta Simmons and Dale Blyth have found that the negative effects of junior high school transitions, especially in combination with other life changes, continue on

into high school, particularly for girls.

Many of the negative effects of transitions and changes seen in our study were tempered when adolescents had particularly positive and supportive relationships with their peers and family. The effects of all these early-adolescent changes were even stronger by the 12th grade than in 8th grade.

Overall, we found that the usual pattern of development in early adolescence is quite positive. More than half of those in the study seemed to be almost trouble-free, and approximately 30 percent of the total group had only intermittent problems during their early teen years. Fifteen percent of the kids, however, did appear to be caught in a downward spiral of trouble and turmoil.

Gender played an important role in how young adolescents expressed and dealt with this turmoil. Boys generally showed their poor adjustment through external behavior, such as being rebellious and disobedient, whereas girls were more likely to show internal behavior, such as having depressed moods. But since many poorly adjusted boys also showed many signs of depression, the rates of such symptoms did not differ between the sexes in early adolescence.

By the 12th grade, however, the girls were significantly more likely than the boys to have depressive symptoms, a sex difference also found among adults. Boys who had such symptoms in the 12th grade usually had had them in the sixth grade as well; girls who had depressive symptoms as high school seniors usually had developed them by the eighth grade.

For youngsters who fell in the troubled group, the stage was already set—and the pathways distinguish-

able—at the very beginning of adolescence. There is an overall tendency for academic decline in the seventh and eighth grades (apparently because seventh- and eighth-grade teachers adopt tougher grading standards than elementary school teachers do). But the grades of boys with school behavior problems or depressive symptoms in early adolescence subsequently declined far more than those of boys who did not report such problems. Thus, for youngsters whose lives are already troubled, the changes that come with early adolescence add further burdens—and their problems are likely to persist through the senior year of high school.

One 12th-grade boy who followed this pathway described the experience: "My worst time was seventh to ninth grade. I had a lot of growing up to do and I still have a lot more to do. High school was not the 'sweet 16' time everyone said it would be. What would have helped me is more emotional support in grades seven through nine." In explaining that particularly difficult early-adolescent period he said, "Different teachers, colder environment, changing classes and detention all caused chaos in the seventh to ninth grades."

We did not find the same relationship between academic failure and signs of emotional turmoil in girls as in boys. For example, those seventh-grade girls particularly likely to report poor self-image or depressive symptoms were those who were academically successful. Furthermore, when these girls lowered their academic achievement by eighth grade, their depression and their self-image tended to improve. These effects occurred in many areas of girls' coursework but were particularly strong in stereotypically "masculine" courses such as

THE VAST MAJORITY OF EARLY TEENS WE STUDIED WERE TROUBLE-FREE OR HAD ONLY INTERMITTENT PROBLEMS. ONLY 15 PERCENT WERE PLAGUED BY TROUBLE AND TURMOIL.

mathematics and science. Like the pattern of problems for boys, the girls' pattern of trading grades to be popular and feel good about themselves persisted into the 12th grade. (Some girls, of course, performed well academically and felt good about themselves both in junior high school and high school.)

We think that for certain girls, high achievement, especially in "masculine" subjects, comes with social costs—speculation supported by the higher priority these particular girls give to popularity. They seem to sacrifice the longer-term benefits of high achievement for the more immediate social benefits of "fitting in." Other studies have revealed a peak in social conformity at this age, especially among girls, and have shown that many adolescents reap immediate, but short-term, social benefits from many

types of behavior that adults find irrational or risky.

Our most recent research is focused

PARENTS LET BOYS GO OUT LATER THAN GIRLS BECAUSE THEY DON'T HAVE TO WORRY ABOUT THEM GETTING RAPED.

---

on exploring further whether the developmental patterns established during early adolescence continue to the

end of high school. We are also trying to integrate our observations into a coherent theory of adolescent development and testing that theory by seeing whether we can predict the psychological status of these students at the end of high school based on their characteristics in early adolescence. Other key concerns include discovering early warning signs of trouble and identifying ways to intervene to improve the course of development.

The biological events of puberty are a necessary—and largely uncontrollable—part of growing up. But we may be able to understand and control the social and environmental forces that make adolescence so difficult for a small but troubled group of youngsters. The adolescent's journey toward adulthood is inherently marked by change and upheaval but need not be fraught with chaos or deep pain.

A Much
RISKIER
PASSAGE

DAVID GELMAN

here was a time when teenagers believed themselves to be part of a conquering army. Through much of the 1960s and 1970s, the legions of adolescence appeared to command the center of American culture like a victorious occupying force, imposing their singular tastes in clothing, music and recreational drugs on a good many of the rest of us. It was a hegemony buttressed by advertisers, fashion setters, record producers suddenly zeroing in on the teen multitudes as if they controlled the best part of the country's wealth, which in some sense they did. But even more than market power, what made the young insurgents invincible was the conviction that they were right: from the crusade of the children, grown-ups believed, they must learn to trust their feelings, to shun materialism, to make love, not money.

In 1990 the emblems of rebellion that once set teenagers apart have grown frayed. Their music now seems more derivative than subversive. The provocative teenage styles of dress that adults assiduously copied no longer automatically inspire emulation. And underneath the plumage, teens seem to be more interested in getting ahead in the world than in clearing up its injustices. According to a 1989 survey of high-school seniors in 40 Wisconsin communities, global concerns, including hunger, poverty and pollution, emerged last on a list of teenage worries. First were personal goals: getting good grades and good jobs. Anything but radical, the majority of teens say they're happy and eager to get on with their lives.

One reason today's teens aren't shaking the earth is that they can no longer marshal the demographic might they once could. Although their sheer numbers are still growing, they are not the illimitably expanding force that teens appeared to be 20 years ago. In 1990 they constitute a smaller percentage of the total population (7 percent, compared with nearly 10 percent in 1970). For another thing, almost as suddenly as they became a highly visible, if unlikely, power in the world, teenagers have reverted to anonymity and the old search for identity. Author Todd Gitlin, a chronicler of the '60s, believes they have become "Balkanized," united less by a common culture than by the commodities they own. He says "it's impossible to point to an overarching teen sensibility."

But as a generation, today's teenagers face more adult-strength stresses than their predecessors did—at a time when adults are much less available to help them. With the divorce rate hovering near 50 percent, and 40 to 50 percent of teenagers living in single-parent homes headed mainly by working mothers, teens are more on their own than ever. "My parents let me do anything I want as long as I don't get into trouble," writes a 15-year-old high-schooler from Ohio in an essay submitted for this special issue of NEWSWEEK. Sociologists have begun to realize, in fact, that teens are more dependent on grown-ups than was once believed. Studies indicate that they are shaped more by their parents than by their peers, that they adopt their parents' values and opinions to a greater extent than anyone realized. Adolescent specialists now see real hazards in lumping all teens together; 13-year-olds, for instance, need much more parental guidance than 19-year-olds.

These realizations are emerging just when the world has become a more dangerous place for the young. They have more access than ever to fast cars, fast drugs, easy sex—"a bewildering array of options, many with devastating outcomes," observes Beatrix Hamburg, director of Child and Adolescent Psychiatry at New York's Mount Sinai School of Medicine. Studies indicate that while overall drug abuse is down, the use of lethal drugs like crack is up in low-income neighborhoods, and a dangerous new kick called ice is making inroads in white high schools. Drinking and smoking rates remain ominously high. "The use of alcohol appears to be normative," says Stephen Small, a developmental psychologist at the University of Wisconsin. "By the upper grades, everybody's doing it."

Sexual activity is also on the rise. A poll conducted by Small suggests that most teens are regularly having sexual intercourse by the 11th grade. Parents are generally surprised by the data, Small says. "A lot of parents are saying, 'Not my kids . . .' They just don't think it's happening." Yet clearly it is: around half a million teenage girls give birth every year, and sexually transmitted diseases continue to be a major problem. Perhaps the only comforting note is that teens who are given AIDS education in schools and clinics are more apt to use condoms— a practice that could scarcely be mentioned a few years ago, let alone surveyed.

One reliable assessment of how stressful life has become for young people in this country is the Index of Social Health for Children and Youth. Authored by social-policy analyst Marc Miringoff, of Fordham University at Tarrytown, N.Y., it charts such factors as poverty, drug-abuse and high-school dropout rates. In 1987, the latest year for which statistics are available, the index fell to its lowest point in two decades. Most devastating, according to Miringoff, were the numbers of teenagers living at poverty levels—about 55 percent for single-parent households—and taking their own lives. The record rate of nearly 18 suicides per 100,000 in 1987—a total of 1,901— was double that of 1970. "If you take teens in the '50s—the 'Ozzie and Harriet' generation—those kids lived on a less complex planet," says Miringoff. "They could be kids longer."

The social index is only one of the yardsticks used on kids these days. In fact, this generation of young people is surely one of the most closely watched ever. Social scientists are tracking nearly everything they do or think about, from dating habits (they prefer going out in groups) to extracurricular activities (cheerleading has made a comeback) to general outlook (45 percent think the world is getting worse and 62 percent believe life will be harder for them than it was for their parents). One diligent prober, Reed Larson of the University of Illinois, even equipped his 500 teen subjects with beepers so he could remind them to fill out questionnaires about how they are feeling, what they are doing and who they are with at random moments during the day. Larson, a professor of human development, and psychologist Maryse Richards of Loyola University, have followed this group since grade school. Although the results of the high-school study have not been tabulated yet, the assumption is that young people are experiencing more stress by the time they reach adolescence but develop strategies to cope with it.

Without doubt, any overview of teenage problems is skewed by the experience of the inner cities, where most indicators tilt sharply toward the negative. Especially among the minority poor, teen pregnancies continue to rise, while the institution of marriage has virtually disappeared. According to the National Center for Vital Statistics, 90 percent of black teenage mothers are unmarried at the time of their child's birth, although about a third eventually marry. Teenage mothers, in turn, add to the annual school-dropout rate, which in some cities reaches as high as 60 percent. Nationwide, the unemployment rate for black teenagers is 40 to 50 percent; in some cities, it has risen to 70 percent. Crack has become a medium of commerce and violence. "The impact of crack is worse in the inner city than anywhere else," says psychiatrist Robert King, of the Yale Child Study Center. "If you look at the homicide rate among young, black males, it's frighteningly high. We also see large numbers of young mothers taking crack."

Those are realities unknown to the majority of white middle-class teenagers. Most of them are managing to get through the adolescent years with relatively few major problems. Parents may describe them as sullen and self-absorbed. They can also be secretive and rude. They hang "Do Not Disturb" signs on their doors, make phone calls from closets and behave churlishly at the dinner table if they can bring themselves to sit there at all. An earlier beeper study by Illinois's Larson found that in the period between ages 10 and 15, the amount of time young people spend with their families decreases by half. "This is when the bedroom door becomes a significant marker," he says.

Yet their rebelliousness is usually overstated. "Arguments are generally about whether to take out the garbage or whether to wear a certain hairstyle," says Bradford Brown, an associate professor of human development at the University of Wisconsin. "These are not earth-shattering issues, though they are quite irritating to parents." One researcher on a mission to destigmatize teenagers is Northwestern University professor Ken Howard, author of a book, "The Teenage World," who has just completed a study in Chicago's Cook County on where kids go for help. The perception, says Howard, is that teenagers are far worse off than they really are. He believes their emotional disturbances are no different from those of adults, and that it is only 20 percent who have most of the serious problems, in any case.

The findings of broad-based studies of teenagers often obscure the differences in their experience. They are, after all, the product of varied ethical and cultural influences. Observing adolescents in 10 communities over the past 10 years, a team of researchers headed by Frances Ianni, of Columbia University's Teachers College, encountered "considerable diversity." A key finding, reported Ianni in a 1989 article in Phi Delta Kappan magazine, was that the people in all the localities reflected the ethnic and social-class lifestyles of their parents much more than that of a universal teen culture. The researchers found "far more congruence than conflict" between the views of parents and their teenage children. "We much more frequently hear teenagers preface comments to their peers with 'my mom says' than with any attributions to heroes of the youth culture," wrote Ianni.

For years, psychologists also tended to overlook the differences between younger and older adolescents, instead grouping them together as if they all had the same needs and desires. Until a decade ago, ideas of teen behavior were heavily influenced by the work of psychologist Erik Erikson, whose own model was based on older adolescents. Erikson, for example, emphasized their need for autonomy—appropriate, perhaps, for an 18-year-old preparing to leave home for college or a job, but hardly for a 13-year-old just beginning to experience the confusions of puberty. The Erikson model nevertheless was taken as an across-the-board prescription to give teenagers independence, something that families, torn by the domestic upheavals of the '60s and '70s, granted them almost by forfeit.

In those turbulent years, adolescents turned readily enough to their peers. "When there's turmoil and social change, teenagers have a tendency to break loose and follow each other more," says Dr. John Schowalter, president of the American Academy of Child and Adolescent Psychiatry. "The leadership of adults is somewhat splintered and they're more on their own—sort of like 'Lord of the Flies'."

That period helped plant the belief that adolescents were natural rebels, who sought above all to break free of adult influence. The idea persists to this day. Says Ruby Takanishi, director of the Carnegie Council on Adolescent Development: "The society is still permeated by the notion that adolescents are different, that their hormones are raging around and they don't want to have anything to do with their parents or other adults." Yet research by Ianni and others suggests the contrary. Ianni points also to studies of so-called invulnerable adolescents—those who develop into stable young adults in spite of coming from troubled homes, or other adversity. "A lot of people have attributed this to some inner resilience," he says. "But what we've seen in practically all cases is some caring adult figure who was a constant in that kid's life."

Not that teenagers were always so dependent on adults. Until the mid-19th century, children labored in the fields alongside their parents. But by the time they were 15, they might marry and go out into the world. Industrialization and compulsory education ultimately deprived them of a role in the family work unit, leaving them in a state of suspension between childhood and adulthood.

To teenagers, it has always seemed a useless period of waiting. Approaching physical and sexual maturity, they feel capable of doing many of the things adults do. But they are not treated like adults. Instead they must endure a prolonged childhood that is stretched out even more nowadays by the need to attend college—and then possibly graduate school—in order to make one's way in the world. In the family table of organization, they are mainly in charge of menial chores. Millions of teenagers now have part-time or full-time jobs, but those tend to be in the service industries, where the pay and the work are often equally unrewarding.

If teenagers are to stop feeling irrelevant, they need to feel needed, both by the family and by the larger world. In the '60s they gained some sense of empowerment from their visibility, their music, their sheer collective noise. They also joined and swelled the ranks of Vietnam War protesters, giving them a feeling of importance that evidently they have not had since. In the foreword to "Student Service," a book based on a 1985 Carnegie Foundation survey of teenagers' attitudes toward work and community service, foundation director Ernest Boyer wrote: "Time and time again, students complained that they felt isolated, unconnected to the larger world . . . And this detachment occurs at the very time students are deciding who they are and where they fit." Fordham's Miringoff goes so far as to link the rising suicide rate among teens to their feelings of disconnection. He recalls going to the 1963 March on Washington as a teenager, and gaining "a sense of being part of something larger. That idealism, that energy, was a very stabilizing thing."

Surely there is still room for idealism in the '90s, even if the causes are considered less glamorous. But despite growing instances of teenagers involving themselves in good works, such as recycling campaigns, tutorial programs or serving meals at shelters for the homeless, no study has yet detected anything like a national groundswell of volunteerism. Instead, according to University of Michigan social psychologist Lloyd Johnston, teens seem to be taking their cues from a culture that, up until quite recently at least, has glorified self-interest and opportunism. "It's fair to say that young people are more career oriented than before, more concerned about making money and prestige," says Johnston. "These changes are consistent with the Me Generation and looking for the good life they see on television."

Some researchers say that, indeed, the only thing uniting teenagers these days are the things they buy and plug into. Rich or poor, all have their Walkmans, their own VCRs and TVs. Yet in some ways, those marvels of communication isolate them even more. Teenagers, says Beatrix Hamburg, are spending "a lot of time alone in their rooms."

Other forces may be working to isolate them as well. According to Dr. Elena O. Nightingale, author of a Carnegie Council paper on teen rolelessness, a pattern of "age segregation" is shrinking the amount of time adolescents spend with grown-ups. In place of family outings and vacations, for example, entertainment is now more geared toward specific age groups. (The teen-terrorizing "Freddy" flicks and their ilk would be one example.) Even in the sorts of jobs typically available to teenagers, such as fast-food chains, they are usually supervised by people close to their age, rather than by adults, notes Nightingale. "There's a real need for places for teenagers to go where there's a modicum of adult involvement," she says.

Despite the riskier world they face, it would be a mistake to suggest that all adolescents of this generation are feeling more angst than their predecessors. Middle-class teenagers, at least, seem content with their lot on the whole: According to recent studies, 80 percent—the same proportion as 20 years ago—profess satisfaction with their own lives, if not with the state of the world. Many teenagers, nevertheless, evince wistfulness for what they think of as the more heroic times of the '60s and '70s—an era, they believe, when teenagers had more say in the world. Playwright Wendy Wasserstein, whose Pulitzer Prize-winning "The Heidi Chronicles" was about coming of age in those years, says she has noticed at least a "stylistic" nostalgia in the appearance of peace-sign earrings and other '60s artifacts. "I guess that comes from the sense of there having been a unity, a togetherness," she says. "Today most teens are wondering about what they're going to do when they grow up. We had more of a sense of liberation, of youth—we weren't thinking about getting that job at Drexel." Pop-culture critic Greil Marcus, however, believes it was merely the "self-importance" of the '60s generation—his own contemporaries—"that has oppressed today's kids into believing they've missed something. There's something sick about my 18-year-old wanting to see Paul McCartney or the Who. We would never have emulated our parents' culture."

But perhaps that's the point: the teens of the '90s do emulate the culture of their parents, many of whom are the very teens who once made such an impact on their own parents. These parents no doubt have something very useful to pass on to their children—maybe their lost sense of idealism rather than the preoccupation with going and getting that seems, so far, their main legacy to the young. Mom and Dad have to earn a living and fulfill their own needs—they are not likely to be coming home early. But there must be a time and place for them to give their children the advice, the comfort and, most of all, the feelings of possibility that any new generation needs in order to believe in itself.

With MARY TALBOT *and* PAMELA G. KRIPKE

Puberty and Parents

Understanding Your Early Adolescent

Dr. Bruce A. Baldwin

Dr. Baldwin is a practicing psychologist who heads Direction Dynamics, a consulting service specializing in promoting professional development and quality of life in achieving men and women. He responds to many requests each year for seminars on topics of interest to professional organizations and businesses.

For busy achievers and involved parents, Dr. Baldwin has authored a popular, positive parenting cassette series and the book, It's All In Your Head: Lifestyle Management Strategies for Busy People. *Both are available in bookstores or from Direction Dynamics in Wilmington, N.C.*

In the large auditorium, concerned parents wait for the program to begin. The speaker appears to talk about the problems of parenting in the eighties. The program begins with a question to the audience: "How many of you would choose to live your adolescent years over if you had the chance?" Relatively few hands are raised and some of them waver indecisively. For just a few, the adolescent years are some of the best. The majority, however, are happy to have reached adulthood and put those tumultuous years behind them.

Then a second question: "How many of you would choose to live your adolescent years over if you had to do it *right now*?" This time, practically no hands are raised. The fact is that in any era, early adolescence is a most difficult time of life. On the other hand, there is ample evidence that this critical period of growth and change for young people is steadily becoming more difficult to negotiate emotionally. Caring parents seem to sense this and they are afraid for their children. Sadly,

their intuitive awareness is quite accurate: what they remember as the simpler world of their own youth has changed irrevocably.

Still, beyond the social environment and value system characteristic of this decade resides the basic adolescent. Understanding the changes that occur and the behaviors that are typical of a young man or woman growing up, regardless of time or place, provides parents with a backdrop of awareness that is most reassuring. It also provides the basis for the necessarily changed relationship with a child who is rapidly growing physically and emotionally. Armed with such understanding, parents can better cope with the many issues that are presented by the changes in their adolescent. At times, they can even manage a knowing smile at the many typical reactions they observe.

Parents who have survived the perils of puberty know, though, that dealing with one or more adolescents is not fun and games. Looking after the kids is relatively easy when they are small and dependent and the immediate neighborhood is their whole world. Three parental apprehensions, however, are forced into the forefront of consciousness by the onset of puberty and fueled daily by powerful adolescent strivings for independence.

Parental apprehension #1: "My adolescent will do the same things I did when I was young." With the wisdom of the years, parents look back at their adolescent antics with a bit of amusement tempered by a fair share of "only by the grace of God . . ." feelings. These parents, now mature individuals, simply don't want their children to take the same chances.

Parental apprehension #2: "The world my teen must live in is much more dangerous than it was years ago." This absolutely valid fear is constantly reinforced by public awareness of high suicide rates in adolescents, life-threatening sexually transmitted diseases and the easy availability of drugs. Mistakes and missteps can be much more serious than they were in the past.

Parental apprehension #3: "My child now has a private life that I can't directly control anymore." A reality is that teens force parents to trust them. Adolescence brings increased mobility and an expansion of time spent outside the sphere of direct family influence. Parents are forced to let go and hope that their teen will handle unknown and possibly dangerous situations well.

With impending puberty, the drama of early adolescence begins to unfold relentlessly. Responsible parents struggle to safeguard their teen's present and future. At the same time, their adolescent precociously lays claim to all adult prerogatives and privileges. In the background, a chosen peer group powerfully influences a child to do its immature bidding. Peers, parents and puberty all interact to produce the conflict-laden "adolescent triangle." It's normal but not easy.

The complex relationships of the adolescent triangle have been a perplexing part of the family life for centuries. It is incumbent upon parents to try to understand the developmental processes being experienced by their growing teen. Only then can they effectively modify their parenting relationship to their child-cum-adult in ways that will promote healthy growth toward maturity. And they must persevere without thanks in the face of active resistance by their teen. To set the stage for effective parental coping, here's an overview of the normal changes that occur during early adolescence.

THE STAGES OF ADOLESCENCE

If the typical individual is asked where adolescence begins and ends, the immediate response is "the teen years." Implicit in this response is the assumption that when the early twenties are reached, adolescence has ended and the individual has become an adult. Nothing could be further from the truth. True, in the past there has been an easy biological marker for the beginning of the adolescent years: puberty. And, in generations past, young men and women became financially and emotionally self-sufficient shortly after leaving home in their late teens.

However, the beginning and end of adolescence have become increasingly diffuse and difficult to define clear-

ly. On one hand, we sometimes see a precocious beginning to adolescence that may predate overt signs of puberty. Children frequently begin to act like adolescents before physical changes begin. At the other end of this growth period, the difficulty is obvious. How do you define the moment when a child has become a true adult? Of course the best way is to use emotional maturity as a gauge rather than more obvious but often misleading criteria such as completing an education, earning a living, marrying or becoming a parent.

In short, adolescence in this society at present spans approximately 20 years. For almost two decades young people struggle to become emotionally mature adults. There are three basis stages of the adolescent experience as it exists today. However, for parents and children the most critical and dangerous is the first.

Stage I: Early adolescence (the rise of tribal loyalties). Age span: 10 or 11 through 17 years. In other words, this most tumultuous stage of growth begins in late fifth or sixth grade and typically ends at about the senior year of high school. During this time, your child joins a "tribe" of peers that is highly separate from the adult world. The peer group (tribe) clearly defines itself as a distinct subculture struggling for identity with its own dress codes, language codes, defined meeting places and powerfully enforced inclusion criteria.

During these most difficult years for both parent and child, the most pronounced changes of puberty occur. The core struggle of the child is to become independent—and that means emotionally separating from parents and forging a new adult identity. Initial attempts are awkward and emotionally naive. In three key areas, here's what the early adolescent is like.

A. Relationship to parents. Suspicious and distrustful, the adolescent begins actively to push parents away and resists their attempts to give advice. Life is conducted in a secretive world dominated by peers. Rebelling, pushing limits and constantly testing parental resolve are characteristic.

B. Relationship to peers. The youth experiences emotionally intense "puppy love" relationships with members of the opposite sex and "best friends" relationships with peers of the same sex. These relationships are often superficial, with undue emphasis placed on status considerations: participation in sports, attractiveness, belonging to an *in* group.

C. Relationship to career/future. Largely unrealistic in expectations of the adult world, the adolescent sees making a good living—and getting the training required—as easy and "no problem." Money made by working is often spent on status items such as cars or clothes or just on having a good time. The future is far away.

Stage II: Middle adolescence (testing adult realities). Age span: about 18 through 23 or 24. Beginning late in the high school years, a new awareness, with a subtle accompanying fear, begins to grow within the adolescent: "It's almost over. Soon I'll have to face the world on my own." A personal future and the hard realities it entails can no longer be completely denied. Shortly after high school, this young adult typically leaves home to attend college or technical school, join the service or enter the work force.

5. ADOLESCENCE AND EARLY ADULTHOOD

While on their own, but still basically protected by parents, middle adolescents are actively engaged in testing the self against the real world in ways not possible while living at home. More personal accountability is required and some hard lessons are learned. These sometimes painful experiences help the middle adolescent learn the ways of the world, but many signs of immaturity remain. In more specific terms, here is what's happening.

A. Relationship to parents. This dynamic is improved but still problematic at times. Middle adolescents still aren't really ready to be completely open with parents, but they are less defensive. During visits home, intense conflicts with parents will still erupt about lifestyle, career decisions and responsibility.

B. Relationships with peers. Frequent visits home may be made more with the intention to see the old gang from high school than to see parents. Good buddies remain at home, but new friends are being made in a work or school setting. A deeper capacity for caring is manifested in increasingly mature relationships with both sexes.

C. Relationship to career/future. The economics of self-support are steadily becoming more important. Sights may be lowered and changes in career direction are common. Meeting new challenges successfully brings a growing sense of confidence and self-sufficiency.

Stage III: Late adolescence (joining up). Age span: 23 or 24 to about 30 years. By the mid-twenties, early career experimentation has ended, as has protective parental involvement. The late adolescent is usually financially self-sufficient and remains quite social. Life is relatively simple because there is minimal community involvement, little property needing upkeep and usually an income at least adequate to meet basic needs. The late adolescent years tend to be remembered fondly as having been filled with hard work and good times.

At first glance, the late adolescent may appear to be fully adult, but this perception is deceptive. Significant adjustments to the adult world are still being made but are less obvious than they were. Many insecurities in relationships and at work continue to be faced and resolved. Spurred by a growing commitment to creating a personal niche in the adult world, the individual continues to change in the direction of true adult maturity. Here's how.

A. Relationship to parents. Over 20 years, the late adolescent has come full circle. Now that he or she is emotionally self-sufficient, a closer relationship with parents becomes possible. Mutual respect and acceptance grow. The late adolescent begins to understand parenting behaviors that were resisted earlier.

B. Relationship to peers. Most high school chums have been left behind and are seen only occasionally. A new group of work-related peers has been solidly established. Love relationships are more mature and show increased capacity for give and take. Commitment to a shared future and to a family grows.

C. Relationship to career/future. Active striving toward the good life and personal goals intensifies. At work, there is a continuing need to prove competency and get ahead. At home, a more settled lifestyle, one that is characteristic of the middle-class mainstream, slowly evolves. Limited community involvement is seen.

EARLY ADOLESCENT ATTITUDES

While adolescents struggle for nearly two decades to attain emotional maturity, the period of early adolescence is clearly the most striking. It is during this critical six or seven years that the growing young adult is most vulnerable to major mistakes. It is an emotional, intense, painful and confusing phase. It is also the time remembered by parents as most trying of their ability to cope.

Because the vulnerability of parents and their children is never so high as it is during early adolescence, it is well to define some of the characteristics of the normal teen during these years. Here are listed 15 of the most common adolescent attitudes that make life difficult for parents and children, but which are entirely normal for this age group. (NOTE: "Teen" in this discussion refers specifically to an early adolescent.)

Adolescent attitude #1: Conformity within nonconformity. The early adolescent attempts to separate from parents by rejecting their standards. At the same time there is an absolute need to conform to peer group standards. It is very important to be like peers and unlike parents.

Adolescent attitude #2: Open communication with adults diminishes. The early adolescent doesn't like to be questioned by parents and reveals little about what is really going on. Key items may be conveniently forgotten as a personal life outside the family is protected.

Adolescent attitude #3: Withdrawal from family altogether. With the advent of puberty, there is increasing resistance to the family. The teen would much rather stay home merely in order to be available or spend time doing nothing with friends than participate in anything with the family.

Adolescent attitude #4: Acceptability is linked to externals. Personal acceptability is excessively linked to having the right clothes, friends and fad items in teen culture. Parents are badgered constantly to finance status needs deemed necessary for acceptance by a chosen peer group.

Adolescent attitude #5: Spending more time alone. Ironically, although early adolescents are quite social most of the time, they also like to spend time by themselves. Often, teens will retreat for hours to a bedroom and tell parents in no uncertain terms to respect their privacy and let them alone.

Adolescent attitude #6: A know-it-all pseudo-sophistication. Attempts by parents to give helpful advice are usually met with a weary "I already know that!" More often than not, however, a teen's information about topics important to health and well-being is incomplete, full of distortions or patently false.

Adolescent attitude #7: Rapid emotional changes. One of the most difficult aspects of early adolescence for parents to cope with is rapid mood changes. A teen is on top of the world one minute and sullen or depressed the next. The emotional triggers for such changes are frequent but unclear and unpredictable.

Adolescent attitude #8: Instability in peer relationships. Early adolescent relationships are marked by intensity and change. Overnight, a best friend may become a mortal enemy because of a real or imagined betrayal. Changing loyalties are often triggered by the incessant gossiping characteristic of teen culture.

Adolescent attitude #9: Somatic sensitivity. In other words, a teen's rapidly changing body is cause for great concern. Frequently, an early adolescent will become obsessed with and distraught over a perceived major physical deformity (an asymmetrical nose, not-quite-right ears, two pimples).

Adolescent attitude #10: Personal grooming takes a spectacular upturn. To parents' astonishment, a lackadaisical preadolescent turns practically overnight into a prima donna who spends hours grooming and checking the mirror to make sure that every feature of personal appearance is letter-perfect.

Adolescent attitude #11: Emotional cruelty to one another. Early teens can be incredibly insensitive to one another. Malicious gossip, hurtful teasing, and descriptive nicknames, outright rejection by the peer group—all are reasons why early adolescence is a time of great pain for so many.

Adolescent attitude #12: A highly present-oriented existence. Parents often learn the hard way that seriously discussing the future with an early adolescent is an exercise in futility. Conflict results when an unconcerned teen insists on continuing a day-to-day, pleasure-oriented way of life.

Adolescent attitude #13: A rich fantasy life develops. The adolescent's world is filled with hopes and dreams: knights in shining armor, great achievements, plenty of money, a life of freedom and fun—all without much personal effort. Such fantasies often help deny true realities.

Adolescent attitude #14: There is a strong need for independence. Translation: "I can make my own decisions by myself." Teens take it as an insult to their maturity to have to ask permission for anything. This leads to circumventing established rules or making decisions without parental knowledge.

Adolescent attitude #15: A proclivity for experimentation. With a new body and new feelings, the early adolescent develops an unwarranted sense of personal maturity. This leads to covert experimentation wth adult behaviors (smoking, drug use, sexual activity) aimed at the achievement of status and the satisfaction of curiosity. The knowledge that this is taking place leads to another legitimate parental fear.

THE EMOTIONAL AROUSAL OF PARENTS

It is a given that early adolescence is difficult for parents. To a degree this is attributable to the erratic and challenging behavior of their teens. It is also true that as long as the child is clearly a child, the parents remain weak or lie dormant. However, once puberty begins, a myriad of powerful feelings wells up in the parents.

In many respects, a child's puberty forces parents to deal actively with emotional issues that promote *their* growth and development if handled well. It is as important for parents to understand their suddenly aroused feelings as it is for them to understand what is happening emotionally within their teen.

Aroused emotion #1: Unadulterated fear. I would not be going too far to say that the parents of teens live with fear and constant worry. "What's happened now?" "What am I going to find out about next?" A child's world is quite small. At puberty, it suddenly expands and the teen is gone much of the time. This occurs at about the same time that a teen becomes evasive about what is going on in his or her world. Fears grow.

Aroused emotion #2: A deep sense of helplessness. Parents grow very uncomfortable as they watch their teen experience all the pain and turmoil that early adolescence usually brings. Because adolescents perceive adults as unable *really* to understand anything of importance to themselves, parents may be pushed away when problems occur. The kids don't realize how helpless parents feel when they see their child suffering emotionally but are relegated to the sidelines.

Aroused emotion #3: High levels of frustration. It is a given that many of the behaviors of an early adolescent trigger parental anger. One of a teen's strongest emotional needs is to be separate emotionally. This need is expressed by constantly confronting parents verbally, violating rules and pushing limits right to the brink. This entirely normal adolescent response pattern takes its toll on parents who become highly stressed, frustrated and tired.

Aroused emotion #4: A growing awareness of loss. With the onset of puberty, parents are forced to recognize that in just a few years, their teen will be going into the world and lost forever to the nuclear family. The undeniable fact that "our little girl/boy is growing up" triggers this deepening sense of loss on the part of parents: the sadness is compounded by the withdrawal of the teen from family life. Often this particular feeling is overwhelmed by fleeting wishes that the child would hurry and grow up so parents can have some peace of mind.

Aroused emotion #5: Personal hurt. Parents of teens struggle to do their very best to guide and protect their children. However, no thanks are forthcoming. In fact, parents' efforts are often resented and they are labeled as old-fashioned or Victorian or old fogies who are obviously completely out of touch with reality. Angry confrontations are the norm. Sullen withdrawal is an everyday occurrence. Continued rejection and hurt feelings make it difficult for parents to continue giving their personal best to an unappreciative teen.

IN THE EYE OF THE HURRICANE

At the center of every hurricane is the eye. That's where there is calm despite the intensity of the storm that swirls around it. This is an excellent way to conceptualize the relationship of effective parents to their children during the tumultuous early adolescent years. At puberty, a teen becomes inexorably swept up in the swift winds of change. To help themselves and their child, parents must remain calm and aware in the eye of the hurricane.

In recent years, much has been written about the changing nature of growing up in America. Some authorities emphasize the group's premature sophistication consequent on the fact that teens these days are exposed to much more at an earlier age than their parents were. Others who study this special group find that beyond the surface precocity of teens, attaining emotional maturity is steadily becoming a more prolonged and difficult process than ever before. The reality that parents must understand is that these seemingly divergent points of view are both absolutely valid and in no way contradict one another.

To be effective, parents must not be fooled by the misleading sophistication of teens and instead respond to the more complex developmental problems that lie beneath this surface veneer. To be of maximum aid in promoting healthy growth toward maturity, parents must make sure that their responses reflect three important teenage needs.

Teen need #1: "Depth perception" by parents. Basically, parents must be able to see accurately beyond the often erratic surface behaviors of an adolescent to the real issues that simply can't be articulated by a teen. Then parents must respond in caring ways to those emotional needs despite protests, confrontations and denials.

Teen need #2: Consistency of parental responses. Teens are notorious for their inconsistency. One of their deepest needs during these years of turmoil is to have parents who are steady and consistent. Such parents become a stabilizing influence and a center of strength—this helps a teen cope effectively with rapid change in every part of life.

Teen need #3: Strength of parental conviction. At no other time during the entire child-rearing process must parents be surer of their values. Teens focus tremendous pressure on parents to convince them they are wrong or that their values are irrelevant. Far too often the kids succeed in compromising solid parental values, to the detriment of the family and themselves.

One of the most emotionally rigorous tasks that parents face during the adolescent years is to keep doing what is right with very little encouragement and without becoming too insecure. And, after all is said and done and those difficult years are over, most teens do mature to join the ranks of respectable adults. Didn't you? And if you parented well, you will be rewarded eventually when your adult son or daughter thanks you directly for all the sacrifices you made in the face of all the obstacles.

But the progress toward the goal is a nightmare. One frustrated parent put up a sign in the kitchen: "NOTICE TO ALL TEENS! If you are tired of being hassled by unreasonable parents, NOW IS THE TIME FOR ACTION. Leave home and pay your own way WHILE YOU STILL KNOW EVERYTHING!"

These days puberty has perils for parents and for the children in grown-up bodies who are in their charge. And adolescence is no time to cut corners and take the easy road. Perhaps it was a wise parent who remarked that "a shortcut is often the quickest way to get somewhere you weren't going." With adolescents, the best road is always difficult but eventually rewarding. Shortcuts too often lead to dead ends. Or dangerous precipices. Sometimes to places you never expected to visit.

JEALOUSY & ENVY

The Demons Within Us

JON QUEIJO

Jon Queijo *is a free-lance writer who resides in West Roxbury, Massachusetts.*

Rick and Liz seemed to have a wonderful marriage; they did everything together. This changed suddenly, however, when Liz's ex-boyfriend began working at her law firm. Besieged by insecurity, Rick began calling Liz's office at odd hours and at night questioned her suspiciously. In a coup de grace, he burst in on her during a business luncheon and falsely accused her of having an affair.

Ann worked extremely hard to achieve success as a real estate agent. Her satisfaction turned sour, however, when a new agent was hired who managed to work less, yet made more sales. Ann hid her dislike of the new agent by offering to take her phone messages while she was out. When Ann began making more sales than her rival, no one made the connection between this turn of events and Ann's tendency to "accidentally" forget to deliver certain phone messages.

The jealous rage of a lover. The shameful actions of envy. Despite our better intentions, most of us feel these emotions dozens of times in our lifetimes. Pulling us apart from lovers, friends, family members, co-workers and even perfect strangers, jealousy and envy can devastate our lives and cause effects ranging from sadness, anger and depression, to estrangement, abuse and even violence.

Beyond our own lives, the power of these emotions has spawned countless works of poetry and prose and triggered numerous historical events. Perhaps for this reason society proclaimed judgment on jealousy and envy thousands of years ago, with the verdict coming down harder on envy. For example, while the pain of jealousy has been forever immortalized in poetry and song, the shame of envy emerges as early as the Ten Commandments: "Thou shalt not covet thy neighbor's house, field, wife or anything that is thy neighbor's." In fact, envy is despicable enough to be considered one of the "Seven Deadly Sins," taking its place alongside pride, gluttony, lust, sloth, anger and greed.

Although we see jealousy and envy arise in numerous situations, their basic definitions are fairly simple: jealousy is "the fear of losing a relationship" (romantic, parental, sibling, friendship); and envy is "the longing for something someone else has" (wealth, possessions, beauty, talent, position).

Despite these definitions and the numerous philosophers, poets and scientists who have pondered these emotions, some remarkably fundamental questions remain: What causes jealousy and envy? Are the emotions actually different? What do they feel like? What are the best ways to cope with these feelings? Why do we often use the terms interchangeably? And what are their implications for society?

Researchers have taken various approaches to answer these questions. The biological view, for example, says that jealousy and envy serve a basic purpose — the emotions lead to biochemical changes that spur the individual to take action and improve the situation. The evolutionary view holds that jealousy may enhance survival by keeping parents together, thus increasing protection of the offspring.

> ## "People who are dissatisfied with themselves are primed for having other people's talents impinge on them. If, on the other hand, you're satisfied with yourself, then what other people have or do won't unduly raise your expectations, and you should be less likely to feel envy."
>
> RICHARD SMITH

Other explanations range from the reasonable — envy stems from parental attitudes that make a child feel inferior; to the bizarre — the emotions begin in infants when the mother withholds breast-feeding.

Probably the most practical understanding of jealousy and envy, however, emerges from the work of social psychologists — researchers who look at the way people react to each other and society. To them, jealousy and envy arise when the right mix of internal *and* external ingredients are present in society.

"I tend to look at jealousy and envy in terms of motivation and self-esteem," explains Peter Salovey, a social psychologist at Yale University. "It's the interaction between what's important to you and what's happening in the environment. The common denominator is this threat to something that's very important to the person — something that defines self-worth."

Richard Smith, a social psychologist at Boston University who has conducted several studies on jealousy and envy, emphasizes external factors, such as how society affects our view of ourselves. "My perspective is from social comparisons," he explains, "which says we have no objective opinion for evaluating our abilities, so we look at others."

Smith, like Salovey, also stresses internal factors — the role of self-esteem, for example — in determining whether we will feel jealous or envious in any given situation. "People who are dissatisfied with themselves are primed for having other people's talents and possessions impinge on them," Smith points out. "If, on the other hand, you're satisfied with yourself, then what other

people have or do won't unduly raise your expectations for yourself, and you should be less likely to feel envy."

Embarrassed by his display of jealousy, Rick apologizes to Liz and they discuss the problem. Soon they realize that while Rick loves Liz and fears losing her, something else is at work here. Because Liz's ex-boyfriend is a lawyer, he possesses skills Rick does not. While Rick is proud of his ability as a store manager, he fears Liz's ex-boyfriend could lure her away with other skills.

Feeling guilty about her actions, Ann calls a friend for support. Ann knows she feels inadequate because the new agent is succeeding in a career that is very important to her, but that doesn't explain everything; others have done better whom Ann has not envied. Then it occurs to her: What bothers her is the way the woman was bettering Ann. She was more outgoing and self-confident — two skills about which Ann has always felt insecure.

As Rick and Ann's situations illustrate, if someone is unsure about an ability — such as Rick and his law knowledge or Ann and her communication skills — then a social situation can bring out that insecurity. "In envy," notes Salovey, "the threat may come from someone else's possessions or attributes. In jealousy the situation is the same, except that the other person's possessions or attributes cause you to fear losing the relationship. Either way, somebody else threatens your self-esteem."

Yet Salovey emphasizes that it is not as simple as saying someone is at risk for these emotions if they have a low opinion of themselves. "It's low self-

esteem in a specific *area*," he explains. "If you have a low opinion about your physical looks or occupation, then that's the area in which you're more likely to be vulnerable. You feel it when you confront somebody else who is superior to you in that respect."

From Smith's point of view, the key is how that person compares him or herself to others. In one study, for example, he found that envy was strongest among people who performed below their expectation in an area that was important to them and then confronted someone who functioned better. In a related study, Smith also found that a person's "risk" for feeling jealous or envious increases with the increased importance they put on the quality.

While much of this may sound like common sense, in fact little research has been done to establish even the most basic ground rules of jealousy and envy. For example, are the two emotions actually different? What do people feel when they are jealous or envious? Despite centuries of long-held assumptions, only recently have researchers begun to answer these questions scientifically.

Smith and his colleagues, for example, recently conducted a study to see if the classic distinctions between the two emotions are actually true. Their findings — presented last August at the annual convention of the American Psychological Association — validated what we have always suspected. Jealous people tend to feel a fear of loss, betrayal, loneliness, suspicion and uncertainty. Envious people, on the other hand, tend to feel inferior, longing for what another has, guilt over feeling ill will towards someone, shame and a tendency to deny the emotion.

The study was not an idle exercise in stating the obvious. It was designed to help clear an ongoing debate about jealousy and envy and our curious tendency not only to mix up the terms, but to experience an overlap of both emotions.

Consider, for example, the following uses of the word jealousy: Bruce was jealous when his girlfriend began talking to another man at the party; the boy cried in a fit of jealousy when his parents paid attention to the new baby; Ellen became jealous when her friend began spending more time at the health club. Nothing unusual with any of these uses of jealousy—they all refer to someone's "fear of losing a relationship."

Now, however, consider these uses: The professor, jealous of his colleague's success, broke into his lab and ruined his experiment; Mary is always complaining of being jealous of her sister's beautiful blonde hair; Mark admits that he is jealous of John's athletic ability. All of these situations actually refer to envy, "the longing for something someone else has." Researchers have noticed the mix-up and it has led them to question how different the feelings really are.

"In everyday language it's clear that people use the terms interchangeably," notes Smith, adding, "For that reason, there's naturally some confusion about whether they're different." In a recent study, however, Smith and his colleagues found the mix-up only works one way, with jealousy being the broader term. That is, jealousy is used sometimes in place of envy, but envy is rarely used when referring to jealousy. So while you might say, "I'm jealous of Paul's new Mercedes," you would never say, "When she left her husband, he flew into an *envious* rage."

Is there an underlying reason for why the terms are used interchangeably? One reason people may use jealousy in place of envy, and not vice versa, is because of the social stigma attached to envy. But Salovey and Smith both point to another reason for the overlap.

Dave and Marcia had been dating for a year when Marcia decided she wanted to see other men. Dave was devastated —not only because he cared for her, but because he was older and feared his age was working against him. One evening he bumped into Marcia, arm-in-arm with another man. As Dave talked to the couple, sarcasm led to verbal abuse, until finally Dave took a swing at Marcia's date—a man at least 10 years his junior.

In case you haven't guessed, Dave wanted back more than his relationship with Marcia; he also wanted the return of his youth. He was feeling a painful mixture of jealousy *and* envy. Explains Salovey, "The same feelings emerge when your relationship is threatened by someone else as when you'd like something that person has. I think one reason is that in most romantic situations, envy plays a role. You're jealous

because you're going to lose the relationship, but you're also envious because there is something the other person has that allows him to be attractive to the person you care about."

Because this overlap occurs so frequently, Salovey has found the best way to understand jealousy and envy is to examine each *situation*. In addition, because jealousy is the more encompassing term, he views envy as a form of jealousy and distinguishes the two by the terms "romantic jealousy," the fear of losing a relationship; and "social-comparison jealousy," the envy that arises when people compare traits like age, intelligence, possession and talent.

Smith agrees with Salovey that one reason people confuse the terms may be that envy is present in most cases of jealousy. Nevertheless, he takes issue with Salovey's use of the term "social-comparison jealousy." "It may be true that there's almost invariably envy in every case of jealousy," he notes, "but it doesn't mean there's no value in distinguishing the two feelings. The overlap in usage only goes one way, so there's no reason to throw out the term 'envy.' "

Salovey counters, "I'm not saying we need to stop using 'envy.' The reason we use 'social-comparison jealousy' is to emphasize that the situation that creates the feeling is important." And one reason

COMPARING OURSELVES TO OTHERS   In Sickness and In Health

Envy, according to Richard Smith, arises when we compare ourselves to others and can't cope with what we see. Indeed, he believes that the way in which we cope with "social comparisons" plays an important role in our physical as well as mental health.

Smith theorizes that we use one of four "comparison styles" to cope with social differences. Two of these styles are "constructive" to well-being, while two are "destructive." "It's a difficult problem to tackle," says Smith, "but we're trying to measure these styles and see if they predict a person's general satisfaction with life or ability to cope with illness." For example, he notes, "There's considerable evidence" that one way people cope with serious illness is by focusing on others who are not doing as well.

Smith has arranged the four comparison styles in a matrix, with the descriptions in each box referring to the characteristics of that style. "*Upward*-Constructive," for example, represents those who compare themselves to others who are better off, and use it as a healthy stimulus. In this category, "You don't feel hostile to others who are better," says Smith, "because you hope to be like them. It suggests that upward comparisons are not necessarily bad."

"*Upward*-Destructive," however, shows how comparing yourself to those doing better can be unhealthy.

Envy, resentment, Type A behavior and poor health all fit into this category. Smith points to a study that looked at personalities of people who had heart attacks, "and the only dimension that predicted heart disease was this jealousy-suspicion trait."

What Smith calls "*Downward*-Constructive," refers to people who compare themselves to those worse off, and use it to feel better about themselves. Such people, says Smith, "realize that others aren't doing so well and how lucky they are. There's some solid evidence in the health literature showing the value of that kind of comparison."

Finally, "*Downward*-Destructive," describes those who get pleasure out of comparing themselves to others who are worse off. "I'd call the effect 'schadenfreude,' or joy at the suffering of others," says Smith. "It's akin to sadism and it's probably not conducive to health."

"What's interesting about all four comparison styles," notes Smith, "is that they don't necessarily have any relation to reality. They reflect what people construe and focus on." While Smith stresses, "This is all speculative," he adds that "my feeling is that 'Upward-Destructive' explains people's hostility in terms of their social comparison context. It shows why their relation to people doing better leads to envy and why they'd feel hostile to begin with."   J.Q.

Salovey stresses the situation—rather than other mood differences—is that romantic jealousy, since it includes envy, is usually very intense, making it difficult to separate distinct feelings.

Nevertheless, Smith believes the distinction should be made, especially because "In its traditional definition, envy has a hostile component to it." Not everyone would agree with that. After all, in envying others, we can also admire *them* and even use *them* as role models to spur ourselves to greater abilities. There is no hostility in that, yet these cases, Smith contends, are not precisely envy. Indeed, Smith believes envy differs from jealousy not only because of its hostility, but because of another distinct ingredient: privacy.

By the time Bill was 40, he was vice president at his firm and owned a luxurious house in an affluent neighborhood. Nevertheless, Bill had never married and was lonely. He envied his brother Jim, who lived a modest but happy life with his wife and children. One day Jim asked Bill to write a reference letter to help him get a bank loan for a new home. Bill said he'd be delighted, but soon realized he could send the letter to the bank without Jim ever seeing it. Bill wrote the letter and his brother, never knowing why, was refused the loan.

Although this anecdote is fictional, Smith has shown in his research that the principles illustrated are probably true. In a recent study, Smith had subjects identify with an envious person. He then gave them the option of dividing a "resource" between themselves and the envied person. Among the many options were: dividing the resource equally; dividing it so the subject kept the most and gave the least to the envied person; and dividing it so they sacrificed the amount they could otherwise keep for themselves if it meant giving the least to the envied person. Most subjects chose the last option, but only when they could do so in private, rather than public, circumstances.

Although Smith admits the findings need to be verified, he believes the results are strongly "suggestive." The envious person's choice, he says, "was unambiguously hostile. Not selfish, but hostile. And the findings verified the conventional wisdom that envy has a secretive quality about it that you wouldn't admit to the person you envy. And under the right circumstances it will lead to actual hostile behavior."

The reason people would be hostile in private seems obvious, given that envy is socially unacceptable. But why the hostility in the first place? Smith theorizes that the envied person's "superiority" emphasizes the envious person's low self-esteem in a specific area—the way the new real estate agent's communication skills affected Ann; Marcia's young date affected Dave; and Jim's happy family life affected Bill. Hostility is a way of putting down the envied person and devaluing his or her "superiority." Whether it takes the form of thought, word or deed, hostility pushes the envied person away, thereby allowing the envious person to restore his self-esteem.

Smith is looking at other implications of envy and hostility in society. For example, "We don't know much about why people are hostile to begin with, but since envy is related to hostility, maybe the way people respond to the way they compare themselves to others is at the root of hostility." And there are other subtle—and even more frightening—implications. For one thing, Smith notes, because envy is socially unacceptable, "It's often not conscious, and as a result people will arrange the details of their situation and their perception of the other person to make envy something they can label as 'resentment'—resentment in the sense of righteous indignation."

Smith goes as far as to propose that many intergroup conflicts in the world—between countries, races and religious groups, for example—may begin with envy. One group is better off economi-

Ranking Jealousy & Envy

What situations are most likely to evoke feelings of jealousy and envy? In a study published in the *Journal of Personality and Social Psychology*, Peter Salovey and Judith Rodin asked subjects to rank 53 situations according to the degree of emotion each would evoke. Below are 25 of those situations, listed in decreasing order, that received the highest "jealousy/envy" ratings:

1 You find out your lover is having an affair.

2 Someone goes out with a person you like.

3 Someone gets a job that you want.

4 Someone seems to be getting closer to a person to whom you are attracted.

5 Your lover tells you how sexy his/her old girl/boyfriend was.

6 Your boyfriend or girlfriend visits the person he or she used to date.

7 You do the same work as someone else and get paid less than he or she.

8 Someone is more talented than you.

9 Your boyfriend or girlfriend would rather be with his/her friends than with you.

10 You are alone while others are having fun.

11 Your boyfriend or girlfriend wants to date other people.

12 Someone is able to express himself or herself better than you.

13 Someone else has something you wanted and could have had but don't.

14 Someone else gets credit for what you've done.

15 Someone is more intelligent than you.

16 Someone appears to have everything.

17 Your steady date has lunch with an attractive person of the opposite sex.

18 Someone is more outgoing and self-confident than you.

19 Someone buys something you wanted but couldn't afford.

20 You have to work while your roommate is out partying.

21 An opposite-sex friend gives another friend a compliment, but not you.

22 Someone has more free time than you.

23 You hear that an old lover of yours has found a new lover.

24 Someone seems more self-fulfilled than you.

25 You listen to someone tell a story about things he did without you. J.Q.

cally, for example, than another, and the "inferior" group feels envy as a result. "But if they're just envious," he explains, "no one is going to give them any sympathy. So they tend to see their situation as unfair and unjust. In this way, envy becomes righteous resentment, which in turn gives them the 'right' to protest and conduct hostile — or even terrorist —activity."

This topic raises questions about what is fair or unfair in our society, how people cope with differences and whether, as a result, they feel envy, resentment or acceptance. Smith points out that coping with envy may depend on how well we learn to accept our inequalities. "I think as people mature, they learn to cope with differences by coming to terms with the fact that life *isn't* fair and that it's counterproductive to dwell on things you can't do anything about."

While some of Smith's ideas on coping with envy are speculative, Salovey has found that there are specific strategies —illustrated in the following anecdotes —that work in preventing and easing jealousy and envy. . . .

Rick and Liz are getting along much better these days even though Liz still works with her ex-boyfriend at the law firm. Rick isn't thrilled by this, but he overcame his jealousy by focusing instead on his relationship with Liz: spending time with her, planning vacations, discussing their future.

Ann no longer feels envy or hostility towards her co-worker at the real estate agency. She put an end to those negative feelings by simply ignoring her rival's superior communication skills and concentrating instead on her own achievements.

As illustrated here and isolated in a survey Salovey and Yale associate Judith Rodin conducted with *Psychology*

Today readers, there are three major coping strategies: *Self-reliance*, in which a person does not give into the emotion, but continues to pursue the goals in the relationship; *Selective ignoring*, or simply ignoring the things that cause the jealousy or envy; and *Self-bolstering*, or concentrating on positive traits about yourself.

Surprisingly, "We found that the first two coping strategies are very effective in helping a person not feel jealousy," reports Salovey. "We thought that self-bolstering would also be good, since if something that's important to you is threatened, then maybe you should think of things in which you do well."

Although self-bolstering was not helpful in preventing jealousy. "Once you were *already* jealous, it was the only thing that kept you from becoming depressed and angry," notes Salovey. "So the first two keep jealousy in check, but if jealousy does emerge, self-bolstering keeps jealousy from its worst effects."

In the same study, Salovey and Rodin also uncovered some interesting data about how men and women experience jealousy and envy. "Men tend to be more envious in situations involving wealth and fame, and women more so in beauty and friendship," reports Salovey, but he emphasizes, "I should put that finding in context. We looked at a lot of variables and very rarely found differences. Men and women were very similar on nearly everything you could measure except that one difference."

Smith and Salovey do agree that while jealousy and envy can be devastating to those experiencing them, in milder forms they can actually be helpful. "I tend to think of jealousy and envy as normal," says Salovey. "In any relationship where you really care about the other person, when your relationship is threatened by someone, you're

going to feel negative emotions. If you don't, maybe you don't care that much."

As for envy, Smith points out that, "I don't think it's a bad thing, necessarily. It's a motivator when it's in the form of admiration and hero worship." He does add, however, that at those levels the emotion may not be envy since envy, by definition is hostile. "It's hard to know where one stops and the other begins," he notes.

Nevertheless, Smith stresses that "Coping with differences is something we all do. Some of us do it in constructive ways and others in destructive, and that has implications for who is going to be happy or unhappy. Envy is a sign of not coping well—maybe." He adds that while "some people have a right to recognize that a situation is unfair, the next question is, what do you do? It may be best to recognize the unfairness and cope with it before it leads to more painful feelings."

Jealousy and envy can have an unpleasant knack of cropping up between the people who care most about each other. Our first reaction is often to blame the other person—my *wife* is the one who is lunching with her ex-boyfriend; my *co-worker* is undeservedly making more sales; why should my *brother* have a happy family *and* a big house? Part of our blame is understandable: life *is* unfair; society and circumstance *do* create differences between us beyond our control.

Nevertheless, the bottom line is not how we view other people, but how we view ourselves. When jealousy or envy become overwhelming, it is as much from passing judgment on ourselves as on others. That's when we owe it to everyone to talk it out, change what needs to be changed and—perhaps most importantly—accept ourselves for what we are.

Development During Middle and Late Adulthood

Perhaps no statistic reflects the changes in the American family across the last generation as effectively as the surge in the number of women who combine family life with careers. Do these dual roles too often prove detrimental to health and happiness? Certainly not, according to "The Myth of the Miserable Working Woman."

Developmentalists hold two extreme points of view about the latter part of the life span. Disengagement theory holds that the physical and intellectual deficits associated with aging are inevitable and should be accepted at face value by the aged. Activity theory acknowledges the decline in abilities associated with aging, but also notes that the aged can maintain satisfying and productive lives.

Extreme views in any guise risk stereotyping all individuals within a category or class as having the same needs and capabilities. Whether one's reference group is racial, ethnic, cultural, or age-related, stereotyping usually leads to counterproductive, discriminatory social policy that alienates the reference group from mainstream society.

Evidence obtained during the past decade clearly illustrates the fallacy of extremist views of middle and late adulthood. Development during adulthood and aging is not a unitary phenomenon. Although there are common physical changes associated with aging, there are also wide individual differences in the rates of change and the degree to which changes are expressed. It is common to think of the changes associated with aging as solely physical and generally negative. The popular press devotes considerable space to discussions of the causes and treatment of such debilitating disorders such as Alzheimer's disease. However, there are also psychological changes associated with aging, and, as is the case at all age levels, some individuals cope well with change and others do not. New research on the aging process suggests that physical health and mental health changes do not correlate well. Although a variety of abuses can hasten physical and mental deterioration, proper diet and modest exercise can also slow the aging process. In addition, one cannot understate the importance of love, social interaction, and a sense of self-worth for combating the loneliness, despair, and futility often associated with aging. Leonard Sagan in his article, "Family Ties: The Real Reason People Are Living Longer," describes how family relationships and dynamics contribute to the good health and longevity of people today.

Behavioral gerontology remains a specialization within human development that is absent from most graduate programs in human development. Perhaps this is partly because of the natural tendency of people to avoid confronting the negative aspects of aging, such as loneliness and despair over the loss of one's spouse or over one's own impending death. Nevertheless, contemporary studies do provide fascinating information about the quality of life in the later years (see "The Vintage Years"). In "On Growing Old," Robert Sapolsky and Caleb Finch review aging research to understand why most species age while others do not.

Does the course of life really progress through an orderly series of universally experienced stages? Anne Rosenfeld and Elizabeth Stark in "The Prime of Our Lives" and Carol Tavris in "Don't Act Your Age!" do not think so and argue strongly against this view. Traditionally, counting birthdays was the only practical way to answer questions regarding the concept of age. In "How Old Are You Really?" we learn that one's true biological age says a lot more about how well we are aging.

Because the proportion of the population represented by the aged is increasing rapidly, it is imperative that significant advances be made in our knowledge of the later years of development. Prolonging life and controlling physical illness should certainly be topics of interest in this regard. However, these biologically and medically oriented topics should be accompanied by studies on the psychological aspects of aging in pursuit of promotion and enhancement of the quality of life for the elderly.

Looking Ahead: Challenge Questions

What are some of the most positive features for women of combining careers with family responsibilities?

Why are the middle adult years, sometimes called the "prime of life," the forgotten years in inquiries into growth and change, relative to both earlier and later life periods?

Do you think that the life of most individuals can be described by a relatively constant sequence of life stages, or are life patterns just too variable for general descriptions to be of use? What are some of the most common stereotypes about aging in our society?

Gerontologists suggest that significantly greater life expectancies are possible even without medical breakthroughs. Control of childhood diseases, better education, better physical fitness, and proper diet are factors that increase the life span. How would your life differ now if your expected life span was 150 years? How do you think your elderly years will differ from those of your parents?

The Myth of the Miserable Working Woman

She's Tired, She's Stressed Out, She's Unhealthy, She Can't Go Full Speed at Work or Home. Right? Wrong.

Rosalind C. Barnett and Caryl Rivers

Rosalind C. Barnett is a psychologist and a senior research associate at the Wellesley College Center for Research on Women. Caryl Rivers is a professor of journalism at Boston University and the author of More Joy Than Rage: Crossing Generations With the New Feminism.

"You Can't Do Everything," announced a 1989 USA Today *headline on a story suggesting that a slower career track for women might be a good idea. "Mommy Career Track Sets Off a Furor," declaimed the* New York Times *on March 8, 1989, reporting that women cost companies more than men. "Pressed for Success, Women Careerists Are Cheating Themselves," sighed a 1989 headline in the* Washington Post, *going on to cite a book about the "unhappy personal lives" of women graduates of the Harvard Business School. "Women Discovering They're at Risk for Heart Attacks," Gannett News Service reported with alarm in 1991. "Can Your Career Hurt Your Kids? Yes, Say Many Experts," blared a* Fortune *cover just last May, adding in a chirpy yet soothing fashion, "But smart parents—and flexible companies—won't let it happen."*

If you believe what you read, working women are in big trouble—stressed out, depressed, sick, risking an early death from heart attacks, and so overcome with problems at home that they make inefficient employees at work.

In fact, just the opposite is true. As a research psychologist whose career has focused on women and a journalist-critic who has studied the behavior of the media, we have extensively surveyed the latest data and research and concluded that the public is being engulfed by a tidal wave of disinformation that has serious consequences for the life and health of every American woman. Since large numbers of women began moving into the work force in the 1970s, scores of studies on their emotional and physical health have painted a very clear picture: Paid employment provides substantial health *benefits* for women. These benefits cut across income and class lines; even women who are working because they have to—not because they want to—share in them.

There is a curious gap, however, between what these studies say and what is generally reported on television, radio, and in newspapers and magazines. The more the research shows work is good for women, the bleaker the media reports seem to become. Whether this bizarre state of affairs is the result of a backlash against women, as *Wall Street Journal* reporter Susan Faludi contends in her new book, *Backlash: The Undeclared War Against American Women,* or of well-meaning ignorance, the effect is the same: Both the shape of national policy and the lives of women are at risk.

Too often, legislation is written and policies are drafted not on the basis of the facts but on the basis of what those in power believe to be the facts. Even the much discussed *Workforce 2000* report, issued by the Department of Labor under the Reagan administration—hardly a hotbed of feminism—admitted that "most current policies were designed for a society in which men worked and women stayed home." If policies are skewed toward solutions that are aimed at reducing women's commitment to work, they will do more than harm women—they will damage companies, managers and the productivity of the American economy.

THE CORONARY THAT WASN'T

One reason the "bad news" about working women jumps to page one is that we're all too willing to believe it. Many adults today grew up at a time when soldiers were returning home from World War II and a way had to be found to get the women who replaced them in industry back into the kitchen. The result was a barrage of propaganda that turned at-home moms into saints and backyard barbecues and station wagons into cultural icons. Many of us still have that outdated postwar map inside our heads, and it leaves us more willing to believe the horror stories than the good news that paid employment is an emotional and medical plus.

In the 19th century it was accepted medical dogma that women should not be educated because the brain and the ovaries could not develop at the same time. Today it's PMS, the wrong math genes or rampaging hormones. Hardly anyone points out the dire predictions that didn't come true.

You may remember the prediction that career women would start having more heart attacks, just like men. But the Framingham Heart Study–a federally funded cardiac project that has been studying 10,000 men and women since 1948–reveals that working women are not having more heart attacks. They're not dying any earlier, either. Not only are women not losing their health advantages; the lifespan gap is actually widening. Only one group of working women suffers more heart attacks than other women: those in low-paying clerical jobs with many demands on them and little control over their work pace, who also have several children and little or no support at home.

As for the recent publicity about women having more problems with heart disease, much of it skims over the important underlying reasons for the increase: namely, that by the time they have a heart attack, women tend to be a good deal older (an average of 67, six years older than the average age for men), and thus frailer, than males who have one. Also, statistics from the National Institutes of Health show that coronary symptoms are treated less aggressively in women–fewer coronary bypasses, for example. In addition, most heart research is done on men, so doctors do not know as much about the causes–and treatment–of heart disease in women. None of these factors have anything to do with work.

But doesn't working put women at greater risk for stress-related illnesses? No. Paid work is actually associated with *reduced* anxiety and depression. In the early 1980s we reported in our book, *Lifeprints* (based on a National Science Foundation–funded study of 300 women), that working women were significantly higher in psychological well-being than those not employed. Working gave them a sense of mastery and control that homemaking didn't provide. More recent studies echo our findings. For example:

7• A 1989 report by psychologist Ingrid Waldron and sociologist Jerry Jacobs of Temple University on nationwide surveys of 2,392 white and 892 black women, conducted from 1977 to 1982, found that women who held both work and family roles reported better physical and mental health than homemakers.

• According to sociologists Elaine Wethington of Cornell University and Ronald Kessler of the University of Michigan, data from three years (1985 to 1988) of a continuing federally funded study of 745 married women in Detroit "clearly suggests that employment benefits women emotionally." Women who increase their participation in the labor force report lower levels of psychological distress; those who lessen their commitment to work suffer from higher distress.

• A University of California at Berkeley study published in 1990 followed 140 women for 22 years. At age 43, those who were homemakers had more chronic conditions than the working women and seemed more disillusioned and frustrated. The working mothers were in good health and seemed to be juggling their roles with success.

In sum, paid work offers women heightened self-esteem and enhanced mental and physical health. It's unemployment that's a major risk factor for depression in women.

DOING IT ALL–AND DOING FINE

This isn't true only for affluent women in good jobs; working-class women share the benefits of work, according to psychologists Sandra Scarr and Deborah Phillips of the University of Virginia and Kathleen McCartney of the University of New Hampshire. In reviewing 80 studies on this subject, they reported that working-class women with children say they would not leave work even if they didn't need the money. Work offers not only income but adult companionship, social contact and a connection with the wider world that they cannot get at home.

Doing it all may be tough, but it doesn't wipe out the health benefits of working.

Looking at survey data from around the world, Scarr and Phillips wrote that the lives of mothers who work are not more stressful than the lives of those who are at home. So what about the second shift we've heard so much about? It certainly exists: In industrialized countries, researchers found, fathers work an average of 50 hours a week on the job and doing household chores; mothers work an average of 80 hours. Wethington and Kessler found that in daily "stress diaries" kept by husbands and wives, the women report more stress than the men do. But they also handle it better. In short, doing it all may be tough, but it doesn't wipe out the health benefits of working.

THE ADVANTAGES FOR FAMILIES

What about the kids? Many working parents feel they want more time with their kids, and they say so. But does maternal employment harm children? In 1989 University of Michigan psychologist Lois Hoffman reviewed 50 years of research and found that the expected negative effects never materialized. Most often, children of employed and unemployed mothers didn't differ on measures of child development. But children of both sexes with working mothers have a less sex-stereotyped view of the world because fathers in two-income families tend to do more child care.

However, when mothers work, the quality of non-parental child care is a legitimate worry. Scarr, Phillips and McCartney say there is "near consensus among developmental psychologists and early-childhood experts that child care per se does not constitute a risk factor in children's lives." What causes problems, they report, is poor-quality care and a troubled family life. The need for good child care in this country has been obvious for some time.

What's more, children in two-job families generally don't lose out on one-to-one time with their parents. New studies, such as S. L. Nock and P. W. Kingston's *Time with Children: The Impact of Couples' Work-Time Commitments,* show that when both parents of pre-schoolers are working, they spend as much time in direct interaction with their children as families in which only the fathers work. The difference is that working parents spend more time with their kids on weekends. When only the husband works, parents spend more leisure time with each other. There is a cost to two-income families—the couples lose personal time—but the kids don't seem to pay it.

One question we never used to ask is whether having a working mother could be *good* for children. Hoffman, reflecting on the finding that employed women—both blue-collar and professional—register higher life-satisfaction scores than housewives, thinks it can be. She cites studies involving infants and older children, showing that a mother's satisfaction with her employment status relates positively both to "the quality of the mother-child interaction and to various indexes of the child's adjustment and abilities." For example, psychologists J. Guidubaldi and B. K. Nastasi of Kent State University reported in a 1987 paper that a mother's satisfaction with her job was a good predictor of her child's positive adjustment in school.

Again, this isn't true only for women in high-status jobs. In a 1982 study of sources of stress for children in low-income families, psychologists Cynthia Longfellow and Deborah Belle of the Harvard University School of Education found that employed women were generally less depressed than unemployed women. What's more, their children had fewer behavioral problems.

But the real point about working women and children is that work *isn't* the point at all. There are good mothers and not-so-good mothers, and some work and some don't. When a National Academy of Sciences panel reviewed the previous 50 years of research and dozens of studies in 1982, it found no consistent effects on children from a mother's working. Work is only one of many variables, the panel concluded in *Families That Work,* and not the definitive one.

What is the effect of women's working on their marriages? Having a working wife can increase psychological stress for men, especially older men, who grew up in a world where it was not normal for a wife to work. But men's expectations that they will—and must—be the only provider may be changing. Wethington and Kessler found that a wife's employment could be a significant buffer *against* depression for men born after 1945. Still, the picture of men's psychological well-being is very mixed, and class and expectations clearly play a role. Faludi cites polls showing that young blue-collar men are especially angry at women for invading what they see as their turf as breadwinners, even though a woman with such a job could help protect her husband from economic hardship. But in highly educated, dual-career couples, both partners say the wife's career has enhanced the marriage.

THE FIRST SHIFT: WOMEN AT WORK

While women's own health and the well-being of their families aren't harmed by their working, what effect does this dual role have on their job performance? It's assumed that men can compartmentalize work and home lives but women will bring their home worries with them to work, making them distracted and inefficient employees.

Perhaps the most dangerous myth is that the solution is for women to drop back—or drop out.

The only spillover went in the other direction: The women brought their good feelings about their work home with them and left a bad day at home behind when they came to work. In fact, Wethington and Kessler found that it was the *men* who brought the family stresses with them to work. "Women are able to avoid bringing the contagion of home stress into the workplace," the researchers write, "whereas the inability of men to prevent this kind of contagion is pervasive." The researchers speculate that perhaps women get the message early on that they can handle the home front, while men are taking on chores they aren't trained for and didn't expect.

THE PERILS OF PART-TIME

Perhaps the most dangerous myth is that the solution to most problems women suffer is for them to drop back—or drop out. What studies actually show is a significant connection between a reduced commitment to work and increased psychological stress. In their Detroit study, Wethington and Kessler noted that women who went from being full-time employees to full-time housewives reported increased symptoms of distress, such as depression and anxiety attacks; the longer a woman worked and the more committed she was to the job, the greater her risk for psychological distress when she stopped.

What about part-time work, that oft-touted solution for weary women? Women who work fewer than 20 hours per week, it turns out, do not get the mental-health work benefit, probably because they "operate under the fiction that they can retain full responsibility for child care and home maintenance," wrote Wethington and Kessler. The result: Some part-timers wind up more stressed-out than women working full-time. Part-time employment also provides less money, fewer or no benefits and, often, less interesting work and a more arduous road to promotion.

That doesn't mean that a woman shouldn't cut down on her work hours or arrange a more flexible schedule. But it does mean she should be careful about jumping on a poorly designed mommy track that may make her a second-class citizen at work.

Many women think that when they have a baby, the best thing for their mental health would be to stay home. Wrong once more. According to Wethington and Kessler, having a baby does not increase psychological distress for working women—*unless* the birth results in their dropping out of the labor force. This doesn't mean that any woman who stays home to care for a child is going to be a wreck. But leaving the work force means opting out of the benefits of being in it, and women should be aware of that.

As soon as a woman has any kind of difficulty—emotional, family, medical—the knee-jerk reaction is to get her off the job. No such solution is offered to men, despite the very real correlation for men between job stress and heart attacks.

What the myth of the miserable working woman obscures is the need to focus on how the *quality* of a woman's job affects her health. Media stories warn of the alleged dangers of fast-track jobs. But our *Lifeprints* study found that married women in high-prestige jobs were highest in mental well-being; another study of life stress in women reported that married career women with children suffered the least from stress. Meanwhile, few media tears are shed for the women most at risk: those in the word-processing room who have no control at work, low pay and little support at home.

Women don't need help getting out of the work force; they need help staying in it. As long as much of the media continues to capitalize on national ignorance, that help will have to come from somewhere else. (Not that an occasional letter to the editor isn't useful.) Men need to recognize that they are not just occasional helpers but vital to the success of the family unit. The corporate culture has to be reshaped so that it doesn't run totally according to patterns set by the white male workaholic. This will be good for men *and* women. The government can guarantee parental leave and affordable, available child care. (It did so in the '40s, when women were needed in the factories.) Given that Congress couldn't even get a bill guaranteeing *unpaid* family leave passed last year, this may take some doing. But hey, this is an election year.

FAMILY TIES

The Real Reason People Are Living Longer

LEONARD A. SAGAN

LEONARD A. SAGAN is an epidemiologist at the Electric Power Research Institute, in Palo Alto, California. His book THE HEALTH OF NATIONS: TRUE CAUSES OF SICKNESS AND WELL-BEING *is published by Basic Books.*

WHEN MODERN MEDICINE made its debut at the Many Farms Navajo Indian community, in 1956, there was every reason to expect decisive results. The two thousand people who inhabited this impoverished and isolated Arizona settlement were living under extremely primitive conditions. Though nutrition was adequate, hygiene was poor, tuberculosis was widespread, and infant mortality rates were three times the national average. To a group of researchers from the Cornell University Medical College and the U.S. Public Health Service, the situation at Many Farms provided a perfect opportunity to introduce modern health care practices and measure the consequences. If the effort proved successful with this target population, they reasoned, it might become an example for underdeveloped communities worldwide.

Almost overnight, the Navajo settlement acquired an array of modern medical resources. The researchers set up a full-service clinic, staffed with physicians and nurses, as well as with public health consultants, a health teacher, and four Navajo health care workers. For medical emergencies, the community got a fleet of radio-equipped vehicles and a light airplane. Over the next six years, ninety percent of the Many Farms residents took advantage of the clinic. Two-thirds of them were seen at least once a year.

The result was a rapid decline in the transmission of tubercle bacillus (the agent that causes tuberculosis) and in the frequency of otitis media (an inflammation of the middle ear). Yet the population's overall health, as reflected in its mortality statistics, was virtually unchanged. Of the sixty-five deaths that occurred during the six-year study period, more than half involved infants, who made up less than four percent of the population. And, despite expert pediatric care, there was no reduction in the pneumonia–diarrhea complex that was the leading cause of childhood illness and death. In the end, the investigators were unsure whether the improved medical care had, on balance, produced any beneficial effect at all.

This outcome would be less unsettling if it were more unusual. Unfortunately, it is not unusual at all. Consider what happened in 1976, when the state legislature of North Carolina sponsored a study to determine the effects of improved maternal and perinatal health care on the state's poorer communities. Researchers identified a number of counties, similar in racial and socioeconomic characteristics, that had suffered high rates of infant mortality over the preceding decades. For the next five years, residents of some of those counties received state-of-the-art treatment at the medical centers of Duke University and the University of North Carolina while, for the purpose of comparison, similar counties were essentially left alone. As expected, infant mortality declined considerably in the areas that received the additional care, but it also declined in the areas that did not. In fact, the researchers found no significant differences between the two groups.

Similar stories can be told about much larger popula-

This article is reprinted by permission of *The Sciences,* March/April 1988, pp. 21-29. Individual subscriptions are $18.00 per year. Write to The Sciences, 2 East 63rd Street, New York 10020 or call 1-800-THE-NYAS.

200

tions. When England established its National Health Service, in 1946, the country's lowest social classes had long suffered the poorest health and the shortest lives—presumably because of economic barriers to adequate health care. The new program effectively removed those barriers. Forty-two years later, however, the disparity in mortality rates remains undiminished; the life expectancy of the most affluent is almost twice that of the least affluent. The economists Lee and Alexandra Benham, of Washington University, in Saint Louis, have noted the similar failure of Medicare and Medicaid to affect mortality rates among the disadvantaged in the United States. This country's least educated classes now experience as much hospitalization and surgery as its most educated classes, yet overall health is still strongly associated with educational achievement.

What are we to make of all this? It is well known that life expectancy has risen dramatically in most societies over the past few centuries. As recently as 1900, the typical American lived only forty-nine years, and one in five children died during infancy. Today we live an average of seventy-five years, and infant mortality has declined to just ten deaths for every thousand births, or one percent. Both physicians and the public credit modern medicine for these bold achievements; we assume, almost reflexively, that people who lack expert medical attention die earlier, and that providing more care is the key to longer life.

Americans, therefore, have invested heavily in medicine. Our expenditures now total more than four hundred billion dollars a year, or eleven percent of the gross national product, the highest rate of any nation on Earth. Yet some measures of ill health, such as the rate of disability due to chronic illness among children, are on the rise. And though life expectancy continues to rise in the United States, it is rising more rapidly in countries that are spending at a lower rate. Many of those countries, including Greece, Spain, and Italy, now enjoy life expectancies greater than our own. And Japan, which leads the world in life expectancy, spends only a third of what the United States spends each year—about five hundred dollars per capita compared with fifteen hundred.

Clearly, we need to take a closer look at the relationship between our efforts at health care, on the one hand, and our actual health, on the other. If the United States is spending more on medicine than any other nation, while suffering poorer health than many, there may be something fundamentally wrong with the country's approach. The urgent questions are: What really makes people healthy? Why do we live so much longer than our ancestors and so much longer than the world's remaining premodern peoples? If medicine is not the source of this blessing, we would do well to find out what is—and to direct our medical and public health efforts accordingly.

THERE IS NO DENYING that modern medicine has accomplished much of value. It has done a great deal to alleviate suffering, and many treatments—including surgery for burns, bleeding, abdominal obstructions, and diabetic coma—undoubtedly save lives. Anything that saves lives would presumably contribute to overall life expectancy. But most therapy is not aimed directly at prolonging life. Rare is the patient for whom death would be the price of missing a doctor's appointment. Moreover, any medical procedure involves some risk; there is always a chance that the patient will have an adverse or fatal reaction to a given treatment—be it surgical, pharmaceutical, or even diagnostic. If treatments were administered only when patients stood to benefit, the net effect on mortality rates might be positive. But physicians have a well-documented tendency to overdo a good thing. And because there are no clear guidelines governing the use of most remedies, the cost of such zeal is that the benefits gained by those who require a particular treatment are often outweighed by the adverse effects on those who receive it unnecessarily. Thus, while such major medical advances as antibiotics, immunization, coronary bypass surgery, chemotherapy, and obstetric surgery all have saved lives, it is impossible to demonstrate that any of them has contributed significantly to overall life expectancy.

The introduction of antibiotics into clinical medicine is generally viewed as the turning point in mankind's war against infectious disease. Clearly, such illnesses as typhoid, cholera, measles, smallpox, and tuberculosis no longer claim lives at the rate they did during the nineteenth century. The decline began at different times in different nations, but it was under way in Scandinavia and the English-speaking countries by the mid-nineteenth century, roughly a hundred years before the first antibiotic drug, penicillin, became available, during the Second World War. By the time streptomycin, isoniazid, and other such agents came into wide use, during the 1940s and 1950s, death rates from the eleven most common infectious diseases had dwindled to a mere fraction of their nineteenth-century levels. Antibiotics did, for a time, hold tremendous therapeutic powers, and had they been used in moderation, they might have remained potent weapons against infection. But overuse has largely destroyed their effectiveness.

The indications that we rely too heavily on antibiotics are myriad. In 1973, scientists at the University of Wisconsin at Madison concluded, after reviewing the findings of other researchers, that enough antibiotics are manufactured and dispensed each year in the United States to treat two illnesses of average duration in every man, woman, and child in the country. The evidence suggests, however, that only once in five to ten years does the average individual experience an infection, such as meningitis or tuberculosis, that antibiotics might help control. The drugs are routinely prescribed for colds and flu, even though there is no evidence they have any effect on such viral ailments, and are given out like vitamins in many hospitals. In one recent survey of hospital patients, the internist Theodore C. Eickhoff, of the University of Colorado Medical Center, in Denver, found that thirty percent were receiving antibiotics—though only half of those receiving the drugs showed signs of infection. Other findings suggest that patients who might actually benefit from an antibiotic frequently receive the wrong one, or an incorrect dose.

One outcome of this overreliance on penicillin and the other so-called wonder drugs is that many bacteria have, through natural selection, become resistant to them, and infections that were easily controlled thirty years ago no longer respond well to treatment. Both gonococcus, the pus-producing bacterium that causes the most common venereal disease, and pneumococcus, a bacterium frequently associated with lobar pneumonia, now show resistance to various antibiotics. And in hospitals, overall infection rates are on the rise. A 1985 study, published by Robert W. Haley and his colleagues at the Centers for Disease Control, concluded that hospital-acquired infections occur in almost six out of every one hundred patients, thereby producing a national toll of four million infections a year, and that this rate is increasing by two percent annually.

Immunization is another therapy widely believed to have reduced death rates from infectious disease. But studies indicate that the use of vaccines and their ostensible benefits are largely unrelated. There is no question that the smallpox vaccine, for one, is effective when properly administered. Historical records show, however, that the number of people dying of smallpox was already falling when the vaccine first became available in Europe, during the early nineteenth century. True, smallpox mortality continued to drop as the vaccine became more accessible, but so did the death rates associated with infectious diseases for which vaccines had *not* been developed. The parallel decline in mortality from typhoid and tuberculosis prompted speculation that the smallpox vaccine was somehow protecting people from those infections, too. But there was never any basis for such a conclusion. A more reasonable inference is that deaths from all three illnesses were declining on account of some other factor.

As in the case of smallpox, vaccines for polio, whooping cough, measles, and diphtheria are effective at protecting individuals from these diseases. As a result, they not only save lives but spare many people permanent disabilities. But the question, for our purposes, is whether such vaccines have caused a significant decline in overall mortality, and the evidence indicates they have not. The historical record shows that death rates for childhood diseases started falling before the vaccines became available, and there is no evidence that forgoing such vaccines shortens people's lives. When concern about the risks associated with the diphtheria vaccine led English physicians to stop administering it during the late 1970s, for example, there was a sharp increase in the incidence of the disease, yet diphtheria mortality barely changed.

L IKE INFECTIOUS DISEASE, cardiovascular illness seems to pose a less dire threat to most of us today than it has in the past. Coronary artery disease appears to be waning both in incidence and in deadliness. A twenty-six-year study of Du Pont Company employees found that the number of people afflicted with the disease declined by twenty-eight percent between 1957 and 1983. Other studies indicate that the rate at which Americans are killed by it fell from about three hundred and fifty for every hundred thousand in 1970 to just two hundred and fifty for every hundred thousand in 1985. If such outcomes could be attributed to medical intervention, they would indeed rank as major accomplishments. But here, as with infectious disease, the link between treatment and health is elusive—whether the treatment is directed at preventing the disease or curing it.

Consider the results of the Multiple Risk Factor Intervention Trial, or "Mr. Fit." In this study, a team of investigators from twenty-two health research centers randomly divided a sample population of nearly thirteen thousand men, aged thirty-five to fifty-seven, into two groups. For the next seven years, members of one group continued to receive routine care from their private physicians, while the other group participated in a therapeutic program to reduce the risk of coronary artery disease. Physicians supervised and monitored efforts to have them avoid smoking, reduce the amount of cholesterol in their diets, and control their blood pressure, using medication if necessary. At the end of the treatment period, the subjects who received the extra medical attention had indeed cut back on cigarettes and cholesterol, and they exhibited less hypertension. But they did not end up living any longer than the subjects who simply went about their business. In fact, their death rate from all causes (41.2 deaths for every thousand subjects) was slightly *higher* than that of the control group (40.4 deaths). The reasons for this failure were not readily evident; the researchers speculated that the ill effects of antihypertensive drugs may have outweighed any benefits derived from the program. Whatever the explanation, such results confirm that the recent decline in death from cardiovascular disease probably is not the fruit of preventive medicine.

If efforts at prevention have not caused the decline, might it reflect the advent of better therapeutic techniques, such as coronary bypass surgery? Saving lives was not the original intent of this operation when surgeons began performing it, during the late 1960s; bypassing portions of coronary arteries that had become partially clogged with fatty deposits was viewed as a way of alleviating the chest pain that accompanies such blockage. But when the operation was found to be effective for that purpose, physicians began touting it as a therapeutic measure—and even a preventive treatment for patients without symptoms—despite an utter lack of clinical evidence. Today coronary bypass is one of America's most commonly performed surgical procedures. Roughly two hundred thousand Americans undergo the operation each year, at a total cost of some five billion dollars. Yet only rarely does it contribute to anyone's survival. A study published in 1983 by the National Institutes of Health concluded that bypass surgery prolongs the life of roughly one bypass patient in ten but that it appears to add nothing to the life expectancies of the other nine.

I S CANCER TREATMENT, another major focus of modern medicine, perhaps the secret of our increased life expectancy? One might guess that it has made a contribution; after all, the average interval between the diagnosis of a malignancy and the death of the patient has increased considerably in recent years. Indeed, the percentage of cancer patients surviving at least five years rose from 38.5 percent in 1973 to 40.1 percent in 1978, an improvement of almost one percent a year. Regrettably, it does not necessarily follow that people with cancer are living longer, let alone that chemotherapy or surgical treatments are extending their lives. Many scientists speculate that earlier detection of the disease merely has created an illusion of increased survival.

There is evidence that physicians are diagnosing cancer at earlier stages of development, thanks largely to more frequent checkups and better diagnostic technology. But there is no indication that earlier treatment has improved patients' overall survival rates. In fact, for some forms of cancer, there is hard evidence that it has not. In one study, sponsored by the National Cancer Institute and published in 1984, a population of adult male smokers, all presumably at high risk of developing lung cancer, was divided into two groups. One group received only annual chest X rays; members of the second group underwent frequent X rays and had their sputum examined regularly for cancer cells. Not surprisingly, there were many more diagnoses of lung cancer among the closely monitored subjects. And because their malignancies were usually detected and treated at early stages, their survival rates from the time of diagnosis were impressive. Even so, the numbers of lung cancer deaths in the two groups were nearly identical. In short, the participants in the early-detection program gained no apparent advantage: they were no less likely to suffer recurrences of the disease, or to die of it, than were members of the control group.

If modern treatments were, on balance, helping cancer patients survive, those patients would be dying at a later average age, and this, in turn, would reduce the average person's chances of dying of cancer at any age. But age-adjusted cancer mortality has not declined at all in the United States during the past fifty years. The death rates have changed for particular forms of cancer (lung cancer mortality has increased, whereas deaths from stomach cancer have declined), and it is possible that treatment has played a role in some of the success stories. The relatively rare cancers of childhood, for example, seem to respond well to treatment. But such situations are the exception, not the rule. Most therapies are introduced without ever being thoroughly evaluated for effectiveness, and they are embraced by physicians and patients who are understandably eager to try anything.

Radical mastectomy, the standard treatment for breast cancer throughout most of this century, is a good example. Studies have shown that patients who have this operation —the mutilating removal of the breast and its underlying tissues—do not, as a group, live any longer than patients who undergo the less radical lumpectomy (removal of the cancerous mass only). In one study, published in 1985 in *The New England Journal of Medicine*, nearly two thousand breast cancer patients were randomly assigned to receive one treatment or the other. Those who had the traditional mastectomy died earlier. Still, most U.S. physicians continue to perform the more extensive operation, and some even recommend it as a preventive measure for women whose cystic (lumpy) breasts place them at a theoretical risk of developing the disease.

The point is not that cancer treatment is never justified, only that it has had no discernible effect on the overall survival rates of cancer patients, let alone the life expectancy of the general population. Indeed, no cancer treatment, however successful, could do much to increase life expectancy, for the disease does little to reduce it. Cancer strikes mostly among the aged. It has long been estimated that even if it were totally preventable or curable, the increase in U.S. life expectancy would be less than two years. Given that life expectancy has increased by twenty-five years during this century, it is impossible that the treatment of cancer has made much of a difference.

If modern medicine cannot be credited with taming infectious disease, cardiovascular illness, or cancer, one might expect to find that it has at least improved the odds that mothers and infants will survive the birth process. Cesarean section has undoubtedly contributed to the rapid decline in maternal mortality during this century. Like so many other medical procedures, however, it is now so grossly overused that it may be costing as many lives as it saves.

The maternal mortality rate had already dwindled to less than one death in ten thousand deliveries by the mid-1970s. Yet, since then, births by cesarean section have increased by three hundred percent in the United States. To confirm that this trend is not making childbirth any safer, one need only consider the survival statistics for societies that rely less heavily on surgical delivery. In 1965, the rate of cesarean births at Ireland's National Maternity Hospital, in Dublin, was equal to that in the United States—about five percent. Since then, the U.S. rate has climbed to twenty percent, but the rate in Dublin has remained stable, and perinatal mortality has fallen faster there than it has in the United States. The Netherlands, meanwhile, which enjoys one of the lowest perinatal and maternal mortality rates in Europe, also has one of the lowest rates of obstetric surgery.

IT SEEMS CLEAR that modern medicine, whatever it has done to save or improve individual lives, has had little effect on the overall health of large populations. Still, the fact is that life expectancy has increased spectacularly during the nineteenth and twentieth centuries. What else might explain such a change? There is no question that sanitation and nutrition, the other factors most often cited, have been beneficial. But neither of these developments accounts fully for the mystery at hand.

It is true that, toward the end of the nineteenth century, improvements in sanitation coincided with a decline in mortality from various infectious diseases in Europe and America. But there is no evidence of a cause-and-effect relationship. Sanitation worsened in many major cities during the Industrial Revolution, as the prospect of work drew hordes of immigrants from rural areas. Rotting meat, fish, and garbage were heaped in the streets of New York and London, and overflowing privies were still far more common than modern toilets in many crowded neighborhoods. Amazingly, though, mortality rates from infectious disease fell steadily over the same period.

Another problem with the sanitation argument is that the *incidence* of infection decreased little during the nineteenth century. What did decline was the frequency with which infections sickened or killed people. As recently as 1940, long after tuberculosis had ceased to be a major health threat, skin tests showed that ninety-five percent of all Americans were still being infected with tuberculosis bacteria by age forty-five. Yet the vast majority managed to fight it off. Even today, most of the microorganisms that caused so much disease and death in pre-modern times, particularly among children, are omnipresent in the environment. No amount of sanitation could eliminate them, for they are passed directly from one person to another. They exist harmlessly, for the most part, both in and on our bodies.

Could it be that improved nutrition has strengthened our resistance? This idea does not withstand scrutiny, either. If eating well were the key to long life, then the most privileged families of old Europe, who enjoyed better nutrition than their contemporaries, should also have enjoyed longer lives. But they died young (as did the first American settlers, for whom the threat of starvation was not a particular problem). Moreover, there is no evidence that the specific dietary changes that are associated with modernization have even been advantageous. Indeed, it is arguable that, on balance, those changes have been harmful.

In the United States—where modernization has been associated with less physical activity, and with increased consumption of white bread, cookies, doughnuts, alcohol, and red meat from fattened animals—an estimated twenty to twenty-five percent of adult men are overweight. Diet and inactivity are not the only factors that contribute to obesity, of course, but they clearly count. In one recent study, the University of Toronto anthropologists Andris Rode and Roy J. Shephard monitored body fat and physical fitness among members of an Eskimo community during a ten-year period of rapid modernization. They found that the community's adoption of a modern diet, along with its increased use of snowmobiles and snow-clearing equipment, accompanied a significant increase in body fat and decreases in several measures of fitness. If these Eskimo follow the usual pattern, modernization will bring about a net increase in life expectancy. But if their overall health improves, it will have improved *despite* the changes in diet and physical activity, not because of them.

I<small>T IS, IN A WORD</small>, impossible to trace the hardiness of modern people directly to improvements in medicine, sanitation, or diet. There is an alternative explanation for our increased life expectancy, however, one that has less to do with these developments than with changes in our psychological environment. We like to imagine that preindustrial peoples endured (and endure) less stress than we do—that, although they may have lacked physical amenities, they spent peaceful days weaving interesting fabrics and singing folk songs. But the psychic stresses of the simple life are, in fact, far greater than those experienced by the most harried modern executive. It is one thing to fret over a tax return or a real estate deal, and quite another to bury one's children, to wonder whether a fall's harvest will last the winter, or to watch one's home wash away in a flood.

To grow up surrounded by scarcity and ignorance and constant loss—whether in an African village or a twentieth-century urban slum—is to learn that misery is usually a consequence of forces beyond one's control and, by extension, that individual effort counts for naught. And there is ample evidence that such a sense of helplessness is often associated with apathy, depression, and death—

whether in laboratory animals or in prisoners of war. The experimental psychologist Martin E. P. Seligman, of the University of Pennsylvania, has designed some remarkable studies to simulate in dogs the experience of helplessness in humans. His classic experiment involved placing dogs in a box in which they could avoid electric shocks by jumping over a barrier upon the dimming of a light. Naïve dogs quickly learned to avoid shocks entirely, leaping gracefully over the barrier whenever the light dimmed. But Seligman found that dogs responded differently if, before being placed in the box, they were confined and subjected to shocks they could not escape. Those dogs, having learned that effort is futile, just lay down and whined.

In many ways, the experiences and reactions of the second group resemble those of people raised in poverty, a shared feature of most premodern societies. Modernization, through such mechanisms as fire departments, building codes, social insurance, and emergency medical care, has cushioned most of us against physical, psychic, and economic disaster. But, more important, it has created circumstances in which few of us feel utterly powerless to control our lives. We now take for granted that we are, in large part, the masters of our own destinies, and that in itself leaves us better equipped to fight off disease.

How did this happen? What are the sources of this sense of personal efficacy and self-esteem? No institution has been so changed by modernization as the family. Until the late eighteenth century, it existed primarily as an economic unit; marriages were arranged for the purpose of preserving property, and children were viewed as a cheap source of labor or a hedge against poverty in old age. Beating and whipping were favored, even among royalty, as tools for teaching conformity and obedience. Then, during the Enlightenment, the standards and goals of child rearing began to change. If children were going to survive in a disorderly and unpredictable world, philosophers began to argue, they could not rely passively on traditional authority; they needed reasoned judgment. And if children were going to develop such judgment, they needed affection and guidance, not brute discipline. It was only gradually, as these ideas took root, that childhood came to be recognized as a special stage of life, and that affection and nurturing replaced obligation and duty as the cohesive forces among family members.

During the nineteenth century, as the upper classes came to view children as having needs of their own rather than serving the needs of the family—and, accordingly, started having fewer of them—their infant and childhood mortality rates began to fall. And as the trend toward smaller families spread to the lower social classes, theirs fell, too. It is unlikely that this was just coincidence, for family size is an excellent predictor of childhood survival even today. Young children of large families continue to suffer more infections, more accidents, and a higher overall mortality rate than the children of small families, regardless of social class. Indeed, as the Columbia University sociologist Joe D. Wray demonstrated in 1971, the effects of family size can outweigh those of social class: an only child in a poor family has about the same chance of surviving the first year of life as a child who is born into a professional-class family but who has four or more siblings.

Why should this be so? One explanation, supported by various lines of evidence, is that the children of small families are strengthened in every way by the extra nurture they receive from their parents. During the past forty years, studies have demonstrated that infants develop poorly, even die, when they are provided food and physical necessities but are denied intimate contact with care givers. In one experiment, orphans placed in an institution at an early age were separated into two groups. Members of one group stayed in the institution while the others were placed with foster parents. At the end of the first year, the children placed in foster homes were better developed, both mentally and physically, than those who received institutional care. And even after the institutionalized children were assigned to foster homes, they remained less developed than their counterparts for a number of years.

Other studies have produced even more arresting evidence. In 1966, Harold M. Skeels, of the National Institute of Mental Health, reported on an experiment that gauged the long-term effect of individual care on retarded institutionalized children. One group of children received routine institutional care, which is often physically adequate but emotionally sterile, while the other children were moved to a special ward to be cared for individually by retarded women. After three years, most of the children in the first group had lost an average of twenty-six IQ points, whereas those in the second group had *gained* an average of twenty-nine points. The differences were even more pronounced thirty years later. None of the children who received routine care had made it past the third grade, and most remained institutionalized. By contrast, many of those cared for by foster mothers had completed the twelfth grade and gone on to become self-supporting.

W E ARE ONLY BEGINNING to understand the mechanisms linking emotional and physical health (the endeavor has of late given rise to a new branch of medicine, known as psychoneuroimmunology). But whatever the connection, the fact stands that the affection and security associated with the modern family are the best available predictors of good health. In the end, it matters little whether sanitation, nutrition, and medical care are crude or sophisticated; children who receive consistent love and attention—who grow up in circumstances that foster self-reliance and optimism rather than submission and hopelessness—are better survivors. They are bigger, brighter, more resistant, and more resilient. And, as a result, they live longer.

It is ironic, in the light of this, that we continue to fret over the quality of our food and the purity of our environment, to spend billions of dollars on medical procedures of no proven value, and to pay so little attention to the recent deterioration of the American family. The divorce rate in the United States, though it appears to have leveled off during the past few years, has increased enormously since the 1950s, from less than ten percent to more than twenty percent today. The number of children being raised by single parents has doubled during the past decade alone, and divorce is not the only reason. Another ominous development is the rise in pregnancy among unwed teenagers. For whites, the rate increased from eight percent in 1940 to twenty percent in 1970, and to thirty percent in 1980. The problem is even worse among blacks, sixty percent of whom are now born out of wedlock. That this, in itself, constitutes a serious health problem is plain when one considers that fetal and infant death rates are twice as high for illegitimate children as for legitimate ones, and that a teenaged mother is at least seven times more likely than an older mother to abuse her child.

All of this suggests that good health is as much a social and psychological achievement as a physical one—and that the preservation of the family is not so much a moral issue as a medical one. Unless we recognize the medical importance of the family and find ways to stop its deterioration, we may continue to watch our health expenditures rise and our life-spans diminish. We will waste precious resources on unnecessary treatments, while ignoring a preventable tragedy.

The Vintage Years

THE GROWING NUMBER OF HEALTHY, VIGOROUS OLDER PEOPLE HAS HELPED OVERCOME SOME STEREOTYPES ABOUT AGING. FOR MANY, THE BEST IS YET TO COME.

Jack C. Horn and Jeff Meer

Jack C. Horn is a senior editor and Jeff Meer is an assistant editor at the magazine.

Our society is getting older, but the old are getting younger. As Sylvia Herz told an American Psychological Association (APA) symposium on aging last year, the activities and attitudes of a 70-year-old today "are equivalent to those of a 50-year-old's a decade or two ago."

Our notions of what it means to be old are beginning to catch up with this reality. During the past several decades, three major changes have altered the way we view the years after 65:

• The financial, physical and mental health of older people has improved, making the prospect of a long life something to treasure, not fear.

• The population of older people has grown dramatically, rising from 18 million in 1965 to 28 million today. People older than 65 compose 12 percent of the population, a percentage that is expected to rise to more than 20 percent by the year 2030.

• Researchers have gained a much better understanding of aging and the lives of older people, helping to sort out the inevitable results of biological aging from the effects of illness or social and environmental problems. No one has yet found the fountain of youth, or of immortality. But research has revealed that aging itself is not the thief we once thought it was; healthy older people can maintain and enjoy most of their physical and mental abilities, and even improve in some areas.

Because of better medical care, improved diet and increasing interest in physical fitness, more people are reaching the ages of 65, 75 and older in excellent health. Their functional age—a combination of physical, psychological and social factors that affect their attitudes toward life and the roles they play in the world—is much younger than their chronological age.

Their economic health is better, too, by almost every measure. Over the last three decades, for example, the number of men and women 65 and older who live below the poverty line has dropped steadily from 35 percent in 1959 to 12 percent in 1984, the last year for which figures are available.

On the upper end of the economic scale, many of our biggest companies are headed by what once would have been called senior citizens, and many more of them serve as directors of leading companies. Even on a more modest economic level, a good portion of the United States' retired older people form a new leisure class, one with money to spend and the time to enjoy it. Obviously not all of America's older people share this prosperity. Economic hardship is particularly prevalent among minorities. But as a group, our older people are doing better than ever.

In two other areas of power, politics and the law, people in their 60s and 70s have always played important roles. A higher percentage of people from 65 to 74 register and vote than in any other group. With today's increasing vigor and numbers, their power is likely to increase still further. It is perhaps no coincidence that our current President is the oldest ever.

Changing attitudes, personal and social, are a major reason for the increasing importance of older people in our society. As psychologist

Bernice Neugarten points out, there is no longer a particular age at which someone starts to work or attends school, marries and has children, retires or starts a business. Increasing numbers of older men and women are enrolled in colleges, universities and other institutions of learning. According to the Center for Education Statistics, for example, the number of people 65 and older enrolled in adult education of all kinds increased from 765,000 to 866,000 from 1981 to 1984. Gerontologist Barbara Ober says that this growing interest in education is much more than a way to pass the time. ''Older people make excellent students, maybe even better students than the majority of 19- and 20-year-olds. One advantage is that they have settled a lot of the social and sexual issues that preoccupy their younger classmates.''

Older people today are not only healthier and more active; they are also increasingly more numerous. "Squaring the pyramid" is how some demographers describe this change in our population structure. It has always been thought of as a pyramid, a broad base of newborns supporting successively smaller tiers of older people as they died from disease, accidents, poor nutrition, war and other causes.

Today, the population structure is becoming more rectangular, as fewer people die during the earlier stages of life. The Census Bureau predicts that by 2030 the structure will be an almost perfect rectangle up to the age of 70.

The aging of America has been going on at least since 1800, when half the people in the country were younger than 16 years old, but two factors have accelerated the trend tremendously. First, the number of old people has increased rapidly. Since 1950 the number of Americans 65 and older has more than doubled to some 28 million—more than the entire current population of Canada. Within the same period, the number of individuals older than 85 has quadrupled to about 2.6 million (see "The Oldest Old," this article).

Second, the boom in old people has been paired with a bust in the proportion of youngsters due to a declining birth rate. Today, fewer than one American in four is younger than 16. This drop-off has been steady, with the single exception of the post-World War II baby boom, which added 76 million children to the country between 1945 and 1964. As these baby boomers reach the age of 65, starting in 2010, they are expected to increase the proportion of the population 65 and older from its current 12 percent to 21 percent by 2030.

The growing presence of healthy, vigorous older people has helped overcome some of the stereotypes about aging and the elderly. Research has also played a major part by replacing myths with facts. While there were some studies of aging before World War II, scientific

A man over 90 is a great comfort to all his elderly neighbours: he is a picketguard at the extreme outpost; and the young folks of 60 and 70 feel that the enemy must get by him before he can come near their camp.
—Oliver Wendell Holmes,
The Guardian Angel.

BY THE YEAR 2030 MORE THAN 20 PERCENT OF THE POPULATION IS EXPECTED TO BE 65 OR OLDER.

interest increased dramatically during the 1950s and kept growing.

Important early studies of aging included three started in the mid or late 1950s: the Human Aging Study, conducted by the National Institute of Mental Health (NIMH); the Duke Longitudinal Studies, done by the Center for the Study of Aging and Human Development at Duke University; and the Baltimore Longitudinal Study of Aging, conducted by the Gerontological Institute in Baltimore, now part of the National Institute on Aging (NIA). All three took a multidisciplinary approach to the study of normal aging: what changes take place, how people adapt to them, how biological, genetic, social, psychological and environmental characteristics relate to longevity and what can be done to promote successful aging.

These pioneering studies and hundreds of later ones have benefited from growing federal support. White House Conferences on Aging in 1961 and 1971 helped focus attention on the subject. By 1965 Congress had enacted Medicare and the Older Americans Act. During the 1970s Congress authorized the establishment of the NIA as part of the National Institutes of Health and NIMH created a special center to support research on the mental health of older people.

All these efforts have produced a tremendous growth in our knowledge of aging. In the first (1971) edition of the *Handbook of the Psychology of Aging,* it was estimated that as much had been published on the subject in the previous 15 years as in all the years before then. In the second edition, published in 1985, psychologists James Birren and Walter Cunningham wrote that the "period for this rate of doubling has now decreased to 10 years...the volume of published research has increased to the almost unmanageable total of over a thousand articles a year."

Psychologist Clifford Swenson of Purdue

University explained some of the powerful incentives for this tremendous increase: "I study the topic partly to discover more effective ways of helping old people cope with their problems, but also to load my own armamentarium against that inevitable day. For that is one aspect of aging and its problems that makes it different from the other problems psychologists study: We may not all be schizophrenic or neurotic or overweight, but there is only one alternative to old age and most of us try to avoid that alternative."

One popular misconception disputed by recent research is the idea that aging means inevitable physical and sexual failure. Some changes occur, of course. Reflexes slow, hearing and eyesight dim, stamina decreases. This *primary aging* is a gradual process that begins early in life and affects all body systems.

But many of the problems we associate with old age are *secondary aging*—the results not of age but of disease, abuse and disuse—factors often under our own control. More and more older people are healthy, vigorous men and women who lead enjoyable, active lives. National surveys by the Institute for Social Research and others show that life generally seems less troublesome and freer to older people than it does to younger adults.

In a review of what researchers have learned about subjective well-being—happiness, life satisfaction, positive emotions—University of Illinois psychologist Ed Diener reported that "Most results show a slow rise in satisfaction with age. . .young persons appear to experience higher levels of joy but older persons tend to judge their lives in more positive ways."

Money is often mentioned as the key to a happy retirement, but psychologist Daniel Ogilvie of Rutgers University has found another, much more important, factor. Once we have a certain minimum amount of money, his research shows, life satisfaction depends mainly on how much time we spend doing things we find meaningful. Ogilvie believes retirement-planning workshops and seminars should spend more time helping people decide how to use their skills and interests after they retire.

A thought that comes through clearly when researchers talk about physical and mental fitness is "use it or lose it." People rust out faster from disuse than they wear out from overuse. This advice applies equally to sexual activity. While every study from the time of Kinsey to the present shows that sexual interest and activity diminish with age, the drop varies greatly among individuals. Psychologist Marion Perlmutter and writer Elizabeth Hall have reported that one of the best predictors of continued sexual intercourse "is early sexual activity and past sexual enjoyment and frequency. People who have never had much pleasure from sexu-

WHILE THE OLD AND THE YOUNG MAY BE EQUALLY COMPETENT, THEY ARE DIFFERENTLY COMPETENT.

ality may regard their age as a good excuse for giving up sex."

They also point out that changing times affect sexual activity. As today's younger adults bring their more liberal sexual attitudes with them into old age, the level of sexual activity among older men and women may rise.

The idea that mental abilities decline steadily with age has also been challenged by many recent and not-so-recent findings. In brief, age doesn't damage abilities as much as was once believed, and in some areas we actually gain; we learn to compensate through experience for much of what we do lose; and we can restore some losses through training.

For years, older people didn't do as well as younger people on most tests used to measure mental ability. But psychologist Leonard Poon of the University of Georgia believes that researchers are now taking a new, more appropriate approach to measurement. "Instead of looking at older people's ability to do abstract tasks that have little or no relationship to what they do every day, today's researchers are examining real-life issues."

Psychologist Gisela Labouvie-Vief of Wayne State University has been measuring how people approach everyday problems in logic. She notes that older adults have usually done poorly on such tests, mostly because they fail to think logically all the time. But Labouvie-Vief argues that this is not because they have forgotten how to think logically but because they use a more complex approach unknown to younger thinkers. "The [older] thinker operates within a kind of double reality which is both formal and informal, both logical and psychological," she says.

In other studies, Labouvie-Vief has found that when older people were asked to give concise summaries of fables they read, they did so. But when they were simply asked to recall as much of the fable as possible, they concentrat-

The pleasures that once were heaven Look silly at sixty-seven.
—Noel Coward,
"What's Going to Happen to the Tots?"

Old age consoles itself by giving good precepts for being unable to give bad examples.
—La Rochefoucauld,
The Maxims.

THE OLDEST OLD: THE YEARS AFTER 85

"Every man desires to live long, but no man would be old," or so Jonathan Swift believed. Some people get their wish to live long and become what are termed the "oldest old," those 85 and older. During the past 22 years, this group has increased by 165 percent to 2.5 million and now represents more than 1 percent of the population.

Who are these people and what are their lives like? One of the first to study them intensively is gerontologist Charles Longino of the University of Miami, who uses 1980 census data to examine their lives for the American Association of Retired People.

He found, not surprisingly, that nearly 70 percent are women. Of these, 82 percent are widowed, compared with 44 percent of the men. Because of the conditions that existed when they were growing up, the oldest old are poorly educated compared with young people today, most of whom finish high school. The average person now 85 years and older only completed the eighth grade.

Only one-quarter of these older citizens are in hospitals or institutions such as nursing homes, and more than half live in their own homes. Just 30 percent live by themselves. More than a third live with a spouse or with their children. There are certainly those who aren't doing well—one in six have incomes below the poverty level—but many more are relatively well-off. The mean household income for the group, Longino says, was more than $20,000 in 1985.

What of the quality of life? "In studying this group, we have to be aware of youth creep," he says. "The old are getting younger all the time." This feeling is confirmed by a report released late last year by the National Institute on Aging. The NIA report included three studies of people older than 65 conducted in two counties in Iowa, in East Boston, Massachusetts, and in New Haven, Connecticut. There are large regional differences between the groups, of course, and they aren't a cross-section of older people in the nation as a whole. But in all three places, most of those older than 85 seem to be leading fulfilling lives.

Most socialize in a variety of ways. In Iowa, more than half say they go to religious services at least once a week and the same percentage say they belong to some type of professional, social, church-related or recreational group. More than three-quarters see at least one or two children once a month and almost that many see other close relatives that often.

As you would expect, many of the oldest old suffer from disabilities and serious health problems. At least a quarter of those who responded have been in a hospital overnight in the past year and at least 8 percent have had heart attacks or have diabetes. In Iowa and New Haven, more than 13 percent of the oldest old had cancer, while in East Boston the rate was lower (between 7 percent and 8 percent). Significant numbers of the oldest old have suffered serious injury from falls. Other common health problems for this group are high blood pressure and urinary incontinence. However, epidemiologist Adrian Ostfeld, who directed the survey in New Haven, notes that "most of the disability was temporary."

Longino has found that almost 10 percent of the oldest old live alone with a disability that prevents them from using public transportation. This means that they are "isolated from the daily hands-on care of others," he says. "Even so, there are a surprising number of the oldest old who don't need much in the way of medical care. They're the survivors.

"I think we have to agree that the oldest old is, as a group, remarkably diverse," Longino says. "Just as it is unfair to say that those older than 85 are all miserable, it's not fair to say that they all lead wonderful lives, either." —Jeff Meer

ed on the metaphorical, moral or social meaning of the text. They didn't try to duplicate the fable's exact words, the way younger people did. As psychologists Nancy Datan, Dean Rodeheaver and Fergus Hughes of the University of Wisconsin have described their findings, "while [some people assume] that old and young are equally competent, we might better assume that they are differently competent."

John Horn, director of the Adult Development and Aging program at the University of Southern California, suggests that studies of Alzheimer's disease, a devastating progressive mental deterioration experienced by an estimated 5 percent to 15 percent of those older than 65, may eventually help explain some of the differences in thinking abilities of older people. "Alzheimer's, in some ways, may represent the normal process of aging, only speeded up," he says. (To see how your ideas about Alzheimer's square with the facts, see "Alzheimer's Quiz" and "Alzheimer's Answers," this article.)

Generalities are always suspect, but one generalization about old age seems solid: It is a different experience for men and women. Longevity is one important reason. Women in the United States live seven to eight years longer, on the average, than do men. This simple fact has many ramifications, as sociologist Gunhild Hagestad explained in *Our Aging Society.*

For one thing, since the world of the very old is disproportionately a world of women, men and women spend their later years differently. "Most older women are widows living alone; most older men live with their wives...among individuals over the age of 75, two-thirds of the men are living with a spouse, while less than one-fifth of the women are."

The difference in longevity also means that among older people, remarriage is a male prerogative. After 65, for example, men remarry at a rate eight times that of women. This is partly a matter of the scarcity of men and partly a matter of culture—even late in life, men tend to marry younger women. It is also a matter of education and finances, which, Hagestad explains, "operate quite differently in shaping remarriage probabilities among men and women. The more resources the woman has available (measured in education and income), the less likely she is to remarry. For men, the trend is reversed."

The economic situations of elderly men and women also differ considerably. Lou Glasse, president of the Older Women's League in Washington, D.C., points out that most of these women were housewives who worked at paid jobs sporadically, if at all. "That means their Social Security benefits are lower than men's, they are not likely to have pensions and they are less likely to have been able to save the kind of money that would protect them from poverty during their older years."

Although we often think of elderly men and women as living in nursing homes or retirement communities, the facts are quite different. Only about 5 percent are in nursing homes and perhaps an equal number live in some kind of age-segregated housing. Most people older than 65 live in their own houses or apartments.

We also think of older people as living alone. According to the Census Bureau, this is true of 15 percent of the men and 41 percent of the women. Earlier this year, a survey done by Louis Harris & Associates revealed that 28 percent of elderly people living alone have annual incomes below $5,100, the federal poverty line. Despite this, they were four times as likely to give financial help to their children as to receive it from them.

In addition, fewer than 1 percent of the old people said they would prefer living with their children. Psychiatrist Robert N. Butler, chairman of the Commonwealth Fund's Commission

> *AMONG OLDER PEOPLE TODAY, REMARRIAGE IS STILL LARGELY A MALE PREROGATIVE, DUE TO THE SEX DIFFERENCE IN LONGEVITY.*

on Elderly People Living Alone, which sponsored the report, noted that these findings dispute the "popular portrait of an elderly, dependent parent financially draining their middle-aged children."

There is often another kind of drain, however, one of time and effort. The Travelers Insurance Company recently surveyed more than 700 of its employees on this issue. Of those at least 30 years old, 28 percent said they directly care for an older relative in some way—taking that person to the doctor, making telephone calls, handling finances or running errands—for an average of 10 hours a week. Women, who are more often caregivers, spent an average of 16 hours, and men five hours, per week. One group, 8 percent of the sample, spent a heroic 35 hours per week, the equivalent of a second job, providing such care. "That adds up to an awful lot of time away from other things," psychologist Beal Lowe says, "and the stresses these people face are enormous."

Lowe, working with Sherman-Lank Communications in Kensington, Maryland, has formed "Caring for Caregivers," a group of professionals devoted to providing services, information and support to those who care for older relatives. "It can be a great shock to some people who have planned the perfect retirement," he says, "only to realize that your chronically ill mother suddenly needs daily attention."

Researchers who have studied the housing needs of older people predictably disagree on many things, but most agree on two points: We need a variety of individual and group living arrangements to meet the varying interests, income and abilities of people older than 65; and the arrangements should be flexible enough that the elderly can stay in the same locale as their needs and abilities change. Many studies have documented the fact that moving itself can be stressful and even fatal to old people, particularly if they have little or no influence over when and where they move.

This matter of control is important, but more complicated than it seemed at first. Psychologist Judith Rodin and others have demonstrated that people in nursing homes are happier, more alert and live longer if they are allowed to take responsibility for their lives in some way, even in something as simple as choosing a plant for their room, taking care of a bird feeder, selecting the night to attend a movie.

Rodin warns that while control is generally beneficial, the effect depends on the individuals involved. For some, personal control brings with it demands in the form of time, effort and the risk of failure. They may blame themselves if they get sick or something else goes wrong. The challenge, Rodin wrote, is to "provide but not impose opportunities. . . . The need for self-determination, it must be remembered, also calls for the opportunity to choose not to exercise control. . . ."

An ancient Greek myth tells how the Goddess of Dawn fell in love with a mortal and convinced Jupiter to grant him immortality. Unfortunately, she forgot to have youth included in the deal, so he gradually grew older and older. "At length," the story concludes, "he lost the power of using his limbs, and then she shut him up in his chamber, whence his feeble voice might at times be heard. Finally she turned him into a grasshopper."

The fears and misunderstandings of age expressed in this 3,000-year-old myth persist today, despite all the positive things we have learned in recent years about life after 65. We don't turn older people into grasshoppers or shut them out of sight, but too often we move them firmly out of the mainstream of life.

In a speech at the celebration of Harvard

> *If I had known when I was 21 that I should be as happy as I am now, I should have been sincerely shocked. They promised me wormwood and the funeral raven.*
>
> —Christopher Isherwood, letter at age 70.

University's 350th anniversary last September, political scientist Robert Binstock decried what he called The Spectre of the Aging Society: "the economic burdens of population aging; moral dilemmas posed by the allocation of health resources on the basis of age; labor market competition between older and younger workers within the contexts of age discrimination laws; seniority practices, rapid technologi-

ALZHEIMER'S QUIZ

Alzheimer's disease, named for German neurologist Alois Alzheimer, is much in the news these days. But how much do you really know about the disorder? Political scientist Neal B. Cutler of the Andrus Gerontology Center gave the following questions to a 1,500-person cross section of people older than 45 in the United States in November 1985. To compare your answers with theirs and with the correct answers, turn to the next page.

	True	False	Don't know
1. Alzheimer's disease can be contagious.	___	___	___
2. A person will almost certainly get Alzheimer's if they just live long enough.	___	___	___
3. Alzheimer's disease is a form of insanity.	___	___	___
4. Alzheimer's disease is a normal part of getting older, like gray hair or wrinkles.	___	___	___
5. There is no cure for Alzheimer's disease at present.	___	___	___
6. A person who has Alzheimer's disease will experience both mental and physical decline.	___	___	___
7. The primary symptom of Alzheimer's disease is memory loss.	___	___	___
8. Among persons older than age 75, forgetfulness most likely indicates the beginning of Alzheimer's disease.	___	___	___
9. When the husband or wife of an older person dies, the surviving spouse may suffer from a kind of depression that looks like Alzheimer's disease.	___	___	___
10. Stuttering is an inevitable part of Alzheimer's disease.	___	___	___
11. An older man is more likely to develop Alzheimer's disease than an older woman.	___	___	___
12. Alzheimer's disease is usually fatal.	___	___	___
13. The vast majority of persons suffering from Alzheimer's disease live in nursing homes.	___	___	___
14. Aluminum has been identified as a significant cause of Alzheimer's disease.	___	___	___
15. Alzheimer's disease can be diagnosed by a blood test.	___	___	___
16. Nursing-home expenses for Alzheimer's disease patients are covered by Medicare.	___	___	___
17. Medicine taken for high blood pressure can cause symptoms that look like Alzheimer's disease.	___	___	___

Alzheimer's Answers — National Sample

	True	False	Don't know
1. False. There is no evidence that Alzheimer's is contagious, but given the concern and confusion about AIDS, it is encouraging that nearly everyone knows this fact about Alzheimer's.	3%	83%	14%
2. False. Alzheimer's is associated with old age, but it is a disease and not the inevitable consequence of aging.	9	80	11
3. False. Alzheimer's is a disease of the brain, but it is not a form of insanity. The fact that most people understand the distinction contrasts with the results of public-opinion studies concerning epilepsy that were done 35 years ago. At that time, almost half of the public thought that epilepsy, another disease of the brain, was a form of insanity.	7	78	15
4. False. Again, most of the public knows that Alzheimer's is not an inevitable part of aging.	10	77	13
5. True. Despite announcements of "breakthroughs," biomedical research is in the early laboratory and experimental stages and there is no known cure for the disease.	75	8	17
6. True. Memory and cognitive decline are characteristic of the earlier stages of Alzheimer's disease, but physical decline follows in the later stages.	74	10	16
7. True. Most people know that this is the earliest sign of Alzheimer's disease.	62	19	19
8. False. Most people also know that while Alzheimer's produces memory loss, memory loss may have some other cause.	16	61	23
9. True. This question, like number 8, measures how well people recognize that other problems can mirror Alzheimer's symptoms. This is crucial because many of these other problems are treatable. In particular, depression can cause disorientation that looks like Alzheimer's.	49	20	30
10. False. Stuttering has never been linked to Alzheimer's. The question was designed to measure how willing people were to attribute virtually anything to a devastating disease.	12	46	42

	True	False	Don't know
11. False. Apart from age, research has not uncovered any reliable demographic or ethnic patterns. While there are more older women than men, both sexes are equally likely to get Alzheimer's.	15	45	40
12. True. Alzheimer's produces mental and physical decline that is eventually fatal, although the progression varies greatly among individuals.	40	33	27
13. False. The early and middle stages of the disease usually do not require institutional care. Only a small percentage of those with the disease live in nursing homes.	37	40	23
14. False. There is no evidence that using aluminum cooking utensils, pots or foil causes Alzheimer's, although aluminum compounds have been found in the brain tissue of many Alzheimer's patients. They may simply be side effects of the disease.	8	25	66
15. False. At present there is no definitive blood test that can determine with certainty that a patient has Alzheimer's disease. Accurate diagnosis is possible only upon autopsy. Recent studies suggest that genetic or blood testing may be able to identify Alzheimer's, but more research with humans is needed.	12	24	64
16. False. Medicare generally pays only for short-term nursing-home care subsequent to hospitalization and not for long-term care. Medicaid can pay for long-term nursing-home care, but since it is a state-directed program for the medically indigent, coverage for Alzheimer's patients depends upon state regulations and on the income of the patient and family.	16	23	61
17. True. As mentioned earlier, many medical problems have Alzheimer's-like symptoms and most of these other causes are treatable. Considering how much medicine older people take, it is unfortunate that so few people know that medications such as those used to treat high blood pressure can cause these symptoms.	20	19	61

cal change; and a politics of conflict between age groups."

Binstock, a professor at Case Western Reserve School of Medicine, pointed out that these inaccurate perceptions express an underlying ageism, "the attribution of these same characteristics and status to an artificially homogenized group labeled 'the aged.'"

Ironically, much ageism is based on compassion rather than ill will. To protect older workers from layoffs, for example, unions fought hard for job security based on seniority. To win it, they accepted mandatory retirement, a limitation that now penalizes older workers and deprives our society of their experience.

A few companies have taken special steps to utilize this valuable pool of older workers. The Travelers companies, for example, set up a job

GREAT EXPECTATIONS

If you were born in 1920 and are a . . .

	. . .white man	. .white woman
your life expectancy was . . .		
at birth	*54.4 years*	*55.6 years*
at age 40	*71.7*	*77.1*
at age 62	*78.5*	*83.2*

If you were born in 1940 and are a . . .

	. . .white man	. . .white woman
your life expectancy was . . .		
at birth	*62.1 years*	*66.6 years*
at age 20	*70.3*	*76.3*
at age 42	*74.7*	*80.7*

If you were born in 1960 and are a . . .

	. . .white man	. . .white woman
your life expectancy was . . .		
at birth	*67.4 years*	*74.1 years*
at age 22	*73.2*	*80.0*

SOURCE: U.S. NATIONAL CENTER FOR HEALTH STATISTICS

bank that is open to its own retired employees as well as those of other companies. According to Howard E. Johnson, a senior vice president, the company employs about 175 formerly retired men and women a week. He estimates that the program is saving Travelers $1 million a year in temporary-hire fees alone.

While mandatory retirement is only one example of ageism, it is particularly important because we usually think of contributions to society in economic terms. Malcolm H. Morrison, an authority on retirement and age discrimination in employment for the Social Security Administration, points out that once the idea of retirement at a certain fixed age was accepted, "the old became defined as a dependent group in society, a group whose members could not and should not work, and who needed economic and social assistance that the younger working population was obligated to provide."

We need to replace this stereotype with the more realistic understanding that older people are and should be productive members of society, capable of assuming greater responsibility for themselves and others. What researchers have learned about the strengths and abilities of older people should help us turn this ideal of an active, useful life after 65 into a working reality.

ON GROWING OLD

Not Every Creature Ages, But Most Do. The Question Is Why

ROBERT M. SAPOLSKY *and*
CALEB E. FINCH

ROBERT M. SAPOLSKY is an assistant professor of biology and neuroscience at Stanford University. CALEB E. FINCH is professor of gerontology at the University of Southern California in Los Angeles. His book LONGEVITY, SENESCENCE, AND THE GENOME *was recently published by University of Chicago Press.*

> *I can do anything now at age ninety that I
> could when I was eighteen. Which shows you
> how pathetic I was at eighteen.*
>
> —George Burns

IT HAS BEEN OBSERVED more than once that human beings are the only creatures on earth haunted by an awareness of their own mortality. People know that life is desperately fragile and that any of myriad intrusions can kill them instantly: an aneurysm, a cerebral hemorrhage or a heart attack; a fire, an earthquake, a traffic accident or a mugger's bullet. And they know that even should they escape sudden disaster, the end remains inevitable. If nothing else, the years themselves take a fatal toll. Muscles weaken, eyesight dims, memories fade, and people become ever more conscious of the discrepancy between what they were and what they have become. In short, they senesce: they age.

To the gerontologist seeking to understand the aging process, the phenomenon of senescence is defined in terms of vulnerability: a "pathetic" eighteen-year-old college student is more likely to survive a certain challenge or insult than is a ninety-year-old curmudgeon. Each one may slip and fall on ice or play host to a single cancerous cell or contract a dangerous fever. Yet the older person is more likely to suffer a broken pelvis from the fall, to develop a malignant tumor from the cancerous cell, to perish from the fever. The risk that an illness or an injury will prove fatal increases with age.

Given such dark prospects, one is tempted to fantasize about living in a sort of never-never land where there is no such thing as senescence, no increase in vulnerability with each passing year. There would be no more crow's feet, sagging jowls or thinning hair and, more to the point, no degenerative heart disease, hardened arteries or Alzheimer's disease. We would all look great and feel wonderful. And we would live forever. Or would we?

The overall risk of mortality in the population at large is lowest at around age eleven. Suppose, magically, that the entire population, with every succeeding year, were somehow able to retain the adolescent's physiological near-invulnerability—in other words, suppose no one ever aged. Then half the people would still be alive by their 600th birthday, but by the same token half would be gone. Certainly that is an improvement, but immortality it is not. The point is that physiological invulnerability goes only so far. Even in a world populated solely with nonsenescing creatures there would be some constant mortality rate, one dependent entirely on the rate of external insults or ecological danger. Such a hypothetical population of Dorian Grays (or Dick Clarks, perhaps) would slowly but steadily decline in size with the passage of time because of airplane crashes, earthquakes or substance abuse. In some unit of time (600 years, for instance) half the population would die from extrinsic causes, in the next unit half the survivors would die, and so on.

For a real aging population the mortality rate increases with time because of an interaction between the rate of extrinsic insults and the extent of internal senescence. As the anatomy deteriorates with age, the person becomes increasingly vulnerable to intrusions by the outside world. Organs, bones and muscles wear out with time, and at age sixty, seventy or eighty, one cannot withstand the same kinds of stresses one sloughed off at eleven. It is all depressingly tragic but certainly not surprising. Things fall apart. How could life be otherwise?

STARTLINGLY ENOUGH, for many species things *are* otherwise. Bristlecone pine trees and rockfish, certain parameciums and some social insect queens, to name just a few, do not senesce. Populations of such plants and animals suffer constant attrition from extrinsic threats. In some insect species a queen dies at the proverbial hands of her minions: when her nuptial sperm supply runs out after many years, she is killed by the workers. But even at an advanced age those organisms do not show any of the usual signs of internal deterioration associated with other representatives of their phyla. For example, unlike most other trees, a bristlecone pine shows no increased sensitivity to insect infestations with age. Although it is unclear how many species are nonsenescers, it is known that there are a great

This article is reprinted by permission of *The Sciences* and is from the March/April 1991 issue, pp. 30-38. Individual subscriptions are $18.00 per year. Write to The Sciences, 2 East 63rd Street, New York, NY 10021 or call 1-800-THE-NYAS.

many of them, particularly in groups such as bony fishes, sea anemones and bivalve mollusks.

One might very well wonder what stroke of evolutionary good fortune, what extraordinary biological innovation, has allowed those species to evade decrepitude. What feature have they evolved that humans and most other animals have not? On closer examination, however, it becomes clear that rockfish, parameciums, mollusks and the like are not the real innovators. Quite to the contrary, such perennially youthful species are typically among the most ancient, primitive organisms. Indeed it appears that nonsenescence was the original state of living things on earth. The mammalian line, one of the latest and certainly the most sophisticated of the chordate classes, can be considered an island of senescence among most of its evolutionary relatives. If, then, aging is a relatively recent development, another question arises: What possible evolutionary advantages are conferred by such a dismal characteristic?

THE ATTEMPT to understand the adaptive benefits of senescence is almost as old as the idea of evolution itself. One of the first to explore the issue was the English naturalist Alfred Russel Wallace, who shares with Darwin the credit for having founded the theory of evolution by natural selection. Darwin and Wallace established that the driving force of evolution is the quest for optimizing reproductive success, a goal best realized by leaving the maximum number of copies of one's own genes for future generations. (As the sociobiologists say, "A chicken is an egg's way of making another egg.")

There are two fundamental strategies for ensuring the proliferation of one's genes: either reproducing a lot or, failing that, doing whatever is possible to increase the reproduction of one's relatives—a kind of genetic altruism known as kin selection. Wallace speculated that aging is a kin-selection strategy; in other words, at some stage in its life the best way for an organism to pass on its genes is for it to senesce and get out of the way, leaving the resources it would otherwise consume behind for its descendants to share as they multiply the genetic line.

Since Wallace's day many other theories of adaptive senescence have been advanced, based on studies of aging patterns in a range of living things. To illustrate one popular recent theory, compare the extremely long lived, nonsenescing rockfish with the short-lived, senescing guppy. As one might expect, the guppy population, subject to both external insult and internal deterioration, dies off at a much faster rate than the rockfish population does. Still, guppies enjoy one crucial advantage over rockfish: earlier in life they fare substantially better at reproduction. In general, species that age follow the same pattern: they die off sooner, but they reproduce earlier in life and more successfully than their nonsenescing counterparts.

For a number of years many biologists have recognized that in senescing species the enhanced fecundity earlier in life and the increased mortality rate later on might express an evolutionary trade-off. The essence of the idea, which has acquired the forbidding label "negative pleiotropy," is that genes have evolved that confer marked advantages on an organism at certain stages in its life, only to extract a cost at certain other stages. Unlike Wallace's notion of altruistic kin selection, negative pleiotropy is a genetically "selfish" mechanism: it would operate solely to maximize the reproductive potential of individual organisms, without regard for the greater good of subsequent generations of the species.

When genes are viewed as negatively pleiotropic, they are double-edged swords. Perhaps the best-known example of this kind of duality—though one not related to aging—is the gene for sickle-cell anemia. The sickle-cell gene can bring about a dreadful, life-threatening disease, in which insufficient oxygen is delivered to the cells of the body. Yet the same gene confers resistance to malaria, a disease that takes a horrendous toll in Africa, where sickle-cell anemia evolved. Whereas senescence may be an instance of negative pleiotropy over time, sickle-cell anemia can be thought of as negative pleiotropy over space: thus the sickle-cell gene offers advantages only in those environments in which malaria is rampant. In the evolution of such trade-offs the critical issue becomes how often the advantage is conferred compared with how often the deleterious bill arrives. Apparently, with sickle-cell anemia the payoffs have led to widespread selection for the trait. That is small comfort to sickle-cell victims who live in, say, urban America, where shored-up resistance to malaria is of little use. Betrayed by geography, American carriers of the sickle-cell gene are forced to pay its price without enjoying any of its benefits.

ALTHOUGH THE IDEA of negative pleiotropy as a driving force in aging looks good on paper, specific examples of the phenomenon have been surprisingly hard to track down. One instance may be Huntington's disease, best known for having afflicted the folksinger Woody Guthrie. People stricken with Huntington's disease generally begin sometime during their forties to suffer from a variety neurological symptoms: flailing and spasms of the limbs, paralysis, rigidity and dementia. Death usually comes after about fifteen years.

A subtle, intriguing feature of Huntington's disease usually manifests itself early on. The illness initially appears to be a psychiatric disorder: the victim's behavior and personality begin to change dramatically before the neurological symptoms emerge. In a few years a quiet and uncontentious person might begin to lose self-control, becoming loud, uninhibited and more aggressive. Clinical lore also holds that a behavioral feature of early Huntington's is hypersexuality; in fact, one recent study indicates that Huntington's patients outreproduce their unaffected siblings. No one has a clue to just how the disease works —especially to why some of the behavioral traits and the neurological symptoms should emerge from the same disorder. Nevertheless, one can speculate that if the gene that accelerates mortality at age sixty also confers increased reproduction by age forty, the gene would work to the overall advantage of the organism in the evolutionary sense. Such a mechanism for the disease would constitute a neat illustration of negative pleiotropy at work in the aging process.

One can imagine any number of other negatively pleiotropic scenarios that give rise to senescence. There could be many genes that confer early advantages in exchange for later costs, each affecting discrete organ systems. One feature of human aging, for instance, is that older men have a much greater chance than younger men of developing prostate cancer. What if such a tendency toward uncontrolled carcinogenic growth were a side effect of a gene that, earlier in life, increased the rate of prostate metabolism and cell division? One result might be that the younger man could produce more seminal fluid, having greater sperm mobility, and thus be a more fertile individual. If the reproductive advantages of better sperm at age thirty outweigh the reproductive disadvantages of dying from prostate cancer at sixty-five, the gene will be selected. Some investigators already consider senescent increases in the frequency of prostate cancer to be a valid example of negative pleiotropy.

Another, more hypothetical example is the potentially adaptive effect of fat stored on the body early in life. In periods of drought or famine fat might act as a buffer, thereby keeping the individual alive through the reproductive years. As a person grows older, however, the advantages of that storage tendency begin to be counterbalanced by the accompanying risk of heart disease and diabetes. In physiology, as in so many other spheres, there are no free lunches; ultimately, the check arrives.

IF NEGATIVE PLEIOTROPY is to account for the emergence of senescence in humans, one would expect to find that certain advantageous traits of youth are genetically linked to whatever turn out to be the mechanisms of decline. Understanding those mechanisms, of course, is one of the central aims of gerontological research. Gerontologists have searched for a single cause of aging—a critical gene, hormone or organ that goes awry. But in the light of the rather sparse evidence in support of that idea, many investigators have adopted another hypothesis: that senescence results from the gradual but steady deterioration of cells, which over time become less proficient at maintenance and self-repair. After all, there is no question that the lives of cells are finite; a cell divides a fixed number of times and then dies. What causes that abrupt cessation? What changes take place in a cell as it approaches the end of its line? These questions are of central concern to gerontologists. And it is becoming increasingly clear that there are no easy answers and that if the key to aging is cellular deterioration, aging is a complex, multifaceted process, perhaps involving not one but a host of regulatory genes.

In the past decade or so a number of theories have been put forward that try to explain what causes cells to wear down. According to one such theory, as it ages a lineage of cells accumulates harmful metabolic "garbage," which can damage nucleic acids, proteins and other vital cellular building blocks. One class of physiological debris may be the oxygen-free radicals: such molecules can lodge in the cell membrane, disrupt and destroy fats and protein by linking them inappropriately, and perhaps impair the functioning of DNA.

Another line of investigation implicates glucose in a process that is severely destructive to animal cells. Glucose can attach itself to proteins via a process called nonenzymatic glycosylation, which binds the proteins together into a nonfunctional yellowish brown mess. (The biochemist Anthony Cerami of Rockefeller University in New York has named such accumulations of disabled proteins "advanced glycosylation endproducts," allowing the acronym AGE.) As animals age, AGE proteins appear to damage vital organs and connective tissue. There is also speculation that, like the oxygen-free radicals, AGE proteins may somehow interact with DNA, causing mutations and obstructing the cell's ability both to repair damage and to replicate. The role of AGE proteins in aging is an intriguing subject for future research. At this point, however, they have been studied only in people and in laboratory rodents. Whether and to what degree other animals accumulate these protein masses may say a great deal about aging patterns across the various species.

TO THE AVERAGE, reluctantly senescing person, aging connotes a gradual, albeit inexorable, slide from summer into autumn and, with any luck, on to winter. But not all the earth's aging creatures necessarily decline and fall in the same way people do. Even in some relatively long-lived species senescence and death can come in a flash, sometimes in a matter of weeks or days. Well-known victims of such sudden death are the five species of Pacific salmon. In the mating season the adult fish heroically fight their way upstream to the pools where they were born in order to spawn—only to die off, en masse, a few days later. Fish captured during the dying-off period typically display enlarged adrenal glands, ulcers and kidney lesions; their immune systems have collapsed and they are teeming with parasites and opportunistic infections.

A similar pattern occurs in about a dozen species of marsupial mice in Australia. Those animals have an annual, synchronized mating season after which, in the course of a few weeks, all the males die. Remarkably the mice exhibit symptoms nearly identical with the symptoms of the salmon. People seemingly age by going to pieces idiosyncratically over decades; one person gets arthritis, another gets diabetes, a third gets cancer. Here instead, an identical pathological switch is thrown in each individual of the species, causing a kind of pansenescence: the population ages almost overnight.

Studies over the past thirty years have traced the sudden-death switch to the adrenal glands, which in times of physical or psychological stress secrete hormones belonging to a class known as the glucocorticoids. Such hormones come in many varieties; in humans they take the form of hydrocortisone, also known as cortisol. Glucocorticoids can be extremely handy in a physical emergency: a lot of energy must be released suddenly when one is, say, sprinting away from an onrushing predator. The hormones work by mobilizing glucose, freeing it from storage sites in the body and sending it into the blood. At the same time they increase the heart rate and raise blood pressure to speed the delivery of the glucose to the muscles. Glucocorticoids also turn off all kinds of long-term, energy consumptive building projects that can be put on hold until the emergency has passed: digestion, growth, reproduction, tissue repair and the maintenance of the immune system, among others.

All these effects are wonderful when you are running for your life, but they are disastrous at other times. In long periods of chronic psychological stress, for instance, the constant mobilization of energy at the cost of storage can waste the muscles away. An increase in cardiovascular tone for a long enough period brings about hypertension. By repeatedly deferring long-term building projects, the body eventually deteriorates: stomach walls ulcerate; growth, reproduction and immunity are irreparably impaired. To a large extent the illnesses that accompany chronic stress are consequences of an overexposure to glucocorticoids.

Pacific salmon and marsupial mice meet sudden death when their bodies loose a veritable flood of glucocorticoids. The phenomenon has been most thoroughly observed in marsupials. Around the mating period three changes take place that guarantee catastrophe. First, far more glucocorticoids than normal are secreted. Second, the concentration of proteins in circulation that can bind glucocorticoids—in effect sponging them up and buffering organs from the effects of the hormones—falls sharply, allowing the glucocorticoids unrestrained access to target tissues. Finally, parts of the brain, as yet unknown, that normally curtail glucocorticoid secretion before too much damage is done, fail to function. How all these steps work is poorly understood, but the result is that massive, pathological levels of glucocorticoids pummel the body. The Pacific salmon and the marsupial mice die from the effects of half the stress-related illnesses on earth, packed into a few miserable weeks.

The most dramatic proof of this account is that if, just after the salmon or the mice have mated, one blocks the secretion of glucocorticoids by removing the adrenal glands, the animals will live on for a year or more instead of the usual few weeks. The procedure demonstrates how drastically the aging process can be accelerated in otherwise diverse creatures that happen to have evolved the same hormonal death switch.

THE EVOLUTIONARY PURPOSE served by such abrupt pansenescence remains unclear. From one point of view Pacific salmon and marsupial mice can be regarded as classic examples of negative pleiotropy: they reproduce in abundance and then pay for their fecundity with their lives. But whether or not there is a pure trade-off of enhanced reproduction for greater mortality later on has not been established. There has been some speculation—and it is no more than that—that ties the Pacific salmon to Wallace's theory of kin selection. Some investigators have suggested that by quickly dying and decomposing in the water, the salmon are contributing nutrients to the ecosystem and hence improving the lot of future generations. The hypothesis is certainly intriguing, but it is still unsubstantiated by experimental evidence.

Are there any examples of greatly accelerated senescence in people? No doubt, devotees of the lurid tabloids ever present at supermarket checkout counters will immediately recall one possibility. Publications of that stripe have a morbid fascination with progeria, a supremely rare hereditary disease that afflicts children. Progerics appear to age incredibly prematurely. By the age of twelve, shortly before their deaths, they may have gray hair or be completely bald, and they manifest the bony chins, beaked noses and dry, scratchy voices common to elderly people. Children stricken with progeria can also suffer from hearing loss, arteriosclerosis or heart disease. When an attempt is made to grow certain cells from their bodies in a laboratory dish, the cells act like the well-worn tissue of a seventy-year-old—that is, they divide very infrequently. The implication seems to be that for a progeric the body's rate of aging has run amuck.

Progeric children, however, are not aged in every respect. For example, they do not show increased tendencies toward dementia or cancer, two major diseases strongly linked to aging. Thus even in progerics there is no single aging clock gone mad, and by the same token, there is no one such timepiece ticking at a normal pace in the rest of us. Instead the development of progeria suggests a mosaic of aging mechanisms, a variety of clocks of which only some are out of joint. Although the macabre disease gives rise to certain features associated with senescence, it is not, by itself, accelerated aging. Almost certainly, many nonprogerics also suffer dire but less spectacular consequences that have been brought on because some, but not all, of their aging clocks have sped out of control: witness the early onset of certain types of cancer in some people. But on the whole there remains sparse evidence of accelerated aging in humans, and even that is not at all like the affliction that befalls Pacific salmon and Australian marsupial mice.

SALMON, MICE AND PROGERICS notwithstanding, there are some species in nature that display determinedly more upbeat patterns of senescence, creatures for which the aging process is greatly slowed down. In spite of our own species' chronic despair about the ephemerality of life, a typical human being comes off next to immortal compared with an average laboratory rat. After only two years the rat is plagued by cataracts, reproductive problems and memory loss. Indeed the maximum human life span of 120 years or so is impressive in almost any context. (Notice that the occasional claims for the existence of substantially older populations such as one in Soviet Georgia usually prove attributable to some blend of bemused exaggeration and the inhabitants' lack of rigor about personal chronology.) There are other species in the range of human longevity—notably apes, elephants, sturgeons, clams and Galápagos tortoises. And there are some that far outstrip us, particularly certain trees such as conifers that can live for more than a millennium. The point is not that such species do not senesce; they do, but they also happen to be long-lived. The decline of a given population comes about quite slowly, over a great many years.

In a few cases species can temporarily arrest the encroachments of age and physical decline and, in effect, achieve suspended animation. One familiar example is hibernation, a dormant state during which the mortality rate of an entire population of animals is essentially frozen. Hibernation has been thoroughly studied in Turkish hamsters. The investigators manipulated the length of hibernation in the laboratory by adjusting the environmental temperature and found, remarkably, that for every day the hamsters hibernated, the animals' life spans were extended by about a day. The hamsters had managed to stop their aging clocks.

Hibernation is only one of several ways senescence can

be temporarily slowed or halted by dormancy. A somewhat more exotic example is the diapause, a holding stage in the development of certain organisms—particularly some insects such as worker bees—which can last for more than a year. If an insect enters diapause, its life span is extended by an equal amount of time. Various African and South American fishes can enter diapause even before they have hatched. As it turns out, the fishes' behavior is opportunistic: They live in ponds that disappear during dry seasons. Rather than start off life just as their homes have been turned into mud flats, unhatched eggs go into diapause amid the dried mud and await the return of the waters—perhaps for a year or more.

People, of course, are desperate for news of any intervention that might forestall decline. Newspapers have recently been filled with reports that the administration of growth hormone apparently reverses some aspects of human aging, in particular the loss of muscle mass and diminution of organ size that typically occur in the elderly. Despite this good news, growth hormone treatment has not been shown to increase the life span. Is there anything in the works, then, that can actually help us live longer?

At the moment, unfortunately, the answer is no. That fact notwithstanding, there are a number of entrepreneurial biologists who—for a handsome price—will contract to freeze you after you die, in the optimistic hope that future scientists will be able to effect your resurrection. Some of these so-called cryobiologists are even lobbying to freeze live but terminally ill patients on the assumption that some later generation of physicians might be able to revive them when a cure is available. (That approach is currently illegal, though a California man with terminal cancer recently initiated a court challenge.) Nevertheless, there is precious little experimental evidence to support any attempt to induce suspended animation in mammals. And there are many reasons such an effort would fail in any organism as large as a human being; for one, the cells could not be frozen quickly enough to avoid severe tissue damage. Even if suspended life were possible, it might not be all that desirable, especially if the hibernation worked as it does in hamsters. It is a safe bet that few of us would care to live on for centuries if all but seventy-two of those years were spent packed in ice. What we presumably want is a full, decidedly nondormant life that lasts beyond the present limits.

REMARKABLY there is one technique that for the past half-century has been known to extend mammalian life. It is not, however, what one would call an inviting alternative. In the 1930s it was discovered that if rats are deprived of nourishment (in this case, 30 percent of calories) indefinitely, beginning just after weaning, they live as much as one-third longer than rats given unrestricted access to food—the equivalent of extending human life expectancy from seventy-five years to a century. Before long a number of investigators had replicated the finding in other rodents, and today an entire branch of gerontology is devoted to studying the benefits of what is variously called dietary restriction or diet optimization.

It is now known that most of what tends to fall apart in an unmolested aging rat does so more slowly in a diet-restricted rat: organs such as the liver, the immune and reproductive systems and possibly parts of the brain such as the hippocampus. Dietary restriction also protects the rat from tumor growth, to which the animal normally becomes progressively susceptible as it grows older. One relatively recent discovery is that dietary restriction need not be as severe as it was in the initial studies in order to prolong an animal's life. Other strategies can be just as effective: cutting back calorie consumption by as little as 30 percent; beginning restriction in adulthood instead of after weaning; or restricting only some dietary constituents such as protein intake instead of the total number of calories consumed.

Gerontologists in this subfield spend most of their time trying to figure out precisely why cutting back on food leads to longevity. One of many attractive answers is that decreasing the diet may slow the accumulation of AGE proteins, the dysfunctional mess slung together over time by glucose. If AGE accumulation is, in fact, one of the basic cellular pacemakers of aging, a delay in its generation might well account for the deceleration of the aging process that dietary restriction seems to effect in so many organ systems.

A number of investigators, however, have raised a somewhat more deflating explanation for the effect. In their view the average laboratory rat, confined to a cage and given unrestricted access to food, eats far more than a normal wild rat does, simply for lack of anything better to do. In the process the animal drives itself into an early grave by contracting some of the diseases that kill millions of Americans. It may well be that dietary restriction is merely a means of getting a bored and gluttonous rat to adopt wild eating habits and thereby live a normal life span. In that circumstance dietary restriction would not change the basic nature of aging, but it would reduce the impact of diet-associated diseases on the aging process. Clarification will come once investigators know more about the eating habits of wild rodents. Only then can one know whether the normal laboratory rat gorges itself on an unrestricted diet.

Assuming, for the moment, that dietary restriction does extend the maximal life span of rodents, should we all start limiting our diets? How general is the phenomenon? Clearly such questions are hard to resolve. For rats or mice that live just a few years it is tedious (not to mention expensive) to manipulate diet over the lifetime of a population. To do the same for creatures that live for decades is far more difficult, and it makes the optimistic assumption that the investigator will live long enough to complete the project. Thus no one knows whether food restriction will work for our pets, our livestock or ourselves.

One observation offers little hope. Actuarial tables show that people with extreme body weights—the thinnest as well as the stoutest—tend to live shorter lives than people who stand somewhere in between. On the other hand, one can retort that some people are thin not because of a lifetime of restricted eating but because of genetics, chronic diseases or any number of other confounding characteristics. At bottom no one yet knows whether eating less means living longer. Nevertheless, the rodent data are sufficiently convincing to have motivated at least one respected gerontologist, Roy L. Walford of the University of California at Los Angeles, to keep himself on a restricted diet for years. Walford's colleagues eagerly—but not too eagerly, of course—await the results of his self-experimentation.

ANY REVIEW of aging research is necessarily somewhat disjointed, an account of what is currently a rather disparate patchwork of unconnected studies. The hope is that a unified theory of senescence will one day emerge. Perhaps there is some thread that draws together AGE production in people, pansenescence in salmon, negative pleiotropy and other anecdotal and hypothetical aspects of aging into the wider context of evolution. On the other hand, senescence may turn out to be resolutely untidy, as complex and varied in its mechanisms as the aging species themselves. Further-more, all the many lines of inquiry into senescence, even if they converge on a fundamental understanding of the phenomenon, may not add a day to human life expec-tancy. Perhaps we will have to content ourselves with curing the prevalent diseases of aging, such as Alzhei-mer's or atherosclerosis, rather than aging itself. That alone would obviously be of incalculable benefit.

But if bristlecone pines, marsupial mice and fishes tell us nothing about our aging problems, why study them? One could as easily ask why anatomists pass their life-times documenting the ways the primate pelvis can be constructed, why ethologists catalogue dialects of bird songs or why geneticists devote study to the hereditary patterns of worms. If we are to understand our place in the scheme of nature, it is perhaps important for us to realize that ours is not the only way to evolve, appear or behave. Or even to grow old.

HOW OLD ARE YOU REALLY?

BIRTHDAYS DON'T COUNT. YOUR TRUE BIOLOGICAL AGE SAYS A LOT MORE ABOUT HOW WELL YOU'RE AGING. AND IF THE TRUTH HURTS, YOU CAN TURN BACK THE CLOCK.

JOHN POPPY

John Poppy is a contributing editor.

Until recently, counting birthdays was the only practical way to answer the mighty questions behind the concept of age: How much more life? How much longer will I stay healthy enough to play this game?

No sports fan would tolerate an official clock as inaccurate as the one we've been using. Some players get to drive cars, write books, and play softball for 90 years and more. Others, even with no detectable disease, lie down decades earlier. Still others come out of the game in baffling condition. When the jazz sax master Charlie "Bird" Parker died, the New York coroner examining Bird's body didn't know how old he was and figured from the look of things that he was 53. According to his birth date, Parker was 34.

The older we get, the more obvious it becomes that not all people age at the same rate. That's why scientists who study aging are replacing the idea of chronological age with a more fluid concept—biological age, a measure of how well a body is working, apart from how many years it has on it.

Why do some people age faster than others? And more to the point, what causes aging in the first place? The answers will emerge, most likely, from two camps of researchers looking in differ-

IT WAS 4:30, AND I WASN'T IN THE MOOD TO SWEAT. OH WELL, WHO KNOWS HOW MUCH GOOD COMES OF ALL THIS ATTENTION TO THE BODY ANYWAY?

ent directions. It's a distinction that calls up one of the oldest debates in biology: nature versus nurture. The nature camp sees the basic processes of aging as genetically determined. If they're right, there won't be much any of us can do to change the rate at which we wear out and move toward death. The nurture camp concedes that we're born with some genetic clockwork, but sees many of the declines that people label "aging" as the results of careless living. If *they* are right, there's a lot we can do about how fast we age.

I'd like to think so. I've been lucky so far. At 5 foot 9 and 136 pounds, I'm no Schwarzenegger. But I can still move pretty much as I did growing up on a farm, playing baseball in cow pastures, and I feel younger than the 56 years my driver's license says I've lived. Lately, though, as I haul brush or walk up our hill with the mail, I've begun to wonder how fast I'm losing speed and stamina.

To hedge my bets, I try to get in some running or fast walking at least three afternoons a week to keep the pipes open, do some push-ups and sit-ups to keep what muscles I have from vanishing entirely, and stretch to stay limber. As for food, I actually *like* broccoli and salads. And ever since the day a surgeon showed me five inches of a patient's artery, clogged with what looked like dog food mashed in with a fork, I haven't used butter on my toast. That—and quitting smoking 30 years ago—sums up the formal attention I've paid to staying alive and well since 1968, the year Kenneth Cooper's *Aerobics* book started a lot of people thinking, "Use it or lose it."

But some days I just don't get around to using it. Like the afternoon not long ago when the clock turned 4:30, the time I like to move around and unwind. That day I had work to finish. By the time it was done, dinner was cooking and I wasn't in the mood to sweat.

Oh well, I thought, who knows how much good really comes of all this attention to the body? Some experts on what turns ordinary aging into successful aging point up the power of the mind—of optimism, humor, an appetite for challenges. That may be, but I still wanted to find out if more tangible things like eating and exercise were changing the way I'd be aging anyway.

Then the mail brought a curious bit of news—a paper describing a desktop computer program called H-SCAN that would, its inventor claimed, reveal one's *biological* age. It sounded like a gimmick. But the paper by the inventor, Richard

Hochschild, looked respectable, packed with statistics and 97 references to previous research. Hoping I might turn out to be a sort of reverse Charlie Parker, I called Hochschild. After some urging—he wants his invention used for research, not to satisfy people's curiosity—he agreed to hook me up and gave me directions to his office in Corona del Mar, south of Los Angeles.

I headed for my plane on test day, wishing I felt stronger. I was harboring the remnants of a cold and the germ of another doubt: Did I really expect to believe H-SCAN? And even if I did, what good would it do me?

"Here's the only thing that interests me about aging," my wife, Julia, remarked as I left. "I want it to quit."

"You mean," I translated, "you want to live forever."

"Absolutely not," she said. "I just want to feel good and look young as long as I *am* alive."

HOCHSCHILD TURNED out to look middle aged, with a little gray in his hair, the spareness of a distance runner, and a strong, steady handshake. I mentioned my cold, and coughed a few times to demonstrate.

As we walked into a spacious, tidy office off a courtyard in his house, he explained how he'd gotten interested in aging. A physicist who quit a Ph.D. program at the University of California at Berkeley to make instruments for testing aircraft parts and metal tubing, he could have retired after selling off two businesses. Instead, he looked for a new project. "The people around you are getting older, and so are you, and the impulse grows to see if you can gain some control over the ways we age," he said. "First, you have to measure the ways."

So he set about developing an instrument to help measure biological age. As an experienced entrepreneur, he didn't mind plunging in alone, without university or government support. Even at a list price of $18,750, though, the H-SCAN hasn't been much of a money-maker. Since he began producing them in 1985, Hochschild has sold only 12—mostly to corporations that use them as part of their health maintenance programs.

When I casually asked a couple of questions hoping to learn his age, Hochschild brought me up short. "I don't want to tell you," he said. "I know it looks funny—I'm in the age game—but I think chronological age is an inaccurate characterization of an individual."

He leaned forward, the cool researcher flushed with intensity. "I disagree with the way age is con-

Testing Your Biological Age

MEDICAL TESTS CAN provide an estimate of your biological age, a measure of how well your body is working—apart from how many years you've lived. Most of us, though, don't have access to the sophisticated equipment required for the job. Here are a few tests you can do on your own to gauge two of the most important components of biological age. They're based on results William Evans has seen in his ten years at the Human Nutrition Research Center on Aging at Tufts University in Boston. He finds them surprisingly accurate. And they have one big advantage over birthdays: They measure the kind of age you can change.

AEROBIC CAPACITY

Aerobic capacity—your body's ability to deliver oxygen to muscles for exertion—provides a pretty good reading of your cardiovascular stamina. In this test, you walk a mile as fast as you can, time the walk, take your pulse, then score your result with a formula developed from tests of hundreds of people at the University of Massachusetts Medical School.

CHECKLIST

If you've ever had a heart attack or have any other reason to suspect that exercise might be dangerous, check with a doctor before taking the test. The results will be more reliable if you're well rested and you avoid nicotine, caffeine, and alcohol for several hours beforehand. Also, medicines that alter your heart rate can affect your score. High blood pressure drugs are a good example: The beta-blockers slow heart rate and can lead you to figure you're more fit than you are.

WHAT YOU'LL NEED

A watch with an easy-to-read second hand. Walking or running shoes. A calculator.

BEFORE THE TEST

Weigh yourself on an accurate scale. Practice taking your pulse. Count it for ten seconds, then multiply by six to get your heart rate per minute. The range for adults at rest is between 60 and 100.

Find a flat, dry, one-mile walking course. Either measure a route with your car's odometer, or better yet, use a quarter-mile track at a high school or college.

Warm up and stretch for five minutes.

THE TEST

Walk the mile as fast as you can. Start off briskly and try to maintain the pace throughout. *Do not jog.* You invalidate the test if you break into a run. When you cross the finish line, note your time to the nearest second and take your pulse immediately. Your heart will start to slow down almost as soon as you stop, so it's important to count the beats per minute right away.

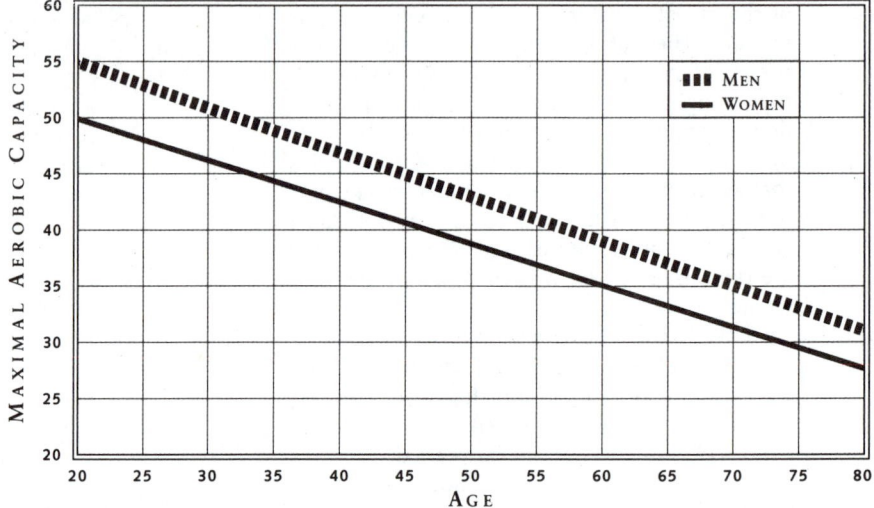

Now you're ready to calculate your aerobic capacity (often called VO_2 max) using the following formula.

Multiply your weight ____ by .08 = ____
Your age ____ by .39 = ____
Your walking time* ____ by 3.26 = ____
Your heart rate ____ by .16 = ____
Add these numbers together = _____

Then subtract your total from one of the following numbers:

132.85	(for women)	
– ____	your total	
= ____	your VO_2 max	
or		
139.16	(for men)	
– ____	your total	
= ____	your VO_2 max	

The number tells you nothing until you compare it with the aerobic capacity of reasonably fit men and women at different chronological ages. On the chart above, find your VO_2 max along the left side. Draw a line straight across to intersect the declining bar for your sex. Draw another line straight down to the age line at the bottom. (Note: Women who score higher than 50 and men who score higher than 55 can assume a biological age of 20.)

The biological age of your aerobic capacity is ____.

To convert the seconds in your walking time to a decimal figure, multiply the number of seconds by .0167. For example, say your time is 15 minutes 30 seconds. Multiply 30 seconds by 0.167 to get .5. Your walking time would be 15.5.

STRENGTH

Evans considers active muscle the key to a longer healthy life. Here you'll gauge arm and leg strength. A measure he uses is the heaviest weight a person can lift with one try (one repetition maximum, or 1RM). In lieu of elaborate equipment, you'll lift a lighter weight as many times as you can to gain an estimate of your 1RM strength.

WHAT YOU'LL NEED

That depends on whether you've been doing any strength training. This test is most accurate when you use a weight you can lift fewer than 15 times, so use a heavier weight if you're reasonably strong, a lighter one if you've done little to build muscle.

If you've done some strength training, you probably have store-bought weights at home or access to a gym. Pick a weight you think is close to the most you can lift, and do a trial run with your dominant arm. If you find you can do more than 15 repetitions, your weight is definitely too light.

If you've done little muscle building exercise, then you may be able to find an object around the house that is heavy enough to provide a challenge. A plastic one-gallon milk or bleach bottle, for instance, weighs about 8 pounds when filled with water. That's a good starting point for women who don't work out. Men—even those who don't lift weights—will probably need a heavier weight. Try starting with 25 pounds. A one-gallon milk bottle filled with sand weighs about 16 pounds. To get a weight you can lift fewer than 15 times, tie two milk bottles together with a soft cloth to fashion a homemade dumbbell. Fine-tune by adding or subtracting water or sand and weigh them on an accurate scale.

The leg-strength test will be easier to do on a leg-extension machine at a gym. But you could try strapping a heavy weight to your ankle—start with about twice as much as you are able to lift with your arms.

THE TEST

For arm strength: **Position 1.** Squat down next to the weight you're going to lift and grasp it with your nondominant arm. Once you have the weight in the proper hand, stand up—be sure to keep your back straight—and hold the weight at your side.

Position 2. Bend your elbow and "curl" the weight to shoulder level. Flex your biceps and use them—try not to use your back muscles—to lift the weight. **Position 3.** Straighten your arm slowly, extending it fully to your side, keeping your shoulder steady.

Move your arm back and forth between positions 2 and 3 as many times as you can. Keep count. Don't stop until your muscles quit on you completely, when you can't lift the weight even one more time.

Don't be surprised if you can't lift as much as you think you should. Many people, especially women, have weak arms—even when they're otherwise fairly active.

Now look at the chart for predicting 1RM, at the top of the next column. Find the number of repetitions you completed along the bottom. Draw a line straight up to intersect with the diagonal line. Then draw a line straight to the left border. Multiply the number you find there by the number of pounds in the weight you lifted and write the result—your predicted one repetition maximum—here: _____.

For leg strength: If you're taking the test at a gym, use the leg-extension machine. If you're at home, sit on a straight-backed chair and tie or strap the weight to the ankle of your nondominant leg (if you're right-handed, it'll be your left leg, and vice

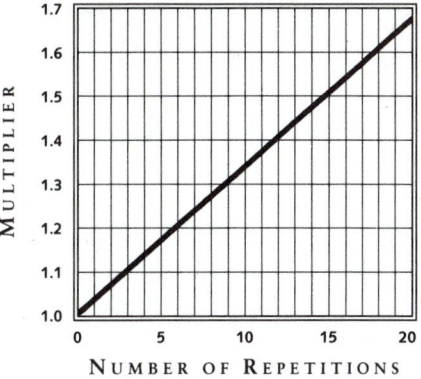

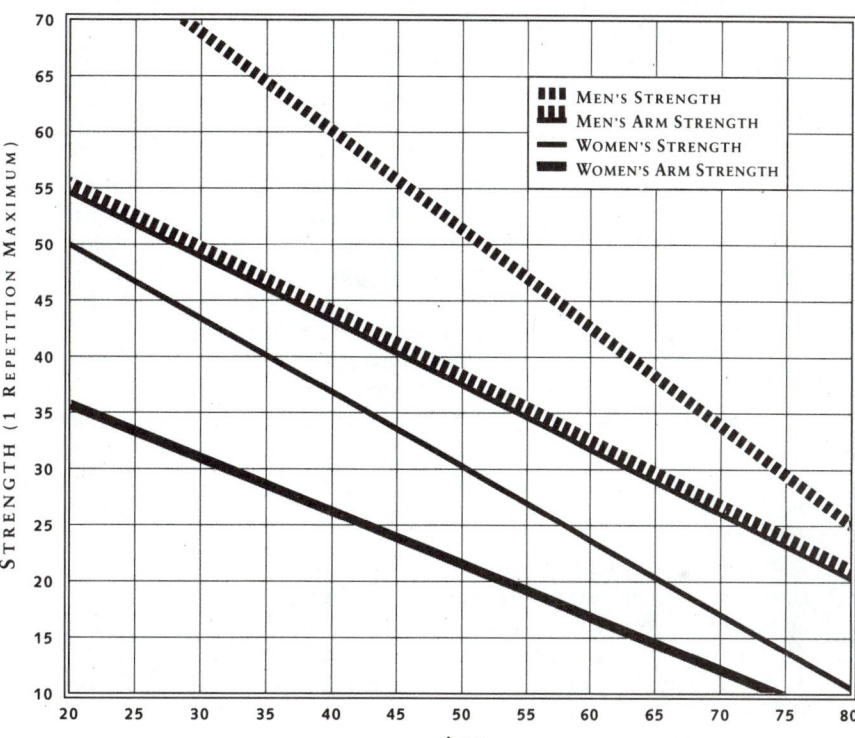

versa).* **Position 1.** Sit with your back straight. **Position 2.** Extend your leg, lifting the weight so it is as straight out in front of you as possible. **Position 3.** Lower your leg back to its starting position. Rest your foot on the floor no more than one second before repeating the lift.

Move your leg back and forth between positions 2 and 3, keeping count, until you can't do it anymore. Just as you did in the arm-strength test, consult the chart (top)

*If you are unable to do the leg-strength test, you can still find out the biological age of your arm strength on the chart.

for your 1RM number, multiply it by the pounds you lifted and write your predicted leg 1RM here: _____.

Now, add your arm and leg 1RM together and divide by two to get your 1RM average.
Arm 1RM _____.
Leg 1RM _____.
Total _____.
Divide by 2 = _____.

Again, the results take on meaning when you compare your scores to those of people who work out regularly. On the chart below, find your 1RM average on the left.

Draw a line straight across to intersect the "strength" bar for your sex. Draw another line down to the age line at the bottom. The biological age of your muscle strength is _____.

(Note: Even if you completed the leg-strength test, you may want to chart your arm strength alone. It could signal that you need some upper-body exercise.)

Keep in mind that these tests measure only certain aspects of your health. They say nothing about the biological age of your liver, brain, bone, and other parts you can't test at home.

Still, you can add up the biological ages you've just calculated and average them:
Aerobic capacity _____.
Muscle strength _____.
Total _____.
Divide by 2 = _____.
The result is a fair idea of your biological age. It's a start.
—J.P.

"PERSONALLY," SPROTT SAID, "I DON'T THINK IT'S AN ACCIDENT THAT THERE ARE NO EIGHTY-YEAR-OLD OLYMPIC POLE-VAULTERS."

stantly used in the media. You can't read a newspaper story without running across 'John Jones, 65.' That immediately creates a picture in a reader's mind of a typical 65-year-old. But biological age testing shows that people have genuine differences that don't depend on chronology. The H-SCAN tells me my biological age is in the early forties. And as you'll see, there's no way I can cheat on it."

What would H-SCAN tell *me?*

I sat in front of a computer wired to various appendages including a blue box the size of a city phone book. The instrument resembled some sort of futuristic lie detector, with wires connected to a tube with a disposable mouthpiece, headphones, and a gray box studded with buttons and lights. I turned it on.

"Let me introduce myself," the screen read. "I am H-SCAN. With a little cooperation from you, I am about to estimate your age . . . An important aspect of aging is the decline of key physiological functions. I will test you on functions that scientists have used to estimate biological age. Your scores will be compared to those of 2,462 male and female office workers . . ."

In 1986, Hochschild sent H-SCANs to 17 insurance companies and asked each company to choose up to 200 employees age 35 and above who were willing to spend an hour with the machine. He had picked his tests—for hearing, vision, lung capacity, and reaction time—because research has shown that those abilities inevitably deteriorate with age. To make the tests fun, he gave H-SCAN the jaunty air of a video game.

First test: reaction time to a sound. H-SCAN told me to put on the headphones. I started to breathe a little faster—that old exam anxiety. "Press Button Six as quickly as you can after you hear a tone," the screen read. My best five out of ten tries averaged .127 seconds. No comment on whether that was young or old for my age.

Next: highest tone I could hear. I knew I'd flunk this. Tinnitus, a high-frequency screech I've had in my ears for years, masked much of the tone.

Fingertip sensitivity. I was to put one finger on a little bar on the gray box and press a button as long as I felt the bar vibrate. Midway through, a scolding on the screen: "The vibration was off, but you held down the button. That scores as miss number one. You are allowed four misses. Try again."

I thought I must be looking pretty old to H-SCAN.

Next: lung capacity. I drew in a deep breath, then blasted it into the tube as forcefully as I could, blowing to the last gasp. This was two tests in one: The amount of air the lungs can expel in the first

second, and the total amount they can hold. The screen showed a curve—the average for my height, age, and sex—as a target. Puffing against nothing was hard; my breath disappeared. But my curve arced above the average. All right! I was looking a little younger.

Coordination: I jumped a finger back and forth 30 times as fast as I could between button one and button six. Relieved to be doing something even remotely athletic, I really attacked this one, whamming my finger back and forth, concentrating on not missing.

After a few more tests, the printout. H-SCAN listed my scores and delivered its verdict. "Your estimated biological age is: 43."

Cool. I liked being 13 years younger.

IT LOOKS AS IF my efforts at a healthy life have paid off, I thought.

Not so fast, said Hochschild as we settled down to debrief. He wasn't so rash as to say he knew whether my running and low-fat diet had anything to do with the positive H-SCAN score. In fact, it turns out that, as far as anyone knows, the H-SCAN tests things that will decline as you get older no matter *what* you do. Your lungs, for example, shrink with age even if you're an elite athlete. Hochschild conceded that I might be in better shape than the average 56-year-old, but that didn't mean I could take credit for it, or that I'd been aging less rapidly than the average person.

"Some of your functions test younger than your chronological age," he said. "But they may or may not be good predictors of an extra-long life. We're still walking, not flying. The big question is which of the things we tested—if any—will turn out to be truly valid biomarkers."

Biomarkers. They're the quarry researchers will be pursuing for years to come as they look for the biological mechanisms that cause aging. They're searching for changes—in DNA, cell division, connective tissue, and so forth—that will provide an accurate gauge of how fast a body is growing older, much as a speedometer reflects the rate of travel in a car by counting wheel revolutions. If you could somehow slow down those changes, you'd slow down aging itself and increase maximum life span —the longest that biologists believe any individual creature in a species can live if it doesn't get killed off by disease or accident. Many now think the upper limit for humans is about 120 years; the oldest confirmed age is 117.

Unfortunately, researchers are a long way from zeroing in on what actually causes aging. "Useful

What you can't change about aging . . . and what you can

"HERE'S OUR REAL take-home message: Aging is a very individual matter," says James Fozard, director of the Baltimore Longitudinal Study of Aging, which tests 2,000 people at two-year intervals to observe what happens to their bodies as they grow older. What have the researchers found? "Extraordinarily 'young' 80-year-olds, along with extraordinarily 'old' 40-year-olds," according to one report. They've even discovered that different parts of the same person decline at different rates—you may have an old heart and young liver, say. Perhaps most reassuring, they've found that while some of the declines we blame on aging may be inevitable, others are partly preventable.

CHANGES YOU PROBABLY CAN'T AVOID

Hearing

High-frequency hearing declines steadily, beginning as early as age 20, but most people don't notice any hearing loss until their sixties, when voices can become less audible as low-frequency hearing also begins to fade. Heredity affects how much hearing you lose, and how quickly, as does exposure to loud music, roaring traffic, and other ear-splitting noise.

Reaction time

Research in Baltimore and elsewhere suggests that reaction time—for putting on the brakes when a car pulls out in front of you, say—slows down as a result of changes in the aging brain and central nervous system. Some nerve cells die off, others lose the receptors needed to receive and relay information. Fast-twitch muscle fibers—the kind you need for quick moves and high-intensity work like lifting heavy objects—start disappearing as early as age 20.

Lung capacity

The amount of air you can take in and force out reflects a true aging process, Fozard says. Lung tissue gets stiffer with age, like a balloon left in the sun, so it won't expand to hold as much air; no matter what size you start with or how much you exercise, your lungs shrink about 40 percent between ages 20 and 80.

Eyesight

The lens of the eye hardens with age, making it more difficult to change focus, especially to see nearby objects.

Memory and learning

Generally, people grow worse at short-term tasks like remembering sequences of words, but remain pretty good at recalling long-ago memories, such as the name of a college friend. Still, a surprising percentage of people remain mentally acute well into old age: One Baltimore researcher found 28 percent of the men over 70 (women have been part of the study only since 1978) doing as well as young men on short-term memory tests.

CHANGES YOU CAN PARTLY PREVENT—OR REVERSE

Muscle mass

The average American adult, a sedentary person, loses about six and a half pounds of lean body mass every ten years. Most of the loss comes from shrinking muscle. For a variety of reasons—mainly too much sitting around—the rate of loss speeds up after age 45. Building muscle may be the best single strategy for a longer healthy life because it increases your strength, so you move around better; edges out fat, thus reducing the risk of developing a chronic disease; increases metabolism, so you burn calories faster; and fine-tunes the body's ability to use insulin, so you're at lower risk of diabetes.

Aerobic capacity

Most men start losing aerobic capacity—the ability to deliver oxygen to muscle during exercise—around the age of 20, and most women in their early thirties. By 65, it declines 30 to 40 percent in both men and women. But the decline is much less in people who exercise regularly.

Cholesterol levels

Although levels of fats in the blood have little direct connection to age, they do tend to rise as we get older, mostly because of the eating and exercise habits we develop. You can lower levels of "bad" low-density lipoproteins (LDLs) with a low-fat diet and raise levels of "good" high-density lipoproteins (HDLs) by exercising, reducing body fat, quitting smoking, drinking moderate amounts of alcohol, or getting off birth-control pills.

Blood pressure

In many places around the world, blood pressure doesn't rise with age, but it does in the United States. While some people are born with a disposition to high blood pressure, others are at risk because they are overweight and sedentary. Many people believe that a low-salt diet is the best defense against high blood pressure, but salt intake increases the risk for only one in five Americans. For most people, shedding fat (if overweight) and staying fit through exercise are the best strategies.

Bone density

Beginning around age 35, bone loss begins to overtake bone growth. Women, on average, lose more than half the density in the top of the femur, the leg bone that joins the hip, and 42 percent from the spinal bones in the small of the back. Men lose two-thirds as much in the femur and only a quarter as much in the spine. So it's best to develop as much bone mass as possible before the loss starts. That's especially true for women, who tend to have thinner bones to begin with, and who face accelerated bone loss after menopause. Researchers generally agree that stressing a bone—with weight-bearing exercise such as walking or running—makes it denser and less prone to fractures. Getting enough calcium—1,000 milligrams for most adults and 1,500 for postmenopausal women—is also key to building bone mass. Studies suggest that exercise may improve the body's absorption of calcium.—*J.P.*

IT'S EASY TO ASSUME THAT GROWING FATTER, WEAKER, AND GETTING BRITTLE BONES ARE THE INEVITABLE CONSEQUENCES OF AGING. BUT THEY'RE NOT.

biomarkers of *aging,* per se?" said Richard L. Sprott, director of the Biology of Aging Program at the National Institute on Aging in Bethesda, Maryland, when I called to ask about his progress. "We haven't found any."

When it comes to the nature versus nurture debate on aging, Sprott is on the nature side of the spectrum. Of course the way you live affects your health, he says. But even if you're in great shape, your body is hard-wired to age in ways that no one yet can remedy—a piece of news so dismaying, considering the faith many of us have in healthy behavior, that it's almost un-American. "Personally," Sprott said, "I don't think it's an accident that there are no eighty-year-old Olympic pole-vaulters."

Sprott believes it may be possible to slow aging— it just might be a while before we know how. A 20-year veteran of biomarker research, he has teams of scientists at universities across the United States and Canada on the chase. He hopes to start experiments with human beings in 1997 or 1998, but for now his researchers are still using mice and rats.

No offense intended to scientists doing DNA-level experiments, but while we wait for God to appear in the details, what are we supposed to do with eyes, hands, legs, and other parts that don't work as well as they used to? What I want to know is this: Are there steps I can take today that will keep me healthy and strong until the day I stop?

I thought it was time to talk to someone who says there are. For a look at the things I *can* change, and a new reading on how old I am, I went to see William Evans.

TWO BLOCKS FROM Boston Common, I looked for 711 Washington Street, figuring I'd find the office where I had an appointment tucked into some corner of the downtown branch of Tufts University, where William Evans runs the physiology lab at the Human Nutrition Research Center on Aging. Surprise: The center occupies an entire 15-story building.

I stepped out of the elevator into Evans's domain with mixed feelings of eagerness and dread. The H-SCAN had felt so much like a video game, I didn't have to take it seriously. But this was the big time: One of the federal government's top research centers, with almost 80 doctorate-level scientists. Now we're really going to see how I'm doing, I thought. That dratted cold . . . I wish I hadn't slacked off my running and push-ups . . .

A soft-spoken, friendly man, Evans has the slightly distracted air of someone doing several things at once. He usually is. In addition to direct-

ing the physiology lab, he's an associate professor of nutrition and physiology at Tufts. If you ask, he'll tell you without hesitation that he's 42.

Evans is one of those scientists who take the hopeful view that exercise and intelligent eating can hold back the hands of the clock, and he practices what he preaches. He runs 20 to 25 miles a week, lifts weights, and he and his wife, Betsy, eat like saints. "I want to enjoy the children as they get older, and their children, and maybe their grandchildren," he said. "I think the only way for me to do that is to continue to be active."

In *Biomarkers,* the book in which Evans and Irwin Rosenberg, director of the research center, write about how to stay vital as you age, they happily admit to focusing on declines that *can* be revived, even reversed. The biomarkers they target —like aerobic capacity, muscle mass, body fat—are measures of how *well* you're aging, not necessarily how fast. Their message: We may not know how to retard aging yet, but we can surely overcome some of its effects. And as Evans paraphrases the wondrously durable Satchel Paige, whose pitching career in baseball stretched from the 1920s to the 1950s, these biomarkers can tell you how old you would be "if you didn't know how old you was."

"Studies have shown all sorts of declines as people grow older—growing fatter, weaker, getting brittle bones," Evans said. "So it's easy to assume those things are consequences of aging. But the premise of what we do here is that many of them are not signs of aging at all, but merely of disuse." Some declines are inevitable, he conceded, at least for now: decreasing lung capacity, slowed reaction times, a dulled sense of taste and smell, to name some. But others are at least partly preventable. While you can't do anything about the genes you were born with, you *can* control how you're treating the body they produced.

Evans's tests would determine how much I'd done with what I'd been given.

"Let's go," he said.

Body fat percentage. In a little room near the south end of the lab, I climbed into a big vat for the classic underwater weighing. I submerged and forced out as much breath as I could—fat floats, and extra air would count as fat—while a computer used my height, land weight, and underwater weight to figure my percentage of body fat.

"Hmmm," said the doctoral student at the computer, "16.3 percent. Pretty lean."

Later, Evans put my results in perspective. "Keep in mind that 85 percent of the population does no

PEOPLE KEEP LOOKING FOR A PILL TO DO WHAT THEY OUGHT TO DO THEMSELVES. YOU WANT A LONGER, BETTER LIFE? THEN JUST DO THESE FOUR SIMPLE THINGS.

regular physical activity." The 15 percent who do, of course, retain more muscle—lean tissue—and less fat. "Men in your chronological age group, fifty to sixty, average 33.3 percent body fat in a study we've been doing around Boston. Your 16.3 percent is what we typically see in college students twenty years old. *Sedentary* college students, but twenty-year-olds nonetheless."

Aerobic capacity. Dried off, I sat while the lab's medical supervisor fitted a blood-pressure cuff on my arm and pasted electrocardiogram leads on my chest. Then I mounted a stationary bike. My nose clipped shut, a breathing tube in my mouth, I pedaled as Evans's crew bumped up the resistance at one-minute intervals. At about six minutes I noticed to my dismay that my legs were going to give out before my lungs. Just past seven minutes my thigh muscles . . . just . . . quit. Oh, disgrace.

"Not bad," Evans said, looking at a printout as I pedaled slowly to cool down. "You maxed out at a little over 43 milliliters of oxygen per kilogram of body weight per minute." The more fit you are, the more oxygen you burn, largely because you have plenty of muscle tissue demanding and using it. The fittest 56-year-old Evans has seen yet in the lab, a marathon runner, used 72 milliliters. "You're average for a sedentary 25-year-old man, or a 49-year-old man who exercises regularly," he said.

Maximum heart rate also figures in the aerobic capacity equation, since oxygen travels to working muscles through the bloodstream. The faster a heart can safely beat, the more oxygen it can force into capillaries and muscle tissue—and the longer and stronger you can keep moving. Fitness trainers usually advise people to rev up their pulse to 60 to 80 percent of their predicted maximum for 20 minutes or more to increase the whole system's efficiency, not the heart's top speed. You can't increase that. To the contrary.

"Your heart's top speed is one of those things that inevitably declines with age, hence the rule of thumb about predicting it by subtracting your age from 220," Evans said. With age, heart muscle cells do lose some of their sensitivity to the adrenaline-like hormones released during exercise, lowering the number of times a minute the heart is capable of beating. "But over the age of forty-five it varies a great deal from person to person, so it's best to measure it, if possible. We just measured yours at 175—that matches the prediction for a forty-five-year-old."

From 20 to 25 to 45 . . . I was growing older as he talked.

Basal metabolic rate. The next morning, I lay quietly for half an hour with my head under a plastic hood while a tube carried my exhalations to an analyzer. The machine figured how many calories my body uses at rest—a measure of basic efficiency at producing energy—and computed how many it would use in 24 hours. The result: 1,543. But most people don't lie around punching the buttons on a remote control all day. To figure a person's actual daily caloric need, physiologists add half again the basal metabolic rate to account for everyday life, plus extra calories for each additional activity. In my case—exercise included—I burn almost 3,000 a day. That gives me license to eat as much as a teenager. The average adolescent boy eats up to 3,000 calories a day, and the average girl 2,200, while staying trim.

"Metabolism is partly genetic," Evans explained. "But there's something else that drives a basal metabolic rate. People's metabolism drops about 2 percent per decade starting at age twenty, almost purely because they let fat replace muscle—the active tissue that burns oxygen and calories.

"Two things determine the number of calories you need: basal metabolic rate and activity levels. 'Activity' doesn't have to be going out and running five miles. It's what people do all day—pacing the floor, walking up stairs, picking up a bag of groceries. Studies in our lab and others show that people who don't move around much tend to be fatter than people who fidget, stand up, and move about. You fidget a lot, besides running and exercising. The muscle you keep toned with that activity explains a lot about why you burn a hefty number of calories just lying down." He gave my metabolic rate a biological age of early twenties.

Strength. An assistant strapped one of my legs at a time onto a machine that measured the power of a push out and pull back from the knee. "This score looks like an average man fifty-five to sixty-four years old, based on a study we did last year," Evans said. "But we also see thirty-five- and forty-year-old people who are sedentary and weak, so the legs could belong to one of them. Obviously, strength is something you could improve just by lifting weights."

Cholesterol levels. Evans took a vial of blood from my arm and sent it down to the research center's lipid lab. The more "good" high-density lipoprotein (HDL) you have, the lower your risk of clogged arteries. The reason may be that HDLs scour other fats off artery walls; or it may be simply that the more of them you have, the fewer your "bad" types of blood fats.

No responsible expert assigns an age, biological or otherwise, to cholesterol levels. Still, the ratio of total cholesterol to HDL is a prime measure of heart disease risk—the lower the better. My total cholesterol, for example, was 199 and my HDL 70. "That's a ratio of 2.84, which is excellent protection from heart disease for a man or woman of any age," said Evans. Anyone beyond middle age is advised to keep that ratio below 4.5.

Blood sugar tolerance. Evans drew another vial of blood, then handed me a bottle of glucose solution that looked like fruit soda. The label read Tru Glu. "This stuff is so sweet, the way I get it down is just chug it fast," he advised. The glucose drink would challenge my body's efficiency at pulling sugar out of the bloodstream—an efficiency that in many people drops with age, thus raising the chance of adult-onset diabetes. One hour and two hours later, he took more blood samples.

I had to catch a plane, so I left without the results of this one. A few days later, Evans called me at home. "Your glucose tolerance curve is excellent, very low—what we'd expect to see in a man in his twenties. And this time I mean an *active,* athletic man. It's better than we see in sedentary men twenty to twenty-five." What he meant was that my body is good at disposing of sugar in the blood because it's using insulin efficiently. Evans sees three causes for the efficiency: a high ratio of lean to fat, lots of exercise, and meals low in fat, high in vegetables and grains.

Now the moment of truth. "If all I had were these printouts and I didn't know your chronologic age," Evans said, "I'd guess that you're a moderately active man thirty-five to forty years old."

Shazam! Even younger than Richard Hochschild's H-SCAN.

Does this mean my life expectancy is greater than the 72 years for the average American male?

"To me it means two things," Evans said. "First, you have a relatively low risk of developing a chronic disease—diabetes, heart disease, stroke, lung cancer, those sorts of killers—so I'd say your life expectancy is greater than the predicted one for a typical man your chronologic age.

"Second, equally or more important: Your *active* life expectancy is much greater than it is for someone of your chronologic age who has the body composition, aerobic capacity, cholesterol levels, glucose tolerance, and so forth of someone typical for his or her age. By 'typical' I mean sedentary, overweight, and out of shape, which is the norm in the United States.

"You have a good chance of seeing your wish come true—a long, healthy life with a pretty short decline at the end."

SO I'VE BEEN TESTED. And I prefer to believe I'm helping my chances of staying vital by the way I've been living. Even Richard Sprott, the skeptical chief researcher at the National Institute on Aging, agrees that Evans's tests are good measures of the effect your way of life is having on the way you age.

"People keep looking for a pill to do what is far better done by changes in behavior," Sprott says. You want to live a better long life? Then, says Sprott, do these four simple things in this order:

1. Fasten your seat belt.
2. Give up smoking.
3. Start a program of regular exercise.
4. Lose some weight (if you're overweight).

"Still," he says, "it's important to recognize that, when you come right down to it, there are no assurances. Life is a crapshoot."

That's right, you can't count on anything. It's too early for a man of 56, or 43, or 40, or whatever I am, to celebrate. Besides, what really matters is how you're doing in everyday life. Work—can you do as much of it as well as you did at 30? Shoveling snow—do you have to stop and rest halfway down the walk? Carrying groceries—can you haul as many sacks as when the children were babies? And what about a friendly game of softball?

A few Sundays after the tests, I played in my first game in years. The hair on the other guys ranged from dark to graying to silver. A quick poll turned up ages from mid-thirties to mid-fifties (chronological). No paunches, though. Some of the silvertops slugged huge home runs and made hard catches in the outfield look easy. Some bent swiftly to scoop up ground balls and threw flat and true. Some younger ones did all that, too, and some didn't.

Me? "It's just a game, it's just a game," I reminded myself when my first at-bat produced a pop-up. I used to hit doubles. Well, I can still run, I told myself in the outfield after making a shoe-top catch of a sinking line drive. "All right!" the regulars yelled. Oops, the next fly ball went over my head; coordination was rusty.

Five runs for the other side, one for ours. Yes, yes, the companionship is what counts, it isn't whether you win or lose . . .

At bat, *another* pop-up, and then some cheery taunts from my fellow male bondees: "Hey, what part of you did they say was under forty?"

I'd have preferred if someone that day had looked at me carrying on as if I still had all my muscle fibers and elasticity and said, "Really. Act your age." Come to think of it, people don't seem to say that as often as they used to. But if the occasion should arise, I guess I'd answer with a question.

"All right," I'd say. "Which one?"

DON'T ACT YOUR AGE!

Life stages no longer

roll forward in a

cruel numbers game

Carol Tavris, Ph.D.

Carol Tavris *is a social psychologist and writer, and author of* Anger: The Misunderstood Emotion.

A friend of mine has just had her first baby. Not news, exactly. It's not even news that she's 45 years old. The news is it's not news that a 45-year-old woman has just had her first baby.

Another friend, age 32, has decided to abandon the pursuit of matrimony and remodel her kitchen instead. The news is that her parents and friends don't think she's weird. They're giving her a Not-Wedding party.

It used to be that all of us knew what we were supposed to be doing at cer-tain ages. The "feminine clock" dic-tated that women married in their early 20s, had a couple of kids by 30 (formerly the baby deadline), maybe went back to work in their 40s, came down with the empty nest blues in their 50s, and faded into grand-motherhood in their 60s. The "mascu-line clock" ticked along as men marched up the career ladder, regis-tering their promotions and salaries with notches at each decade.

Nowadays, many women are fol-lowing the masculine clock; many men are resetting their schedules; and huge numbers of both sexes have stopped telling time altogether. This development is both good news and bad.

The good news is that people are no longer expected to march in lock step through the decades of life, making changes on schedule. "No one is doing things on time anymore," says Dr. Nancy Schlossberg, an adult develop-ment expert at the University of Maryland, and the author of the forthcoming *Overwhelmed: Coping with Life's Ups and Downs* (Lexington Books). "Our lives are much too irreg-ular and unpredictable. In my classes I've seen women who were first-time mothers at 43 and those who had their first baby at 17. I just met a woman who is newly married—at age 65. She quit her job, and with her husband is traveling around on their yacht writing articles. You can bet she won't be hav-ing an age-65 retirement crisis. She's having too much fun."

The bad news is that without time-tables, many people are confused about what they're "supposed" to be doing in their 20s, 30s, 40s and be-yond. They have confused *age* (a bio-logical matter) with *stage* (a social matter). Women ask: "When is the best time to have children—before or after I've started working?" Men want to know: "Since I can't make up my mind about marriage, work, children and buying a dog, is it possible I'm hav-ing a midlife crisis even though I'm only 32?"

Although confusion can be unset-tling, I prefer it to the imposed phoni-ness of the "life stage" theories of personal development. Actually, I date my dislike of stage theories to my childhood. My parents used to keep Gesell's *The First Five Years of Life* and *The Child From Five to Ten* on the highest shelf of their library (right next to Rabelais), and I *knew* they were consulting these volumes at regular in-tervals to check on my progress. I was

NO ONE IS DOING THINGS ON TIME ANYMORE.

indignant. For one thing, a 9¾-year-old person finds it humiliating to be lumped with six-year-olds. For an-other, I was sure I wasn't measuring up, though what I was supposed to be measuring up to I never knew.

I survived Gesell's stages only to find myself, as a college student in the '60s, assigned to read Erik Erikson's theory of the eight stages of man. Ev-ery few years in childhood, and then every 10 years or so after, Erikson said, people have a special psychologi-cal crisis to resolve and overcome.

The infant must learn to trust, or will forever mistrust the world. The toddler must develop a sense of auton-omy and independence, without suc-cumbing to shame and doubt. The school-aged child must acquire compe-tence at schoolwork, or will risk life-long feelings of inferiority. Teenagers, naturally, must overcome the famous "identity crisis," or they will wallow in "role confusion" and aimlessness. Once you have your identity, you must learn to share it; if you don't master this "intimacy crisis," you might be-come lonely and isolated. To Erikson, you're never home free. Older adults face the crises of stagnation versus generativity, and, in old age, "ego in-tegrity" versus despair.

It turned out, of course, that Erikson meant the ages of "man" literally, but none of us knew that in those days. We female students all protested that our stages were out of order—but that was just further evidence, our instructor said, of how deviant, peculiar and irritating women are. Erikson's theory, he said, was a brilliant expansion of Freud's stage theory (which stopped at puberty). If women didn't fit, it was their own damned fault.

In the 1970s, stage theory struck again with an eruption of popular books. (Stage theories recur in predictable stages.) Journalist Gail Sheehy published *Passages: Predictable Crises of Adult Life* (no one asked how a crisis, by definition a "turning point" or "a condition of instability," could be predictable). Harvard psychiatrist George Vaillant, now at Dartmouth, studied privileged Harvard (male) students, and concluded that men go through orderly stages even if their lives differ. Yale psychiatrist Daniel J. Levinson, in *The Seasons of a Man's Life*, argued that the phases of life unfold in a natural sequence, like the four seasons. This book had nothing to say about women's seasons, possibly because women were continuing to irritate academics by doing things unseasonably.

By this time I was really annoyed. I wasn't having any of my crises in the right order. I hadn't married when I was supposed to, which put my intimacy and generativity crises on hold; leaving my job created an identity crisis at 32, far too late. My work-linked sense of competence, having reached a high of +9, now plunged to -2, and I was supposed to have resolved *that* one at around age seven.

I had only to look around to realize I was not alone. All sorts of social changes were detonating around me. Women who had been homebodies for 35 years were running off to start businesses, much to the annoyance of their husbands, who were quitting their businesses to take lute lessons. People who expected to marry didn't. People who expected to stay married didn't. Women who expected never to work were working. Men who expected never to care about babies were cooing over their own. Expectations were out the window altogether.

LIFE AS A FAN

Eventually, stages no longer mat-

EXPERTS CAN'T AGREE ON WHERE TO LOCATE "MIDLIFE."

tered, either. Psychological theories—which follow what people actually do—have had to change to keep up with the diversity of modern life. In recent years, researchers have discovered a few things that, once and for all, should drive a stake through the idea of fixed, universal life stages:

The psychology and biology of aging are not the same thing. Many of the problems of "old age" stem from psychological, not physical, losses. They would afflict most people at any age who were deprived of family, close friends, meaningful activity, intellectual stimulation and control over what happens to them. Today we've learned to distinguish the biology of normal aging from the decline caused by illness: Conditions once thought inevitable— osteoporosis, senility, excessive wrinkling, depression—can result from poor nutrition, overmedication, lack of exercise, cell damage or disease. For example, only 15% of people over 65 suffer serious mental impairment, and half of those cases are due to Alzheimer's disease.

These findings have played havoc with the basic definition of "old." It used to be 50. Then it was 60, then 70. Today there are so many vibrant octogenarians that "old" is getting even older. Researchers can't even agree on where to locate "midlife" (30 to 50? 40 to 60? 35 to 65?), let alone what problems constitute a midlife crisis.

Although children progress through biologically determined "stages," adults don't. Children go through a stage of babbling before they talk; they crawl before they walk; they wail before they

they can say, "Can we discuss this calmly, Mom?" These developments are governed by maturational and biological changes dictated by genes. But as children mature, genes become less of a driving force on their development, and the environment has greater impact.

Bernice Neugarten, a professor of behavioral science at the University of Chicago, observes that the better metaphor for life is a fan, rather than stages. When you open a fan, you can see all its diverse pieces linked at a common point of origin. As people age, their qualities and experiences likewise "fan out," which is why, she says, you find greater diversity in a group of 70-year-olds than in a passel of seven-year-olds.

The variety and richness of adult life can't be crammed into tidy "stages" anymore. Stage theorists such as Erikson assumed that growth is fixed (by some biological program or internal clock), progressive (you grow from a lower stage to a higher one), one-way (you grow up, not down; become more competent, not less), cumulative (reflecting your resolution of previous stages), and irreversible (once you gain a skill, there's no losing it).

Yet it has proven impossible to squash the great variety of adult experience into a fixed pattern, and there is no evidence to support the idea of neat stages that occur in five- or 10-year intervals. Why must you master an "identity crisis" before you learn to love? Don't issues of competence and inferiority recur throughout life? Why is the need for "generativity" relevant only to 30-year-olds?

EVENTS AND NONEVENTS

For all these reasons, new approaches to adult development emphasize not how old people are, but what they are doing. Likewise, new studies find that *having* a child has stronger psychological effects on mothers than the age at which they have the baby. (New mothers of any age feel more nurturing and less competent.) Entering the work force has a strong positive effect on your self-esteem and ambition, regardless of when you start working. Men facing retirement confront similar issues at 40, 50 or 60. Divorced people have certain

THE NEW APPROACH: NOT HOW OLD YOU ARE, BUT WHAT YOU ARE DOING.

common problems, whether they split at 30 or 50.

In their book *Lifeprints* (McGraw-Hill), Wellesley College psychologists Grace Baruch and Rosalind Barnett and writer Caryl Rivers surveyed 300 women, ages 35 to 55. They found that the differences among the women depended on what they were doing, not on their age. A career woman of 40, for example, has more in common with a career woman of 30 than with an unemployed woman her age.

At the heart of *Lifeprints* is the heretical notion that "there is no one lifeprint that insures all women a perpetual sense of well-being—nor one that guarantees misery, for that matter. American women today are finding satisfying lives in any number of role patterns. Most involve trade-offs at different points in the life cycle."

Instead of looking for the decade landmarks or the "crises" in life, the *transitions* approach emphasizes the importance of shifting from one role or situation to another. What matters are the events that happen (or fail to happen) and cause us to change in some way. Maryland's Schlossberg describes four kinds of transitions:

■ **Anticipated** transitions are the events you plan for, expect and rehearse: going to school, getting married, starting a job, getting promoted, having a child, retiring at 65. These are the (previously) common milestones of adult life, and because they're predictable, they cause the least difficulty.

■ **Unanticipated** transitions are the things that happen when you aren't prepared: flunking out of school, being fired, having a baby after being told you can't, being forced to retire early. Because these events are bolts from the blue, they can leave you reeling.

■ **Nonevent** transitions are the changes you expect to happen that

don't: You don't get married; you can't have children; you aren't promoted; you planned to retire but need to keep working for the income. The challenge here is knowing when to accept these ongoing events as specific transitions and learning to live with them.

■ **Chronic Hassle** transitions are the situations that may eventually require you to change or take action, but rumble along uncomfortably for a long stretch: You aren't getting along with your spouse; your mother gets a chronic illness and needs constant care; you have to deal with discrimination at work; your child keeps getting into trouble.

There are no rules: An anticipated change for one person (having a baby) might be unanticipated for another. An upsetting "nonevent" transition for one person (not getting married) can be a planned decision for another and thus not a transition at all. And even unexpected good news—you recover despite a hopeless diagnosis—can require adjustment. This approach acknowledges that nonevents and chronic situations cause us to change just as surely as dramatic events do, though perhaps less consciously.

Seeing our lives in terms of these transitions, says Schlossberg, frees us from the old stereotypes that say we "should" be doing one thing or another at a certain time in our lives. But it also helps us understand why we can sail through changes we thought would be traumatic—only to be torpedoed by transitions expected to be a breeze. Our reactions have little to do with an internal clock, and everything to do with expectations, goals and, most of all, what else is happening to us.

For example, says Schlossberg, people have very different reactions to "significant" birthdays. For some, 30 is the killer; for others it's 50. For an aunt of mine, who breezed through decade markers without a snivel, 70

was traumatic. "To determine why a birthday marker creates a crisis," says Schlossberg, "I'd ask what was going on in the person's life, not their age. How old were they when their last parent died? How is their work going? Have they lost a loved one?" If they see a birthday as closing down options, then the event can feel negative, she adds.

"All of us carry along a set of psychological needs that are important throughout our lives, not just at one particular age or stage," says Schlossberg. "We need to feel we *belong* to a family, group or community, for example. Changing jobs, marriages or cities often leaves people feeling temporarily left out.

"We also need to feel we matter to others, that we count. At some phases of life, people are burdened by mattering too much to too many people. Many women in their 30s must care for children, husbands and parents, to say nothing of working at their paid jobs. At other phases, people suffer from a sense of mattering too little."

In addition to belonging and "mattering," says Schlossberg, people need to feel they have a reasonable amount of control over their lives; they need to feel competent at what they do; they need identity—a strong sense of who they are; and they need close attachments and commitments that give their lives meaning.

These themes, says Schlossberg, reflect our common humanity, uniting men and women, old and young. A freshman in college and a newly retired man may both temporarily feel marginal, "out of things." A teenager and her grandmother may both feel they don't "matter" to enough other people, and be lonely as a result. A man may feel he has control over his life until he's injured in a car accident. A woman's identity changes when she goes back to school in midlife. A newly divorced woman of 30 and a recently laid-off auto worker of 40 may both feel inadequate and incompetent. When people lose the commitments that give their lives meaning, they feel adrift.

"By understanding that these emotional feelings are a normal response to what is going on in your life, and not an inevitable crisis that occurs at 23 or 34, or whatever," says Schlossberg, "people can diagnose their problems more accurately—and more important, take steps to fix them." If you say, "No wonder I'm miserable; I'm having my Age 30 Decade Panic," there's nothing to do but live through it—getting more panicked when you're still miserable at age 36½.

But if you can say, "No wonder I'm miserable—I don't feel competent at work, I don't feel I matter to enough people, I feel like a stranger in this neighborhood," then more constructive possibilities present themselves. You can learn new skills, join new groups, start a neighborhood cleanup committee, and quit whining about being 30.

None of this means that age doesn't matter, as my 83-year-old mother

A WOMAN'S IDENTITY CHANGES WHEN SHE GOES BACK TO SCHOOL.

would be the first to tell you. She mutters a lot about irritating pains, wrinkles, forgetfulness and getting shorter. But mostly my mother is too busy to complain, what with her paralegal counseling, fund-raising, organizing programs for shut-in older women, traveling around the world, and socializing. She knows she belongs; she matters to many; she has countless commitments; she knows who she is.

And yet the transitions approach reminds us that adult concerns aren't settled, once and for all, at some critical stage or age. It would be nice if we could acquire a sense of competence in grammar school and keep it forever, if we had only one identity crisis per lifetime, if we always belonged. But adult development is more complicated than that, and also more interesting. As developmental psychologist Leonard Pearlin once said, "There is not one process of aging, but many; there is not one life course, but many courses; there is no one sequence of stages, but many." The variety is as rich as the diversity of human experience.

Let's celebrate the variety—and leave stages to children, geologists, rocket launches and actors.

The Prime of Our Lives

*WHAT SEEMS TO MARK OUR ADULT YEARS
MOST IS OUR SHIFTING PERSPECTIVE
ON OURSELVES AND OUR WORLD. IS THERE A
COMMON PATTERN TO OUR LIVES?*

Anne Rosenfeld
and Elizabeth Stark

*Anne Rosenfeld and Elizabeth Stark, both
members of* Psychology Today *'s editorial staff,
collaborated across cohorts to write this article.*

"My parents had given me everything they could possibly owe a child and more. Now it was my turn to decide and nobody ... could help me very far...." That's how Graham Greene described his feelings upon graduation from Oxford. And he was right. Starting on your own down the long road of adulthood can be scary.

But the journey can also be exciting, with dreams and hopes to guide us. Maybe they're conventional dreams: getting a decent job, settling down and starting to raise a family before we've left our 20s. Or maybe they're more grandiose: making a million dollars by age 30, becoming a movie star, discovering a cure for cancer, becoming President, starting a social revolution.

Our youthful dreams reflect our unique personalities, but are shaped by the values and expectations of those around us—and they shift as we and our times change. Twenty years ago, college graduates entered adulthood with expectations that in many cases had been radically altered by the major upheavals transforming American society. The times were "a-changin'," and almost no one was untouched. Within a few years many of the scrubbed, obedient, wholesome teenagers of the early '60s had turned into scruffy, alienated campus rebels, experimenting with drugs and sex and deeply dissatisfied with their materialistic middle-class heritage.

Instead of moving right on to the career track, marrying and beginning families, as their fathers had done, many men dropped out, postponing the obligations of adult life. Others traveled a middle road, combining "straight" jobs with public service rather than pursuing conventional careers. And for the first time in recent memory, large numbers of young men refused to serve their country in the military. In the early 1940s, entire fraternities went together to enlist in World War II. In the Age of Aquarius, many college men sought refuge from war in Canada, graduate school, premature marriages or newly discovered medical ailments.

Women were even more dramatically affected by the social changes of the 1960s. Many left college in 1967 with a traditional agenda—work for a few years, then get married and settle down to the real business of raising a family and being a good wife—but ended up following a different and largely unexpected path. The women's movement and changing economics created a whole new set of opportunities. For example, between 1967 and 1980, women's share of medical degrees in the United States rocketed from 5 percent to 26 percent, and their share of law degrees leaped from 4 percent to 22 percent.

A group of women from the University of Michigan class of 1967 who were interviewed before graduation and again in 1981 described lives very different from their original plans. Psychologists Sandra Tangri of Howard University and Sharon Jenkins of the University of California found that far more of these women were working in 1981 than had expected to, and far more had gotten advanced degrees and were in "male" professions. Their home lives, too, were different from their collegiate fantasies: Fewer married, and those who did had much smaller families.

Liberation brought problems as well as opportunities. By 1981, about 15 percent of the women were divorced (although some had remarried), and many of the women who "had it all" told Tangri and Jenkins that they felt torn between their careers and their families.

Living out our dreams in a rapidly changing society demands extreme flexibility in adjusting to shifting social realities. Our hopes and plans, combined with the traditional rhythms of the life course, give some structure, impetus and predictability to our lives. But each of us must also cope repeatedly with the unplanned and unexpected. And in the process, we are gradually transformed.

For centuries, philosophers have been trying to capture the essence of how people change over the life course by focusing on universally experienced stages of life, often linked to specific ages. Research on child development, begun earlier in this century, had shown that children generally pass through an orderly succession of stages that correspond to fairly specific ages. But recent studies have challenged some of the apparent orderliness of child development, and the pattern of development among adults seems to be even less clear-cut.

When we think about what happens as we grow older, physical changes leap to mind—the lessening of physical prowess, the arrival of sags, spreads and lines. But these take a back seat to psychological changes, according to psychologist Bernice Neugarten of Northwestern University, a pioneer in the field of human development. She points out that although biological maturation heavily influences childhood development, people in young and middle adulthood are most affected by their own experiences and the timing of those experiences, not by biological factors. Even menopause, that quintessentially biological event, she says, is of relatively little psychological importance in the lives of most adult women.

In other words, chronological age is an increasingly unreliable indicator of what people will be like at various points. A group of newborns, or even 5-year-olds, shows less variation than a group of 35-year-olds, or 50-year-olds.

What seems to mark our adult years most is our shifting perspective on ourselves and our

*S*TAGE THEORIES ARE A LITTLE LIKE HOROSCOPES—VAGUE ENOUGH TO LET EVERYONE SEE SOMETHING OF THEMSELVES IN THEM. THAT'S WHY THEY'RE SO POPULAR.

world—who we think we are, what we expect to get done, our timetable for doing it and our satisfactions with what we have accomplished. The scenarios and schedules of our lives are so varied that some researchers believe it is virtually impossible to talk about a single timetable for adult development. However, many people probably believe there is one, and are likely to cite Gail Sheehy's 1976 best-seller *Passages* to back them up.

Sheehy's book, which helped make "midlife crisis" a household word, was based on a body of research suggesting that adults go through progressive, predictable, age-linked stages, each offering challenges that must be met before moving on to the next stage. The most traumatic of these transitions, Sheehy claimed, is the one between young and middle adulthood—the midlife crisis.

Sheehy's ideas were based, in part, on the work of researchers Daniel Levinson, George Vaillant and Roger Gould, whose separate studies supported the stages of adult development Erik Erikson had earlier proposed in his highly influential model (see "Erikson's Eight Stages," next page).

Levinson, a psychologist, had started his study in 1969, when he was 49 and intrigued with his own recent midlife strains. He and his Yale colleagues intensively interviewed 40 men between the ages of 35 and 45 from four occupational groups. Using these interviews, bolstered by the biographies of great men and the development of memorable characters in literature, they described how men develop from 17 to 65 years of age (see "Levinson's Ladder," this article).

At the threshold of each major period of adulthood, they found, men pass through predictably unstable transitional periods, including a particularly wrenching time very close to age 40. At each transition a man must confront issues that may involve his career, his marriage, his family and the realization of his dreams if he is to progress successfully to the next period. Seventy percent to 80 percent of the men Levinson interviewed found the midlife transition (ages 40 to 45) tumultuous and psychologically painful, as most aspects of their lives came into question. The presumably universal timetable Levinson offered was very rigid, allowing no more than four years' leeway for each transition.

Vaillant's study, although less age-bound than Levinson's, also revealed that at midlife men go through a period of pain and preparation—"a time for reassessing and reordering the truth about adolescence and young adulthood." Vaillant, a psychiatrist, when he conducted his study at Harvard interviewed a group of men who were part of the Grant Study of Adult Development. The study had tracked almost 270 unusually accomplished, self-reliant and healthy Harvard freshmen (drawn mostly from the classes of 1942 to 1944) from their college days until their late 40s. In 1967 and 1977 Vaillant and his team interviewed and evaluated 94 members of this select group.

They found that, despite inner turmoil, the men judged to have the best outcomes in their late 40s "regarded the period from 35 to 49 as the happiest in their lives, and the seemingly calmer period from 21 to 35 as the unhappiest." But the men least well adapted at midlife "longed for the relative calm of their young adulthood and regarded the storms of later life as too painful."

While Levinson and Vaillant were completing their studies, psychiatrist Roger Gould and his colleagues at the University of California, Los Angeles, were looking at how the lives of both men and women change during young and middle adulthood. Unlike the Yale and Harvard studies, Gould's was a one-time examination of more than 500 white, middle-class people from ages 16 to 60. Gould's study, like those of Levinson and Vaillant, found that the time around age 40 was a tough one for many people, both personally and maritally. He stressed that people need to change their early expectations as they develop. "Childhood delivers most people into adulthood with a view of adults that few could ever live up to," he wrote. Adults must

confront this impossible image, he said, or be frustrated and dissatisfied.

The runaway success of *Passages* indicated the broad appeal of the stage theorists' message with its emphasis on orderly and clearly defined transitions. According to Cornell historian Michael Kammen, "We want predictability, and we desperately want definitions of 'normality.'" And almost everyone could find some relationship to their own lives in the stages Sheehy described. Stage theories, explains sociologist Orville Brim Jr., former president of the Russell Sage Foundation, are "a little like horoscopes. They are vague enough so that everyone can see something of themselves in them. That's why they're so popular."

But popularity does not always mean validity. Even at the time there were studies contradicting the stage theorists' findings. When sociologist Michael Farrell of the State University of New York at Buffalo and social psychologist Stanley Rosenberg of Dartmouth Medical School looked for a crisis among middle-aged men in 1971 it proved elusive. Instead of finding a "universal midlife crisis," they discovered several different developmental paths. "Some men do appear to reach a state of crisis," they found, "but others seem to thrive. More typical than either of these responses is the tendency for men to bury their heads and deny and avoid all the pressures closing in on them."

Another decade of research has made the picture of adult development even more complex. Many observations and theories accepted earlier as fact, especially by the general public, are now being debated. Researchers have espe-

Erikson's Eight Stages

According to Erik Erikson, people must grapple with the conflicts of one stage before they can move on to a higher one.

BONNIE SCHIFFMAN

	1	2	3	4	5	6	7	8
Old Age								Integrity vs. Despair, Disgust
Maturity							Generativity vs. Self-absorption	
Young Adulthood						Intimacy vs. Isolation		
Adolescence					Identity vs. Identity Confusion			
School Age				Industry vs. Inferiority				
Play Age			Initiative vs. Guilt					
Early Childhood		Autonomy vs. Shame, Doubt						
Infancy	Trust vs. Mistrust							

SOURCE: ADAPTED FROM "REFLECTION ON DR. BORG'S LIFE CYCLE": ERIK H. ERIKSON, DAEDALUS, SPRING 1976.

Oh, God, I'm only twenty and I'll have to go on living and living and living.
—Jean Rhys, *Diary*

At thirty a man should know himself like the palm of his hand, know the exact number of his defects and qualities, know how far he can go, foretell his failures—be what he is. And above all accept these things.
—Albert Camus *Carnets.*

cially challenged Levinson's assertion that stages are predictable, tightly linked to specific ages and built upon one another.

In fact, Gould, described as a stage theorist in most textbooks, has since changed his tune, based upon his clinical observations. He now disagrees that people go through "formal" developmental stages in adulthood, although he says that people "do change their ways of looking at and experiencing the world over time." But the idea that one must resolve one stage before going on to the next, he says, is "hogwash."

Levinson, however, has stuck by his conceptual guns over the years, claiming that no one has evidence to refute his results. "The only way for my theory to be tested is to study life structure as it develops over adulthood," he says. "And by and large psychologists and sociologists don't study lives, they study variables."

Many researchers have found that changing times and different social expectations affect how various "cohorts"—groups of people born in the same year or time period—move through the life course. Neugarten has been emphasizing the importance of this age-group, or cohort, effect since the early 1960s. Our values and expectations are shaped by the period in which we live. People born during the trying times of the Depression have a different outlook on life from those born during the optimistic 1950s, according to Neugarten.

The social environment of a particular age group, Neugarten argues, can influence its so-

WHAT WAS TRUE FOR PEOPLE BORN IN THE DEPRESSION ERA MAY NOT HOLD FOR TODAY'S 40-YEAR-OLDS, BORN IN THE UPBEAT POSTWAR YEARS.

cial clock—the timetable for when people expect and are expected to accomplish some of the major tasks of adult life, such as getting married, having children or establishing themselves in a work role. Social clocks guide our lives, and people who are "out of sync" with them are likely to find life more stressful than those who are on schedule, she says.

Since the 1960s, when Neugarten first measured what people consider to be the "right" time for major life events, social clocks have changed (see "What's the Right Time?" this article), further altering the lives of those now approaching middle age, and possibly upsetting the timetable Levinson found in an earlier generation.

As sociologist Alice Rossi of the University of Massachusetts observes, researchers trying to tease out universal truths and patterns from

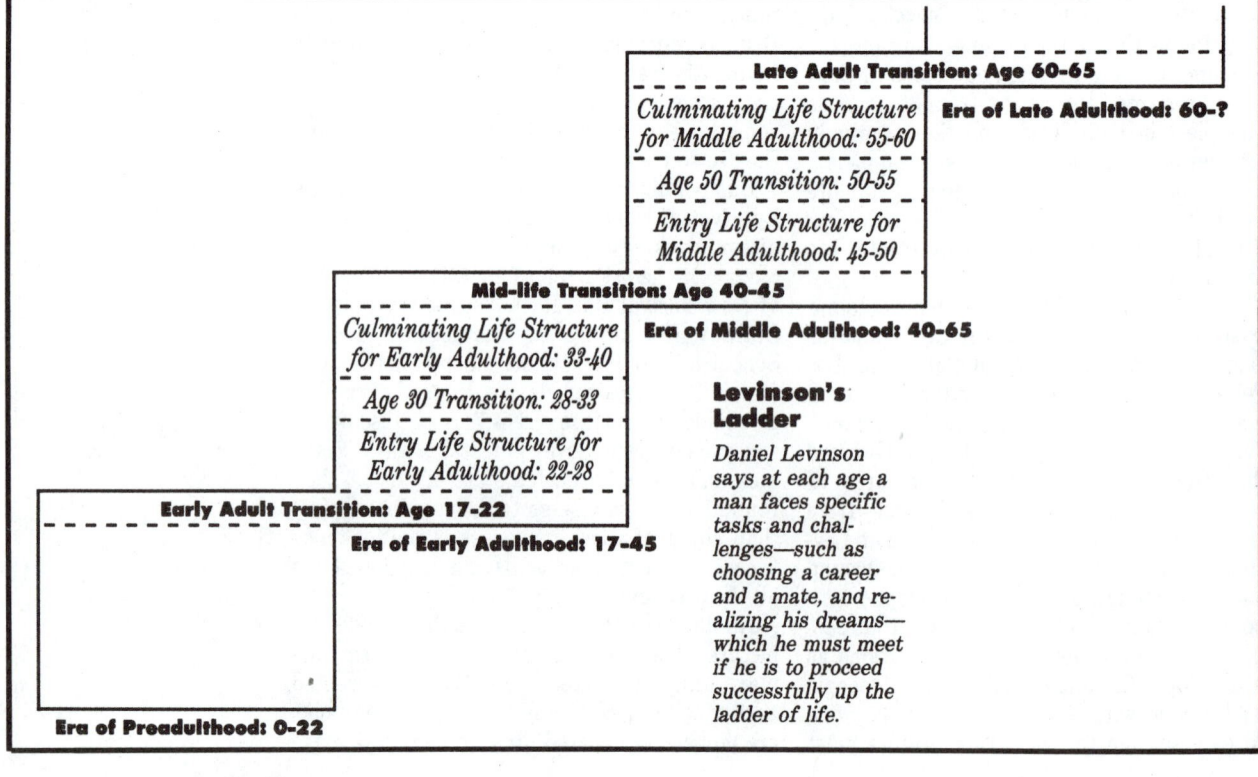

Late Adult Transition: Age 60-65

Culminating Life Structure for Middle Adulthood: 55-60

Era of Late Adulthood: 60-?

Age 50 Transition: 50-55

Entry Life Structure for Middle Adulthood: 45-50

Mid-life Transition: Age 40-45

Culminating Life Structure for Early Adulthood: 33-40

Era of Middle Adulthood: 40-65

Age 30 Transition: 28-33

Entry Life Structure for Early Adulthood: 22-28

Levinson's Ladder

Daniel Levinson says at each age a man faces specific tasks and challenges—such as choosing a career and a mate, and realizing his dreams—which he must meet if he is to proceed successfully up the ladder of life.

Early Adult Transition: Age 17-22

Era of Early Adulthood: 17-45

Era of Preadulthood: 0-22

the lives of one birth cohort must consider the vexing possibility that their findings may not apply to any other group. Most of the people studied by Levinson, Vaillant and Gould were born before and during the Depression (and were predominantly male, white and upper middle class). What was true for these people may not hold for today's 40-year-olds, born in the optimistic aftermath of World War II, or the post baby-boom generation just approaching adulthood. In Rossi's view, "The profile of the midlife men in Levinson's and Vaillant's studies may strike a future developmental researcher as burned out at a premature age, rather than reflecting a normal developmental process all men go through so early in life."

Based on her studies of women at midlife, Nancy Schlossberg, a counselor educator at the University of Maryland, also disagrees that there is a single, universal timetable for adult development—or that one can predict the crises in people's lives by knowing their age. "Give me a roomful of 40-year-old women and you have told me nothing. Give me a case story about what each has experienced and then I can tell if one is going to have a crisis and another a tranquil period." Says Schlossberg: "What matters is what transitions she has experienced. Has she been 'dumped' by a husband, fired from her job, had a breast removed, gone back to school, remarried, had her first book published. It is what has happened or not happened to her, not how old she is, that counts.... There are as many patterns as people."

Psychologist Albert Bandura of Stanford University adds more fuel to the anti-stage fire by pointing out that chance events play a big role in shaping our adult lives. Careers and marriages are often made from the happenstance of meeting the right—or wrong—person at the right—or wrong—time. But, says Bandura, while the events may be random, their effects are not. They depend on what people do with the chance opportunities fate deals them.

The ages-and-stages approach to adult development has been further criticized because it does not appear to apply to women. Levinson claims to have confirmed that women do follow the same age-transition timetable that men do. But his recent study of women has yet to be published, and there is little other evidence that might settle the case one way or the other.

Psychologists Rosalind Barnett and Grace Baruch of the Wellesley Center for Research on Women say, "It is hard to know how to think of women within this [stage] theory—a woman may not enter the world of work until her late 30s, she seldom has a mentor, and even women with lifelong career commitments rarely are in a position to reassess their commitment pattern by age 40."

But University of Wisconsin-Madison psychologist Carol Ryff, who has directly compared the views of men and women from different age groups, has found that the big psychological issues of adulthood follow a similar developmental pattern for both sexes.

Recently she studied two characteristics highlighted as hallmarks of middle age: Erikson's "generativity" and Neugarten's "complexity." Those who have achieved generativity, according to Ryff, see themselves as leaders and decision makers and are interested in helping and guiding younger people. The men and women Ryff studied agreed that generativity is at its peak in middle age.

Complexity, which describes people's feeling that they are in control of their lives and are actively involved in the world, followed a somewhat different pattern. It was high in young adulthood and stayed prominent as people matured. But it was most obvious in those who are now middle-aged—the first generation of middle-class people to combine family and work in dual-career families. This juggling of roles, although stressful, may make some men and women feel actively involved in life.

Psychologist Ravenna Helson and her colleagues Valory Mitchell and Geraldine Moane at the University of California, Berkeley, have recently completed a long-term study of the lives of 132 women that hints at some of the forces propelling people to change psychologically during adulthood. The women were studied as seniors at Mills College in California in the late 1950s, five years later and again in 1981, when they were between the ages of 42 and 45.

Helson and her colleagues distinguished three main groups among the Mills women: family-oriented, career-oriented (whether or not they also wanted families) and those who followed neither path (women with no children who pursued only low-level work). Despite their different profiles in college, and their diverging life paths, the women in all three groups underwent similar broad psychological changes over time, although those in the third group changed less than those committed to career or family.

Personality tests given through the years revealed that from age 21 to their mid-40s, the Mills women became more self-disciplined and committed to duties, as well as more independent and confident. And between age 27 and the early 40s, there was a shift toward less traditionally "feminine" attitudes, including greater dominance, higher achievement motivation, greater interest in events outside the family and more emotional stability.

To the Berkeley researchers, familiar with the work of psychologist David Gutmann of Northwestern University, these changes were not surprising in women whose children were mostly grown. Gutmann, after working with Neugarten and conducting his own research, had theorized that women and men, largely

SUDDENLY I'M THE ADULT?

BY RICHARD COHEN

Several years ago, my family gathered on Cape Cod for a weekend. My parents were there, my sister and her daughter, too, two cousins and, of course, my wife, my son and me. We ate at one of those restaurants where the menu is scrawled on a blackboard held by a chummy waiter and had a wonderful time. With dinner concluded, the waiter set the check down in the middle of the table. That's when it happened. My father did not reach for the check.

In fact, my father did nothing. Conversation continued. Finally, it dawned on me. Me! I was supposed to pick up the check. After all these years, after hundreds of restaurant meals with my parents, after a lifetime of thinking of my father as the one with the bucks, it had all changed. I reached for the check and whipped out my American Express card. My view of myself was suddenly altered. With a stroke of the pen, I was suddenly an adult.

Some people mark off their life in years, others in events. I am one of the latter, and I think of some events as rites of passage. I did not become a young man at a particular year, like 13, but when a kid strolled into the store where I worked and called me "mister." I turned around to see whom he was calling. He repeated it several times—"Mister, mister"—looking straight at me. The realization hit like a punch: Me! He was talking to me. I was suddenly a mister.

There have been other milestones. The cops of my youth always seemed to be big, even huge, and of course they were older than I was. Then one day they were neither. In fact, some of them were kids—short kids at that. Another milestone.

The day comes when you suddenly realize that all the football players in the game you're watching are younger than you. Instead of being big men, they are merely big kids. With that milestone goes the fantasy that someday, maybe, you too could be a player—maybe not a football player but certainly a baseball player. I had a good eye as a kid—not much power, but a keen eye—and I always thought I could play the game. One day I realized that I couldn't. Without having ever reached the hill, I was over it.

For some people, the most momentous milestone is the death of a parent. This happened recently to a friend of mine. With the burial of his father came the realization that he had moved up a notch. Of course, he had known all along that this would happen, but until the funeral, the knowledge seemed theoretical at best. As long as one of your parents is alive, you stay in some way a kid. At the very least, there remains at least one person whose love is unconditional.

For women, a milestone is reached when they can no longer have children. The loss of a life, the inability to create one—they are variations on the same theme. For a childless woman who could control everything in life but the clock, this milestone is a cruel one indeed.

I count other, less serious milestones—like being audited by the Internal Revenue Service. As the auditor caught mistake after mistake, I sat there pretending that really knowing about taxes was for adults. I, of course, was still a kid. The auditor was buying none of it. I was a taxpayer, an adult. She all but said, Go to jail.

There have been others. I remember the day when I had a ferocious argument with my son and realized that I could no longer bully him. He was too big and the days when I could just pick him up and take him to his room/isolation cell were over. I needed to persuade, reason. He was suddenly, rapidly,

Richard Cohen is a syndicated columnist for The Washington Post.

locked into traditional sex roles by parenthood, become less rigidly bound by these roles once the major duties of parenting decline; both are then freer to become more like the opposite sex—and do. Men, for example, often become more willing to share their feelings. These changes in both men and women can help older couples communicate and get along better.

During their early 40s, many of the women Helson and Moane studied shared the same midlife concerns the stage theorists had found in men: "concern for young and old, introspectiveness, interest in roots and awareness of limitation and death." But the Berkeley team described the period as one of midlife "consciousness," not "crisis."

In summing up their findings, Helson and Moane stress that commitment to the tasks of young adulthood—whether to a career or family (or both)—helped women learn to control impulses, develop skills with people, become independent and work hard to achieve goals.

older. The conclusion was inescapable: So was I.

One day you go to your friends' weddings. One day you celebrate the birth of their kids. One day you see one of their kids driving, and one day those kids have kids of their own. One day you meet at parties and then at weddings and then at funerals. It all happens in one day. Take my word for it.

I never thought I would fall asleep in front of the television set as my father did, and as my friends' fathers did, too. I remember my parents and their friends talking about insomnia and they sounded like members of a different species. Not able to sleep? How ridiculous. Once it was all I did. Once it was what I did best.

I never thought that I would eat a food that did not agree with me. Now I meet them all the time. I thought I would never go to the beach and not swim. I spent all of August at the beach and never once went into the ocean. I never thought I would appreciate opera, but now the pathos, the schmaltz and, especially, the combination of voice and music appeal to me. The deaths of Mimi and Tosca move me, and they die in my home as often as I can manage it.

I never thought I would prefer to stay home instead of going to a party, but now I find myself passing parties up. I used to think that people who watched birds were weird, but this summer I found myself watching them, and maybe I'll get a book on the subject. I yearn for a religious conviction I never thought I'd want, exult in my heritage anyway, feel close to ancestors long gone and echo my father in arguments with my son. I still lose.

One day I made a good toast. One day I handled a headwaiter. One day I bought a house. One day—what a day!—I became a father, and not too long after that I picked up the check for my own. I thought then and there it was a rite of passage for me. Not until I got older did I realize that it was one for him, too. Another milestone.

According to Helson and Moane, those women who did not commit themselves to one of the main life-style patterns faced fewer challenges and therefore did not develop as fully as the other women did.

The dizzying tug and pull of data and theories about how adults change over time may frustrate people looking for universal principles or certainty in their lives. But it leaves room for many scenarios for people now in young and middle adulthood and those to come.

People now between 20 and 60 are the best-educated and among the healthiest and most fit of all who have passed through the adult years. No one knows for sure what their lives will be like in the years to come, but the experts have some fascinating speculations.

For example, Rossi suspects that the quality of midlife for baby boomers will contrast sharply with that of the Depression-born generation the stage theorists studied. Baby boomers, she notes, have different dreams, values and opportunities than the preceding generation. And they are much more numerous.

Many crucial aspects of their past and future lives may best be seen in an economic rather than a strictly psychological light, Rossi says. From their days in overcrowded grade schools, through their struggles to gain entry into college, to their fight for the most desirable jobs, the baby boomers have had to compete with one another. And, she predicts, their competitive struggles are far from over. She foresees that many may find themselves squeezed out of the workplace as they enter their 50s—experiencing a crisis at a time when it will be difficult to redirect their careers.

But other factors may help to make life easier for those now approaching midlife. People are on a looser, less compressed timetable, and no longer feel obliged to marry, establish their careers and start their families almost simulta-

> The first forty years of life furnish the text, while the remaining thirty supply the commentary.
> —Schopenhauer, Parerga and Paralipomena.

neously. Thus, major life events may not pile up in quite the same way they did for the older generation.

Today's 20-year-olds—the first wave of what some have labeled "the baby busters"—have a more optimistic future than the baby boomers who preceded them, according to economist Richard Easterlin of the University of Southern California. Easterlin has been studying the life patterns of various cohorts, beginning with the low-birthrate group born in the 1930s—roughly a decade before the birthrate exploded.

The size of a birth cohort, Easterlin argues, affects that group's quality of life. In its simplest terms, his theory says that the smaller the cohort the less competition among its members and the more fortunate they are; the larger the cohort the more competition and the less fortunate.

Compared with the baby boomers, the smaller cohort just approaching adulthood "will have much more favorable experiences as they grow

WHAT'S THE RIGHT TIME?

Two surveys asking the same questions 20 years apart (late 1950s and late 1970s) have shown a dramatic decline in the consensus among middle-class, middle-aged people about what's the right age for various major events and achievements of adult life.

SOURCE: ADAPTED FROM "AGE NORMS AND AGE CONSTRAINTS TWENTY YEARS LATER": P. PASSUTH, D. MAINES AND B.L. NEUGARTEN. PAPER PRESENTED AT THE MIDWEST SOCIOLOGICAL SOCIETY MEETING, CHICAGO, APRIL 1984.

Activity/Event	Appropriate Age Range	Late '50s Study % Who Agree		Late '70s Study % Who Agree	
		Men	Women	Men	Women
Best age for a man to marry	20-25	80%	90%	42%	42%
Best age for a woman to marry	19-24	85	90	44	36
When most people should become grandparents	45-50	84	79	64	57
Best age for most people to finish school and go to work	20-22	86	82	36	38
When most men should be settled on a career	24-26	74	64	24	26
When most men hold their top jobs	45-50	71	58	38	31
When most people should be ready to retire	60-65	83	86	66	41
When a man has the most responsibilities	35-50	79	75	49	50
When a man accomplishes most	40-50	82	71	46	41
The prime of life for a man	35-50	86	80	59	66
When a woman has the most responsibilities	25-40	93	91	59	53
When a woman accomplishes most	30-45	94	92	57	48

up—in their families, in school and finally in the labor market," he says. As a result, they will "develop a more positive psychological outlook."

The baby busters' optimism will encourage them to marry young and have large families—producing another baby boom. During this period there will be less stress in the family and therefore, Easterlin predicts, divorce and suicide rates will stabilize.

Psychologist Elizabeth Douvan of the University of Michigan's Institute for Social Research shares Easterlin's optimistic view about the future of these young adults. Surprisingly, she sees as one of their strengths the fact that, due to divorce and remarriage, many grew up in reconstituted families. Douvan believes that the experience of growing up close to people who are not blood relatives can help to blur the distinction between kinship and friendship, making people more open in their relationships with others.

Like many groups before them, they are likely to yearn for a sense of community and ritual, which they will strive to fulfill in many ways, Douvan says. For some this may mean a turn toward involvement in politics, neighborhood or religion, although not necessarily the religion of their parents.

In summing up the future quality of life for today's young adults and those following them, Douvan says: "Life is more open for people now. They are judging things internally and therefore are more willing to make changes in the external aspects. That's pretty exciting. It opens up a tremendous number of possibilities for people who can look at life as an adventure."

Index

Credits/ Acknowledgments

Cover design by Charles Vitelli

1. Genetic and Prenatal Influences

Facing overview—WHO photo. 19—Illustration by Lewis E. Calver. 20—(top right) Hank Morgan—Rainbow; (middle left and bottom right) Courtesy of Buchsbaum; (middle right) Dan McCoy—Rainbow; (bottom right) Howard Sochurek. 21—(top & middle) Courtesy of Haier & Buchsbaum; (bottom) Courtesy of Buchsbaum.

2. Infancy and Early Childhood

Facing overview—WHO photo.

3. Childhood

Facing overview—United Nations photo by John Isaac.

4. Family, School, and Cultural Influences

Facing overview—United Nations photo by L. Barns.

5. Adolescence and Early Adulthood

Facing overview—WHO photo by J. Mohr.

6. Middle and Late Adulthood

Facing overview—United Nations photo by F. B. Grunzweig.

ANNUAL EDITIONS ARTICLE REVIEW FORM

■ NAME: _____ DATE: _____

■ TITLE AND NUMBER OF ARTICLE: _____

■ BRIEFLY STATE THE MAIN IDEA OF THIS ARTICLE: _____

_____

_____

_____

_____

■ LIST THREE IMPORTANT FACTS THAT THE AUTHOR USES TO SUPPORT THE MAIN IDEA:

_____

_____

_____

_____

_____

■ WHAT INFORMATION OR IDEAS DISCUSSED IN THIS ARTICLE ARE ALSO DISCUSSED IN YOUR TEXTBOOK OR OTHER READING YOU HAVE DONE? LIST THE TEXTBOOK CHAPTERS AND PAGE NUMBERS:

_____

_____

_____

_____

_____

_____

■ LIST ANY EXAMPLES OF BIAS OR FAULTY REASONING THAT YOU FOUND IN THE ARTICLE:

_____

_____

_____

_____

■ LIST ANY NEW TERMS/CONCEPTS THAT WERE DISCUSSED IN THE ARTICLE AND WRITE A SHORT DEFINITION:

_____

_____

_____

_____

*Your instructor may require you to use this Annual Editions Article Review Form in any number of ways: for articles that are assigned, for extra credit, as a tool to assist in developing assigned papers, or simply for your own reference. Even if it is not required, we encourage you to photocopy and use this page; you'll find that reflecting on the articles will greatly enhance the information from your text.

ANNUAL EDITIONS:
HUMAN DEVELOPMENT 93/94
Article Rating Form

Here is an opportunity for you to have direct input into the next revision of this volume. We would like you to rate each of the 49 articles listed below, using the following scale:

1. **Excellent: should definitely be retained**
2. **Above average: should probably be retained**
3. **Below average: should probably be deleted**
4. **Poor: should definitely be deleted**

Your ratings will play a vital part in the next revision. So please mail this prepaid form to us just as soon as you complete it.
Thanks for your help!

Rating	Article	Rating	Article
	1. Suffer the Little Children: Shameful Bequests to the Next Generation		28. The Lasting Effects of Child Maltreatment
	2. The Gene Dream		29. Children of Violence
	3. A New Genetic Code		30. Children After Divorce
	4. Mapping the Brain		31. Biology, Destiny, and All That
	5. Nature or Nurture?		32. Why Japanese Kids Are Smarter (or Are They?)
	6. Making Babies		33. Alienation and the Four Worlds of Childhood
	7. Sperm Under Siege		
	8. What Crack Does to Babies		34. Culture, Race Too Often Ignored in Child Studies
	9. War Babies		
	10. A New Perspective on Cognitive Development in Infancy		35. Tracked to Fail
			36. Why We Need to Understand Science
	11. The Child Yesterday, Today, and Tomorrow		37. The Myth About Teen-Agers
			38. Girls' Self-Esteem Is Lost on Way to Adolescence, New Study Finds
	12. Preschool: Head Start or Hard Push?		
	13. How Three Key Countries Shape Their Children		39. Those Gangly Years
			40. A Much Riskier Passage
	14. The Day Care Generation		41. Puberty and Parents: Understanding Your Early Adolescent
	15. Sizing Up the Sexes		
	16. The Good, the Bad, and the Difference		42. Jealousy and Envy: The Demons Within Us
	17. Your Loving Touch		
	18. The Miracle of Resiliency		43. The Myth of the Miserable Working Woman
	19. How Kids Learn		
	20. A Head Start Does Not Last		44. Family Ties: The Real Reason People Are Living Longer
	21. Now We're Talking!		
	22. Clipped Wings		45. The Vintage Years
	23. Tykes and Bytes		46. On Growing Old
	24. Same Family, Different Lives		47. How Old Are You Really?
	25. Putting Children First		48. Don't Act Your Age!
	26. Can Your Career Hurt Your Kids?		49. The Prime of Our Lives
	27. Life Without Father		

(Continued on next page)

ABOUT YOU

Name_____ Date_____

Are you a teacher? ☐   Or student? ☐

Your School Name _____

Department _____

Address _____

City _____ State _____ Zip _____

School Telephone #_____

YOUR COMMENTS ARE IMPORTANT TO US!

Please fill in the following information:

For which course did you use this book? _____

Did you use a text with this Annual Edition?   ☐ yes   ☐ no

The title of the text? _____

What are your general reactions to the Annual Editions concept?

Have you read any particular articles recently that you think should be included in the next edition?

Are there any articles you feel should be replaced in the next edition? Why?

Are there other areas that you feel would utilize an Annual Edition?

May we contact you for editorial input?

May we quote you from above?

ANNUAL EDITIONS: HUMAN DEVELOPMENT 93/94

BUSINESS REPLY MAIL

| First Class | Permit No. 84 | Guilford, CT |

Postage will be paid by addressee

The Dushkin Publishing Group, Inc.
Sluice Dock
DPG **Guilford, Connecticut 06437**